cd

THE COLLECTED PAPERS OF BERTRAND RUSSELL
VOLUME I

THE COLLECTED PAPERS OF BERTRAND RUSSELL

The McMaster University Edition

Volume 1   *Cambridge Essays, 1888–99*

Bertrand A. W. Russell, B.A., age 21, at Cambridge, 1893. (*BBC Hulton Picture Library*)

BERTRAND RUSSELL

# Cambridge Essays
## 1888–99

Edited by
Kenneth Blackwell
Andrew Brink
Nicholas Griffin
Richard A. Rempel
John G. Slater

London
GEORGE ALLEN & UNWIN
Boston     Sydney

**George Allen & Unwin (Publishers) Ltd.**
**40 Museum Street, London WC1A 1LU, U.K.**

George Allen & Unwin (Publishers) Ltd.
Park Lane, Hemel Hempstead, Herts HP2 4TE, U.K.

Allen & Unwin Inc.,
9 Winchester Terrace, Winchester, Mass. 01890, U.S.A.

George Allen & Unwin Australia Pty Ltd.
8 Napier Street, North Sydney, NSW 2060, Australia

First published in 1983

Funds to edit this volume were provided by a major editorial grant from the Social Sciences and Humanities Research Council of Canada and by McMaster University.

**British Library Cataloguing in Publication Data**

Russell, Bertrand
    Cambridge essays.—(The Collected papers of Bertrand Russell; v.1)
1888–99
1. Philosophy
I. Title     II. Blackwell, Kenneth     III. Series
192     B1649.R94
ISBN 0–04–920067–4

**Library of Congress Cataloging in Publication Data**

Russell, Bertrand, 1872–1970
    The Collected papers of Bertrand Russell
Includes Indexes
1. Philosophy—Collected Works     I. Blackwell, Kenneth     II. Title
B1649.R91     1983     192     83–15865
ISBN 0–04–920095–X (Set)

Set in 10 on 12 point V.I.P. Plantin by
The Bertrand Russell Editorial Project, McMaster University
and printed and bound in Great Britain by
William Clowes Limited, Beccles and London

THE COLLECTED PAPERS OF BERTRAND RUSSELL

# Contents

# Illustrations

Plates I and III–VIII are photographs of documents in the Bertrand Russell Archives at McMaster University. All but VIII are shown reduced from their original size, which is given at the head of each set of textual notes.

# Abbreviations

To GIVE THE the reader an uncluttered text, abbreviations and symbols have been kept to a minimum. The few necessary to the referencing system are as follows.

The papers printed in the volume are given a boldface number for easy reference. For example, the "Locked Diary" is Paper **9**. Angle brackets in the text distinguish rare editorial insertions from Russell's more common square brackets.

Bibliographical references are usually in the form of author, date and page, e.g. "Russell *1967*, 20". Consultation of the Bibliographical Index shows that this reference is to *The Autobiography of Bertrand Russell, 1872–1914*, Vol. I (London: Allen & Unwin, 1967), p. 20.

The location of archival documents cited in the edition is the Bertrand Russell Archives at McMaster University ("RA"), unless a different location is given. File numbers of documents in the Russell Archives are provided only when manuscripts of papers printed here are cited or when files are difficult to identify. "RA REC. ACQ." refers to the files of recent acquisitions in the Russell Archives.

Cross-references to annotations are preceded by "A" and followed by page and line numbers (as in "A5:14").

Cross-references to textual notes are preceded by "T". Further abbreviations are used in the Textual Notes, but they are identified at the beginning of each set of notes.

# Introduction

"THREE PASSIONS, SIMPLE but overwhelmingly strong, have governed my life: the longing for love, the search for knowledge, and unbearable pity for the suffering of mankind." It is characteristic of Russell to analyze the complex pattern of a long life in a single sentence, the opening sentence of his *Autobiography* (*1967*, 13). The analysis, too, is characteristically accurate. Each of the passions he there identifies originated at an early point in his life and persisted through all the subsequent mutations of his thought and actions.

His lonely childhood and his early, unsuccessful marriage to Alys Pearsall Smith, bitterly opposed by his family, are the starting points of a long quest for love and happiness. The speculations about God, freedom of the will and immortality in the "Greek Exercises", the journal he kept at the age of fifteen and sixteen, are the real beginning of his quest for philosophical knowledge, even if he did not officially take up philosophy at Cambridge until he had completed three years of mathematics there. His description of the human condition in the journal is deeply pessimistic. Nevertheless, and not surprisingly in the light of his family traditions, his pessimism is modified by a sense of compassion and a political commitment to do all he could to improve the lot of his fellow human beings. His political concern is revealed in the fact that he came near to choosing a topic in economics rather than in philosophy for his fellowship dissertation, as it also is in the fact that in the last years of his life, after he had completed his major contributions to philosophy, he devoted so much time and energy to the cause of nuclear disarmament. The search for love, for knowledge, for means of alleviating human suffering—these were indeed his life-long passions governing the conduct of his life, providing the impulse for his writings.

Writing came naturally to Russell, in a manner that is nowadays rare. In his formative years he regularly recorded, whether in letters or journals, his reactions to his unusually extensive reading. He would extract the essence from what he had read and organize it rigorously to aid his retentiveness. In his journals, too, he writes out what others might have been content privately to think. Yet when he came to write his articles and books, he did not let his pen run away with him. Although he revised to a greater degree than is sometimes suggested, his general habit was to compose in detail in his mind before he wrote. That is one reason why he exhibits a decisiveness and degree of clarity seldom conjoined with such profundity of thought. He was fully prepared, nevertheless, to change his mind; he valued truth above consistency over time. His writings, numerous as they are, provide us with a continuous record of the way in which his ideas developed on any particular topic. At each stage, he writes so clearly that the changes are readily discernible to an unusual degree. Such public exposition took confidence, which only rarely deserted Russell—not only in his technical writings but also when he was confronting great public issues. Few philosophers of his time attempted such a confrontation. Russell was never content to be a philosopher's philosopher. More lucid than Coleridge, more balanced than Carlyle, more profound than Ruskin, Russell carried single-handedly the tradition of the Victorian sage into the twentieth century. In an age which had ceased to believe in progress, he still proclaimed the liberal values and the self-confidence of an earlier age.

A reader may be interested in Russell as a philosopher or as a mathematical logician. Russell's views may be sought on the political issues of his time or on ethics or on political theory. Or the reader may simply venerate Russell as a sage. For whatever purpose a reader consults Russell's writings, he has several different kinds of source available to him. The first, and most accessible, is, of course, Russell's published books. Secondly, given the manner in which Russell developed his ideas, a letter often provides inside information about the way his mind was working. Thirdly, there is the great mass of his shorter writings, not always easy of access even when they are already in print. The aim of this edition is to bring together all the shorter writings that record Russell's own thoughts, whether or not they have been previously published. Scholars will now be able to find, in a compact, accessible form, most of the material that needs to be added to his published books for a full understanding of his views. Personal letters will not be included, because the process of collecting them has not yet been completed.

His shorter writings are of many different kinds. There are papers published in specialized periodicals, essays and articles for the general reader, letters to the editors of newspapers, political statements, pamphlets and speeches. There are also contributions to other authors' books, such as prefaces or introductions, and there are reviews, diaries and a small amount of fiction. We have included unpublished drafts of books only when they are not the direct antecedents of published versions. Each headnote to previously unpublished material indicates that this is its first appearance in print and where the manuscript can be located. A comprehensive bibliographical index to the collection will be contained in the last volume. Published in conjunction with the *Collected Papers* is a full bibliography of Russell's published writings.

Whoever wishes finally to judge Russell on any topic on which his opinions changed will need access to all his extant writings on that topic. This is especially true of his views on authority and the individual, on war and peace, and on marital relations, because they were all modified by time and events, but it is also true of his views in philosophy and logic. It will now be possible to base such judgments on a complete, annotated collection of his shorter writings. No doubt, some volumes will be singled out because they contain items of special interest. For example, Volumes 1 and 12 each contains a diary that has not been printed in full before, and the hitherto unpublished part of *Theory of Knowledge* in Volume 7 is indispensable for understanding why Russell's dream of collaborating with Wittgenstein was never realized.

After the first volume, *Cambridge Essays, 1888–99*, the edition divides into two parallel series. The first series, Volumes 2–11, contains Russell's philosophical, logical and mathematical papers. Here we can watch him struggling out of his early allegiance to neo-Hegelianism towards the "analytic" philosophy with which he is normally identified. As well, we can see emerging those ideas about the philosophy of mathematics and its relation to logic which bore fruit in his great writings on the foundations of mathematics. Systematic papers in ethics are also included in the series. The subsequent volumes, starting with 12, contain his writings on the many other subjects which absorbed his attention. The range of his interests as displayed in the second series is indeed enormous. It covers international relations from World War I to the Vietnam War, and political campaigns for Free Trade, women's suffrage and unilateral disarmament. It also includes political theory, literary commentary, history, biography, and papers on religion, education and practical ethics.

## II. VOLUME I, "CAMBRIDGE ESSAYS"

*Cambridge Essays* includes nearly all Russell's available shorter writings down to 1899. The exception is a group of philosophical papers written after mid-1896, which appear in Volume 2, because they are concerned with problems in the philosophy of mathematics covered by that volume. The editors have divided *Cambridge Essays* into seven parts. Part 1 contains his earliest surviving writings, although not such documents as the questions and answers on English constitutional history dictated to him by his aunt, Lady Agatha Russell, which are not original compositions—for all that they do indicate how seriously she took his education in the family political tradition.

The first piece in the collection is "Greek Exercises", a journal begun when Russell was fifteen and written in English but using Greek characters for the sake of secrecy. Published here in full for the first time, it shows how early his passion for truth developed. He himself made this point much later in his retrospective account of his philosophy: "There is only one constant preoccupation: I have throughout been anxious to discover how much we can be said to know and with what degree of certainty or doubtfulness" (*1959*, 11). His inquiry into the grounds for his beliefs soon began to undermine the Christian dogmas imparted by his grandmother, Countess Russell, who had assumed the responsibility for his upbringing and education after the three-year-old Bertrand had been left an orphan in 1876. His parents, Lord and Lady Amberley, had been firm supporters of such unpopular causes as birth-control, women's rights and universal suffrage and had intended their children to be educated as freethinkers. They were certainly not. Countess Russell was a sternly evangelical moralist who became a convert to Unitarianism. The young Russell attended, from time to time, Anglican, Presbyterian and Unitarian churches, in itself a somewhat bewildering experience for a youth in search of a settled religious position.

That he wrote his diary in the disguise of the Greek alphabet indicates to what a degree he came to find himself at odds with the religious atmosphere surrounding him at Pembroke Lodge. In his first entry he wrote that he once had a tutor, Mr. Ewen—an acquaintance of Karl Marx's daughter, Eleanor—to whom he had been able to speak freely, "but now I cannot let out my thoughts to any one, and this is the only means I have of letting off steam" (5: 11–13). Not until he went up to Cambridge was Russell able to claim his full intellectual inheritance, to speak out with the freedom of his parents. Much later, in 1937, with the help of his third wife, Patricia Spence, he published *The Amberley Papers* as a monument to their memory.

Half-way through "Greek Exercises", he wrote: "It is extraordinary how few principles or dogmas I have been able to become convinced of. One after another I find my former undoubted beliefs slipping from me into the region of doubt" (16: 5–7). He asked himself whether, as he had supposed, the quest for truth is an unmixed blessing. He suggested that, perhaps, the discoverer of certain kinds of truth is a martyr whose unhappiness is the price paid for the happiness of others. The thought is already extraordinarily mature and the style that gives it exact expression is already well developed.

"Greek Exercises" is followed by a set of essays written while Russell was preparing to sit the scholarship entrance examinations at Trinity College, Cambridge. The topics are nearly all social or political. Presumably they were chosen by his tutor at Southgate, the cramming school in London to which he was sent to prepare for Cambridge. The essays demonstrate the unusual extent of his reading and also reveal the degree to which Liberal politics and a sense of his country's history had been infused in him at Pembroke Lodge. His paternal grandfather, Earl Russell (better known by his earlier title of Lord John Russell) had been the architect of the great Reform Act of 1832 and subsequently Prime Minister and Foreign Secretary. So he had played a very full part in British political life even if he lived, during Bertrand's early boyhood, in retirement and relative seclusion at Pembroke Lodge in Richmond Park at the edge of London. Countess Russell was as noted for her political radicalism as for her evangelical convictions. George Santayana, who knew both Russell and his older brother Frank as young men, perceptively summed up Countess Russell's decision to keep her younger grandson directly under her guidance: "Bertie at least must be preserved, pure, religious, and affectionate; he must be fitted to take his grandfather's place as Prime Minister and continue the sacred work of Reform" (*1953*, 28). Russell was also very conscious of the fact that John Stuart Mill was his "secular godfather".

The main item in Part II is "A Locked Diary", which is published here for the first time. Russell kept it from 1890 to 1894 and showed it only to his Quaker wife, Alys. (That she was a Quaker explains why "thee" is the preferred form in their correspondence.) The diary starts with an account of life in Pembroke Lodge. In an early entry he writes, "I really must become less reserved, and say rather more what I think. Even if it does make many people hate me, the few I like best will like me the better for it" (49: 37–9). Several pages later there is a good example of his reserve. His comment on his brother's unhappy marriage was evidently not made to his family but confined to the diary. The passage runs: "This sort of case makes me think that divorce should be made much easier, and should be divested of all the scandal which now accompanies it" (51: 17–19). His interest in politics, already deep, is not very prominent in the diary, but there is a well-observed account of a dinner-party at which he defended Home Rule without the support of John Morley, who had been invited but was detained at the House of Commons (p. 54). It is notable that this dinner-party was held at the house of his Liberal Unionist maternal grandmother, Lady Stanley, where discussion was subject to fewer limitations than at Pembroke Lodge.

Later, when he looked back from the freedom of Cambridge on his life at Pembroke Lodge, he painted a picture in darker colours than is perhaps entirely just. In 1894, during his six months' engagement to Alys, he wrote, "P.L. is to me like a family vault haunted by the ghosts of maniacs, especially in view of all that I have recently learnt from Dr. Anderson" (66: 6–8). The doctor had told him that there was madness in his family. Russell had already suspected as much, and in the year before his engagement he wrote, "I dreamt last night that I was engaged to be married to Alys, when I discovered that my people had deceived me, that my mother was not dead but in a madhouse: I therefore had of course to give up the thought of ever marrying" (61: 39–62: 1). The account in this part of the diary of his courtship of Alys and his feelings for her is very direct and revealing.

Part III contains all the extant papers that Russell read to the Apostles, the Cambridge Conversazione Society founded in 1820, whose members kept strict secrecy about its proceedings. At Cambridge the atmosphere was one of free and open discussion, but the Society gave Russell the special advantage of being able to discuss on his own intellectual level. The papers the members read to each other often combined higher flippancy with deep seriousness, a characteristic English blend which he found congenial. In a paper in which he argued for the election of women to the Society he wrote:

> Of course before electing any woman some member would have to promise that she was perfectly ready to discuss unnatural vice in case the subject should come up, and not merely to discuss it, but to discuss it in a perfectly unartificial manner, without the feeling of doing anything unusual or perhaps a little naughty. And where this could be promised, I think one may safely say that freedom of discussion *would* be antagonistic to the beginnings of love. (85: 14–20)

So two problems would be solved together: freedom of discussion would not be impaired by the admission of women and the serenity of the Apostles would not be disturbed by inappropriate passions.

Looking back in his *Autobiography*, he wrote that from the time that he entered Cambridge "everything went well" (*1967*, 56). His new friends included several of his most distinguished contemporaries. Among them were the historian G. M. Trevelyan who much later, in 1944, as Master of Trinity College, would bring him back to Cambridge, and G. E. Moore who was to exert a profound influence on his philosophy. However, his first three years at the University were devoted to mathematics. Alfred North Whitehead, who had admired his scholarship papers, soon became a friend, and in the next decade was his collaborator on *Principia Mathematica*. After completing the first part of the Mathematical Tripos in 1893 as seventh wrangler, Russell spent a fourth year working with equal success for honours in Moral Sciences (i.e. philosophy). His tutors included James Ward, G. F. Stout and Henry Sidgwick. He also absorbed Hegelian idealism (the diluted British mixture) from J. M. E. McTaggart. Sidgwick, Ward, Whitehead, Moore, McTaggart and Trevelyan were all Apostles.

Parts IV and V contain the surviving papers written by Russell while he was reading for the Moral Sciences Tripos. His student papers on epistemology and the history of philosophy make up Part IV. His papers on ethics are placed in Part V, which also contains three essays on ethical topics written after Russell had taken his final examination in June of 1894.

In the epistemological essays in Part IV his philosophy is not yet directed on the course that it eventually took. That was not to happen until Moore persuaded him that the human mind really is in direct contact with things outside of it and until Russell's own interest in à priori knowledge and necessary truth had extended from the special problems of geometry to the general question whether all branches of mathematics stem from logic.

Most of the essays on ethics in Part V were written for Sidgwick. Russell paid close attention to Sidgwick's comments in class. There is an excellent example of such a comment, relating to the points of issue between Utilitarian and Kantian ethics, in the headnote to **33**. The paper itself is short but searching; students of ethics will find it well worth reading today. There is also a very good, related paper, written for Alys (**31**). A long discussion of freedom and determinism (**37**) sets out the controversy with exceptional conciseness.

The ethical papers are notable performances, although they were mostly written in the year in which Russell first received tuition in philosophy. Their range, the sureness of his judgments, the sharpness of his statements and the lucidity of his arguments mark him out as someone who might already have been tutoring others. Of course, he had begun his acquaintance with philosophy while he was still at home, and given that already aroused interest, his mastery of the subject must have been developing during his first three years at Cambridge, for all that they were officially devoted to mathematics. Even if his achievement is not quite miraculous, it is certainly remarkable.

Part VI contains the papers and reviews that he wrote on the philosophy of geometry in 1895 and 1896. In almost all of them he confronts a problem posed by the existence of non-Euclidean geometries. Kant's explanation of the necessity of Euclidean geometry, which he took to be the geometry of perceived space, was that this particular system of spatial relations is generated in the mind of the perceiver and projected onto what is perceived. Evidently, no such explanation will work for non-Euclidean geometries. Russell made use of nineteenth-century advances toward the unification of geometry in order to argue that, while neither Euclidean nor non-Euclidean geometry could properly be considered à priori, a generalized geometry which included both was necessary, in the Kantian sense of being presupposed by all external perception. He was soon to abandon this qualified defence of Kant (see the papers on geometry in Volume 2).

It is worth remembering that Russell deliberated whether to take his fellowship examination in philosophy or in economics. In 1895 he made two lengthy visits to Berlin to study economic theory and German Social Democracy. He even dreamed, while walking in the Tiergarten, of following two parallel courses of study, one in the philosophy of the sciences, from pure mathematics to physiology, and the other in political and social philosophy. However, his main reason for studying economics was a practical one. He contemplated going into politics, for which he believed a knowledge of economic theory to be indispensable. In a paper read to the Apostles in 1893 on the question, "Can We Be Statesmen?" (**12**), although he assumed that "most of us take our stand on Utilitarianism" (79: 7), he pointed out the difficulty of applying it to "that larger class of political questions which affect the nation first and the individuals through the nation" (81: 16–17). He also argued that, though Political Economy gives some help, it still leaves many political issues undecided. Nonetheless, Russell remained confident that the help it could offer was well worth securing.

In the papers printed in Part VII, only one of which (**49**) has previously been published in English, he writes both as a practical politician and as a theoretician, as if he might not only adapt Gladstone's liberalism to the twentieth century but also bring Mill's moral and political philosophy up to date. He studied economic theory in order to discover the best way to apply his liberal principles, and recent German history in order to choose the most effective party of reform.

Completed lives often present a delusive appearance of inevitability. Russell could well have followed the Whig tradition into which he was born and gone into politics. In his later prolific writings on social and political questions, his firm conviction that he knew what was best for his country is sometimes concealed by the wit with which he mocked his opponents; but his conviction is never far below the surface and emerges most clearly at the end of his life in his support of the campaign for nuclear disarmament. Georgiana Blakiston sums up the character of the Russell family very accurately:

> Integrity coupled with a love of country and a natural acceptance of service to the state initially kept the name of Russell to the fore. A martyr in the family helped to fan the embers of youthful pride and give a whiggish direction to latent patriotism. From the security of settled wealth and power an independent and liberal outlook developed, manifested by a stubborn opposition to the power of the Crown.... As individuals they tend to show in diverse ways a disregard for accepted attitudes, each pursuing his course in his own way with no timid apprehension of being thought different from his fellow-men. (*1980*, 2–3)

Pembroke Lodge was indeed a gloomy place, for the series of blows that the Russells experienced would have daunted even the most enlightened, resourceful and secure of families. Besides the premature deaths of the Amberleys, Lord John and his wife suffered further disasters in the early

1870s. Their second son, William, became incurably insane, and Rollo was forced to give up a promising career in the Foreign Office because of deteriorating eyesight. Countess Russell was further burdened in 1884, when Agatha collapsed with a nervous breakdown during her engagement and had to forego all hopes of marriage. Moreover Frank, who is depicted in *The Amberley Papers* (Russell and Russell *1937*) as nearly uncontrollable even before his parents' deaths, was soon viewed by his family at Pembroke Lodge as completely intractable. He was sent off to a preparatory school at Cheam and then to Winchester School in 1879.

Frank's absence allowed the Russell family to concentrate its attention on Bertrand. He affirmed that this attention was important in his development and he "vividly" remembered his grandfather's exemplary political career (*1956a*, 109). Bertrand's family, throughout the time he lived at Pembroke Lodge, steadily impressed upon him the tradition of public service he had inherited and was obliged to uphold. With all the other Russell males either dead, incapacitated or unacceptable, he alone could be expected to wear his grandfather's mantle.

It is not only his Whiggish political convictions which Russell derived from family tradition. Even his method of argument resembles that of Lord John Russell, whom the Victorian historian W. E. H. Lecky described as noted for "his admirable terseness and clearness of expression.... Beyond all men I have ever known, he had the gift of seizing rapidly in every question the central argument, the essential fact or distinction" (Reid *1895*, 335).

### III. SOURCES OF THE TEXT OF VOLUME I

The main source is the material in the Bertrand Russell Archives at McMaster University. Russell's large collection of manuscripts and letters, acquired from him in 1968, is the nucleus and the University has since made many additions to it, particularly by acquiring the second part of the archives in 1972. The collection also includes about 3,500 books from his library, many of them dated and annotated in his own hand. There is a catalogue of the original Russell Archives (Feinberg *1967*); a periodical, *Russell*, published at McMaster records later acquisitions.

When this edition was first planned, in 1969, two bibliographies were available: the fourth edition of Denonn's bibliography (*1963*) and the unpublished bibliography by Kenneth Blackwell and Harry Ruja, whose collaboration began in 1967. Russell kept no bibliography of his own. The Archives' search for papers to be included in *Cambridge Essays* began in 1969. Before the archives were acquired only six of the papers contained in this volume were available. Thirty-nine more came from the archives. Then in 1977 three new unpublished papers (**9**, **10** and **31**) were found in the Pearsall Smith family archives, now owned by Barbara Strachey Halpern.

The discovery of **9** was a very welcome surprise; Russell had written (*1967*, 82) about keeping "a locked diary" during his engagement to Alys, but it was not until the late 1970s that it became known at McMaster that her papers had survived. A perusal of Ernest Samuels' life of Bernard Berenson (1979) led to yet another addition (**11**), and, in 1981, a collation of the notebook containing **41** with *An Essay on the Foundations of Geometry* resulted in the final addition (**41d**).

When the editors compiled Volume 1, all papers satisfying the criteria for inclusion and known to be extant were available to them. However, others are known to be lost. Naturally, the papers that Russell wrote for examinations at Trinity College, Cambridge had been destroyed, but a surviving entrance paper, headed "Examination for Major and Minor Scholarships, Exhibitions and Sizarships" (15 Dec. 1890), has his notes on the questions that he decided to answer. In a letter to Alys (3 Sept. 1894) he mentioned a paper "on Elizabethan Lyrics" which apparently has not survived. In *Russell Remembered* Rupert Crawshay-Williams, a friend and neighbour in Russell's later years, says that he "told us once he had written masses of extremely purple passages in his early twenties, and had destroyed them all" (*1970*, 47). He was evidently selective in what he allowed to survive from his childhood and youth. Even so, and even allowing for the Victorian propensity to hoard, the density of material extant for Russell's early years is unusual.

Three of his papers read to the Apostles have vanished and one essay for his tutors in philosophy is known to be lost. It is probably not the only one (see the general headnotes to Part III and to Parts IV and V). His lost fellowship dissertation seems to have had the title "The Metaphysical Basis of Geometry" (see a report in *The Inquirer*, 19 Oct. 1895). The syllabus of the lectures based on it is printed in Appendix 1.

In his correspondence with Alys during the long separation forced upon them in 1894 by Countess Russell, he mentioned several papers, written or only planned. On 22 August he sent her a paper that he described rather uninformatively as "written just after a fortnight's separation". On 5 September he told her that he would enjoy writing essays and notes for her on difficult passages in Bradley (probably from *Appearance and Reality*, which he had been reading). On the 12th he said he would like to send her a history of his knowledge of sexual matters from his boyhood to the time he fell in love with Caroline FitzGerald (see A45: 4), and on the 17th he did send "a few reminiscences". On 11 October he mentioned a paper on Adolf Wagner's theory of motivation, which he had sent to her two days before (see headnote to **33**). None of these papers has apparently survived.

The last missing paper, which there is, perhaps, some hope of finding, "Socialism as the Consummation of Individual Liberty", was read by him at Bryn Mawr College in November 1896, and he then sought the aid of the

President, Carey Thomas, in getting it published in a periodical (according to his letters to her on 1 Dec. 1896 and 15 Jan. 1897).

The descriptions and histories of these missing papers have been given in some detail, because it is still possible that some of them may be discovered.

## IV. PRESENTATION OF THE TEXT OF VOLUME I

The editors' primary duty has been to provide an accurate, readable text of Russell's own words, unencumbered by textual apparatus. However, certain factual questions inevitably arise, not only when Russell alludes to persons, places, events, and writings unfamiliar to the modern reader but also in relation to the provenance and establishment of the texts. These questions, or at least all the more crucial ones, are answered in headnotes and annotations and in the chronology of his life, reference to which facilitates the reading of the papers in the order of their composition.

The headnotes are of two kinds. Each paper has its own headnote and there are also general headnotes for most of the seven parts of the volume. The headnote for an individual paper records what is known about its origin, the versions in which it survives and, where applicable, the history of its publication. The general headnotes supply the broad context of the papers which follow.

In the annotations almost all Russell's allusions are explained. Particular care has been taken to identify the sources of material quoted, but not attributed, by him. All quotations have been checked for accuracy; substantive errors are noted in the annotations. Any errors in bibliographical references are corrected in the text.

There are two appendices. The first contains abstracts of two papers printed in this volume, published summaries of some lost papers and an outline of a series of lectures. The second appendix contains "What Shall I Read?", Russell's selective record of what he (and occasionally Alys) read between 1891 and 1902.

Finally, there are textual notes, a bibliographical index and a general index. The "Textual Principles and Methods" explain and justify the selection, emendation and regularization of the copy-text. The extensive textual notes that follow include the alterations that Russell made in his manuscripts, which will help readers to understand how he wrote.

# Acknowledgements

THIS VOLUME COULD not have been completed without the generous assistance of McMaster University and the Social Sciences and Humanities Research Council of Canada. The Council's award of a Major Editorial Grant, beginning in July 1980, has been of crucial significance for our plan to publish the *Collected Papers*. Without this grant the Russell Editorial Project could not have obtained the extensive released time needed for the editors, and assembled the staff and equipment to produce this volume and the many volumes that are planned for the future.

McMaster University released time from teaching to its faculty editors and helped with financial and technological requirements both before and after the award of the Major Editorial Grant. We are grateful, in particular, to the following University administrators: the late William Ready, University Librarian 1966–79, who brought the Russell papers to McMaster; Alwyn Berland, former Dean of Humanities, Chairman of the Project's Board of Management and of the Bertrand Russell Archives Academic Advisory Board and McMaster's negotiator with our publisher and the Bertrand Russell Estate; and Assistant Vice-President Alan C. Frosst, our adviser on budgetary matters. Other administrators have been helpful: former President A. N. Bourns, Associate Vice-President J. P. Evans, Vice-President Leslie J. King, President Alvin A. Lee, former Acting Dean S. M. Najm and Associate Dean Chauncey Wood.

We wish to thank the Bertrand Russell Estate for permission to publish those papers in which the Estate holds copyright. Our thanks are also due to George Allen & Unwin Ltd. for their advice on the design of the volume and for the confidence they have shown in our own design and typesetting initiatives. The Project has profited from the interest of Rayner Unwin for many years and the advice of Keith Ashfield since 1977.

The late Countess Russell encouraged this Project and sustained the editors with her support until her death in 1978.

Members of the Advisory Editorial Board have keenly supported our editorial work. In particular, Katharine Tait, Bertrand Russell's daughter, has provided much useful advice. John M. Robson, general editor of the *Collected Works of John Stuart Mill*, has encouraged us at all times but especially when the plan for the edition was first being formulated. David Pears provided us with a most helpful and detailed critique of the Introduction. Jock Gunn, an editor of the *Letters* of Benjamin Disraeli, and Colin Matthew, editor of *The Gladstone Diaries*, have also been very helpful. Philip Gaskell, Librarian of Trinity College, Cambridge, and author of *A New Introduction to Bibliography* (1972) and *From Writer to Reader* (1978), has advised us on textual bibliography. Assistance on mathematical questions has been given by Ivor Grattan-Guinness.

We have drawn upon consultants from outside the Advisory Editorial Board, including the late Lloyd Woollon on phototypesetting.

Many people and institutions in Canada, the United States, Britain and Europe have generously provided advice and, in some cases, vital material for Volume I. Barbara Strachey Halpern has kindly made available to us Russell's "Locked Diary" that is in her possession and has shared with us the massive correspondence between Russell and his first wife. Through her goodwill a microfilm of the correspondence is available in the Russell Archives. The British Library has made its resources available in the search for Russell's fugitive writings. The Library of Trinity College, Cambridge, has put at our disposal the correspondence of philosophers with whom Russell was in contact in his early years at Cambridge, as has the Cambridge University Library. The Nuffield College Library, Oxford, has provided details on Russell's association with the Fabian Society. The Biblioteca Berenson, at the Harvard University Center for Italian Renaissance Studies, Villa I Tatti, Italy, has helped us in regard to Pearsall Smith family connections; and the Bibliothèque de la Ville, La Chaux-de-Fonds, Switzerland, has permitted us to quote from Russell's letters to Louis Couturat in its possession. Lucy Fisher West, Archivist of Bryn Mawr College, has kindly sent us copies of the correspondence of Carey Thomas with Mary E. Garrett, with her father, James Carey Thomas, and with Alys Russell. M. C. Beecheno of The Johns Hopkins University Library researched Russell's early lecture series there for us. Walter Ong, S.J., of St. Louis University, helped us with many obscure references in Paper **25**.

Fred Keay, his assistant Joan Johnson, and Peter Smith have clarified obscure allusions in source materials available only in Britain. Jo Ann Boydston of Southern Illinois University at Carbondale, general editor of John Dewey's *Works*, has provided advice on editorial theory and practice. Kirk Willis of the University of Georgia contributed a number of suggestions, and Peter Mühlhäusler of Linacre College, Oxford, has made clear some points of nineteenth-century German orthography.

At McMaster, we have had the cooperation of the entire library staff. In particular, the University Librarian, Graham R. Hill, and the staffs of Archives and Research Collections, Interlibrary Loan, Reference and Serials deserve acknowledgement. Kenneth Blackwell, the Russell Archivist since the arrival of the papers at McMaster in 1968, has been responsible for preparing and extending the resources of the Archives for the undertaking of the edition. The Assistant Russell Archivist, Carl Spadoni, and the Archival Assistant in the Russell Archives, Cheryl Walker, have attended to our multitudinous requests for archival materials. Among faculty members at McMaster, G. M. Paul and Howard Jones of the Classics Department have given expert advice on Russell's "Greek Exercises", while an alumnus, Christopher Dean, helped to transliterate them. Thomas Willey in History and William Hunter in Economics have advised us on aspects of Russell's political and economic writings. Bruce Kinzer in History advised us on the General Index. Gerald Field in Mathematical Sciences made the drawing in the annotations. McMaster's Audio-Visual Services worked to decipher cancelled passages in "What Shall I Read?" The translations from German in the annotations are the work of Murray Miles of Toronto.

This list could be extended considerably, and we hope that all others who have helped with this volume will accept our thanks and apologies where we have inadvertently failed to list them.

On the Project itself, we have been fortunate in our research staff: Gregory H. Moore, an historian of mathematics, and Margaret Moran as postdoctoral Research Associates; Paul Gallina, the Bibliographical Assistant; Sheila Turcon, who drafted the General Index and researched the Chronology; and Catherine Funnell, a librarian.

The Major Editorial Grant has allowed us to employ graduate students to work on the Project. We thank especially John King of McMaster for his detailed and precise work, particularly on the compilation of Textual Notes, and for checking the bibliographical references and quotations. Marilyn Mason from McMaster, who has also been with us for two years, has ranged widely in her duties and has been especially vigilant in keeping us alert for factual errors in annotations. Other graduate students who have helped are James Dianda from McMaster and Bernd P. Frohmann and William G. Stratton from the University of Toronto. A number of undergraduate students have helped in researching for the annotations, in collating, and in proofreading. We thank Maria Forte, Daphne Jarvis, Catherine Johnson, James O'Meara, Don Ross, Alan Siaroff, Hilary Turner and Ben Zipursky. The Philosophy Department assigned the following students to work on the Project: Sitwat Ansari, Wayne Borody, David Brown, Earl Darlington, Rashida Khan and Steve Sommerville. The McMaster Arts Research Board funded Karen Zizzo for some months.

The production of camera-ready copy for *Collected Papers* I has been supervised by the Production Manager, Diane M. Kerss, with typesetting and paste-up by Joy Drew, Jacqueline S. Hassan, Nancy Scott, Patricia Sorrell-Yates and Carmen Stermann. Hugh Fraser has proofread the volume in camera-ready copy. On questions of production, much of the character of Volume I has depended on the Textual Editor, who has chief responsibility for typographical design, and Diane Kerss, who carried out the exacting task of implementing the design. Myrna-Gail McDonald has cheerfully typed correspondence and drafts of the annotation.

Our work has been greatly facilitated by McMaster's Printing Services, managed by Don Henwood. Sue Fletcher has patiently processed our galleys.

For permission to use materials in their copyright, gratitude is extended to the following: BBC Hulton Picture Library, for the frontispiece photograph; Cambridge University Press, for passages from *An Essay on the Foundations of Geometry* quoted in the Textual Notes to Papers **42** and **44**; Barbara Strachey Halpern, for the Alys (Pearsall Smith) Russell letters; John Russell Lloyd, for the Rollo Russell quotation; John Russell, for the passage from Logan Pearsall Smith's letter; and Harriet Whitehead, for extracts from the Alfred North Whitehead correspondence.

Acknowledgement is made to the following publishers and journals who previously published some of the papers printed here: Atlantic–Little, Brown (parts of Paper **1**, in Russell's *Autobiography*, Vol. I); *The Economic Journal* (Paper **49**); *Mind* (Papers **40**, **42** and **43**); *Proceedings of the Aristotelian Society* (Paper **44**); and Simon and Schuster (Paper **16**, in Russell's *Why I Am Not a Christian*, and parts of Paper **1**, in *My Philosophical Development*).

# Chronology:
# Russell's Life and Writings, 1872–99

| | Life | Writings |
|---|---|---|
| 18 May 1872 | Born at Ravenscroft, near Trelleck, Monmouthshire; second son of Lord and Lady Amberley. | |
| 28 June 1874 | Death of Lady Amberley. | |
| 3 July 1874 | Death of sister Rachel. | |
| 9 Jan. 1876 | Death of Lord Amberley. | |
| Feb. 1876 | Sent with brother Frank to live with grandparents, Earl and Countess Russell, and their grown children, Rollo and Agatha, at Pembroke Lodge, Richmond. | |
| Autumn 1877 | Frank is sent away to school. | |
| 28 May 1878 | Death of Earl Russell; Frank becomes 2nd Earl. | |
| 9 Aug. 1883 | First lesson in Euclid from Frank. | |
| 3 Mar. 1888 | | First entry in Paper 1. |
| 9 May 1888 | Enters Green's at Southgate to prepare for Trinity College scholarship examinations; stays eighteen months. | |
| June 1888 | Awarded book prize (Macaulay *1883*) for Cambridge University Local Examinations written in London. | |
| 1889 | | 2–8 written at Southgate. |
| Apr. 1889 | | Last entry in 1. |
| Summer 1889 | Meets Alys Pearsall Smith at Friday's Hill, the Pearsall Smith house. | |
| Aug. 1889 | First independent trip abroad (to Paris and Switzerland with the FitzGeralds). | |
| Autumn 1889 | Shares lodgings with FitzGerald at Southgate. | |
| Dec. 1889 | Wins Minor Scholarship to Trinity. | |

| 18 May 1890 | Eighteenth birthday. | First entry in **9**. |
|---|---|---|
| Oct. 1890 | Enters Trinity to study mathematics for three years. | |
| 27 Feb. 1891 | Joins Cambridge Moral Sciences Club. | |
| 4 June 1891 | Moves "Women should be admitted to equal political rights with men" at Magpie and Stump Debating Society. | |
| 27 Feb. 1892 | Elected to the Apostles. | |
| Spring 1892 | Helps found *Cambridge Observer*. | Lost paper on Elizabethan lyrics perhaps written. |
| 6 May 1892 | Moves that "The ending or mending of the House of Lords is desirable" at the Magpie and Stump. | |
| Sept. 1892 | Receives Joachim's reading list on philosophy. | |
| 5 Dec. 1892 | | Last entry in first section of **9**. |
| 18 May 1893 | Comes of age with inheritance of £20,000. | |
| 17–20 May, 1–4 June 1893 | Sits Mathematical Tripos (Pt. I). | |
| 9 June 1893 | Bracketed 7th wrangler in Mathematical Tripos (Pt. I), proceeding B.A. Attends temperance demonstration with Alys. | |
| 21 June 1893 | Correspondence with Alys begins. | |
| July 1893 | Commences year of study of Moral Sciences at Trinity. | **30** written. |
| 21 July 1893 | | First entry in new section of **9**. |
| Aug. 1893 | | **10** written. |
| c.15 Sept. 1893 | Proposes to Alys at Friday's Hill. | |
| c.28 Sept. 1893 | | **31** written. |
| Oct. 1893 | | **32** written. |
| Nov. 1893 | Contributes to coalminers' strike fund. | **18, 19, 20, 33, 34** written. |
| 18 Nov. 1893 | | **12** read to Apostles. |
| Jan. 1894 | | **35** written. |
| Feb. 1894 | | **13, 21, 22, 23, 36** written. |
| 3 Mar. 1894 | | **13** read to Apostles. |
| 15 Mar.–7 Apr. 1894 | Travels to Rome with Aunt Maude Stanley, later joining the Pearsall Smiths in Paris. | |

| | | |
|---|---|---|
| Apr. 1894 | | **24, 25** written. |
| May 1894 | | **26, 27** written. |
| Spring? 1894 | | **28, 29** written. |
| 21–3 May 1894 | Sits Moral Sciences Tripos (Pt. II). | |
| 31 May 1894 | Engagement announced. | |
| 2 June 1894 | | Reads lost paper to Apostles. |
| 5 June 1894 | Receives reading list on economics from Alfred Marshall. | |
| 8 June 1894 | First class with distinction in Moral Sciences Tripos (Pt. II) announced. | |
| 10 June 1894 | Thesis topic chosen. | |
| 21 June 1894 | Signs pledge of British Women's Temperance Association. | |
| 16 July–17 Aug. 1894 | Lives with Pearsall Smiths at Friday's Hill. | Begins thesis research. |
| 17 Aug. 1894 | Three months' enforced separation from Alys begins. | |
| 10 Sept.–1 Dec. 1894 | Honorary attaché, British Embassy, Paris. | |
| Oct. 1894 | | Last entry in **9**; **14** written. |
| 9 Oct. 1894 | | Lost paper on Wagner's "fifth motive" written. |
| 3 Nov. 1894 | Weekend trip to Cambridge. | **14** read to Apostles. |
| 9 Nov. 1894 | | "Geometrical Axioms" (now lost) read to Moral Sciences Club by Sanger. |
| 10 Nov. 1894 | | Lost paper on free will written. |
| 17–20 Nov. 1894 | Brief visit to England to see Alys, ending their separation. | |
| 13 Dec. 1894 | Marries Alys in London. | |
| 14 Dec. 1894 | Honeymoon at The Hague for three weeks. | |
| Jan.–Mar. 1895 | Studies economics at the University of Berlin. | Keeps notebook on economics lectures attended. |
| early 1895 | | **45** perhaps written. |
| 16 Feb. 1895 | Death of Lady Stanley of Alderley, his maternal grandmother. | |
| Feb. 1895 | | **40** probably written. |
| Mar. 1895 | Visits Italy. | Starts writing **41**. |

| | | |
|---|---|---|
| Apr. 1895 | | **40** published. |
| Spring 1895 | At Friday's Hill. | Works on thesis. |
| 6 June 1895 | | **41** completed in draft. |
| 8 June 1895 | | **37** completed. |
| Aug. 1895 | | Submits thesis for Trinity prize fellowship. |
| 10 Oct. 1895 | Trinity prize fellowship won. | |
| Nov.–Dec. 1895 | In Berlin studying German social democracy. | |
| Nov. 1895 | | **43** probably written. |
| 4 Nov. 1895 | | Correcting proofs of **42**. |
| Christmas 1895 | At The Hague. | Writing lectures on German Social Democracy. |
| early 1896 | | **38** and **39** perhaps written. |
| Jan. 1896 | | **42** and **43** published. |
| Feb. 1896 | With Alys, starts the Cambridge and Westminster Club in London. | |
| 1 Feb. 1896 | | Alys sends outline of "The Foundations of Geometry" lecture series to Bryn Mawr. |
| 6 Feb.–13 Mar. 1896 | | Lectures on German social democracy at London School of Economics. |
| 14 Feb. 1896 | | **46** read to Fabian Society. |
| 17 Feb. 1896 | Joins Aristotelian Society. | **47** completed. |
| Mar. 1896 | | "Review of Hannequin" (Vol. 2) probably written. |
| 1 Mar. 1896 | | **44** completed. |
| 30 Mar. 1896 | | **44** read to Aristotelian Society. |
| Apr. 1896 | Visits Italy. Takes possession of The Millhangar. | |
| 2 June 1896 | | "On Some Difficulties of Continuous Quantity" (Vol. 2) completed. |
| July 1896 | Russell Research Studentship at L.S.E. awarded for first time. | **44** and "Review of Hannequin" (Vol. 2) published. |
| 23 July 1896 | | **48** completed. |
| late July 1896 | Attends International Socialist Congress, London. | |

| | | |
|---|---|---|
| Aug. 1896 | | "Review of Couturat" (Vol. 2) probably written. |
| Sept. 1896 | | Reading proofs of *German Social Democracy*. |
| 28 Sept. 1896 | | Date of agreement with Cambridge University Press for *An Essay on the Foundations of Geometry*. |
| 3 Oct.–23 Dec. 1896 | In U.S.A. with Alys. | |
| 2–20 Nov. 1896 | At Bryn Mawr College. | Delivers six lectures on "The Foundations of Geometry". |
| 22, 24 Nov. 1896 | At Bryn Mawr College. | "Socialism as the Consummation of Individual Liberty" (now lost) read. |
| Dec. 1896 | | *German Social Democracy* published. |
| 2–11 Dec. 1896 | At The Johns Hopkins University. | Delivers five lectures on "The Foundations of Geometry". |
| early 1897 | | **11** probably written. |
| Jan.–July 1897 | At The Millhangar. | Working on philosophy of mathematics. "Various Notes on Mathematical Philosophy" (Vol. 2) written 1896–98. |
| Jan. 1897 | | "Review of Couturat" (Vol. 2) published; **49** probably written. |
| 14 Jan. 1897 | Proceeds M.A. | |
| 6 Feb. 1897 | Resigns from active membership in Apostles. | **15** read to Apostles. |
| Mar. 1897 | Joins Fabian Society. | **11, 49** published. |
| 5 Apr. 1897 | | "On the Relations of Number and Quantity" (Vol. 2) read to Aristotelian Society. |
| Easter 1897 | Spends two weeks in Italy. | |
| 20 May 1897 | | *An Essay on the Foundations of Geometry* published. |

| | | |
|---|---|---|
| July 1897 | At Friday's Hill. | "On the Relations of Number and Quantity" (Vol. 2) published. |
| Oct.–Nov. 1897 | Visits Italy. | |
| Dec. 1897 | | "Review of Love" (Vol. 2) perhaps written. **16** read to Apostles. Takes extensive notes at McTaggart's lectures on Lotze. |
| 11 Dec. 1897 | First evidence of break with idealism. | |
| Jan.–Feb. 1898 | At Cambridge working in the Cavendish Laboratory. | |
| 17 Jan. 1898 | Death of Dowager Countess Russell. | |
| 25 Feb. 1898 | | "The Constitution of Matter" (now lost) read to Moral Sciences Club. Writes "An Analysis of Mathematical Reasoning" (Vol. 3). |
| Mar.–July 1898 | At The Millhangar. | |
| 14 Mar. 1898 | | "Review of Love" (Vol. 2) read to Aristotelian Society. |
| Spring 1898 | Donation of £1,000 to Cambridge and £1,000 to Newnham. | |
| July 1898 | At Friday's Hill. | "Review of Love" (Vol. 2) published. "Are Euclid's Axioms Empirical?" (Vol. 2) written. |
| Aug. 1898 | | "Review of Goblot" (Vol. 2) probably written. |
| Sept.–Nov. 1898 | Visit to Italy via Germany. | |
| Oct. 1898 | | "Review of Goblot" (Vol. 2) published. |
| Nov. 1898 | | "Are Euclid's Axioms Empirical?" (Vol. 2) published. |
| 6–8 Nov. 1898 | First visit to Couturat at Caen, France. | |
| Jan.–Feb. 1899 | At Cambridge. | Gives course of lectures on Leibniz. |
| 27 Jan. 1899 | | "The Classification of Relations" (Vol. 2) read to Moral Sciences Club. |
| 11 Feb. 1899 | | **17** read to Apostles. |

Part I

Adolescent Writings

# 1

# Greek Exercises [1888–89]

DURING HIS ADOLESCENCE Russell came increasingly to doubt the Christian faith he had been taught by his family, especially his grandmother, Lady Russell. At first he attempted to discuss his doubts with her; but because the attempt merely provoked her ridicule, he found life with her "only endurable at the cost of complete silence about everything that interested me" (Russell *1967*, 46). Russell began keeping a diary to unburden himself of the thoughts and anxieties about which he could not speak. The "Greek Exercises" are that diary. Written entirely in Greek characters, but headed "Greek Exercises" in the Roman alphabet, the entries were designed to conceal his thoughts from anyone who might casually glance at the diary.

Russell's earliest known reference to the diary is in a letter to Alys Pearsall Smith, his fiancée. He told her that he had been "looking at my old speculations on theology when I was fifteen; they amuse me now, especially the tremendous struggle I made to free myself from sentiment in forming my opinions" (12 April 1894). Later, when Alys inquired of his religious development, he mentioned his

> old journal in the Greek letters, headed "Greek Exercises" and written mostly in pencil. I put down most of my religious experiences there while they were fresh and I might copy them into plain English for thee, supplementing them by memory where they need it. (7 Sept. 1894)

The extracts (from entries 1–2, 9, 12–13, 15 and 17) with the commentary that Russell made for Alys survive in their correspondence and have been drawn upon in the Annotation and Textual Notes. In telling Lady Ottoline Morrell of the diary's existence, he disclosed his belief that his grandmother never learned of it: "To make quite sure, I even invented a system of phonetic spelling of my own" (letter 198, 28 Sept. 1911). Russell first mentioned the diary in print in "My Religious Reminiscences" (*1938*, 5), where he quoted from entry 5; and he remarked on the autobiographical importance of the "Greek Exercises" in "My Mental Development" (*1944*, 8).

The diary consists of twenty-two entries, all but one written in 1888. The first is dated 3 March 1888 and the last April 1889. Russell published extracts from eleven of the entries in *My Philosophical Development* (1959); in the first volume of his *Autobiography* (1967) he included a longer, and less philosophically oriented, selection from fifteen of the entries. Russell never published any extracts from entries 2,

3

10, 13, 14, 21 and 22. His principles of choice are unknown—many of the omitted entries are as interesting philosophically and biographically as those he selected. The relevant annotation (A5: 14–27) indicates that as early as 1894 Russell expressed dissatisfaction with entry 2. He may have omitted entry 22 (written at the height of his period of nature worship) because of what he may have come to regard as the sentimentality evident in it.

The text is more than English written in Greek characters. The early entries contain numerous Greek words and constructions, and Russell's progress in learning Greek is evident. Details of his use of Greek vocabulary and grammar will be found in the Textual Notes. Later he disclosed that he learned the least amount of Greek compatible with his entering Cambridge—adding that the amount was more than worth his while (*1930*, E1). His phonetic system of transliteration may reflect his aristocratic Victorian accent. Some examples (all culled from entry 21) are ὠρλρεδι ("already"), φηα ("fair") and χαμφετιν ("comforting").

The copy-text is the manuscript. Russell made an interlinear transliteration of most of the entries in 1948 or 1949. The text presented below, however, is a new transliteration and translation. The new version is considerably closer at many points to the copy-text than is Russell's interlinear version, especially in its published forms, with all of which it has been collated.

The "Greek Exercises" are in a black exercise book that has been rebound with beige tape (RA 220.010010). The notebook has ninety-six pages, of which the journal occupies the first forty-nine; the first page carries the title as well as the first entry, and the title appears to be contemporaneous. Russell used the other end of the notebook for a variety of purposes over a considerable period of time. First there are eleven pages of arithmetic. Next there is a short translation (Xenophon's *Anabasis*, I.i.8), followed by calculations on lines tangent to ellipses. Then there are four pages of exercises on infinite series and De Moivre's theorem, taken from Chaps. 19 and 20 of Todhunter's *Plane Trigonometry* (1859). Some lines from Wordsworth's "Ode: Intimations of Immortality" and Cowper's poem "To Mary" follow. Between them are six stanzas of Goethe's "Mason-Lodge" as translated in Thomas Carlyle's *Past and Present*, Bk. III, Chap. 15. Following the poetry is a scrawled message about bad eyesight (a condition noted by Wood *1957*, 22). Finally there are two notes (dated 1888) on Grimm's law with classified lists of Greek, German, Latin and English vocabulary. (For a quotation from these notes, see A18: 7.) The handwriting, in conjunction with the dated notes on Grimm's law, suggests that all these pages (except for the early arithmetic exercises) were written over the same period in 1888, extending possibly to early 1889.

EIGHTEEN EIGHTY-EIGHT. *March 3.* I shall write about some subjects especially religious ones which now interest me. I have in consequence of a variety of circumstances come to look into the very foundations of the religion in which I have been brought up. On some points my conclusions have been to confirm my former creed, while on others I have been irresistibly led to such conclusions as would not only shock my people, but have given me much pain. I have arrived at certainty in few things but my opinions, even where not convictions are on some things nearly such. I have not the courage to tell my people that I scarcely believe in 10 immortality. I used to speak freely to Mr. Ewen on such matters, but now I cannot let out my thoughts to any one, and this is the only means I have of letting off steam. I intend to discuss some of my puzzles here.

2

*9th.* I read an article in the *Nineteenth Century* today about genius and madness. I was much interested by it. Some few of the characteristics mentioned as denoting genius while showing a tendency to madness I believe I can discern in myself. Such are, sexual passion which I have lately had great difficulty in resisting, and a tinge of melancholy which I have often had lately and which makes me anxious to go to this tutor's as there I shall 20 probably be too much occupied to indulge such thoughts. Also he mentions a desire to commit suicide, which though hitherto very slight, has lately been present more or less with me in particular when up a tree. I should say it is quite possible I may develop more or less peculiarity if I am kept at home much longer. The melancholy in me is I think chiefly caused by the reserve which prompted the writing of this, and which is necessary owing to my opinions.

3

*19th.* I mean today to put down my grounds for belief in God. I may say to begin with that I do believe in God and that I should call myself a theist if I 30 had to give my creed a name. Now in finding reasons for belief in God I shall only take account of scientific arguments. This is a vow I have made, which costs me much to keep and to reject all sentiment. To find then scientific grounds for a belief in God we must go back to the beginning of all things. We know that if the present laws of nature have always been in force, the exact quantity of matter and energy now in the universe must always have been in existence; but the nebular hypothesis points to no distant date for the time when the whole universe was filled with undifferentiated nebulous matter. Hence it is quite possible that the matter and force now in existence

may have had a creation, which clearly could be only by divine power. But
even granting that they have always been in existence, yet whence come the
laws which regulate the action of force on matter? I think they are only
attributable to a divine controlling power, which I accordingly call God.

4

*March 22.* In my last exercise I proved the existence of God by the
uniformity of nature, and the persistence of certain laws in all her ways.
Now let us look into the reasonableness of this reasoning. Let us suppose
that the universe we now see has as some suppose grown by mere chance.
10 Should we then expect every atom to act in any given conditions precisely
similarly to another atom? I think if atoms be lifeless, there is no reason to
expect them to do anything without a controlling power. If on the other
hand they be endowed with free will we are forced to the conclusion that all
atoms in the universe have combined in the commonwealth and have made
laws which none of them ever break. This is clearly an absurd hypothesis,
and therefore we are forced to believe in God. But this way of proving his
existence at the same time disproves miracles and other supposed manifestations of divine power. It does not however disprove their possibility for of
course the maker of laws can also unmake them. We may arrive in another
20 way at a disbelief in miracles. For if God is maker of the laws, surely it would
imply an imperfection in the law if it had to be altered occasionally, and such
imperfection we can never impute to the divine nature. (As in the Bible,
God repented him of the work).

5

*April 2nd.* I now come to the subject which personally interests us poor
mortals more perhaps than any other. I mean, the question of immortality.
This is the one in which I have been most disappointed and pained by
thought. There are two ways of looking at it. First, by evolution, and comparing man to animals, second by comparing man with God. The first is the
30 more scientific, for we know all about the animals, but not about God. Well,
I hold that, taking free will first to consider, there is no clear dividing line
between man and the protozoon. Therefore if we give free will to man, we
must give it also to the protozoon. This is rather hard to do. Therefore
unless we are willing to give free will to the protozoon, we must not give it to
man. This however is possible, but it is difficult to imagine, if, as seems to
me probable, protoplasm only came together in the ordinary course of nature, without any special providence from God, then we and all living things
are simply kept going by chemical forces and are nothing more wonderful
than a tree (which no one pretends has free will) and even if we had a good

enough knowledge of the forces acting on anyone at any time, the motives pro and con, the constitution of his brain at any time, then we could tell exactly what he will do. Again from the religious point of view, free will is a very arrogant thing for us to claim for of course it is an interruption of God's laws, for by his ordinary laws all our actions would be fixed as the stars. I think we must leave to God the primary establishment of laws which are never broken and determine everybody's doings. And not having free will we cannot have immortality.

6

*Monday April 9.* Miss Bühler has been here for nearly a fortnight now. 10 Yesterday we went to a Unitarian Chapel at Ealing. There were very few there and it was children's service. Yet Mr. Muirhead managed to make himself very agreeable. He preached on service. I was much struck by the way of conducting the service. The children were running about till just as it was beginning. Then immediately they all became silent and remained so till the end of the service. I do wish I believed in the life eternal. For it makes me quite miserable to think man is merely a kind of machine endowed unhappily for himself with consciousness. But no other theory is consistent with the complete omnipotence of God, of which science I think gives ample manifestations. Thus I must either be an atheist or disbelieve in immortal- 20 ity. Finding the first impossible, I adopt the second, and let no one know. I think, however disappointing may be this view of man, it does give us a wonderful idea of God's greatness to think that he can in the beginning create laws which, by acting on a mere mass of nebulous matter perhaps merely ether diffused through this part of the universe, will produce creatures like ourselves, conscious not only of our existence but even able to fathom to a certain extent God's mysteries! All this with no more intervention on his part! Now let us think whether this doctrine of want of free will is so absurd. If we talk about it to any one, they kick their legs or something of that sort. But perhaps they cannot help it, for they have something to prove 30 and therefore that supplies a motive to them to do it. Thus in anything we do we always have motives which determine us. Also there is no line of demarcation between Shakespeare or Herbert Spencer and a Papuan. But between them and a Papuan there seems as much difference as between a Papuan and a monkey.

7

*April 14th.* Yet there are great difficulties in the way of this doctrine that man has not immortality, nor free will, nor a soul, in short, that he is nothing more than a species of ingenious machine endowed with consciousness. For consciousness in itself is a quality quite distinguishing men from dead 40

matter. And if they have one thing different from dead matter, why not another, free will? (By free will I mean, that they do not for example obey the first law of motion, or at least that the direction in which the energies they contain is employed depends not entirely on external circumstances). Moreover, it seems impossible to imagine that man, the great man, with his reason, his knowledge of the universe; and his ideas of right and wrong, man, with his emotions, his love and hate, and his religion, that this man, should be a mere perishable chemical compound, whose character, and his influence for good or for evil, depends solely and entirely on the particular
10 motions of the molecules of his brain, and that all the greatest men have been great by reason of some one molecule hitting up against some other a little oftener than in other men! Does not this seem utterly incredible, and must not any one be mad who believes in such an absurdity? But what is the alternative? That (accepting the evolution theory, which is practically proved), apes having gradually increased in intelligence, God suddenly, by a miracle, endowed one with that wonderful reason which it is a mystery how we possess. Then is man, truly called the most glorious work of God, is man destined to perish utterly, after he has been so many ages in evolving? We cannot say; but I prefer that idea to God's having needed a miracle to
20 produce man, and now leaving him free to do as he likes.

8

*April 18th*. Accepting then the theory that man is mortal, and destitute of free will (which is as much as ever a mere theory, as of course all these kinds of things are mere speculations), what idea can we form of right and wrong? Many say, if you make any mention of such an absurd doctrine as predestination (which comes to much the same thing, though parsons don't think so), why what becomes of conscience, etc. (which they think has been directly implanted in man by God). Now my idea is that our conscience is in the first place due to evolution, which would of course form instincts of
30 self-preservation, and in the second place, to civilization and education, which introduces great refinements of the idea of self-preservation. Let us take for example the ten commandments as illustrative of primitive morality. Many of them are conducive to the quiet living of the community, which is best for the preservation of the species. Thus what is always considered the worst possible crime, and the one for which most remorse is felt, is murder, which is direct annihilation of the species. Again, as we know, among the Hebrews it was thought a mark of God's favour to have many children, while the childless were considered as cursed of God. Among the Romans also widows were hated, and I believe forbidden to remain unmar-
40 ried in Rome more than a year. Now why these peculiar ideas? Were they not simply because these objects of pity or dislike did not bring forth fresh

human beings? We can well understand how such ideas might grow up when men became rather sensible, for if murder and suicide were common in a tribe, that tribe would die out, and hence one which held such acts in abhorrence would have a great advantage. Of course among more educated societies these ideas are rather modified; my own I mean to give next time.

9

*April 20th.* Thus I think that primitive morality always originates in the idea of the preservation of the species. But is this a rule which a civilized community ought to follow? I think not. My rule of life, which I guide my conduct by and a departure from which I consider as a sin, is to act in the manner which I believe to be most likely to produce the greatest happiness, considering both the intensity of the happiness and the number of people made happy. I know that Granny considers this an impractical rule of life and says that since you can never know the thing which will produce greatest happiness, you do much better in following the inner voice. The conscience however can easily be seen to depend mostly upon education (as for example common Irishmen do not consider lying wrong), which fact alone seems to me quite sufficient to disprove the divine nature of conscience. And since, as I believe, conscience is merely the combined product of evolution and education, then obviously it is an absurdity to follow that rather than reason. And my reason tells me that it is better to act so as to produce maximum of happiness than in any other way. For I have tried to see what other object I could set before me, and I have failed. Not my own individual happiness in particular, but everybody's equally, making no distinction between myself, relations, friends or perfect strangers. In real life it makes very little difference to me as long as others are not of my opinion, for obviously where there is any chance of being found out, it is better to do what one's people consider right. My reason is, for this view, first that I can find no other, having been forced, as everybody must who seriously thinks about evolution, to give up the old idea of asking one's conscience, next that it seems to me that happiness is the great thing to seek after, and which practically all honest public men do seek after. As an application of the theory to practical life, I will say that in a case where nobody but myself was concerned (if indeed such a case exist), I should of course act entirely selfishly, to please myself. Suppose for another instance that I had the chance of saving a man whom I knew to be a bad man who would be better out of the world. Obviously, I should consult my own happiness better by plunging in after him. For if I lost my life, that would be a very neat way of managing it, and if I saved him I should have the pleasure of no end of praise. But if I let him drown, I should have lost an opportunity of death, and should have the misery of much blame, but the world would be the better for his loss, and, as I have some slight hope, for my life.

10

*April 25th.* I have begun reading Argyll's *Reign of Law*, and have read about half his chapter on the supernatural. I am much interested by it, but I think there are lots of fallacies in it. For example he seems to assume that there are lots of laws of nature, of which God chooses the ones necessary for his purpose, and by suitably choosing them performs an apparent miracle. But I think, very likely, that first, there is only one ultimate law of nature (since fresh discoveries tend to diminish their number, as gravitation reduced Kepler's laws to one, and as I hope before long all the inverse squares will be reduced to one law, and as I hope all elements will reduce to one, ether, their differences, on the vortex theory, being caused by different kinds of vortices), which law of nature is really pretty much the same as God (bearing about the same relation as the Logos in the gospel according to John); secondly, God, I should say, lets his laws act for themselves, and choosing them out in that way would be in itself an act of divine interven-tion, which I should have called a miracle. Many other things in the book struck me as unsound but perhaps I didn't understand them. I think this visit of Miss Bühler's has had a very good effect upon me; I don't often have fits of melancholy now, and I don't morosely cogitate over the idea which is now no longer an empty dream to me, but a grim truth:

> Life is but an empty dream
> For the soul is dead that slumbers
> And things are not what they seem.

I do hope they won't change their minds again about Southgate, for I feel being where there is some life would do me so much good, leaving me no time to cogitate and get melancholy and morose.

11

*April 29th.* In all things I have made the vow to follow reason, not the in-stincts inherited partly from my ancestors and gained gradually by them owing to a process of natural selection, and partly due to my education. How absurd it would be to follow these in the questions of right and wrong. For as I observed before, the inherited part can only be principles leading to the preservation of the species, or of that particular section of the species to which I belong. The part due to education is good or bad according to the individual education. Yet this inner voice, this God-given conscience which made Bloody Mary burn the Protestants, this is what we reasonable beings are to follow. I think this idea mad, and I endeavour to go by reason as far as possible. What I take as my ideal is that which ultimately produces greatest happiness of greatest number. Then I can apply reason to find out the course most conducive to this end. In my individual case, however, I can also go more or less by conscience, owing to the excellence of my education. But it is curious how people dislike the abandonment of brutish impulses for reason. I remember poor Ewen getting a whole dinner of argument owing to his running down impulse. Today again at tea Miss Bühler and I had a long discussion because I said that I followed reason not conscience in matters of right and wrong. I do hate having such peculiar opinions, because either I 10 must keep them bottled up, or else people are horrified at my scepticism, which is as bad with people one cares for as remaining bottled up. I shall be sorry when Miss Bühler goes, because I can open my heart easier to her than to my own people (strange to say).

12

*May 3*. Miss Bühler is gone and I am left again to loneliness and reserve. Happily however it seems all but settled that I am going to Southgate, and probably within the week. That will save me, I feel sure, from morose cogitations during the week, owing to the amount of activity of my life, and novelty at first. I do not expect that I shall enjoy myself at first, but after a 20 time I hope I shall. Certainly it will be good for my work, for my games, and my manners, and my future happiness I expect.

I am beginning to understand a possibility of the existence of free will. I am reading over again Argyll's chapter on the supernatural. I am much interested by his idea of miracles. He says they may be produced not by breaking through the laws of nature, but by the use of laws not commonly brought into play, i.e. of peculiar circumstances. Now may not we apply this argument to man and the animals? May we not say, in the ordinary course of nature, when the constituent parts of protoplasm came together, by a law at present quite beyond us, the compound formed was endowed 30 with a germ of consciousness certainly and possibly of free will? This germ, if it existed in the protozoon, may easily be conceived of as developing itself more and more until it has evolved into the marvellous product of nature which we behold in man. Even man may be only a prelude to something grander and more gifted still, which may even now be in process of evolution. I don't believe in the Duke when he says there is an obvious purpose running through all animals, which received its final attainment in man. For is there not just as much an evolution from the Papuan to a philosopher or a Newton, as from the monkey to the Papuan? May not this process of evolution continue until a being is evolved differing greatly from the man of 40 today? A being perfectly reasonable, without superstition, ?(able possibly to

comprehend the infinite,) and in many other, perhaps as yet inconceivable ways, superior to the greatest of modern philosophers? This loophole about free will, (which does not at all convince me of its actual existence, but only of its possibility) does not however affect my views on immortality. For there is another very strong argument which I did not insert in its place, namely, that the soul here below seems so inseparably bound up with the body, growing with it, weakened with it, sleeping with it, and affecting the brain and affected in return by anything abnormal in the brain. Wordsworth's "Intimations" are humbug, for it is obvious how the soul
10 grows with the body, not as he says, perfect from the first.

### 13

*May 4th.* I must write about prayer today, for that is a subject in which I feel that I do wrong every night. I think Argyll exactly hits it when he says that the apparently universal reign of law seems to show that God has subjected us also to its reign, and will therefore leave us to what it produces without leaving any room for prayer to alter our inexorable fate. Well let us go back to the very beginning of all things, that is, to the time when the present order of things began to exist. There existed then I suppose matter, of the same amount as now, but diffused through space, and perhaps resembling rather
20 ether than the present familiar forms of matter. Then probably force began to act on it, the energy in the universe being exactly equal to that in it now, when energy first existed. This force was controlled in its action, from the first I suppose, by Law. This law which we see now in nature is to my mind the great argument for the existence of God. For why, even presupposing the existence of force and matter in the universe, should the latter act on the former according to a general law, unless controlled by an all wise and all powerful Being? Now Law was, I should think, created so as to produce his purpose without any more interference on his part, for such is the highest wisdom. Now among other things which law did, it produced man, and to
30 the present day it rules him. Now we have no certain evidence that law ever has been broken by God, hence we infer that it never is. Therefore is it likely that God will break it just because we ask him? Prayer has no doubt, through the imagination, a good effect on those who believe in it, but not on others. Therefore I do not wish to spread my opinion on the subject.

### 14

*May 6th.* We went to Ealing again today, and Mr. Muirhead gave us a most excellent sermon; the subject was immortality, and especially the bearings it has had, and ought not to have, on practical morality. All the practical part of the sermon was splendid, in other words, I quite agreed with it. He said faith in immortality might be shaken by science, and hence it was bad to make morality rest on this doctrine, which moreover supplies a selfish motive for all good actions in holding out a future reward. He said also that it was held out to the poor and ill used as a justification of injustice, since all would be rectified hereafter. Although he believed in immortality, he said, he thought these uses should not be made of the doctrine, though why not I don't know, being logical consequences of it, whose absurdity ought properly to condemn their ground, which is belief in immortality. The moment he came to his grounds for belief, however, his excellence, to my mind, completely vanished. He said, for example, that owing to the advances of 10 science, immortality was now a matter of faith, not of demonstration. I should like to know what he meant. The only meaning I could think of was that though his reason told him the contrary, his "inner consciousness" told him of the falsehood of its conclusions. It is said that even such people as the Unitarians have not got over all old superstitions, and come to follow pure reason. I can understand a reasonable man believing in immortality, but evidently reason was not what convinced him. Argyll alludes to a very strong argument against immortality, which is the inseparable connection of brain and mind. I think this almost makes it plain that the mind retains memory only by storing up motions or possible motions of atoms of the 20 brain, which by being let loose, or by some arrangement or other now quite beyond science, produces recollection. I am getting quite resigned now to the idea of extinction after death, were it not for the restraint upon my speaking out which it imposes. I think there is much in Buddha's nirvana, where the good sleep in peace. For is not a good night a most pleasant thing? And is not a really sound sleep temporary cessation of the action of the mind? We are delivered from all troubles and anxieties, and are entirely forgetful of our existence. If this then is a happy state may we not wish to arrive in nirvana after death, and not dread it so? Also it makes goodness a much finer thing, as it takes from it all possibility of reward beyond internal 30 satisfaction. For this reason also it makes goodness harder to practise, and is therefore not a religion I should wish to spread among the masses, who might relapse into excesses of immorality.

15

*May 8th*. What a much happier life mine would be but for these wretched ideas of mine about theology. Tomorrow I go, and tonight Granny prayed a beautiful prayer for me in my new life, in which among other things she said: may he especially be taught to know God's infinite love for him. Well that is a prayer to which I can heartily say amen, and moreover it is one of which I stand in the greatest need. For according to my ideas of God we have 40 no particular reason to suppose he loves us. For he only set the machine in working order to begin with, and then left it to work out its own necessary consequences. Now you may say his laws are such as afford the greatest possible happiness to us mortals, but that is a statement of which there can be no proof. Hence I see no reason to believe in God's kindness towards me, and even the whole prayer was more or less a solemn farce to me, though I was truly much affected by the simple beauty of the prayer and her earnest way in saying it. What a thing it is to have such people! What might I be, had I been worse brought up!

By the way, to change to a more cheerful subject, Marshall and I had an awfully fine day of it. We went down to the river, marched into Broom Hall, bagged a boat of Frank's we found there, and rowed up the river beyond Kingston Bridge, without anybody at Broom Hall having seen us, except one old man who was lame. (Who the dickens he was I haven't the faintest idea). Marshall was awfully anxious to have some tea, and we came to an $n$th rate inn, which he thought would do. Having however like idiots left our jackets in the boat-house at Teddington, we had to march in without coats, and were served by the cheekiest of maids ever I saw, who said she thought we were the carpenters come to mend the house. Then we rowed back as hard as possible, and got home perspiring fearfully, and twenty minutes late, which produced a small row.

By the way, Horace has exactly Granny's idea of opinions like mine in his lines

> Parcus deorum cultor et infrequens
> Insanientis dum sapientiae
> Consultus erro.

16

*May 20th.* Here I am, home again for the first time from Southgate. It seems a pleasant place, but it is sad really to see the kind of boys that are common everywhere. No mind, no independent thought, no love of good books, nor of the higher refinements of morality, it is really sad that the upper classes of a civilized and (supposed to be) moral country can produce nothing better. I am glad I didn't go away from home before, as I should never have come to my present state had I done so, but should have been merely like one of them. (By the way, how terribly pharisaical I'm getting). I think the six months since Baillie went have made a great alteration in me. I have become of a calmer, thoughtfuller, poeticaller nature than I was. One little thing I think illustrates this well. I never before thought much of the views in spring, whereas this year I was so simply carried away by their beauty that I asked Granny if they were not more beautiful than usual, but she said not. I like poetry much better than I did, and have read over Shakespeare's historical plays with great delight, and long to read *In*

*Memoriam.* What beautiful lines for one who has a religion (which would that I had) are those in the motto to *The Reign of Law*:

> Let knowledge grow from more to more
> But more of reverence in us dwell
> That mind and soul according well
> May make one music as before
> But vaster....

I think those just about the finest lines I know. Would that wish were answered in me! I should like to believe my people's religion, which is just what I could wish, but alas, it is impossible. I have really no religion, for my  10
God, being a spirit shown merely by reason to exist, his properties utterly unknown, is no help to my life. I have not the parson's comfortable doctrine, that every good action has its reward, and every sin is forgiven. My whole religion is this: do your duty, and expect no reward for it, either here or hereafter.

17

*May 27th.* As I said last time, I attempt to work according to my principles, without the smallest expectation of reward, and even without using the light of conscience blindly as an infallible guide. Today I acted in a way which in my calm moments I know to be wrong, and which would for ever ruin my  20
character among my people. As Mr. Mauchlen tried to prove today, it is very difficult for anyone to walk aright with no aid from religion, by his own internal guidance merely. I have tried, and I may say, failed. But the sad thing is that I have no other resource. I have no helpful religion. My doctrines, such as they are, help my daily life no more than a formula in algebra. But *the* great inducement to a good life with me is Granny's love, and the immense pain I know it gives her when I go wrong. But she must I suppose, die some day, and where then will be my stay? I have the very greatest fear that my life may hereafter be ruined by my having lost the support of religion. I desire of all things that my religion should not spread, for I, of all  30
people, ought, owing to my education and the care taken of my moral wellbeing, to be of all people the most moral. So I believe I might be, were it not for these unhappy ideas of mine, for how easy it is, when one is much tempted, to convince oneself that only happiness will be produced by yielding to temptation, when, according to my ideas, the course one has been taught to abhor immediately becomes virtuous. If ever I become an utter wreck of what I hope to be, I think I shall bring forward this book as an explanation. We stand in want of a new Luther, to renovate and invigorate Christianity, and to do what the Unitarians would do if only they had a really great man such as Luther to lead them. For religions grow old like trees,  40

unless reformed from time to time. Christianity of the existing kinds has had its day. We want a new form in accordance with science and yet helpful to a good life.

18

*June 3rd.* It is extraordinary how few principles or dogmas I have been able to become convinced of. One after another I find my former undoubted beliefs slipping from me into the region of doubt. For example, I used never for a moment to doubt that truth was a good thing to get hold of. But now I have the very greatest doubt and uncertainty. For the search for truth has
10 led me to these results I have put in this book, whereas, had I been content to accept the teachings of my youth, I should have remained comfortable. The search for truth has shattered most of my old beliefs, and has made me commit what are probably sins where otherwise I should have kept clear of them. I do not think it has in any way made me happier; of course it has given me a deeper character, a contempt for trifles or mockery, but at the same time it has taken away cheerfulness, and made it much harder to make bosom friends, and worst of all, it has debarred me from free intercourse with my people, and thus made them strangers to some of my deepest thoughts, which, if by any mischance I do let them out, immediately be-
20 come the subject for mockery which is inexpressibly bitter to me, though not unkindly meant. Thus, in my individual case, I should say, the effects of a search for truth have been more bad than good. But the truth which I accept as such, may be said not to be truth, and I may be told that if I get at real truth I shall be made happier by it, but this is a very doubtful proposition. Hence I have great doubts of the unmixed advantage of truth. Certainly truth in biology lowers one's idea of man, which must be painful. Moreover truth estranges former friends and prevents the making of new ones, which is also a bad thing. One ought perhaps to look upon all these things as a martyrdom, since very often truth attained by one man may lead
30 to the increase in the happiness of many others, though not to his own. On the whole, I am inclined to continue to pursue truth, though truth of the kind in this book (if that indeed be truth) I have no desire to spread, but rather to prevent from spreading.

19

*July 15th.* My holidays have begun about a week now, and I am getting used to home and beginning to regard Southgate as an evil dream of the past. For although I tell people I like it very much, yet really, though better than I expected, life there has great trials and hardships. I don't suppose anybody hates disturbance as I do, or can so ill stand mockery, though to outward
40 appearance I keep my temper all right. Being made to sing, to climb on

chairs, to get up for a sponging in the middle of the night, is to me fifty times more detestable than to others. I always have to go through, in a moment, a long train of reasoning as to the best thing to say or do (for I have sufficient self-control to do what I think best), and the excitement, which to others might appear small, leaves me trembling and exhausted. However, I think it is an excellent thing for me, as it increases my capacity for enjoyment, and strengthens me morally to a very considerable extent. I shan't forget in a hurry their amazement that I had never said a damn, which, with things like it, goes near to making me a "fanfaron de crimes". This, however, is a bad thing to be, when only too many real crimes are committed, as example is 10 the best possible thing for chaps like Williams, who, with a home education, might have made a pretty decent chap.—I am glad I didn't go to school before; I should have wanted strength, and have had no time for the original thought, which, though it has caused me much pain, is yet my chief stay and support in troubles. I am always kept up by a feeling of contempt, erroneous though it may be, for all who "despitefully use me and persecute me". I don't think contempt is misplaced when a chap's habitual language is about something like "who put me on my cold cold pot, whether I would or not? My mother", sung to the tune of "thy will be done". Had my education, however, been the least bit less perfect than it is, I should probably have 20 been the same. But I feel I enjoy myself at home much better than ever before, which, with an imaginary feeling of heroism, reconciles me to a great deal of unhappiness at Southgate.

20

*30th July 1888.* In numbers fifth, sixth and seventh I have treated of free will and immortality. Now however I should not say what I then said, that without free will, immortality is impossible. Force and matter are most likely wanting in free will, yet they have immortality. So that argument is done for. In fact, since then, the question of free will has only grown clearer and clearer to me, while immortality remains wrapped in uncertainty. I will 30 here make an exposition of my views about free will, and in the next, say what I can about the other.

There are about three different, though comerging, ways of looking at this question of free will, first, from the omnipotence of God, second, from the reign of law, and third, from the fact that all our actions, if looked into, show themselves as caused by motives. These three ways we see at once to be really identical, for God's omnipotence is the same thing as the reign of law, and the determination of actions by motives is the particular form which the reign of law takes in man. Let us now examine closely each of these ways.

First, from the omnipotence of God. What do we mean, in the first place, 40 by free will? We mean that where several courses are open to us, we can choose any one. But according to this definition, we are not ruled by God, and alone of created things, we are independent of him. That appears unlikely, but is by no means impossible, since his omnipotence is only an inference. Let us then pass on to the

Second, from the reign of law. Of all the things we know, except perhaps the higher animals, it is obvious, that law is completely the master. That man is also under its dominion, appears from a fact such as Grimm's law, and again from the fact that it is possible sometimes to predict human actions. If man, then, be subject to law, does not this mean, that his actions are
10 predetermined, just as much as the motions of a planet or the growth of a plant? The Duke of Argyll indeed speaks of freedom within the bounds of law, but to me that's an unmeaning phrase, for subjection to law must mean a certain consequence always following in given conditions. No doubt different people in the same circumstances act differently, but that is only owing to difference of character, just as two comets in the same position move differently because of differences in their eccentricities.

The third, from the consideration of motives, is about the strongest. For if we examine any action whatsoever, we find always motives, over which we have no more control than matter over the forces acting on it,
20 which produce our actions. The Duke of Argyll says we can present motives to ourselves, but is not that an action, determined by our character, and other unavoidable things.

The argument for free will from the fact that we feel it, is worthless, for we do not feel motives which we find really exist, nor that mind depends on brain, etc. But I am not prepared dogmatically to deny free will, for I have often found that good arguments don't present themselves on one side of a question till they are told one. My nature may incline me to disbelieve free will, and there may be very excellent arguments for free will which either I have never thought of, or else have not had their full weight with me. All my
30 arguments may be answerable, but my present opinion is that free will is a delusion, arising from the imperceptibility of the bonds that hold us. It is however a hard thought, and one which causes one at first much pain, for it reduces man to the level of a conscious steam engine or electric battery. It is impossible for us to imagine, although we find we must be, that we are

... only cunning casts in clay,

and we may say with the poet

Let science prove we are, and then
What matters science unto men?

We can scarcely continue to believe that "life is real, life is earnest", and it is difficult not to become reckless and commit suicide, which I believe I should do but for my people.

21

*July 31st.* I now come to that most difficult of subjects, immortality, a question I have already tried to answer in this book, but, as now seems to me, on false lines of reasoning. We cannot hope to answer it till all the prejudice which naturally settles round such a subject, all the natural yearning of our hearts to retain so comforting a doctrine ⟨is overcome?⟩. This aspect of the question is beautifully set forth in *In Memoriam*, so as almost to convince one that it is a true way of looking at it, where he says:    10

> ... and he, shall he,
> Man, her last work, who seemed so fair,
> ... etc. ...
> Be blown about the desert dust,
> Or sealed within the iron hills?
> No more? A monster, then, a dream,
> A discord....
> Oh life as futile, then, as frail,
> Oh for thy voice to soothe and bless
> What hope of answer or redress?    20
> Behind the veil, behind the veil.

He is right in one thing at least, that redress must be sought behind the veil, but he might add that it is a veil never to be lifted.—But to come to a serious discussion.—First, what is the soul? Very few most likely could answer such a question. My own answer is that it is anything distinguishing man utterly from dead matter, not merely as a steam engine differs from a lump of rock, but something impossible to suppose evolved from dead matter, which, if evolution from dead matter did take place, must have had a beginning at some definite time. We see at once that consciousness is included in this definition. It may be objected, that, if Clifford's hypothesis be true, 30 dead matter has "mind-stuff", or dormant consciousness. But that is no objection; for then inorganic matter is not dead, but has a soul. Accepting this definition, we see that man has a soul, for consciousness is undeniable, whatever else may be attacked. One of the many poetic arguments for immortality is that force and matter is immortal, and the soul is surely greater than these. The soul would hardly include vital force, for that is evolved by purely material processes from chemical force. But the soul, whatever its nature, is so bound up with the body, weakening with it in illness, strengthening with returning health, "mens sana in corpore sano", that

without the body we can hardly conceive of it. Trances, sleep, and such things, show how a suspension of the action of the body means suspension of that of the soul as well. The soul moreover is always connected with one permanent structure, the nerves, as life with protoplasm. All these facts tend to make one imagine that the bond of body and soul is indissoluble, both living and both dying together. Of course the resurrection of the body gets one out of this, but is manifestly absurd, for we see it rot in the ground. Let us not however dogmatically deny man's immortality, for innumerable "poetic" arguments may be urged in its favour, as that from man's great-
10 ness, (ably put forth by Tennyson in the piece a bit of which I quoted above,) and poetic arguments often have something in them. But let us despise those whose reason tells them they know nothing about it, but who fall back on "faith", which seems to me always to mean belief in something unreasonable, and is a most cowardly thing to call down upon us all as a divine gift.—
*Note.* Wordsworth's idea of immortality before death, that

> The soul which rises with us, our life's star,
> Has had elsewhere its setting, and cometh from afar,

seems to me to be utterly disproved by the fact of mental inheritance, which
20 *is* a perfectly well established fact. This shows, surely, that our soul comes from our parents, not, as Wordsworth says, from God.

⟨22⟩

*April '89*. Nature-worship. When it first occurred to me to doubt the existence of God I contented myself with the answer that order and government prevail throughout nature, showing signs of a ruling intelligence; that observed phenomena are the result of laws which themselves are the results of more general laws; that thus converging lines are built up, which must meet in a head, or first cause, which first cause we call God. This argument still appears to me perfectly satisfying to the intellect, but to the soul it is in-
30 sufficient. It makes belief in God a mere intellectual inference, which has no more bearing on practical life than the conservation of energy, or any other great scientific generalization. It cannot feed the soul or sustain it in times of despondency; indeed it does not even give any insight into the attributes of God, beyond a manifestation of infinite power and immutability.—But as I grew fonder of nature, and came more into harmony with her spirit, till I could fancy I heard the music of the spheres, a new aspect of God burst in upon me. In the calm of the moon, in the peace and silent vastness of the stars, in the boundless freedom of the ocean, in the holy tenderness of dawn, in the soothing sweetness of spring woods, in all these a soul appeared, with

which my soul could commune, if but imperfectly; this seemed as the eye, through which the beauty of the soul within shone forth; then could I "hold converse with nature", not as a mere lifeless machine, but as a living soul, a soul perfect in all those things which our highest aspirations seek after; perfect in wisdom, love, power, beauty, harmony, constancy, tenderness; a soul whose voice can be heard when that of the world is hushed, speaking to man through nature, more and more clearly as he becomes more and more one with nature, until it seems to transcend all earthly voices and to be the one certain reality.—

Herein indeed lies the beauty of nature, and the comfort it can afford 10 when the spirit is vexed with doubt, when peace seems a thing never more to bless the soul; then the blessed influence of the stars or the moon descends like balm upon the soul; a peace and calm seem to reign over all, and all jar and discord flee away—and is it reasonable to suppose such influence to lurk in mere lifeless matter? What is the beauty in art, in painting or sculpture, unless it be the soul that manifests itself in the canvas or the marble? And is not the same true of nature? Can inanimate speak to animate? Is not rather the soul which is manifested in nature as much more perfect than the soul of painter or sculptor, as nature is more perfect than art? In human handiwork perfection can never be attained; in nature, perfection appears at every turn, 20 manifesting the perfect soul of the creator.—Thus God has become a part of my life, an ever present influence, moulding my action and my thought, comforting me in dejection and soothing me in inquietude.—Whether this faith be mere poetic sentimentalism, as a year ago I should have pronounced it to be, I know not; but this I do know, that it brightens my life, and harmonizes with all my highest. Let it then remain and bear fruit.

## 2–8

# Essay Notebook [1889]

TO PREPARE FOR the scholarship examination at Trinity College, Cambridge, in December 1889, Russell attended "an Army crammer at Old Southgate" for eighteen months (Russell *1967*, 42). At this school, B. A. Green's University and Army Tutors, in Southgate, London, he wrote various papers, seven of which survive in a notebook in his archives. The titles appear as follows:

2 How far does a country's prosperity depend on Natural Resources (pp. 1–3)
3 Evolution as affecting modern Political Science (pp. 6–11)
4 State-Socialism (pp. 16–21)
5 The Advantages & Disadvantages of Party Government, / & the conditions necessary for its Success (pp. 22–31)
6 "The Language of a Nation is a monument to which every / forcible individual in the course of ages has contributed a stone." (pp. 32–9)
7 Contentment; its good & bad points (pp. 40–3)
8 Destruction must precede Construction (pp. 44–50)

Given his age and the nature of the school, it is unlikely that Russell chose these topics himself, but the pertinence of the contemporary social and political allusions in the papers shows that the topics were congenial to him.

The papers bear alterations in two hands. Most likely his tutor made the stylistic changes in Paper 7, and the same hand has written the title for Paper 8—taking over a phrase Russell himself used towards the end of 7. But most of the alterations are in Russell's hand, and the large number of word and phrase substitutions are evidence of an early determination to develop his style.

When he was revising the draft of his *Autobiography* late in the 1940s, Russell intended to insert two of the papers in the second chapter of Volume I. He wrote at the end of the paragraph that he added on Southgate (*1967*, 46): "I wrote essays as part of the preparation for the Scholarship Examination; one, on 'Evolution as affecting modern political science', and another on 'State-Socialism', will show what my opinions were" (RA 210.007050–F1). The papers were first shifted to the end of the chapter and then deleted altogether, along with the passage referring to them (see Russell's letter of 21 September 1949 to Rupert Crawshay-Williams and RA 210.007052–F1).

The copy-text is the notebook (RA 220.010020), which is bound in a soft, green cover with the ink inscription "B. Russell / Essay" on the front. The year, 1889, has been added in pencil—perhaps late in the 1940s, when Russell was working on his archives. (His typescripts of **3** and **4** are both annotated "written in 1889" in his secretary's hand.) In the same notebook are several untitled translations from Latin (Virgil, *Aeneid*, IX.424–45; Cicero, *De amicitia*, 100; Phaedrus, *Liber fabularum*, 3.357–74; and Livy, *History*, 22.49.6–12). These exercises are not printed here. On p. 12 of the notebook Russell made a list that may have been a plan for **4**: "I. History. II. Theoretic aspects. III. Future of Socialism." The single sentence, "Since it lessens nothing of our pain, why do we uselessly wish to be shameful?", is found at the top of p. 14. It may be a translation or it may be an autobiographical remark.

## 2  How Far Does a Country's Prosperity Depend on Natural Resources [1889]

THE QUESTION OF the causes which produce the social state of a country is a very complex one, and it is often very difficult to unravel the multitude of coexistent and often conflicting agencies which, combined, bring about the existing condition of things. The only way in which we can hope to form an estimate of the relative importance of these agencies is by a careful study of History, a study, that is, not of the history of kings and wars merely, but of the history of peoples. It may indeed be
10 possible to establish some few economic laws by abstract reasoning, but in general such reasoning will be found not to have foreseen all the forces which will be brought into play, and it is therefore not so safe a guide as History. By a study of History we shall be brought to the conclusion that Natural Resources are certainly one, though probably not one of the most powerful, of the forces which tend to bring prosperity to a people.

Before going further, it may be well to examine the exact meaning which we attach to the term Natural Resources. We might at first sight be inclined to include under this head only the natural fertility or habitability of the soil, and in dealing with an uncivilized community this might be a sufficiently
20 wide definition. But as a nation becomes more civilized, and acquires a greater dominion over Nature, Natural Resources become more numerous and more complex. We have now to take into account the suitability for commerce (which is in itself the result of many causes), the suitability for manufactures, (which requires mines of iron and coal), and other causes; before which the natural fertility of the soil sinks into insignificance. Climate must also be included as a separate cause, since it affects character, and character is one of the most important agents.

These are the principal Natural Resources, and their importance may be at once seen by a comparison of the nations of modern Europe. England,
30 which possesses almost all the natural resources possible to a country (except extreme fertility, which, in tending to produce lethargy, is rather an obstacle than a help to prosperity), is by far the wealthiest of modern European states; while states, such as Austria, which have a small sea-coast and no coal, are comparatively very poor.

But among European nations, other causes of prosperity are to a great extent equally strong; civilization, knowledge, fiscal administration; in these there is no very great difference between them, and therefore the difference between Natural Resources has a clear field for producing its results. If we compare two nations at a very different level in civilization, we
40 shall see at once how much more important this is than Natural Resources. When England, with all the resources which it has now, was nothing but a

24

forest thinly populated with uncivilized tribes which lived on fruits and berries and the produce of the chase, the cities of Assyria and Egypt, in the midst of what are now vast wildernesses, with no advantage but the energy and superior civilization of their populations, were full of magnificent palaces stocked with masses of wealth such as no modern sovereign can boast and abounding in luxuries and comforts such as are now unknown even to the most luxurious.—Natural Resources are then useless until civilization has given man a control over them; when this control has been acquired, they minister to his comfort and wealth in a way which would before have seemed impossible. Our object, then, must be to acquire this control as far as possible; the manner of acquiring it is to endeavour to discover Natural Laws, and then to act as far as possible in conformity with them. And here we see, almost more clearly than anywhere else, the truth of the saying: Knowledge is Power.

## 3   Evolution as Affecting Modern Political Science [1889]

THE SCIENCE OF Politics is probably of all Sciences the most complex. For the complexity of a Science depends upon the complexity of the object of its speculations. Thus organic chemistry is more complex than inorganic, Biology is more complex than Physics, and a Science which deals with Man, the most complex of all the known works of Nature, is necessarily the most complex of all Sciences.—In the Science of Politics, the object in view is so to investigate the motives of human action and the causes of human happiness as to be able to present such motives to each individual and to each community as shall tend most to the happiness of the race. It is a necessary part in this investigation to discover what causes tend most to happiness, and this question is that which is most usually understood under the name of the Science of Politics.

This question is one of great difficulty, and one on which at different times very different opinions have been entertained. It has usually been held that civilization is a producer of happiness, and that increase of knowledge is increase not of sorrow, but of happiness. Whether this be so or not, we may for the moment consider the object of legislation to be increase of civilization, and accepting this view, we shall see how it comes that Evolution has so profoundly affected the political thought of certain philosophers of the day.

For, accepting the theory of Evolution, we are brought at once to the fact that Nature, if left to herself, constantly causes a developement and differentiation of life, and by a gradual but continual progress produces a higher type from a lower. We say then, by a very safe Induction, that Nature

left to herself will continue her process of developement with Man, and will perfect his mind more and more, until possibly a new type may be produced, with a mind capable of ideas which to the present mind are inconceivable. The obvious application to practical Politics is that State Interference is useless, nay, even harmful, since it interferes with the Struggle for Existence, and this Struggle is the means by which Nature produces her developements. The whole Science of Politics is thus reduced to the question of how free competition may be best encouraged, so as best to secure the Survival of the Fittest. This is the aim of Herbert Spencer's *Sociology*, and in
10 the light of abstract reason there seems little to be said against it. But in a question such as Politics, it is well to test our results by their practical application, for a false assumption or hypothesis at the outset will vitiate all results deduced from it, and an entirely true hypothesis is very difficult to obtain. In practice, most unprejudiced people will agree that State Interference may sometimes be useful even where it does interfere with the Struggle for Existence; for instance, in the case of the Factory Acts. At the time of their passing the old "laissez-faire" school of politicians was still strong, but in the face of the revelations of Commissions of Enquiry it became impossible to stop interference any longer. The Modern Evolutionist "laissez-faire"
20 takes its stand on slightly different grounds from the old Economists, since the fierceness of competition is the very means by which it looks for the attainment of its ends; but if a system would lead us to allow the continuance of such a state of things as existed formerly among factory hands, we are inclined to question the system, and indeed it will have to be considerably modified if it is to be applied to practice.

But if this inductive investigation do not agree with the deductive, then, since the deduction from our first principle was clearly logical, it follows that our first principle was at fault. This first principle was, that the sole object of government is progress in civilization. We cannot then take this as
30 the sole object of government, although we may still consider it the principal object. It will be found necessary to take some account of present happiness, and to mitigate the hardships of competition to a certain extent. It may be found possible to effect this without ultimately interfering with the survival of the fittest, but the means of combining the two do not come within our present subject.

On the other hand some interference to encourage the Survival of the Fittest might be put into operation, and thus hasten the working of Nature, which operates so slowly that its progress is almost imperceptible. Interference in the form of compulsory education also is conducive to the aim of
40 Evolutionists, by making the Fittest still more fit.

State Interference would then seem to be desirable to a certain extent, but in general private enterprise and cooperation should be preferred, since it calls beneficial influences into play in obtaining its end, whereas State Interference acts as a discouragement to energy and even puts a premium on inactivity. Some things, however, cannot be done by private enterprise unless there be a union and cooperation throughout the whole country, and in such a case it would seem fair that the majority should force the minority to comply with the interests of the whole. In fact it is acknowledged now by all practical politicians that State Interference must sometimes be resorted to, and every year stronger cases of Interference occur, until even Free Contract is broken, as in the case of the Irish leaseholds. Socialism in some form or other seems inevitably coming on, and although it is clearly a retrograde movement, it may be a necessary stage in the progress towards perfect lib- 10 erty, when, as among Swift's Houyhnhnms, government shall no longer be necessary, but all shall work together for the good of the whole.

The Individualistic theories of Evolutionists, then, can clearly not be rigidly carried out in practice; and even if we accept their view of the operation of Nature as a developer, we may surely seek to find gentler and rapider methods than that of the Survival of the Fittest, which is more cruel in its operation than the most bloodthirsty of tyrants. Indeed the whole object of government is to prevent the hardships which Nature would cause, and the Evolutionist policy is an acknowledgement of utter failure on the part of government which does not appear to find any warrant in History.—Our 20 conclusion is, then, that so long as men have not sufficient self-restraint and wisdom to neglect their individual interests in favour of those of the community, perfect individual freedom cannot be allowed them; that the Struggle for Existence should rather be mitigated than fostered; and that Civilization and Education must be sought by other means, if anything is to be left of either. Nevertheless, we may learn a lesson from Nature's methods, and endeavour to make our march towards wisdom as sure and continual as Nature's developement of ever higher and higher types, and not disgrace her by letting the progress stop at its present stage.

## 4   State-Socialism [1889]                                                30

I N THE LAST century there has been a great movement and stirring of minds on the subject of government, and many ancient principles which had not been doubted from the times of the ancient Greeks have been overthrown, and a science of Political Economy has begun to grow up and to bear fruit in practical legislation. This Science, however, is hitherto only in its infancy, and its principles are not yet very fixed or certain. The result of the overthrow of old theories is to foster the rise of many new theories, most having a certain element of truth which causes their acceptance among a certain class of people. Let us briefly glance at the rise of this Science and these theories, and endeavour to see by their practical working how far they are true or false.

The Science of Political Economy can scarcely be said to have existed before Adam Smith. His book was the first which treated the subject in anything like a scientific spirit, and he was the first who dared to attack the principle of State Interference, which had until then always received a larger or smaller share of acceptance among Politicians. His principles were eagerly taken up by Pitt, but owing to the French War, they were, with all
10 other reforms, put off for many years, and were not put into practice until theory had advanced a long way beyond the stage at which Adam Smith left it. His fundamental principle, the doctrine that Nature, if left to herself, will tend to prosperity and comfort, (which he based chiefly on religious considerations) had been denied by Malthus and Ricardo, but his deduction, that the best government is that which allows most individual freedom, had been confirmed on other grounds. It was said that the population always rises to the highest level at which existence is possible, and that any legislation made with the object of improving the condition of the working classes could only stimulate the increase of population, but could not per-
20 manently raise those whom it was desired to benefit. Nature was no longer regarded as a beneficent agent, but it was thought that legislation could only aggravate the evil it was designed to mitigate. "Laissez-faire" was then the wisest policy of a ruler, although things would not naturally tend to good. This doctrine was so gloomy that it caused the Science to be hated by all who knew but little of it; but its gloominess made it impossible it should last long. The fact that the population tends to increase until wages fall to starvation level seemed undeniable, but the second principle, that State Interference must always be rendered nugatory by this increase, did not seem equally certain. It seemed that the tendency to increase of population might
30 be lessened by raising the standard of education and comfort of the working classes, and that such a rise was possible could be seen by cases which had occurred in history. For example, after the Black Death, in spite of the two Statutes of Labourers, the scarcity of labour caused a rise of wages which raised the standard of comfort of the working classes generally, and which caused that higher standard to be permanently maintained.—This rise had been effected, it is true, not by State Interference, but by an external accidental cause; nevertheless by State Interference it was thought that something might be done, and this gave rise to the Socialist school of Economists. Even those who refused to accept Socialism, and looked on Competition as
40 the great producer of all improvement, acknowledged that State Interference might sometimes be useful, and the rigid "laissez-faire" doctrine is now abandoned by all who have any connection with practical work. Indeed of late years socialistic legislation has become very common, and the State

now recognises in England hardly anything with which it may not interfere. It compels Education, it regulates hours of labour, it forces landowners to sell their land to railways and to let it in allotments to labourers who wish to give their spare time to agriculture, it interferes between landlord and tenant and even breaks leases. In some respects, however, the "laissez-faire" doctrine has had a practical lasting effect; for example, in the question of Pauperism. This most difficult question first came into notice under Elizabeth, when the Poor Law was passed, whose disastrous effects formed a strong point of attack for the Individualists. In concession to them workhouses were made much less comfortable, outdoor relief was greatly re- 10 stricted, and the condition of a pauper was made much less enviable. This legislation doubtless had a very good effect, but it is doubtful whether it went far enough. The mere existence of workhouses is to many a great encouragement to idleness or extravagance, and many labourers who receive good wages save nothing for illness or old age, but count on ending their days in the workhouse or the hospital. So long as workhouses exist it is impossible to make such men thrifty, but to abolish workhouses would seem a step backwards towards barbarism, and few would say that the poor and destitute should in no way be provided for. The question is, however, so intricate and difficult that it cannot be decided here, and any abstract prin- 20 ciple, such as the Survival of the Fittest, by which we attempt to solve it, is almost sure to be found to fail in its application to details.

In the question of Pauperism, then, Socialistic legislation has hitherto been prevented; but in most other Economic questions it has been steadily creeping in in practice, and Socialistic ideas have been steadily gaining ground among theorists. A narrow section of theorists, indeed, following Herbert Spencer and the Evolutionists, have raised the standard of thorough "laissez-faire" once more, but at present they have no disciples among practical politicians, and their ideas do not seem to be in any way gaining ground. On the contrary, in practical politics State Interference is 30 becoming commoner and commoner, and although some of the great principles of the "laissez-faire" school have been permanently established, yet Socialism both in theory and practice seems to be a growing force. The immense harm which it may do has been shown in the case of such Socialistic institutions as have from time to time been established (as the Poor Law for example); but if judiciously carried out it may improve the moral and intellectual as well as the physical condition of the poor, and it may prevent the evils of a floating population of unemployed. It is more likely, however, to produce apathy and laziness among labourers, to make their work less efficient, to remove the stimulus to improvement which is afforded by com- 40 petition, and to sap our civilization at its foundation. It should, then, be fought against by all who wish sturdiness and energy to be maintained, and those forces which have produced our civilization to continue to perfect it.

## 5  The Advantages and Disadvantages of Party Government, and the Conditions Necessary for Its Success  [1889]

I N DISCUSSING THE merits of any system of government it is well to
determine first what we consider to be the object of government. Its
most immediate object, of course, is the protection of peaceable citizens
and the maintenance of order; but this is secured by any government which
is strong, and the advantages of any system must therefore be judged by its
efficiency in securing further objects. These further objects are very different in their relative importance in different times and places. In the small
10 states of ancient times, the most important had relation to war; the protection from foreign attacks and the increase of fighting power were the ends at
which most policies aimed. But when states became larger and civilization
produced new phases of society, war occupied a smaller portion of mankind, while new questions arose out of the new state of society. These social
questions grew in importance, until today they occupy the most earnest
attention of both practical and theoretic politicians. In the government of
such a country as England, foreign policy, though still an important part, is
by no means the most important part of the functions of government. Questions of internal polity, questions of a social nature, are the really pressing
20 questions; though others may for a time supplant them, and put them out of
sight, they are sure soon again to obtrude themselves on our notice, all the
more forcibly for the temporary neglect of them.

Thus the functions of government change with changing time and place;
and it is natural that a change of function should cause a change in system
also. This change, where natural growth has not been hindered, has taken
place very generally in modern times; in some countries it has taken the
form of a gradual developement, in others of a sudden revolution. The
change has been from the government of a man or of a class to the government of the people. It is clearly the result of the change in the functions of
30 government; for while foreign policy was the principal thing, a continued
policy and prompt action were the most important objects for successful
legislation. But now, when the improvement of the condition of the people
and the settling of the Social Problem are the vital questions, the Government most likely to secure this end is a Democracy, where the legislators
express the spirit of those for whom they legislate. This form of government, however, is very ill suited for a resolute foreign policy, for conducting
great wars or forming firm alliances, for the people are always changing, and
a policy begun today may tomorrow be broken off in favour of its exact
opposite. Thus it is only the modern state of society which has produced
40 Democracy, and as a necessary corollary, Party Government. For Democracy without Party Government has never yet been known and is scarcely

conceivable. When a number of men meet together to undertake Government, there are certain to be some prominent questions which form the policy of the day, and on these questions men are sure to combine into camps according to their opinions, regardless of differences on other subjects. In the supreme desire of securing these objects, other objects in themselves important will be sunk so as to gain the strength of unity in opposing those with opposite objects; and thus Party Government is at once the result.

Its advantages in a Democratic country are very great; but its disadvantages are also considerable, at least in its present form. Its advantages are, that it enables a policy to be carried out in its minor details when it is in the main agreeable to the people; that it to a certain extent enables the leaders of a party (whose views are usually wider than those of their followers) to carry measures which, if judged independently by each member of the party, would be most certainly rejected. Thus, for example, Disraeli was enabled to pass the Reform Bill of '67, to which very nearly the whole Conservative Party would, but for his influence, have been opposed; but which, as it was, was resisted only by a few of the more independent. Thus also Peel passed the Repeal of the Corn Laws, which was never voted for by the people, and which, but for his individual influence, would very likely not have been passed to this day.

On the other hand the evils of Party Government are considerable, but they are mostly of a nature which can be remedied by a modification of the system, without necessitating any radical change. The greatest of the evils is, that in a partizan zeal for party, patriotism is often neglected; provided the interests of the party be furthered, it matters not at what cost to the nation or by what manner of means the furtherance be accomplished. It is thought and said, or at least assumed, that nothing good can be found in the aims of one party, nothing bad in the aims of the other; provided anything be taken up as a party cry, it is accepted without further thought by the members of the one party, and decried by those of the other. Also Party strife gives rise to canvassing and electioneering and wire-pulling, where principles are lost sight of in the battle of petty personalities and trivial animosities. Moreover party lessens a practical politician's independence, ties his hands to certain definite lines of policy, a desertion of which will infallibly deprive him of office and make him the butt of endless abuse for his inconsistency, as though any thinking man could be expected through years of changing circumstances to be always consistent, which assuredly is "the virtue of fools". Instead of leading the party to the wiser aims of its leader, it often drags the leader down to the level of his party, as in the case of the late Egyptian war, to which Gladstone was always opposed, but to which he was driven by party pressure. Owing to the iron rod of party, independent thought has no chance of affecting government except slowly

by moving the minds of party-leaders, which can seldom be done within the generation of the thinker. Many a thoughtful man is entirely prevented from taking part in practical politics by the inability to adhere to either party through thick and thin, and the unwillingness of all electioneering wire-pullers to have any candidate who is not certain always to stand by the party which elected him. The entire thoughtlessness with which even members of the House of Commons follow Party ties was well shown a short time ago by the case of the Allotments Bill. This was first introduced by the Liberals, and vigorously opposed by the Conservatives; but after the passing of the
10 Second Reading it was dropped until the new Parliament met. It was then introduced, substantially unaltered, by the Conservatives, and passed by their votes through a very Conservative House.—This case shows how Party Government blinds many even intelligent men to principles, and makes them judge a question solely by the party which brings it up.

Party Government has then many and great evils, but some form of it appears indispensible to Democracy. It would be much improved by being lessened in rigidity; if men were more encouraged to think for themselves, to choose their party after due reflection, and not to consider themselves bound thoughtlessly to accept the policy of their party, except where a re-
20 sistance to party on a minor point would entail graver consequences whose avoidance is of more importance than any minor question. In foreign affairs it might be well to allow a continuous policy to be carried out by one party so long as it is not of a nature to place the country in any serious danger, or to cause any serious injustice to be done; but in home questions, where a continuous policy is less essential, all who have thought much about any question should be listened to by all parties, and rigid adherence to party ought neither to be asked nor offered. Elections ought to be contested on principles, not simply because one man pledges himself, whatever changes may occur, always to support one party, while another pledges himself equally to
30 support another party. Party will still in the main be adhered to, for it is the result of a man's nature and lies deep ingrained in his character and modes of thought, so that the removal of all restrictions would still leave men supporters of the party which suited them, while it would prevent such strange distortions as the Tory Democrat, which result from the dislike of deserting party.

With some such modifications, Party Government might become the most efficient machine for turning the wheel of progress, and might enable Thought to establish a sway over Thoughtlessness which would be the grandest form of Government ever yet seen on this earth.

## 6 "The Language of a Nation Is a Monument to Which Every Forcible Individual in the Course of Ages Has Contributed a Stone." [1889]

IN THE STUDY of Language no less than in the study of History we are struck by a national character which marks different races and which feels any great wave of feeling which may move the minds of men. So clear does our perception of this character and its changes in time become that it may be used to supplement History where her more certain light fails us. Let us look more closely at the way in which this national character of the language arises, and the way in which it may be studied to most advantage. 10

The growth of Language, although its earlier stages are still to a certain extent a matter of doubt, may in its later developements be easily watched in any modern literature, and still better by a comparison of modern language with the primitive speech of such races as have never come in contact with civilization. Among these latter, there are no names for colours, for abstract nouns, for anything in short except the most concrete and tangible of daily surroundings. Something of this character may still be observed in the primitive literature of a nation first emerging from barbarism. Abstractions are few; the words are adapted for expressing broad meanings rather than fine shades of feeling; the language has few words for mental phenomena, 20 for emotions, thoughts, ideas; it is, in short, objective rather than subjective. If we now compare this language with that of a modern Poet, such as Shelley for example, we find an extraordinary developement of words which express abstract ideas; there is more capability of putting into words the deepest emotions of a feeling soul; although it must always be true to some extent that "language is but a broken light on the depths of the unspoken", still this is much less true with a cultured modern language than with one such as the mediaeval romance languages or the early Latin, as would soon be seen by the utter inability of the latter to express modern thought, and by the new meanings which have been put into old words. And this growth has 30 been effected mostly, if not wholly by those who have first conceived new ideas and first felt the want of a word to express it. Where an emotion is strongly felt, men will not remain long content without means of expressing it, although the expression of it will remain unintelligible to all who have not experienced the feeling. Thus literature is the great fertilizer of civilized language, for in literature a word becomes stereotyped for all future generations, and even if the author of the word be too much before his time for its immediate acceptance into common language, the word remains, and those who imbibe the ideas of its inventor will adopt the words expressing them also. Thus we have seen coined a multitude of philosophical words within 40 the last century, which express ideas before unknown, and also a host of

scientific words; which new words remain a monument to all time of the advance of thought and knowledge in the period corresponding to their developement. Another tendency which is an exponent of the age has been to give a more abstract meaning to words; to use words formerly only applied to express qualities of concrete things as expressing ideas of the mind quite apart from the actual world; such words as Beauty, or Thought, are abstracted and almost personified; Nature, again, has in modern poetry a meaning much deeper and greater than it ever had before; such a title as "Hymn to the Spirit of Nature" could not before have been understood, and
10 is now only clear in its entirety to those who have made Nature an object of study and even worship. Thus the growth of a new Idea is shown by the growth of a new mode of expression, and the first to express the Idea has contributed a stone to the Monument, which remains a part so long as the language is understood.

Again, we may study the character of a people by the ideas which its language best expresses. The French, for instance, contains such words as "spirituel", or "l'esprit", which in English can scarcely be expressed at all; whence we naturally draw the inference, which may be confirmed by actual observation, that the French have more "esprit", and are more "spirituel"
20 than the English. In reading Molière this character of the French language continually strikes us, and the impossibility of translation into English. On the other hand, the simple grandeur of Milton or the homely beauty of Cowper, as they are typical of the English character, are utterly unable to be put into the light frivolous French dress. And as the character of a nation changes, the language adapts itself to the new character, and thus we find that periods of transformation in History correspond to periods of transformation in language. So long as a nation remains undisturbed by foreign interference, so long as its social condition remains unchanged, its language also is stagnant, as may be seen in the case of the Semitic races of today,
30 whose language is hardly changed since the time of Mahomet or even further back. On the other hand any violent disturbance is sure to produce a change in language, as, for example, after the downfall of Rome, when the old civilization was swept away, and the old races infused with new blood. At this time the old Latin gave way, and though forming the foundation of the new romance languages, these soon became so different from their parent that it had to be studied as a dead language. The new states which grew up, so long as they remained unsettled, preserved a changing chaotic language; it was not till the end of the Middle Ages, when the Renaissance had restored civilization and a settled state of things began, that modern lan-
40 guages settled down into the type in which they are now fixed so long as the present nations exist. Thus mediaeval languages preserve a record of mediaeval developement, and in their gradual approach to the modern form we see the gradual approach of mediaeval thought and feeling to their mod-

ern type. The immense influence of individuals in fixing language may be
seen perhaps more clearly than anywhere else, in the Italian, which was
virtually made by Dante. Before his time it was not a written language; it
had no fixed grammar and was continually changing; by his writing it was
fixed for all time as a language worthy of study and capable of expressing
beautiful ideas. Future generations read Dante, and wrote in his language;
an outburst of poetry which followed close upon him still further determined its permanent form. Language is thus a living monument of great
men's thoughts; and its study shows the modes of thought of our ancestors.
The great have thus an influence on future generations even beyond that 10
directly exercised on their readers; for many who know nothing of them use
expressions due to them, and are influenced by them in their ideas; and thus
in a still wider sense than merely as applied to books, the great live on in
their words.

## 7 Contentment; Its Good and Bad Points [1889]

AT FIRST SIGHT it might appear that contentment is the best gift that
man can possess, and so indeed it is, according to a certain view of
life. But our opinion of it must depend directly upon our idea of the
object of life. Also contentment may be of different kinds, one, that of a log,
the other, that which springs from the consolation of religion and the peace 20
of mind given by a well-regulated life. The contentment which is com-
monest is the former; it springs simply from ignorance and apathy, and is
the great prop of tyranny and oppression and the great obstacle to progress.
It is equally powerful in fortune and misfortune; nothing but a sudden
change can disturb it, and then the inherent indolence of mind murmurs
against the exertion of change. It is common among all who have little mind,
and it is for this reason that in countries where the poor are very much
oppressed, the outcry against the oppression has usually begun from above,
where education has opened men's eyes to the evils of the existing state of
things. Those who possess this kind of contentment, if they cannot be said 30
to be unhappy, can certainly not be said to be happy; they are simply passive
instruments of fate, and are no more happy than inanimate objects. If the
object of life be simply to avoid pain, then these may be envied; but if there
be anything great or noble in the undertaking arduous labours for human
advancement, if we would feel any of the deep emotions which make a life
worth the name, if there be anything preferable to the existence of a mere
tree or stone, then these are objects of contempt, and every advance removes
us farther and farther from this blank content. As education increases, as

the view becomes wider and the imagination expands, the miserably unsatisfactory state of the actual world comes more and more clearly before the
mind, and its own weakness and smallness stand out before the ideal conceptions which it is able to raise out of the mines of thought. It struggles to
realise the ideal, to conceive the inconceivable, and its failure is an almost
certain cause of discontent, except where a strong faith in the continual
march to higher and higher things, and in something over all and beyond
our comprehension, produces a cheerful view of the future and a hope that
some day the Ideal may become the Actual. This state must however be
10 preceded by a state of discontent, and this discontent is the incentive to all
the highest thought and all the greatest actions. The first step towards
knowledge is the discovery of one's own ignorance, and the first step towards truth is the discovery of error. The beginning of any great work must
be negative; the destructive must precede the constructive, and in the interval between the beginning of the negative and the beginning of the positive
work there is sure to be a period of discontent, a groping after truth, a
seeking for new gods to replace old fetishes; this discontent is the necessary
power to drive the engine of progress through the accumulated rubbish of
effete institutions and systems on to new institutions and systems fit for the
20 requirements of the present. Discontent is then a great power for good; but
it should cease with its cause, and should be succeeded by a higher contentment than can ever be known to those who have not passed through the
night of discontent.

## 8    Destruction Must Precede Construction [1889]

I T IS A common thing to reproach Nihilism and Anarchism because they
have no system to offer in exchange for that which they combat. A bad
system, it is said, is better than no system; we must therefore oppose
these wild enthusiasts who see no evils beyond the present ones.

As with Nihilism, so with other movements of emancipation. Those who
30 wish to sweep away an old institution or religion are looked upon as anarchists or iconoclasts, as spreaders of dangerous ideas, and disturbers of the
peace. And such, no doubt, the earlier stages of a reform movement always
must be. Although Nihilism may at present be a mere wild struggle to sweep
away everything, all that could be a reminder of the old abuses, yet in the
day of success it must develop into a system, which, though possibly wild
and impracticable at first, is certain soon to mould itself to the requirements
of the time. And although the first steps of a reform are usually directed
against old superstitions, yet, when these are overcome, there succeeds a

new element to replace that which has been destroyed, one more suited to the cravings of the time and more in harmony with the best thought of the day.

Thus in all cases of regeneration, we see that the first steps are destructive; construction can only begin after a clear field has been won for fresh action. This, however, is only the case with regeneration; with generation the case is entirely different. It is only where there is a system already that destruction is necessary; if a new system is to be built up where there was no need of one before, there is no destruction, but everything is peaceful and easy. To take a very simple illustration from our system of weights and measures, it is clear that it grew up naturally and gradually among a not highly civilized people, and that having nothing to replace there was no difficulty in introducing it. But now, when a more perfect and logical system is required, it is very difficult to remove the old one, and thus the necessity for destruction before the possibility of construction is an impediment so great as to prevent any improvement whatever. In France it was accomplished by the Revolution, in which no extent of destruction was shrunk from, but was rather looked upon as an end in itself instead of merely a means of securing fresh construction. But the difficulty of the change of system is clear when we consider that the old weights and measures still exist in England, though the immense advantage of the decimal system has been clear for years to every intelligent man in the kingdom. Or again, to take another instance from Astronomy. The first connected theory of the Solar System was the Ptolemaic, which, having none to replace, was accepted by all Astronomers and taught for nearly two thousand years without a dispute. But when the Copernican System arose, although it was clear that the old theory was inadequate, and that the new one had reason on its side, yet from the necessity of destroying the old Theory it was long before the new one became definitely established.

As with Science, so with Religion. Most civilized countries have at some time had a first great teacher who, like Moses among the Jews, has been acknowledged as a Lawgiver even in his own time, and whose teaching has been peacefully accepted. But when later prophets have arisen, to supplement old teachings and adapt them to the time, they are cried down as heretics and destroyers of religion; while in reality they only wish to destroy old religions in so far as destruction is a necessity for the introduction of a purer faith.

Thus it is in some ways an advantage for any great teacher if he has no former theory to replace, and the fewer old institutions there are in a country, the easier it is to apply modern research in practical government. In the words of Herbert Spencer: "Continued growth implies unbuilding and rebuilding of structure, which becomes therefore in so far an impediment." And thus when a country has acquired a certain degree of structure, its growth usually ceases, and in time decay sets in, which usually ends either in a great upheaval such as the French Revolution, or in a slow death of inanition, as was the case with the Roman Empire. Our structure must therefore be watched with the utmost care, and although we have now arrived, in most nations of western Europe, at a state of stability, where changes are small and gradual, we should beware of allowing our institutions to fall behind the age, and no destruction should be shrunk from if it be a necessary preliminary to construction of better and more efficient systems.

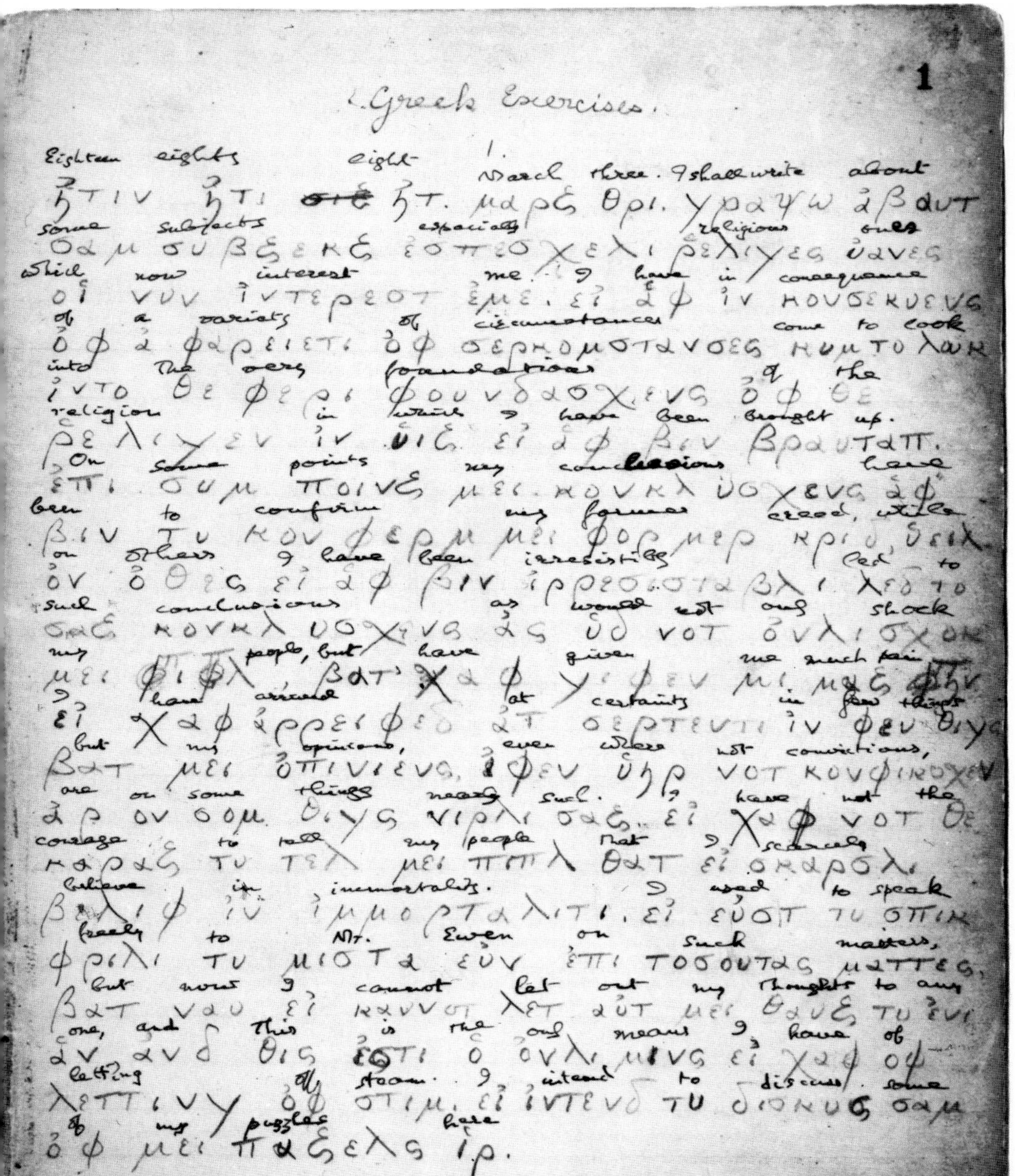

*Greek Exercises.*

PLATE I. The first page of Paper **1**, "Greek Exercises", showing the entry of 3 March 1888 and Russell's later interlinear transliteration. See 5: 1–13.

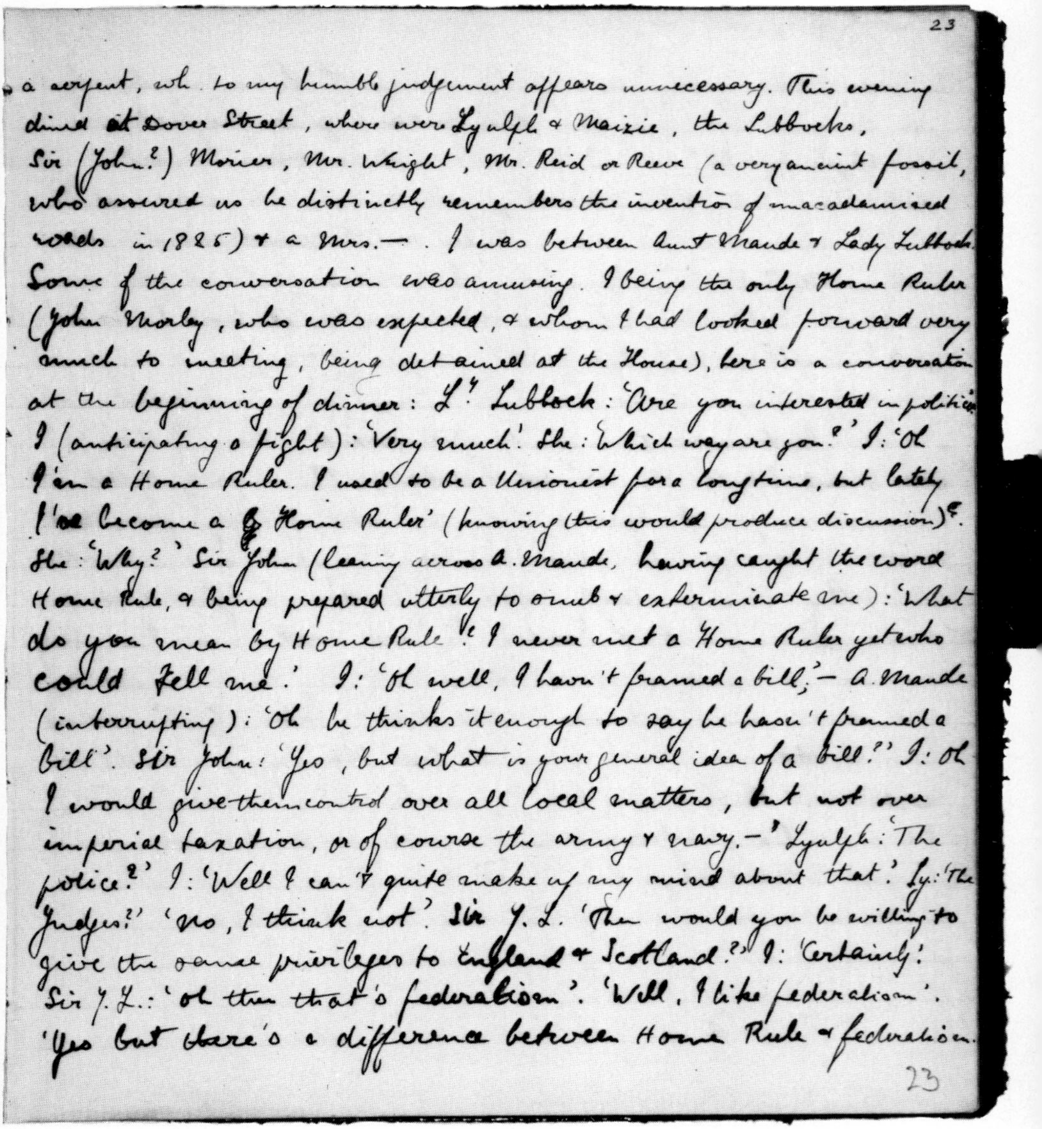

23

a serpent, wh. to my humble judgement appears unnecessary. This evening dined at Dover Street, where were Lyulph & Maizie, the Lubbocks, Sir (John?) Morier, Mr. Wright, Mr. Reid or Reeve (a very ancient fossil, who assured us he distinctly remembers the invention of macadamised roads in 1825) & a Mrs.— . I was between Aunt Maude & Lady Lubbock. Some of the conversation was amusing. I being the only Home Ruler (John Morley, who was expected, & whom I had looked forward very much to meeting, being detained at the House), here is a conversation at the beginning of dinner: Ly Lubbock: 'Are you interested in politics? I (anticipating a fight): 'Very much'. She: 'Which way are you?' I: 'Oh I'm a Home Ruler. I used to be a Unionist for a long time, but lately I've become a Home Ruler' (knowing this would produce discussion). She 'Why?' Sir John (leaning across A. Maude, having caught the word Home Rule, & being prepared utterly to snub & exterminate me): 'What do you mean by Home Rule? I never met a Home Ruler yet who could tell me'. I: 'Oh well, I haven't framed a bill;— A. Maude (interrupting): 'Oh he thinks it enough to say he hasn't framed a bill'. Sir John: 'Yes, but what is your general idea of a bill?' I: 'Oh I would give them control over all local matters, but not over imperial taxation, or of course the army & navy.—' Lyulph: 'The police?' I: 'Well I can't quite make up my mind about that'. Ly: 'The Judges?' 'No, I think not'. Sir J. L. 'Then would you be willing to give the same privileges to England & Scotland?' I: 'Certainly'. Sir J. L.: 'Oh then that's federation'. 'Well, I like federation'. 'Yes but there's a difference between Home Rule & federation.

23

PLATE II.    Record of a dinner conversation at the home of Russell's Grandmother
Stanley, from the entry of 26 June 1890 in Paper 9, "A Locked Diary".
See 54: 7–31. The broken lock is shown. (*Courtesy of Barbara Halpern*)

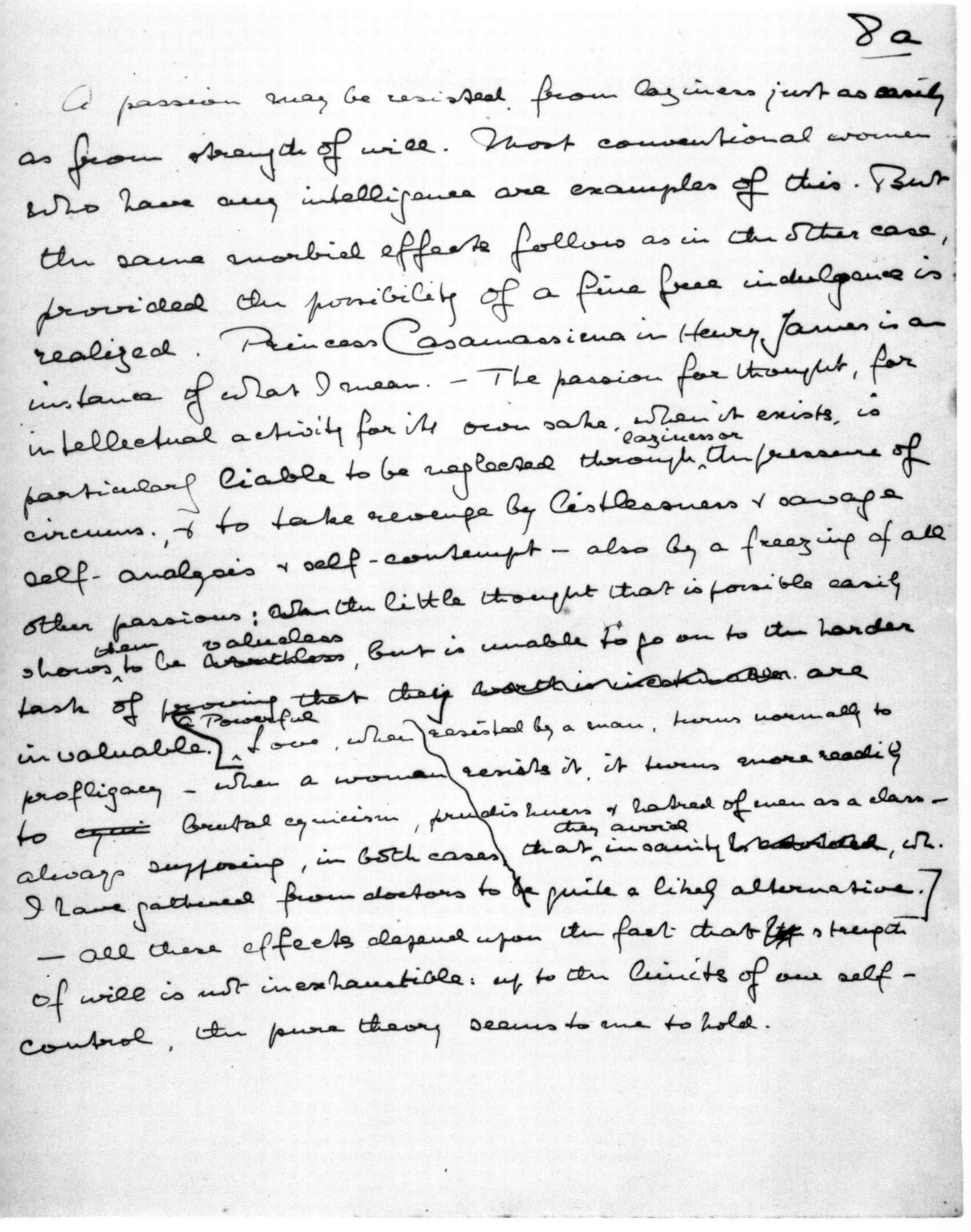

A passion may be resisted from laziness just as easily as from strength of will. Most conventional women who have any intelligence are examples of this. But the same morbid effects follow as in the other case, provided the possibility of a fine free indulgence is realized. Princess Casamassima in Henry James is an instance of what I mean. — The passion for thought, for intellectual activity for its own sake, when it exists, is particularly liable to be replaced through laziness or the pressure of circums., & to take revenge by listlessness & savage self-analysis & self-contempt — also by a freezing of all other passions; when the little thought that is possible easily shows them to be valueless, but is unable to go on to the harder task of showing that they are invaluable. A powerful love, when resisted by a man, turns normally to profligacy — when a woman resists it, it turns more readily to brutal cynicism, prudishness & hatred of men as a class — always supposing, in both cases, that they avoid insanity, which I have gathered from doctors to be quite a likely alternative.

— all these effects depend upon the fact that strength of will is not inexhaustible: up to the limits of our self-control, the pure theory seems to me to hold.

PLATE III.   The second of three inserted leaves in Paper **14**, "Cleopatra or Maggie Tulliver" (1894), illustrating Russell's deletion of personal examples. See 96: 12–24.

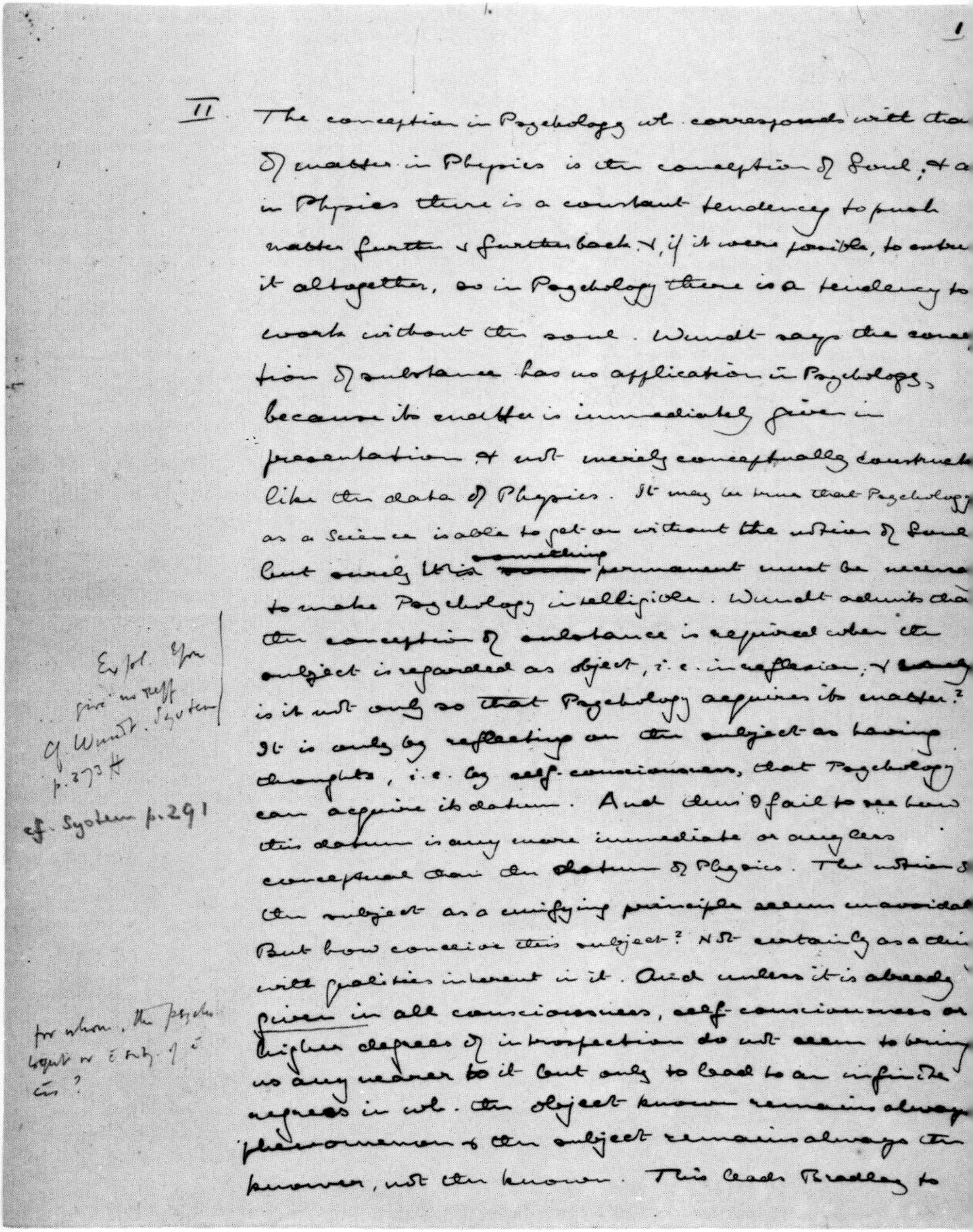


PLATE IV. Paper 22, "Paper on Epistemology III" (1894), the 4th folio (the 2nd numbered "1"). See 148: 13–33. Note the comments by James Ward, and Russell's response to one of them.

× The imagined approbation of God must be — a prominent motive in such self of fanatical asceticism. [not merely 'self']

Still he imagined that his mortification of the flesh was in a special sense in harmony with god's will

Those whose lives are spent in mathematical investigations become notoriously so rapt up in their intellectual pleasures as to be almost unconscious of the external event of their life: those who make it their aim to attain the × pleasures of self-approbation become at last so impressed with the nothingness of all other pleasures that they are able, like Simon Stylites, to spend 40 years on a pillar; for it can scarcely be supposed that that fanatic imagined heaven unattainable on easier terms ×. — Of pain fortunately this proposition does not hold: mental pain as well as physical loses its edge by long continuance: a certain energy seems essential to the possibility of intense pain as of intense pleasure, & this energy is in time destroyed by the very pain wh. requires it ×. Besides in the case of mental pain there is a tendency gradually to acquiesce in one's surroundings however loathsome, or in one's misfortunes, however severe, as 'custom inures one to them, wh. is inconsistent with the long continuance of mental pain in its original intensity. At the same time every increase of susceptibility to any source of pleasure (except perhaps the purely intellectual) of course involves an increase in susceptibility to pain.

### III

Possibility of making pleasure the end of rational action.

There are two classes of objection to Hedonism wh. may conveniently be considered separately, especially as the 1st class apply strictly speaking to Utilitarianism as well as to Egoistic Hedonism, while the 2nd class are at least different in the two cases. These may be called the practical & the theoretic objections.

(1) Practical objections. These depend upon the impossibility of a strict numerical estimate of the relative values of pleasures. I shall therefore here use pleasure in the sense indicated in

PLATE V. Paper 30, "On Pleasure" (1893), fol. 3. See 203: 15–40. Note Henry Sidgwick's method of tutorial comment.

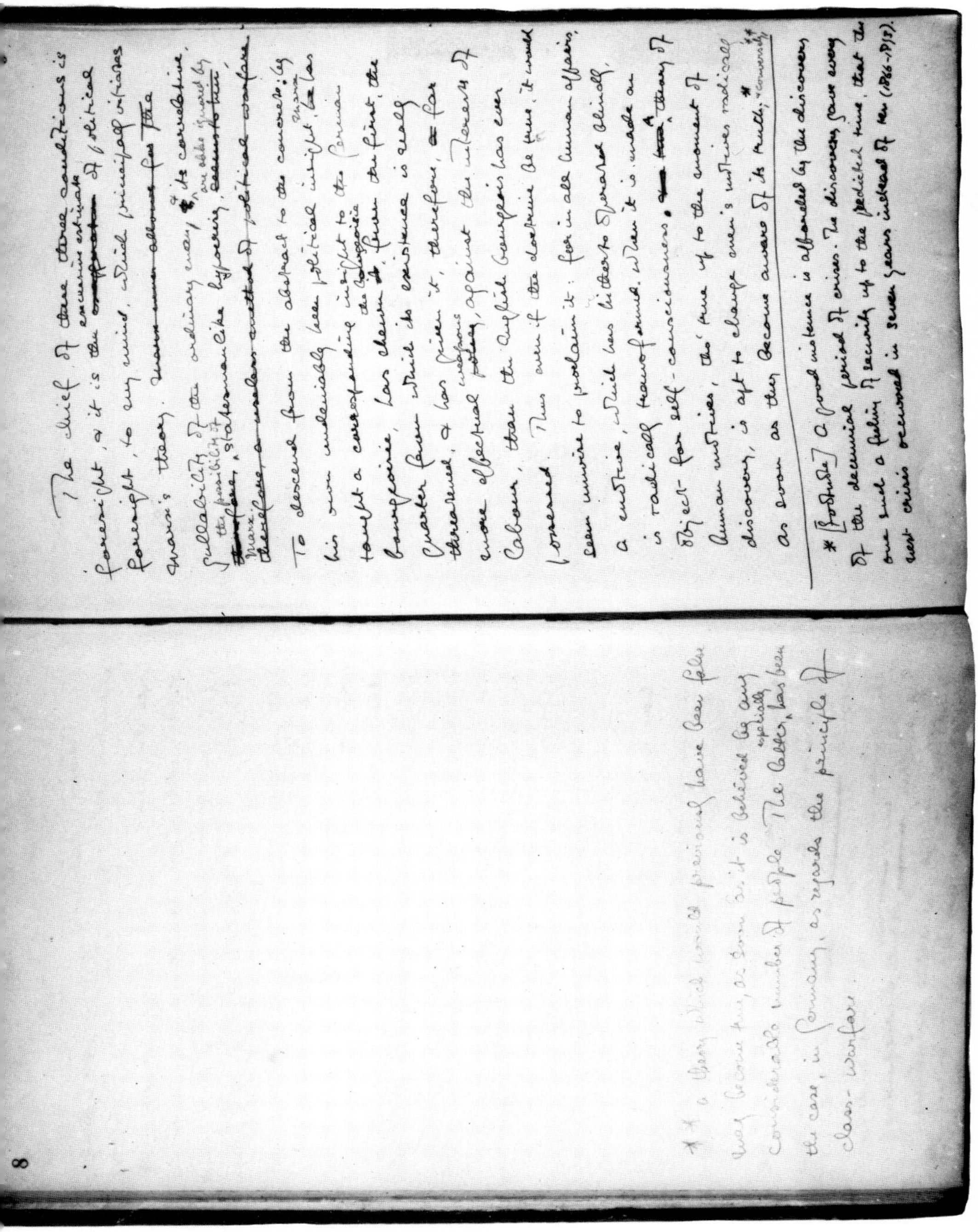
8

** a theory which would previously have been false may become true, as soon as it is believed by any considerable number of people. The latter, especially, has been the case, in Germany, as regards the principle of class-warfare.

The chief of these three conditions is foresight, & it is the excessive estimate of political foresight, to my mind, which principally vitiates Marx's theory. The fallibility of the ordinary man, & its correlative, the possibility of statesmanlike hypocrisy, are alike ignored by Marx.

To descend from the abstract to the concrete: by his own undeniably keen political insight, Marx has taught a corresponding insight to the German bourgeoisie, has shewn the bourgeoisie, from the first, the quarter from which its existence is really threatened, & has given it, therefore, far more effectual weapons, against the interests of Labour, than the English bourgeois has ever possessed. Thus even if the doctrine be true, it would seem unwise to proclaim it: for in all human affairs, a motive, which has hitherto operated blindly, is radically transformed when it is made an object for self-consciousness. A theory of human motives, tho' true up to the moment of discovery, is apt to change men's motives radically as soon as they become aware of its truth;* & conversely**

* [footnote] A good instance is afforded by the discovery of the decennial period of crises. The discovery gave every one such a feeling of security up to the predicted time, that the next crisis occurred in seven years instead of ten (1866–1873).

PLATE VII. A number of Russell's characteristic methods of revision are apparent on these opposing pages of the "Mit Gott" notebook containing Paper **46**, "German Social Democracy, as a Lesson in Political Tactics" (1896). See 312: 39–313: 13.

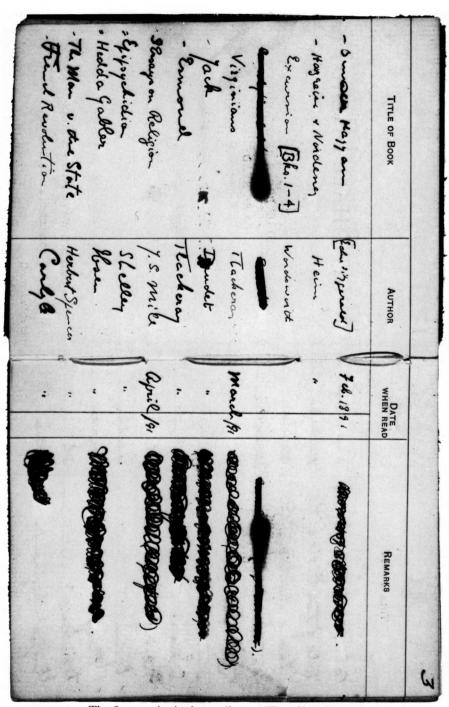

PLATE VIII.   The first entries in Appendix II, "What Shall I Read?" Some of the
obliterated remarks are deciphered on p. 347.

Part II

Later Personal Writings

# 9

# "A Locked Diary" [1890–94]

IN HIS *Autobiography* Russell mentions that at the time he proposed to Alys he "kept a locked diary which I very carefully concealed from everyone" (*1967*, 82). This hitherto unpublished diary enriches the account in his *Autobiography* of his late adolescence at Pembroke Lodge, friendship with Edward FitzGerald, undergraduate years at Cambridge, courtship of Alys Pearsall Smith and stay at the Paris embassy. Interspersed with these topics are numerous references to family members and other aristocrats, political controversies (especially Irish Home Rule), books read, concerts attended, games played and moods experienced.

When Russell wrote of the diary many years later, his memory appears to have played him false on two occasions. He claimed that in the diary he had "recorded my conversations with my grandmother about Alys and my feelings in regard to them" (*1967*, 82). There are no entries recording these conversations in the diary and no leaves have been removed. Instead of recording these conversations in the diary, he seems to have written them out in letters to Alys (see those of 13 Nov. and 19 Dec. 1893 and 4 Feb. 1894). In the other instance, Russell asserted that the reflections printed in the *Autobiography* had been shown "to nobody, not even Alys, until a much later date" (*1967*, 84). The reflections are printed there from a single sheet of pencilled manuscript (RA 710.055228) dated 20–1 July 1894 and are virtually identical to the version in the diary. An entry by Alys (who had been keeping the diary since February) on 21 July reveals that Russell showed the diary version of the reflections to her that day.

Russell had left the diary with Alys at the beginning of their three months' separation, i.e. before he went to Paris on 10 September 1894 to take up the position of honorary attaché at the British Embassy. He wrote her on 28 September: "I am seized with a great wish to see what thee has been writing in the Journal all this time—would it be possible to send me it and its key? I would return it a day or two after getting it." Alys responded: "I have written very little in our Journal, nothing of interest, but will send it to thee.... Thee might keep it and write it for the remaining ⟨period of their separation⟩, as so much more happens to thee than to me" (30 Sept.). Russell made a very brief entry in the diary on 3 October and acknowledged its receipt to Alys on the 4th, commenting:

> I am *so* glad to have the Journal, but I think I shall send it back soon, as I shouldn't write anything in it—when I've written to thee there's nothing left

to write. But it is lovely to have the heavenly times we've had together in the Book—they all come so vividly before me as I read. I only wish I'd gone on keeping the Journal till I gave it to thee—some chronicle of this time last year would have been very nice.—But it is sad to see how many entries there are since August 17 of thy having cried thyself to sleep, looked at my photo and felt sad and depressed and wept, and so on.

On 12 October Russell wrote Alys: "I am returning the journal ... in today's bag. I have nothing to write in it myself, since I express everything to thee. I send the key with this." He did in fact make one long entry in the diary during the nine days he had it—the entry of 6 October.

The diary falls into several sections. Only three complete sections and part of a fourth are printed here, since the rest are in Alys's hand. (1) The first of Russell's sections is untitled. It consists of twenty-nine entries from 18 May 1890 (Russell's eighteenth birthday) to 5 December 1892, ending at the bottom of the thirty-fifth page. (2) The second section is titled "A History of My Friendship for Fitz." It runs for four unnumbered pages. (3) The third section, which starts at the top of the next page following seven blank pages, begins on 21 July 1893 and is titled "Occasional Journal". Russell's entries run for six pages, the last of the five prose entries being dated 16 September 1893. Alys's many entries begin on 6 February 1894 on the bottom half of a new page on which Russell has carefully copied out the second stanza of a poem—in contrast to the much less careful handwriting of the previous page, which probably marks the end of the entry of 16 September. Hence the poem appears here as a separate, undated entry. (4) The fourth section, beginning on 20–21 July 1894, consists of four entries by Russell scattered among Alys's intentionally "dry" entries (as he characterized them in a letter of 12 April). His final entry, made in Paris sometime between 6 and 12 October, is a Shakespearean sonnet.

Subsequent sections consist of entries by Alys, beginning with her note that she had received the diary at Friday's Hill on 15 October. She restricted herself in these sections almost entirely to recording trips, publications and the like. She also kept formidable annual lists of books she and Russell read, but they duplicate the information in "What Shall I Read?" After the break-up of their marriage in all but name in 1902 there are two intensely personal entries by Alys in 1907 and 1909. They are quoted in Barbara Halpern's book on her family (Strachey *1980*, 222–3). Russell, for his part, resumed keeping a diary in 1902, but in another notebook. It will be found in *Collected Papers* 12.

The "locked diary" is a black notebook, the clasp, which is still locked, having been forcefully removed from the front cover and depending from the back. The flyleaf is inscribed "Bertrand Russell / Pembroke Lodge." The notebook is in the possession of Mrs. Halpern. A microfilm is in the Russell Archives (REC. ACQ. 434). The printed text has been read against the copy-text (the original notebook).

Sunday may 18. 1890. My birthday. One of the pleasantest I have ever spent. A beautiful day. The hyacinths, may, and lilac in full bloom and the nightingale in full song. How delightful, as compared with last birthday, and still more the birthday before last, the feeling of repose in being established at home, instead of having Southgate like a nightmare always before one. My hopes for the coming year are that I shall become less introspective, less shy, more genial, less cynical, more firm and steadfast of purpose. My fears are that I shall become more conceited, more argumentative, more conventional, that I shall lose whatever poetic feeling I may have had, that my conceit will prevent my making friends at Cam- 10 bridge. Conceit is at present my great danger, and Pharisaism, which is closely allied to it, is another. I have been too happy the last few months not to feel some of the bad effects which happiness always has upon me.—

This morning I went to Channing Hall where Mr. Farrington preached one of his usual see-saw sermons, from which very little is to be learnt, though today he did say many very true and useful things, as that it is bad to be always examining the state of one's own soul. Miss Bühler came to luncheon, and in the afternoon Ribblesdale and Addy Lister came, and in the evening a large Burdett party. After dinner we read aloud out of Boswell, from where Uncle Rollo and I had stopped. Mr. Mahoney and his two 20 dreadfully shy boys came early in the afternoon and I played fishponds with them, which seemed to amuse them.—As presents I had from Granny O'Brien's novel, from Auntie, *New Aids to Reflection*, from Miss Bühler *Der Trompeter* by Scheffel. Of course I had no time for reading any of them. I got a letter from Frank at Granny's instigation to say he regretted the old affair of the breakfast-letter. His moralizing sentences did not sound very real; they seemed to come out of the Latin *Principia*. However I dare say it was only a little awkwardness in expressing things he is not used to.

*May 19.* Did a three-hour conics paper in the morning, and a little of the Rigid in the afternoon. Sat out with Granny in the evening, and played 30 tennis with Miss Fraser. Dined at Lady Sophia Melville's with Auntie and Uncle Rollo, and heard Brandram recite afterwards, which was of course delightful. He recited Henry the V's speech before Agincourt, Macaulay's "Horatius", a very funny piece about a bishop and a caterpillar, and Poor Wichard's proverbs. He seemed to put a totally new life into Macaulay, whom I had never half appreciated before.

*May 20.* In the morning worked at the Rigid but only got one example out. In the afternoon, ditto. In the evening went to Petersham with Uncle Rollo to see the flags and arches for Dysart's reception, which were certainly very pretty, though the whole affair showed more of the feudal spirit than I like 40 to see. It is really extraordinary that here should be a man who has spent

£40,000 on his own house before doing a thing for the Sanitation of Ham, and that he, when he returns, in spite of his heresy and of his being so destitute of agreeable qualities, should receive all this ovation. Really people ought to learn to look more at the man and less at the wealth and rank.— Granny and Auntie dined with Lord Dysart, as did Lilly Blyth, who is staying here a day or two, and Uncle Rollo went to dine in town, so I was left alone, and read Ruskin's *Modern Painters*. The book is *most* interesting to me as a study of mind; his mind is so exactly the antitype of the mathematical that I have great difficulty in entering into it. He has a certain artistic
10 want of logic and sturdiness, which latter I should think must be almost inseparable from such a stationary pursuit as art appears to be, if not retrograde. However, his religiousness and deductive reasoning from the nature of God are delightful after more modern modes of thought. Of the purely artistic parts of the book I can of course say nothing.

*May 22*. Yesterday Rochat arrived to luncheon, having got a few days' holiday from Belgium. I was delighted to see him again after so many years. He is very shy, and owing to his rigid orthodoxy many subjects are excluded from conversation, as I should not like to hurt him by revealing the state of my own opinions. However he has by this time become much more conver-
20 sational, and there is always a good deal to say about old reminiscences, etc. I lent him *Past and Present* to read while I was at work this morning, which seemed to amuse him mightily. Yesterday afternoon I wired to Robson to say I wasn't coming and took Rochat out on the Pond in Metrodora and then played tennis with him, which I did again this afternoon with the addition of Miss Fraser. Yesterday evening we read Boswell, and this evening we played lines, which was particularly amusing with Rochat, whose word was almost always obvious from his manner. I have been working at the Newton, having got stuck in Routh.

*May 23*. In the morning rolled the tennis-court and worked. In the after-
30 noon went to Robson who elucidated several problems in Routh, by normal and tangential resolutions instead of horizontal and vertical. Most of them however temporarily stumped him. At dinner described to Granny the miseries I used to suffer from being oddly dressed as a child, the subject having come up à propos of Baby. She seemed vexed, and evidently thought I exaggerated.—In the evening read Boswell, and were much amused by a most furious letter from Johnson to M'Pherson.

*May 24*. (Saturday). In the morning did a three-hour Mechanics Paper (Trinity) wherein I did seven out of ten questions. In the afternoon we had tennis, with Mr. Ross the Elphinstones' friend, and Maud Burdett, who
40 with Rochat and me made up a four. It was a magnificent day but very hot,

so our best sets were after tea. The court is very lively and in excellent order. After dinner went out in the grounds with Rochat and discussed graphology, which he quite got me to believe in. He says he knows very little about it, but I showed him a letter from Caroline Fitzmaurice with which he got on very well. He guessed that she had imagination, was of a nervous disposition, unselfish, well educated, energetic in mind, etc. I mean to show him a great many and see what he can make of them. There is certainly no abstract reason against it, for the difference between different hands can only be the result of character or education or both, and as education affects character, it may be supposed entirely determinate when the character is known.          10

*May 26*. Yesterday morning had an uninteresting sermon almost entirely destitute of practical bearings on life and principally devoted to the narration of the origin of Pentecost. Mr. Farrington always seems afraid to let himself out.—In the afternoon had Fitz and Fred for tennis, and had some rather good games. The day was very hot and fine. Poor Fitz! I never think of trying any serious subject with him now; he has been entirely spoilt by the conventional and unintellectual atmosphere of Southgate. I also have been spoilt by the unwholesome atmosphere of my own mind, so that I have helped to shut him up almost as much as he has me. However, it is no longer, thank goodness, what it was last autumn when I had not yet got over          20 the disappointment of discovering that he was not that ideal friend I have always looked for and still hope to find. This morning did some work, and this afternoon had a lot of very good sets of tennis with the Hamiltons and a friend of Fred's called Dickens and Maud Burdett and Miss Fane.—Rochat has been reading *Modern Painters*, apparently with great delight. Played a long game of chess with him in which I ultimately won.

*May 28*. Yesterday morning had a long talk with Rochat on various subjects. He told me much that was interesting about the social and political and religious condition of Belgium. The latter, if one can trust at all to his account, appears to be very bad. The Protestants seem to be a very small          30 sect, and the nation is therefore divided between abject Catholicism and militant atheism. The two parties are, it seems, so evenly balanced that they hold office alternately. The Jesuits seem to have most of the education and all old spinsters' fortunes. The labouring classes, by his account, are improvident, ignorant, usually engaged in labour which incapacitates them for further exertion after a few years, mostly atheistic socialists, and utterly without organizations such as our unions. The drunkenness appears to be terrible, so much so that Rochat has become an entire prohibitionist, which I should be too if I thought it could be carried, particularly as it would affect the rich as well as the poor.—Saw Rochat off and then went down to the          40 Simeons at Datchet for a day on the river, which is very pretty about there.

Met some friends of theirs, Irish people called Dennehy, with whom we shared our tea on an island.—Dined with the Simeons and saw his translations from German, French and Italian, by which he says he can already make £100 a year. Got home about midnight.—This morning worked, and in the afternoon went up to Robson, having solved three problems in the Rigid, which I am beginning to look upon as quite a good record. Met Miss Bühler on the hill and walked back here with her, after which she went.

*May 29*. In the morning read Routh, the Chapter on Motion in three Dimensions, with more comprehension than before, and got out several examples. I am really beginning to get a certain amount of grip of the subject. Directly after luncheon, went onto the river with Auntie, in compliance with Dr.'s orders, and had a very nice row up to Kingston, where we had tea, and returned *presto presto* double sculling I and the boatman. Ady Villiers arrived to luncheon, before which Granny and I read a little of Dante, in the bolge of the hypocrites. After dinner Auntie read us one or two lovely little poems of Hamilton Aïdé's; I was astonished the apparently finniky little man should have so much in him. Ady was very nice, and told amusing stories about Earl's elder brother, not like what I should have imagined him. It turns out he is a cousin of theirs after all, though he didn't know it.

*May 30*. (Friday). In the morning had a lesson from Robson, and after coming home began a three-hour Trinity Geometry (Euclid and Conics) paper, which I mean to finish tomorrow. After luncheon read some of Ruskin and wrote to Boughey about rooms; then played tennis with Maud Burdett and afterwards with Uncle Rollo too. In the evening went over to the Kew Coteries to hear Uncle Rollo read a paper on Lowell. The paper was interesting, being almost entirely quotations. The people who spoke in the discussion ran him down dreadfully as a poet, one man saying he supposed a dozen men now in London could write as good verse as Lowell, and another saying, what I think is rather true, that the great want in him as a poet (and a *very* great want it is) is the want of genius. However I think they all made a mistake in placing the *Biglow Papers* above the best of his poetry, which is occasionally grand and always sturdy and strengthening. However I know nothing about him and so cannot say. "John P. Robinson" is very amusing, particularly the verse where

> John P. Robinson he
> Said they didn't know everything down in Judee.

Rather a good answer to the parsons on other points, by the way. Which reminds me of a good case of ecclesiastical bigotry in this "so-called" nineteenth century which I heard of from the Simeons, of all people. Their parson, a "most excellent fellow" as every body always is according to them, went to see an unfortunate woman down at Datchet three days after her baby had died, unbaptized. And this parson forsooth tells the poor woman that it will "make a very serious difference to her baby in the next world" not having been baptized. He won't quite say it's damned, but it will make a very serious difference! What a church to support with all the wealth it has! Naturally the woman has not been to church again.

*May 31st.* (Saturday). In the morning finished up my three-hour paper, wherein I only did seven out of twelve. However geometry never was my strong point. Afterwards got out several questions in Routh about angular momentum. In the afternoon, played tennis with Maud Burdett who was the only person who arrived for tennis. After dinner had a talk with Uncle Rollo on the Church and the Salvationists and the question of selfishness with respect to a future life. He seemed doubtful whether the motives of salvationists and of some methodists could be selfish, but they seem to me as purely so as anybody's. As I once heard a salvationist put it, "you put down a penny and you take up a thousand pounds". Uncle Rollo said such ideas made him glad that to thinking men there was no certainty or definiteness about a future state, by which I fancy he only meant about our mode of being, not about our being at all, for he always seems to have a firm belief in immortality of some kind. To me the absolute perfection which is usually attributed to angels does not seem such a beautiful idea as the gradual approach to perfection such as I believe the Buddhists affirm, ending at last in Nirvana or absolute repose and perfection. However I am afraid there are no very strong reasons for belief in either. During the last three years, I have looked at the question from many different points of view, but all the arguments for immortality seem to me to be of a vague poetic nature, such as that put forward in Wordsworth's ode, while the arguments on the other side, though scarcely convincing, are I am afraid far more scientific. So that, much as I detest the faintest tinge of materialism, and intensely painful as it is to think of utter annihilation after such a short and imperfect life as is possible here, I have not been able, except for moments now and then, to believe in any future state, at least combined with memory, which is an essential for any comfort in the doctrine.—Later on we discussed capital punishment, on which Auntie had a meeting last night. Of course Auntie thinks, as women almost always do, principally, of the effect of punishment on the man after committing the crime, rather than of its deterrent effect on those who avoid the crime. Another point of view from which she seemed inclined to regard it was the point of view of abstract justice; saying, that Society causes crime, and therefore Society has no right to punish crime. This no doubt is true as regards the first clause, at least up to a certain point, but the second does not seem to me to follow. I think expediency should be the sole ground of a settlement. If there are more murders without capital punishment, I would keep it on; but without an appreciable excess, I would abolish it, especially considering the chance of false convictions.

*June 2*. (Monday). Heard a very good sermon from Mr. Farrington, the first of three on the Word of Reconciliation, this time between God and Man. He spoke of the ancient system of sacrifices and the modern system of Calvinism, and showed how both rested on a wrong theory of the relation between God and Man; how the real relation is not one of antagonism, but of
10 agreement, and how man has evolved and developed, and is still doing so, so that ultimately he may rise to a different level altogether.—After luncheon Fitz came and I played seven sets of tennis with him, all singles. In all but the first he gave me thirty, but I won all but the last with that arrangement, by which time I was getting fagged. He seems to have gone ahead with the Calculus tremendously.—This morning went to Robson, and this afternoon played tennis with Maud. Baby went to see a Punch at the Moretons in Petersham, with which he seems to have been less delighted than might have been expected.—In the evening we read Johnson, and were amused by his view of America, that all Americans are convicts, and ought to be grate-
20 ful to us if we let them off without hanging. It reminds one of what is said about Ireland nowadays.

*June 5*. (Thursday). Mabel came the day before yesterday, and Frank yesterday, and they go tomorrow. Poor Mabel! She seems very nice by nature, but from education utterly without firmness or moral courage. She always has to give in to Frank in every little discussion they have, as I noticed first the first time I ever saw her, the day after their engagement, when Frank absolutely refused to give in to her, and she had to content herself with shrugging her shoulders and saying "Just as you like". The day before yesterday went on the ponds with Aunt Agatha in the morning, and in the
30 afternoon cycled over to call on the Levens and the Freres, the latter of whom I found and got tea from and an invitation for tennis yesterday, but as it poured all day I didn't go. Yesterday went to Robson in the morning, and read Ruskin for about an hour in the afternoon, and afterwards read Dante with Granny. Afterwards did some work, and in the evening sat in the schoolroom with Frank and Mabel, as the rest were having a committee. They both smoked, and Frank read us several bits of Browning, which with the benefit of his reading sounded some of them very fine, especially "Abt Vogler", which really is grand. Mabel of course pronounced them all "sweet". Today she said Granny was "worried, poor thing", which was
40 almost as annoying as Ady seemed to find it her having called Granny "sweet". Today Baby was ill, his temperature being 102°, so the Kinder-

garten had to go on without him. In the morning saw Frank's new works at
Teddington, and in the afternoon did a lot of Rigid, and everything came
out. In the evening, same as yesterday. Day before yesterday, heard from
Boughey; answered him today, saying I would go Thursday to see rooms.

*June 7*. (Saturday). Yesterday went to Robson in the morning, and when I
got home began a Conics paper, which I finished this morning, having only
done six out ⟨of⟩ eleven, but those six were the hardest. Yesterday afternoon there were lots of people here; Lady Elizabeth Biddulph with three
Adeane daughters; Lady S. Palmer, Dysart and Lady Huntingtower and
several more. Uncle Rollo was afraid to go in to tea alone with all the people, 10
and I hadn't meant to go at all there being so many, but he got me to go in at
last. Before all the people came, we had O'Brien down with Madame and
Miss Raffalovich, which was very interesting, as none of us except Auntie
knew him before. She is certainly dreadfully ugly, but apparently nice.
Yesterday evening Arthur seemed to have bronchitis but today he seems
well. This morning drove in the pony carriage and did a very nice problem
about vis viva and angular momentum. This afternoon did several easier
ones, and played tennis with Uncle Rollo as I did also yesterday. Maud
Burdett was here too this afternoon, and enquired very particularly about
Channing Hall. I told her, as best I could without shocking her feelings, 20
what Unitarians believe. She is practically, though not theoretically, broad,
and I always think the practical breadth the more important.—Wrote to
Frank about his letter, which I forgot to speak about.—Read Boswell both
evenings. Heard particulars from Boughey about meeting on Thursday.

*June 8*. (Sunday). Had Mr. Farrington's second sermon on the Word of
Reconciliation, this time between Nature and Grace. After entering very
fully into Calvinistic theories of original sin and atonement, he went on to
say that he believed Nature and Grace to be not antagonistic but identical.
Miss Bühler was there and came up with us to luncheon. We played chess,
and halma. Did several questions in Vis Viva, which is the easiest thing I 30
have yet come to in Rigid. In the evening, had a small dinner, Maie and
Maud Burdett, Clarke and Swift MacNeill M.P., who was very Irish, very
amusing and *very* nice. The Irish heartiness is such a relief from English
stiffness and sameness. Sat next Maud, and assured her that if I appear
flippant or indifferent, it is only put on as a defence, and not real. However,
the crust is growing so thick that I am almost beginning to doubt which is
my real self. I really must become less reserved, and say rather more what I
think. Even if it does make many people hate me, the few I like best will like
me the better for it.—

*June 10*. (Tuesday). Yesterday morning, Robson. In the afternoon read 40 some of *Modern Painters*, a part which was almost entirely about mediaeval painters. Tintoret seems his favourite, at least in respect of Imagination Penetrative, as he calls it. I dislike his theory of suitably combined imperfections resulting in perfection, or uglinesses in beauty, as he himself appears to do in his maturer years by a note. It seems to me that the features in a beautiful face are individually beautiful, and if any are not so, that by so much they take off from the beauty of the whole. In landscape again, any object in itself ugly spoils the view as a whole, at any rate as far as what Ruskin calls typical beauty is concerned. It seems to me also that on his hypothesis a simple gradation of colour without form, such as in the blue of the evening sky or of a calm sea, could not be beautiful, for every tint is in itself equally perfect, and should therefore according to him be the work of an unimaginative artist, which it certainly is not.—In the evening yesterday I went on the river with Uncle Rollo and after dinner read Boswell. Today drove the pony in the morning and worked in the afternoon. Read a canto of Dante with Granny about the ladre. Uncle William (Minto) was here to tea looking very well in spite of a bad cold.

*June 12*. (Thursday). Yesterday morning went with Aunt Agatha to O'Brien's wedding, which was most interesting and beautiful. It seemed a pity to have the ceremony in such an out of the way place as Ogle Street, and in such a small church. But no doubt it was a more Irish neighbourhood than Brompton, and a more Nationalist church.—The music was most beautiful, particularly the Hallelujah which was very well sung. Never having been inside a Catholic Church before, I was much struck with the peculiar soft dreamy music without clear beginning or end, *of* which I had often heard though I had never heard it. Poor O'Brien and still more poor Dillon looked dreadfully nervous, Dillon actually miserable, but as the ceremony went on they brightened up. As for the bride she was beaming all through, particularly at the end, when all her relations, male and female, came up to her in the church before every one and kissed her, that being, I suppose, either a Russian or a Jewish custom. In the course of the wedding O'Brien had to kiss her twice, which he did very shyly, and which made Protestant members smile.—The press coming out of church was frightful, but we were reconciled by being just behind Dillon and hearing and seeing the enthusiasm of the Irish, which they could not restrain even in the church. Such handshaking he got from them on the way down that one wonders he had a whole bone left in his arm. The poor terrorized and oppressed people whom Balfour is so nobly struggling to liberate from National League tyranny were all tumbling over each other to get a handshake with their cruel oppressor, and full of such ejaculations as "God bless the lad", "I've shaken hands with the lad", "Bless his dear face", etc., all uttered in the strongest brogue which it did one's heart good to hear.—On our way home we stopped ten minutes at the Alexandra Hotel and went up and shook hands with O'Brien, and I was introduced to Parnell, who shook hands and said he was glad to make my acquaintance. There is some distinction about knowing Parnell, as he is usually so invisible.—In the church, I was next Mrs. Cobb, and close to Swift MacNeill, and several other people I knew were not far off.—On getting home, there was the news of Mr. Buller's engagement, which I should think a very ⟨sic⟩ thing.— There was also sadder news, about Mabel, who was very ill. Granny and Agatha telegraphed for, drove over to Walton; said she was utterly miserable, and could not stay with him any longer at present. Today she is come here, we hope to stay a long time. They say she is much better already than yesterday. I heard nothing from her about it, but she did not seem at all well or in at all good spirits. Poor thing! what misery people do submit themselves to without serious thought! However I think all the blame lies with the mother, who I feel sure strongly urged her to accept him, and who, however she may cant about love for her daughter, cannot have much when she allows her to make such a marriage.—This sort of case makes me think that divorce should be made much easier, and should be divested of all the scandal which now accompanies it.—Today I went to Cambridge for the day. I went by Broad Street and Liverpool Street and returned by St. Pancras and King's Cross Met. Arrived there 12.15, went to Trinity, saw Boughey and the rooms which will be vacant, of which I preferred Hurst's, G Whewell's Court. Then went with Boughey to his house, lunched there, looked about the place, discussed the Little-go and rolled his tennis-court with him, then went and called on the Butlers, found Mrs., who gave me tea and talked about Grandmama, and about Miss Fawcett of course; then went off to the station and caught the 4.42, which brought me here in time for dinner. After dinner we began *Deerbrook*, which is to be our book during Mabel's stay.

*June 14.* (Saturday). Yesterday was a wet morning which I spent at Robson's, but fair afternoon, which enabled me to play tennis over at Mr. Ross's, where there was a large party, among others the Elphinstones, and two parsons, one of whom was always swindling about the score (it is to be hoped not intentionally, but only from the natural clerical bias). The ground was very dead, but we got on fairly well. This morning did five out of ten of a Dynamics paper, Rigid and Particle. Got out two Rigid problems, which in a three-hour paper rather pleased me, being a very different thing from examples in a book. This afternoon had five very good sets of tennis, with Maud and Fred, and Mabel, who plays very well. After dinner Mabel sang Tosti's "Goodbye" most beautifully. I think it is a song which ought to be put on quite a different level from any other I ever heard. It seems to me absolutely perfect of its kind, and only to be compared to some of Shelley's short lyrics. She also sang several other songs, but in comparison with that they seemed nothing at all, though the "Convent Gate", also Tosti's, is very beautiful indeed. Both nights we read *Deerbrook*, which I like very much; the character of Miss Young is very nicely done.

*June 16.* (Monday). Yesterday morning had an unsatisfactory sermon from Farrington, the third on the word of reconciliation, this time Reason and Faith. He seemed to me not to reconcile them at all, for he ended by saying that certain fundamental propositions dare to stand without proof, and that is as much as saying that in the most important matters Reason is to be
10 superseded by, not reconciled to, Faith. My own mind is in such a haze about fundamental axioms that I have absolutely no positive opinion on the subject, though I rather lean towards the opinion that nothing is to be ac-cepted which is incapable of experimental or inductive proof, except perhaps such laws of thought as no person could at first sight have any hesitation in accepting.—It is clear that the argument of many orthodox theologians, that God exists because we feel that he exists, is no argument to an atheist, and therefore no sound argument to any person.—In the after-noon spent about two hours on a Rigid problem, which I spent three hours on again this morning, and finally did not solve, because I could get no first
20 integral of my equations except the energy equation, and two were neces-sary for the solution. After tea played tennis with Fred, and in the evening read *Deerbrook*, without Mabel, who was kept in bed almost all day by a most frightful headache, a remnant of her illness. Today she seemed much better, went to Windsor and back, sang beautifully in the evening and lis-tened to *Deerbrook*. It is most fortunate, as Aunt Agatha was saying, that her nature is not a deep one; if it were, she must be almost broken-hearted by the prospect of life-long misery which is apparently all there is before her.—Today I finished *Modern Painters*, Vol. II; I have been more in-terested in it than I should have supposed possible for me to be in any book
30 about art. Of course the style is not comparable to that of his later books, *Sesame and Lilies* for example; but his thought is fine, and for an artistic person, wonderfully sturdy.—I began *Der Trompeter* but am very doubtful whether I shall read it regularly just yet.

*June 20.* On Tuesday I worked in the morning, and played tennis with Mabel in the afternoon. Wednesday, Robson, who showed me that my Sunday's Rigid Problem required no first integral at all, being an initial $\rho$, and obtainable from the formula $\rho = y^2/2x = (\eta^2 t)/\xi$ if $\eta$, $\xi$ be initial accel-erations. Yesterday was a very full day. In the morning I did three hours' work at Rigid; then went to town and dined at Dover Street, where Grand-
40 mama was very kind and apparently fairly well, and Aunt Maude asked me to accompany her to Switzerland for three weeks in a month's time, which I

hope to do, and fortunately for me they asked nothing about Mabel; then I came back here, played tennis with Mabel, read some more of the *Trompeter*, supped and went up to meet Uncle Rollo at the Bedfords' box at Covent Garden. He brought Mr. and Miss Pearsall Smith and two lady friends of theirs. The opera was Gounod's *Roméo et Juliette*. It was my first Opera, strange to say, and of course I enjoyed it immensely. Madame Melba and Jean de Reszke were the principal singers. I just caught the last train down, and got here about 1 A.M. Today, Robson morning, tennis afternoon, Uncle Minto to dinner in the evening, played lines after dinner, and then read *Deerbrook* after he was gone. When everybody else was in bed, Uncle Rollo and I had a most interesting talk about Faith and Reason, in which he agreed with me wonderfully, condemning Faith in its ordinary sense altogether, and acknowledging only Reason. We got to speaking about illogical people, e.g. Salvationists, whom Uncle Rollo does not apparently consider selfish.

*June 23*. (Monday). On Saturday had Mr. Spencer Holland to tennis, and F.G.H. of course. On Sunday, Silas Farrington's friend Rowland Hill preached, well except for one or two slight wants of taste. Miss Bühler spent the day here. A large number of people came in the afternoon, George Russell, George Lefevre, H. H. Fowler M.P., Uncles Minto and Henry Elliot, Ethel Portal, Herbert Paul and others. Played tennis in the evening. Today Robson in the morning. After Miss Fraser went away. I am very sorry she is gone; there is always an awkwardness about a new person in the house, and Miss Fraser was very nice in her way. I spent almost the whole afternoon at work, till dinner. Mabel has gone to Windsor, but we expect her back here before very long. No improvement in her relations with Frank, which now evidently the world is finding out all about, which accounts for Grandmama not asking anything on Thursday.—We have been reading *Deerbrook* steadily. I do not agree with Miss Martineau in thinking Hope makes such a mistake in thinking he ought to marry Hester.

*June 25th*. (Wednesday). Today and yesterday tremendously hot, too much so for exercise till the evening. Consequently I did a lot of work yesterday; almost all the problems I had to do came out by Lagrange's equations, which are very agreeable for examples in small oscillations. Robson today acknowledged that my Saturday's paper (in which I had done very little) was about the vilest he ever saw. Being a Trinity June First-Year Problem Paper, it ought not to have been so bad, but everything was a grind, nothing came to a nice solution and some questions were insoluble. Yesterday and today played tennis in the evening, today with Maud Burdett. We have been going ahead with *Deerbrook*, which is apparently going to be tragic. Today I read some more of the *Trompeter* which is very pretty, and excellent practice in German, being brimfull of out-of-the-way words.

*June 26.* This morning did one or two easy questions about motion under no forces, and then got stuck over one about motion under any forces. I spent some hours on it again this afternoon, but could not solve my equations, the path of the Centre of Gravity being required and second integrals being therefore necessary. Also read some of Dante with Granny, containing a minute description of the transformation of a serpent into a man and a man into a serpent, which to my humble judgement appears unnecessary. This evening dined at Dover Street, where were Lyulph and Maizie, the Lubbocks, Sir (John?) Morier, Mr. Wright, Mr. Reid or Reeve (a very ancient fossil, who assured us he distinctly remembers the invention of macadamised roads in 1825) and a Mrs. —. I was between Aunt Maude and Lady Lubbock. Some of the conversation was amusing. I being the only Home Ruler (John Morley, who was expected, and whom I had looked forward very much to meeting, being detained at the House), here is a conversation at the beginning of dinner: Lady Lubbock: "Are you interested in politics?" I (anticipating a fight): "Very much". She: "Which way are you?" I: "Oh I'm a Home Ruler. I used to be a Unionist for a long time, but lately I've become a Home Ruler" (knowing this would produce discussion). She: "Why?" Sir John (leaning across Aunt Maude, having caught the word Home Rule, and being prepared utterly to snub and exterminate me): "What do you mean by Home Rule? I never met a Home Ruler yet who could tell me." I: "Oh well, I haven't framed a bill;"—Aunt Maude (interrupting): "Oh he thinks it enough to say he hasn't framed a bill". Sir John: "Yes, but what is your general idea of a bill?" I: "Oh I would give them control over all local matters, but not over imperial taxation, or of course the army and navy. —" Lyulph: "The police?" I: "Well I can't quite make up my mind about that". Lyulph: "The Judges?" "No, I think not". Sir John Lubbock: "Then would you be willing to give the same privileges to England and Scotland?" I: "Certainly". Sir John Lubbock: "Oh then that's federalism". "Well, I like federalism". "Yes but there's a difference between Home Rule and federalism. The one means giving privileges to one part of the Empire which you deny to the others. The other means giving equal privileges to all". "Oh, I'd rather not favour any part particularly". Aunt Maude (taking pity on me): "There, you see, he has his answers all ready". Later on the conversation took a more peacefully amusing form. Sir — Morier (who suffers very much from the gout) having first explained how he never put himself on diet for gout, preferring the pain and the good eating and drinking to no pain with simple fare, next went on to a gratis lecture on the iniquity of temperance, thus: "If there's one beast I hate, it's the teetotaller. The impiety of the thing is the great objection". (Lyulph, most gravely: "Yes, that is the great objection —.") Morier: "Well I'm glad you agree with me. Why, it says clearly, after the flood, when God had given them plenty of water, he said 'now I'm going to give you plenty of wine'. He didn't say he'd mix water with their wine, but wine with their water". Grandmama: "Where does it say that?" Morier: "Oh Lady Stanley, you ought to read your Bible". Lyulph: "Don't you remember, Mama?" (Followed by a detailed proof that it is so, with a hint that some few people in these days don't accept the Bible as infallible). There was more amusing conversation if I could remember it.

*July 14th.* Am going to give up keeping a regular journal and only to write now and then.—I have just been reading that wonderful chapter in the *Mill on the Floss* where Maggie finds Thomas à Kempis. I wish I could take his lesson to heart even in the misunderstood way in which Maggie does. For although she is still perhaps in some sort selfish in her self-renunciation, as is proved by her yielding to the first temptation worth the name which comes across her path, still she does carry some sort of holiness about with her throughout that time, and her life is calmer and unquestionably happier. Like her, I feel that all my life has been selfish: even my best acts have had some background of selfish motives, as my miserable habit of introspection shows me; but unlike her, though convinced of the truth of the blessedness of self-renunciation, I have not enough self-control nor enough steadiness of purpose to be able to practise it for any length of time. I always hanker after a fuller life, after a satisfaction of my highest wants which I know to be inconsistent with the highest life. Of course the want of faith, which I feel to be no fault of mine, does increase the difficulty of life for me; but even so, if I could put away that miserable longing for happiness, I might instead thereof find blessedness. For with the faith in immortality and in a reward for virtue hereafter, the utter and entire self-denial of those who do good without that hope is much diminished.—I am convinced it is useless to try and crush out all the higher parts of my nature (besides being wicked and impious) as I have been trying to do since Christmas; I cannot permanently occupy my thoughts with work so exclusively as never to feel that there are other things needful; and the longer other thoughts are kept down, the wilder and the more painful they will be when they do arise. The foundation of all my unhappiness is I believe that same selfishness which was in Maggie; but it is so mixed up with other feelings that it is difficult to get at the root of it. At one time I fancied it was caused solely by religious questions; but since last Autumn I know that that is not the case, for then I was more unhappy than ever before or since, and yet I hardly gave any thought to religious matters. And even that part of it which is due to this cause is to some extent selfish. Why should I wish myself to be immortal? If I do my duty here, the hereafter can be no concern of mine. In any case I shall have rest, and freedom from struggle, both with myself and with the outside world. Why should I wish to believe myself a free agent? If I am not, I ought to rejoice in that I have no responsibility, not to be hurt by wounded pride and by the disappointment of the conceited and blasphemous wish to help God's work, as though he were not able to do it himself.—When I have eliminated the selfish element from all my troubles and when I have cured my morbid self-analysis, I shall certainly find a very small residuum, and may hope, if I ever succeed in this, to be of some use to others instead of being always fully occupied with the spectres of the mind.

*August 31st.* Alas! the only shred of faith I had left in me is, for the time at least, gone. I did believe in a Deity, and if I did have to close my eyes to the fact that His moral qualities did not manifest themselves with the same clearness as His intellectual, still I derived immense comfort from the belief, and from the necessary deduction that a world governed by an all-wise and all-powerful Being must be tending to good always. But now!—I have begun to feel that the reasoning which always convinced me before, for a long time so as to preclude even comprehension of doubt, has lost its cogency. I began by seeing that the existence of evil really cannot, at least in the present state of knowledge, be reconciled by any straight-forward reasoning with the government of a perfectly beneficent and perfectly wise God; I was finally overturned by some passages in Mill's *Autobiography*, in which he puts this argument very clearly. With regard to my old argument, a necessary prime Cause and Law-giver, I see that it affords no explanation of the mystery but merely offers one permanent unchangeable Mystery in the place of the many which Science now is unable to answer. This argument Mill puts clearly in speaking of the education he got from his father: "He told me that the question, Who made me? cannot be answered, because it immediately suggests the further question, Who made God?" I still think that the hypothesis of an almighty First Cause affords a consistent explanation of the Universe, and therefore has the same kind of probability as the theory of the Ether, but the degree of its probability must depend upon its explanation of a large number of particular facts, on which I am not qualified to give an opinion.—The loss of certainty, is however the great pain which results from the change. To feel that the universe may be hurrying blindly towards all that is bad, that humanity may any day cease its progressive development and may continually lose all its fine qualities, that Evolution has no necessarily progressive principle prompting it; these are thoughts which render life almost intolerable. Indeed I doubt whether, if I do not regain my old faith, I shall long be able to hold out against the frightful thoughts that crowd in upon my mind. I remember an instant of the same pain at Southgate once in thinking of the sadness which is always suggested by natural beauty, when the idea flashed across my mind that when most in harmony with Nature I felt most sad, and that therefore the spirit of Nature must be sad and the Universe a mistake. Then I could not have borne it another instant, for though it came and went like a flash I felt as though I had been stabbed; but now I am more inured to mental pain, and I am comforted by the thought that Humanity will probably improve, for it has usually done so in the past, and also by the thought that Agnosticism is not, at least according to Mill, necessarily productive of moral evil even if wide-spread, or is even a great agent for good. Moreover I believe that to those brought up in Agnosticism it cannot be the agony that it is to one coming to it after having known the repose of the other theory.

*November 20*. (Cambridge). It is strange, on looking back to what I wrote on August 31, to see the pain with which I came to Agnosticism; for now I have become quite reconciled to it, and have even found some increase of 10 repose in the feeling of having nothing to lose. Since coming here, I have of course had no time to think, since work and society have divided practically the whole of my time among them. Strange, how completely I have changed in the last two years. I am now not perceptibly shy, I am fond of fairly agreeable society, I read no poetry or literature of any sort, I do no thinking, I can look with comparative indifference on natural beauty; on the other hand I have lost almost all my cynicism (though a small dose of disagreeable society would bring it back). I have on the whole certainly deteriorated more than could at all have been expected, though to most outsiders I suppose I have seemed to improve. I certainly have more social powers than I had; I 20 actually find people willing to recognise my existence. The people I have hitherto met here are every one of them unsatisfactory; the least so are the Llewelyn Davies's, but even they have a want of sturdiness in some things. The dons are sad specimens of wasted power, and have persuaded me that emoluments for mere academical distinction are a very pernicious institution. Among undergrads, there seems a large agnostic element, characterized by a flippancy which entirely prevents my having any sympathy with them. In fact flippancy strikes me as *the* besetting sin of the whole place, perhaps of the whole country or of the whole world. Up here, however, the amount of learning leads one to expect some wisdom, but there seems to 30 exist but little of it.—Short of the highest excellence there are great numbers, however, whose society is rather pleasant than otherwise, and with whom one has some subject of common interest. Altogether, I feel that much enjoyment is to be had here, and perhaps the friend I look for may appear in time; perhaps the fault lies rather in me.

*December 15*. (Cambridge). The last evening of my first term. On looking back I am struck by the fact that it has been ever so much more successful than I expected. I have made acquaintance with such people as Trevelyan, the Llewelyn Davies's, and McTaggart, who are all a great acquisition and all tend to engender in me a more healthy view of life and of humanity than I 40 have ever taken since going to Southgate. Among those whose society is

extremely agreeable are Waldegrave, Buckler, Crawford and many others, but almost all third or fourth-year men. My acquaintance among freshmen seems to be limited to the mathematical set, and I do not see quite how it is to become more extensive. In the mean time, however, my society is exactly what I should wish it; not very large, but almost entirely composed of men of ability and of a quiet mode of life. A larger acquaintance would interfere more with my work than I should wish, besides which it would scarcely be so select. The most curious character I have come across is Gaul. Though a wonderful mathematician, he is in every other respect vulgar and childish
10 and materialistic and selfish. It is a pity to see such a person brought to the fore by the cram system, and I think an extension of the system introduced in the Scholarship Essay and General Paper would be a great advantage. A certain percentage in these two papers should I think be necessary no matter how well a man might do in his special subject. This would prevent the ignorant uncultured specialist from succeeding in the way he does now and would also prevent overwork to a great extent and encourage general intelligence, which is to my mind far more useful than great knowledge entirely restricted to one subject.

*January 18. 1891.* (Cambridge). I here insert two sonnets written at differ-
20 ent times and imitating I think (though at the time unconsciously) Shelley's two "Ye hasten to the dead" and "Lift not the painted veil". I insert them merely from the psychological point of view, and not as having in themselves the very minutest merit. They seem to me to throw light on what may be called the dynamics of psychology, though of course the first was written under the influence of feelings over which the intellect had for the moment lost control.
(1). December 1889.

O weary soul, that seekest for more light,
And find'st but broken fragments of the truth,
30 That feel'st a vague and undefined desire
For something greater than this earth can give,
A striving after perfect blessedness
And fuller life than here is granted thee:
Think not this want shall never be supplied
Dream not that death will quench that spark of light
Which makes thee long for more; but trust in God,
Who, as he gave thee thoughts which seek for him,
Will, when this life's short struggle is no more,
Fulfil thy noblest hopes, and satisfy
40 That restless striving after perfect life
Which while thou liv'st doth ever drive thee on.

(2). September 1890.

> How hateful is the light of day to me
> And all the weary tasks of daily life,
> Without that faith which ever led me on
> And gave me hope through thickest clouds of pain!
> The faith, that One above doth rule the world
> In perfect equity and perfect love,
> For all his creatures toiling here below
> For then I felt that good must ever come
> From all the misery and sin around,                                    10
> And I did trust that man must ever move
> Upward and onward toward the perfect life.
> But now I know not whither the world moves;
> Evil may come of good, and sin and death
> Hold sway as long as man shall live to suffer pain.

When I look back to the state of mind that produced these two sonnets, and
still more when I look back to Southgate in the spring of 1889, when I
worshipped nature with an emotional pantheism and felt my faith renewed
by "sunset and its gorgeous ministers, and solemn midnight's tingling silentness" and by "spring's voluptuous pantings, when she breathes Her    20
first sweet kisses" and by every beautiful thing I saw; when I look back to
these states of feeling, I despair of ever regaining the moral and intellectual
elevation which I had then reached; I find myself daily becoming more vulgar and more conventional; I find (which proves the most frightful degrada-
tion) that even Agnosticism is become not unpleasant to me; in fact, I have
acquired happiness by brutification, and as for a time I endeavoured to do
so, I can scarcely complain now that my desire is accomplished. I believe a
very large amount of solitary leisure, such as I had at Southgate, is absolutely necessary to the maintenance of a high moral and intellectual standard, with me at least. A life without leisure, such as the life here (for one's   30
exercise is as little leisure as one's work), is absolutely fatal to mental development. Happiness also is bad for moral and perhaps for intellectual
health, and I have not yet found an antidote to these unwholesome conditions. (By "unwholesome" I mean adverse to the highest development; in
the ordinary sense of the word, my mind is a thousand times healthier now
than at Southgate; but the ordinary sense of the word implies absence of
extreme views on any subject, which is incompatible with the highest development). The sense in which I have lost is that expressed in
Wordsworth's ode, though I have deteriorated rather before my time: "at
length the man perceives it die away and fade into the light of common day".   40

*December 5. 1892.* 1 a.m. O God forgive me; I have sinned grievously. What the others did, that I did also for fear lest I should seem to set myself up above them, for fear lest I should seem a prig. How ought I to glory in that name, could I indeed deserve it! How weak and foolish seem now the paltry motives, the mean fears which I vainly endeavoured to mistake for a broad-minded freedom from prejudice. How vain a thing it is to hope to lead others to a knowledge of the highest when in my own acts I evince a folly no less than that of whatever companions chance or the moment has assigned to me! Ah My God in Thy mercy grant if thou carest for us poor weak erring
10 mortals and not for the saints only, grant that I may henceforth have strength to stand out against the insidious advances of folly, to draw the line justly between harmless merriment and vicious jesting. May I no more do that which in my heart I abhor to win the paltry and ephemeral good will of those whose respect I forfeit by the very course which deference to them has led me into. Give it to me O Lord, if thou canst, to stand out from the follies of my friends no less than from the vices of my enemies; to resist the intoxication of mirth and preserve a sane mind among pleasures as among sorrows. Grant this O Lord and I will serve thee with my might, for the will I have but the courage I sorely need.

20                    A HISTORY OF MY FRIENDSHIP FOR FITZ

It began when I made his acquaintance, in the autumn of 1888. I saw him first at Green's. I had then been some time at Green's without finding *any* intellectual or moral sympathy; I had lived a life of complete solitude, often passing whole days without exchanging any avoidable words with any one. At the same time, I had been awaking to all the larger interests of life, I had begun to read Carlyle, Tennyson, Shelley, Byron; in short, to take a keen interest in literature, and poetry in particular. I had awakened to the love of Nature, and had emerged from the base materialism into which my Theology had sunk me. At the same time, I had no companions outside my own
30 home; I had been taught to look out for a friend in whom I should find similarity of tastes, a high standard of morality, and faults indeed, but such as could be mutually reproved and pointed out without endangering friendship. At this time, when I had begun to think all young men in England were steeped in brutish stockish materialism, Fitz appeared on the scene. I saw that he mixed little with the others, that he had a refined intellectual face over which an interesting melancholy seemed to brood; that he was shy (a quality which I then considered an invariable accompaniment to any agreeableness in young people); and that he did not swear or talk smut, and in short appeared generally quiet and respectable. Attracted by these
40 things and by the dislike which the others felt towards him, I bethought me how to make a more intimate acquaintance with him. To others this would

not have been difficult; but to me, owing to shyness, it was no easy matter.
He lodged some way off from Green's, and I used to walk down that way and
catch him up or be caught up by him in a casual accidental sort of manner
(whereat and at my shyness generally he was naturally much amused).
However I did not get far into his friendship in his first term; he spoke so low
and indistinctly that I could not make out a word he said, and we were both
too reserved to find out much about each other. However at the end of the
term we went away in the train together and he was very agreeable and polite
and asked me to call on his people in town (which of course I didn't do) and
generally made a favourable impression on my simplicity. In the following 10
term I was thrown much more together with him owing to our going three
times a week to Notting Hill together to coach with Robson, and to my often
on those occasions lunching with his people. I discovered that he had read
all Shakespeare (a thing which seemed to me then quite to establish a literary
reputation); that he knew *Hamlet* very well; and that he had read *Paradise
Lost*. With this foundation I rapidly advanced in knowledge of his reading,
and he played upon my gullibility for his amusement by pretending to be
very poetic and a great admirer, though not worshipper (as I then was), of
Nature. These ideas I was the more ready to accept, as I was making the
acquaintance of his sister, who seemed to me the ideal of young woman- 20
hood. In her I found liberalism in politics and religion, complete emancipation from vulgar prejudices, great culture and wide reading (which I then
believed to be even greater and wider than they really were). Moreover I
found (or thought I found) high moral aims in her, which I was willing to
believe were reflected in him. She has apostatized since. The birth of my real
friendship with him was on a certain evening when he came here from
Saturday to Monday and disclosed to me that he was an atheist, that he was
purely selfish, in short, that he was destitute of all which would have recommended him to most people. To me however, who was at that time a firm
believer in a God and in a rigid utilitarian code of morality which I deduced 30
from my belief, this seemed an occasion for the conversion of one whom I
then believed to be an honest though erring seeker after truth. I had boundless faith, and as for selfishness I did not believe him but put it down to
excessive humility. From this night onwards we had frequent theological
discussions; that a person should be unorthodox I regarded as an essential to
friendship, and the particular shade being different from mine only made
our intercourse the more interesting.

OCCASIONAL JOURNAL

*July 21. 1893.* I dreamt last night that I was engaged to be married to Alys,
when I discovered that my people had deceived me, that my mother was not 40
dead but in a madhouse: I therefore had of course to give up the thought of

ever marrying. This dream haunts me. (Alys's birthday.)

I think of Alys all day long. Like Neschdanoff in Turgenjeff, I am haunted by a doubt of my real feelings. Still more horrible, I half fear the amusement of my relations. What a curse it is to have so keen a sense of humour! But of course the whole business is ridiculous and I ought to get it out of my head as soon as possible; and above all keep it quite to myself. I incline to think that my passion is imaginary when I reflect that I "love Love" just now and envy those who have a mutual love. But I think it has been genuine, not only now, but ever since I first met her, when I reflect on the minute recollection I have of every detail of my meetings with her. In particular when they asked me to recite and I said I knew only Shelley and *she* asked me to recite "I can give not what men call Love". I believe they were surprised at the amount of feeling which Art (as they supposed) put into my repetition of those lines: but it was natural enough. She did not know either why it was the happiest day of my life when she asked me in the boat last month if it was not. To suppose a miserable Tripos List could make me happy! And yet I could not undeceive her.—But Walt and work will I hope help me through and I suppose I shall grow reconciled and reasonable again in time. One thing thank God I gain by my habit of self-analysis: I know Lust has absolutely no share in my passion.

*August 12. 1893.* The greatest day of my life hitherto. Alys and a cousin came to stay a night and she staid afterwards by herself: we went *tête-à-tête* in a canoe and discussed love and marriage. How absurd to an older person it would seem to have to argue and argue on a question of social ethics before acquiring the minutest right to speak of one's own feelings! I gave her my little essay on the immorality of not marrying if in any way above the average: this led to a discussion. I explained how in my view love, sympathy, friendship (whichever you like) was the greatest thing attainable, was indeed the only thing ultimately worth having; she maintained independence; I tried to prove this a means to a higher end. We agreed to a large extent that marriage gave the best opportunity for such spiritual love and that a pure friendship between man and woman is impossible. But I found, what I had always imagined in women, an aversion to sexual intercourse and a shrinking from it only to be overcome by the desire for children. I then tried to argue it was neither good nor bad and neither added to nor subtracted from a spiritual communion.—But whether she remained blind to my feelings throughout I know not: I fear I hinted them unintentionally once or twice. She said with no other man would she have gone about alone as she was doing. I regretted her departure. However we shall meet again she said as though the thought were pleasant. I trust my arguments made some impression, and she consented to occasional correspondence by which much may be done.—Never before was she so *vertraulich*. I intended to shew her some of the more intelligible passages in McTaggart's paper, about love in its philosophical aspect: was it an omen that on our returning home it had mysteriously disappeared?

*August 25. 1893.* Have received two letters from Alys and written two. Any place seems to me now endurable, as I can reach her by letter, which is next best to her society. We still discuss marriage: I am confident of converting her in time with patience and conversation, but then will be only the time to begin what is important to me. The ridiculous elements in my position, which used to obtrude themselves so painfully on my thoughts, have vanished in comparison of the keenness of my love, which has become a clear and certain fact to me. She dwells in my thoughts from morning till night and in my dreams from night till morning. I dreamt Miss Stephens flirted furiously with me in the wood here: I found myself almost forced to put my arm round her waist and kiss her, but in doing so I said: You mustn't imagine I wish to marry you, as I am in love with another. When I am awake my relation to her seems so much more real than my relation to anybody else that what others may do and say appears of no importance. Ah when shall I be able to speak, and will she be horrified and regard all my present conduct as selfish and me as a fool? For me no happy issue I am sure is possible. But to resist is now become impossible to me: I no longer tear up her letters with a gulp and a jerk as I used to do, but treasure them up, and read them constantly. Fool! Fool! Fool!

[*August 29. 1893.* Lunched with Frank and his Spanish-American friend Santayana, a charming cosmopolitan with whom I discussed much philosophy, poetry and art; also German Universities. Berlin everyway best, especially as to professors. Good lodgings neighbourhood of Unter den Linden, Friedrichs- or Wilhelmstrasse. Summer semester in a small place e.g. Tübingen. This was his advice.] Shakespeare's sonnets and the one Drayton are the greatest love poetry in the world.

*September 16. 1893.* All is accomplished: my wildest hopes had not imagined such success. I have been two days at Friday's Hill: the first morning she and I went up into the Bôw-Tree: I said I made few demands on life and those were not to be granted: she said all wishes could be obtained by perseverance: I felt certain she knew what I meant so felt encouraged but could hardly believe my good fortune. So I talked about friends in general and said I always cared more about them than they about me. *She*: You don't trust them. *I*: I don't.—After a pause, and with the greatest hesitation, after a concentrated struggle in myself, I said: I am sure you don't care for me as I care for you. *She*: No but I have entire sympathy with you and what more can you want. I wish you could take our friendship calmly like any other: I

think this makes a defect in the relation. *I*: I have tried but it isn't like any other; I have fought hard but cannot take it calmly. Then there was a long pause. At last she said in a rather unsteady voice: I think if I were conscientious I should put an end to this friendship, for your sake; but I care about it too much myself. *I* interrupting: Oh you couldn't do that: it's the only thing that makes life valuable to me. *She*: Well fortunately I'm not conscientious. After a pause and with some hesitation (as no word of marriage had yet been said) I told her my dream with which this journal begins. After some talk about it she said: I wish you would put away the thought of marriage:
10 friendship is so much nicer, I don't want to marry, at least for a long long time. [Before this talk began I found her views were changed on the general question of marriage]. *I*: I will try and be calm, and I could be more easily if I saw more of you. *She*: We ought to see each other oftener if we are ever to think of it (marriage I suppose).—Then we were long silent: when for the first time I felt an intense happiness with all but no admixture of pain.— Next morning we went onto the beech hill before breakfast: it was a glorious morning when everything seems young and innocent. We sat down and looked into the wood. *She*: I feel we ought to discuss our friendship once more before beginning it: I am not sure if you are entering on it with your
20 eyes open. You see if we were to grow very very intimate and I not to fall in love with you at the end it would give you such intense pain. *I*: But it's my only chance. I can answer for my love remaining unchanged: it is too late if you wish to save me pain in a separation. If it must come, the longer it is postponed the better: seeing my love cannot grow greater than it is. *She*: But people develop so much after your age. *I*: Yes I think it would be wrong not to wait years before marriage.—But we are to meet as often as is at all possible: talk little of our friendship (having made our positions quite clear to each other) but try and get to know each other intimately: as we of course both feel that without great intimacy it is folly to become engaged. She
30 promises nothing after years of intimacy; but these are in themselves a prospect full of joy; and I have promised (what is within my strength) even if the worst should happen I would not be in any way foolish. I assured her that for the present she had made me happy as I had never believed I could be: and she said she was much happier than before our explanation. *Et depuis je ne me sens plus de joie.*

But what a curse the conventions necessitated by folly and bestiality are to those who like ourselves must disregard them if we are to act honestly, and yet ought not, however we might desire it, *openly* to disregard them, as this would lessen our influence and power of doing good and would besides
40 cause both her relations and mine considerable pain, and be completely misunderstood. Hence concealment and all its attendant dangers. However I have practised it so long at home that I must by now be inoculated against its bad effects. Oh that there could be one morality for the prudent and one

for the fools!

⟨*Undated*⟩

>O Love they wrong thee much
>Who say thy sweet is bitter
>When thy rich fruit is such
>As nothing can be sweeter
>Fair House of joy and bliss
>Where truest pleasure is
>I do adore thee
>I know thee what thou art                          10
>I serve thee with my heart
>And fall before thee.

*July 20–21,* ⟨*1894,*⟩ *midnight.* This night is the anniversary of my dream about Alys, and also of her birth. Strange coincidence, which, combined with the fact that most of my dream has come true, very strongly impresses my imagination. I was always superstitious, and happiness has made me more so. It is terrifying to be so utterly absorbed in one person. Nothing has any worth to me except in reference to her. Even my own career, my efforts after virtue, my intellect (such as it is), everything I have or hope for, I value only as gifts to her, as means of shewing how unspeakably I value her love.  20 And I am happy, divinely happy. Above all, I can still say Thank God Lust has absolutely no share in my passion.—But just when I am happiest, when joy is purest, it seems to transcend itself and fall suddenly to haunting terrors of loss—it would be so easy to lose what rests on so slender and unstable a foundation! My dream on her birthday; my subsequent discovery that my people had deceived me as in that dream; their solemn and reiterated warnings; the gradual discovery, one by one, of the tragedies, hopeless and unalleviated, which have made up the lives of most of my family; above all, the perpetual gloom which hangs like a fate over P.L., and which, struggle as I will, invades my inmost soul whenever I go there, taking all joy even out of 30 Alys's love; all these, combined with the fear of heredity, cannot but oppress my mind; they make me feel as though a doom lay on the family and I were vainly battling against it, to escape into the freedom which seems the natural birthright of others. Worst of all, this dread, of necessity, involves Alys too; I feel as though darkness were my native element, and a cruel destiny had compelled me, instead of myself attaining to the light, to drag her back with me into the gulf from which I have partially emerged. I cannot tell whether this destiny will take the form of a sudden blow, or of a long-drawn torture, sapping our energies and ruining our love; but I am haunted by the fear of the family ghost, which seems to seize on me with clammy 40 invisible hands to avenge my desertion of its tradition of gloom—

All these feelings of course are folly, solely due to chocolate cake and sitting up late; but they are none the less real, and on the slightest pretence they assail me with tremendous force. Painful as it will necessarily be to them, I must for some time avoid seeing more than a very little of my people, and of P.L., otherwise I really shall begin to fear for my sanity. P.L. is to me like a family vault haunted by the ghosts of maniacs, especially in view of all that I have recently learnt from Dr. Anderson.—Here, thank heaven, all is bright and healthy, my Alys especially; and as long as I can forget P.L. and the ghastly heritage it bequeaths to me I have no forebodings, but only the pure joy of mutual love; a joy so great, so divine, that I have not yet ceased to wonder how such a thing can exist in this world which people abuse. But oh I *wish* I could know it would bring joy to her in the end, and not teach her further, what alas it has already begun to teach her, how terrible a thing life may be, and what depths of misery it can contain.

*Wednesday. October 3.* Received at Paris with joy. B.R.

*Paris. October 6. 1894.* Was interrupted in my evening's letter to Alys by a d—d cypher telegram asking if France would cooperate with England, Germany, U.S.A. and Russia in intervention between China and Japan, former to pay indemnity for expenses of war.—Phipps heard that Rosebery had considered it touch-and-go that we might have had a regular diplomatic rupture with France.—In that case I should have gone to Cambridge and told the tale, to Sanger's intense interest—how selfish I am! I could hardly help regretting it had not come about, as it would have been so pleasant for me.—Read Wagner on Psychology of Economic Action, and felt his Ethics to be amateurish. I almost think I could have written a better account of the matter myself! Wrote to Alys about abstract intellectual nature of my passions—I grow more abstract every day—I believe I'm drying up, like Spinoza in Pater—but perhaps it's only a phase, due to self-preservation— any more human passions cannot be satisfied here.—I'm glad to be cheerful—it makes me feel a brute to see how often my depressed letters have brought Alys to tears.—Got Photo of group containing Alys, which called up her half-forgotten features to my memory and made me very happy in consequence. I have discovered in reading James that almost all my psychical life is carried on in auditory and tactile images—I suppose that is why I can't read without pronouncing every word as I go. This has led me to a psychological generalization about aesthetics and intellect—the temporal arts appeal to the ear, the spatial to the eye—what appeals to the ear is necessarily successive because the ear is not capable of taking in a large number of simultaneous impressions, what to the eye, mainly simultaneous. Hence the visualizing type should go with a life of present impressions, i.e. with a non-intellectual, so-called artistic temperament—the type which thinks in sounds on the other hand should like the temporal arts, music and literature—must therefore have a coordinating, remembering mind, not wholly absorbed in the present—must in short be more intellectual. In music, one who attends only to each passing note misses most of the beauty, which lies in the sequence—so in literature. This idea strikes me as suggestive, but I suppose it is either false or old.

Looking back to what I wrote on July 20–21, I am amazed how much happier I am now than then—I have no doubts whatever about the rightness of our decision or the possibility of our marriage being all it ought to be. Every day I become more convinced that marriage, so far from making our relation deteriorate, will make it deeper and better. We have met each other half way in our theories, and I am more and more impressed by Alys's power of developing and broadening and abandoning long-cherished theories. There only remains religion, and in that there are signs of our soon coming into sympathy, which *would* be a joy to me. A little patience, and a little sympathy, has always been all that has been needed—but I can understand how in marriage an utterly unsympathetic rejection of a woman's opinions, theoretically and practically, would harden her in crude views, and how the woman's-rights people get their hatred of men. The more sympathetic people can be, the more they suffer from absence of sympathy—and that is why women are harder and cruder than men when they have a Cause at heart.—Abstract again! My mind has got to the stage where it refuses to remain a moment in the concrete. It *is* shocking!

[Returned to Alys October 12]

> How like a winter hath my absence been
> From thee, the pleasure of the fleeting year!
> What freezings have I felt, what dark days seen,
> What old December's bareness every where!
> And yet this time removed was summer's time,
> The teeming Autumn big with rich increase,
> Bearing the wanton burden of the prime
> Like widow'd wombs after their lord's decease.
> But this abundant issue seemed to me
> But hope of orphans and unfathered fruit,
> For Summer and his pleasures wait on thee,
> And thou away the very birds are mute—
>     Or, if they sing, 'tis with so dull a cheer
>     That leaves look pale, dreading the winter's near.

August–November 1894.

# 10

# Die Ehe [1893]

"THE GREATEST DAY of my life hitherto" is how Russell described 12 August 1893 in the preceding diary (at 62: 21). He and Alys had gone canoeing alone at Cambridge and discussed love and marriage. In the same entry Russell commented:

> How absurd to an older person it would seem to have to argue and argue on a question of social ethics before acquiring the minutest right to speak of one's own feelings! I gave her my little essay on the immorality of not marrying if in any way above the average: this led to a discussion.

"Die Ehe" ("Marriage") is the essay referred to. It is found in Barbara Halpern's files of Russell's correspondence with Alys following his letter of 9 August 1893, although the letter makes no reference to the essay. An undated half leaf in Russell's hand following the essay discusses "wishes and opinions"—a more personal continuation of their discussion of marriage. The title of **10** may reflect Russell's reading of Ibsen in German in June and August 1893. His copy of the German translation of *Nora* (or *A Doll's House*) survives in his library. This play portrays a marriage in which an independent woman finally leaves her husband.

Alys responded to "Die Ehe" on 16 August with an essay of her own, presenting reasons why certain kinds of women should not marry. Russell's letter from Holyhead of 19 August shows that he was considering Alys's argument. There the exchange ended, with Russell writing on 25 August from Pembroke Lodge that he cannot think of any new arguments to "fill a new paper". He continued, however, to send Alys passages from Whitman, a favourite poet of theirs and from whose *Leaves of Grass* he quotes at the beginning of "Die Ehe".

The copy-text is the manuscript; it consists of three leaves. A microfilm of it is in the Russell Archives (RA REC. ACQ. 434).

Unfolded out of the folds of the woman man comes unfolded and is
    always to come unfolded
Unfolded only out of the superbest woman of the earth is to come the
    superbest man of the earth
Unfolded out of the friendliest woman is to come the friendliest man
Unfolded only out of the perfect body of a woman can a man be
    formed of perfect body
Unfolded only out of the inimitable poems of woman can come the
    poems of man (only thence have my poems come)
Unfolded out of the strong and arrogant woman I love only thence      10
    can appear the strong and arrogant man I love
Unfolded by brawny embraces from the well-muscled woman I love,
    only thence come the brawny embraces of the man
Unfolded out of the folds of the woman's brain come all the folds of
    the man's brain duly obedient
Unfolded out of the justice of the woman all justice is unfolded
Unfolded out of the sympathy of a woman is all sympathy
A man is a great thing upon earth and through eternity but every jot
    of the greatness of man is unfolded out of woman
First the man is shaped in the woman, he can then be shaped in      20
    himself.

W.W.

IT IS AN unfortunate result of the present transitional position of women
in this country that the best of them, those who in most respects best
understand the new and wider duties which a woman now ought to fulfil,
have, as is not unnatural, a determination not to marry. This I suppose
springs from two causes, (1) an objection to the present permanence of the
marriage contract (2) the aversion to temporary loss of usefulness in the first
years of marriage. The second objection is perhaps the more strongly felt,
but the first appears to me the only one which is really serious. I will there-  30
fore endeavour to obviate the second first. That (say) as much as ten years at
the beginning of a woman's married life are liable to be, as far as public work
is concerned, wasted, is very true; but in what sense can these years be
supposed really wasted? Suppose a family of four, three of whom survive
and in their turn become workers: these are extremely likely to become
thoroughly useful members of the community, being *ex hypothesi* born of
parents endowed with the social qualities to an unusual degree (otherwise
the objection to marriage to meet which this argument is designed could
never have existed), and being educated in liberal traditions. Further these
children in the new generation are almost certain to be centres of liberalism  40
and to advance the cause of unprejudiced opinion and of toleration, to which
few things are so great an assistance as a good body of opinion sufficient to

compensate for the odium incurred with the multitude. There is yet another argument: it is doubtful whether a woman's sympathies can ever develope at all fully without marriage and whether in her old age she is not likely to become narrow and bigoted, as appears to be the usual fate of old maids. And on the husband's side too: he is condemned either to marry a woman who is mentally his inferior, who does not share his enthusiasm or his opinions, with whom therefore it is impossible to have any real sympathy and who is very likely to pervert him and bring up her children conventionally and whose children in any case are likely to be greatly inferior to those of a
10 better woman: or he is condemned to celibacy, in which case *his* superiority also is lost from a hereditary point of view. As a minor argument, it may be observed that a married couple not under the tyranny of Respectability and Conventionality have much more power of befriending those who practically rebel against these than either a single man or a single woman. Are not all these advantages, but of course chiefly that of producing children, sufficient to weigh against ten years' work? Our parents occupied in the last generation the position which we occupy in this: had they not married the present generation would have been destitute of all who lead the van of progress, of all its Pioneers.
20     The other argument, arising from an objection to the permanence of the marriage contract, appears to me more serious. For any man or woman engaged in any sort of philanthropic or public work it is of course out of the question to indulge, at least openly, in extra-connubial sexual intercourse; on the other hand it is difficult to see how the cause of freedom is advocated by a monkish celibacy. In fact one who lives a life of celibacy would by many be considered to have no right to an opinion on questions of sexual intercourse and could certainly be much less competent to judge of such subjects than he or she might otherwise be. Again if both parties to a marriage are agreed as to the inadvisability of permanent contracts there may easily be an
30 extra-legal understanding that so far as the disapproval of society can be either faced or avoided, freedom on both sides should be allowed. This is no doubt a very unsatisfactory system, but supposing (as the present argument necessarily must) the inadvisability of permanent marriage contracts it might to some extent obviate the evils arising from them.—But apart from the possible methods of circumventing the law as it stands, surely the best way of operating towards a change of both law and opinion on such a subject is to conform to custom in acts though not in words and to bring up a family in the freer creed of the parents. If all who hold this creed in the present generation abstain from marriage the number who hold it in the next will,
40 instead of being as it should be much greater than in the present, be on the contrary much smaller, and no improvement either in law or in public opinion can be hoped for. And all the advantages mentioned above are to be weighed against the apparent inconsistency of marrying while disapproving

of marriage, which does not, to me at least, appear to be a real inconsistency, as many bad customs are best altered by submitting to them in act while rebelling against them in speech. For those, however, whose utility does not depend upon the esteem of the multitude (such as artists and men of science), it is of course better, if they hold the views above stated, to inaugurate the change by practice as well as theory and endeavour to force public opinion to admit their virtue by other more recognized forms of self-denial.

# 11

# Self-Appreciation [1897]

THIS PAPER APPEARED under the heading "Self-Appreciations. / 1. Orlando" in *The Golden Urn*, no. 1 (March 1897): 30–1. The *Golden Urn* was edited by Logan Pearsall Smith (Alys's brother) with the collaboration of Bernard Berenson. It was printed at Oxford but privately issued from Fiesole; there were just three numbers. The aim was to print the most perfect lines of poetry and prose and "some impressions of art and life, some experiments in letters" (no. 1: 1). The editors welcomed "above all the loving or ironic study of the human soul, treasuring the expression of an exquisite mood far more than any excitement of drama or action" (*ibid.*). In an undated letter apparently to Alys (Library of Congress; copy in RA REC. ACQ. 178), Pearsall Smith wrote of potential contributions to the *Golden Urn*:

> Also it would be interesting for a few self-conscious people to make studies, or rather sum up the studies they must always be making—of their own sensations, what things in life come to them most vividly and appealingly. It would be amusing if nothing more.

Apparently Pearsall Smith requested contributions in the form of responses to questions (now lost) that he had posed, for in a letter of 9 February 1897 thanking Alys for her and Russell's "Self-Appreciations" he put several "new questions" (L. P. Smith *1950*, 68). Certainly Russell's contribution is in the form of a series of responses (though there are no replies to the new questions).

The self-appreciation by "Orlando" is not otherwise signed. It is followed by one by "Florizel", who remains unidentified. Orlando is identified as Bertrand Russell by Samuels (*1979*, 272–3). The identification is undoubtedly correct, although the only evidence is internal. It is not known whether Russell or Pearsall Smith chose the pseudonym "Orlando". Its pertinence may be that Orlando is the somewhat depressive, slighted younger brother in Shakespeare's *As You Like It*. Also like Orlando, Russell might be described as "never schooled and yet learned" (1.i.175–6).

Pearsall Smith's letter of 9 February 1897 probably dates the paper's composition as early 1897, since as late as Christmas 1896 the Russells were en route from America (Russell *1968*, 156), where they had spent two months. Since no manuscript has been found, the copy-text is the version in the *Golden Urn*.

YES, I THINK of the Universe as a whole—several times a day at least. But I have no image, only the word universe with certain predicates, or the proposition Universe = God.

Nature seldom speaks to me, though it used to very much. Metaphysics, not science, interest my soul.

I am quite indifferent to the mass of human creatures; though I wish, as a purely intellectual problem, to discover some way in which they might all be happy. I wouldn't sacrifice myself to them, though their unhappiness, at moments, about once in three months, gives me a feeling of discomfort, and an intellectual desire to find a way out. I believe emotionally in Democracy, though I see no reason to do so. Progress I believe in both emotionally and scientifically, though not metaphysically. I am very patriotic. I believe in several definite measures (e.g. Infanticide) by which society could be improved. My ideal of government is the Fabian ideal of the English Government. I feel a duty to society, but chiefly negatively, i.e. I couldn't do anything I thought harmful to it, such as living too expensively.

I live most for myself—everything has for me, a reference to my own education. I care for very few people, and have several enemies—two or three at least whose pain is delightful to me. I often wish to give pain, and when I do, I find it pleasant for the moment. I feel myself superior to most people, and only pity myself at rare intervals, when I am tired out. I used to pity myself at all times and deeply. I believe in happiness and I am happy. I enjoy work immensely. I wish for fame among the expert few, but my chief desire—the desire by which I regulate my life—is a purely self-centred desire for intellectual satisfaction about things that puzzle me.

I do change as I grow older. Desires do grow duller; many are satisfied, or in process of continuous satisfaction; others have died from impassibility; those in process of satisfaction have become constant, and permanently dominate my actions. I feel myself now the same person that I was when I was a child; though at sixteen and seventeen I felt quite a different person.

My faults are a tendency to nagging, and to overestimating my own importance, so that what thwarts my pursuits seems wicked, though essential to other people's happiness. Also dogmatism. I used to try and improve my character, and I used to succeed. Now I only care for efficiency.

I think Spinoza and Lassalle attract me as much as any one in history.

Psychologically, sin has a meaning to me, and I love to see sinners punished. Logically I can find no meaning for the word Sin.

The fact of my own and human existence is simply amazing to me: sometimes I burst out laughing over it, when I am alone—perpetually, when my thoughts are free, I wonder about it. I don't feel that there is a future life, and I don't particularly wish to, as it would not prove this world to be righteous.

# Part III
# Apostolic Essays

# General Headnote

RUSSELL WENT UP to Cambridge at the beginning of October 1890. On 27 February 1892 he was elected to "The Cambridge Conversazione Society", or "the Apostles", as this secret, mainly undergraduate, discussion group is more generally known. Russell's *Autobiography* (*1967*, 68–9) recalls his delight at being elected to the active membership of twelve. Among them he found high regard for the pursuit of truth and complete speculative freedom. He "took wings", i.e. resigned from active membership, on 6 February 1897, the same day he read Paper **15**.

During his early years as an Apostle, the members (or "brothers") with whom he was most in contact were J. M. E. McTaggart, G. E. Moore, Charles Percy Sanger, Crompton and Theodore Llewelyn Davies, Robert Trevelyan and Edward Marsh. (A long list of members is given in Levy *1979*.) Weekly meetings at Cambridge were of intense interest, but surprisingly attendance was often small and papers sometimes had to be coaxed from reluctant members. Russell himself was less prolific of papers than might be expected, yet he loved the debates and entered them spiritedly. Surviving correspondences with such contemporaries as Sanger, Crompton Llewelyn Davies and Marsh show that when Russell was absent from Cambridge he craved news of the Society, which the brothers gladly sent. He took pleasure in sometimes attending the annual dinners, in London, for the active and retired members.

Russell wrote to Alys that "There are a few bits of Society-slang I will explain: *Real* is what relates to this Society, *phenomenal* everything and everybody else. We all have to speak in turn, and lots are drawn as to the order: and we all speak from the *hearthrug*" (25 Feb. 1894). Meetings, held Saturday evenings during term, were based on a paper written for the occasion. By convention the title bore little relation to the paper's content. Members were sometimes given a short list of topics to choose from, or sometimes one paper simply suggested the next. The reader was called the "moderator", and comments, like the paper itself, were delivered from the hearthrug. To terminate each meeting, a question, usually arising from the discussion rather than the paper's argument, was put to the vote. "Angels", i.e. members who had taken wings, were entitled to attend meetings and give papers.

The heading "Apostolic Essays" groups six papers clearly written for delivery to a sympathetic audience. Only one (Paper **16**) has been previously published. Russell characteristically wrote "A." on the first leaf of an Apostolic essay, followed by the date of delivery. There were three other recorded moderations by Russell (2 June

1894, 25 January 1895 and 10 March 1900), for which the papers have not survived. It is just possible that the papers read on the latter two dates were old ones on deposit in the "Ark"—the Society's archives. The titles of the three papers are unknown, although a paper on Mr. Bennet (probably the character in Jane Austen's *Pride and Prejudice*) is mentioned in a letter to Alys of 3 June 1894: "I was very glad, as it turned out, that they had chosen Mr. Bennet for me to write on, as ⟨Henry⟩ Sidgwick and two other angels turned up, and the other subjects were too intimate to read about before an old man like Sidgwick." Topics cannot be suggested for the other two papers. Since Russell had gone to Germany well before the end of January 1895, it is reasonable to suppose that if there was a paper of 25 January it was read *in absentia* by one of the brothers. The date, however, is doubtful because the 25th was a Friday and Edward Marsh wrote Russell on 28 January 1895 that he had read on the 26th on a topic of his own. It is possible that Russell read further papers as an angel.

Throughout these papers Russell's striving for clarity of argument is evident in the many cancelled passages and inserted leaves. Some of his most characteristic concerns as an essayist—for example, politics, the relation of the sexes, and religious belief—occur in this group written for the Cambridge friends among whom he found such delight and stimulation.

# 12

# Can We Be Statesmen? [1893]

RUSSELL READ THIS paper to the Society on 18 November 1893. On the 17th he wrote Alys:

I have been writing a paper for the Society which I have called Can we be Statesmen? by which I meant Can our political opinions be determined on reasonable grounds? I have come to the conclusion that it is quite impossible and I fear everyone will agree with me.

This conclusion was also expressed by him in writing to Alys on 7 October after G. Lowes Dickinson had invited him to join a political theory society. He told her then that he did not know what theoretical basis his political opinions had or could have. "I believe we shall find that political differences depend ultimately on differences of temperament", he remarked. After reading the paper, Russell responded to a query from Alys and told her of the paper's reception:

What I meant was what I fear would annoy you, that every one's political opinions are and must be sentimental, because the questions of politics are too difficult for reason to deal with, and would remain so even if we had a much more perfect Science of Politics. I have tried every way I know of to settle political questions reasonably and all of them seem quite inadequate. Every one agreed with me except the youngest brother and the two eldest: and as one of the latter is in the Treasury he must be regarded as prejudiced. I had both McTaggart and ⟨Nathaniel⟩ Wedd on my side so the other side was rather weak. The only question which did seem clear was Vaccination.— Ever since I came up I have been gradually discovering that Reason in most things if pushed too far refutes itself: so I don't see any ground for lamenting that one more subject should be abandoned to sentiment. (21 Nov. 1893)

The copy-text is the manuscript (RA 220.010130). Its eight leaves include the addition of whole leaves and the deletion of several sentences.

IF OUR BROTHER Sidgwick were moderator tonight he would probably content himself with first defining the word Statesman and then making an enquiry into the psychological causes of existing political opinion. I shall not attempt the first nor should I wish to content myself with the latter; but I think it would be useful to consider briefly how we do come by the opinions which most of us, as a matter of fact, hold, and hold strongly. I suppose most of us take our stand on Utilitarianism, and proceed to make deductions, largely influenced by personal idiosyncrasies, as to the kind of Government most likely to secure the general happiness; or rather as to the particular changes in the existing Government which would most benefit the existing community. One of us for example is very anxious to be allowed personal liberty in the satisfaction of his desires, whether because these have at some time been unduly restrained or because they conflict with positive morality and seem in danger of being restrained by law. Another, whose desires have seldom been thwarted and can be satisfied without his incurring censure from public opinion, is less impressed with the value of liberty and perhaps, having himself found the desires of others inconvenient or positively harmful, is more inclined to believe in State-Interference. Such considerations would I imagine largely influence a decision on such questions as for example Local Option: both would appeal to Utilitarian principles, but, having no Hedonimeter except their own consciousness, would attach different Hedonistic values to the pleasures and pains involved.

A rather more systematized method proceeds by means of middle axioms. These axioms are like proverbs: no one offers a proof for them, but they are accepted as an epitome of past political experience. No method of proof could be offered which would not be empirical: when one is attempted it is usually a hasty generalization from some one or two instances: for example my *Chronicle* tells me this morning that by the Coal-Strike we have learnt "not from the mouths of the wise but from the endurance and sacrifice of rough uncultured men, that right must be done though the heavens fall and mines are closed". It seems a pity so much endurance and sacrifice should have been wasted on proving a tautology: but it is clear the author of the article supposed it not a tautology but a valuable lesson of experience, so it may serve to illustrate the current method. Principles such as Mill's, that the State ought not to interfere with a man for his own good, in the first place are not susceptible of proof, and in the second are never clearly applicable. They are not susceptible of proof: for the only proof attempted is from experience, and not only are no two cases ever alike, but wholly new classes of cases arise from time to time, in which there is no experience at all to guide us. And even within experience, it can never be clearly shewn that a course which was not actually adopted would have been better or worse than that which was adopted. Further they are never clearly applicable: in the case considered for example, no action can affect only one individual: every one who stands in any relation to him is affected by his well-being: if he is a drunkard, his family are affected; if he has no family there is still the work which he would do better if he were sober; if he would in any case be idle, there are at least the brewer and publican who profit by his custom. I believe the particular principle in question, if a case could be discovered in which it was clearly applicable, would probably cease to be true, since it is the indirect bad effects of such interference on which Mill lays most stress and which in practice are the most important.—In the same way the value of any other such middle axiom may I think be reduced to zero.

10    The difficulty of measuring pleasure seems inherent in any application of a purely empirical hedonistic method: so that it seems useless to attempt to found a philosophic view of Politics on any such considerations. Of course to apply such a method correctly we ought to take account not only of all existing nations, but of all posterity. If we assume that every man is able to form a fairly correct estimate of his own interest, a Democracy is likely, on the assumption that every voter is purely selfish, to lead to Government in the interest of the majority; but as unfortunately there seems no way of giving votes to posterity and yet they are affected very materially by our acts, there is no reason why a Democracy should not purchase present gain
20 at the expense of the next or even of all future generations. And so we cannot say that although no voter can form an estimate of the general interest, Democracy is a machine for getting it done. A philosophic statesman cannot therefore like Gladstone accept the maxim *Vox Populi Vox Dei* and reserve his whole reasoning faculties for the discovery of the people's mandate. We must then abandon all purely empirical methods and somehow introduce an à priori element into our discussion. But how is this to be done? Perhaps something might be done by substituting the idea of progress for that of happiness. Of course progress is not ultimate, it must be progress towards an ideal in which there is no progress, but politically we need not be much
30 troubled by the thought of coming to an end of possible progress. The ideal will hardly be one realizable in an existence involving birth and death, but might perhaps be used as pointing the directions in which we must move sooner or later if we are to approach it at all.

Progress must be more or less similar in a race and in an individual; now our ideas of individual progress, of our own development, are pretty definite: such progress consists I suppose in increase of sensitiveness, involving intellectual and moral education as means to it. Increase of sensitiveness in the individual is probably, at least at first, attended by increase of pain: but is yet to be regarded as good even from the individual's point of view, as
40 being the only means of self-development, the only way of obtaining whatever may give existence any value. Can we apply a similar criterion in politics? I think to many questions we can. For although laws can hardly directly aid individual development, they can remove hindrances to it, and

can provide means for those willing to use them. We can condemn the drunkard however he may glorify the pleasures of drink, and however we may be convinced that without drink he would be miserable. For such individual development as we recognize to be desirable is impossible to any one who is a slave to pleasures of sense. Whether we can therefore vote for Local Option is another matter: but at least we shall have done everything that can be done à priori for the settlement of this question and shall have removed it from the quagmire of empirical estimates of the joys of alcohol. We shall also be able to give ground for the desirability of education for everyone. And generally I think we ought to be able to determine on some such principles 10 all questions that affect the individuals first and the nation only through the individuals. Of course we must remain rather vague and not attempt a rigid demonstration any more than we do in regulating our own lives. But as here we know in the main how best to forward our own development so I think in the main we can see what is desirable for other individuals.—But when we come to that larger class of political questions which affect the nation first and the individuals through the nation, such as Home Rule, no such method seems applicable. Here there is no idea of progress involved, and we seem reduced to empirical Hedonism again. It is easy in this instance to say that the whole century has been tending to the formation of nation-states: but 20 even if we are so rigidly optimist that we regard every event as fortunate, we still get no presumption even from such an argument: for the tendency is not irresistible since it is we who have the decision: and our optimism will only persuade us that the tendency is good where it conquers, not that it is always good. And arguments from analogy are almost sure to be worthless in politics because of the complexity of the conditions. I cannot see any possible method then of deciding such a question reasonably; perhaps the discussion may suggest one.

And I do not believe that any Social Science of the kind to be looked for at present would really be of any great avail. Let us consider the only branch of 30 it, Political Economy, which can be regarded as actually existing. Let us admit for the sake of argument that it provides perfectly definite laws, that as Science its conclusions are incontrovertible. Still these conclusions do not give certain *practical* results; for they are not conclusions as to pleasure, directly at least, but as to sources of pleasure. And when we consider what very unequal amounts of pleasure different people derive from the same source, and how impossible it is to estimate these differences, it becomes Utopian to expect very definite practical guidance from such laws. If you give one man a fortune he will drink himself to death and so convert it into a misfortune: another will enjoy it rationally and perhaps make it a means of 40 permanent benefit to the community. It is of course easy to prove mathematically that a given sum of money is most felicific when distributed equally throughout the community: but this assumes every one's capacity equal and ignores all indirect results. No one would maintain that Darwin's fortune would have been more felicific if it had been distributed equally all round, by which he would have been reduced to the state of a labourer or artisan.—We must then always make some perfectly unwarrantable assumptions in deciding political questions: these ought to be as nearly true as possible but are sure to be very wide of the mark. I cannot see how one assumption is any more plausible than another and it seems that short of a detailed theory of development there is no way of getting even a presumption on either side.

10     If we had a Hegelian Philosophy of History developed in considerable detail, we should know what must be the next movement of the dialectic, and to accelerate it would be our whole political duty. But as I gather that such a Philosophy is for practical purposes non-existent, this method is at present at least impossible.—And yet since all of us who use our votes do make up our minds, it is plain that there are methods more or less fallacious and I would not be so pessimistic as to suppose all methods equally so. There must therefore be some method at present available which is less misleading than any other, and I suppose there ought to be some criterion for deciding the relative value of the different methods: but I am unable to 20 see what they are: perhaps this point too may be elucidated by discussion.

# 13

# Lövborg or Hedda [1894]

"Lövborg or Hedda", which was read to the Society on 3 March 1894, discusses the advantages and disadvantages of admitting women as members. The title (despite its dismissal in the paper's first sentence) poses the conflict between male and female in Ibsen's *Hedda Gabler* (1890). Hedda, a spoiled, eccentric meddler, destroys the intellectual Eilert Lövborg. Russell first read the play in April 1891, and after delivering his paper he and Crompton Llewelyn Davies reread *Hedda Gabler*. While the essay shows Russell's attraction to Ibsen, several of whose plays he read in this period, it also prefigures his practical concern with women's rights—a cause inherited from his parents and his "godfather", John Stuart Mill.

In a letter to Alys of 22 February 1894 Russell said that he had agreed to write a paper for the Society on the admission of women, though that would be a "*very* unapostolic proceeding". He enclosed an abstract (printed as Appendix 1.1) of the arguments, asking for Alys's comments on the psychology presupposed by them. Her reply, sent 24 February, argued that including women would almost certainly ruin the Society. On the 25th Russell reported that he had worked in her rather pessimistic suggestions. In her response of that date Alys retracted somewhat, saying that she had exaggerated "the proneness of intellectual women to fall in love" and thus to upset the Society's pursuits. Yet she insisted that young people of opposite sexes were not helped by discussing sexuality. Russell's letter of 28 February takes her retraction as supporting his position that women should be admitted. (In general Alys did believe in women's rights, and her article "A Reply from the Daughters", a plea for the dignity of womanhood, was about to be published.)

Russell's letter of 4 March discusses reactions to the reading of his paper the previous night and conveys the seriousness of his wish to persuade the Apostles that women should be admitted to membership. He reported that after the paper the Society divided on the question "Should we like to elect women?", and that all but Lowes Dickinson voted in favour of it. It was not, however, until 1970 that a woman was admitted (Levy *1979*, 128).

The copy-text is the manuscript (RA 220.010230), consisting of eleven leaves. Russell did not carry out an intention to rewrite the paper. He told Alys: "⟨Ralph⟩ Wedgwood discovered the point I mentioned, that my end contradicted the beginning, but I invented a subtlety which reconciled them" (4 March). The many revisions reveal how much Russell was willing to alter at the age of twenty-one, and how important it was to him to polish his writing for a Society audience.

THE SUBJECT OF my paper has no connection with its title, and it would be a waste of time to explain how I came to think it had. What I wish to discuss is whether, from the point of view of the Society alone, it would be a good or a bad thing if women could be elected. I shall not consider either the phenomenal advantages or the phenomenal difficulties of such a step, though I believe the former incalculable and the latter (for the present at least) insuperable. I don't know whether any one will be found to deny that there may be apostolic women, whom apart from the accident of sex we should feel to be a gain to the Society. If any one will be found to maintain that view, he will have to maintain also that no woman would ever be elected, and therefore his opinion will be irrelevant, as I wish merely to discuss whether, supposing such women to exist, it would or would not be a gain to the Society to have them as sisters. This seems to me to depend on two questions: (1) How far the sexual point of view would come in (2) How far it would spoil discussion if it did. These are purely psychological questions, and in dealing with them one must of course remember that the answers to them would be utterly different with different people, and to some extent different with the two sexes. One must remember also that we are not dealing with the average man or woman, but with men and women whose intellectual interests are *ex hypothesi* abnormally strong, and whose intellectual side is abnormally well-developed. This of course is by no means incompatible with a very strongly-developed emotional side, rather the reverse if anything: but it has this importance in the argument, that in people of strong intellectual interests the nature and effects of passion would probably be usually rather different from what they would be in other cases. This applies especially to the women who might be elected, as women normally derive their intellectual from their personal interests: they are usually not interested in any question of theory until it has somehow connected itself with their personal affections. But just as some men resemble women in this respect, so some women resemble men; and it seems scarcely too much to suppose that the women who might be elected would have at any rate the possibility of purely intellectual interests and of looking at things through other spectacles than those of love or hate.—Thus much by way of preliminary.

First: as to how far the sexual point of view would come in at all. There seem to me several reasons which make it less likely to come in than in any other gathering of young men and women, similar to the Society in the eyes of Mrs. Grundy. (1) The intellectual frame of mind necessary for following and taking part in an argument is very antagonistic to the sexual and emotional: few things are so liable to kill passion for the moment, or to ward off its first attacks, as a purely reasoning attitude towards the proceedings: that is, if it can be got or maintained; and on the election of a new member it must be supposed some time would elapse before he or she became unable to maintain this attitude of mind; so that during this time passion would make slow advances, and would probably in many cases never get the upper hand at all. Again the absolute freedom of discussion, the absolute unreserve on all matters, sexual or otherwise, when once it is firmly established in any one's mind and has become a matter of course, is hostile to the beginnings of sexual feeling, which are immensely helped by mystery and reserve and consequent curiosity. Of course while such free discussion is rare, and is only possible with (say) one member of the opposite sex, it gives that one member an exceptional position and makes him or her fill a larger share in the thoughts of her or him than would otherwise be the case; particularly if the advisability of such discussion is at all keenly felt. There is also the pleasure of satisfied curiosity, and of forbidden fruit probably on the woman's side at least. But this is a transitional and temporary state of things, and if we had women in the Society it would *ipso facto* cease. Of course before electing any woman some member would have to promise that she was perfectly ready to discuss unnatural vice in case the subject should come up, and not merely to discuss it, but to discuss it in a perfectly unartificial manner, without the feeling of doing anything unusual or perhaps a little naughty. And where this could be promised, I think one may safely say that freedom of discussion *would* be antagonistic to the beginnings of love. (2) Also the frequent meetings on a basis at least in theory non-flirtatious would accustom people to meeting members of the opposite sex, who were intelligent and presumably more or less agreeable, without the main object of their meeting being (as it is in general society) love, with a view to marriage. It would be impossible for a sister to fall in love with all the brothers at once, and she would probably have got so accustomed to meeting a number of men (with almost any of whom individually she might have fallen in love) before love had arisen, that such meeting would have become normal and she would no longer be so prone to passion as monasticism would now make her. And the same would apply to men if there were several sisters. Our present separation of the sexes, our monasticism in the Varsity, makes us far more likely to fall in love when an opportunity occurs than we should be if we met people of the opposite sex constantly. The extreme case, the *reductio ad absurdum* of monasticism, is to be found in the stories of early Christian hermits who went into the desert and devoted their whole lives to the killing of lust and measured their holiness by the meagreness of their diet: yet these men (if one may trust Gibbon, which I don't wish to affirm) used to be perpetually haunted by visions of naked harlots dancing before them and tempting them to sin. Just as the life of the hermit led to the arousing of the coarsest form of sexual passion on so slight a stimulus as the mere idea, so the contrary course makes a continually greater stimulus necessary, and makes the form taken by the passion a better and healthier one.

These reasons make me think the sexual feeling would arise much less

easily than it might otherwise be expected to do: but that it would arise occasionally it would of course be absurd to deny. In many people normally, and in most people at times, there is a difference of mental attitude towards *any* member of the opposite sex who is fairly young (unless physically repulsive); but this merely stimulates to greater activity and to greater interest in such a person's sayings and doings, and both in men and women, if the thing aimed at is serious discussion, has I think, so far as I have been able to observe, an unmitigatedly good effect on the argument. This however is merely a sort of sub-conscious instinct, and is not what seems to me the
10 danger. The second question I wished to discuss was how far discussion would be spoilt by definite love of one member of the Society for another. First, there is unreciprocated love: this I think requires to be rather differently treated according as it is on the part of a man or of a woman. In the former case, I believe it would be rather beneficial than harmful: the man would not wish to appear to disadvantage; he would pay keen attention to the argument if only for that reason; and when it came to his turn to be on the hearthrug, he would *not* talk for effect, for that would be contrary to the traditions of the Society and would be viewed with universal disfavour, but he *would* endeavour if possible to contribute something to the argument.
20 But in a woman, unless she were even more man-like than I have a right to suppose, love might destroy intellectual interests and produce a sort of mental lassitude: only the object of her affection would engross her and however she might struggle when on the hearthrug, ideas would fail her, or if they did not, they would either be a mere echo of those of the man she loved, or the exact opposite, to shew her independence and conceal her love. Either of which would be equally fatal. At least this would be the case with a fairly new subject of discussion: on a subject on which one already has any coherent ideas it is *always* possible to express them if the motive for doing so is strong enough, as in the case supposed it would be.
30     This however would be by no means universally the effect of unreciprocated affection on the woman's side. I have heard that among women whose intellectual interests are keen there are many who regard love merely as a nuisance, like an attack of the measles; and in whom it never becomes powerful enough, at least when one-sided, to interfere with their ordinary pursuits or interests at all. And when women *are* of this hard practical nature, they are apt to outdo almost all men in the power of pursuing chosen ends whatever may come in their way. In such women (and I imagine this type would be much commoner in the Society than in the world), such feeble love as would be likely to arise would in no way interfere with their power of
40 discussion or with their interest in the subject discussed.
    But the most dangerous case would be that of reciprocal love, so strong as to make everything else seem worthless. This would make a meeting of the Society a very difficult occasion for the pair: it would probably be their chief

opportunity of meeting and would of course come to be regarded in that light rather than as a meeting of the Society: they would wish to see each other and to talk to each other, but the nature of the case would make very little talk together possible; and probably the desire for more intimate intercourse than would be possible would be very strong in them all the time and would be annoying them and making the proceedings more or less of a blank. Also their interest in each other would very likely become so great as to destroy all intellectual interests except in questions immediately relating to the relations of the sexes. The incentive which would be strong in the case of one-sided love would be absent here, since each would know that he or she would not be judged by his or her hearthrug by the one whose opinion would be valued. At the same time, they would probably be anxious not to prove the election of women a mistake, and this would lead them when on the hearthrug to endeavour to shew as much appreciation of the proceedings as possible. In the case of men, this effort would certainly often be completely successful: and in the case of women such as would be likely to be elected I see no reason why it should not fairly often be successful too. In some *men* certainly the exhilaration of mutual love would so sharpen all their faculties, so rouse them to life, that their intellects would be even better than usual and they might reach a penetration which at other times would be absent. I fancy in most women this effect would not be likely to occur: their faculties would be likely to be entirely absorbed in sympathy and emotion.

There is one more danger which might perhaps be feared, but which I believe does not exist at all; that is the danger of degenerating into sentimentality, into something resembling the phenomena known as the Souls. I believe such sentimentality is only *possible* where the women are fools. No apostolic woman would submit to the insult of being foolishly sentimentalized about: any love which might arise would have to be real, to be passion; I cannot imagine entertaining a Goetheish fancy for anybody one respected. This kind of feeling seems to me to depend essentially upon regarding its object as a plaything, a toy to amuse the leisure from more serious pursuits, not as an equal human being. Of course many men at the present day hold this view about women in general, but the days when apostolic men could do so are rapidly passing away, if not already passed. If however a man belonging to this class were apostolic and were elected, such a man would be forced to modify his views on election, as these views depend either upon meeting only foolish or uneducated women, or upon so treating all women as to make it impossible anything not purely frivolous should come to the surface; both of which election would render impossible.—I am convinced then that if love should arise it would be love of the best kind, such as would have absolutely nothing silly about it and would not tend to sentimentality but rather to its utter destruction.

So far I have dwelt almost solely on the dangers and difficulties involved

in the election of women: I must now mention a few very important advantages which it seems to me we should be likely to gain. In the first place, in
all questions not purely metaphysical, our views are apt to be one-sided, and
would very likely be much ameliorated by hearing the opposite one-
sidedness of women's views. I do not mean that views on (say) social questions are inherently sexual, but that our opinions are largely the result of our
education, and women's education being different their opinions would
probably be different: and the truth presumably lies between the two. I am
prepared to maintain, (and I think every one whose view is not jaundiced,
10 like McTaggart's, will agree with me,) that opinions on practical questions,
as we found last Saturday, depend on personal idiosyncrasies far more fundamentally than on reason. McTaggart's Absolute, before which as before a
Juggernaut car we are expected to prostrate ourselves, would be very useful
perhaps if we were appointed architects of heaven: but as G.A. has not
thought fit to confer that dignity upon us, we are it seems to me compelled to
leave heaven and metaphysics out of the question, and we shall then always
be unable to decide anything by reason alone. Our education and personal
tastes then come in to help us to decide, and therefore our decisions are
bound to be one-sided as long as women are excluded. Again we sometimes
20 discuss definitely sexual subjects, and the inadequacy of discussions by one
sex alone then becomes glaring: when we divided last term on "Can we love
those we copulate with" the presence of women in the discussion would
have been invaluable. And in a vast number of questions, an opinion is
almost worthless unless based on actual personal experience. It seems to me
that the majority of the questions we have discussed of late have required for
their adequate discussion some experience of emotion or passion in some
form or other: and in any case such experience is highly desirable, both as a
good in itself and as a help in the formation of character, or self-realization as
McTaggart would prefer to call it.—The argument that our one-sidedness
30 might be corrected seems to me very important: as we most of us by the
time we take wings have more or less crystallized in our opinions, and it is
only after that time that most of us grow intimate with women, when it is too
late to profit by this intimacy. And I suppose no one will maintain that a
woman's point of view is *per se* less worthy of consideration than a man's,
where they differ.

Finally: it is absurd to pretend that the attitude of most of us towards
other members is now purely intellectual: our best friends are very likely to
be in the Society, and it is difficult in discussion not to be more influenced by
the arguments of those we like best than by the arguments of others. [Nor is
40 even a physical interest absent, for most of us care more or less about bodies,
some of us care a great deal.] Our brother Trevelyan confessed to me once
that he was more interested in the brothers than in what they said, and in
this I agree with him. Personally I look forward to Saturday nights more as

an occasion when I meet my friends in the pleasantest possible way than as
an occasion for the intellectual exercise of following an argument and contributing to it. Indeed I believe much of my interest in the argument would
cease if I were not interested in the arguers. But I have not found that this
frame of mind destroys the discussions of the Society, though I believe most
of the other members feel as I do. Of course (though McTaggart will deny
this) sexual love is immeasurably more powerful than friendship, but it is
not radically different in kind, and its occurrence in the Society would not
introduce a totally new element, but only greatly intensify one which already exists and which, in my opinion, so far from detracting from the value 10
of the Society, gives it a great part of that value. Thus in spite of the dangers,
I should on the whole be very strongly in favour of electing women: but I
shall be glad to hear the opinion of the brethren on these dangers in the
discussion.

# 14

## Cleopatra or Maggie Tulliver [1894]

THIS PAPER, ON controlling the passions and the relationship of desire and knowledge, was read to the Society on 3 November 1894. The title draws a contrast between Shakespeare's voluptuary heroine Cleopatra and George Eliot's Maggie Tulliver, a figure of sensitivity and self-control in *The Mill on the Floss* (1860). (For Russell's initial reaction to Maggie Tulliver, see 57: 10.) On 17 October Russell wrote from Paris to Charles Sanger, informing him that he would write "on Marsh's question Maggie Tulliver or Cleopatra, which I've been thinking about a good deal both from the practical exigencies of life and from my reading of Wagner and James's *Psychology*".

Russell wrote often to Alys of the paper and the doubts he had about it:

> It will be an immense pleasure to go to Cambridge and read a paper and enjoy the Society again.... I shall read them a paper on controlling our passions, in which I shall point out that we can't, and that the greater they are the less we ought to though the more easily we can—This sounds paradoxical but isn't.   (20 Oct.)

Soon after he wrote that he was "very much dissatisfied" with his draft (22 Oct.), for "neither the theoretical nor the practical part of it will come straight" (23 Oct.).

The paper was completed on 24 October, and Russell sent it to Alys for criticism. He was still not happy with the paper. His correspondence shows his difficulty in deciding what to say:

> —By the way, I mean to cut out all the practical part of my paper, about Anna Karenina—it is too commonplace and wishy-washy. If thee can give me any better example I will try and work it up. My own life, between thee and my Grandmother, affords an admirable instance—but that is too personal—thee will see I have avoided everything which has the remotest bearing on myself. The Dilemma at the end has puzzled me for a year—I think there is no solution short of the Hegelian Dialectic. I am thinking of saying more on the independence of desire and knowledge: how they form coordinate realms, and how just as no isolated truth is wholly true, so no isolated object of desire is wholly good—and as thought leads one on dialectically to the Absolute, so desire, by alternate satisfaction and disappointment, leads one on to the Ab-

solute Good. And then I might discuss how to bridge the gulf between knowledge and desire—i.e. how to pass from morality to religion. But I'm inclined to leave this to McTaggart, as I've never understood the transition myself. (26 Oct., 10.30 a.m.)

Alys mistook the theory of the interdependence of knowledge and desire for Russell's view that they are independent. He commented:

I'm glad thee likes my paper, but sorry thee has no criticism to make. It was not the *inter*dependence but the *in*dependence of knowledge and desire I wanted to write about—*logical* independence of course, not *psychological*. My paradox ... has been to me for years a worry—a solution would be a real solid addition to my happiness. (29 Oct., 10 a.m.)

Alys liked the practical points, while Russell thought that the paper's "value lay in the theoretical emphasising of desire and analysis of virtue, and in the statement of the difficulty about transcending the Self in Ethics. I think they won't like it at Cambridge—they'll think it too moral and edifying" (29 Oct., 9 p.m.).

On 31 October Russell told Alys of major revisions he had made: "I wrote three more sheets for it, which I think I will put in place of Anna and Wronsky—I have got in Raskolnikow and Princess Casamassima who seem to me more instructive because less obvious examples." The three new sheets must be the new fol. 8, supplemented by fos. 8a and 10a. (Fol. 10a has a cancelled signature at the bottom, as if the essay had originally ended there, but the quotation from the letter of 26 October shows that Russell had already written about "the Dilemma at the end", i.e. as far as fol. 12.) Other additions were made on fos. 3a and 11a.

On 4 November Russell reported to Alys on the paper's reception:

We had a large meeting last night—McTaggart and Dickinson and Wedd came, at which I couldn't help feeling flattered. Thee will be glad to hear that several of them thought my paper too theoretical, though McTaggart and I between us persuaded them in time that there was nothing definite to be said about practical conduct.... McTaggart spoke first, and was excessively good, as I had hoped. I said in my paper I would probably accept anything he said, and so I did. For my sake he left out immortality, and reconciled my dilemma at the end without it. I can't put what he said in a letter, but I dare say I shall bring it out in conversation some day.... Most of them were pleased with my paper, and were glad of my making Good and less good my terms instead of right and wrong. The beginning also amused them a good deal.

The Society divided on the question "Duty or Passion?" (Levy *1979*, 139). Russell voted on both sides, qualifying his vote with "according to circumstances".

The copy-text is the manuscript (RA 220.010290); it has seventeen leaves.

WHAT SHALL WE do with our passions? Slay them, say Stoicism and Mediaevalism: fix our minds on the sovereign contemplation of virtue, or the Deity, and live a calm, unchanging unruffled life. This is Descartes's "remède souverain contre les passions": its ideal is calm, in which perhaps some joy may be found, but for which the real recommendation is that it avoids pain. Mrs. Grundy's answer is different: to hold our tongues about them and draw down the blinds before we indulge them is her gospel. To her, there is no harm in them if the blinds are thick enough and we don't allow the indulgence to interfere with dinner and Success—but to make any sacrifice to them is improper and shows that one is not "safe". Above all it is shocking to admit their existence.—As a reaction against both these, the French, and the English aesthetes of the last generation, admit them and glory in them—to indulge them beautifully is morality, to be able to resist them is to be Machiavellian and disgusting; to feel the appropriate passion at the critical moment is the acme of virtue—and passions in this Ethic are judged aesthetically, not by their practical consequences. It is amusing to compare this, the creed of all that Mrs. Grundy abhors, with her own sentimental professions, which agree exactly with this if we substitute the word sentiment for the word passion. Only with her they are merely professions, while with the others they are real beliefs.—I ought to mention too the Whitmaniacs, whose views on the subject are none of the above: they have two gods, tolerance and sanity: hence they have a derived worship for all those passions which the sane and healthy man or woman feels—these are great Nature, and to be ashamed of them is to be ashamed of sane and normal humanity. Hence they too, like the French, glorify passion: but unlike the French, they glorify it only when it makes for health, when, in Mr. Carr Bosanquet's words, it is "sane lusty and adequate". "Without shame the woman I love avows the deliciousness of sex" says Walt: but also—spite of his tolerance—"no diseased person, no venereal taint", is with us ("Song of the Open Road").

Sidgwick would admit then that there is here no "consensus of common sense"—let us therefore abandon common sense and define our terms. If I don't use them quite in the ordinary way, that will be only for the sake of precision. I shall then define a *passion* as a body of particular desires coordinated by direction to a single end or to a closely related system of ends. I shall use *Emotion* as the State of Mind accompanying the fruition or frustration (final or temporary) of a Passion, with special reference to its aspect of pleasure and pain.

Starting from these definitions I shall maintain (1) That, as Spinoza says, a passion can only be overcome by a stronger passion (2) That the greatest passions, those which most influence our actions, are not necessarily those of greatest intensity (3) That from an ethical standpoint, the greater a passion is the more it ought to be followed, and that the problem of self-control

92

is to give the victory to the great and permanent passion rather than to the small and temporary one.

Before beginning the regular discussion of these points, I may observe that it follows from my definition that a passion cannot be valuable for its own sake, though an emotion may. For the essence of passion is desire, and desire is consciousness of imperfection, of contrast between the ideal and the actual—thus a passion is only the *condition of an attempt* to realize the Good, and is not intrinsically good in itself; it is a means, not an end. But as a means it can hardly be valued too highly—the passions for knowledge, for beauty, for love are the very condition of all development, of all that is good—if the Good is that which satisfies, the desire is essential to the struggle after it, and to imagine the Good, to be conscious of it, is to desire it—hence a passion may be ethically defined as a more or less imperfect conception of the Good, combined with the consciousness of its absence and the consequent desire for its realization.

After this parenthetical remark, I will try to tackle my question—being ethical in form, I fear it will be necessary to plough through some rather dry ethical theory first, before attempting any more practical conclusions.

I will begin by a classification of desires, which I put forward subject to criticism, though I shall state it dogmatically. Lowest in the scale are immediate desires for physical objects for their own sakes—*on account*, doubtless, of some quality they possess, but without conscious isolation of this quality as that which gives them value. To this class belong animal appetites, for food and drink, etc.; a jackdaw's love of a shilling and a savage's love of beads. Next come desires for particular states of mind in ourselves, desires relative to our own psychical life. These involve self-consciousness and therefore stand on a distinctly higher plane than the first class. They are in the first place no doubt desires for pleasure. And the wish for pleasure has peculiar importance, because, since *every* satisfied desire is pleasant (even if the thing desired be pain, which may be the case in moods of morbid sentimentality), the desire for pleasure reinforces every other, though not in equal degrees—for not all satisfactions are equally pleasurable. But this class does not consist exclusively of desires for pleasure—we may equally desire knowledge or a particular kind of volition for their own sakes. The last indeed cannot be an immediate motive in action, because volition is not the proximate effect of volition—however, defining *virtue* as a *potentiality* of desirable volition, the desire for virtue can be a motive, since every volition affects our power of making future volitions. This however involves self-consciousness in the second degree, and is a complex and presumably rare motive.—Third come desires relative to other people's psychical life; these certainly exist pure—e.g. hatred is a desire for another's pain for its own sake—indeed I am inclined to think that it is normal to desire for others—for our friends, our acquaintances, even perhaps our relations—everything

we desire for ourselves—this constitutes sympathy, and it seems to me an ultimate and unanalyzable fact. I do not mean of course that sensible people desire every particular thing for others as for themselves—because as desires grow complex we like things for their uses more often than for their own sakes—but whatever we regard as intrinsically and *per se* good for us we cannot but desire also for our friends, though in most cases less intensely than for ourselves. Then come desires for relations between ourselves and other people, or between ourselves at one time and at another—even, as is shown by the match-making instinct in women, between others, without
10 reference to self.—Thus in the development of desire we get further and further from the passing moment, and from wishes which can be gratified immediately—we have to search for means, and when the object of our desire is abstract, e.g. power (which consists in a relation between our volitions and those of others), no particular thing can wholly satisfy the desire, which thus prompts to a long series of actions all directed to one end. This sort of desire is what I have called a Passion and generally speaking, the further a desire is removed from sense, the higher it comes in my scale, the more extended is its universe, and therefore the more commendable it is, ethically considered. The intensity of a passion may be very slight, that is,
20 our desire at any moment for the particular thing to be attained by the act we are deliberating about may be weak, and yet, being reinforced by the thought of all the future occasions where similar desires will recur, and of the lasting loss if we let the passing moment slip by, the passion may acquire great power in deciding us, and may overcome a much more intense desire less bound up with our future. But we *must* always do as we wish—this is a mere tautology—the stronger desire is that which conquers; and if we are capable of realizing the future, a passion will overcome an isolated desire, and a passion with a larger universe will overcome one with a smaller universe. Self-control, a strong will, a firm character, etc., are all names for the
30 power of vividly bringing to mind the larger and perhaps remoter universe of the less intense desire, and so resisting the more intense but more limited one. I will say nothing for the moment as to "selfish" and "unselfish" desires and the like vague terms, because they seem to me to have no ethical importance at any rate at our present level. The thing that *has* ethical importance is the extent of a desire's universe, because the larger its universe, the more permanent is its possible satisfaction, and the more self-consistent can the life be made which is regulated by it. Although in my phraseology this is a plea for indulging the larger passion, it is in common language the plea of morals for what it calls "resisting one's passions"—it is the command
40 to "scorn delights and live laborious days", to resist passing allurements and be what the world calls passionless.

So far so good: this is theoretical and I hope sound, but when we try to apply such principles to practice—and the question we started with was a practical one—many things have to be considered which make our problem far more complex than before. I don't know any general principles invariably applicable here—one can only indicate a few broad lines along which to conduct the process of balancing by which practical questions have to be decided. First of all—there are two different conditions which make it possible to resist one's passions: strong will, or weak desires. It is because we are apt to imagine the latter (which is wholly despicable) that we feel a sort of contempt sometimes for people who renounce happiness for what they believe to be their duty—women who sacrifice intelligence to family or to child-bearing, children who obey their parents, etc. For nothing can be ac- 10 complished without powerful passions—the most efficient men are the men wholly in the grip of some great passion which carries them over difficulties and obstacles and makes them neglect all but what conduces to their end: the Napoleons and Newtons and men of single powerful purpose. And here lies the danger of too rigid repression of passing passions: in time our desires sicken and die: we become purposeless anaemic beings, saints perhaps, but totally incapable of any achievement. Like Mr. Gilfil in George Eliot, we cease to take an interest in anything but our whiskey and soda if we are men, or our tea if we are women: or worse still, a person who has resisted a great passion and prevented it from venting itself in action may come to regard 20 with hatred all those who do not so resist, even where there are no grounds for resisting—such a person is apt to idolize pain, to regard all enjoyment as wicked, and to become in consequence the most fiendish person imaginable in daily life. The passion remains, and not being allowed to take its natural course, it turns to mute rage against all who are more fortunate, and leads to the most ghastly morbid developments. It is therefore very necessary to gauge one's own strength before denying any really strong craving, and the dangers involved in doing so may make it well worth while to indulge a passion even where it seems to interfere with some wider and nobler one. It is necessary to keep the spring of desires fresh, otherwise the character dries 30 up—the energy and life goes out of it, and it loses perhaps the very passion for which it made the sacrifice. Also the amount of self-control of which a person is capable at any time is limited, and by a too great exercise of it in one direction one loses the power of using it in others.

The effects of too great repression of passions are somewhat curious and interesting. First comes an extraordinary lassitude—a complete absence of will or desire. Then, in this void, arise various instinctive impulses, chiefly trivial, which may have existed before, but were never attended to because of the energy of other thoughts which drove them out. Now however, owing to the mind's emptiness and weariness, it has not the energy to drive them 40 out, and they persist—partly morbid, partly belonging to a more primitive state, a reversion to which is a common symptom of degeneracy. At first they are *mere* ideas—what little vigour remains is spent in keeping them so—but gradually they work like madness in the brain, and it becomes impossible to resist. Where, as in Dostojewski's *Crime and Punishment*, the impulse is not trivial, it produces pronounced mania—where, as is more usual, there are a number of trivial impulses, they merely turn to eccentricity or ill-temper or nagging or nervousness. A very common result, and one of the earliest, is an unreasoning hatred of almost every body, and a joy in giving and watching pain. Superstitious dread, of one knows not what, or of some trivial thing such as one fly getting to the top of a pane before another, is also common.—And unless some strong and healthy passion is found to replace the one resisted, these impulses are apt to grow more frequent and more dominant, until, at worst, they develop into insanity.

A passion may be resisted from laziness just as easily as from strength of will. Most conventional women who have any intelligence are examples of this. But the same morbid effects follow as in the other case, provided the possibility of a fine free indulgence is realized. Princess Casamassima in Henry James is an instance of what I mean.—The passion for thought, for intellectual activity for its own sake, when it exists, is particularly liable to be neglected through laziness or the pressure of circumstances, and to take revenge by listlessness and savage self-analysis and self-contempt—also by a freezing of all other passions: the little thought that is possible easily shows them to be valueless, but is unable to go on to the harder task of proving that they are invaluable.—All these effects depend upon the fact that strength of will is not inexhaustible: up to the limits of our self-control, the pure theory seems to me to hold.

From a practical point of view, when once a passion is given, there is not much more to be said—I suppose a moraliser would propound the education of the passions and a close watch over the birth and growth of those that may prove dangerous—but this involves an amount of self-consciousness and an absence of spontaneity which I shudder to think of. The only solution then would be an education of them by others by which I am sure very much may be done—but if others have neglected this duty, the problem for the individual seems insoluble. No ethical theory is likely to have any permanent effect in the presence of an intense passion, so that the only hope lies in a correct psychology to strangle an inconvenient one in its infancy—but it is just in infancy that passions are often so alluring, and few people's estimate of themselves can stand out against such seductions. Since I am going away tomorrow, why not make the most of today? When tomorrow comes, today has been made such good use of that it is impossible to go away, and so the last chance is gone. Here we stumble against the ghastly question of free-will: many acts would be desirable, but they *can't* be done unless the agent desires them. I have hitherto spoken as if only a conflict of passions presented difficulties because only then is deliberate choice possible: but many passions—like Iago's hatred of Othello—may exist perfectly pure and yet be ethically condemned.

I am afraid this forces me to revise part of my theory.

This necessity is annoying, the more so as I see no very satisfactory way of revising it. McTaggart will say that all my difficulties arise from the attempt to make goodness an ultimate point of view—and so no doubt they do—but in an ethical discussion one is forced to take up this position, and only where a definite dilemma compels one to rise above the level of the Science in question is one justified in using this method of escape—short of this, the objections to what James calls making capital out of our intellectual defeat are good. I will then briefly recapitulate my former theory: Just as truth is true, ultimately, because we cannot but believe it if we judge at all, so the Good is good because we cannot but desire it if we desire at all. But as there may be error in belief, so there may be error in desire—a desire is erroneous when and in proportion as the attainment of its object will not bring satisfaction, i.e. when the desire conflicts with the general body of desires.

No reason can, at bottom, be given for desires—Desire and Knowledge are separate and independent realms, which may, I suppose, be brought together by a Metaphysic, by proving that what we desire must be real, and that Reality must be what Desire pronounces good—though I confess I have never understood any metaphysic which proves the world ethically as well as logically perfect. Knowledge is concerned with fact—Desire can (and does) damn facts, and construct an utterly different world of its own, a self-subsistent world, for which the ultimate and entire justification is that it is desired, and would satisfy desire if it were actual. As soon as we *talk* about desire, we are no longer in the *realm* of Desire, but in that of Knowledge, which is apt to cause confusion—we are dealing with the desire, which is a fact, not with its object, which is not a fact—that is why knowledge cannot judge desire as a whole, but only postulate that desires should form a harmonious system, otherwise they must, partially at least, defeat their own end of satisfaction, since the satisfaction of one is inconsistent with that of another. If we leave the Self out of account here, and require that Desires should not clash anywhere, whether in the same or in different individuals, we have the whole, it seems to me, that ethics can say on conduct: for since we do as we wish to do, judgments on conduct are reducible to judgments on desires. But how to prove, à priori, that the satisfaction of the individual is necessarily that of the Universe, I do not see, and this is to me *the* fundamental difficulty of Ethics.

So far I had not raised the question: Satisfaction to whom? and with this question a host of difficulties arise. The desires are of the Self, and hence, it seems, the satisfaction should be of the Self too. If, with McTaggart, we bring in personal immortality and a progress towards perfection (waiving the difficulty about Time), this limitation to the Self involves no great difficulties, for with higher sensibility comes acuter sympathy, and so personal satisfaction cannot be perfect until it is shared by all. But with a more Bradleian view of the Subject this theory becomes unsatisfactory—though it is difficult to see how Ethics can be expected to transcend the Self. But how, without such transcendence, are we to condemn a Iago or a Napoleon? They acted in the way most conducive to personal satisfaction, and common sense condemns them only because their gain was others' loss. I am vastly tempted to regard the Subject, as apparently Bradley does, as a mere fluid nucleus of Feeling, of uncertain and constantly changing boundaries, and so adopt an almost Spinozistic monism, in which our terms become merely Desire on the one hand and Satisfaction on the other—this would obviate all these ethical difficulties, and reduce Hatred and similar passions to my former case of a conflict, for reciprocal hatreds do not form a harmony like reciprocal loves, and cannot both be satisfied. Also all I said in the early part of my paper about desires with large universes would hold—the harmonious passions bring satisfaction to their objects as well as to the agent. An object such as knowledge or beauty, whose attainment is a gain to all, has obviously a wider universe than dinner, which is a gain only to the eater and to those who profit by his subsequent good-humour; and it has a larger universe than (say) power, which is limited to the individual. Thus if I am allowed, in estimating a desire's universe, to consider things outside the agent himself, all becomes easy. And yet Conduct is *my* Conduct, and therefore Virtue is *my* Virtue—so that nothing can be plainer than the egotistic nature of the whole question. McTaggart may draw what conclusions he will from this dilemma, and I shall probably accept them—only it is not my business now to draw them.

However we are to get out of this maze fairly, *I* shall do it by climbing over the hedges. I shall simply state dogmatically that though the Desires are of the Self, the Satisfaction required to make them ethically good is *not* necessarily of the Self. The problem of Ethics is to produce a harmony and self-consistency in Conduct—but mere self-consistency within the limits of the individual might be attained in many ways—there must therefore, to make the solution definite, be a universal harmony; my conduct must bring satisfaction not merely to myself, but to all whom it affects, so far as that is possible. In the face of what may be called the disharmonious passions (hatred, malice, etc.) this is not completely possible—and this would make one person's virtue necessarily incomplete so long as others are not completely virtuous—but to this conclusion I see no theoretic objection.—The practical modification of the previous results then would be that it is better to sacrifice personal consistency than to obtain it from desires directly opposed to those of the others whom they affect—so that desires themselves can be judged ethically according as they are such as can be satisfied universally or such as must conflict in different individuals—this is really only the old Kantian rule, and is an eminently commonplace conclusion for so long an argumentation. But having got back to common sense, I feel it is quite time I should hold my tongue.

# 15

# Is Ethics a Branch of Empirical Psychology? [1897]

RUSSELL READ THIS paper to the Apostles on 6 February 1897. The original title, "On Ethics as a Branch of Empirical Psychology", may have been altered after the manuscript was lengthened. Folios 1–6 form a complete essay; for folios 7–10 Russell used different paper and ink (beginning at 102: 7). In writing the essay Russell made use of one of his earlier writings on ethics, as the summary paragraph (104: 13–31) is taken, with a few stylistic changes, from his "Note on Ethical Theory" (Paper **38**), probably written the previous year. The invitation to give the paper came from G. E. Moore, then secretary of the Apostles, and conversations with him may have inspired the addition of the last four folios. Russell wrote to Moore on 31 January 1897:

> I had not meant to read a paper, as I wanted to find out what the Society is thinking about—but as you are in difficulties, I will read, if you like, on "Is Ethics a branch of Psychology?" I can't read on practical things, as I think little about them, and cannot prove the few opinions I have in any valid manner.

By this time Russell was no longer a regular attender of Apostolic meetings, and at the meeting at which the paper was read he took wings.

On the verso of the final leaf Russell wrote: "Shall we spell {Good/good} with", to which the reply in Moore's hand is: "Good = good". Also on this leaf is a reference to "Sigwart's *Logic*, Eng. trans. Appendix C." Sigwart's *Logic* has an "Appendix C" in both of its volumes. Neither appendix is relevant to the topic of this paper, but it seems likely, in view of his interests at the time, that Russell was referring to Appendix C in the second volume, which deals with non-Euclidean geometry.

The copy-text is the manuscript (RA 220.010560), which consists of ten leaves.

BETWEEN THE FOUNDATIONS of ethics and the foundations of Epistemology, a certain analogy may be traced. The one is a theory of the good, the other a theory of the true. Both are due, in a sense, to the existence of states of consciousness with an objective reference. In desire, as in knowledge, we have a mental state with a reference to something other than itself. The two differ in the *manner*, but agree in the *fact*, of reference. In knowledge, we distinguish the act of knowing from the thing known: in desire, we distinguish the act of desiring from the thing desired. In the theory of knowledge, we isolate the thing known, as the objectively true, from the act of knowing: in ethics—so it is usually held—we can isolate the thing desired, as the objectively good, from the act of desiring.

But let us examine a little more closely the justification, in the theory of knowledge, for this isolation from the fact that we know. The psychological investigation of belief or cognition, as we know, analyses the causes of belief, and assigns, empirically, many causes which cannot, by logic, be regarded as valid grounds. Why does not this undermine our faith, as it undermined Hume's, in the correctness of our logical postulates? The reason is, that the results we obtain by empirical psychology are themselves knowledge, and therefore postulate the correctness of our methods of cognition. To call in question the correctness of these methods, on the ground of results obtained by postulating them, is therefore a vicious circle.

To put the matter otherwise: knowledge, in the concrete, has two aspects, the objective fact asserted, and the psychological fact of assertion. But any study of the psychological fact of assertion can only lead to fresh knowledge, having the same two aspects, with the logically irrelevant difference that now the objective fact asserted is that I previously made an assertion. Hence again, the validity of knowledge has to be postulated, before our manner of knowing can be investigated: this investigation cannot, therefore, shake our belief in the validity of knowledge. Thus the theory of knowledge is, in its foundations, independent of empirical psychology, and the objective reference of our judgments can be studied apart from the fact that we know.

In the same way, it is suggested, we can study the objects of desire apart from the fact that we empirically desire them. The primary assertion would thus be: "This is good", and only psychological reflection would lead to: "I desire this". But to this view there is a fundamental objection. The state of mind in which I desire an object does not, abstractly considered, contain an assertion or a cognitive element: to say, "This is good", is not the same as to desire this. Reflection is involved in the transformation of the desire into the assertion: the assertion is made on the ground of the desire, and is not itself the same mental state as the desire. Thus the two statements: "This is good", and: "I desire this", are strictly equivalent to one another: both are made by a reflection on the desire, and both assert one and the same fact. This is not the case with the previous couple: "This is true", and: "I believe this". Here the first assertion actually *is* the state of mind of the person believing, while the second assertion asserts the existence of that state of mind. In the ethical couple, on the contrary, neither assertion is the original state of mind, but both, as the result of reflection, assert that state of mind.

Put briefly, the distinction is this. When we reflect on knowledge, the result is fresh knowledge: when we reflect on desire, the result, so far as ethics is concerned, is not fresh desire, but knowledge. For an ethical proposition, considered as a psychical occurrence, is not a desire, but a cognition. In reflecting psychologically on desires, therefore, we are not bound to postulate beforehand the ethical justification of all desires, since the result of our reflections is not itself desire, but knowledge. The result of psychological reflection on knowledge is to know our manner of knowing: the validity of this result therefore presupposes the validity of knowledge. To obtain a strict parallel in ethics, we should have to consider an attitude towards our desires which led to our desiring our manner of desiring. If this were the result of psychological reflection on desires, the objective reference of desires would remain ultimate and irreducible: in the practical sphere, where desire is ultimate, this is the case: but in the theoretical sphere, where only knowledge is ultimate, we cannot establish any such contention. Now ethics belongs to the theoretical sphere: it is *knowledge* of the practical sphere, and thus not itself practical. Knowledge of desire is as little practical as desire for knowledge is theoretical.

Thus the relation of ethics to desire is quite different from the relation of the psychology of cognition to knowledge. Ethics asserts the desire for an object, whereas the psychology of cognition asserts the assertion of an object. Thus the objection to psychology as a legitimate method in the theory of knowledge does not exist in the ethical sphere. The practical fallacy, parallel to this theoretical fallacy, would be to take desire for virtue as our criterion of the good, where virtue is defined as the possession of those desires which we desire to have. This would be plainly absurd, for if our desires are ever a criterion of the good, they must be so equally whether their objective reference is to other desires or not. Thus for ethics, the primary assertion is the knowledge that something is desired, which is already at the psychological level. The unreflective level does not, as in the theory of knowledge, afford any component of ethics, but self-knowledge is an indispensable condition of ethical judgments.

Thus the only method for ethics, it would seem, is to investigate as best it can the nature and objects of our desires. It cannot investigate the objects of desire, without at the same time and in the same terms investigating desire itself, since the objects referred to by desire are not cognitively referred to, and are therefore only *known* as objects of desire by a distinct reflective act. An à priori system of desires, independent of reference to psychology, would have to be primarily desired, not known, and could be known only empirically, by reflection on the state of mind in which it was desired. Unless, therefore, the good can be defined otherwise than in terms of desire, ethics, properly studied, must always remain, it would seem, purely a branch of empirical psychology, dependent through and through on investigation of the things which people desire or find to satisfy their desires. From this conclusion there seems no escape.

If, then, the good is the desired, it follows that ethics is a wholly empirical study, that ethical judgments have not any objectivity or permanence in ascribing goodness to things, and indeed that goodness is a relation to ourselves which varies with our every whim. We may take this result either as condemning ethics, or, as our brother Moore will certainly take it, as condemning the identification of the good and the desired. There are several ways, historically, of escaping from this identification. We may regard the good, as the Hedonists mostly intend to regard it, as the pleasant; or we may regard it, with Mr. Bradley, as that which satisfies desire. There is very little to choose between this and the Hedonist definition: as soon as we have amended pleasure into the pleasant, it becomes practically the same as that which satisfies desire; except that Mr. Bradley's definition omits those pleasures which come unsought, and omits them with little apparent justification. It is to be observed that what satisfies desire is very different from what is desired: it excludes all foolish desires, whose attainment is disappointing; it affords an ethical meaning for error, and it makes the good less dependent on the particular degree of knowledge of the person desiring, since what would satisfy desire is more constant than what is actually desired. Moreover, if there be a dialectic of desire, to be gone through in practice, Mr. Bradley's definition places the good in the ultimate goal, and not in the ever-changing will-o'-the-wisp which we pursue on the way. These are solid advantages; but it seems impossible not to challenge the premiss. Why should I call good what satisfies desire, rather than what I desire?

The ultimate premiss of any subject should have an evidence which cannot be questioned. The premiss of Logic and Metaphysics is that truth is true of reality, and that some knowledge is true. This depends on the ontological argument, which again depends on the impossibility of total scepticism. But where are we to find corresponding evidence for an ethical premiss? We have it, if we define the good as the desired, but not, so far as I can see, on any other definition. A man needs no argument to convince him that what he desires is good: he can accept no argument to prove anything else good. When Sigmund refuses Valhalla because Sieglinde will not be there, it is useless to argue that he will forget her, that he will have satisfaction of desire, etc., etc.: the fact remains that his present desire is for Sieglinde, not for Valhalla, and to speak of error in his estimate of the good seems absurd. It is to be observed that in Economics, the only science worth the name which deals with human nature, the same definition of goods prevails. Goods are whatever people desire. Brackish water which could be disposed of as fresh, for example, would come under the head of goods, though it would not satisfy desire. We cannot escape by saying people desire things because they believe they will give satisfaction: that would plunge us into the fallacies of psychological hedonism. With any other definition of the good, it is open to us to say Why? People said Why? to pleasure, as soon as it became evident that the desired was not always pleasure. Similarly, one may say Why? to that which satisfies desire. If we do not happen to desire it, there is no way of convincing us that we ought to do so. It may be said, nothing can satisfy desire unless it is desired. True; but the desire presupposed is here a hypothetical one, or else Mr. Bradley's definition becomes mine. There seem to be three ways of defining the Good by reference to desire: (1) The satisfaction of desire (2) That which satisfies desire (3) The desired. (1) The first is open to all the objections to Hedonism: it places the good in a mere frame of mind, not in a state of the universe. But for these objections, it would lead, in a few moves, to a satisfactory and beautiful ethic. For it would lead us to assert that those things only ought to be desired which the Universe will let us have, since only so can our desires be satisfied. This would place virtue in submission to, or harmony with, the universal will—a very pious doctrine, which I should like extremely to believe. It would prove, also, that the Universe is neither good nor bad, since both good and bad exist only in our attitude towards the Universe. But, unfortunately, it affords no argument against the man who stubbornly desires what the Universe will not give, and its definition is wholly arbitrary.

(2) The second definition, as that which satisfies desire, also allows of moral error, not now in our estimate of the world, but in our estimate of ourselves. The first definition placed the good in that which, if we desired it, we could obtain. The second places it in that which, if we obtained it, would satisfy our desires. Error, here, consists in a wrong estimate of the things which would give lasting satisfaction. All the banal objections to the man of pleasure, all the homilies on the vanity of human wishes, fall under this definition. These things, it is said, turn to dust and ashes as soon as they are attained. But if this is used as an argument for a change of life, it presupposes that what people really want is desires for things which can give lasting satisfaction: if they retort, But I desire human things, though I know they will prove a disappointment, the unhappy moralist is left shocked and speechless, but without arguments.

(3) The third definition alone, it would seem, needs no argument to prove it—and this is fortunate, since all argument in proof of a definition of the good is impossible. The good, we say, is simply the desired. Since people always act from desire, this destroys the possibility of moral error. But, oddly enough, it does not destroy the possibility of bad conduct. For good

conduct, on our definition, is desired conduct, and our conduct is only too often not such as we desire. The habitual drunkard normally desires to keep sober, and drunkenness is therefore bad conduct. Since many of our desires, in short, have other desires for their objects, we can distinguish good and bad among all those desires which are themselves objects of desire or aversion. The desires we desire to have are good; those we desire not to have are bad. In general, the desires we wish not to have are those which interfere with our master passions: the drunkard objects to his desire for drink, because it interferes with work or worldly success. Thus good desires will be
10 those which form a harmonious system *inter se*, and bad desires those which clash. Though this will be only approximate and empirical, it is odd to see so old an ethical friend returned from so anarchical a quarter.

To sum up: An ethic which merely says: The good is the desired, leaves the good a prey to changing fancies. An ethic which says: The good is the satisfaction of desire, is open to all the objections to Hedonism: it chooses an aspect of the good, a mere result of desire, as the whole good. On the other hand, since we always do act from desire, an ethic which takes all desires as equally ultimate loses all criterion, all standard of judging action: all acts become alike good or alike bad. Now morality is exhibited only in action,
20 and action springs only from desire. Therefore moral judgments must discriminate between desires. But since all contrast of ideal and actual rests on desire, since all goodness, all morality, rest on the contrast of ideal and actual, desire alone can supply the criterion among desires. The criterion must be supplied, therefore, by the contrast between ideal and actual desires, by the contrast between desires we desire and desires we dislike. Whether we have them or not, for example, most of us desire a wish for the good of humanity, and dislike a craving for drink or morphia. In fact, the desired has as wide a range in conduct as in feeling. The man, then, who desires always and only what he wishes to desire, is perfectly good in his
30 conduct: in all that depends upon himself there is no conflict, but the most perfect harmony possible.

That my conclusion is satisfactory, I do not pretend. If our brother Moore will give me an unexceptionable premiss for his definition of the good, or even a hint of where to find one, I will retract. At present, I see no way of distinguishing between the good and the desired. I regard the good, therefore, as totally devoid of objectivity, and as matter for purely psychological investigation.

# 16

# Seems, Madam? Nay, It Is [1897]

THIS PAPER WAS read to the Society on 11 December 1897. The title quotes Hamlet speaking in a moment of grief for the loss of his father, the king (*Hamlet*, I.ii.76f.). The loss of paternal assurance resembles loss of metaphysical assurance, the essay's topic. Russell wrote to Moore, who was still secretary of the Apostles, on 7 December:

> I will write you a paper, as you seem badly in need of it. But I fear it will be rather a scratch sort of paper, as I am having what revivalists call a "dry time". I have called it "Seems, Madam? Nay it is"; the gist of it being, that for all purposes which are not *purely* intellectual, the world of Appearance is the real world—agin McTaggart's notion of getting religion out of Philosophy. I have never thought out my ideas on heredity, and cannot write a paper on it at such short notice.

"Seems, Madam? Nay, It Is" marks the beginning of Russell's break with neo-Hegelianism.

The paper was first published, at Russell's suggestion, in *Why I Am Not a Christian* (1957), edited by Paul Edwards. Edwards's historical headnote (p. 94), which was based on information he received in a letter from Russell of 6 March 1956 (RA REC. ACQ. 190), erroneously states that it was written in 1899. The error can be traced to Edith Russell's misreading of the date on the last leaf as "Dec. 11. 1899" and to Russell's failure to correct the mistake when he read her typescript. The manuscript (RA 220.010600), which has fourteen leaves, has been collated with Edith Russell's typescript and the first edition of *Why I Am Not a Christian*. The manuscript is the copy-text.

PHILOSOPHY, IN THE days when it was still fat and prosperous, claimed to perform, for its votaries, a variety of the most important services. It offered them comfort in adversity, explanation in intellectual difficulty, and guidance in moral perplexity. No wonder if the Younger Brother, when an instance of its uses was presented to him, exclaimed with the enthusiasm of youth

> How charming is divine Philosophy!
> Not harsh and crabbed, as dull fools suppose,
> But musical as is Apollo's lute.

10    But those happy days are past. Philosophy, by the slow victories of its own offspring, has been forced to forego, one by one, its high pretensions. Intellectual difficulties, for the most part, have been acquired by Science—philosophy's anxious claims on the few exceptional questions, which it still endeavours to answer, are regarded by most people as a remnant of the dark ages, and are being transferred, with all speed, to the rigid Science of Mr. F. W. H. Myers. Moral perplexities—which, until recently, were unhesitatingly assigned by philosophers to their own domain—have been abandoned by McTaggart and Mr. Bradley to the whimsies of statistics and common sense. But the power of giving comfort and consolation is
20    still supposed by McTaggart to belong to philosophy. It is this last possession of which, tonight, I wish to rob the decrepit parent of our modern gods.

It might seem, at first sight, that the question could be settled very briefly. "I know that philosophy can give comfort," McTaggart might say, "because it certainly comforts me." I shall try to prove, however, that those conclusions which give him comfort are conclusions which do not follow from his general position—which, indeed, admittedly do not follow, and are retained, it would seem, only *because* they give him comfort.

As I do not wish to discuss the truth of philosophy, but only its emotional
30    value, I shall assume a metaphysic which rests on the distinction between Appearance and Reality, and regards the latter as timeless and perfect. The principle of any such metaphysic may be put in a nutshell. "God's in his heaven, all's wrong with the world"—that is its last word. But it seems to be supposed that, since he is in his heaven, and always has been there, we may expect him some day to descend to earth—if not to judge the quick and the dead, at least to reward the faith of the philosophers. His long resignation, however, to a purely heavenly existence, would seem to suggest, as regards the affairs of earth, a stoicism on which it would be rash to found our hopes.

But to speak seriously. The emotional value of a doctrine, as a comfort in
40    adversity, appears to depend upon its prediction of the future. The future, emotionally speaking, is more important than the past, or even than the

present. "All's well that ends well" is the dictum of unanimous common
sense. "Many a dull morning turns out a fine day" is optimism; whereas
pessimism says:

> Full many a glorious morning have I seen
> Flatter the mountain tops with sovereign eye
> Kissing with golden face the meadows green
> Gilding pale streams with heavenly alchemy;
> Anon permit the basest clouds to ride
> With ugly rack on his celestial face
> And from the forlorn world his visage hide          10
> Stealing unseen to west with this disgrace.

And so, emotionally, our view of the universe as good or bad depends on the
future, on what it will be; we are concerned always with appearances in
time, and unless we are assured that the future is to be better than the
present, it is hard to see where we are to find consolation.

So much, indeed, is the future bound up with optimism, that McTaggart
himself, while all his optimism depends upon the denial of time, is compelled to represent the Absolute as a future state of things, as "a harmony
which must some day become explicit". It would be unkind to urge this
contradiction, as it is mainly McTaggart himself who has made me aware of   20
it. But what I do wish to urge is, that any comfort, which may be derived
from the doctrine that Reality is timeless and eternally good, is derived only
and exclusively by means of this contradiction. A timeless Reality can have
no more intimate connection with the future than with the past: if its perfection has not appeared hitherto, there is no reason to suppose it ever
will—there is, indeed, every likelihood that God will stay in his heaven. We
might, with equal propriety, speak of a harmony which must once *have been*
explicit; it may be that "my grief lies onward and my joy behind"—and it is
obvious how little comfort this would afford us.

All our experience is bound up with time, nor is it possible to imagine a   30
timeless experience. But even if it were possible, we could not, without
contradiction, suppose that we ever *shall* have such an experience. All experience, therefore, for aught that philosophy can show, is likely to resemble the experience we know—if this seems bad to us, no doctrine of a Reality
distinguished from Appearances can give us hope of anything better. We
fall, indeed, into a hopeless dualism. On the one side we have the world we
know, with its events, pleasant and unpleasant, its deaths and failures and
disasters—on the other hand an imaginary world, which we christen the
world of Reality, atoning, by the largeness of the R, for the absence of every
other sign that there really is such a world. Now our only ground for this   40
world of Reality is, that this is what Reality would have to be if we could

understand it. But if the result of our purely ideal construction turns out so very different from the world we know—from the real world, in fact—if, moreover, it follows from this very construction that we never shall experience the so-called world of Reality, except in a sense in which already we experience nothing else—then I cannot see what, as concerns comfort for present ills, we have gained by all our metaphysicizing. Take, for example, such a question as immortality. People have desired immortality either as a redress for the injustices of this world, or, which is the more respectable motive, as affording a possibility of meeting again after death those whom they have loved. The latter desire is one which we all feel, and for whose satisfaction, if philosophy could satisfy it, we should be immeasurably grateful. But philosophy, at best, can only assure us that the soul is a timeless reality. At what points of time, if any, it may happen to appear, is thus wholly irrelevant to it, and there is no legitimate inference from such a doctrine to existence after death. Keats may still regret

> That I shall never look upon thee more,
> Never have relish in the fairy power
> Of unreflecting love

and it cannot much console him to be told that "fair creature of an hour" is not a metaphysically accurate phrase. It is still true that "Time will come and take my love away", and that "This thought is as a death which cannot choose But weep to have that which it fears to lose". And so with every part of the doctrine of a timelessly perfect Reality. Whatever now seems evil—and it is the lamentable prerogative of evil that to seem so is to be so—whatever evil now appears may remain, for aught we know, throughout all time, to torment our latest descendants. And in such a doctrine there is, to my mind, no vestige of comfort or consolation.

It is true that Christianity, and all previous optimisms, have represented the world as eternally ruled by a beneficent Providence, and thus metaphysically good. But this has been, at bottom, only a device by which to prove the future excellence of the world—to prove, for example, that good men would be happy after death. It has always been this deduction—illegitimately made of course—which has given comfort. "He's a good fellow, and 'twill all be well."

It may be said, indeed, that there is comfort in the mere abstract doctrine that Reality is good. I do not myself accept the proof of this doctrine, but even if true, I cannot see why it should be comforting. For the essence of my contention is, that Reality, as constructed by metaphysics, bears no sort of relation to the world of experience. It is an empty abstraction, from which no single inference can be validly made as to the world of appearance, in which world, nevertheless, all our interests lie. Even the pure intellectual

interest, from which metaphysics springs, is an interest in explaining the
world of appearance. But instead of really explaining this actual palpable
sensible world, metaphysics constructs another fundamentally different
world, so different, so unconnected with actual experience, that the world
of daily life remains wholly unaffected by it, and goes on its way just as if
there were no world of Reality at all. If even one were allowed to regard the
world of Reality as an "other world", as a heavenly city existing somewhere
in the skies, there might no doubt be comfort in the thought that others have
a perfect experience which we lack. But to be told that our experience, as we
know it, is that perfect experience, must leave us cold, since it cannot prove 10
our experience to be better than it is. On the other hand, to say that our
actual experience is not that perfect experience constructed by philosophy,
is to cut off the only sort of existence which philosophical reality can have—
since God in his heaven cannot be maintained as a separate person. Either,
then, our existing experience is perfect—which is an empty phrase, leaving
it no better than before—or there is no perfect experience, and our world of
Reality, being experienced by no one, exists only in the metaphysics books.
In either case, it seems to me, we cannot find in philosophy the consolations
of religion.

There are, of course, several senses in which it would be absurd to deny 20
that philosophy may give us comfort. We may find philosophizing a pleasant way of passing our mornings—in this sense, the comfort derived may
even, in extreme cases, be comparable to that of drinking as a way of passing
our evenings. We may, again, take philosophy aesthetically, as probably
most of us take Spinoza. We may use metaphysics, like poetry and music, as
a means of producing a mood, of giving us a certain view of the universe, a
certain attitude towards life—the resulting state of mind being valued on
account of, and in proportion to, the degree of poetic emotion aroused, not
in proportion to the truth of the beliefs entertained. Our satisfaction, indeed, seems to be, in these moods, the exact opposite of the metaphysician's 30
professions. It is the satisfaction of forgetting the real world and its evils,
and persuading ourselves, for the moment, of the reality of a world we have
ourselves created. This seems to be one of the grounds on which Bradley
justifies metaphysics. "When poetry, art and religion", he says, "have
ceased wholly to interest, or when they show no longer any tendency to
struggle with ultimate problems and come to an understanding with them;
when the sense of mystery and enchantment no longer draws the mind to
wander aimlessly and love it knows not what; when, in short, twilight has no
charm—then metaphysics will be worthless." What metaphysics does for us
in this way is essentially what, say, *The Tempest* does for us—but its value on 40
this view, is quite independent of its truth. It is not because Prospero's
magic makes us acquainted with the world of spirits that we value the *Tempest*; it is not, aesthetically, because we are informed of a world of spirit that

we value metaphysics. And this brings out the essential difference between the aesthetic satisfaction, which I allow, and the religious comfort, which I deny to philosophy. For aesthetic satisfaction, intellectual conviction is unnecessary, and we may therefore choose, when we seek it, the metaphysic which gives us the most of it. For religious comfort, on the other hand, belief is essential, and I am contending that we do not get religious comfort from the metaphysic which we believe.

It is possible, however, to introduce a refinement into the argument, by adopting a more or less mystical theory of the aesthetic emotion. It may be contended that, although we can never wholly experience Reality as it really is, yet some experiences approach it more nearly than others, and such experiences, it may be said, are given by art and philosophy. And under the influence of the experiences which art and philosophy sometimes give us, it seems easy to adopt this view. For those who have the metaphysical passion, there is probably no emotion so rich and beautiful, so wholly desirable, as that mystic sense, which philosophy sometimes gives, of a world transformed by the beatific vision. As Bradley again says: "Some in one way, some in another, we seem to touch and have communion with what is beyond the visible world. In various manners we find something higher, which both supports and humbles, both chastens and supports us. And, with certain persons, the intellectual effort to understand the Universe is a principal way of thus experiencing the Deity.... And this appears", he continues, "to be another reason for some persons pursuing the study of ultimate truth".

But is it not equally a reason for hoping that these persons will not find ultimate truth? if indeed ultimate truth bear any resemblance to the doctrines set forth in *Appearance and Reality*. I do not deny the value of the emotion, but I do deny that, strictly speaking, it is in any peculiar sense a beatific vision, or an experience of the Deity. In one sense, of course, all experience is experience of the Deity, but in another, since all experience equally is in time, and the Deity is timeless, no experience is experience of the Deity—"as such" pedantry would bid me add. The gulf fixed between Appearance and Reality is so profound, that we have no grounds, so far as I can see, for regarding some experiences as nearer than others to the perfect experience of Reality. The value of the experiences in question must, therefore, be based wholly on their emotional quality, and not, as Bradley would seem to suggest, on any superior degree of truth which may attach to them. But if so, they are at best the consolations of philosophizing, not of philosophy. They constitute a reason for the pursuit of ultimate truth, since they are flowers to be gathered by the way; but they do not constitute a reward for its attainment, since, by all that appears, the flowers grow only at the beginning of the road, and disappear long before we have reached our journey's end.

The view which I have advocated is, no doubt, not an inspiring one, nor yet one which, if generally accepted, would be likely to promote the study of philosophy. I might justify my paper, if I wished to do so, on the maxim that, "where all is rotten, it is a man's work to cry stinking fish". But I prefer to suggest that metaphysics, when it seeks to supply the place of religion, has really mistaken its function. That it can supply this place, I admit; but it supplies it, I maintain, at the expense of being bad metaphysics. Why not admit that metaphysics, like science, is justified by intellectual curiosity, and ought to be guided by intellectual curiosity alone? The desire to find comfort in metaphysics has, we must all admit, produced a great deal of fallacious reasoning and intellectual dishonesty. From this, at any rate, the abandonment of religion would deliver us. And since intellectual curiosity exists in some people, it is probable that some attempts would still be made to understand the world, and it is possible that they would be freed from certain hitherto persistent fallacies. "The man", to quote Bradley once more, "whose nature is such that by one path alone his chief desire will reach consummation, will try to find it on that path, whatever it may be, and whatever the world thinks of it; and if he does not, he is contemptible."

# 17

# Was the World Good before the Sixth Day? [1899]

RUSSELL READ THIS paper to the Apostles on 11 February 1899. It is unusual among Russell's contributions for the amount of playful Apostolic argot in its opening paragraphs. The paper was written in response to Moore's view that beauty has intrinsic worth, a position taken in the "The Elements of Ethics"—a course of lectures he had delivered at the London School of Ethics and Social Philosophy in the autumn of 1898. Russell's marginalia on Moore's typescript of the lectures reveal his familiarity with them. For further information concerning the marginalia, see Rosenbaum *1969* and the typescript in the Moore papers in the Cambridge University Library.

According to Levy (*1979*, 204), Russell's paper resulted in the members voting on two questions: (1) "Is matter beautiful?" and (2) "Is matter good?" Question (1) was carried unanimously. On (2), only Moore and one other member voted yes, while Russell and two others voted no. Levy quotes Moore as commenting on both questions: "The whole thing is absurd, the question has never been raised."

The manuscript (RA 220.010580), which consists of nine leaves, is the copy-text.

OUR BROTHER MOORE has been engaged, by order of the Society, in a heroic work, involving the very highest degree of danger and difficulty. He has been endeavouring—I believe with success—to corrupt still further (an arduous task) the morals of those phenomena who frequent the shallow abyss known among shadows as "The London School of Ethics and Social Philosophy". As the glory of God is enhanced by the damnation of the wicked, by which they are rendered still more wicked than they intended to be, so the glory of the Society is enhanced by increasing the phenomenality of phenomena. And as it is the mark of the Society to be wise and good, so it is the mark of phenomena to be foolish and wicked. Moore has been endeavouring, then, to render these shadows even more foolish and more wicked than they naturally are. That this is difficult, is certainly undeniable; but the difficulty seems to have been successfully overcome. For according to an emissary, sent by the Society to report upon Moore's success, he persuaded the assembled phenomena that their so-called lives were of such value to each other, that, if they saw one of the wise and good drowning, they ought not to risk death in an endeavour to save him. The danger of Moore's mission, however, was even more overwhelming than the difficulty, and has, I greatly fear, been less effectually avoided. It is well-known that whatever is dangerous to a brother is unreal, and that contact with the unreal may entail fatal consequences. What, then, was my horror, when I discovered that these views, designed for the corruption of the non-existent, had—I shudder at the thought—infected our lamented brother himself. To free him from these dreadful toils is my purpose tonight.

Moore contends that God, when he looked upon the world in its early stages, was right in maintaining it to be good—that it was already good in and for itself, and would have continued so even if God had not been looking. A world of matter alone—so says our misguided brother—may be good or bad. For it may certainly be beautiful and ugly, and beauty is better than ugliness. It cannot be said—so the argument proceeds—that beauty is good only as a means to the production of emotion in us. For we judge the man who is moved by beauty to be better than the man who is equally moved by ugliness. This judgment can only be valid, if beauty is good *per se*; for in this case, the man who enjoys ugliness more is to be condemned for liking what is bad. But if beauty were only good as a means, ugliness would be equally good if it produced the same effect; this, however, is manifestly false. Hence beauty is good *per se*, and a purely material world, with no one to contemplate it, is better if it is beautiful than if it is ugly.

Such is the argument which, though invented for the further perdition of shadows, has, alas! deceived our brother himself. Let us now endeavour to persuade him that this sophism, like the world of matter, can only be good as a means, and must never be taken as an end.

There are several lines of argument, commonly taken as regards beauty,

which I shall avoid. Many would urge that beauty is purely subjective, and exists only in the spectator, or begins when a spectator is seen to be coming. This is rather like the Berkeleian theory, that when a house is tumbling down, it doesn't begin to make a noise till some one comes along the road, and then only if the some one is not deaf. This theory I shall not adopt. I shall admit that beauty is a quality of the object, and that persons of bad taste—if there be any such—are those who are unable to see this quality. Another course which might be taken, would be, to admit that ugliness *is* as good as beauty if it produces as much pleasure. This course would be un-
10 avoidable for a utilitarian, and is much to be commended as a method of ir-ritating hedonistic but fastidious art-critics. The objection to it is, as Moore says, that it makes the person of bad taste as good as the person of good taste, provided only he enjoys bad art as much as the other enjoys good art—a proviso which, one must admit, is fully satisfied by the facts. To maintain that "Home Sweet Home" gives less pleasure than a Bach fugue, would only be possible for one in bondage to a theory. Nor shall I adopt the really radical puritanical view, that beauty is good neither as means nor as end, but is an invention of the fiend to tempt us to damnation. This is a view I have much sympathy with, and should like, outside the Society, to advocate. But
20 for the present I will adopt another and less thorough-going argument.

That nothing is good or bad in itself except psychical states, is a position which could only be maintained by omniscience. For we do not know of what nature other possible existents than mind or matter may be, and of what we do not know we cannot judge whether it is good or bad. But it is possible to maintain, and I intend to maintain, that among the things we know there is nothing good or bad except psychical states. Of matter I affirm, that it can only be good or bad as a means. When a smut falls on my nose, it is bad as a means; when it falls on the bald head of the Vice-Master, it is similarly good; but in neither case is it an end in itself. But how, then,
30 are we to account for our ethical judgment that the man who sees and enjoys beauty is better than the man who enjoys ugliness? It seems to me that Moore's argument on this point presupposes, what he would be the last to affirm, that psychical states can only derive value from the pleasure they contain. For the pleasure derived from ugliness may certainly be greater than that derived from beauty; but no evidence is offered that there are not other differences between the state in which the fastidious man perceives beauty and that in which the other perceives ugliness. No evidence is possi-ble, since indeed the opposite is the case. The man who knows beauty when he sees it is *ipso facto* different from the man who does not. There is no
40 reason to deny, therefore, that there is a specific aesthetic emotion, only to be had by the man who consciously perceives beauty; just as there is a feel-ing of red only to be had by the man who looks at something red, and does not, through colour-blindness, take it to be blue. If there be such a specific

emotion, there is no ground for denying that beauty is to be valued as a means to this emotion, and that this emotion is good *per se* in a degree quite out of proportion to its pleasurableness.

Let us examine this possibility more minutely. We will suppose two people, $A$ and $B$, the first having perfect taste, the other having the very reverse. We will suppose two objects, $\alpha$ and $\beta$, the first perfectly beautiful, the other utterly hideous. Then $A$ gets from $\alpha$ the aesthetic emotion, which is good, and from $\beta$ he gets its opposite, which is bad. $B$, on the other hand, being a person of bad taste, judges $\alpha$ to be horrid and $\beta$ to be quite lovely. Are we bound to hold that $B$ gets the aesthetic emotion from $\beta$? I do not see that we are. For there is no reason to suppose the emotion the same merely because the judgment is the same. We may maintain, on the contrary, that only beautiful objects can give the aesthetic emotion, and only people who perceive their beauty can feel this emotion. People of bad taste, before an ugly object, we shall say, falsely judge it to be beautiful, and falsely judge that they feel the aesthetic emotion. In this I see no more difficulty than in the fact that some people mistakenly think themselves in love. Indeed it would be very curious if the emotional effect of beauty on one person were exactly the same as that of ugliness on another, nor do I see the shadow of a reason for such an assumption. It does not follow, because a person *thinks* he sees beauty, that he will have the same emotions as he would have if he really saw it. Indeed, even though it be admitted that beauty is objective, we may still regard the beautiful as that which *can* produce the aesthetic emotion, though this is of course no definition of it. And there is no reason to suppose all people capable of this emotion or of the perception of beauty. That many people, when they use the word, have no idea of what it means, seems a plausible way of accounting for the disputes which rage about it. We learn what *red* means by having red things pointed out to us. But if the vast majority of mankind, when a red thing was pointed out, saw in it only hardness, smoothness, shape, etc., and not colour, great disputes would doubtless rage as to what was red. One man would pitch on hardness, and call all hard things red; another on smoothness, and so on. Thus we may suppose most people use the word beauty in some wholly irrelevant sense, and do not, when they use the word, mean by it at all what should be meant.

But even when they mean the same, it is quite likely that they are subject to a sheer error, and do not obtain the same emotion from many of the things they call beautiful as the more cultivated obtain from things which really are so. You may think so-and-so a very amusing fellow, through mere lack of self-consciousness, when, as a matter of fact, you are bored to death whenever he is in the room. And the same may happen with regard to beauty.

Thus broadly, the people of bad taste are of two kinds. There are first those who don't know what the word means, but are ignorant even of their own ignorance. The judgments of these are quite irrelevant. Secondly there are those who know what the word means, but through defective perception sometimes apply it falsely. There remains the question why these two classes are less good than the faultless critic.

As regards the first class, who do not know even what beauty means, they are to be condemned because, first, they are ignorant, but secondly because they have never felt the aesthetic emotion, which, it is contended, is *sui generis* and good as an end. The second class are less condemnable. They have at some time seen beauty and felt its charms. But they have not seen it clearly enough to recognize it when they saw it again, nor yet felt its charms
10 strongly enough to recognize the feeling when they felt it again. These people may again be of two kinds. They may always feel the appropriate emotion, without recognizing it as such, or recognizing the beauty of the object. Such people are essentially people of good taste: their error is purely intellectual, and is no greater than that of people who can't do sums. But— and this is probably the more common case—they may be very seldom capable of aesthetic emotion, and feel it only slightly when they have it. In this case the slightness of their sensibility is the source both of their bad taste and of their ethical inferiority.

If then, we admit a specific aesthetic emotion, which can only be pro-
20 duced by beautiful objects, and then only in those who are not aesthetically blind, there is no reason, even though we admit the objectivity of beauty and the inferiority of those who have bad taste, to admit so monstrous a paradox as the possible goodness of a purely material world. There is a sense, I admit, in which such a world is *bad*, since it contains nothing good; but this applies equally to all such worlds, and does not distinguish the beautiful from the ugly. That the good is confined, as far as objects of experience are concerned, to what is psychical, is a conclusion, then, if there be an aesthetic emotion, which the objectivity of beauty cannot alone destroy. Whether any other arguments exist against this view, I do not know, but I expect to be
30 soon informed.

# Part IV
# Graduate Essays in Epistemology
# and the History of Philosophy

# General Headnote to Parts IV and V

THE PAPERS IN this Part, and several in Part V, are among those that Russell wrote for his tutors as a Moral Sciences student at Cambridge in the academic year 1893–94. During this year Russell attended courses by James Ward ("Metaphysics" and "History of Philosophy"), by Henry Sidgwick ("The Elements of Philosophy" and "Ethics"), and by G. F. Stout ("History of Philosophy"). He began his work as a philosophy student immediately after the completion of Part I of the Mathematical Tripos, by attending Sidgwick's lectures on ethics which started in the Long Vacation of 1893. With the exception of Sidgwick's course on the elements of philosophy, Russell took lengthy notes of the lectures he attended in two thick lecture notebooks (1: RA 220.010040; and 2: RA 220.010050). In addition there are various loose sheets (RA 220.010050) found in these noteboooks. These sheets consist mainly of notes Russell made of his reading for these papers.

For most papers, the questions set by the tutors have been preserved either as a result of being taken down in dictation at lectures, or on sheets distributed by the tutors. Where the questions are extant, a full record is supplied in the headnotes. (All abbreviations have been expanded in their transcription.) In addition, the lecture notebooks sometimes contain an account of comments by Russell's tutors on the papers, but it is often hard to determine whether these were general remarks addressed to the entire class or comments specifically about Russell's papers. Only when there is clear evidence that they were directed to Russell's papers have they been included in the headnotes.

The papers themselves often bear comments by the tutors. Sidgwick's comments are by far the most extensive though often hard to decipher and sometimes difficult to set into type because they involve a network of lines drawn across the entire page. (See the Illustrations.) Comments by Ward, who exerted a considerable influence on Russell's early philosophical thinking, though less frequent, are usually concise. Stout seems never to have written anything on the papers. None of Russell's tutors wrote synoptic comments. In deciding which comments to include in the annotations, mere requests for further explanation and such enigmatic marks as underlinings, marginal lines, queries and crosses have been ignored. Only those comments have been included which make a substantial point about a particular passage or to which Russell added his reply. In addition, of course, there is the limitation of what it is possible to decipher and represent intelligibly in print. Abbreviations have been expanded and doubtful readings are followed by "⟨?⟩". (In the case of some of

Sidgwick's remarks these readings represent little more than best guesses.) Russell's papers, notably those for Stout, contain occasional pencilled alterations, often in a very crabbed hand. They seem to have been made by Russell, who may have read these papers aloud in tutorials and corrected them as he read. This would also explain the lack of written comments by Stout.

It was a common practice in setting the topics for the papers to group several questions together. Accordingly most of the papers Russell wrote for his tutors consist of several sections, each in answer to one of the set questions. It was Russell's practice to number the sheets by section, and to start each section on a new leaf. Thus the manuscripts have the appearance of being several short papers gathered together. However, the first leaf of each paper usually bears the title, as does the verso of the final leaf together with Russell's name and the date. In two cases (**20**, **25**) the first section is missing, and in one (**28**) the verso of the final extant leaf lacks Russell's usual identification, suggesting that the paper may not be complete. No answer is extant to one of the set questions in the cases of **19** and **27**—although there is no way of telling whether Russell answered these questions. Where Russell used section headings, he usually wrote them in the left-hand margin with their number (printed here in small capitals as centred section headings). In addition he sometimes used marginal subheadings within a section, usually following the divisions of a multi-part question. These have been printed as subsection headings in italics against the left-hand margin.

Not all the papers Russell wrote for his Moral Sciences courses have survived. In a letter to Alys Pearsall Smith of 2 May 1894 he mentions an essay on Kant which is not among his papers. Its loss is particularly unfortunate since Russell's fellowship work was concerned with Kant. The lecture notebooks also contain several sets of questions for which there are no corresponding papers. Since students were clearly not required to answer all the questions, there is no means of knowing which (if any) of these sets of questions were answered by Russell. Another notable gap is the absence of any papers written for Sidgwick's course on the elements of philosophy. Of the surviving papers, those printed in Part IV relate to Ward's metaphysics course (**18**, **19**, **22**, **29**), Ward's history of philosophy course (**21**, **23**), and Stout's history of philosophy course (**20**, **24**, **25**, **26**, **27**, **28**). Papers Russell wrote for Sidgwick's course on ethics are printed in Part V, together with other papers on ethics written at about the same time. Papers in both parts are arranged in chronological order in so far as that can be determined.

During the 1950s Russell's first biographer, Alan Wood, had typescripts (now in the Russell Archives) made of **18**, **19**, **22**, **29**, **35** and **36**. Wood intended to use the papers for a comprehensive study of Russell's philosophy, but he died before completing the work (see Russell *1959*, 5). The typescripts have no textual authority, and their collation with the manuscripts revealed nothing worth reporting.

# 18

# Paper on Epistemology I [1893]

THIS PAPER WAS written for Ward's course on metaphysics. The verso of the last leaf of the otherwise untitled manuscript reads "*B. Russell / Paper on Epistemology I. / Nov. 1893.*" The manuscript bears a number of markings in blue pencil by Ward; apart from one or two requests for elucidation, most are underlinings or vertical lines in the margin. Russell's lecture notebook for the course contains a loose sheet (RA 220.010050) in Russell's hand with the questions set for this paper.

*Paper to be done*
I. What's a theory of knowledge? What its data, assumptions, method? How would you estimate comparative worth of two different theories of knowledge? Is it true till knowledge complete, theory of it cannot be complete? If so wherein lies incompleteness? If not, why is not completed theory absolutely certain?
II. Examine conception of matter and form applied to knowledge. Is matter of knowledge knowledge? Is form subjectively imposed on matter? Reference to concrete and abstract; variable and constant.
III. What are sense-particulars? Discuss attempt to make epistemological generalizations about them.
IV. Briefly characterize our concrete experience of temporal relations and consider how get from these to conception of time.

The copy-text is the manuscript (RA 220.010160), which consists of four leaves.

# I

A THEORY OF knowledge must accept existing knowledges as its data: its problem must be to unify them, to make a self-consistent whole of the various Sciences, to interpret these in such a way as to overcome their apparent contradictions. Every Science deals necessarily with abstractions: its results must therefore be partial and one-sided expressions of truth. These results must be criticized by Epistemology, their one-sidedness if possible corrected, so that the results of the different Sciences may be exhibited as consistent with each other and as parts of a whole of knowledge. Epistemology, though it must criticize and interpret knowledges, cannot adopt even hypothetically a completely sceptical position with regard to them, for they are its data and cannot be made to derive their validity from it: it will have to explain how they are possible, not prove that they are possible. It must assume that the world is intelligible, that it is one, that knowledges can be unified. The comparative worth of two theories of knowledge would have to be tested by their success in harmonizing and rendering intelligible existing knowledges: just as two scientific hypotheses are compared by their success in explaining the phenomena which they are invented to account for.

A theory of knowledge can in any state of knowledge have relative completeness: that is, it can perform its task completely so far as existing knowledge is concerned: but such a theory is liable to require revision when a new branch of knowledge arises. A theory such as Descartes', invented to account for Mathematics and Physics, may be complete so far as it goes; but may break down as soon as Biology has to be considered. Thus the theory of knowledge must be always undergoing modifications as fresh knowledge arises to be explained.

# II

The distinction of matter and form is that of a manifold and its relations. The datum of knowledge is a manifold of perceptions connected by spatial and temporal relations. The most primitive knowledge is expressed in judgments about immediate sense-particulars. But such interjectional propositions hardly amount to knowledge: rather we must suppose the understanding to have so far operated on sensation as to have produced such judgments before sensations can be regarded as the matter of knowledge: i.e. the true matter of knowledge is not the actual sensations, but the expression of them in judgment. Knowledge must deal with the relations of these: no knowledge can be pure matter. In distinguishing form from matter, there are according to Wundt two marks to be sought: (1) The independent variation of the material and formal elements (2) The constancy of the gen-

eral properties of the purely formal elements. Now the matter of perception can vary without variation of space and time. And again the general properties of space and time are invariable and independent of their content. Thus space and time would constitute the forms of perception. But of course these forms are empty abstractions: they express relations, which suppose things related: space and time, in the sense in which their general properties are constant, are space and time in conception, not in perception. Kant's arguments for the apriority of space and time from the certainty and universality of their properties apply only to the concepts, not to space and time as they
10 occur in perception. In this, they are not infinitely divisible, time does not advance uniformly, etc. His argument for their independence of experience as percepts à priori will therefore not hold.

### III

Sense-particulars are particular sensations to which the mind attends as they pass. Sense-particulars are not individuals: they are not completely differentiated one from another: in sensation there is nothing discrete, but one sensation merges into another. The constituents of sense-particulars may be arranged in classes, heat, colour, etc.; and each of these classes is a continuum, not a genus containing species. Mere sense-particulars cannot con-
20 cern epistemology: we cannot make judgments about them until we have performed a process of abstraction, until we have concepts, which must be universals. Words can never give mere particulars: words express concepts, and until we have so far transcended sense we cannot make even existential judgments such as It's hot. We must have got beyond mere difference of sensations to unity before we can have the conception *hot*. This implies memory and abstraction; and it is only after sense-particulars have been so far operated on by thought that we can properly be said to have knowledge about them and that they can concern Epistemology. On the level of mere sense we must remain dumb.

30                                    IV

Our concrete experience is made up of successive acts of attention: the interval between two such acts of attention must be regarded psychologically as the ultimate time-unit: concrete time-experience must regard time as no further divisible. What we attend to in these successive acts are changes: the elements in sensation which remain unchanged do not enter into presentation. We thus have a series of presentations with temporal relations: time has in concrete experience three modes, succession, intensity and duration. In a psychological unit of time there is no succession but only intensity. The specious present must consist partly in memory, otherwise we should not have the idea of succession and therefore of time. All these characteristics are absent in the conception of time, which is perfectly linear: intensity no longer has any meaning here, but time is an equi-crescent one-dimensional continuum. This conception can only have been derived from comparison of the experience of different people: when it was found that certain events, notably the rising and setting of the heavenly bodies and the course of the seasons, recurred periodically in every one's experience, and that a good many of these appeared to agree (approximately at any rate) in the intervals between their successive occurrences, it was natural to take such intervals as objective units of time, and further to sup- 10 pose the diurnal motion of the sun and stars uniform, so as to give a means of subdividing the unit *ad lib*. It was then possible in thought to abstract this objective time from the successions which had suggested it and so arrive at astronomical or mathematical time. But equi-crescence is a pure conven-tion: no meaning can be attached to it: mathematically it only amounts to saying that time is taken as the (or an) independent variable.

# 19

# Paper on Epistemology II [1893]

THIS PAPER WAS written for Ward's course on metaphysics. The verso of the last leaf reads: "*B. Russell. | Paper on Epistemology II. | Nov. 1893.*" On 2–3 December 1893 Russell wrote Alys that he had written a paper for Ward "in ... which I tried to defend Kant against Metageometry ⟨i.e. non-Euclidean geometry⟩ and Ward." Russell's lecture notebook for this course indicates a substantial attack on Kant by Ward (I: 89–90), and the defence of Kant in this paper anticipates some features of Russell's more restricted defence in his fellowship dissertation and in *An Essay on the Foundations of Geometry* (1897), which arose out of the dissertation. The manuscript bears a number of pencilled markings by Ward, but only one extended comment. The verso of the first leaf has some calculations by Russell on a problem in dynamics. Russell's lecture notebook contains a loose sheet (RA 220.010050) in his hand with the questions for this essay:

*Paper*
1. Analyse *conception* of time and expound mutual relations of its constituents and discuss connection of time and change. What understand by measurement of time?
2. Discuss (a) meaning (b) possibility of mentally representing other space-relations than those of Euclid.—Explain (look at Helmholtz) and discuss Helmholtz's distinction between geometry based on transcendental intuition and geometry based on experience. [*vide* in Paper what means: *Mind*. Vol. III, p. 222–end ⟨Helmholtz *1878*⟩. Also *Mind* Vol. I, p. 301 ⟨Helmholtz *1876*⟩. *Read* Land in Vol. II ⟨1877⟩.]
3. Give what Kant would call (a) metaphysical (b) transcendental exposition of number (relations of number to space and time come in here); examine his position that $7 + 5 = 12$ synthetic.
4. Discuss nature of logical evidence and enquire into relation of algorithmics to (1) Mathematics (2) Formal Logic.

In a week: i.e. Thursday 30th.

There is no evidence that Russell answered the fourth question.

The copy-text is the manuscript (RA 220.010170), which consists of eleven leaves.

THE CONCEPTION OF time appears to differ as it appears in mathematics or in relation to reality. In the former time is perfectly simple and homogeneous, a one-dimensional continuum with no distinction of past, present and future, no necessity to traverse it in one direction rather than the other. Its mathematical treatment differs in nothing from that of a straight line: as in this, the origin of measurement is perfectly arbitrary, and times measured in one sense are positive, in the other negative.

But as soon as we imagine the content of time to be real, we have one point of time given as present, as real; the past is what conditions the present, and 10 the present conditions the future; only through this conditionment do past and future exist. This marked point, the present, is continually moving and time is conceived as growing, as advancing. It is necessary here to imagine a varying content: succession has no meaning unless the events which succeed each other are different. We are not here considering time as a whole, from the point of view of a consciousness not in time, (as we can in mathematics), but the actual time-series, a varying content with temporal relations. But since the time can remain unchanged while the content is different, this content may, in a purely conceptual treatment of time, be varied at will; although we must imagine the content a changing one, it is arbitrary in the 20 investigation of the conception of time. And hence we arrive at astronomic time, equi-crescent and one-dimensional. This has for its content the motion of the heavenly bodies, and is measured with reference to this.

Time can only be measured by means of space: some motion has to be assumed as uniform or as varying according to a known law, and then times can be measured by the spaces described in them. It seems arbitrary what motion we assume as our standard: our choice is therefore guided by motives of convenience. Since the rising and setting of the heavenly bodies recur continually and are visible to everybody and important in the regulation of practical life, it is convenient to take the motion of these as our 30 standard, and so it is the velocity of the earth's rotation which is assumed uniform,[1] and on this assumption it would appear that the other motions recognized as more or less uniform depend. I do not know if there is any ground except convenience for this basis for time-measurement: I am unable to see what other is possible. The laws of motion, and the whole of mathematical Physics, presuppose the possibility of measuring time; so that Physics only supplies another motive of convenience.

---

[1] This assumption is plausible as it makes the length of the year and the periods of rotation and revolution of the other planets also constant.

2

In Euclidean geometry certain axioms are assumed (such as especially the axiom of parallels) which depend upon the nature of space and which are held to derive their validity from the impossibility of picturing a case in which they fail. This impossibility is denied by Meta-Geometry: it proposes to substitute for certain axioms certain others, either general forms of which Euclid's are a particular case, or fresh axioms arbitrarily assumed as a basis for hypothetical systems. By this method Lobatchewsky succeeded in building up a geometry in which the propositions were proved synthetically
10 as in Euclid, while the results were consistent with each other but different from Euclid's. An easier and safer method is by analysis: the possibility of moving bodies without distortion being found to depend on the constancy of the measure of curvature, and being I suppose considered as proved by experience, we can take, as a space resembling our own in this respect, any space in which this condition (the constancy of the measure of curvature) is fulfilled. Hence we have spherical and pseudo-spherical space; our new geometry can be worked out by analysis: that is, having made certain changes in the (algebraical) data, we arrive at new (algebraical) conclusions. These by a sort of dictionary we proceed to translate into the language of
20 geometry, and our results of course form a self-consistent system, being translations, according to a fixed rule, of a series of valid propositions in algebra. This seems to be the meaning of non-Euclidean geometry.

But whether our results, even when obtained by Lobatchewsky's method, can be correctly called geometry, may be questioned. In analytical geometry, the letters employed are symbols, not, as in algebra, of *any* kind of quantity, but of spatial quantities only; and as such, if they are to retain their *meaning* as symbols, they must remain subject to certain restrictions which would not be imposed on them in algebra. When we remove these restrictions, or substitute others for them, there is no *primâ facie* reason for
30 supposing the symbols to be capable of geometrical interpretation. If we can picture to ourselves a space different from Euclid's, in which this new geometry would hold, then we have a right to employ analytical methods for getting our results, and to interpret the symbols geometrically. But unless at the beginning of the process we can picture to ourselves what our symbols symbolize, we have no right to regard them as symbols of spatial relations. Helmholtz endeavours to make pseudo-spherical space imaginable by an elaborate analogy with the space inside a sphere: but I imagine the way this analogy has been obtained has been by giving to the symbols a new meaning, so that all the algebraical results have two interpretations, one for the one
40 space and one for the other. But when the question at issue is whether the first of these meanings can be given to the symbols, it does not seem a good way of deciding it to give them another.

The question turns on the imaginability of other spaces. Helmholtz defines this as the power of representing the sense-impressions we should have in such spaces. It is not altogether clear what is meant by *representing* these sense-impressions: if Helmholtz means, what would seem the only adequate meaning, actually picturing them, intuiting them, then I should have thought such spaces were not imaginable: but at the same time if Helmholtz should say that he can picture them, I see no way of disproving his assertion. But there appears to be a confusion in Helmholtz's mind, or else he has used the word *represent* in a different and more conceptual sense; for he recurs to his analogy with the inside of a sphere, in which he has eliminated just the essential elements (essential, that is, from an epistemological point of view: from a mathematical point of view it is of little importance what meaning we give to the symbols). To take spherical space: how can I picture a three-dimensional space in which two straight lines enclose a space, or in which the line of sight, if unimpeded, ends on the back of my head? The analogy of flat-fish living on the surface of a sphere seems irrelevant, if only because we are not flat-fish; and I do not see why the line of sight of such a flat-fish should not be just as much a Euclidean straight line as ours.—And if we are engaged in working with such spaces, the restriction to those in which bodies can be moved without distortion seems to have no justification except mathematical simplicity; the bodies we have to deal with in experience are not rigid; W. K. Clifford even hints, in his wild enthusiastic way, that changes of shape such as we ascribe to changes of temperature, etc., might possibly be explicable as due to changes in the measure of curvature of space; this suggestion is of course rather preposterous but may serve to shew how arbitrary such a restriction is.

Finally then: I do not see how we can avoid the conclusion, that geometry, to be geometry, whether synthetic or analytical, must depend ultimately on space-intuitions, though these are of course not necessary at every stage of the argument, nor even in interpreting geometrically an algebraical result: further that such space-intuitions are *for us* necessarily Euclidean; and that therefore the speculations of meta-geometry have no epistemological importance.

---

Helmholtz's distinction of geometry based on transcendental intuition and geometry based on experience seems hardly relevant as against Kant: the whole point of Kant's argument is that geometrical experience is determined by the constitution of the mind, is à priori and transcendental and not imposed from outside. In this case, if Kant is right, the two geometries are one and the same. Helmholtz says that Kant's proof of the apriority of spatial intuition is insufficient because other spaces can be mentally rep-

resented. If by this he means that they can be pictured or intuited, I have endeavoured to maintain that this is not the case: if he only means that they can be conceived and reasoned about, Kant's position is not affected thereby. But, he says, allowing this transcendental intuition, what warrant have we for expecting it to coincide with experience? When I prove by Euclidean geometry that a certain pair of straight lines are equal, what warrant have I for assuming that measurement will verify my proof? since meta-geometry has shewn that other spaces are possible, in which these two lines will not be equal. This meta-geometry, he maintains, has proved the possi-
10 bility of a consistent series of sensible pictures; though it is difficult to see how operations with symbols representing numbers (as algebraical symbols do) can prove anything as to sensible pictures unless their applicability to such pictures can at some point in the argument be perceived or intuited, so that we know the symbols will bear a geometrical meaning. He says accordingly that if Kant is right in his assumption of a transcendental intuition of space, we shall require two geometries, whose axioms are based, the one set on this transcendental intuition, the other on measurement. Even the first axiom, that things equal to the same thing are equal to one another, will have to be arrived at by measurement if it is to be applied in practice or in science:
20 indeed no application to the external world can possibly be made of the Kantian geometry. In order to avoid a crude realism, he says he will assume only the law of causation: he uses this to prove that there must be something in objective reality which determines the position in space which we assign to an object. This something he calls a "topogenous moment" to avoid the appearance of identifying it in any way with perceptual position. He then says the geometry which practice and science would be concerned with would be that which referred to these topogenous moments; and this geometry would require measurement as the foundation of its axioms, and equivalence in it would not necessarily correspond with equality in the
30 transcendental geometry, even if the results obtained by the two geometries were the same.

I am not here concerned to defend Kant's argument, but only to attack Helmholtz's attack on it: and does it not miss the point of Kant's argument to assume any such thing as "topogenous moments"? Surely the argument maintains that space is an à priori form into which we fit perceptions, so that this form is not a mere chimera with which we amuse our leisure while sitting in our studies. That axioms were historically elicited by experience, Kant might admit: that they could be contradicted by experience he could hardly admit. Helmholtz's distinction becomes impossible to maintain
40 when Kant's position is admitted: the results of our measurement, in so far as we can make this accurate, must fit into the transcendental form of our space-perceptions. If we measure two things with a foot-rule and find them apparently the same length, but find on comparing them that they are not

the same length, we shall not reject the first axiom, but shall suppose an alteration due to change of temperature or an inaccuracy in our measurement or any of the many possible sources of error: but I do not see how any experience could force us either to reject the first axiom or to alter our view of the nature of space. That other space than ours can be intuited does not seem to me to be proved by meta-geometry: and this seems to be all that Kantians need maintain against it.

3

*(a). Metaphysical exposition of number*

The motive to number is in the first instance interrupted sensation; 10 number is not produced by this, but the occasion is given for the exercise of a free activity. When we hear a clock strike, the relations of our sensations give rise to number; but these are not themselves sensations. Mill thought number was derived by abstraction from numerable things: but there is nothing common to all the constituents of a collection which could be abstracted as number: the number is neither in any one of them nor in the collection as a whole. Counting presupposes that each of the things counted is *one*: it also involves a spontaneous conscious passage of the attention from one member of a collection to the other. Number is thus a free creation of our thought. Counting is presupposed in numbers: these arise from the 20 gathering of a plurality into a unity. Until we apprehend a plurality as a unity, we cannot apprehend it as a plurality. Successive acts of gathering of this sort give the series of natural numbers.—Thus number is completely à priori: it springs from a spontaneous activity ⟨of⟩ a purely formal nature.

*(b). Transcendental exposition of number*

We have here to discuss the nature of the evidence for arithmetical propositions and the possibility of synthetic propositions à priori about numbers. The definitions of the natural numbers $(3 = 1+2)$ are synthetic, since they require the gathering of a plurality into a unity: $1+2$ does not involve the conception of three; we are at liberty to think of one and two without 30 apprehending the result as a unity. From these definitions the rest of arithmetic follows: $5+2 = 5+\overline{1+1} = \overline{5+1}+1 = 6+1 = 7$ and so on. We require only the possibility of gathering a plurality into a unity, and of analysing a unity into a plurality; which was presupposed in the definitions. This depends on the possibility of attending to successive sensations, of noting our acts of attention and assembling them by memory in one whole. In this process time is involved: psychologically counting involves time, but not logically. The evidence of arithmetical propositions must be logically independent of time and space, since these are continuous and number is essentially discrete. Number indeed is strictly inapplicable to space and 40 time; in measuring these we have to deal with quantity, not number.

The proposition $7+5 = 12$ involves an act of unifying which is not involved in 7 or 5 or in $7+5$. We can think of 7 things and 5 things without reflecting that they can be made into a whole of 12 things. No analysis of $7+5$ will give us the single conception of a whole 12. The proposition would seem then to be synthetic.

# 20

# Paper on Bacon [1893]

RUSSELL WROTE THIS paper for Stout's course on the history of philosophy. The verso of the last leaf reads "*B. Russell / Paper on Bacon / Nov. 1893.*" Stout did not write any comments on the paper. Russell's lecture notebook (2: 102–3) for the course contains the following list of questions for the paper:

*Paper to be done* by Wednesday

1. Account of Bacon's classification and encyclopedia of Sciences especially suggestions for new lines of enquiry.
2. What did Bacon mean by induction? Compare with method of Galileo.
3. Discuss Bacon's doctrine of forms and compare with Locke's doctrine of real and nominal essence. [⟨Locke's *Essay*⟩ Bk. III. Chap. 3. §15]
4. "(1) Bacon ignores plurality of causes" (2) "Bacon entertained radically false view of nature of causality in as much as treated logical and scientific problem as if one of coexistence." Discuss these criticisms.
5. What was Bacon's theory of constitution of matter: what did he mean by latent configuration and latent process?
6. Give an account of striking, constitutive, comformable instances, and of instances of finger-post (instantiae crucis). What ⟨is⟩ general aim of that part of Bacon's work which deals with prerogative instances?
7. Discuss Bacon's relation to Aristotle, Plato and Democritus; also Telesius (vide Valerius Tannius (?)).
8. Give a full account of Bacon's doctrine of idols.
9. Discuss Bacon's anticipations of modern science.

The reference to "Valerius Tannius" is Russell's mistranscription of "Valerius Terminus", a pseudonym used by Bacon for a fragmentary work, "Of the Interpretation of Nature". To the left of question 9 Russell put a question mark. There is no evidence that he answered questions 1 and 9.

The copy-text is the manuscript (RA 220.010140), which consists of fifteen leaves.

ACON'S INDUCTION BEGINS with the collection of instances, designed to throw light on some particular phenomenon and methodically chosen as suitable to this end. There must be not only instances where it is present, but also instances where it is absent: the latter, however, being infinite in number, are only to be noted if they have some affinity with a positive instance: as for example, the moon, which is bright and a heavenly body, does not give heat, though the sun does. A detailed account is given of Prerogative Instances, i.e. instances particularly valuable in the investigation. The instances are to be particulars, individuals; not species, as with Aristotle. The Baconian induction is applied to the investigation of forms, but there seems no reason why this should be in any way essential to the method. A certain nature, e.g. heat, is being investigated, and it is assumed to have a certain form, always present when heat is present and absent when heat is absent. The collections of instances then by elimination will gradually exclude irrelevant forms, until when a sufficient number of suitable instances have been obtained, all forms except the true one have been excluded. If $A$ is the nature to be investigated, $a$ its form, we have as our series of instances

$$
\text{positive instances}
\begin{cases}
ABC & abc \\
ADE & ade \\
AFG & afg
\end{cases}
\text{etc.}
\quad \text{and} \quad
\begin{cases}
B'C' & b'c' \\
D'E' & d'e' \\
F'G' & f'g'
\end{cases}
\text{etc.}
\quad
\text{negative instances}
$$

leaving no form to satisfy the required conditions except $a$. When it is assumed that the number of possible forms is finite, this method leads to a certain conclusion: but when, as is the fact, there is an infinite number of possibilities, it becomes Mill's method of Agreement and Difference. Some of his classes of Prerogative Instances introduce also Concomitant Variations.

## Comparison with Galileo's Method

Galileo's Method is very different from the above: it is that of Mathematical Physics, whereas Bacon's is rather that of Biology. Galileo's method requires also to begin with a certain number of related facts, as for instance successive positions of a planet: but the number of these instances is indifferent. They are only required to suggest a hypothesis which shall explain them: this hypothesis can not be framed by any method but must be simply guessed at. If it is found to explain the data, it is made the basis of a deduction as to hitherto unobserved phenomena: or where experiment is possible, as to the results of experiments. These deduced results are then tested by experiment or observation (as the case may be), and if found to be correct the hypothesis stands: but it remains liable to be upset by any phenomenon which is found to contradict the deductions made from it. As Galileo understood induction, quantitative exactness was necessary throughout. He was completely modern in taking as the aim of Science to explain *how* a thing takes place, rather than why; to seek for uniformities in phenomena rather than for any ground of their happening. It was for this characteristic of the Astronomy of his day that Bacon complained of it; but every other aim has been more and more excluded from Science since his time.                                                                      10

Galileo's method was far more fruitful in the science of his time than Bacon's: and wherever quantitative precision is attainable, wherever deduction tested by experiment or observation is possible, there Galileo's method must be the best; but in Sciences like Biology a large number of instances do become almost the only way of testing a hypothesis and the Baconian method (excluding the doctrine of forms) becomes applicable. But owing to his notion that there were a finite number of forms, by which everything could be explained, he omitted almost the most essential and difficult part of Induction, the framing of a hypothesis to suit the facts.

### III. BACON'S DOCTRINE OF FORMS                                    20

The word *Form* Bacon derived from Aristotle and the schoolmen: but the sense which he gives to the word is completely his own. There is some ambiguity in his use of it: sometimes it appears to denote the true specific difference of a quality, sometimes the law underlying the phenomena, sometimes the real process in bodies which is the cause of the sensible appearance. He seems hardly to have distinguished between these meanings: the last appears most prominently in his investigation of the Form of Heat, and may be taken perhaps as the most fundamental. He thought there was a limited number of simple natures, each with its corresponding form: that the complexity of phenomena was due to the mixture of these forms in  30 varying degree: and that the aim of Science should be the investigation of the forms of simple natures; the immediate practical result of which would be the power of inducing any desired nature on any body by the production of the required form. He appears to have thought that forms consisted in motions of the small parts of a body: as in the case of heat, which consists in a motion outwards and upwards of the particles. He was modern in his idea of the nature of forms; but the scholastic point of view appears in his belief that there was a finite number of such forms, which could be discovered and made the basis of all scientific explanation. Forms are continually becoming and ceasing to be: but yet they are the fixed and persistent constituents of  40 things, the essence of the qualities which appear.

*Comparison with Locke's Doctrine of Real and Nominal Essence*

*Real Essence* in Locke seems to have much the same meaning as *form* in Bacon: but he avoids the false view of forms as finite in number: as he states the nature of real essence it appears unobjectionable: "a real but unknown constitution of their insensible parts: from which flow those sensible qualities which serve to distinguish them one from another": this might almost serve as a definition of the Baconian *Form*: in this sense the real essence of a thing can be destroyed with the thing: nominal essence on the other hand is an abstract idea, which constitutes species and is independent of change, of
10 becoming and ceasing to be.

### IV. MILL'S OBJECTIONS TO BACON'S VIEW OF CAUSE

(1) *Plurality of Causes*. Mill's objection here overlooked the distinction between formal causes on the one hand and material and efficient causes on the other. The formal cause is not a cause in the sense of a necessary antecedent: rather it is the actual configuration and condition of a body which is the ground of the appearance: it is the reality behind the phenomena. In this sense plurality of causes becomes impossible: any change in the formal cause, since this is the reality underlying the phenomenon, and not another phenomenon as Mill's cause is, must involve a corresponding change in the
20 phenomenon. The forms are the real constituents of nature: to a definite form must correspond a definite nature, and to a definite nature a definite form.

(2) The same mistake is apparent in Mill's objection that Bacon treated causality as a problem of coexistence: the formal cause and the phenomenon must coexist. As regards material and efficient causes Bacon recognized plurality of causes and succession in time.

### V. LATENT CONFIGURATION AND LATENT PROCESS

Bacon appears to have had no clear view of the constitution of matter: although in an early work he criticizes the atomic theory as too gross, and
30 seems to lean to the view of matter as constituted by centres of force, yet in the *Novum Organum* he rejects atoms from the opposite point of view, and says (Aph. 8) analysis will not lead us to atoms, but to "real particles, such as really exist". It is apparently the relations and motions of these real particles which he calls latent configuration and latent process. Latent Process he says (Aph. 6) is a process perfectly continuous, which for the most part escapes the sense; it should be enquired in all alterations and motions, for all natural action depends on things infinitely small. Latent Configuration has the same function in statical explanation that latent process has in dynami-

cal: it is to be discovered by separation and solution of bodies, not by fire, as is the manner of the alchemists, but by reasoning and true induction.—The investigation of both is subordinate and preliminary to the investigation of forms.

VI

*Striking Instances*

Striking Instances are those which exhibit the nature in question in the highest degree, and standing alone, without the admixture of other natures. They are, according to Bacon, of special importance, because where several natures meet in a body they interfere with each other and the individual 10 forms are obscured. But they are to be used with caution: whatever exhibits the form too conspicuously is to be held suspect. Thus suppose Weight to be the nature investigated: Quicksilver is a better example than Gold, because although lighter it has not the consistency and solidity of gold, which might be supposed to be essential to weight.

*Constitutive Instances*

Constitutive instances are those which make a single species of the proposed nature into a sort of Lesser Form. The particular forms should be diligently investigated, because the genuine forms lie deep and are hard to find. They are of great use in framing definitions and in the division of 20 natures. But care must be taken, when many of these lesser forms have been investigated, not to rest in them to the neglect of the real fundamental forms.

An instance which Bacon gives is that a man with a bad cold in his head can't taste rancid or putrid tastes, but if he blows his nose violently he can: the inference being that the sense of taste is in part a sort of internal smell.

*Conformable Instances*

Conformable Instances represent resemblances and conjunctions of things not in lesser forms but in the concrete. They constitute the first and lowest step in the investigation of nature, and are of great use in revealing 30 the fabric of the parts of the Universe, though of little service for the discovery of forms. Examples of such resemblance are the eye and a looking-glass, the ear and places which give an echo, the Old and New World, etc.

*Instances of the Finger-Post*

Instances of the Finger-Post decide between two or more natures, where previous instances had left it doubtful which of these was the cause of the nature in question. Suppose previous instances exhibited in the form

*ACD*                             *abcd*
*AEF*                             *abef*
*AGH*                             *abgh*
                    *etc.*

leaving us in doubt between *a* and *b*, a crucial instance would be

*AKL*                             *akl*

shewing that *A* depends on *a* and not on *b*.

An instance which Bacon gives is taken from magnetism: a needle pointing north and south becomes in time magnetic and points the same way
whenever it is free to turn: to determine if this is due to terrestrial magnetism, place a needle pointing east and west over a larger magnetic mass, so
that it becomes in time magnetic: if then on being removed and left free to
turn, it turns to the north, there will be evidence that its doing so is due to
the earth.

The general aim of Bacon's list of Prerogative Instances is to give rules for
facilitating the exclusion of irrelevant natures in the investigation of any
nature: this being the aim of all collections of instances, and some instances
being more useful for this purpose than others.

VII

### Bacon's Relation to Aristotle

Bacon himself appears to have thought that he was completely emanci-
pated from the Aristotelian and scholastic point of view, and at first sight he
might seem to be so. He rejected entirely the classificatory view of nature,
the view of the fixity of species, of types as final causes tending to realize
themselves in nature. (Though he appears to have allowed final causes in
Metaphysics, but not in the Aristotelian sense). He rejected also the Aristotelian view of induction, which consisted in the enumeration of positive
instances only, of *species* having some particular quality, which by induction
is then affirmed of the *genus*. Bacon insisted that we ought to pay just as
much attention to negative as to positive instances: that our procedure
should not be by mere enumeration, but by a careful choice of examples
most suitable to the process of elimination: and that in this process we must
start with individuals, not with species.

But in his doctrine of forms he is clearly under the influence of Aristotle:
he regards the form, as Aristotle does, as the true specific difference, as the
essence of a thing. With Aristotle this essence was merely logical, but was at
the same time the real essence because Aristotle regarded nature as constituted by types tending to realize themselves. With Bacon the form was also

the real essence, but this with him consisted in a difference of configuration and molecular motion, i.e. in a physical difference which had to be investigated, not in one constituted by logic. This real analysis into forms however corresponds to the logical, into qualities; this logical analysis, hypostasized, has to be combined with the forms in investigating nature.

### Bacon's Relation to Plato

An analogy to Plato and to the ancient point of view may be traced in Bacon's view of the relation of a thing and its qualities: like the ancients he believed a thing to be constituted by qualities inherent in it, not by relations. These qualities with Bacon are his forms: so that he regards it as possible to transform one body into another by inducing new natures upon it. The forms may be compared to Plato's Ideas, as being the permanent constituents of nature: they are opposed to the world of becoming as Plato's Ideas were.

### to Democritus

Bacon seems to have entertained a high opinion of Democritus and his school, because they went direct to nature, and because they investigated molecular constitution and changes, what Bacon would have called Latent Configuration and Latent Process. In one passage he says "to resolve nature into abstractions is less to our purpose than to dissect her parts: as did the school of Democritus, who went further into nature than the rest." On the other hand he censures them for being "so concerned with the particles that they hardly attend to the structure."

### VIII. DOCTRINE OF IDOLS

The idols are errors or prejudices which influence opinion unduly. They are of four kinds, those of the Tribe, the Cave, the Market-Place and the Theatre. The real way of avoiding them, says Bacon, is by the formation of ideas and axioms by true induction; but it is useful to point them out for avoidance. Those of the Tribe have their origin in human nature itself: for it is false that the sense of man is the measure of all things: the mind is like a false mirror, which distorts the images it receives. These idols are common to the race, but those of the cave are peculiar to each individual, his personal equation in modern phraseology; they are due to his education and character. Those of the market-place arise from the vague and inaccurate use of words in common talk: and those of the theatre arise from the dogmas of false philosophies and from wrong modes of demonstration: they are so called because all received systems are according to Bacon so many stage-plays representing an imaginary world after an unreal and scenic fashion.

### Idols of the Tribe

Of the idols of the tribe Bacon gives several examples. The first is the supposition of too much order and regularity in the universe, which leads people to neglect instances that seem to conflict with a previous opinion. Again we are more moved by affirmatives than by negatives; we tend to believe also what we wish to think true, whence spring Sciences as one would. Also we are most impressed by the things which strike our imagination most forcibly, and expect other things to resemble them. But the most important error in this class springs from trusting the senses too far, and not
10 investigating the things not obvious to the senses: here I suppose Bacon was thinking of his latent configuration and latent process chiefly.

### Idols of the Cave

These are peculiar to each individual and cannot therefore be briefly pointed out. A few can however be noted. For example when a man has invented or greatly perfected a Science he is apt to think it will explain everything and to neglect other branches of knowledge. Again some are prone to note resemblances, some, differences; and in both directions it is easy to err by excess. Again some like antiquity, some novelty. Generally we ought to be suspicious of whatever we seize on with particular satisfaction.

20 ### Idols of the Market-Place

But the most troublesome class of idols are those of the market-place. These says Bacon have crept in through the alliances of words and names. For the understanding does not completely govern words, but words also react on the understanding. The meanings of words are fixed by the vulgar, at least if the words are in common use; and this gives rise to difficulties for a more acute or diligent understanding. This class of idols spring from words of two kinds: names of things which do not exist, such as the Primum Mobile, and names confused and ill-defined. In this kind there are degrees of distortion; the most accurate being usually the names of substances,
30 especially of very special kinds of substances; the next best, the names of actions; and the worst the names of qualities, as hot and cold.

### Idols of the Theatre

The idols of the theatre are not innate nor do they steal in secretly, but they are taught and impressed in the schools. They are the more dangerous, as stories invented for the stage are more compact and elegant and more as one would wish them to be than true stories out of history. Philosophies either get a great deal out of a few carefully observed instances, or very little out of a great number of inaccurate instances. Thus Rationalists have a variety of instances neither duly ascertained nor diligently examined, and
40 leave the rest to speculation: of these Aristotle is an example, who corrupted

natural philosophy by fashioning the world out of Categories. The Empiricists on the other hand have made a few careful experiments, and have to wrest everything else into conformity with the theories they have based on these, whence spring results even more "monstrous and deformed" than in the former case, since their opinions are in no way based on common sense, as the others are in some degree. Of these Bacon mentions the alchemists as an example; but he thinks in his day there are none left unless perhaps Gilbert. There is a third kind of these philosophical idols, the mixture of theology with philosophy. This misleads by flattery and is the most pernicious of the three. Nothing is so mischievous as the apotheosis of error 10 which thus arises.—Again there are errors arising from faulty subject matter, especially in natural philosophy. To this class belongs the investigation of types as final causes; also of quiescent principles wherefrom, not moving principles whereby, things are produced. Both positive and negative dogmatism Bacon also regards as Idols of the Theatre.

The pointing out and removing of these idols was preliminary to the true Induction; it was the negative, destructive work necessary before beginning the constructive part of his method.

# 21

# Paper on History of Philosophy [1894]

THIS PAPER WAS written for Ward's history of philosophy course. The verso of the last leaf reads "*Paper on History of Philosophy / Feb. 1894. / B. Russell.*" The manuscript bears a number of pencilled notations by Ward. The questions for this paper have not survived, but Russell's lecture notebook (2: 39), carries the following note: "[Make analysis of Hume's argument on cause. *Observe* how shifts: raises one question, drops it and takes up another. Sections 2. 3. 4. 5. 6. 7.]" This is presumably the topic set for section IV of the paper. The references are to Hume's *Treatise*, Bk. I, Pt. iii, which Russell quotes in section IV.

The copy-text is the manuscript (RA 220.010210); it has ten leaves.

D ESCARTES HAD LEFT the conception of substance in a very unsatisfactory condition: mind and matter were substances relatively to each other, i.e. could each exist independently of the other; but yet he allowed interaction between them, and made both dependent on God, who was therefore really the only substance. The imperfect nature of this doctrine called for elaboration: Spinoza took the step of definitely asserting God as the only substance, and mind and matter as attributes of the one substance. In this one substance all individuality was swallowed up, all being was in God and individuals had no independent reality. The whole 10 time-series in the world of phenomena was the development of a logical series in the world of thought: everything proceeded by logical necessity, there was no room for final causes, no loophole in rigid Determinism. There was no distinction whatever to Spinoza between a thing and its idea and his rationalism was thus complete.

Leibnitz, as individualist, appears certainly as at the opposite pole from Spinoza: his windowless monads, each independent of all the others, and able to exist and continue as before if all the others were annihilated, seem like a recoil from Spinozistic monism, in which the individual can hardly find a place. We have here just as undue a preponderance of the individual as 20 we had before of the universal: here the difficulty is to see why these monads should mirror the world, what function God can perform in such a world, how a monad is to know, if it has no windows, that the world it knows is a picture of the real world, and so on; in short, to get away from the individual to the universal. Every individual monad seems like a Spinozistic world in itself.—But Leibnitz is still a rationalist: his introduction of the principle of sufficient reason is an advance on the reliance on mere Identity and Contradiction, but he entertains no doubt that his principles of thought find themselves carried out in the world of reality: and he deduces the existence of God from his essence in a thoroughly Cartesian or Spinozistic manner. 30

II

DesCartes rejected final causes entirely in Physics, and even in Physiology and Biology. Everything was to be explained by mechanical action and reaction, even the bodies of men and animals were to be completely explained in terms of motion and mechanics. But he allowed free will, and he seems to have allowed purpose in God; so that his denial of final causes was not complete. In this his rationalism was half-hearted, and Spinoza was far more consistent. In him final causes are nowhere admitted: the Deity acts from logical necessity, and the whole development of the universe flows from the principle of contradiction. This view is the logical outcome of 40

141

DesCartes: admitting the clearness and distinctness of an idea as a test of existence, the distinction between thought and its object ought to vanish, so that the real order of events becomes the logical order of ideas, and all is reduced to necessity.

The addition of the Principle of Sufficient Reason by Leibnitz was a revolt against Spinoza's thorough-going rationalism: although Leibnitz is just as decided as DesCartes in rejecting final causes in Physics, he requires them doubly in Metaphysics: for each monad has free will, and God has arranged the pre-established harmony between the world and the pictures of it in the minds of the monads. Also in choosing the actual out of all the various possible worlds God was ethically and not logically determined. And Leibnitz throughout requires a satisfaction of ethical requirements not to be got from Spinoza. Although Leibnitz tries to regard the principle of sufficient reason as a purely logical principle, there is always in his mind the idea that the sufficient reason is finally that God perceives the actual occurrence to be ethically the best possible: in short that existence cannot be accounted for on purely logical grounds.

III

### Locke's idea of substances

Locke uses the word *substances* almost as equivalent to *things*. A piece of gold is a substance, a man or a vegetable is a substance: he says: "The complex ideas that our names of the species of substances properly stand for are collections of such qualities as have been observed to coexist in an unknown substratum, which we call substance" (IV.6.§7). But he protests, in a manner that reminds one of Bacon, against the fixity of species, the classificatory scholastic view. He says a changeling may be fitly described as between man and beast, for we have no ground for confining things within the limits of the species marked out by such words as *man* and *beast*, and refusing to allow the possibility of intermediate forms which do not fit into any species.—He adheres entirely to the old view of a thing with qualities inherent in it: the thing is a *substance*, the qualities constitute its essence.

### Locke's idea of substance

In all such things, we require a substratum for these qualities to inhere in: this substratum is substance, and is self-subsistent (except in relation to God). It may be material or spiritual or both: we have no ground for supposing any contradiction in the idea of thinking matter, only such matter would at the same time be spirit. Thus he says: We experiment in ourselves thinking, which is inconsistent with self-subsistence, and therefore has a necessary connexion with a support or subject of inhesion: the idea of that support is what we call substance, and so from thinking experimented in us

we have a proof of a thinking substance in us, which in my sense is spirit....
The general idea of substance being the same everywhere, the modification
or power of thinking makes it a spirit, whatever other modifications it has:
and similarly solidity makes it matter. (IV.3, Note).

Thus Locke's idea of substance is practically DesCartes's, with this important difference, that he thinks thought and extension (or solidity as he
would say) can be combined in one subject, in one substance, this being
nothing but a substratum for qualities, and all qualities not logically contradictory being (in thought at any rate) combinable in one thing. This
would remove the difficulty about interaction of mind and matter; but it    10
seems rather cutting the knot to combine such incompatible qualities in one
substance. Of course Locke's view of things as each containing a substratum
of reality, a self-subsistent entity, making it independent of all other things,
ought to have led him to monadism if it had been consistently carried
through: he would certainly admit a plurality of reals, but the difficulties
involved in this view do not seem to have occurred to him. And of course to
his substances, as to DesCartes's, the objection suggests itself that relatively
to God they are not substances at all.

### IV. ANALYSIS OF HUME ON CAUSE

Causation, in the first place, is the only relation by which we can get beyond    20
what is immediately given to the senses. The difficulty with Hume is to see
how this is effected. If we examine into the nature of causation, we see that
the important element in our conception of it is *necessary connexion*. Hume
tries to discover how experience can give rise to such an idea, but he sees
very clearly the difficulties involved in such an explanation and avoids at-
tacking the question directly. That the necessity of a cause for every event is
not intuitively known appears to him evident from the fact that we can at
least conceive a thing beginning to exist without a cause. If we admit this, it
is difficult to avoid Hume's view that we derive our idea of causation from
experience. When he has brought us face to face with the difficulty of this    30
view, he takes up fresh points, as why such particular causes should have
such particular effects. From this enquiry it appears that all reasonings
about cause and effect must be ultimately based upon an impression or the
memory of an impression. Thus there are three distinct elements in inferences of this kind: (1) The original impression (2) The transition to the idea
of the cause or effect connected with it (3) The nature and qualities of the
idea of causation itself. (2) can only be effected by experience, never by mere
impressions: experience being defined as the observation of frequent
coexistence or succession. But at this point Hume seems to see the futility of
his whole attempt: he says (p. 389): From the mere repetition of any past    40
impression, even to infinity, there will never arise a new original idea such as

necessary connexion. This reasoning however he simply puts aside as inconvenient: we do, he says, as a matter of fact, infer from one object to another, and perhaps the idea of necessary connexion depends on this inference and not vice versa. He then examines into the method by which experience leads us to make this inference: if by the understanding, then the uniformity of nature is presupposed; and probability is unable to help us out here, since it depends itself on the assumption of the uniformity of nature. Thus there remains only the imagination. We are left then with a purely psychological explanation depending on the Association of Ideas: such an explanation has no logical or epistemological bearing whatever, and except from the psychological point of view leaves us quite unrelieved from our first ignorance.

Throughout the discussion Hume is continually being brought face to face with the question how experience can produce such an idea as necessary connexion: several times he seems on the point of recognizing that it is this idea alone which makes experience possible, so far from being itself produced by it: but such a conclusion would be so alien to his habit of mind that he always shies at it and takes up with some fresh point until he has worked this up till it brings him again to the same impossibility.—Since he sees in belief only a greater liveliness in the idea, he converts all questions of belief into psychological questions and ought to explain all knowledge psychologically as he explains causation.

V

One might be tempted, in reading Hume's criticism, to compare him with Hylas (towards the end of the second Dialogue), as Fraser does in a note. Hylas too found no conviction from the arguments of Philonous, but had to admit that this absence of conviction sprang merely from difficulty in giving up a belief so long held as the belief in material substance. Indeed, to a sensationalist, there seems scarcely any possibility of an answer to Berkeley, and an absence of conviction would probably be due simply to the fact that such philosophers are in general characterized by an inordinate passion for common sense, which Berkeley struggles hard to bring over to his side, but in vain. —Berkeley maintains that all knowledge rests upon sensation, but allows inferences from sense-knowledge such as are necessary to make such knowledge self-consistent. He does not reject matter merely because it is not perceived but because any conception of it which can be framed appears to him self-contradictory. He allows the inference from my consciousness of Self to the existence of other Spirits, and of God, whose perceptions supply the permanence required to explain the external world; and he admits that he has no *idea* (= sensible idea) of Self or of other spirits, but maintains that he has a *notion* of these.—The permanence of external things, their existence even when unperceived by any finite mind, Berkeley apparently takes simply from common sense: and since *esse* is *percipi*, this requires a mind in which such things are always perceived, i.e. God. But why not, if all knowledge depends solely on sense, reject this existence when unperceived by any finite mind, and define matter, with Mill, as a "permanent possibility of sensation"? Whether such a phrase has any meaning or not, it seems about as much as sensationalism allows us to assume. But Berkeley's arguments are an odd blend of common sense and sensationalism, which no doubt would make them difficult for Hume to answer: while their spiritualism is so much opposed to common sense that it would be impossible he should accept them.

# 22

# Paper on Epistemology III [1894]

LIKE PAPERS 18 and 19, this paper was written for Ward's course on metaphysics. The verso of the last leaf reads *"B. Russell / Paper on Epistemology III. / Feb. 1894."* Apart from requests for clarification, the manuscript carries several longer comments by Ward, sometimes with Russell's replies. These are given in the annotations. Russell's lecture notebook for the course contains a loose sheet (RA 220.010050) in Russell's hand giving the questions for this paper:

### Paper on Epistemology, III

I. "Problem of physical enquiry so to define conception of matter that phenomena can be deduced from it without contradiction." Discuss, and explain how would define matter for this purpose.

II. Has psychologist an analogous problem? If so, how solved? if not, why not?

III. "Principle of Causality provisional device of scientific method useful till science reaches deductive stage, as dynamics e.g. has done: here causal relations are superseded by equations." Examine this statement of Laland ⟨Lalande *1890*⟩.

IV. Explain what you take to be the meaning of the problem of External Perception and why the problem has hitherto proved so intractable.

The copy-text is the manuscript (RA 220.010190), which consists of nine leaves.

I

A CONCEPTUAL TREATMENT of phenomena requires, as Kant shewed, a permanent substratum to which changes are referred. If a change occurs, it must be regarded as a change of something, which something must therefore be regarded as permanent. It would be impossible to conceive or speak about mere flow of becoming in which there is not something which becomes. The original conception from which that of substance is elaborated is the conception of Thing. But for the purposes of physical Science this conception immediately shews its inadequacy: things shew no permanence throughout changing states, so that we have to assume a substance or substances which remain when the thing is transformed. The further determination of the conception of substance has to be guided by the needs of physical Science: the problem is to combine these needs with the metaphysical postulate of permanence in changing states.

When we try to formulate a hypothesis which shall account for phenomena it becomes very difficult to exclude contradictions. Science contents itself with different views for different Sciences, and this procedure is of course perfectly legitimate so long as these different views all afford good working hypotheses. But when we try to synthesize the different views, many difficulties present themselves. Physics endeavour to exclude action at a distance by the hypothesis of a continuous ether, in which ponderable matter is formed by vortices. But chemistry requires its atomic hypothesis, so that these vortices have to be of as many different kinds as there are chemical elements. Again the conception of vortices in a perfect fluid, though mathematically very tractable, seems to involve difficulties. It has of course the advantage of accounting for the constancy of the quantum of mass and of energy (since a vortex in a perfect fluid is indestructible): but how then are we to conceive the ether which forms the vortices? Shall we let this consist of fresh atoms? If not, if it is completely continuous and undifferentiated, what would be meant by its motion? How could we fix on any one element and say "This is moving in such and such a manner"? How would Ether differ from empty space? Thus the possibility of explaining matter by vortex-rings seems illusory.

If we adopt the view of atoms as consisting of centres of force, we avoid many difficulties which beset us before. We avoid the absolute hardness or perfect fluidity, one or other of which the atomic theory compels us to adopt: we have to accept action at a distance, but if this gives us a more consistent explanation there seems nothing but prejudice against it. It is said action by contact is the only kind of physical action we can intuit: but that seems no reason against accepting action at a distance in a conceptual treatment of matter. But when we regard atoms as *merely* centres of force we are replacing substance by cause; we have lost the permanent substratum we required for the conception of physical phenomena. Force is usually defined in Dynamics as that which produces or tends to produce a change of motion: it is an essentially relative notion, and presupposes something moveable, so that to make this something moveable merely a centre of force seems to involve us in a circle. On the other hand the moment we allow our atom to be any thing more than a centre of force we are again involved in all the difficulties of the atomic theory: is it extended or unextended? If the latter, it seems meaningless: if the former, is it absolutely hard or more or less elastic? Since space is infinitely divisible, an extended atom is divisible in thought and the limit to actual divisibility must be arbitrary. And so the difficulties multiply, and no theory seems satisfactory.

## II

The conception in Psychology which corresponds with that of matter in Physics is the conception of Soul; and as in Physics there is a constant tendency to push matter further and further back, and, if it were possible, to extrude it altogether, so in Psychology there is a tendency to work without the soul. Wundt says the conception of substance has no application in Psychology, because its matter is immediately given in presentation, and not merely conceptually constructed like the data of Physics. It may be true that Psychology as a Science is able to get on without the notion of Soul, but surely something permanent must be necessary to make Psychology intelligible. Wundt admits that the conception of substance is required when the subject is regarded as object, i.e. in reflexion; and is it not only so that Psychology acquires its matter? It is only by reflecting on the subject as having thoughts, i.e. by self-consciousness, that Psychology can acquire its datum. And thus I fail to see how this datum is any more immediate or any less conceptual than the datum of Physics. The notion of the subject as a unifying principle seems unavoidable. But how conceive this subject? Not certainly as a thing with qualities inherent in it. And unless it is already given in all consciousness, self-consciousness or higher degrees of introspection do not seem to bring us any nearer to it but only to lead to an infinite regress in which the object known remains always phenomenon and the subject remains always the knower, not the known. This leads Bradley to regard the subject as a "felt background" in all consciousness, and when any element of this "felt background" enters into definite consciousness it passes over into the object. But I am unable to understand what is meant by this view.—If we regard the Self as essentially activity, we have removed it from the category of substance to that of cause, shewing the same tendency as leads to the view of matter as constituted by centres of force. But do we not require something active, as we require, in matter, centres as well as force?

III

The principle of Causality, until further defined, is more or less ambiguous. In one sense it means the postulate that every event must have a cause; this is the sense of the Kantian category; in another sense it means the methodological postulate of uniformity. This principle of uniformity of course implies no assumption as to the actual recurrence of the same event, but postulates that if the same event could recur, it would be followed by the same result: i.e. that successions can be reduced to general laws, applicable throughout space and time and independent of these: such as Gravitation. When this meaning is given to Causality, cause also assumes a peculiar meaning: causes are always events and are homogeneous with their effects, which are fresh events and become causes in their turn. In this sense the principle of Causality is not absent from Pure Physics: all the equations used involve the postulate of uniformity in the laws of succession of phenomena. But cause in the sense of efficiency is certainly extruded entirely. Force, which was originally used to denote cause in this sense, has now become a purely auxiliary conception, only used as an abbreviation and involving no assumption of efficiency whatever. And even this auxiliary use is being continually minimized and is not the least essential to Dynamics.

But this possibility of extruding efficiency seems to me to depend not on the perfection of Physics, but on its abstractness and the homogeneity of its matter. As soon as such a conception as that of an individual comes in, or of an organism, it seems difficult not to suppose causes heterogeneous from their effects. In Psychology especially, activity seems incommensurable with other psychical elements, and seems to afford the very type of a cause in the sense of efficiency. A psychology which omits it, and endeavours to reduce all to presentations, and so to approximate psychology to physics, seems ineradicably defective.

IV

Historically the problem of external perception arose out of that of the relation of body and mind: this problem was found intractable when directly attacked, and hence it was asked: But after all how do we know about our bodies? Our knowledge of matter is mental, and what warrant have we for assuming anything beyond perceptions and of what nature shall we assume such external existence to be?

In answer to this question, Locke adopted the view of common sense, that things exist outside us, and our perceptions are copies of them. Our ideas of substances, according to him, have their archetypes without us. But the secondary qualities are referred to the perceiving subject. From this position it was a natural step for Berkeley to refer the primary qualities also

to the percipient and identify *esse* and *percipi*. The transition from Des-Cartes to Malebranche is similar to that from Locke to Berkeley.—Leibnitz occupied a more or less unique position, in denying the perception of external things while admitting them to an independent reality. What the monad perceives is not external things, but internal modifications, which mirror external things according to a pre-established harmony. Kant first on the rationalist side clearly saw the distinction between knowledge of relation of ideas and knowledge of existence. The problem of external perception merges in the question as to the possibility of such knowledge of existence.
10 Kant holds that all our knowledge is of phenomena, and is rendered possible by the moulding of these by the mind. *We* make phenomena what they are, and it is only of the *form* contributed by the subject that we have knowledge. He admits the *Ding an Sich* as an unknown something, but all knowledge is of phenomena, not of noumena.—

The intractability of the problem of external perception is I suppose due to its ultimateness. Unless the object is given from the first, at least obscurely, it is impossible ever to get to it. Unless in sensation there is already implicit the distinction of subject and object, it is impossible to arrive at this distinction by thought. The distinction, and the problem of
20 external perception, are only rendered explicit by inter-subjective intercourse. When other subjects are distinguished in the external world, and these are found to perceive the same objects, the same sun and moon, etc., as I do, it becomes necessary to assign to these some existence not dependent merely on my perceiving them. But when we ask What sort of existence? Of what nature are these objects? we get the whole problem of the relation between thought and things, and as we have only thought by which to attack this problem, we are tied to a circle which we can travel round and round but cannot get out of.

# 23

# Paper on Descartes [1894]

THIS PAPER WAS written for Ward's course on the history of philosophy. The verso of the last leaf of the manuscript is marked: "*B. Russell / Paper on Descartes / Feb. 1894*". The manuscript bears a number of pencilled notations by Ward, many of them requesting further explanation. Russell's lecture notebook (2: 35) records the questions as follows:

### *Paper on DesCartes*
1. Examine meaning and purport of DesCartes's cogito ergo sum.
2. Is DesCartes guilty of circle of passing from his criterion to the Divine existence (and veracity) and then resting criterion on same Divine existence (and veracity)?
3. "But for his logical inconsequence DesCartes would have been an idealist". Discuss this, examining in particular DesCartes's handling of "sense-knowledge".
4. Expound and criticize the Cartesian Dualism. How are particular bodies and particular minds related to Matter and Mind as substances and how is the human body related to the human mind?
5. Discuss the relation of conception of self to conception of God in DesCartes's philosophy.

The copy-text is the manuscript (RA 220.010270), consisting of six leaves.

## I. MEANING AND PURPORT OF THE "COGITO ERGO SUM"

THE "COGITO ERGO SUM" must not be regarded as a syllogism proceeding from some such major as "whatever thinks, is": such a major would rather be inferred from the "cogito ergo sum". This is really an analytical inference: it might be exhibited thus: I think = I am thinking = I am [thinking]. In the very moment of most extreme doubt, the very doubt itself implies a doubter: and all my thinking, all the psychical processes of which I am conscious, involve a thinking subject.—The chief importance of the "cogito ergo sum" in his system is as affording an epis-
10 temological criterion of knowledge. I know my own existence at any rate: how? By its clearness and distinctness. This then is the test of knowledge: whatever I clearly and distinctly know is to be accepted.

## II. HAS DESCARTES COMMITTED A CIRCLE IN RESTING GOD ON HIS CRITERION OF CLEARNESS AND DISTINCTNESS, AND THIS AGAIN ON GOD?

Descartes does not seem to me to have been guilty of a circle in his argument: he first gets his criterion by a criticism of "cogito ergo sum", his criterion then leads him to God, and when he has proved the existence of God from his criterion he finds that God affords a reason for the truth of his criterion. This criterion he had held formerly simply as a result of criticism
20 from the one firm piece of knowledge he possessed: he was forced to accept the criterion, but was unable to shew deductively why it was true. Now that he has demonstrated the existence of a veracious God, he can return to his criterion and shew how it flows deductively from this dogma. The argument seems to me no more circular than that of Newton in proving the Law of Gravitation by Kepler's Laws and then proceeding immediately to deduce these from the Law of Gravitation.—But the issue is confused in Descartes by the fact that he uses his criterion for no other purpose than to establish the existence of God until this has been established: and he does speak as if his criterion had acquired new certainty when he has shewn that it follows
30 from God's nature. Perhaps there may have been some such thought in his mind; but it does not seem essential to his system that there should have been. He himself in answer to objections distinguishes the criterion as the "principium cognoscendi" of God and God as the "principium essendi" of the criterion, which seems satisfactorily to answer the objection.

## III

Descartes's argument for the material world is briefly this: Whatever I clearly and distinctly conceive is true; now when I examine some material object, such as a piece of wax, I find that I can conceive it as retaining its identity though all its sensible qualities should change: but the one quality of extension I cannot think away from it; further I have no clear conception of colour, etc., except as my sensations, but of extension I have a clear conception as belonging to external objects, and further I have an irresistible impulse to believe that there really is such an external extended world as I so conceive. Hence it would be contrary to God's veracity if no such world existed. Descartes appears to argue also (though herein the inconsistency is more glaring) that imagination alone, by which material things are conceived, can persuade me of their existence: for imagination is an application of the cognitive faculty to the body which is intimately present to it, and which therefore exists (Med. VI). 10

It is sufficiently evident that the above argument gives no ground whatever for believing in a material world as distinct from the spiritual: there is no reason why extension should not have gone the way of colour and taste and been referred to the perceiving subject alone. His veracious God is in any case rather a *pis-aller*: and it is very difficult to apply him systematically: either he gives too much or too little, and in this case he has certainly been made to give too much. All science is unaffected by idealism: and having started with consciousness as the fundamental principle, it seems an absurd and useless complication to introduce this unnecessary dualism. Even had Descartes been an occasionalist his position would have been less palpably absurd: but the theory of interaction between mind and body (developed most fully in the treatise on the Passions) is utterly inconsistent with the rest of his doctrine, about the two independent substances. 20

Descartes's entire rejection of sense as a source of knowledge makes his subsequent dualism even more surprising. He points out the possibility of deception by the senses, in dreams for instance, and when pains are felt in amputated limbs: from these he ought to have concluded that we have no right to affirm a world of extended objects, but he fails to take the final step and considers only the secondary qualities as due to the imagination. Indeed his inconsistency is so great that it can only be attributed to his overpowering fear of ecclesiastical censure. 30

IV. CARTESIAN DUALISM

According to Descartes there are two substances, mind and matter: these are substances in the sense that either could exist entirely independently of the other: we can at least in thought separate mind and body and imagine either existing without the other. But this independence is only relative: both exist only in God, or by a continual exertion of God's power. Thus relatively to God neither is a substance; God alone has independent being, and the Cartesian dualism breaks down. 40

*Relation of particular bodies to matter as a substance*

Space is a plenum in the Cartesian physics: extension is the one universal characteristic of matter, and where there is no matter there is no extension. This matter, when once set in motion (whether by the will of God or by whatever other means might be adequate) will necessarily maintain the same amount of motion throughout all time, since no particle can move without pushing some other before it. Particular bodies are merely denser or rarer portions of this plenum (though in what sense such all-pervading matter could be denser or rarer does not seem to me clear).

10 *Relation of body and mind*

Descartes was not an occasionalist, as appears from many passages, most clearly perhaps in the *Passions de l'Âme*. He believed imagination and memory and the passions to be due to the action of the body on the soul by means of the animal spirits, but he thought pure thought, pure intellection, was not thus affected by the body. The soul also could act on the body: it could not alter quantity of motion, for that according to Descartes's physics was a constant, but it could alter direction, and this was what occurred when a limb was moved by volition for instance.

V. RELATION OF CONCEPTION OF SELF TO CONCEPTION OF GOD IN
20                              DESCARTES

Descartes's three proofs of God's existence, which he uses indiscriminately and seems to regard as all equally valid, make it confusing to know what really he did regard as the relation of self to God. But if we take what is perhaps the proof he lays most stress on: I exist, and I form the idea of a perfect Being; therefore my existence must be contingent, for otherwise I could have given myself all the perfections I lack; therefore I owe my existence to a perfect Being—if we take this proof, we can hardly say that either self or God is logically prior: they are implied in each other. My own existence is finite and contingent: it can be contingent only on some other existence and thus there must be some Being who exists necessarily, and such a
30 being must be complete, for he could have no bounds set him except by some other being by whom he would then be conditioned. My own finitude can thus only be conceived in opposition to God's infinity and as soon as I have formed the conception of myself as existing, I am driven on to conceive God, as the complete and necessary being.

# A Critical Comparison of the Methods of
# Bacon, Hobbes and DesCartes [1894]

RUSSELL, IT SEEMS, did not always do his assignments on time. While this paper, which was written for Stout's history of philosophy course, is dated April 1894, Russell's lecture notebook for the course has the note: "*Do* by March 8: *Essay* on Critical comparison of the Methods of Bacon Hobbes and DesCartes in philosophy" (2: 155). The verso of the last leaf reads "*B. Russell / Essay on Methods of Bacon, Hobbes, and DesCartes. / April 1894.*" The longer title used here is from the head of the first leaf. The paper bears no written comments by Stout, although at one point (160: 26–7) Russell noted in the margin: "[Not true, or at any rate greatly exaggerated, says Stout.]"

The copy-text is the manuscript (RA 220.010260), which consists of fifteen leaves.

BACON AND HOBBES seem at first sight to stand at opposite poles as regards method; but when we come to compare both with a philosopher of such a very different stamp as DesCartes, the greater contrast brings out a certain amount of resemblance; a resemblance rather in what they omit to consider than in the positive opinions they profess, in their limitations rather than in their constructive work.

## Differences between Bacon and Hobbes

As to the differences between Bacon and Hobbes, they are easily pointed out. Bacon thought all knowledge depended on induction; Hobbes allowed no place to induction in his method. Bacon began with observation of particulars, and from these gradually built up species and genera, none of them fixed, but as fluid as any Darwinian could desire. Knowledge must rest on observation; no other basis seemed to him possible. Hobbes on the other hand insists on the uncertainty of any such knowledge; everything certain must rest on deduction; deduction requires some fundamental propositions from which to start; these fundamental propositions must (says Hobbes) be definitions. In such a method observation can at best serve only as affording suggestions; everything must logically be dependent on names. Hobbes insists that our first principles must be self-evident, and this he seems in some way to believe definitions to be. In urging the importance of self-evidence he seems at times to speak almost like DesCartes, but his meaning is not really that of the principle of clearness and distinctness; it is only required at the outset, and is a clearness connected only with the meanings of words, whereas DesCartes's is applied throughout any chain of reasoning, and to objective facts as well as to verbal propositions.—To point out the resemblances between Bacon and Hobbes it will be necessary to consider each more in detail, and then pass on to DesCartes.

## Bacon

Almost alone among the philosophers of his age, Bacon appears to have been almost ignorant of mathematical method, and quite indifferent to it. This is what gives his method its individuality and makes it a corrective to the one-sidedness of almost all subsequent methods for some time after him. Bacon did not believe that investigation can begin with self-evident propositions and proceed in a rationalistic manner from these to construct new truths about existence; and it was existence alone which interested him. His aim was practical, he wanted to increase man's power over nature. He therefore cared nothing for idealistic systems or for investigations not bearing in some visible manner on the actual world. He wished to know causes, in order that he might be able to control nature by bringing suitable causes into operation. He quarrelled with the astronomy of his day because it only described instead of accounting for the motions of the heavenly bodies. He wished to get

rid of all presuppositions or Idols, and collect facts patiently until uniformities became manifest. At least this was what he wished his method to be: but
some rationalistic basis was necessary to make it possible to interpret his facts,
and even to make his facts possible at all. Although he says that the tables are
to contain particular facts, and not facts about whole species as in Aristotle's
induction, it would of course be impossible to get facts of any value for inductive purposes unless the observed particulars were interpreted as being true
somehow of species, or unless phenomena were somehow classified mentally
so as to give a principle of coordination among observations. This need does
not seem to have been present to Bacon's mind consciously, because as soon as
it arose, it was set at rest by his doctrine of Forms, which for some reason or
other he never questioned, and seems to have always considered self-evident.
It is this doctrine which supplies the rationalistic basis on which induction
must rest if it is to give indubitable and general results; but unfortunately
Bacon chose a very bad basis, very likely because he was so little conscious
how indispensable some such basis was to his system. It is this doctrine of
forms which connects him most closely with Aristotle and the schoolmen; he
thought there were a finite number of such forms, whose mingling in various
degrees gave rise to the variety of phenomena. To every form corresponded
some outward and visible nature, but the form itself was hidden from sense
and had to be discovered by induction. He appears to have thought the true
nature of forms consisted always in some molecular motion; this at any rate is
his result in the case of heat. The forms being finite in number, when we wish
to discover the cause of any phenomenon we have only to collect instances to
see which form is always present when the phenomenon in question occurs,
and absent when it does not occur. We have a disjunctive syllogism to begin
with, and if we can exhaust every alternative but one, the remaining one is
therefore the true one. His lists of various kinds of Prerogative Instances all
have the better performance of this elimination in view. They are valuable as
aids to all induction, quite independently of the doctrine of forms; but when
that is gone we require some new way of supplementing the mere collection of
instances, and some new principle on which to group the facts.

## Hobbes

When we come to Hobbes, we find a resurrection of the Aristotelian syllogism and a return to scholastic nominalism. Hobbes, as far at any rate as
method is concerned, is an uncompromising rationalist. He uses the word
*cause* as equivalent to *logical ground* and interchangeable with it: thus he
speaks of the *cause* of equality or of angle, expressions which in Bacon would
have no meaning. His definition of Philosophy is "the knowledge we acquire,
*by true ratiocination*, of appearances, or apparent effects, from the knowledge
we have of some possible production or generation of the same; and of such
production as has been or may be, from the knowledge we have of the effects".

His definition of method in philosophy is accordingly: The shortest way of finding out effects by their known causes, or vice versa. But owing to his rationalistic view of the meaning of the word *cause*, these definitions do not lead to a Baconian induction, but to a system of ratiocination, necessarily preceded by an analysis of things (or rather concepts) into their most universal elements, but preceded by this analysis only in order to discover where deduction is to start from. The analysis meant is similar to that pursued by a geometrician endeavouring to discover a synthetic proof for a proposition, who begins by analysis to discover a suitable starting-point. Thus *square*
10 being defined as "a plane, terminated with a certain number of equal and straight lines and right angles", we analyse the idea of square into those of "line, plain, terminated, angle, straightness, rectitude, and equality"; and, says Hobbes, "if we can find out the *causes* of these, we may compound them altogether into the cause of a square". By thus analysing, we come at last to universal things, and when we have the causes of these, we go back by ratiocination to the causes of particular things. But now comes the pill disguised in the jam of all this logic. The causes of universal things, we are told, where they have any, are manifest of themselves, so they need no method, but have one universal cause, namely *motion*. This statement must have appeared to
20 Hobbes self-evident, but he says elsewhere that only definitions are primary and universal propositions, and I fail to see how the above principle can by any stretch of imagination be called a definition.

### Resemblances between Bacon and Hobbes

If we now consider the likeness between Bacon and Hobbes, I think we shall be able to find a good deal. Both considered motion the cause of everything: Hobbes says, in a thoroughly Baconian spirit, that in Physics we must first know the motions in the smallest parts of bodies; that Moral Philosophy has to consider the motions of the mind, as desire and aversion, etc.; that these have their causes in sense and imagination, which are the subject of Physics;
30 so that Physics must be first studied before proceeding to Psychology. Both Bacon and Hobbes appear to have thought the possibilities of method exhausted by the antithesis of induction or deduction, and both were forced tacitly to go beyond their professions and make assumptions unwarranted in the one case by observation, in the other by definition. Neither imagined any possible difference of method between philosophy and science, only the one took Mathematics as the type while the other took the Sciences of observation. In all these respects DesCartes far exceeded them both, and transcended their opposition to a great extent, though as a rationalist and a mathematician he stands nearer to Hobbes than to Bacon.

### 40 DesCartes

When we come to consider DesCartes's method, we are met on the threshold by much greater difficulties than in the cases of Bacon and Hobbes. These seem to me to be largely due to the fact that when DesCartes writes about method, he usually has Science, and especially mathematical Science, in his mind; but when he comes to treat of metaphysics, he abandons the mathematical method almost entirely, though apparently almost without recognizing that he does so. That he should have abandoned it is of course a pre-eminent merit, but it is a pity that in his *Règles pour la Direction de l'Esprit* and in other places he should have treated of it so exclusively. Let us consider first his method in science, and then see how far his metaphysical method differs from it.                                                                          10

### Scientific Method

DesCartes had revolutionized mathematics by the introduction of the method of analysis which is known as Cartesian Geometry: this revolution, whether or not it would have occurred even if DesCartes had not brought it about, was essential to all modern developments of mathematics, and the new method was used by DesCartes himself with the most felicitous results. It was therefore natural that he should be greatly impressed by the importance of right method, and especially of his method. Analysis in everything is urged by him as of the utmost importance, not as ultimate, but as an indispensable pre-liminary. In the *Règles*, he develops very fully the method of analytical    20 geometry, as the universal method of science. Like all his contemporaries, also, he was deeply impressed by the progress of mechanics, and held that all Science was reducible to mechanical laws. He grasped quite as firmly as Hobbes the view of the world as a mechanism; consistently with this view, he referred all the secondary qualities of objects to the percipient, leaving to ex-ternal things nothing not quantitatively estimable in terms of matter and mo-tion. And this view he applied also to the human body, and even to the imagi-nation and the passions, being, as far as these are concerned, as materialistic as Hobbes. He explained all these, to use his own phrase, "selon les règles de la méchanique, qui sont les mêmes que celles de la nature". But in his view of    30 these laws of mechanics and of the grounds of their validity he shewed his superiority to his contemporaries both in insight and in method. He recog-nizes two sources of knowledge, deduction and *intuition*. The latter is neces-sary, not only to supply the basis for deduction, but also, in a sense, at every step of a deduction; it is the intuitive certainty of logical connexion which justifies it.—He allows induction too, but in a peculiar mathematical sense, merely as the reduction of complicated to simpler questions, and so as a help to deduction. Intuition is allowed by DesCartes not only in purely conceptual thinking, but also as applied to objects of sense. He has constantly in his mind its use in Geometry, and he knew how this depends on sense.                         40

Although he thus mentions deduction and intuition as the only sources of knowledge, he recognizes a possible scientific experience in an almost Kantian sense. The understanding, he says, can be deceived by no experience, if only it contents itself with the experience itself and does not proceed to unjustifiable inferences, as that the sensible qualities perceived faithfully portray the objects of sense. And he recognizes, to some extent at least, the importance of experiment in Science.

In Rule XII, he makes a very Baconian analysis of things into simple natures, which he says are known by intuition, and whose composition gives actual things. These simple natures may be compounded either by ourselves, or because experience shews such compounds. In the former case, the result
10 will be valid only if the composition proceeds by deduction. As an example of composition given by experience he mentions investigations on the nature of the magnet; we must, he says, assemble all possible experiments about it, and then try to deduce what mixture of simple natures will produce all the effects we have seen. This passage might have come bodily out of Bacon; but he is not really putting forward anything like the doctrine of forms: his simple natures are unanalysable conceptions, such as motion, will, etc. He divides them into three classes, the purely intellectual, the purely material, and the common. They are all known of themselves and can contain nothing false. He mentions among the first class some axioms, and he allows a necessary connexion be-
20 tween simple natures, such as extension and figure, even where the one concept does not contain the other; in short he allows what Kant called synthetic judgments à priori; but how these are possible he does not explain.

*Metaphysical Method*

When we come to Metaphysics, we find, however, a complete abandonment of the method of the *Règles*. He no longer analyses difficulties into their simplest elements, or speaks of simple natures to be found. His difficulties are too fundamental now to be met in any such manner. The problem for him is largely epistemological: like Kant he is puzzled to know how knowledge at all is possible, and to a great extent his method consequently is critical. It seems
30 as if a little more criticism, a little more of the method of doubt, might have led him on almost to Kant. DesCartes's doubt, though no doubt true biographically, is in the *Méthode* and the *Méditations* nothing but a method of sifting out the grounds of certainty. As a method it already involves implicitly a criterion of truth, that whatever cannot be doubted is true. And it is able to lead to an ontology as well as to an epistemology, since the first proposition which cannot be doubted, his own existence, is ontological. When DesCartes has got hold of this first piece of certain knowledge, he proceeds to ask, quite in the manner of Kant's *Prolegomena,* how it is that this fact comes to be known. And he finds that what distinguishes it from facts he can doubt is its
40 clearness and distinctness. He therefore proceeds to take clearness and distinctness as a criterion of truth, but of course this criterion was already implicit in his method of doubt. It then becomes the basis of his epistemology,

while the *cogito ergo sum* remains the basis of his ontology. He gives, in answer to the second objections to his *Méditations*, the reasons why he did not adopt the geometrical method, or why, as he puts it, he adopted analysis rather than synthesis. He says the former is more suitable for teaching, but his chief reason for rejecting the geometrical method is that the first notions in metaphysics are the principal difficulty, and therefore it is not convenient to set out with definitions and axioms, but rather to arrive at definitions after mature consideration of the things dealt with. The ideas of mathematics, he says, are objects of sense, and are therefore easily known and defined; those of metaphysics on the contrary are not objects of sense, but are very difficult to detach from prejudices due to sense. And this, he tells us, is why he called his book *Méditations*, in order to approach the subject gradually and get the mind of the reader sufficiently detached from everything sensible to be able to consider adequately the conceptions of metaphysics. In his ontology he has a tendency to fall back on scholasticism, and at the height of his doubt he assumes such principles as that an effect cannot have more reality than its cause, to which at such a level of doubt he seems hardly entitled. But in the main his method is critical, and this is how he succeeded in establishing consciousness as more fundamental than motion or anything else.

*Conclusion*

In conclusion, then, we cannot help being struck by certain broad characteristics in which all three philosophers are at one with each other and with their age. All are most anxious to discover *the* true method; all are much impressed by the advance of Science, and hope to be able to solve all questions connected with the physical world in terms of matter and motion alone. If we were to take DesCartes only as he appears in the *Règles*, the resemblance between the three might perhaps be pushed even further. But in Metaphysics, he made the enormous advance of beginning from the side of mind, from consciousness, instead of trying, as Bacon and Hobbes did, to reach this from the side of physical Science and explain it in terms of mechanical laws. This it was which enabled DesCartes to become the founder of continental rationalism, and indeed of modern philosophy generally, while Bacon and Hobbes remained more or less isolated, standing midway between the medieval and the modern. DesCartes held as firmly as Hobbes that the physical world is wholly explicable on mechanical principles: he recognized, with Bacon, the need of experiments, and of crucial instances where several causes are possible; but he saw that a different method was required in metaphysics, and so laid the foundations both of epistemological and of ontological rationalism.

# 25

# Paper on Bacon [1894]

THIS PAPER WAS almost certainly written for Stout's course on the history of philosophy. The verso of the last leaf of the manuscript reads "*Paper on Bacon. / April 1894*". The date is surprising since Stout's course ran for two terms (Michaelmas 1893 and Lent 1894), and the material covered in the paper was studied at the beginning of the first term, as Russell's lecture notebook for Stout's course makes clear. It might have been expected, therefore, that this paper would precede the other paper on Bacon (**20**), which covers material in the lecture notebook immediately following that dealt with in the present paper. No questions for this paper have been found in the notebooks or among the loose sheets Russell kept. There is, however, a sheet of preparatory notes (RA 220.010050) on Digby made from a reading of Charles de Rémusat's *Histoire de philosophie en Angleterre* (1875). This sheet was obviously used in section III of the paper.

The manuscript itself is incomplete. It starts with section II, above which there is the pencilled annotation in Alan Wood's hand: "(No answer I)". The copy-text is the manuscript (RA 220.010250); it consists of fourteen leaves.

ETER RAMUS REPRESENTS essentially an age of transition. He
maintained in his thesis that all Aristotle had taught was false, but yet
his own views did not differ very widely from those of Aristotle. He
upheld Plato as greater than Aristotle, and used to commend the Socratic
search for definitions. But himself he maintained that deduction is the only
true road to knowledge, and Logic was the branch of Philosophy which
most interested him. He invented the doctrine of method in Logic, and
attacked some points in the doctrine of the Syllogism; he rejected the fourth
figure (in this respect returning to Aristotle), and later on he attacked the 10
third also. But his chief characteristic was his manner of instruction, and the
spirit in which he gave it. Like Bacon, he held that knowledge was to be
valued on account of its practical utility: he was a Humanist, and used to
urge the search for philosophy by the investigation of "nature", meaning
however by this chiefly the works of the ancients. He taught Logic in
teaching Vergil and Cicero. He did not free himself really from the authority
of the ancients, but he endeavoured to free men's minds from the blind
bondage to Aristotle, particularly to the Aristotle of the schools, into which
the Middle Ages had fallen. He was a devotee of Mathematics, to which he is
said to have devoted fifteen years of study. His chief achievement was that 20
by producing a ferment and by boldly defying the authority of Aristotle and
the schools he set men thinking more freely than formerly and paved the
way for the revolution which he himself cannot be said to have effected.

In this general way Bacon was doubtless influenced by him, not directly,
but through Temple, who was a professed Ramist and was at Cambridge
when Bacon was an undergraduate. Possibly a more definite influence may
be traced in Bacon's utilitarian view of the value of knowledge.

# III

The two chief men in Cambridge when Bacon was an undergraduate were
Digby and Temple. Of these Digby was the older, and adhered to Aristotle; 30
Temple was a follower of Ramus; his writings are mostly of a controversial
character and directed against Digby.

*Digby* was a fellow of St. John's College: he made himself unpopular by
his leanings to Catholicism and was therefore finally expelled from the College (in 1587) for eccentricity in blowing a horn all day and going fishing
during chapel-time. He was a mystic, and an adherent of Aristotle as seen
through the eyes of the schoolmen. He attacked Ramus passionately for his
opposition to Aristotle, whom he upholds as above everyone else and whose
authority he quotes as beyond appeal. (Yet in the matter of Metaphysics, he
allows himself to criticize Aristotle: he says the highest principles of Met- 40

aphysics were only in germ in him). Digby is in no way original: all his views are supported by reference to authorities. Like all the philosophers of his age, he thought knowledge was only to be had by following a fixed method, and that the discovery of the true method was of fundamental importance. His view of method was, that starting from the data of sense we must proceed gradually upwards by abstraction to the highest principle, and then descend again by deduction to the particulars of sense, which cannot be explained except by reference to the highest principle. Sensation is for him the beginning of knowledge: it frames pictures of objects, which the imagi-
10 nation retains and from which conceptions arise by abstraction. The soul is for him a *tabula rasa*, and he admits no innate ideas. But sensible objects alone cannot produce knowledge, because it is not in them to produce. We need also a spiritual force: the understanding is a spontaneous but impeded activity. Digby in all this is merely scholastic: he sums up his position in the maxim that the second substance, the universal, has its existence only in the first, the individual, while the first has its essence only in the second.—The highest knowledge, says Digby, is the knowledge of God: and this is to be obtained only through faith. He wrote much on theosophical subjects, and was very full of cabalistic and mystical writers. He was throughout an
20 eclectic, little troubled by the fact that his thoughts are often inconsequent. He owed little to the Renaissance except his good style and his Greek quotations. He was the first who spread Neo-Platonic doctrines in England, and also the first who dealt systematically with the whole of theoretic philosophy.

He appears to have had some influence on Bacon: the mention of Philosophia Prima and the connection with Logic and Metaphysics which Bacon gives it may be due to Digby: also a mention he once makes of the hierarchy of angels. A more important influence is perhaps traceable in Bacon's view of the twofold way of knowledge, from the particular to the
30 universal, and then, using this as the principle of explanation, back to the particular again; and in regarding the universal as at once the Platonic immanent idea and the Aristotelian Form.

*Temple* was rather younger than Digby: when Digby's authority in Cambridge was at its height, Temple (though not yet M.A.) began his attack on him, at first anonymously under the pseudonym of Mildapettus. He is not original any more than Digby, but his authority is Ramus instead of Aristotle. Almost all his writings are polemical, and he was the first who introduced Ramism into England (though about the same time it had been introduced into St. Andrews by Buchanan). Temple upholds a simpler pro-
40 cedure as against the scholastic, and common sense as against mysticism. He is very moderate in his judgment of the ancients, and unlike Digby is usually temperate and polite in controversy, though his language about the schoolmen and their representatives in his time is not always as mild as it

might be. He holds with Ramus that Logic should start with observation of nature, that it should not deviate from life and hide itself in the schools, but should guide and rule our practice. He admits the necessity of starting from particulars to get to universals, but he regards this as a process which takes place of itself and is not reducible to method, and on this ground he attacks Digby's twofold way of knowledge, holding that Logic is concerned with Deduction alone.—He also attacks Aristotle's Physics and Metaphysics, but not at such length; his chief interest is in Logic. The Ethics, however, he attacks at some length, and here he is independent of Ramus. He objects to Aristotle's conception of the Supreme Good, and says it is rather a Supreme 10 Evil.

Nevertheless, although scarcely any sharper criticism has been directed against Aristotle and Scholasticism than that of Temple, and although his criticism was on many points well founded, he was still, like Ramus, really unfreed from Scholasticism. The universal is still better known to nature than the particular, and is therefore the principle of knowledge. The universal is necessary to explain the particular, but the particular is not required to explain the universal. Thus deduction is the only road to knowledge. But Temple is not a realist: the universals have not real existence like Plato's Ideas.                                                                                 20

In other respects also Temple was not modern: he was quite free from the pantheistic and naturalistic tendencies of his time: he coordinated faith and knowledge, and was full of religion.

Temple made Cambridge the chief seat of Ramism, so that in 1600 it was recognized as such even on the Continent: Bacon grew up during the controversy between him and Digby, and this controversy must have set his mind at work, especially in the direction of the investigation of the true method, which was the chief question at issue.

IV

Aristotle meant by "perfect Induction" an enumeration of all the species of 30 a genus as having a certain predicate, leading to the conclusion that the genus had the same predicate. It depended entirely on the classificatory view: what belonged to all the species could not constitute the differentia of any one of them and therefore belonged to the genus. It would naturally arise in the search for definitions: suppose for example we are seeking a definition of justice: we examine various classes of just acts until we hope to have exhausted all such classes: the common quality or qualities in them all constitute the definition of justice. Or, to take a more Aristotelian example: suppose we have a class of animals, such as the ruminants, clearly marked off from other animals by certain prominent characteristics such as chewing 40 the cud: we find by examining each separate species of these ruminants, that all of them have horns, and are therefore able to predicate horns as a quality of the genus.

This procedure differed entirely from the Baconian induction; for as Bacon rejected the classificatory view of things such a notion as perfect induction became in his system inapplicable. In Bacon, what was sought was causes of phenomena: phenomena could it is true be roughly collected into groups, but not rigidly classified. Bacon thought however that their diversity was explicable as the mixture, in varying degrees, of fixed "forms": and to discover the nature of these forms was his aim in investigating phe-
10 nomena. This enabled the Baconian induction to lead to certainty, just as much as the Aristotelian, for it was always possible to begin with a disjunctive proposition as major premise, exhausting all the possible forms; and if all but one were found inadequate, the remaining one was the true cause of the nature in question.

V

In Plato and Aristotle, the permanent was conceived as an Idea, a type, to which actual things tried to approximate. To every class of things belonged such a regulative type, and the final causes by which everything was explained were constituted by these types. The fleeting was constituted by
20 the diversity of the actual things and their divergence from the Idea or type.

In Bacon on the other hand the permanent was the Forms.[1] These were not tied down to this or that particular thing, but their passage from one thing to another produced the flux of phenomena. This view had great advantages as compared with the Aristotelian: it allowed for continuity in phenomena, since the forms could vary continuously in intensity: and though it did not really get rid of the classificatory view, it removed it from the actual objects and as leading to a method of scientific investigation was far more fruitful than the old one.

VI

30 The old view of nature was anthropomorphic in several ways. It sought to explain phenomena teleologically; it cared little for analysis of the sensible world on the physical side into the minute processes which Bacon regarded as the causes of what appeared; its "Dinglichkeit", its *thing* with qualities and activities inherent in it, was obviously constructed on the analogy of man. In all these respects Bacon found fault with the ancients, though as to the *thing* he was really very little better than they were. But as to final causes,

---

1 *Novum Organum*, Bk. II, Aph. IX: "Forms ... are, in the eye of reason at least, and in their essential law, eternal and immutable."

he utterly rejected them in all Sciences except such as have to do with human action (*Nov. Or.*, Bk. II, Aph. 2); and as to latent process and latent configuration, he is careful to urge that they are "perfectly continuous and for the most part escape the sense" (Aph. 6), and that it is the investigation of these and their causes, not of the immediate data of sense, which is the business of Science. In thus urging continuity and investigation of the minute portions of matter, Bacon is also sapping the foundations of the thing-with-qualities, although he never himself got free of this view.

### VII

If we omit the doctrine of Forms, we can find in the Baconian Induction everything that Mill afterwards embodied in his four canons. In his lists of prerogative instances all four methods are suggested. Conformable instances, or instances of Analogy, correspond roughly speaking with the method of Agreement: the Solitary and the Crucial Instances seem both to be included in the method of Differences: and Migratory Instances combine this method and that of Concomitant Variations. And in the general account of his method, Bacon dwells on the importance of Negative as well as Positive Instances, as against the Aristotelian view of Induction. The collecting of positive instances would only give Mill's method of agreement, which according to Mill himself cannot be made the basis of a certain induction; but by methodical collection of negative instances, i.e. collection of instances resembling as far as possible the positive instances, Bacon arrives, where possible, at the method of Difference, or at least at what Mill calls the Joint Method of Agreement and Difference.

The basis for Mill, by which he is able to raise Induction above the level of mere enumeration, is Causation; the basis for Bacon is the Doctrine of Forms. As an account of induction in Sciences of Observation, Bacon's method does not seem to me to be vitiated at all by this Doctrine: except that it led him to omit perhaps the most important step, though it is one which cannot very well be reduced to method: that is, the framing of a hypothesis to account for the facts already collected, and to serve as a guide in the collection of fresh observations and experiments, especially the latter. For Bacon, the hypothesis was supplied ready-made in his Forms, or at least a finite number of possible hypotheses were supplied, and all that Induction had to do was to decide between these. In this respect Galileo's theory of Induction was certainly superior to Bacon's.

### VIII

Galileo's view of Induction was derived solely from the physical Sciences, especially Astronomy. As an account of the method of Physics it was almost faultless, but it was only applicable where quantitative exactness could be obtained. He aimed only at obtaining an answer to the question *how* a thing takes place, not *why* it should be so and not otherwise. Like Bacon, he begins with the collection of facts; but unlike Bacon, he needs these only as a help to analysis; they are not necessarily collected according to method, and it will often be quite unnecessary to have large numbers of them. What he wants them for is merely in order to make a quantitatively exact analysis of them: when this had been done the next step is to frame a hypothesis as to how they happen. Then we proceed by deduction to deduce the results of some imagined set of conditions from our hypothesis, and to verify these results by experiment or observation.

I have mentioned above one respect in which Galileo's method is superior to Bacon's; another very important merit is the quantitative exactness of its results; at least this is a merit where quantitative exactness is possible, i.e. in the mathematical sciences, but elsewhere it makes the method inapplicable, thus giving Bacon's method the merit of greater universality. There is a third respect in which Galileo is superior to Bacon, that is, in his view of the importance and use of the facts to be gathered before framing a hypothesis. Bacon, owing largely to his Forms, thought the mere methodical collection of instances all-important: Galileo saw that these instances were really only needed to suggest a hypothesis, and that the important thing was the subsequent verification of the hypothesis by fulfilment of deduced results as tested by experiment or (where that was impossible) by observation. Also in asking how, rather than why, things occurred, Galileo was more at one with modern Science than Bacon; but this is perhaps hardly a question of method. Generally speaking, Galileo's method is best in the mathematical Sciences, Bacon's in the rest.

seem to have clearly realized how motion was to be measured; the usual
meaning of quantity of motion in his day was what is now called momentum, but momentum, unlike energy, has direction as well as magnitude,
and Descartes believed that direction of motion could be altered without the
interference of other matter. He probably meant momentum independently
of direction; the product of mass into velocity summed throughout the universe ($\Sigma mv$).

Although he laid little stress on it, Descartes had some notion of experiment; in the *Method* for instance (Chap. VI) there is a passage where he refers
to crucial instances as in some cases the only way of deciding between two or
more possible explanations. But he regards experiment as a *pis aller*, as a last
resource when those of reasoning have been exhausted. He began his researches into nature, he tells us, by examining what were the most general
causes of things which he drew "from certain seeds of truth which are naturally in our souls"; [these appear to have been certain simple natures, not
like Bacon's forms, but unanalysable concepts and propositions, such as
extension, will, and Euclid's first axiom]. He then proceeded to deduce the
most general effects possible from these simple natures, and to look about
him at phenomena with his à priori principles at hand for explaining them.
He thus began his explanations of nature from within, from his intuitive
certainty as to fundamental principles; observation and experiment came at
a later stage, to help him in the application.

IV

Matter and mind can interact in Descartes, but each can be conceived without relation to the other and does not depend in any way upon the other for
its existence. The dependence of each is only upon God; God is the only true
substance, the only self-subsistent reality. God ought to have been conceived pantheistically, but whether from fear of ecclesiastical censure or
from some other cause, this was not the case. Matter and mind had for
Descartes a real existence, and God was not immanent in the world; he was
regarded as an external Creator.

In this view there are obvious inconsistencies, most of which are not to be
found in Spinoza. In Spinoza there is one substance only, i.e. God. God has
two attributes, thought and extension; God is immanent in the world, and is
the whole of what is; finite minds and finite portions of matter exist only in
so far as they are God. Mind and matter no longer interact because they run
completely parallel: any one fact about God may be viewed either under the
attribute of extension or under that of thought, and there are no longer two
substances but one only. Nevertheless Spinoza's monism is not so complete
as it might be, since extension, for us, exists only as thought about, and the
two attributes of God are therefore unnecessary; thought alone would have

been sufficient.

## V

Locke's polemic seems to rest on a misunderstanding. Descartes' innate ideas are not necessarily always present to the mind, but are only ideas which the mind has in itself the power of producing (*v.* replies to Hobbes's objections). They are compared by Descartes to hereditary gout, that is, they are tendencies or faculties which are elicited when a suitable occasion arises, not ready-made ideas existing in the mind of the infant, or persisting (as Hobbes would have it that they ought to do) in deep sleep.

10     Thus stated, the doctrine is one which Locke himself held. What Locke would seem to have denied is, that we have any ideas which *in time* precede experience; for he acknowledges that we have ideas not derived *from* experience, though elicited *by* it. Ideas of relation generally, and the idea of substance (which is not for Locke an idea of relation) are he says "the inventions and creatures of the understanding", though they are obtained by comparison of ideas which arose from sensation. The confusion in Locke's mind of the psychological genesis of knowledge with the enquiry into its logical order and validity when once it has sprung into existence, is probably the cause of this misunderstanding of Descartes, and it seems to be on a pure 20 misunderstanding that the whole controversy rests.

## VI

Descartes' views on ethical subjects depend on his division of psychical processes into those depending on the body and those produced by the pure activity of the soul. The latter as a rule are nobler and more joyous, for he seems to think that moral excellence is always accompanied by joy, and that grief is on the whole a sign of moral weakness. I am not quite sure whether this doctrine extends to his illustration of the man who weeps for his deceased wife because of the physical effect of the apparatus of mourning, while in his inmost heart he feels a great joy, which is purely intellectual and 30 unadulterated by any physical admixture; but Descartes' language certainly suggests that the latter feeling is more commendable than the former.—His duality is carried through consistently, and applied to perceptions, passions and volitions; all these may be either due to the influence of the body, in which case they are confused and untrustworthy; or to the soul alone, in which case they are noble and good. Passions of the second class he prefers to call emotions; and as to the will, it is only the will determined by purely intellectual motives which can rightly be called free; this freedom is not the liberty of indifference, on the contrary the will is never so little indifferent as when it is moved by pure perception of the good; thus his liberty is that of 40 self-determination, and it is in moral action only that freedom is completely realized. I do not know of any place where his ethical views are very clearly stated, but at the end of the second and third sections of the *Passions* he speaks as if virtue consisted in freeing ourselves from the bodily passions and devoting ourselves to a life of pure contemplative intellect, in which our actions are all determined by pure reason; this doctrine, if worked out, would lead to a theoretic asceticism, though it might allow practically such indulgence in the pleasures of sense as the reason was willing to permit, provided these were never pursued for their own sakes but always only after the reason had had its say. His doctrine seems to contain the germ of Spinoza's intellectual love of God and indeed of Spinoza's ethical system generally; but it is not logically worked out, and is only here and there hinted at in a fragmentary fashion; and fear of the church, if nothing else, would have kept him from pushing it to its logical conclusions.

In the *Discours* Descartes gives three provisional rules of conduct, but these do not constitute an Ethic, for they were only accepted as rules while he doubted everything, and were palpably not regarded as necessarily valid but only as more convenient than any others for a person without settled convictions.

### VII

Geulinx's modifications of Descartes were mostly in the direction of Spinozism; he tried to bring more consistency into the doctrine of substance and of God. Finite things exist only by negation; God is the only Reality, and finite spirits are only limitations of his being. But God is Spirit only, so that extension is contained in him only *eminenter*; and here Geulinx has some difficulty, not having the courage to say, like Spinoza, that God *is* also material. The relation of finite spirits to God is quite different from that of finite portions of extension to him. The former are self-limitations of God and differ from him only by their limitations; remove these, and they become God. But as to extension, Geulinx speaks, like Spinoza, of Body as one, of which finite bodies are portions; strictly speaking, Body is indivisible, and this removes one of Descartes' difficulties in including it in the nature of God. But Geulinx left the question of extension in rather a muddle, and led the way for Spinoza's two coordinate attributes.

The chief advance of Geulinx on Descartes was his occasionalism. This arose from the proposition that nothing can be truly regarded as a cause unless it not only knows the effect it will produce but also how it will produce it. Thus not only can there be no interaction between mind and matter, but even between different bodies there can be none. God is the only efficient cause; on the occasion of our volition he moves our bodies in the way we will. This does not preclude human activity altogether, but such activity can only affect the active spirit itself. The soul appears to be as rigidly confined within itself as a Leibnitzian monad. Geulinx's occasionalism is not to be confounded with the Pre-established Harmony of Leibnitz, but in a note to his *Ethics* there is a passage suggesting the latter doctrine. He gives the Leibnitzian illustration of the two clocks for the correspondence of soul and body. This passage appears however (Bouillier, p. 288, Vol. I) to be by the editor of the *Ethics* and not by Geulinx himself. It is certainly not quite consistent with occasionalism.

In one point he approaches Malebranche rather than Spinoza. He denies that God has the power of altering eternal truths, such as that $2+3 = 5$. If we allow God this power, we must allow him the power of making himself
10 non-existent, for the one is no more impossible than the other.

IX

All the developments of Cartesianism turn on the doctrine of substance; Geulinx, Malebranche and Spinoza had taken hold of the God of Descartes and given him undue prominence, to the final destruction of the individual in Spinoza; Leibnitz, by a natural reaction emphasized the Self, to which Descartes had given in his system a prominence quite as great as that of God. The mark of substantiality in Leibnitz is activity; we know ourselves as active, and therefore as substances. Thus there is not one substance, but many; every individual is a substance, self-existent and independent of all
20 others. It is true Leibnitz says we all owe our existence and preservation to the continual exertion of the creative power of God, and praises the schoolmen for regarding preservation as just as great an exertion of divine power as creation; but this has rather the air of an after-thought, and it is difficult to see what there is left for God to do in Leibnitz's world, unless it be to set a-going the pre-established harmony. By emphasizing the individual to such an extent he is forced to sacrifice the universal; his monads are windowless, and though they picture the world none of them would know the difference if they went on picturing while the rest of the world was destroyed.
30    Leibnitz accepts Descartes' ontological proof, which he regards as the only valid one; but he tries to improve it by substituting the word *necessary* for the word *perfect*. From the mere idea of a necessary being, if only such a being be possible, it follows that such a being must exist.—But although in this matter he is as purely rationalist as his predecessors, he naturally combines with his worship of activity a revolt against the purely logical world of Spinoza; he adds the principle of Sufficient Reason to that of Contradiction, and allows God to be ethically determined instead of only logically.—Many passages in Descartes would countenance this view; indeed his whole argument from the veracity of God rests on it. Thus Spinoza and Leibnitz are
40 both latent in Descartes, and by removing Descartes' inconsistencies either of them can be derived, according as we begin from God or from the Self.

# 28

# Paper on Hobbes [1894]

THIS PAPER WAS written for Stout's course on the history of philosophy. The manuscript is undated but was probably written in the spring of 1894. The absence of Russell's usual method of identifying his term papers suggests that the text is not complete. Since the questions set for this paper are not known, it is possible that there was an additional section or sections. The manuscript has no marginal comments by either Russell or Stout.

The copy-text is the manuscript (RA 220.010300), consisting of seventeen leaves.

HOBBES WAS BORN at Malmesbury in 1588; he received a good classical education at school, and afterwards went to Magdalen Oxford, where Scholasticism was still rampant. The nominalism which he retained to the end of his life may perhaps be due to his education at the university. In 1608 he was engaged as tutor to the son of Lord Hardwicke (afterward Lord Devonshire), with whom he went to France in 1610, and apparently made the acquaintance of many of the leading men in Paris. On his return he became one of Bacon's secretaries, and is said to have helped
10  Bacon in translating his works into Latin. It is remarkable that in spite of this connection and of the fact that Bacon used to speak of him as his favourite secretary, Hobbes never once mentions him in all his writings, and his philosophy bears very little trace of Bacon's influence. About this time also Hobbes translated Thucydides, in whom he was probably specially interested as being opposed to democracy. He was in all five times in Paris, and appears to have profited much by his intercourse with prominent men in that city. During his third journey, about 1640, he began Euclid, having picked him up by accident one day. He opened him at the 47th Proposition and was immediately fascinated by him. "By God, this is impossible" he
20  exclaimed, and read the earlier Propositions to which reference was made in the proof. From this time onwards he was much interested in Geometry: the manner of proof especially struck him as admirable, and he tried as far as possible to use the mathematical method in his Philosophy. It was during the third journey also that motion first occurred to him as the principle on which to explain the world; this may have been due to his intercourse with Gassendi. In 1639 he wrote (after his return to England) the *Elements of Law*, published in 1650 in two parts under the titles *Human Nature* and *de Corpore Politico*. Soon after writing this treatise, he went to France to escape the turmoil of the Civil War, and remained there until about 1651, in which
30  year the *Leviathan* appeared. The *de Corpore* was published in 1655, the *de Homine* in 1658, thus both during the Protectorate. *Behemoth*, a dialogue on the Civil War, appeared shortly before his death, against his wish. He died in 1679, at the age of ninety-one.

II

Hobbes defines Philosophy as "the knowledge we acquire, by true ratiocination, of appearances or apparent effects, from the knowledge we have of some possible production or generation of the same; and of such production as has been or may be, from the knowledge we have of the effects." Thus to philosophize is to reason; the word *cause* in the above definition is used not
40  in a Baconian but in a Spinozistic sense, as equivalent to logical ground.

Cause and effect are coexistent in Hobbes, and their connection must be transparent to reason; thus the revolution of a line of constant length about one of its ends is the *cause* of a circle: there is no empirical conjunction of events, but rather cause and effect are the same fact viewed from different points of view. This conception is quite different from Bacon's, and the inverse procedure is quite different from Bacon's induction: it consists in assigning hypothetical conditions from which if realized the phenomena would flow; but here we are confined to hypothesis, as owing to plurality of causes we can never be sure these conditions were actually those from which the phenomena did flow.—Thus philosophy is for Hobbes entirely a matter  10 of Logic, of logical analysis and synthesis, or addition and subtraction as he calls them; he is as purely rationalist as Spinoza.

III

Hobbes has been accused of making truth a mere matter of naming, but this is not really the case, though his words often lend themselves readily to such an interpretation. Generality, he says, is not in things, but in our mode of considering them. He defines a *name* as "the voice of a man arbitrarily imposed for a mark to bring to his mind *some conception concerning* the thing on which it is imposed", having previously defined a *mark* as a *sensible* thing of which we make use at pleasure to call up to mind a *thought* similar to one we  20 have had before. Thus words register our thoughts and help us to recall them, since names are easily recalled. Names are "signs of our conceptions"; one universal name is imposed on many things for their similitude in some quality or other accident. Thus universality is not only in names, but also in conceptions. For every conception we have a separate name, and many conceptions of the same thing are possible, so that many names of the same thing are also possible. Thus, he says, "of two appellations, by the help of the little verb *is*, we make affirmation or negation"; and such affirmation is true if the later name signifies all that the former does. The truth of a judgment is thus not merely a matter of naming, for names corre-  30 spond to conceptions, and universality in conceptions depends on some common quality in things themselves. It is true Hobbes says "true and false are attributes of speech, not of things" and "the first truths were arbitrarily made by those that first of all imposed names on things, or received them from the imposition of others", but all he means is that truth and falsehood are concerned with judgment, and that judgment is impossible without names. *Error*, which he distinguishes from falsity, is possible without names; as "when we expect the thing which shall not be". The same doctrine is of course easily extended to syllogism: *A* and *B* are names of the same thing, and so are *B* and *C*; therefore *A* and *C* are names of the same  40 thing.

Thus as to the function of names in reasoning Hobbes seems on the whole to have been in the right; his error lay in supposing that there was no universality in things. Thus the names which he regards as individual, such as Socrates, are really names for a thing pursued through many variations; they involve a synthesis of many particulars, and so are universal; and the same holds of *things* altogether.

IV

The fundamental principles of philosophy are definitions, says Hobbes; now a definition resolves the subject when it may; when it cannot, it exemplifies it. Thus the fundmental concepts cannot be resolved: their definitions can only exemplify them. He seems to hold that one concept, motion, is the most fundamental of all; and whenever he can, he explains others by means of this one, which is the key of the universe.

In his account of *space* he is inconsistent with his materialistic opinions; if he had pursued the method pursued here he could hardly have continued to regard motion as more ultimate than consciousness. To discover the nature of space he begins by feigning a world in which everything is annihilated except one mind, which he supposes to see phantasms of external things, in memory or imagination. These phantasms, he says, must appear as external, as in space: "if we consider not that the thing was such and such, but only that it had a being without the mind, we have presently a conception of what we call space; an imaginary space, indeed, because a mere phantasm, but yet that very thing men call so." "No man calls it space for being already filled, but because it may be filled." Hence his definition of space is "the phantasm of things existing without the mind simply", which seems almost the same as Kant's "form of the external sense".—In this exposition he does not so much depart from his analytic method of discovering definitions as from his principle that "the causes of universal things, where there are any, are manifest of themselves ... they have one universal cause, motion." And from his account of space it ought to have followed for him that Geometry is independent of the conception of motion.

*Body*

Hobbes defines body as that which, having no dependence upon our thought, is coincident or coextended with some part of space. The extension of a body is the same as its magnitude or real space, but this is not dependent on our cogitation as imaginary space is. The accidents of a body do not really belong to it, though some (such as extension) are inseparable from the conception of it: but an accident is "the manner by which any body is conceived".

## Motion

Although everything else was to be explained by motion, Hobbes provides us with a definition of motion. It is "the continual relinquishing of one place and acquiring of another". Of course it is impossible to define space, motion and time; and by the word *continual* Hobbes has to introduce time, thus making his definition depend on space and time, and later on he makes this dependence on time explicit, though he had formerly defined time as "the phantasm of before and after in motion". Of course such circles are unavoidable if definitions are taken as fundamental principles, and fundamental concepts are thought to need formal definitions.—But here he says, 10 referring to this definition of time, that it is impossible to conceive motion without time, for, time being the phantasm, i.e. conception, of motion, this would be to conceive motion without motion.—What is moved is not in the same place for any time, however short, by which Zeno's antinomy is solved. Line, surface and solid are defined by motion, starting from the point. Quantity of motion is defined as what is now called *momentum*, as in Newton's Second Law. Newton's first law, that a body will continue to be at rest or in uniform motion except in so far as it is compelled to alter its state by action from without, is stated; the action from without being however restricted to contact-action. This law, though known as Newton's, was 20 discovered by Galileo, from whom I suppose Hobbes learnt it.—Generally the chapter on motion seems to shew some acquaintance with the Physics of his day and is in the main sound.

## Cause

A body is said to *act* on another when it generates or destroys some accident in it. The accident generated is called the effect, and the accident in the generating body owing to which the effect was generated is called the *cause*. But this is a partial view of the cause, for the final effect is different according to the varying accidents of the body on which it is produced as well as to those of the agent. Hence "cause simply taken is the sum of all the accidents 30 both of agents and patients, how many soever they be", from which the effect follows *necessarily at the same instant*, and without any of which the effect couldn't follow. The aggregate of accidents in the agent is called the *efficient* cause, in the patient, the *material* cause. Both these are partial, and either alone may fail of its effect. But the *entire* cause must produce its effect instantaneously as soon as it is present; and every effect has a *necessary* cause. Also the same cause, if repeated, must always produce the same effect.—Formal and final causes Hobbes dismisses as both really efficient.

This is the account which Hobbes gives when he is definitely discussing causation; but elsewhere he uses the word in a sense which at any rate seems 40 at first sight more rationalistic. In the "Computation or Logic" it is throughout equivalent to logical ground; while in the above it sounds much

more like the modern scientific view of cause, as homogeneous with its effect, both being phenomena. However if we lay stress on the fact that in the
above Hobbes regards the effect as contemporaneous with its cause, and as
following from it necessarily (i.e. by a logical, not merely a physical, necessity), the two views will be found perhaps to be essentially the same. "All
mutation is motion" he says, and also no motion is communicated except by
contact-action; and probably he thought this manner of communicating
motion self-evident, so that when motion was produced by impact it might
be regarded as deducible by a logical necessity, and as of a certainty in its
10 operations equal to that of Geometry. This may have been the manner in
which the two accounts were reconciled in his mind.

### Possibility

Possible, says Hobbes, is merely another name for our ignorance; there
can be no sphere of real possibility. If all the conditions of an effect are
present, the effect follows necessarily; if not, it is impossible. This view was
of course unavoidable with his rationalistic view of causation, and was
applied by him to mental as well as to physical phenomena. He is throughout as thoroughly determinist as Spinoza.

V

20 Hobbes distinguishes the *real* space of a body, or its magnitude, from its
*imaginary* space or place; the former it carries about with it and maintains
independently of us, the latter is phantasmal and depends on the subject. To
prove that the former is real and that there is a real external world, Hobbes
appeals to causality. The phantasm exists in us and must have some cause;
and it is a fundamental precept with Hobbes that the ultimate cause of everything is motion. Hence the phantasms must arise through motion, and
presuppose real bodies as their cause.

Of course this argument is a very palpable *petitio principii*; it assumes that
body is more ultimate than consciousness, that motion is the fundamental
30 principle; that is, it assumes Hobbes's materialism.

VI

The body, throughout Hobbes's writings, is always put first, as being prior
to the mind in scientific explanation. Thus he says that all conceptions
spring from external things; these external things act on the senses by producing motions in the bodily organs, and the impressions of the senses produce *conceptions*. While the action of the thing is present, the conception is
also called sense; but afterwards the conception remains, but decays by little
and little. Hobbes uses the words *conception* and *image* as interchangeable;

he never regards a conception as anything but a mental picture, arising from sense. He states four propositions in which he refers the secondary qualities to the percipient: they are as follows:

(1) The subject in which colour and image inhere is not the object perceived.
(2) There is nothing without us which we call image or colour.
(3) "The image or colour is only the apparition unto us of the motion, agitation, or alteration which the object worketh in the brain or spirits or some internal substance of the head".
(4) And the same holds of the other senses besides sight.　　　　10

The third of these rules gives about as clearly as any passage Hobbes's view of the relation of Body and Mind; he never questioned that all was to be referred to motion (though in his psychology he often forgot it), but he did not endeavour, like DesCartes, to manufacture any careful physiological theory as to the manner of the interaction of mind and body, because it did not occur to him, as to DesCartes, that such interaction involved any difficulty or perplexity.

As to Association of Ideas, Hobbes enunciated the essential points in the doctrine, but without the sweeping generality of later Associationists. He says "Not every thought to every thought succeeds indifferently. But as we 20 have no imagination whereof we have not formerly had sense, in whole or in parts, so we have no transition from one imagination to another whereof we never had the like before in our senses. The reason whereof is this. All fancies are motions within us, the relics of those made by the sense: and those motions that immediately succeeded one another in the sense continue also together after sense, insomuch as that the former coming again to take place, and be predominant, the latter followeth, by coherence of the matter moved." But he allows that Desire may provide a thread to guide the train of Ideas, so as to choose between various transitions which have formerly occurred in sense. With this modification the above passage seems to give the 30 doctrine of Association of Ideas in its barest form, as allowing no connection except that of actual sense-perception. Hobbes is careful to observe, however, that so many different successions occur in sense that it might seem perfectly arbitrary which thought succeeds which, so many different successions are possible while still following sense. Of course if one wished to criticize Hobbes and the Associationists generally, one might say that the same succession never recurs; the same idea (if taken on its psychical or on its sensuous side if it is sensuous) never recurs; the idea is the same only in its *meaning*, which it does not derive from sense.

Conceptions, as we have seen, are only internal motions in the head; these motions, when they proceed to the heart, either help or hinder the vital motion; in the former case they give pleasure, in the latter, pain. The *motion in which consists* pleasure and pain, says Hobbes, is *endeavour*; and this endeavour is desire or aversion according as it is towards or away from the thing which is causing the motion. Thus all delight is appetite, and presupposes a further end; there is no contentment but in proceeding. Felicity consists in prospering, not in having prospered. We suppose a thing will be
10 only in so far as we know of a power which will produce it; therefore expectation of pleasure to come involves belief in one's own power. Power is for Hobbes the supreme object of desire; it consists only in the excess of one man's above another's, for equal powers destroy each other. Thus life is like a race, in which we have no goal but to outstrip others: all the passions are deduced from this one desire.—In all this Hobbes closely resembles Spinoza; except that Spinoza throws a tinge of mysticism into his whole account and into his view of power. Like Spinoza, Hobbes simply studies the passions scientifically, without praise or blame; like him, he regards power as the aim of all our striving, and human life as essentially constituted
20 by striving; as in Spinoza, pleasure consists in the acquisition of power, or in passing from a lower to a higher perfection (for to Spinoza power and perfection are synonymous). They agree also in the view of the opposition between the claims of the individual and those of society, in their universal enmity between individuals, and in the impossibility of attainment except at another's expense; but Hobbes has no hint of the ascetic self-abnegation by which alone Spinoza thinks this continual striving can be overcome. For Hobbes the remedy consists merely in a compromise, in a social contract; all are to agree to give up their power to a sovereign, so that they may live in peace with each other and be subject to no vexations except those of the
30 king. A settled order of society seems impossible for Hobbes except by some such contract; he recognizes no *social* desires, none which can be satisfied otherwise than at the expense of others; though in all this he is not nearly so sweeping or so definite as Spinoza. But this analysis of the passions is very defective; it has purchased unity and simplicity at the expense of truth. Of course passions arise from unsatisfied desires, and would therefore be impossible if there were no limitations to our powers; but it does not therefore follow that they *are* desires for power. If we wish for a clue to a classification of passions, it is well to begin with simple cases, as the passions of a civilized man are so complex as to seem at first quite impossible to classify. But if we
40 take even animals, their passions are not only those that spring from desire for power; if this class be roughly identified with those that belong to self-preservation, there remains still the sexual instinct, and in females the ma-

ternal instinct. These give rise to desires and passions just as powerful as those connected with self-preservation, but are radically distinct, and irreducible to the former. Perhaps the passions of human beings might be classified biologically as products and bye-products of these instincts, though even then it is hard to see where (for instance) artistic pleasures are to be placed. And even if we succeeded, having begun at the lower end of the scale we should have missed the most interesting aspect of the passions; for as these point into the future, and depend on an imagined good not represented as actual, the better way to view them would be as a striving after some perfection in which all desires are represented as satisfied, not extinguished by asceticism as in Spinoza, but allayed by attainment. Such a state is of course inconceivable if life is really a race with no goal but to outstrip our neighbours; for if we are satisfied our neighbours are not, and vice versa. But if (as seems at least possible) we could combine the satisfaction of our own desires with that of other people, as is the case with love and benevolence (which come in awkwardly in Hobbes's list), then this opposition ceases, and self and the world are brought into harmony. And the partial realization of such a state of things would seem a more natural way of accounting for the existing social organism than Hobbes's social contract.

Hobbes's account of *pity* is one of the most ingenious in all the list of the passions. "Pity is the imagination or fiction of future calamity to ourselves, proceeding from the sense of another man's calamity". And hence we pity the undeserving most, because where calamity is undeserved it seems more likely to happen to ourselves. For the same reason we pity those we love more than other people, because we think them deserving of felicity.—In all these statements there is a great deal of truth, but it is only one-sided, and has missed the altruistic element which makes pity interesting and which is really the most important side of it. Of course it is true that we do not pity people simply in proportion to their sufferings, but that sufferings which seem likely to occur to ourselves move us more than others. But in explaining hardness of heart, which he says proceeds from slowness of imagination, Hobbes seems to have accidentally and inadvertently hit on a much truer explanation of this fact. We cannot thoroughly pity a person suffering from toothache if we have never had it ourselves, and no doubt in this case we do not think this calamity likely to befall us; but the reason we are unable to feel pity is because we are unable to realize the other person's sufferings, and probably think he is making a great fuss about nothing; which no one who has had toothache is likely to think.

The emotion accompanying laughter, says Hobbes, "hath no name but is always joy; and in what we triumph when we laugh hath never yet been declared by anybody". We laugh only from what is sudden and unexpected; this is either some unexpected defect in others, or some unexpected ability in ourselves. In the simile of the race, "to see another fall is disposition to laugh".—This account seems to me admirable and thoroughly sound so far as it goes except that I doubt if an unexpected ability in ourselves makes us laugh, unless it is very minute; but it omits a good many things which make us laugh. I suppose Hobbes might account for our laughing at a pun by saying that in others we regard it as an unexpected defect and in ourselves as an unexpected ability; but in others it is often sadly the reverse of unexpected, and yet we still feel disposed to laugh, when we read Hood say.— Also Hobbes does not observe what seems very characteristic of laughter, that it only accompanies small emotions (with the curious exception of very intense and sudden grief). I believe the only element which is common to all the things that make us laugh is unexpectedness or incongruity; and this not normally unless the surprise is either agreeable or neutral, which is the reason why the small defects of others are peculiarly amusing, for that they are a source of pleasure it would be absurd to deny. But I don't know how to account for standing jokes, which are often the most amusing. However, as to these, Hobbes's account is equally inadequate.

# 29

# On the Distinction between the Psychological and Metaphysical Points of View  [c. 1894]

THIS PAPER WAS probably written for Ward's course on metaphysics in the spring of 1894. Although its subject matter corresponds very closely with part of that course, it is impossible to be certain that it was an assigned paper since no record of the assignment has survived and the manuscript bears no tutorial comments. Moreover, the paper's format is different from that of Russell's other tutorial papers. That the paper was handed in to a tutor is suggested by its being labelled "Distinction between Psychological / and Metaphysical Points of View" on the verso of the last leaf, and its being signed "B. Russell" at the foot of the last leaf. The title used here is found at the head of the first leaf.

The copy-text is the manuscript (RA 220.010310), which consists of seven leaves.

I N THE SCIENCE of Psychology we are concerned with mental states as such; we analyse them into their simplest constituents, we study the laws of their generation and decay; if possible, we find out their physiological antecedents or concomitants (though this strictly speaking belongs to Psychophysics). We accept every mental state, or psychosis, as a fact, just as in Astronomy we accept the motions of the heavenly bodies. We try to discover causal laws as to the succession of such states, and to discover what, in isolation from the outer world, their true nature and composition may be.

But, besides their existence and their nature, our ideas have what we may
10 call *meaning*. This word is used to denote their objective reference, that is, their reference to something beyond themselves, to something which they are not, but with which they are intimately concerned. And this aspect of our ideas is more interesting to the plain man, is indeed altogether more that which presents itself in every-day life, than the psychological aspect. This may be illustrated by pretty nearly every state of mind, though in the case of pure sensation this distinction between subject and object is perhaps hardly as yet explicit, and the reference to anything beyond itself is very vague. If I lie in a field on a hot day with my eyes shut, and feel sleepily the heat of the sun, the buzz of the flies, the slight tickling of a few blades of grass, it is
20 possible to get into a frame of mind which seems to belong to a much earlier stage of evolution; at such times there is only what Bradley would call "a vague mass of the felt"; I do not reflect on the outside causes of the various blurred and indistinct sensations, nor on the fact that I am feeling these sensations. Perhaps we may hope that there are also possible states of mind where we are above the distinction of subject and object, as in pure sensation we are below it; but to pursue such a possibility would be to plunge into mysticism, from which for the present we shall do well to keep free.

Neglecting, then, such extreme cases, and confining ourselves to more normal states of consciousness, whether cognitive or volitional, we see that
30 it is the objective reference which first attracts our attention. If I see a table, the normal reflection is "There is a table", not "I am in a state of mind in which a table appears to my sight." Indeed in each of these I have transcended the immediate datum, in the one case by judging that there is a table, in the other by judging that I have a certain perception (which, be it observed, is an entirely different frame of mind from that in which I have the perception, and contains knowledge only obtainable by memory and retrospection). It is extremely important to realize that the psychological reflection is a transcending of the given every whit as much as the physical; indeed even more if anything. It was the failure to notice this which led to
40 Berkeley and Subjective Idealism, and made people suppose their knowledge of their own states of mind was more certain and ultimate than that of the outside world. The experience is originally given as one whole, a subjective idea with an objective reference; thought splits the whole into two parts,

196

relegating the one to Physics, the other to Psychology; Metaphysics endeavours, somewhat lamely, it is to be feared, to undo the work of thought and restore the original concrete unity; or, as has been said, to stitch Cassim together again after the robbers have hewn him asunder.—The above instance was from a cognitive element of consciousness: similar remarks apply to the volitional. Suppose I desire to eat an apple: there is here (1) a subjective state of mind, springing from certain causes, hunger, gourmandise or what not; this is what interests the psychologist (2) an objective reference, to the apple namely; this latter is what interests the student of Ethics. The state of mind *is* (to the psychologist) a state of tension accompanied or produced by a certain state of the body, having definite causal antecedents and consequents just like any other event, physical or mental; but it *means* (to the student of Ethics) a felt want, a contrast between the ideal and the actual, the craving for a fuller self-realization, the momentary identification of the apple with my Good; and he has to discuss how far such identification is moral, just as the Physicist has to discuss how far our perception is correct. Here again the metaphysician endeavours to combine the two; for him the absolute chasm between the ideal and the real, which Ethics has produced by abstraction, has somehow to be bridged: the desire and the desired have somehow to be brought into harmony.—But to pursue this idea would take us too far from our subject.

We have thus seen how a psychosis has three aspects under which it may be viewed: (1) Its existence (2) Its content (3) Its *meaning*. Psychology deals with the second alone, and in doing so it is of course perfectly justified; like every Science, it has to proceed by abstraction. But—and here lies the peculiarity of this Science—every idea in Psychology, when it comes into the mind of the discoverer or the learner, is itself a fresh idea, with all the three sides to it, whereas we are very apt, unless we take care, to regard it as the old idea which forms our matter. Let us take an instance in which this is particularly glaring, the act of belief. Any particular act of belief exists, and it has meaning; the meaning, indeed, is here evidently of overwhelming importance; but, in accordance with the principle of Psychology, we abstract from these two sides of belief, leaving it merely as a psychical phenomenon. It follows that we can no longer be concerned with the logical grounds for any belief, since these have reference to its meaning, but only to the psychological causes. But every result we obtain as to these causes is itself a proposition demanding our belief, and if we subject it to a similar criticism to that which produced it, we only get a fresh proposition, and so on *ad infinitum*, so that our procedure is circular. Of course it is none the worse for that: philosophical procedure is necessarily circular; but this affords an instance of the slipperiness of psychological reasoning, for until this point has been made clear, it might seem as if such criticism were giving valuable aid in deciding what we should believe and what not, whereas in reality it of necessity takes its stand within the matter it is criticising, and cannot therefore have any such value (directly at any rate). The same criticism applies (though less obviously) to a psychological treatment of desire, for desire is an ever-present element in every psychosis, and but for it we should not go on reading about Desire in our Psychology-books. Of course I do not mean that Psychology is not a valuable study, full of important results; I only mean, that, being from the first one-sided, its results throughout are necessarily one-sided; and that its criticism, like every criticism of fundamentals, is of necessity not thorough, and can have no direct bearing on our views as to the correctness of beliefs or the morality of desires, except on purely psychological subjects.

Metaphysics then endeavours to bridge the chasm between physics and psychology. Seeing that the objective reference of an idea is known as intuitively and immediately as its subjective nature (if not more so), it frankly accepts both; it allows a world other than the individual mind, concerning which we have knowledge and desire; its criticism is not of these themselves, but of a world concerning which they are possible: *given* Self and the world in relation, the problem is to make each term and their relation intelligible; and Self and the World are given, because the only alternative is blank and absolute scepticism.

# Part v

# Graduate Essays in Ethics

# On Pleasure: Its Definition,
# Its Causes and Conditions, and the Possibility
# of Making It the End of Rational Action  [1893]

THE EARLIEST OF Russell's writings as a Moral Sciences student, this paper was written for Sidgwick's course on ethics. The verso of the last leaf reads "*B. Russell / Essay on Pleasure / July 1893*"; the shorter title used here comes from the heading on the first leaf. Russell's notebook for Sidgwick's lectures records the assignment thus: "Write *Essay* on Pleasure: causes and conditions and possibility of making maximum pleasure end of rational action. Definition also. For Monday" (I: 8). The manuscript bears a number of critical remarks by Sidgwick, mostly concerned with section II. The verso of the first leaf bears some fragmentary pencilled notes in Russell's hand, possibly some rough working for an example in syllogistic.

The copy-text is the manuscript (RA 220.010100), which has six leaves.

# I. DEFINITION OF PLEASURE

IN POPULAR USAGE, a pleasure denotes a desirable feeling: and abstracting from this, pleasure may be used to denote the quality of agreeableness in such feeling, or more loosely agreeable feeling in general. For quantitative purposes pain may be considered as negative pleasure: in this case we may define pleasure more generally as the (positive or negative) quantity of desirability in feeling: but this use of the word does not accord at all with that in common use and should therefore only be used where it is necessary to balance pleasures and pains quantitatively considered, as it may then take the place of the longer phrase "excess of pleasure over pain". Except for the purposes of such discussion pleasure may then be defined as agreeable or desirable feeling: that is feeling which when present we (implicitly or explicitly) wish to prolong or, when absent, to produce.

# II. CAUSES AND CONDITIONS OF PLEASURE

The ordinarily recognised sources of pleasure and the means to its attainment by normal people are largely formulated by proverbs and common maxims, whose original purpose would seem to be usually to embody an experience of worldly wisdom in a pithy sentence. But such maxims belong in their origin to a state of society much less highly organized than the present, and it would therefore be erroneous to expect them to yield even approximately true results in any of the more complex of the relations of modern life. Some few maxims, such as that health is essential to happiness, are no doubt at all times true in the majority of cases: but where mental activity is very great this may be by no means true.—Perhaps the most obvious guiding principle in a classification of sources of pleasure would be to take them in the order of their evolutionary development: thus the satisfaction of the purely bodily appetites would come lowest, the love of ornament and brilliancy (such as the lowest savages, and even, if there be any truth in the theory of sexual selection, birds and possibly insects experience) would come next, and so on. But this method could not be rigorously carried out, as a *logical* classification would necessarily include pleasures widely apart in their origin in the same class: it would be difficult logically to separate a jackdaw's love of a gold coin from a painter's appreciation of the colouring of a Veronese. The ordinary division into physical and mental, though like most divisions its boundaries are doubtful, seems more possible to carry out: and, although not strictly, it would roughly coincide with an evolutionary distinction. There is about this division also the chief requisite of a classification: as many qualities as possible are common to all the members of either class besides that which furnishes the definition. For example all or almost all physical pleasures obey the law of diminishing return: it is a commonplace to observe how weary those who indulge purely in sensual pleasures become of these, and how they lose their power of enjoyment: indeed from a habit of inaccurate speaking which often restricts the word pleasure to sensual pleasure, this characteristic has been thought to belong to all other sources of enjoyment: but when we come to mental pleasures the contrary would rather seem to be the case. In the artistic pleasures, which form the transition from the sensual to the more purely mental, there is a mixture: while the increased knowledge derived from study increases the appreciation of the technique and so the enjoyment of the art as distinguished from its product, the enjoyment of this product *per se* probably 10 diminishes as a rule: which explains the fact that connoisseurs take pleasure in a work of art almost solely according to the skill of the artist and not according to any inherent beauty or charm about the subject. But the purely mental pleasures, the intellectual and still more the moral, grow continually keener by exercise. Those whose lives are spent in mathematical investigations become notoriously so wrapt up in their intellectual pleasures as to be almost unconscious of external events: those who make it their aim to attain the pleasures of self-approbation become at last so impressed with the nothingness of all other pleasures that they are able, like Simon Stylites, to spend forty years on a pillar; for it can scarcely be supposed that that fanatic 20 imagined heaven unattainable on easier terms.—Of pain fortunately this proposition does not hold: mental pain as well as physical loses its edge by long continuance: a certain energy seems essential to the possibility of intense pain as of intense pleasure, and this energy is in time destroyed by the very pain which requires it. Besides in the case of mental pain there is a tendency gradually to acquiesce in one's surroundings, however loathsome, or in one's misfortunes, however severe, as custom inures one to them, which is inconsistent with the long continuance of mental pain in its original intensity. At the same time every increase of susceptibility to any source of pleasure (except perhaps the purely intellectual) of course involves an in- 30 crease in susceptibility to pain.

### III.  POSSIBILITY OF MAKING PLEASURE THE END OF RATIONAL ACTION

There are two classes of objections to Hedonism which may conveniently be considered separately, especially as the first class apply strictly speaking to Utilitarianism as well as to Egoistic Hedonism, while the second class are at least different in the two cases. These may be called the practical and the theoretic objections.

  (1) *Practical objections.* These depend upon the impossibility of a strict numerical estimate of the relative values of pleasures. I shall therefore here use pleasure in the sense indicated in defining the term, i.e. as excess (posi- 40 tive or negative) of pleasure over pain. That it is impossible to obtain a

numerical estimate of a pleasure referred to some standard pleasure as unit is of course true: also it is true that for a mathematically accurate hedonistic calculus nothing short of this would be necessary. Let us consider whether a rough estimate of the comparative value of two pleasures, such as we all make fifty times a day, is likely to be sufficiently accurate to warrant our relying upon it. If so we shall be able to regulate our life upon hedonistic principles without fear of serious error. First of all: there are many cases where the balance is by no means doubtful, where yet owing to greater remoteness in the one term of the comparison there is a tendency to choose
10 the nearer good. So for example many people put off going to the dentist though they know they will have to go sooner or later and very likely have a great deal of toothache, and much more pain when they finally do go, all of which additional pain might have been avoided. So many old-fashioned Christians yield to temptation and live in fear of Hell. I once met a man who dreaded to die suddenly and unprepared as, like Mr. Worldly Wiseman, he intended to repent on his death bed: but it is obvious that on hedonistic principles the mere chance of infinite pain should have outweighed the certainty of finite pleasure. These then are cases where the comparison can be effected and yet is not acted upon: they prove that at least it would be possi-
20 ble to set up the rational pursuit of maximum pleasure as an ideal, which would in some cases at least give a definite result for a moralist to preach. In fact the comparison of pleasures of the same kind or of pains of the same kind is easy as a rule: but more complicated cases present great difficulties. In the first place one term at least of the comparison can only be represented in imagination: it may even, and in the most important decisions of life usually must, be a pleasure never yet experienced and therefore judged of by the report of others. Both these sources of inaccuracy may be minimised: the first by observing, on each occurrence of the pleasure in question, whether it is more or less pleasant than we had anticipated (e.g. most people
30 I believe find that in their recollection of a long walk the weariness and discomfort are lost sight of, as being less easily represented by the imagination, in comparison with the pleasure of the view or the conversation or other mental enjoyments); the second by taking the opinion of a person whom we have usually found in agreement with ourselves where comparison has been possible. In the second place where the terms of the comparison belong to very different classes of pleasures it is almost impossible to imagine both in the same frame of mind: when I am thinking of a soft melody of Schubert it is impossible to imagine the more brutal pleasure of physical exercise and vice versa. This is a more serious objection and I doubt
40 if it is possible to compare satisfactorily two pleasures of widely different classes. I know that my own choice in such a case depends entirely upon my frame of mind at the moment of choice, as this determines which of the two pleasures I can most completely represent in imagination. This would lead

to the establishment of differences of quality among pleasures, and Hedonism would need to be helped out by preferring some as higher to others as lower pleasures, as Mill does. However the difficulty seems to depend merely upon a defect of imagination or of recollection, which can be remedied and therefore cannot form a fatal objection to the Hedonistic theory. A further objection may be based upon the fact that a satisfactory comparison of pleasures requires considerable self-analysis and introspection, and that this habit of mind is supposed to defeat its own end and destroy happiness. No doubt if such a habit of mind becomes very persistent it does destroy pleasures, but it also destroys pains; unless either is very 10 intense. In place of pleasure, it puts the neutral feeling: Now I am enjoying myself; and instead of pain it puts: Now I am suffering pain; and neither of these is either pleasant or unpleasant. But such comparisons need not very often be gone through, since a little reflection enables us to form general rules to cover the vast majority of cases (the middle axioms of Hedonism); there seems therefore no reason why the introspective attitude should become habitual: indeed it may well be questioned whether introspection is not sure to take place frequently in some minds and seldom in others whether encouraged or not; since few things are so little under control as thoughts. Moreover as most of the best pleasures are in a high degree excit- 20 ing, these will not be interfered with unless the habit is very strong.

The second, the theoretic class of objections are directed against the whole view that happiness or pleasure is the ultimately desirable, the absolutely good: but these go so much deeper that I will say nothing further about them here.—The conclusion then as far as the practical objections are concerned would seem to be that though beset with difficulties and necessarily inaccurate a hedonistic Calculus may for practical purposes be regarded as possible: the more so as we do not require to know by how much one pleasure exceeds another, but only that it does exceed it.

# 31

# On the Foundations of Ethics [1893]

ALTHOUGH THIS PAPER is the second by Russell on ethics during his graduate year, it was written not for a tutor but for Alys Pearsall Smith. Like Paper **10**, it was meant to be a statement of views that would lead to more correspondence with her. Russell was then attending Sidgwick's lectures on ethics and as a result was reading T. H. Green's *Prolegomena to Ethics* (1883). On 25 September 1893 he wrote Alys:

> I have all but finished Green: I think it a very fine book but differ on one or two absolutely fundamental points so that I can accept very few of his conclusions though granted the few points where I disagree the rest seems logical enough. If it would amuse you I would set these forth in a little essay and if you agree with him you might answer it by another. I am told by my director of studies at Cambridge that in reading a philosophical book one should be as critical as possible.

Russell's director of studies was probably Ward.

Three days later Russell had written the essay and seems to have enclosed it with his letter of 28 September, in which he comments on the paper:

> I find on reading over what I wrote about Green (1) that I have been portentously dry, which I think does not call for an apology (2) that instead of systematically criticising Green I have set forth my own views, which I think does. It was the last thing I intended doing, as they have absolutely no philosophic interest. However I believe (though I am not sure) that the view I have put forward is that of most of the younger men at Cambridge. I was greatly shocked to perceive that it might almost be enunciated by a broad churchman as the modern form of the doctrine of heaven and hell; but it is really independent of personal immortality though the practical deductions from it might depend to some extent upon one's belief or disbelief in that dogma. The statement of my own creed has served one purpose, however, that of clearing up my own views. I used to hold every pleasure, of whatever kind, valuable; and only to be forgone if entailing greater pain. This doctrine is partly responsible for some of my most regrettable actions; though I see now that it did not really justify them itself. [One must distinguish a true ethical doctrine from one which leads to virtuous acts: for a true doctrine may

lend itself easily to sophistical reasoning].

Alys replied on 1 October that she was very interested in the paper, especially as it contained Russell's own views; but before she could criticize it she would have to finish reading Green herself. She did criticize the paper, in a letter of 27 October.

The manuscript, which is the copy-text, belongs to Mrs. Halpern; a photocopy is in the Russell Archives (REC. ACQ. 410). She has annotated it: "Sent to Alys Pearsall Smith 25.9.1893", but Russell's letter of three days later and Alys's acknowledging reply of 1 October indicate 28 September as the date the manuscript was sent. It has five leaves.

THE ART OF Living, with which Ethics is concerned, includes, in its widest sense, every other art.[1] It must therefore be based upon a Science which shall include every other Science, or at least be logically prior to every other Science; that is, it must be based on Metaphysics. Before we can determine what ought to be done, we must, if our proceeding is to be logical (which of course is not an obvious requirement), first determine what end we should consider desirable if attainable. If it be said that our moral sense is prior to Science and that this gives us direction as to particular duties, without any consideration of ends, I should admit the first
10 proposition, but should maintain that our moral sense is in itself an empty form, merely telling us that we have a duty; that the filling of this form must be (and is) derived from experience and knowledge. [This process would be similar to that by which the Categories (which are supplied à priori) derive their content from experience, so that all knowledge is subsequent to experience although some elements of it are logically prior to experience]. Such an à priori element there must be in morality: since the idea of duty is obviously not derived from phenomena. But the filling of the idea of duty must be got from considerations not purely ethical and the true procedure would seem to be

20 (1) To determine the most perfect form into which it is metaphysically possible for the universe to develop
(2) To discover (if we can) the best means to the attainment of this end.

[It is clear how we require the moral sense at this stage to make us pursue our idea of perfection however the pursuit may conflict with irrational desires]. The second of the above steps is a matter of detail in any particular branch of conduct, depending upon particular sciences: it does not concern us as philosophers, but only as actors. Let us consider further the first of these steps to a philosophic Ethic.

Green throughout considers the ultimate ideal to be a universe of perfect
30 virtue; and supposes the true end of action to be the attainment of a virtuous character by ourselves and those whom we can influence. There is undoubtedly in this view, something which commends itself to the virtuous mind: but in philosophy we must rid ourselves of the bias of virtue as of every other. And when we have effected this, we shall I think be bound to confess that Virtue can be only a means to an end, not itself an ultimate end. For what is Virtue? A disposition to obey the dictates of Ethics. These dictates must themselves then derive their sanction from some consideration which

___

1 Art is here used, in its technical sense, as a series of rules, for the guidance of practice, based upon the laws of the corresponding Science: as e.g. the Art of Engineering on the Science of
40 Mechanics.

is not ethical. Or again: the perfect state must be timeless: for any change would *ex hypothesi* mar the perfection which had been attained. There will therefore be no action in the perfect state, for action is a process in time; virtue being then that which prompts to right action must also disappear. Or again, if the last argument appears too mystical, virtue depends upon the necessity of acting, and the necessity of acting depends upon the possibility of ameliorating something; and in the perfect state this possibility will cease to exist. Or I might appeal to McTaggart's pamphlet for the proof that emotion alone would remain possible: desirable emotion for all spirits must therefore be the end of action. [The proof of this in the pamphlet depends in no way so far as I can see upon Hegelian metaphysics]. This doctrine is really Utilitarian; but by the assumption of the perfectibility of the universe it has been made to assume quite a different aspect from that of the Utilitarianism which regards every separate pleasure as of intrinsic value. This view would estimate the goodness of an act by its tendency to promote absolute harmony among spirits; since this harmony when established would involve the eternal happiness of all spirits, the passing pleasures and pains of our present existence in time would be of no account to it; and its precepts would often lead to acts which might increase human misery for a time, though it would reckon on an ultimate recompense.

As an example of the great difference between this doctrine (which yet considers happiness the one thing desirable *per se*) and ordinary Utilitarianism I may perhaps parenthetically quote another theorem of McTaggart's, of which I do not know the proof but which we can all verify approximately from our own consciousness. He says that if $y$ be our actual attainment at any given time and $x$ our greatest possible attainment in the time, our unhappiness may be represented by the product $y(x-y)$. This is largest when we have attained half as much as we might; and is zero when we have attained nothing or everything. With those whose developement is less than half what it might be it becomes our duty then to make them unhappy, as the only means to greater happiness.

To return from our digression: we can by an ethic of the above kind get out of the circle in which Green is involved in Bk. III, Chap. II; at least so far as the determination of our duty is concerned: though of course if we ask why we should do our duty, the circle reappears and must reappear if the moral sense is part of the "à priori furniture" of our minds, as I have supposed. But Green's ethic gives no method by which two conscientious people who hold different views about a particular duty can argue the question on which they differ: unless we assume, as he is inclined to do, that self-sacrifice is a good in itself. The fact that his theory suggests this result ought almost to be enough to condemn it; self-sacrifice I suppose means the performance of an action from which we expect more pain than pleasure to ourselves: and although so long as evil exists such actions will be necessary, it is difficult to see how in itself self-sacrifice can be anything but an evil. The view that I have advocated is suggested as an ameliorated Utilitarianism in §360 and objected to in §361 apparently solely on the ground of indefiniteness: this objection is largely removed by such considerations as McTaggart brings forward in his pamphlet, and it seems to me that all the ordinary duties are easily deducible from it, while it draws the limit better than Green's view between valuable self-denial and that which is purely waste, of which there is unfortunately so much just now.

But it must not be supposed that this view in any way minimises the importance of virtue: it is clearly only by action that our condition can be ameliorated, and this must always require virtue: but the more perfection is approached, the less often will self-sacrifice be necessary. When sympathy is more developed no person will be able to feel happiness in the pursuit of his own selfish pleasures if he knows he might be improving the condition of another, and thus gradually selfishness and unselfishness will become indistinguishable, the end of each will be the end of all. Previous virtue is no doubt a condition of the attainment of this state; and of course entire absence of irrational action is necessary. But in the perfect state we shall be neither virtuous nor vicious, any more than the soul is either round or square: the words will have lost their meaning.

Green is to my mind very conclusive against psychological Hedonism[2] (the doctrine that we always do act for pleasure); but this, so far from being logically involved in ethical Hedonism, is strictly speaking (as Sidgwick points out) inconsistent with it. If we always do act for our own greatest pleasure there is no point in saying we ought to do so, and no use in saying we ought not. But as this doctrine had already been rejected by Sidgwick, who kept to Ethical Hedonism, it seems almost superfluous to object to a form of the doctrine which had already been rejected by the champion of Hedonism. I do not entirely understand his objection that a sum of pleasures cannot be enjoyed all at once, but am inclined to agree with it. This objection does not apply to the form of Hedonism I have advocated.

On Free Will Green appears to me not to prove his contention at all. Of course there is in action a non-natural element (using natural as Green does) but so there is in every phenomenon, unless we arbitrarily abstract the mechanical element from the element of consciousness, which latter is just as essential to the intelligibility of the phenomenon (as indeed Green himself sees). But this does not prevent the mechanical explanation of the motion of matter; nor need it interfere with a scientific account of the determining of the will. What Green does prove is that Spirit is the ultimate reality, and that Spirit as a whole is therefore free (i.e. undetermined by anything else, there being in fact nothing else to determine it); but that in no way interferes with

---

2 Art. 221 appears to me especially acute.

the reciprocal determination of individual spirits so far as I can see. I think however that the doctrine has scarcely any ethical importance. But this is too big and too difficult a subject to discuss at the end of this little essay.

# 32

# The Relation of What Ought to Be
# to What Is, Has Been or Will Be  [1893]

THIS PAPER WAS written for Sidgwick's course on ethics. The verso of the last leaf reads: "*B. Russell / Relation of What Ought to be to What is. / Oct. 1893.*" The longer title used here is taken from the top of the first leaf. The manuscript bears a number of pencilled comments by Sidgwick, and Russell's lecture notebook (2: 22) has more extensive comments taken from Sidgwick on the topic, though these do not appear to relate specifically to Russell's paper.

The copy-text is the manuscript (RA 220.010110), consisting of three leaves.

THE QUESTION IS: When we say "*A* ought to be done" or "I ought to do *A*", do we *mean*, if we are logical, to make any assertion about the real world? It is obvious that such an assertion is *implied* in either proposition, namely the assertion of our opinion; but it is equally obvious that this is not what we mean; an opinion, of whatever kind, is not the same as the assertion that we hold the opinion; such an assertion narrates a fact, which fact is true whether we choose to narrate it or not, and indeed could not otherwise be narrated as a fact. The assertion then that *A* ought to be done is not a statement of a psychological state; it involves (whether justifiably or not) an objective element; it is supposed true for all minds. But we do not mean to state that the opinion is universally held any more than we mean to state that we hold it; it may be held only by ourselves, but whoever does not hold it is regarded as in error, and it is regarded as just as much a statement of a truth as a proposition of Euclid. But what sort of truth is it? We obviously do not mean to assert that *A* ever is done or not done; nor that under any imaginable circumstances *A* would be done. Do we mean that certain consequences will follow if *A* is done? That the agent or any other person or body of persons will derive any sort of satisfaction from the performance of *A*? This is plainly not our meaning: it may be that the particular duty in question is held because we believe that the performance of *A* will lead to some result, but if so we must regard the result attained as desirable. If we call the result attained *B*, then we have not got rid of our *ought* but merely shifted it onto *B*, thus: Acts tending to *B* ought to be done. And if we consider the matter from the point of view of formal logic, it is plain that there are only two alternatives: either (1) we hold the view that "*A* ought to be done" unreasoningly as an immediate intuition or (2) it has been obtained as the conclusion of a syllogism in which one premise must have been of the same form as itself, i.e. must have asserted that something ought to be done. Thus it is plain that propositions of the kind considered are *formally* irreducible to propositions about reality: some one or more propositions ethical in form must be regarded as axiomatic, unless such propositions are materially equivalent to some assertion about what is, has been, or will be. Thus we might attempt to found our ethics on psychology: we may say "because pleasure always is desired therefore pleasure is desirable and ought to be sought". But even accepting the premise the conclusion cannot by any method be derived from it. It is involved in the notion of "ought" that there is a power in the agent of choice between two or more courses of action; not necessarily of free choice, since we may suppose the additional motive derived from conscience to determine the will in the direction of the moral precept considered; but a power of choice is involved, that is it must be supposed that a change in the agent's will would produce a change in the resultant action and that such change might be brought about by circumstances; it would be palpably absurd to say e.g. that the earth ought to remedy the obliquity of its axis, however much we may be convinced it would be a good thing if it did so. Therefore to say that we do desire pleasure as a matter of fact lands us in this dilemma: either we must suppose it impossible we should do otherwise and then the word *ought* becomes meaningless; or we must suppose it possible to desire other things than pleasure, and then we find that psychological facts give no indication as to the rightness of following such other desires. And here pleasure of course may be replaced by any other hypothetical object of desire without affecting the argument.

The notion of *ought* implies more than that the prescribed action will
10 realize some end which is considered desirable: for a moral judgment is objective and would not be renounced if we found that the end we considered desirable was not so considered by others. Moreover the fact that some end is desirable or desired may lead to action but cannot lead of itself alone to a precept about action. I may say "True; I desire pleasure; but I see no reason why I *ought* to pursue pleasure as an end. I pursue pleasure because I desire it, but if any other person chooses to pursue some other end, well and good." And in reflecting on our self-consciousness it becomes clear that the sense of duty is entirely distinct from the sense of an end to be attained by action (though of course a particular duty may be determined by reference
20 to a desired end); that it enjoins action immediately and not the pursuit of whatever may be desired (though of course we can only act in accordance with desire: but desire may be determined by duty). Thus there seems no relation whatever between what ought to be and what is, has been, or will be.

# 33

# The Relation of Rule and End [1893]

THIS PAPER WAS written for Sidgwick's ethics course. The verso of the last leaf reads: "*The Relation of Rule and End in Ethics. / Nov. 1893.*" Russell's lecture notebooks (1: 21) contain the following, in a list of five essay topics: "(4). Rule and end, and relation of the two. (Interesting in connection with Kant)." Below is the injunction: "(Leave margin of good breadth in Essays)." Russell's left-hand margins in this essay are, in fact, much wider than previously, and Sidgwick's comments correspondingly more extensive (see the Annotation). Russell also took down the following comments from Sidgwick:

> *Relation of Rule and End In Ethics.* I agree, can't will only in order that volition subjectively right, but can make this indispensable part of my volition; in fact this state I believe normal with man of developed moral consciousness. Kant allows empirical element in every actual volition. Do not admit desire involves imagined imperfection. A will to decide by morality in a case of perplexity is a good will even I think in Kantian sense. (Lecture notebooks, 2: 30)

Nearly a year later, Russell sent Alys a paper (now lost) on Adolph Wagner's theory of motivation. (See the Introduction, sec. III.) In his covering letter he compared the new paper with "The Relation of Rule and End":

> If either thee or Logan is at all interested in my Essay, there is another at Friday's Hill, treating the same point more ethically and less psychologically, called "Relation of Rule and End in Ethics"—with Sidgwick's comments in the margin. It was much the best Essay I ever wrote on Ethics.... In spite of the pencil comments, it pleased Sidgwick very much, and he said in class that he had been observing his own motives closely for days to test a certain point in it. That was a petty triumph for me! (12 Oct. 1894)

As Alys liked the paper on Wagner, Russell referred her again to this paper: "I'm glad my Essay interests thee! The one at Friday's Hill is better, much—it's about the best bit of work I ever did in the way of close reasoning, though there are several fallacies in it, which Sidgwick has spotted" (13 Oct.).

The copy-text is the manuscript (RA 220.010150), which consists of three leaves.

WRITERS ON ETHICS may be divided into those who consider the Good to be of the nature of Will and those who consider it to be of the nature of Feeling. These two views might possibly be harmonized as far as results are concerned: but in theory they must remain fundamentally distinct. If we adopt the former view, a good Will has worth in itself and apart from the consequences of the act willed: the logical procedure then will be first to determine if possible the nature of a good Will, and the rules by which it must be guided: and then, if we choose, to try to discover some End or Ends which will be furthered by the performance of acts dictated by these rules. The rules are thus logically prior: the ends (if they exist) have only a relative worth, dependent on the worth of the Will which tends to their realization. But if we regard the good as of the nature of feeling, the value of a good Will becomes dependent; the goodness of the Will is not ultimate, but contingent on its effort to realize the End, namely the kind of feeling regarded as the Good. In this case the End is logically prior to the rules, these being determined as prescribing conduct conducive to the End. [An ethical theory might be proposed which regarded a good Will as the ultimate good, and made the production of a virtuous disposition an End: such a theory would come under the second head, but would differ radically from the Kantian view, since the excellence of particular moral acts would have to lie in their tendency to perfect character and not in the volition itself].

The question, then, whether Rule or End is the more ultimate depends upon the following: Is a moral act absolutely good *per se*, or good only as promoting some other Good? Moral praise or blame are bestowed on a man considered as an agent, i.e. as having Will. Moral Good is therefore of the nature of Will: it is the actual volition which is morally good or bad. Thus the question becomes: is moral good Good *per se*, or Good only as means to an end? According to Kant the good Will is the ultimate good itself: but it is impossible to regard it as such in acting, for the will cannot will itself: it must will some imagined result of the act willed, and this result must be regarded as good, and must be the cause of the volition. [This objection might perhaps be made clearer by imagining a perfect universe constructed on Kantian principles: this would be a universe in which every individual was willing rationally. But volition implies desire, desire implies imagined imperfection; thus a perfect universe could only exist if every rational being in the universe believed it to be imperfect.] It may be said, in objection to the above view, that when we will simply for the sake of conformity to the dictates of the moral law we are not willing any result of our volition: but such a volition requires a previous volition in which we will that virtue shall be our sole determining motive in deciding the particular practical question we have in hand: and this volition is determined by an end, namely our conformity to virtue in the immediate future. More clearly thus: suppose a

216

contingency arises in which two courses of action, A and B, are open to us and we have to decide which to follow: in order that our action may be virtuous in the Kantian sense we require first a volition (V say) in which we decide that our choice shall be influenced only by the dictates of the moral law, and then a volition (W say) in which one of the two courses, A or B, is chosen. The first of these two volitions, V, is not made as being good in itself, but as a means to the further good of choosing virtuously between A and B. Thus in willing we must always have some good in view other than the excellence of the volition, and it is impossible for us at the moment of willing to regard our volition as an end in itself. We must therefore have, in willing, some end in view other than momentary conformity to virtue: we must therefore suppose moral action not to be good in itself, but to be good only as tending to some further result. And this result must be sought as a part of the Good or as an indispensable means to a part of the Good; and this Good cannot be regarded as of the nature of Will. The Good will be our end, and the rules of Ethics will be rules for its attainment: we shall obey them, when we act consciously morally, not because they appeal to us immediately, but because we believe duty to consist in the pursuit of the Good and our rules to direct this pursuit.

# 34

# On the Definition of Virtue [1893]

THIS PAPER WAS written for Sidgwick's course on ethics. The verso of the last leaf reads "*B. Russell. / Essay on the Definition of Virtue. / Nov. 1893.*" The title used here heads the first leaf. Russell's lecture notebook (1: 39) has the essay topic: "*Essays* ⟨:⟩ Discussion of Points of Controversy between myself ⟨i.e. Sidgwick⟩ and Martineau, by Monday: *or* definition of Virtue". Russell's paper has a number of pencilled comments by Sidgwick, and his lecture notebook (1: 52) contains a brief note of some further comments from Sidgwick in answer to this question. The latter do not appear to relate specifically to Russell's answer.

The copy-text is the manuscript (RA 220.010120), which consists of six leaves.

IN DEFINING A term in such common use as the word Virtue it is important to depart as little as possible from popular usage, for fear of becoming misleading and apparently paradoxical: on the other hand if Ethics is to be at all philosophical, it is important to attach a clear and definite meaning to the word, so far as this may be possible.

That the popular conception of virtue is far from clear, appears at once when we consider the various contradictory propositions about it to which the plain man could with a little ingenuity be got to assent. For example if I say it is more pleasant to me to do wrong than to do right, I shall be supposed to be uttering an immoral sentiment: but again if I say I always do as I like, it will be supposed that I am not in the habit of performing virtuous actions. If I profess that the exercise of kindness is irksome to me, I shall be censured, and should be commended if such exercise sprang from benevolent inclination: on the other hand it will perhaps be said that there is no virtue in merely following inclination. Common sense is also not always clear as to whether subjective or objective rightness is to be made the test: a persecutor, whatever his motive, would usually be censured, while on the other hand it would be easy to make the plain man admit that what the agent honestly believes to be his duty it is virtuous, and alone virtuous, for him to do.

If then we try to get a self-consistent conception of virtue as nearly as may be in accordance with common sense, we shall be forced to make our definition very complicated and full of reservations. There is something tempting about the simplicity of Kant's view of virtue, as consisting solely in the will to do right; and I think we shall have to admit all acts that come under this definition as virtuous. But if we are to avoid paradoxes, it will be necessary to widen our definition considerably. For it is an acknowledged consequence of this view, that for example a kind action done from affection and not from regard for duty is not virtuous; but common sense would probably regard it not only as virtuous but as more virtuous than in the former case. In the family for example it is supposed that mutual forbearance and sacrifice ought not to be the result of a conflict of impulses in which a sense of duty finally conquers, but rather of an emotional desire for the well-being of others which is so strong as to exclude selfish considerations altogether. Yet a man who had reached this state would according to Kant be unable to perform any virtuous acts.

This brings out an important distinction between two different meanings of the word Virtue which common sense seems to allow confusedly to coexist, although they are very apt to come into conflict. According to one view, "virtuous" is applied to acts considered separately and regarded as separate victories of the sense of duty over inclination. Thus temperance is considered virtuous in one who is strongly tempted to over-indulgence in alcohol, while in another who has no such temptation it is not so considered,

though perhaps it might be regarded as praiseworthy in the same way as other non-moral excellences are. This view leads to the paradox (which apparently the plain man shuts his eyes to) that the more irrational desires I have the more virtue I display in living rightly: the man who hates his neighbour and yet acts benevolently is more virtuous than the man who so acts from kindliness. And so we come to the other view, that virtue consists not in particular acts but in the whole disposition and character. On this view it is necessary to have some standard of objective rightness first: it then appears that certain impulses tend to promote acts objectively right, others
10 to discourage them: a character in which the former class of motives is strong is then virtuous, while one in which the latter is strong is at least less virtuous. And common sense would admit probably that a perfect man could have no conflict of impulses but would act rightly without effort; just as in the orthodox view God is not regarded as liable to temptation. And I think it could hardly be maintained that the conflict of impulses would cease because the moral sense had become so overpowering that all other desires were negligeable compared to the desire of doing right: rather we should look for such an ordering of the other desires that they should always prompt of themselves to the action which the moral sense would approve. It
20 is for this reason that emotions, such as Benevolence and Sympathy, are commonly reckoned among virtues: because they normally afford a motive tending to facilitate the performance of duty, and if they become strong enough may in most cases be safely allowed to supersede conscious conformance to the moral code. But it is thought dangerous to allow conscience to be altogether in abeyance: as Wordsworth says

> There are who ask not if thine eye
> Be on them: who in simple truth,
> Where no misgiving is, rely
> Upon the genial sense of youth:
30　　 Glad hearts, without reproach or blot,
> Who do thy will and know it not,
> O if through confidence misplaced
> They fail, thy saving arms dread power around them cast.

But some virtuous acts can only be performed impulsively, their performance requiring immediate action, without time for reflection: such acts can hardly arise from conscious virtue, but must spring from an impulse, which would be regarded as virtuous. Indeed sometimes common sense would disapprove of reflection even where it could be performed: for example when Godwin censures Fénelon for his effort to rescue his housekeeper
40 from his burning house, on the ground that his life was more valuable than hers, we feel that although, if Fénelon had stopped a moment to reflect, he

might have seen the justice of the argument, it was more virtuous to rush in and be burned. This view may be erroneous, but I think it would certainly be the view of common sense. And generally, even in deliberate action, where the agent incurs considerable pain by his act, this act is usually regarded as virtuous although perhaps mistaken. This may be explained by the consideration that the disposition shewn in such acts is one which would in general lead to conduct such as the moral sense would approve, although the particular act may be Quixotic.

In conclusion then: Virtue will apparently be defined most nearly in accordance with common usage if applied to disposition or character, as man-  10 ifested in acts: it being supposed that the moral sense is able to decide, or at least that the decision can somehow be made, as to what conduct is moral and what immoral. The virtuous disposition or character is then that which is most prone to moral acts, that in which the desires (including among these the desire to act morally) are so graduated as always to prompt to the best action; and further in which some acts are performed without conscious reference to the moral sense (though it must always be supposed that the moral sense would approve if it judged at all); indeed the perfectly virtuous disposition would I suppose *always* find sufficient motive for moral action without calling in the moral sense, though this must be supposed strong. We  20 should then call a person more or less virtuous according as he approximates more or less to this ideal.

# 35

# The Ethical Bearings of Psychogony [1894]

THIS PAPER WAS written for Sidgwick's course on ethics. The verso of the last leaf reads "*B. Russell / The Ethical Bearings of Psychogony. / Jan. 1894*". The paper, however, can be dated more exactly. The last entry in Russell's lecture notebook (1: 52) for Sidgwick's course in the Michaelmas Term 1893 reads "For Monday after Jan. 17 ⟨i.e. for 22 Jan. 1894⟩: The Ethical bearings of Psychogony"; and on 10 January Russell mentioned, in a letter to Alys, that he was writing the paper, "in which I have pointed out the very serious advantages of Suttee". The manuscript bears a number of pencilled comments by Sidgwick, who demurred, in one of them, as to the advantages of Suttee. Later in the lecture notebook (1: 56), Russell recorded Sidgwick's more general comments, probably from a tutorial, on his and another student's papers: "*My Essay*. Savages can overeat themselves without being the worse for it. Don't want to take responsibility for all your illustrations. Morality of civilized societies not wholly due to natural selection".

The copy-text is the manuscript (RA 220.010180), which comprises six leaves.

A T FIRST SIGHT we might be tempted to say that Psychogony, being concerned with what is and what has been, cannot possibly have any bearing on what ought to be: and in this opinion we should be at least so far justified, that of itself no mere history of the moral sentiments or science of their development can afford any ground for a belief in their ethical validity or invalidity as they at present exist. But on a closer inspection we may find that Psychogony has considerable indirect bearings on Ethics, that it is important, if not as a constructive, at least as a negative and regulative force. Let us first see briefly what Psychogony can tell us about the moral sentiments.

If we accept an Evolutionary account of the development of this as of every other set of impulses, we can easily point out the importance of many simple virtues both to the primitive tribe and to the still more primitive family. In the struggle for existence it would be an advantage to a family if the father protected the mother until she ceased to bear children and if the parents protected the children until they grew up. In the primitive tribe it would be essential to its existence that some feeling of patriotism, of self-surrender for the good of the whole, should exist; and as soon as it did exist in any tribe, this tribe would be able to exterminate its enemies with comparative ease. Even a certain amount of mutual forbearance within the tribe might possibly be advantageous, as an aid to cooperation against common enemies and also as facilitating the propagation of the species and the maintenance of children. And as society became more complex, more and more of such cooperation would be required and this would introduce the need for more and more action of the kind usually known as virtuous. Also with greater stability comes in the possibility of excessive self-indulgence and therefore the necessity of prudence and self-control.

Thus it is easy to see how the existing virtues are on the whole and in the main of use in the Struggle for Existence and may have been produced by Survival of the Fittest. But in the first place it by no means follows that morality has been developed precisely in the way most adapted to its original evolutionary purpose: what are known to the biologist as morbid bye-products may have been produced along with the directly useful virtues, and perhaps the race would prosper better without these bye-products. For example it is difficult to see what use a woman is to society, from an evolutionary point of view, when she has ceased to bear children, or at least to bring them up. The Indian custom of Suttee seems far more suitable than ours: why waste the means of sustenance on one who can serve no longer for the preservation of the species? Again the humanitarian habit of carefully preserving the lives of weak and sickly members of the community, and of even allowing them to propagate their weakness and sickliness, is undoubtedly the result of sentiments which must be put in the category called *moral*: and yet I suppose no one will deny that on the whole it is a disadvantage from

223

the evolutionary point of view, and that the Spartan habit of exposing sickly babies was far preferable. But secondly: even if we were to admit that all our moral sentiments are such as tend to the maximising of Life (in Herbert Spencer's phrase), or if we construct or could construct a morality which should serve this end, what warrant have we for accepting it as ethically valid? Because evolution has brought forth a certain morality tending on the whole to the maximising of Life, why accept this end as ours? Since we have survived, we have of course bodies and minds which are liable to survive: but how does the mere fact of our survival prove us ethically superior to those whom we have succeeded in exterminating? The murderer is not usually considered more virtuous than the man he murders: yet on the principle of survival he ought to be, having proved himself the stronger. For his position is in reality not materially different from that of a tribe which by superior patriotism and courage has succeeded in exterminating another tribe and so in propagating the virtues which led to its success. Nothing compels us to regard life in itself as valuable and alone valuable: this must of course appear the end of nature since those organisms only which best attain this end survive: but why blindly follow nature? why survive? or if we choose to survive, why not endeavour to attain some other end beside mere life? These questions belong to Ethics, and no account of the origin of ethical opinions can answer them.

So far, then, Psychogony would not seem to give us much help in Ethics. But when we have determined the most fundamental questions of Ethics, we may be helped in details by Psychogony. For psychogony can give some light as to the ends which will be served by following the morality of common sense; and therefore in so far as we consider these ends desirable or undesirable we shall accept or reject this morality. If for example we consider happiness the end of moral action, and if we hold further with Mr. Herbert Spencer, that pleasure springs from life-preserving actions, existing morality will no doubt help us in ordinary circumstances. But the more we examine into such indirect bearings of Psychogony on Ethics, the more evanescent they seem to become. Apart from the glaring fallacies involved in the proof of the proposition quoted above from Mr. Herbert Spencer (among which Psychological Hedonism is prominent), we cannot at all trust that moral sentiments will be always life-preserving in their character: for in so far as they have arisen through evolution, they are likely to be adapted, as most of our other impulses are, to a much more primitive state of society: and they are bound always to lag a little behind the needs of the age. It is true that those whose moral sentiments are too grossly out of touch with these needs will be unable to propagate their quixotism (if examples were needed one might instance a curate who leaves the church in consequence of religious scruples and is therefore unable to afford marriage): but these people are genuinely following their moral impulses, and so we can never be sure in acting (as we think) virtuously that we shall not become those very victims of imperfect adaptation who are eliminated in the struggle. Such cases are similar to those of death or loss of health from excessive sensual indulgence: here too a man is following an impulse originally produced by natural selection, but which owing to the altered conditions of civilized society has become more powerful than it need be for evolutionary purposes. These instances shew how dangerous it is in a complex and changing society to trust to impulses which originally had a life-preserving or life-producing tendency: they may be slightly injurious, but not to the extent of loss of life; or again they may be normally so restrained by self-control as to fail of the destructive effects which they cause when not so controlled. On the whole then it would seem that even the indirect bearings of Psychogony are very limited and doubtful.

# 36

# Ethical Axioms [1894]

THIS IS THE last of the papers Russell wrote for Sidgwick's course on ethics. The verso of the last leaf reads: "*B. Russell / Essay on Ethical Axioms / Feb. 1894*". The title used here heads the first leaf. Russell's lecture notebook (1: 69) for Sidgwick's course contains a short note giving the essay topic: "Ethical axioms, with special reference to Bk. III. Chap. 13." The reference is to the chapter "Philosophical Intuitionism" in Sidgwick's *The Methods of Ethics*, although Russell's paper makes no reference to this work. The manuscript bears a number of pencilled comments by Sidgwick, mainly requests for clarification. The paper obviously led to further discussions with him, since Russell wrote to Alys: "I am also carrying on an Ethical controversy as to Ethical Axioms: I have revolted from pure Hedonism which has annoyed Sidgwick" (24 Feb. 1894).

The copy-text is the manuscript (RA 220.010220), consisting of four leaves.

WE MAY TAKE as our datum here that we do make moral judgments, as a matter of fact; and that we regard these, like judgments as to what is, as liable to truth and falsehood. Hence there must be some criterion, implicit or explicit, to which we refer such moral judgments: if we allow the possibility of error, we must regard propositions as to what ought to be as deducible from some one or more fundamental ethical maxims, not themselves based on any further propositions. Of course in framing any particular moral precept, Do this or Avoid that, our premisses are partly matter of fact, or may be; but one premiss at any rate, if we have any premisses at all, must be ethical, and thus finally we are brought to the necessity for ethical maxims which have no further basis. And however impossible we may find it to compel everyone to accept such maxims, however unfounded the whole structure may appear, we are precluded from scepticism by the mere fact that we will and act: for to choose one action rather than another, where two or more courses are open to us, or even to abstain from acting, involves some ground for preference of our choice, and thus involves the distinction of better or worse: volition must imply a good presented to the imagination as possible but not actual, a contrast, that is, between what is and what ought to be.

Thus some basis *must* be found for ethical judgments. And it is sufficiently obvious that such a basis cannot be sought in any proposition about what is or has been. No theory of the origin of the moral sentiments, no general consensus of common sense can afford even the shadow of an ultimate ethical axiom, being themselves concerned with what is and not with what ought to be.

But where are we to find the axioms we are seeking? Unfortunately the immediate dictates of conscience are always more or less particular: they may prohibit lying or murder, they may enjoin kindness to my neighbour, but such precepts are not sufficiently general for our purpose. Can we then find axioms as self-evident as those of Arithmetic, on which we can build as on a sure foundation, which could be shaken only by a scepticism which should attack the whole fabric of our knowledge?

It becomes important here to distinguish between formal and material axioms. The Kantian maxim, which Kant himself apparently regarded as sufficient, is purely formal: it gives no indication as to the sort of conduct we ought to will to become universal. I see no reason why an astute pick-pocket in galloping consumption should not will picking pockets to become the universal rule: for he might thus avoid spending his last days in prison and might be so convinced of his superior skill as to be certain of making more by picking the pockets of others than he lost by having his own picked: and though society would rapidly fall into ruin, he might hope to be dead before this result followed.—But as a formal rule, Kant's precept really amounts to no more than that moral judgments claim objective validity, (since there is no knowing what perverseness a man might shew in willing universal laws of conduct). And this objectivity of moral judgments is involved in their liability to truth and error: if they were merely statements of a psychological state, and claimed to be nothing more than this, they could not err (except by the speaker's mistaking his own feelings). This one formal axiom, then, as soon as its meaning is clear, must I think be admitted as self-evident by all who pass moral judgments.

But when we come to seek a material precept the case seems to me very different. No maxim of this kind has obtained the universal consent of moralists, and therefore we can scarcely hope to find one which shall command our assent by its self-evidence. Let us endeavour to find out the sort of axiom we should require.

As was said above, all action implies an imagined good sought by the agent: where we may define the Good as that which satisfies desire. This good which is sought must be, strictly speaking, the agent's own good: though he may of course find this in any object of desire, as for example in complete self-surrender to the good of others. But from the above definition it follows that the agent must seek his own imagined good by his act, since all action must aim at the satisfaction of desire. There may be error in his view of his own good, for the frequent failure to find satisfaction in the attainment of our desires is a commonplace of moralists. But if in all action I necessarily seek what I imagine to be my good, the difference between moral and immoral action must consist in the difference of the conception I form of my own good. The good for me is obviously dependent on myself and my surroundings, but is not dependent upon my idea of it at any moment, since it is that which *will* satisfy desire, and not that which I merely believe will satisfy desire. Thus the material axiom which we are seeking will have to contain a precept that we are to seek our own good, with a definition of this good, more or less partial of course. Our duty will consist in self-realization, but self-realization may of course be best attained by what is commonly called self-sacrifice: and so long as we live in a society, our own development must be closely connected with that of the society we live in. But in what more particularly self-realization would consist I cannot here discuss: this is a metaphysical rather than an ethical question.

## 37

# The Free-Will Problem
# from an Idealist Standpoint [1895]

RUSSELL DATED THIS paper 8 June 1895 on the final leaf. At this time he and Alys were living at Friday's Hill, and he was concentrating on his fellowship dissertation. Late the previous year he had written a paper (which must be considered lost) on the free-will problem for Alys's sister, Mary Costelloe, who had been visiting him during his stay in Paris. He told Alys of his satisfaction with the result:

> Yesterday Mariechen was away all day, and I wrote her an Essay on the Free-Will Controversy, which we are both much pleased with. I have never written anything (except my Essay on Scepticism in the Tripos) which seemed to me to accomplish its object so well. I will bring it on Saturday and thee can read it when I'm gone. It puts the reconciliation of Freedom and Determination in very simple and yet accurate language—I am more conceited than ever! (11 Nov. 1894)

The present paper also takes a reconciliationist position but cannot be identical with this earlier effort, for Balfour's *Foundations of Belief*, with which the present essay deals in part, was not published until February 1895. (Russell may not have read the whole book, but only the chapter on idealism, for the title does not appear in "What Shall I Read?") It remains a mystery why he returned to the free-will problem after the publication of Balfour's book, especially when he considered his earlier attempt so successful.

From two allusions in the text, as well as from its general tone and level of exposition, what he referred to as "this article" (237: 43) appears to have been intended for a more popular audience than that of a professional journal. At 230: 22–4 Russell says that it has "seemed worth while, perhaps, to state popularly the chief points of the accepted Idealist solution [to the problem of free-will]"; and at 231: 34–5 he comments that "it may not be fruitless to render popularly the chief points on which the solution depends." Several references to the thinking of the "plain man" and the "up-to-date scientist" reinforce this assumption. No trace of the paper's publication has been found, nor any other reference to its composition or intended audience, though there is some textual evidence (T231: 32) to suggest that it may have been intended for an audience outside Britain.

The copy-text is the manuscript (RA 220.010510), which has twenty-nine leaves. They show extensive alterations by Russell.

AMONG THE COUNTLESS readers of Mr. Balfour's *Foundations of Belief*, there must have been many who, after appreciating to the full his very able criticism of Naturalism, have felt a certain disappointment at the brevity and inconclusiveness of his Chapter on Idealism.[1] There is a cardinal weakness, to begin with, in the choice, as the representative of English Idealists, of the late Mr. T. H. Green, who can scarcely, at this date, be regarded as a satisfactory champion. It is a canon of criticism—at any rate if criticism is to be conclusive—to criticize the *best* of a school. But we cannot deny, however we may honour Mr. T. H. Green as a pioneer, that
10 the school which he founded has, since his day, made very material advances in several directions. Mr. Balfour complains of the non-appearance of "original work which shall represent the constructive views of the younger school of thinkers". Mr. Bradley's *Appearance and Reality* might, one would think, have answered very accurately to this description; but Mr. Balfour dismisses this epoch-making work with the remark that "he does not know whether it has yet commanded any large measure of assent from the few who are competent to pronounce a verdict upon its merits." His criticism of Idealism cannot, therefore, be regarded as touching the more modern work of those to whose views this name applies.
20     As a large part of Mr. Balfour's objections, both to Naturalism and to Idealism, are founded on their treatment of the Free-Will problem, and the supposed insufficiency of that treatment as a basis for Ethics, it seemed worth while, perhaps, to state popularly the chief points of the accepted Idealist solution of this problem, and to trace, briefly, the effects of that solution on the foundations of Ethics. Such a statement seemed the more desirable, as Mr. Balfour's only allusion to this view, in a foot-note, contains, if I am not mistaken, an error as to the nature of law in the psychical world, which a discussion of this problem is calculated to remove.
     The question of Free Will is one in which we must all feel some interest,
30 whether we are metaphysicians or "plain men". Many people have an uneasy sense that Science has destroyed the possibility of Freedom, and yet they cling passionately to their belief in it—so passionately, sometimes, as to dread all discussion of it, for fear their faith might be shaken. Some, indeed, who are of a scientific turn of mind, and anxious to be "up to date", reject it scornfully, as a metaphysical mystery, fit only for the Middle Ages. These men will tell you boldly that all your actions are due to processes in the brain, that life is nothing but protoplasm, and matter is the only ultimate reality. But from these the "plain man" shrinks; he cannot face "that moral impoverishment which", as Mr. Balfour says, "determinism is calculated to
40 produce". He falls back, usually, on the supposed self-evidence of freedom; "why, I *know* I can do whatever I choose", he says, "and it is simply absurd

1 *Loc. cit.*, Bk. II, Chap. II, pp. 137–155.

230

to tell me I couldn't have done otherwise if I had wanted to." "No doubt", you might retort, "you can do whatever you choose, but can you *choose* at hap-hazard? Your choice always has a motive, which is determined by your whole nature, and your nature came to you partly through inheritance, partly through education. At any rate, you have it now, for better or worse, and such as it is, you cannot alter it." But if you made such a retort, you would not convince him; you would only bring down upon you a vehement abuse of Metaphysics. In this abuse, if in nothing else, the "up to date" scientist would be ready enough to join. He would join the more readily, if you previously applied the same process of questioning to him. You would easily, by suggesting a few metaphysical abstractions, get him to refuse belief to anything which was not evident to his senses, and from this point his ruin would be easy. "How so?" you would rejoin, "you allow nothing to exist except what is evident to the senses? How about matter which no one sees? How about the world before the germ of life appeared?" At this point he would begin to be puzzled, and if you pushed your advantage home, and urged that such a world, by his own definition, was impossible, and therefore mind must be just as ultimate as matter—if you urged all this upon him, he would join with the plain man in abuse of Metaphysics, and say, with mock humility, that, for his part, he preferred to confine himself to the plain teachings of Science.

Thus the "plain man" and the "up to date man" both abuse Metaphysics, and yet there is no other way out of their difficulties. They cannot hope finally to settle the problem—so important to them both—except by Metaphysics, that "unusually obstinate attempt to think clearly", as Mr. Bradley has called it. To make such an attempt, however imperfectly, in connection with the question of Free Will; to point out that, in the main, each of the men we have been cross-questioning is right in what he asserts, but wrong in what he denies; to supply a positive doctrine, in which each of them shall find all that he really values in his view—this is the object of the present Essay. The solution which will be suggested is no new one in philosophy, but philosophy is so apt, in this country at any rate, to be crowded out by science, and has been, on this question, so hardly used by Mr. Balfour, that it may not be fruitless to render popularly the chief points on which the solution depends.

First of all, what is the meaning of our terms? Freedom and Determination are both ambiguous, have both a stricter and a wider sense—determination, in the narrower sense, means fatalism, and freedom, the freedom of caprice. This ambiguity is a very fruitful source of controversy, the stricter sense being usually the one attacked, while the wider sense is the one defended. Thus the arguments on *both* sides are apt to be irrefutable, and by sufficient care in avoiding definitions, the discussion can be prolonged *ad infinitum*. The fact is, as we shall see, that in their narrower senses

both are false, while in their broader senses both are true—the reconciliation of these broader senses, however, belongs to that domain of which the
plain man entertains a vague though vivid horror, the domain of
"metaphysical subtleties".

To begin with Determinism: What its opponents usually mean by it is the
doctrine—more properly called fatalism—that, struggle as you will, you are
fatally and irrevocably compelled, from *without*, to a certain type of actions
and of thoughts. Your whole soul may rebel against the acts you commit,
and yet, as in some horrid nightmare, you are driven by that vague power,
the force of circumstances, into this, that or the other course.

> If we are doomed to die, we are enow
> To do our country loss; and if to live,
> The fewer men, the greater share of honour.

What need of more men, since heaven has ordained our victory or defeat,
and our efforts cannot alter the eternal decrees? Of late, this doctrine has
acquired a pseudo-scientific sanction, from such works as Ibsen's *Ghosts*;
the sins of the fathers are supposed, without any acquiescence of our own, to
lead us, blindly and helplessly, along the downward path. But, whatever
may be said by crude interpreters of science, the doctrine of Fatalism,
though it has led to some of the most heroic episodes in the world's history,
is manifestly false; we cannot reasonably doubt, however much our actions
may be determined by previous causes, that those causes lie partly within
ourselves. We know that, in different characters, similar circumstances lead
to different actions, and this alone shews that our character, however acquired, counts for something in determining what our acts shall be. The
only sense, therefore, in which Determinism deserves our consideration, is
the sense in which it asserts that all our actions have a cause. Our own
character and disposition, however, is always a part of that cause and can
never be neglected without error. So much as to the two meanings of Determination.

There remain the two meanings of Freedom. The freedom of caprice—or
Liberty of Indifference, as it was called—though formerly the only sort of
freedom contemplated, has now been almost universally abandoned. It was
supposed, by those who held this view, that a man could, by a sheer act of
will, in the presence of any motives, act in any way whatever; no knowledge
of his previous character, not even the most perfect, and no knowledge of
the motives at present soliciting him, would enable the onlooker, according
to these people, to decide with certainty as to the course of conduct which
the man will pursue. And this inability to predict does not spring from the
insufficiency of the data, or from the complexity of the problem, but simply
from the fact that Will is exempted from the domain of Causation. This view

was upheld by Kant, and formed the basis of his whole Ethic. The pure or moral Will, in his view, was never determined by external causes, was never, in short, an effect, but always itself a new cause breaking in upon the series of events—it was the beginning of a new chain of causes and effects, but never a link in the middle of the chain. Kant admitted that the Will was often determined by previous causes, but he regarded actions so caused as base, and held that it is always possible to prevent the natural effect on the Will from taking place. He imagined a Transcendental Ego sitting aloft, in eternal calm, above the realm of passion and of sense, and able, despite all the solicitations of the phenomenal world, to determine, by the light of pure reason, what it should do and what it should avoid. Such an Ego has, however, become impossible now-a-days; we know enough about Psychology to be sure that volitions always obey the law of causation, and that, like all other events, they are at once effects of what precedes, and causes of what follows. Further, even if such capricious acts of will *were* possible, we should not be bound to restrict the notion of Freedom to these; indeed, there is much to be said for denying that such volitions would be free at all. Pure caprice, if it could exist, would involve that the agent did not necessarily pursue his own ends, for his ends, since he desires them, are motives, and if he pursues them, his will is *caused* by them. We may even go further, and say, if there are to be real cases of caprice, that the agent *cannot* always pursue his own ends—but this, surely, is not freedom, but the most intolerable bondage! Not only, then, is this Liberty of Indifference, philosophically impossible, but, even if it could exist, it would not really be Freedom.

But if not this, what *do* we mean by Freedom? The true meaning seems to be, absence of *external* compulsion. A man is free, when the laws he follows are self-imposed, when he is "a law unto himself". Such laws—being, in truth, nothing but the resolution consistently to pursue certain ends—will in no way limit our freedom—the power of making them *is*, indeed, that very freedom which we all desire.

But how, in the face of science and its demands, can we maintain that such a freedom is real? On this point, let us hear Mr. Balfour, who has condescended, for this occasion only, to make himself the mouthpiece of science.

> Mankind, it seems, are on this theory free, but their freedom does not exclude determinism, but only that form of determinism which consists in external constraint. Their actions are upon this view strictly prescribed by their antecedents, but these antecedents are nothing other than the characters of the agents themselves.
>
> Now it may seem at first sight plausible to describe that man as free whose behaviour is due to "himself" alone. But without quarrelling over words, it is, I think, plain that, whether it be proper to

call him free or not, he at least lacks freedom in the sense in which freedom is necessary in order to constitute responsibility. It is impossible to say of him that he "ought", and therefore he "can". For at any given moment of his life his next action is by hypothesis strictly determined. This is also true of every previous moment, until we get back to that point in his life's history at which he cannot, in any intelligible sense of the term, be said to have a character at all. Antecedently to this, the causes which have produced him are in no special sense connected with his individuality, but form part of the general complex of phenomena which make up the world. It is evident, therefore, that every act which he performs may be traced to pre-natal, and possibly to purely material, antecedents, and that, even if it be true that what he does is the outcome of his character, his character itself is the outcome of causes over which he has not, and cannot by any possibility have, the smallest control.[2]

How are we to answer this argument? This question is, as Mr. Balfour rightly points out, the crux of the Free-Will problem, but I believe, contrary to Mr. Balfour's view, that it is a question which Idealism is able to answer.

The apparent cogency of the above argument depends upon an insufficient criticism of the nature of those causes and laws with which science deals. To make this plain, let us consider some science, such as Astronomy, in which the "Reign of Law" has been thoroughly established, and chance and caprice have long ago disappeared. A cause may have, here, in popular language, two meanings, but only one of these, as the following discussion will shew, can be admitted by philosophy.

(1) Cause may denote a more general law, such as the Law of Gravitation, under which the particular phenomenon can be subsumed: the fall of Newton's apple, we say, was *caused* by gravitation. This sense, however, is very loose. It regards the law as something existing independently of the phenomena, just as a human law exists on the statute-book, whether or not there are any cases to which it applies. Hence we get the notion that natural laws *govern* phenomena, as human laws govern states, but this notion rests, at bottom, on no better foundation than the double meaning of the word Law. The law of Gravitation was *discovered* by *observing* the phenomena. Newton saw the apple fall, and he saw the moon go round the earth; he found that the one formula, of the earth's attraction, would describe both these facts. Finally, he discovered that attraction all round, according to the same formula, would also describe the motions of the planets round the sun. Thus the law is nothing but a compendious description of these various motions. Without the motions, it would be nothing; it is a uniformity ana-

2 *Loc. cit.*, p. 147.

lysed out of the phenomena, and has no existence apart from the phenomena which exemplify it. Hence it can no more *control* the phenomena than a census controls the population. It is, therefore, only in a very loose and popular sense, that a law can be regarded as the *cause* of the phenomena to which it applies.

(2) But, again, we say that a phenomenon is *caused* by some phenomenon which immediately preceded it—gunpowder explodes because we put a match to it, a man dies because he has taken arsenic, a billiard-ball moves because we hit it, and so on. In this sense, the notion of cause has still a function in science. In Physics, cause and effect are phenomena of the same kind, and are quantitatively equal. One billiard-ball is in motion, it hits another, and communicates its motion to that other; the total amount of motion is the same after the impact as it was before, and the former motion is the cause of the latter. In this sequence of cause and effect, there are certain uniformities by which, when we know the cause, we can discover the effect, and when we know the effect we can discover the cause. These uniformities are the laws of science. But these laws only tell us *how* phenomena follow each other—they do not shew us *why* phenomena should choose that particular mode of sequence. Nor do they give us any more reason for regarding the future as determined by the past, than for regarding the past as determined by the future. From the present state of the heavenly bodies, we can discover past eclipses and transits, just as easily as those to come. The fact is, that, in the most perfect sciences, any two phenomena have to each other a perfectly determinate relation. We cannot say that the cause determines the effect, without admitting, at the same time, that the effect determines the cause—had the effect been different, we should have inferred a different cause. Neither, in any way that we can see, compels the other—all we can say is, that, as far as our experience goes, the one can be inferred from the other, by certain rules which, in all hitherto observed sequences, have been found to hold.

If, then, Psychology is to have laws like those of Physics, we must not expect those laws to be such as to *control* psychical phenomena—they will only be laws which the phenomena themselves contain. If people, on certain occasions, act in certain ways, that is no ground for saying they *could* not have acted otherwise—we cannot say this even of the heavenly bodies—all we can say is, that people *do* act in these ways. Again, we saw that it was just as reasonable to regard the future as determining the past as it was to take the opposite view, and when we come to examine the nature of will, we shall see how important this way of regarding things may be.

When we start from the later phenomenon, and regard it as determining the earlier one, we call the one which comes last an *End*, and that which went before a *means*. This way of looking at things does not upset the causal relation, but supplements it—and in dealing with will, at any rate, it is essential to any complete account of the facts. My putting the kettle on the fire *causes* it to boil, but it is also the *means* I adopt to the *end* of making it boil. Now in any act of will, we always have some end in view; hence we may regard the end, which is future, as determining the will, which is the means to its attainment. The will, however, regarded as cause, also determines, as its effect, the occurrence of the end which it has in view; thus neither will nor the end it has in view outweighs its alternative in the relation, but each, as an event in the time-series, would enable an ideally perfect Psychology to infer the other.

10     After this, I fear, somewhat tedious series of definitions and distinctions, let us see what consequences they will lead to in the metaphysical discussion of Free Will. We have, here, the inestimable advantage of direct introspection—we may hope, therefore, to get a deeper insight into the nature of laws and sequences than was possible where, as in the physical sciences, we had only outward observation to guide us.

The meaning which we found above for Freedom was, it will be remembered, the absence of *external* compulsion. Where our acts follow no laws save those of our desires—where we are able, always, to pursue what seems to us our highest good—there, surely, it would be out of place to complain of

20 want of freedom. There are cases where such a complaint would be justified—cases where the outer world, breaking in upon our hopes, interposes some impassible obstacle between ourselves and our desires. The death of a friend, the deafness of a Beethoven, the defeat of a cause to which all life's energies had been devoted, these are real limits to liberty, in these the world does definitely declare itself hostile to our cherished ends; but where we are freely able to work out the realization of our desires, there, surely, it would be unreasonable to complain because our desires cannot be other than they are. Such a complaint would be the more unreasonable, as this inability to be different is, at bottom, only the law of identity. If they *are*

30 such and such, it would be a contradiction to suppose them anything else; but if we *choose*, we can make of our desires what we will. Whatever appears to us desirable, we desire; what appears otherwise, we surely should not wish to desire.

But to what extent does such freedom fall to our lot? And what are the conditions of our attaining to the fullest possible development of it? To answer these questions, it will be necessary to consider man's relation to his environment, and his share in the life of the whole.[3]

---

3 I ought to point out that, in what follows, I have departed somewhat from the traditional meaning of freedom. We may distinguish freedom in volition and freedom in attainment.
40     Whenever our volition has, as to some extent it always has, an end in view which is not wholly dependent on ourselves for its possibility, there, though our volition proper may be free—as, indeed, we have just seen that it must be—yet, as beings with ends to attain, we are *not* wholly free. We cannot, that is, attain to any end we may desire—even our most

Since freedom consists of the absence of external compulsion, it is clear that the Universe, as the sum of all that is, must be free, for there is nothing outside it by which its freedom could be interfered with. Nevertheless, since the universe is amenable to science, since the world, so far as we know it, is an orderly world, this freedom, which the universe enjoys, is not Liberty of Indifference—on the contrary, we must regard the universe as imposing laws upon itself, and these laws must be regarded as flowing from its own nature. We have thus, in the universe as a whole, a combination of perfect freedom with perfect determination. The determination is self-deter- mination—that is, it comes from within, and may be regarded as an expres- sion of the Universal Will—but it is none the less perfect on that account, for no one, now-a-days, would maintain that there is any part of the universe not amenable to law.

But, further, the Universe is an organism—that is, it is a whole, in which all the parts are interrelated, so that a change in any one part involves a change in every other. Even in physical science, this interdependence may be seen—laws such as Gravitation and the Conservation of Energy, which apply to the whole world, make the motion of every single particle depen- dent on the motions and attractions of all other particles throughout the material universe—so that we cannot give a full account, even here, of any one portion of the whole, without considering, at the same time, its relation to every other portion. And when we come to the human world, this inter- dependence is infinitely more varied and more intimate—each of us has a thousand points of contact with the world of his fellow-men, and is depen- dent on them in a thousand ways in every part of his life. How can such dependence, we may ask, be compatible with Freedom?

The laws of the universe, as we saw, are self-imposed laws. Now the universe is only the sum of all the beings in it, so that every being must have some share in determining what the laws shall be. As a participator in the nature of the whole, every finite spirit must, to some extent, participate in the freedom of the whole; we each and all of us add our votes in the con- struction of the whole, and every one of us, by his will, makes the world, to some extent, a different place from what it would have been without that will. The whole sum of such wills constitutes the whole activity of the uni- verse. We shall be free, then, when the activity we propose to ourselves is one which the universe as a whole allows, when the law we impose upon ourselves is the same as the law of the whole. A limitation to our freedom will only occur when we set ourselves in opposition to the General Will; in

---

immediate volitions, which have only bodily motions in view, may be impeded by paralysis or bodily infirmity. The will, then, in the strict sense, is always free, but we are not always free to work out the effects which we hope from our volitions. The latter sort of freedom, which I may call freedom in attainment, is that considered throughout the subsequent parts of this article.

such a case, we shall find our activity impeded from without, and our actions will no longer be completely self-determined. Hence, finally, we are free in proportion as we are self-determined, and we are self-determined in proportion as we are in harmony with the whole. To be in harmony with the Universal Will is, therefore, the full and sufficient condition of our freedom.

We have now arrived at the end of the discussion of Free Will, which is the more special subject of this Essay. We have seen in what sense man has freedom, how far that freedom extends, and how to make its extent as great as possible. But it may not be out of place, before taking leave of the subject, to add a few words as to the ethical bearing of our solution.

Ever since the time of Kant, the dependence of freedom upon virtue has been recognized in some sense or other, but owing to Kant's faulty psychology of volition, his own account of this dependence is no longer completely adequate. For we saw that liberty, to him, meant Liberty of Indifference; the will, according to his view, was only moral when it had no motive outside itself, when, as he expressed it, the action sprang from pure respect for the moral law as such. The moral will, in such an act, was supposed to have no end in view—it was not determined by any prevision of consequences—the pure love of virtue alone determined it, and virtue lay, not in any prevision of desirable consequences, but in the will alone. Such a pure, unmotived will was possible to a believer in Liberty of Indifference, but to us, with our vastly improved psychology, a will which has no purpose in view has become a chimera. The only acts which are not determined by a prevision of the end to be attained are purely instinctive or reflex acts, and these, unfortunately, are precisely the acts which Ethics and common sense agree in regarding as outside the pale of the moral judgment. The acts which we judge good or bad are deliberative acts—choices between two or more courses which lie open to us, each presenting some advantageous features which the other lacks. In these cases, we estimate, as best we can, the consequences of either course, and judge which of the two sets of consequences we most desire. The motives to will, even in what are called acts of self-sacrifice, are always desires—desires, namely, for the consequences of the volition in question. We can desire the happiness of another just as truly, and in just the same sense, as we desire our own happiness—when we sacrifice our own pleasure to another's, we do so because our desire for the other's pleasure is stronger than that for our own. It may be, indeed, that the conquering desire is not, by itself, so strong as that which it conquers, but secures the victory by seeking allies among other desires which point to the same act. Thus we may sacrifice our own pleasure to another's because we desire to cultivate what is called an unselfish disposition, or because we desire the other's esteem; these desires will reinforce that for the other's happiness, and may make it prevail, even though singly it was weaker than the desire for our own happiness. Thus stated, in fact, the doctrine that the strongest desire always conquers, becomes a truism, for, as in the Survival of the Fittest, the test of superior strength lies only in the conquest. The only part of the doctrine which is not a truism, is the psychological fact that our actions, except when they are purely reflex, always spring from the desire for their consequences.

In all deliberate action, then, what we seek is the *satisfaction of desire*. If this is so, if all that seems good to us appears as the realization of desired ends, the fundamental principle of Ethics must be to obtain as much of this satisfaction as the world can yield. But here it becomes necessary to guard against a probable error. Satisfaction of desire is not to be confounded with pleasure. As I pointed out above, we may desire another's pleasure just as much as our own; we may desire truth, or beauty, or posthumous fame, or a thousand other things besides our own pleasure. If any one of these objects is attained, the desire for it is satisfied, and what seemed to us good is, so far, realized in the world. Every object of desire, it is true, gives us, when attained, a greater or less degree of pleasure, but this pleasure is not itself the object which we desired. The satisfaction of desire is to be understood as meaning, not the mere feeling of attainment, but the concrete realization, in the actual world, of the object of our desire.

We may, therefore, state our fundamental moral principle thus: In any case of a conflict of desires, that desire is to be followed which will bring with it the largest satisfaction—the satisfaction being great in proportion to the possibility of fully realizing the object of the desire. From this point, it is easy to see the bearing, on morals, of our proposed solution of the Free-Will problem.

A man is free, as we saw, when he is unimpeded in his activity, that is, when his desires are such as can be progressively realized by his actions. But we also saw that his activity is unimpeded in proportion as he is in harmony with the universe as a whole. Hence a man will attain to the satisfaction of his desires in proportion as he is in harmony with the world. Our principle of morals, therefore, reduces itself to the precept of harmony with the Universal Will, and such harmony, as we saw, constitutes freedom. The moral law, therefore, has turned out to be the one and only law "whose service is perfect freedom". Virtue consists in harmony with the will of the Whole, and in harmony with the Whole lies the secret of perfect freedom.

In this conclusion the "plain man", would, I hope, be ready to acquiesce, even if he thought the argument by which it was reached unnecessarily tedious. If the edifying nature of my result does anything to reconcile him to the "metaphysical subtleties" of my method, I may hope to have done something, however slight, towards reconciling him to that "obstinate attempt" in which Philosophy consists.

# 38

# Note on Ethical Theory [*c.* 1896]

THIS NOTE IS found in one of the two large notebooks Russell kept during the 1890s (RA 210.006550–FI). The notebooks are not titled by Russell in any way, but the title-pages bear the printed words "Mit Gott" in large Gothic type, and below them in smaller Gothic type the name and address of the printer (Heinrich Schultze, Königlicher Hoflieferant, Berlin W., Behren-Strasse 28). Both left- and right-hand pages of the notebook have been number-stamped 1 through 200. Russell, in addition to writing on the right-hand pages through this sequence, turned the notebook upside down and wrote on the unused left-hand (now right-hand) pages, starting from the back (now the front). It is in this second sequence that the "Note on Ethical Theory" occurs, on page 164, between "Note on Economic Theory" (Paper 45) and "Note on the Logic of the Sciences" (to be included among other material on this topic in *Collected Papers* 2). Russell used the second paragraph of the "Note" (with minor changes and the deletion of the last sentence) as the conclusion to "Is Ethics a Branch of Empirical Psychology?" (Paper 15, 104: 13–31).

The "Note on Ethical Theory" is printed here from the manuscript, which is the copy-text. It is not dated, but since the notebook was evidently purchased during one of Russell's two visits to Germany in 1895, and since Paper 15 was written early in 1897, the likely year of composition is 1896.

ETHICS REQUIRES A criterion among desires, and yet seems unable to avoid regarding desires as ultimate. Can we say: Virtuous desires are those I *desire* to have? Put the matter thus: the Good is the desired, therefore good conduct is desired conduct, good desires are desired desires.

An ethic which merely says: the Good is the desired, leaves the Good a prey to changing fancies. An ethic which says: the Good is the Satisfaction of Desire, is open to all the objections to Hedonism: it chooses an aspect of the Good, a mere result of desire, as the whole Good. On the other hand, since we always do act from desire, an ethic which takes all desires as equally ultimate loses all criterion, all standard of judging action: all acts become 10 alike good or alike bad. Now morality is exhibited only in action, action springs only from desire. Therefore moral judgments must discriminate between desires. But since all contrast of ideal and actual rests on desire, since all goodness, all morality, rests on contrast of ideal and actual, only desire can supply the criterion among desires. The criterion is supplied, therefore, by the contrast between ideal and actual desires, by the distinction between desires we desire, and desires we dislike. Whether we have them or not, for example, we desire a wish for the good of humanity, and we dislike a craving for drink or morphia. In fact, the desired has as wide a range in conduct as in feeling. The man, then, who desires always and only 20 what he wishes to desire, is perfectly virtuous: in all that depends upon himself, there is no conflict, but the most perfect harmony possible. What want of harmony may remain, will be the fault of the world; a conflict of desires would no longer be possible.

Even in such a man, of course, intellectual error would remain: what he wished to desire he might wish as a means, and might be mistaken in thinking it a means. But what would a man with perfect knowledge wish to desire? Obviously he would wish to desire those things which would lead to the greatest possible harmony, inside and outside himself. For only in harmony could he avoid disappointment, and avoid a conflict in which some desires 30 would be unsatisfied. He would wish to desire, therefore, what he could get, i.e. what the whole desired. He would wish so to organize his own desires that they might be in harmony with those of the world. If the world were such as to make this impossible, he would wish for such desires as might lead the world to make it as possible as he could.

[This last paragraph is shaky, and needs enlarging].

# 39

# Are All Desires Equally Moral? [c. 1896]

THIS PAPER WAS written on three loose sheets inserted between pages 164 and 165 of the same "Mit Gott" notebook in which Paper **38** is found. The manuscript is undated. It was most likely written soon after Russell finished composing the lectures published as *German Social Democracy*, i.e. early in 1896, since the verso of the last leaf was apparently part of the draft of the bibliography of that book. It is numbered "4" in the top left-hand corner and carries details of three works on the German socialist movement, the third of which was published in 1894. This paper is a development of the issue of universal harmony among desires raised in the final paragraph of **38**, which Russell thought to be "shaky, and needs enlarging".

The copy-text is the manuscript (RA 210.006550–F9), consisting of three leaves.

ETHICS MUST HAVE a postulate, which cannot be disputed. This postulate is, that the Good, for me, at any moment, *is* what I want, and cannot be other: that it is useless, therefore, to say it *ought* to be other. I always shall act from desire, and it is a counsel of perfection to urge that I had better act otherwise. I desire objects which will satisfy desire, but not, except derivatively, the satisfaction of desire. Therefore the Satisfaction of Desire is *not* the Good, but the things desired *are* the Good. But what then becomes of morals? *All* acts are virtuous, since they pursue the Good. May it be that vice lies in a bad choice of means? That desiring $A$, I regard $B$ as a means, and commit an act $\beta$ which brings $B$, but turns out not to bring $\phantom{}$ 10 $A$ with it? This gives the Socratic maxim, that no man sins wittingly. It brings into relief the distinction between *primary* desires, for ends, and *secondary* desires, for means. In this way, the Good, the object exclusively of the primary desires, might acquire some permanence amid the changing secondary desires. And this is essential: if Ethics is to be a definite body of knowledge, the Good must be a fixed standard, by which to test the moral worth of acts.

Is it essential to the goodness of a desired object that its attainment should really bring satisfaction? This satisfaction seems logically involved in the desire, and yet it is a platitude that attainment brings disgust. This platitude $\phantom{}$ 20 is true, I believe, only because most of our desires are secondary, and our choice of means is often bad. If we desire a thing truly for its own sake, and not as a means, its attainment *must* bring satisfaction, by the very meaning of terms.

This seems a theoretically possible ethic: *primary* desires are *not* subject to moral praise or blame, being the data, in morals, for the construction of the Good; but *secondary* desires are immoral, when they are mistaken, i.e. will not attain the ends to which their objects are supposed to be means.

The problem of Ethics then becomes: What things do we desire for their own sakes? The problem of practical morals becomes: How are we to get $\phantom{}$ 30 these things? If we fail to adopt the right means, *we* are immoral: if the world does not provide any possible means, the *world* is immoral.

If Ethics could prove that the only primary desire is the desire for *harmony*, we should have a Good which would be the same for all, which therefore, given adequate knowledge, all would attain. But how prove that this is the only primary desire?

If it were proved that desire for harmony is the only primary desire, further constructions as to the Universal Will would follow of themselves. For the Universal Will would be desire for universal harmony, and submission to it would be the best way of attaining individual harmony. But how $\phantom{}$ 40 prove this?

Desires may be classified as

I. Immediate desires for some relation to objects of sense.
II. Desires for a state of ourselves as to
   1. Feeling
   2. Knowledge
   3. Volition—the latter, however, a derivative desire.
III. Desires for states of mind in other people, known to ourselves,
   1. Having no direct reference to ourselves
   2. Having direct reference to ourselves
   A compound of II and III 2 gives desires for certain relations between
10 ourselves and others. A complication of III gives desires for relations between others.

As regards I, the relation desired must be one which gives pleasure, and must therefore be a harmonious relation. As regards II.1, pleasure results directly from harmony, 2 is a harmony, 3 depends on a previously established standard of virtue, and is thus irrelevant in discussing what is virtue. III is the crux.

We may say, straight off, desire is always for a harmony between idea and existence, and this seems to settle the question. But what idea?

# Part VI

# Fellowship and First Professional Papers

# General Headnote

RUSSELL'S WORK ON geometry falls into a number of distinct phases. The first, centred around the writing of his dissertation, ended with the publication of *An Essay on the Foundations of Geometry* (1897), where the position advanced in Papers **42** and **44** finds its fullest expression. Shortly thereafter his position began to change, as the geometrical writings in *Collected Papers* 2 show. This Part includes all of Russell's extant papers, published and unpublished, on the philosophy of geometry through 1896. Also included are Russell's first two published reviews, both of which devote considerable attention to geometry. The first review (Paper **40**) is also of interest as an early statement of Russell's objections to psychologism and of his position on the philosophy of dynamics (a topic on which he planned to write more extensively after completing his work on geometry). The reviews initiate Russell's considerable series in *Mind* of reviews of foreign authors. Russell's former tutor, G. F. Stout, was at this time the journal's editor, and doubtless his personal knowledge of Russell's abilities led to the review assignments.

When Russell completed his Moral Sciences Tripos in the spring of 1894, he was uncertain whether to write the dissertation required for a Cambridge fellowship on philosophy or economics (see the headnote to Part VII). Soon after writing his Tripos essays, Russell conferred with Ward and as a result decided upon the philosophy of geometry. This topic remained a major research interest of his until the turn of the century, despite occasional hints as late as 1895 that he would abandon philosophy and switch to economics or even do dissertations in both fields. He reported in a letter of 10 June 1894 to Alys that Ward had been impressed by his Tripos essays and was optimistic about Russell's chances of a fellowship:

> We discussed a lot of possible subjects and finally seemed to fix on the Epistemological Bearings of Metageometry, which sounds well at any rate. I then went on, at Ward's recommendation, to a somewhat younger member of the Society, named Whitehead, another Trinity don, who has worked at this subject from the mathematical side, and he instructed me in the Bibliography of the subject. I may write on the meaning and validity of the differential calculus instead, but I think that would be harder and less exciting. In either case I shall be able to utilize both my Triposes, and so, I hope, make my dissertation unintelligible to all my examiners, in which case I shall be safe.

246

Both the subjects mentioned by Russell were important areas of controversy in nineteenth-century philosophy of mathematics. From the point of view of Russell's later work, the foundations of the differential calculus and the real number system (to which Cantor's work in set theory was an important contribution) might have seemed more appropriate. But Russell himself said later (*1959*, 39) that at this stage he was ignorant of the mathematical work being done in this area. In any case, the philosophy of geometry soon led him to Cantor's work, through the problems of spatial continuity (see *Collected Papers* 2). In the latter part of the nineteenth century, however, non-Euclidean geometry was much closer to the mainstream of philosophical debate.

The admission of non-Euclidean geometries raised major questions about the status of geometrical (and, more widely, mathematical) propositions and about the concept of truth in mathematics. Although non-Euclidean geometries were first published in 1829, they had received comparatively little attention until, in the 1860s, the publication of Riemann's "Ueber die Hypothesen, welche der Geometrie zu Grunde liegen" (1867) and Gauss's letters (Gauss *1860–65*) brought them into prominence. Philosophical interest was generated because the widespread recognition of non-Euclidean geometries coincided with a revival of interest in Kant's philosophy. On geometry, Kant had maintained that the propositions of Euclidean geometry were synthetic, but known with à priori certainty. The admission of non-Euclidean geometries was *prima facie* in conflict with this position. Russell's fellowship dissertation (of which no copy can be traced) and his first philosophical book, *An Essay on the Foundations of Geometry*, which arose out of it, were concerned with the problem of what could be salvaged of a Kantian position on geometry in view of the recent developments in the subject.

It is clear that Russell started working on geometry at least as early as the month he spent at the Pearsall Smiths' home in July and August 1894. His reading of Frischauf *1872*, Killing *1885* and Klein *1893* at the time is one indication. Another is that soon after he left Friday's Hill he wrote Alys asking her to send him Lotze's *Metaphysik*, Wundt's *System der Philosophie*, Kant's *Kritik der reinen Vernunft* and "The few loose sheets of manuscript headed *Geometrical Axioms* and those headed *Absolute Position* (1 page) and *Congruence* (3 pages) (all these were lying on my desk when I left Friday's Hill)" (24 Aug. 1894). Unfortunately, none of these notes survives among Russell's papers. The first note led to the paper "Geometrical Axioms", which was probably Russell's first paper to the Cambridge Moral Sciences Club and which was read on 9 November 1894 by C. P. Sanger in Russell's absence. According to the minutes, the paper led to "a very mathematical discussion" (Min. IX.41, p. 2, Cambridge University Library). This paper is also lost, and no other details of its contents are known. There does survive a brief entry in a notebook (RA 220.010500) which Russell kept during his visit to Berlin early in 1895. The book's contents are primarily notes taken by Russell at Adolph Wagner's economics lectures, but there are also fourteen pages of notes on Riemann *1867*, after which Russell has written the following, starting a fresh page (61), under the heading "Notes on Geometrical

Axioms":

> Observe unless space be nothing but relations, points in general and the *here* in particular are very hard to understand. If space *be* mere relations, *here* is only one term in the relation, *there* being the other term and the distance being the relation.

This is the earliest known statement by Russell of the relational theory of space, which underlies all the geometrical writings in this volume.

The topic of congruence was of considerable importance to Russell's work and continued to trouble him for some time. In a letter to Sanger (29 Sept. 1894) from Paris he asked about Euclid's method of establishing congruence for three-dimensional figures, since the method of superposition used for plane figures was inappropriate. This problem related clearly to the axiom of congruence (or free mobility) which figures prominently in Russell's account of the à priori parts of geometry (see Papers **42** and **44** and his *1897*, §§143–57).

In discussions with his fellowship examiners Russell was encouraged to publish parts of the dissertation. Paper **42** is certainly one result. **44** is also based on the dissertation, although it is more substantially revised (see the respective headnotes). Throughout much of 1895–97 Russell must be assumed to have been working on the dissertation and then turning it into a book. Chapter 1 of the book exists in a first draft. The differences between the draft and the book reveal that Russell made many substantial alterations as well as a host of stylistic ones. Together with the papers in this Part, they show him developing his professional capacity both philosophically and stylistically.

## 40

# Review of Heymans, *Die Gesetze und Elemente des wissenschaftlichen Denkens* [1895]

THIS REVIEW WAS published in *Mind*, n.s. 4 (April 1895): 245–9. By Russell's own account it was the first time his name had appeared in print as an author (Denonn *1943*, 15). Russell also wrote to Lady Ottoline Morrell: "One's first publication is rather an event. I well remember my first ... a review of a Dutchman" (letter 976, *c*.21 Jan. 1914). Gerardus Heymans (1857–1930) was a Dutch philosopher and psychologist who held a chair at the University of Leiden. His other books deal with issues in ethics, metaphysics and psychology. The two volumes of his *Die Gesetze und Elemente* were published in 1890 and 1894, respectively.

Russell read *Die Gesetze und Elemente des wissenschaftlichen Denkens: ein Lehrbuch der Erkenntnisstheorie in Grundzügen* [The Laws and Elements of Scientific Thought: A Textbook in Basic Theory of Knowledge] in February 1895 and almost certainly wrote the review that month. In working on it he sought advice from A. N. Whitehead on the line he should take with regard to absolute direction. Whitehead replied on 13 February 1895:

> As to absolute direction authorities differ: Newton, Clerk Maxwell ... and your Dutchman affirm that "absolute" *direction* can be determined: Mach and a large following deny. For the purposes of a review you can take whatever side you please without putting your foot into it, or you may hedge. As to my own view: I incline with much hesitation to believe that the dispute hinges on an ambiguity in the term "absolute".

According to Whitehead, if the axioms of dynamics are to hold, "it is necessary to assume certain axes as fixed in direction.... The controversy seems to be, whether this ... sense is properly called 'absolute'." And this controversy, he claimed, "broadens out into the wider question as to whether Science is merely descriptive or is explanatory." Whitehead made his own views clear by declaring "a strong personal preference for the free unsophisticated use of 'cause and effect' ideas in Science" and a fear that a purely descriptive view of science would check scientific progress. On the narrower question he claimed that

> Mach does not seem to have realized that the determination of the "fixed" axes is really involved in the Dynamical axioms: his arguments really come to the statement that if the Universe were different to what it is, we could not be

249

sure a priori that the Dynamical axioms would hold. This is a truism, unless you believe that the Dynamical axioms are a priori evident and need no verification—which is rather a large order.

Although Russell did not discuss absolute direction in his review, he did consider the related question of absolute motion (254: 16–32), where he comes down on the side of Heymans and the absolutists. He declared Heymans's treatment of mechanics "much the best section of the book" (254: 33). Subsequently, in *The Principles of Mathematics* (*1903*, 489) Russell referred to Heymans's book as one which "revived and emphasized" Newton's argument for absolute space and time from absolute rotation.

It is possible that Russell had sent Whitehead a draft of his review, for Whitehead's letter contains a postscript:

> I rather object to your paragraph on time-measurement. Why pitch on the Earth's rotation *alone*? Why not King Alfred's candle? Surely the *consistency* of innumerable alternative methods is important and gives a basis from which any one method may be corrected—e.g. the Earth is believed by Astronomers to be slowing off.

Russell's published review contains no paragraph on time-measurement, and it is possible that he omitted it in response to Whitehead's criticism, or that Whitehead was referring to some other writing by Russell. (Russell's account of time-measurement in Papers **42** and **44** incorporates Whitehead's point.)

From the mistake in the page number at 251: 33 (see the Textual Notes), it seems likely that the printer set type from Russell's handwritten manuscript. Since the manuscript is not known to be extant, the copy-text is the version in *Mind*. Russell made no corrections to the review in his copy of *Mind*.

*Die Gesetze und Elemente des wissenschaftlichen Denkens*. By Dr. G. Heymans. Leiden: S. C. Van Doesburgh; Leipzig: Otto Harrassowitz. Vol. I: 1890. Pp. xii, 270. Vol. 2: 1894. Pp. vi, 271–478.

"THE SUBJECT OF this book", we are told in the Preface, "is two-fold: for non-philosophers it is a text-book of Epistemology, while for philosophers it forms a treatise on method, illustrated by examples. The endeavour to combine the two in a single book springs from my conviction that the empirical method of investigation and proof, which I wish to advocate towards my fellow-philosophers, is precisely the method of presentation best fitted for introducing men of scientific culture to philosophy." 10

This two-fold object necessitates a good deal of matter (for example the accounts of the Syllogism and of Mill's Canons of Induction) which except for the purposes of a text-book would be superfluous; and there is through-out an endeavour to avoid whatever would be too technical for the unphi-losophical reader. Our author has, however, allowed himself one exception to this rule, in connection with the relation of Epistemology to Psychology, to which he addresses himself at a very early stage. His position on this question is one which might have been owned by Hume: Epistemology is a "Psychology of Thought", and is formally defined as "The exact determi- 20 nation and explanation, by means of the empirical investigation of given thought, of the causal relations which condition the occurrence of convic-tion in consciousness" (p. 3). Whatever may be thought of its philosophical merit, I cannot but think that a position so generally disputed must make the work somewhat unsuitable as a text-book; the more so, as the solutions proposed, at any rate throughout the first volume, are strictly in accordance with this view of the problem—i.e. they are solutions which account psychologically for our beliefs, instead of giving grounds for their validity. Accordingly the ultimate test of certainty is the "Gedankensexperiment"; the laws of Contradiction and Excluded Middle are regarded as "irreducible 30 psychical laws suffering no exception", and are based on the impossibility which we feel (*empfinden*) of simultaneously affirming two contradictory propositions (p. 69). Similarly the laws of Arithmetic refer not to things, but to thoughts; they are purely psychological laws. And Geometry is regarded as established by explaining the genesis of space-perception through motor-sensations; these are subjective, and produced by our volitions, and appear to account by this property for the à priori certainty and exactness of the Euclidean system, in relation to which Dr. Heymans adheres to the position of the Transcendental Aesthetic.

In all this there is, it seems to me, a confusion between the psychologically 40 subjective and the logically à priori; the apriority of Logic, Arithmetic and Geometry being proved merely by referring them to subjective psychical processes. But no ground is shewn for regarding the result as less empirical in the case of a "Gedankensexperiment" than in the case of any other kind of experiment. I fail to see how, except by the previous assumption of the whole array of the canons of inductive science, we can have any assurance that two such experiments will give the same result, nor how we can set any limits to the efficiency of the White Queen's practice in "believing as many as six impossible things before breakfast". In order to get a theory of knowledge out of psychology, it has been necessary to leave out of account the various emotional and pathological causes of belief, which certainly come under the above definition; it is throughout assumed that no *causes* of belief are possible except the evidence of the senses, logical reasoning, and certain fundamental à priori laws, i.e. the *grounds* of *correct* belief. In short the psychology of belief appears to be rather that which would apply to an intellectually ideal man than to men liable to error; accordingly error is regarded as springing only from deficient analysis, and this is the only answer we obtain to the question how the laws of thought can be at the same time norms for correct thinking and psychological laws for all thinking.

To illustrate this general criticism of the first volume, let us examine more in detail our author's views on Geometry, to the discussion of which a considerable space is devoted. Here Dr. Heymans maintains a Kantian position, which he supports by Riehl's hypothesis of the generation of space-perception from motor-sensations. It is somewhat cavalierly assumed, as though no one had ever disputed it, that the propositions of Geometry are exact and of apodeictic certainty, and therefore à priori. The value of metageometry is taken to consist solely in the fact that it has proved the axiom of parallels to be independent of the others and essential to the Euclidean system. The indispensable axioms are regarded as five in number: Every point is determined by three coordinates; these vary continuously; bodies can be moved without distortion; through any two points only one straight line can be drawn; and through any point only one parallel can be drawn to a given straight line (p. 188). These axioms are regarded as all necessarily deriving their evidence in the same way, and are not discussed separately; though the results of non-Euclidean Geometry would seem to necessitate a division into three classes, omitting the second, which is in my opinion involved in the third, since the idea of mobility is only applicable to a continuum. As to the other four, the first deals with a purely sensuous quality of given space, which has no *logical* importance; the extension to four or *n* dimensions would not invalidate three-dimensional Geometry any more than the third dimension invalidates Plane Geometry. In fact this axiom might almost be called statistical; the number of dimensions must be a positive integer, so that we are not in the realm of approximations any more than in counting the number of people in a room, and accuracy can therefore hardly be taken as evidence of apriority. The third, the axiom of

Congruence or free mobility, on the contrary, has, I think, no *sensuous* import; for, as Dr. Heymans observes in answer to Helmholtz, any apparent exception to it on the part of actual bodies is always to be regarded as due to physical rather than geometrical causes. But its *logical* importance is such that without it Geometry in every form would be impossible; no means would exist of discovering *how* objects changed their shape in moving from place to place, since the change would affect the measure as much as the thing measured. There is also a philosophic absurdity in denying this axiom, for if shapes were changed by mere motion, they must depend on absolute position, and bodies would be determined by their relation to empty space. Between these two extremes come the fourth and fifth of the above axioms, which seem to answer pretty closely to Klein's definition of axioms in general, that they are postulates by which we rise from the inexactness of sense to the perfect exactness of Mathematics. For, as every one knows, they are equivalent to the assumption that the measure of curvature of our space is zero; and since here it is logically possible, by supposing the measure of curvature small, to make *small* departures from such an assumption, (which was not possible with the first axiom), it is difficult to see how sense can give us accuracy beyond the limits of the errors of observation.

These considerations seem to me to necessitate a separate discussion of the different classes, but Dr. Heymans treats them as all alike exact and certain; this certainty, however, must, he thinks, refer to something other than given objects, since mental images suffice to give perfectly correct results, though they can never accurately reproduce those objects. This something is the motor sense, in terms of which he tries to explain all his five axioms. Motor-sensations are subjective, and they are brought forth by our own volitions; these facts are supposed to establish Geometry on a Kantian à priori basis.

Apart from the psychological validity of Riehl's hypothesis, this theory of Geometry seems to me very inadequate to Dr. Heymans' contention; if Geometry really does deal with motor-sensations, it must, one would think, be merely a branch of empirical psychology. I fail to see in what sense motor-sensations are less phenomenal or more à priori than any other sensations, and I should have supposed Hume's difficulties with the *minimum sensibile* would have rendered so sensational an account impossible, unless one were willing to throw to the winds all claim to exactness on the part of Geometry. The entire theory seems to me to rest on the confusion of the à priori with the psychologically subjective, which underlies the whole first volume.

The second volume, which deals with Causation and Mechanics, is for the most part free from this confusion, and consequently appears to me to be of much greater epistemological value than the first. In Logic, Arithmetic and

Geometry, we had not yet, in Dr. Heymans' view, got beyond self-knowledge; our judgments always referred to our own thoughts and feelings. But with the consideration of the real category of cause, we rise to the problem of the knowledge of Not-Self. All Induction rests, directly or indirectly, on Causation, on the definition of which much care is bestowed. After an excellent criticism of the views of Mill and Jevons, Dr. Heymans declares in favour of Hamilton's hypothesis: causation is equivalent to the axiom that a real creation or destruction is impossible. Having chiefly Mechanics in view, he shews that this axiom accounts for the equivalence of
10 cause and effect, and explains their connection with the logical couple of ground and consequent. The latter being, in accordance with the first volume, taken as a case of psychological causation, our knowledge of the cause is, assuming Hamilton's principle, the ground of our knowledge of the effect, which essentially is nothing but the perpetuation of the cause (p. 387).

The view of Causation thus gained is now applied with great success to Mechanics. The laws of motion cannot be wholly empirical, for they refer to absolute motion, which is not a possible object of experience. (This is proved by the following argument: If the whole universe were rotating with uniform angular velocity, the laws of motion would require the appearance
20 of centrifugal forces, causing quite a different distribution of matter from that which would otherwise exist; but such a motion could never directly appear to the senses.) The à priori element is Hamilton's principle. But the laws are not *wholly* à priori; the first law for example may be thus formulated: The changeless state which, in the absence of any disturbing cause, a body must preserve is not rest, but uniform motion. Hamilton's principle leaves both these alternatives as possible, in fact the former *was* taken by the ancients and by the Aristotelians; the function of experience has been to decide in favour of the latter. (It may be observed that the alternative only exists on the assumption that the law refers to *absolute* motion: in relative
30 motion there is no difference between rest and uniform velocity.) The other laws are similarly explained by the application of Hamilton's principle to experience, and this is, in my opinion, much the best section of the book.

As regards Mechanics, Causation in the above sense is probably all that the science requires, being quite superfluous in the sense of efficiency, as is shewn by the superannuation of the idea of force and its supersedence by that of energy. Also it is noteworthy that the mechanical properties of the universe as a whole, its mass, momentum, and energy, are regarded by Mechanics as constant. Of course, the principle is only what Kant would call regulative, not constitutive; we search for as much constancy as possi-
40 ble, but a thorough carrying out of the principle, if applied, as Mechanics requires, to attribute as well as to substance, would involve the task of explaining away all change; the effect cannot be regarded as *identical* with the cause, or all happening must disappear. The use of the principle in

Mechanics involves the abstraction of motion from the moving matter; these two are regarded as separately constant, though the motion is allowed to be transmitted from body to body; in fact, the orthodox mechanical doctrine might be compared to the Transmigration of Souls. Thus the principle is not applied to the real, but to an intellectual and abstract construction of the real, resting on the distinction of substance and attribute. Its efficiency in Mechanics, which depends throughout on this distinction, is thus comprehensible; but it remains a question whether some theory in which cause and effect are less homogeneous, in which there is still some idea of activity, might not be necessary in other sciences, e.g. Psychology; at any rate, Psychology is not yet in the state where its laws can be *seen* to flow from the indestructibility of existence. Dr. Heymans has not discussed any other sciences than Pure Mathematics and Mechanics; it would have been interesting to see how far it was possible elsewhere to apply the same view.

The chief value of the book seems to me to lie in the analysis of the laws of motion, and in the exposition of the à priori elements contained in them. The whole account is thoroughly self-consistent, and shews a distinct superiority to his opponents, Mach and others, who maintain a more empirical position. In the first volume there is some good critical work, for instance in connection with Lange's geometrical theory of formal logic; but the constructive work is impregnated with his psychological view of Epistemology, and I must therefore regard the discussion of Mechanics as the portion of the book best worthy of attention and of most permanent value.

# 41

# Observations on Space and Geometry [1895]

THE EARLIEST SURVIVING account of Russell's research on the foundations of geometry is to be found in a small, water-damaged black notebook (RA 210.006551). One end begins "January 26. Schmoller, Prussian History" and has five pages of notes on Gustav Schmoller's lectures at the University of Berlin. The other end is headed "Observations on Space and Geometry" and is dated "Berlin, March 1895" on the title-page. Below the date are the two quotations printed here above the first section. As with most of his notebooks from this period, Russell wrote mainly on the right-hand pages, reserving the facing pages for occasional insertions and footnotes. When all the right-hand pages were full, Russell turned the notebook upside down and continued, beginning six leaves from the end on the unused left-hand pages. Altogether 134 pages (some of them unnumbered) are filled with his observations. The final page is dated "June 6. 1895". The "Observations" are divided into the following six sections (which are not numbered in the notebook):

1  1. Introduction. (fos. 1–6)
2  Alternative or Supplementary Introduction. (versos of fos. 3–5)
3  Note. On the meaning of Apriority as applied to space. (fos. 7–13)
4  Criticism of Lotze's attack on Metageometry. (fos. 14–29)
5  *Erhardt* Metk. Kap. v, pp. 226–258 (fos. 30–8)
6  Mathematical History of Metageometry. (fos. 39–121)

On the verso of the title-page, facing the start of the first introduction, Russell wrote:

*Note.* The Introduction will require considerable alteration, as it does not agree with the view of Kant's Transcendental Aesthetik in the next section. A judicious substitution of *intuition* for *sensation* might do much.

Of the six sections listed above only the two introductions, the note on apriority and the section on Erhardt are printed here. The criticism of Lotze is essentially that of *An Essay on the Foundations of Geometry*, §§85–97, although in its original form it seems to have been regarded as an appendix (see p. 73 of the notebook). The published version contains many (primarily stylistic) alterations. The "Mathematical History of Metageometry" is Russell's first draft of Chap. I, "A Short History of Metageometry", of the *Essay*. The published version, however, is considerably expanded and several passages in the notebook version, especially those dealing with topics in the second and third periods of the development of non-Euclidean geometry, have been replaced by new material in the book.

The four sections printed in this volume as Paper **41** do not occur in any form in the *Essay*. The discussion of Erhardt was omitted presumably because of the similarity between Erhardt's position and Lotze's, while the note on apriority was replaced by the discussion with which the *Essay* opens. Neither introduction was used in the book, and it is not known whether either was used in Russell's dissertation, since the note on the need for alterations in the first introduction is not dated. The Alternative Introduction does not make the suggested alterations.

The copy-text is the notebook. Authorial alterations are on at least two levels. First there are ink alterations made simultaneously with the initial composition of the "Observations". Secondly there are a number of pencil alterations, which appear to have been made at a later stage. They are carefully made, possibly for typing or copying by someone else. (It is not known whether Russell employed a typist at this time, though three years later, in a letter of 20 July 1898, he recommended his own typist to Moore.) The pencil alterations appear only in sections **41a** and **41c**.

Quelle blague que la Géométrie!

Flaubert, *Education Sentimentale*, p. 258.

The whole science of Geometry may be said to owe its being to the exorbitant interest which the human mind takes in lines. We cut space up in every direction in order to manufacture them.

W. James, *Principles of Psychology*, II, p. 150n.

## 41a Introduction

THE ONLY MANNER in which we are immediately affected by the outer world is *Sensation*. Whatever surpasses mere Sensation springs from Thought—it is thus psychologically subjective and its laws cannot be determined from without. In this sense, then, every *explanation* of empirical facts of the *outer* world—i.e. of sensations—rests on subjective needs and proceeds by subjective laws. Apart from thought, our sensations might be passively accepted in their succession—the consciousness of this succession being itself the product of thought—and no need could be felt for their explanation or classification. There is thus in all thought a volitional element—if we could make up our minds to accept our sensations passively as they come to us, without any desire for insight into future sensations, none of the problems of knowledge could arise, because knowledge, if it could be said to exist at all, could only be of the actual present sensation; this sensation, being purely factual, could contain nothing logically contradictory to any other sensation, and no other sensation could be present in imagination save by the activity of the mind. But even *sensation*, though we regard its immediate cause as something external to the soul (I use this word without any questionable implication), is itself a psychical phenomenon—it is therefore natural to suppose that its nature is composite, in part due to the external cause, in part to the nature of the subject affected—just as the melting of wax by the fire is partly due to the heat, partly to the nature of the wax. In all those elements of sensation which spring from the latter, we might expect a certain similarity, in that they have a common ground, which there is no reason to suppose in the external causes. Hence we arrive at something like the Kantian standpoint—the *matter*, which varies with every fresh sensation, would be regarded as due to the object, while the form, in which the matter is ordered, would be ascribed to the subject.—There is certainly something fascinating in the apparent simplicity of this view and in the insight it appears to afford; space and time, as universal forms, are subjective, and being independent of particular sensations, are not merely factual, but are unvarying forms into which all the diversity of externally-caused sensation has to be moulded. This gives to our knowledge of them a more than empirical certainty, since they spring from our own natures and therefore have constant properties and can be exhaustively known to us in a manner not dependent on, though elicited by, experience. Geometry and Kinematics are thus supposed to be established on a firm basis, quite apart from observation and induction.

At the same time, even accepting the *subjectivity* of space and time, it does not really follow that we can have apodeictic certainty about them. Aesthetic value is on all hands admitted to be purely subjective, and yet judgments about it have become a bye-word for their uncertainty—*de gustibus* etc. Or, to give a more direct criticism, how can we know, except by that very obser- 10 vation and induction whose necessity was to be obviated, that the subjective forms are the same in different individuals, or, in the case of space, in the same individual at different times? Further, space is given us primarily in sensation, or at best in sensuous imagination—it is, in its primitive form, as Kant himself insists, *Intuition*, not Conception. Hence reflective knowl- edge, such as Geometry professes to give, can be derived only by psychol- ogy, primarily introspective and always empirical. It follows that as an ob- ject of thought, crystallized into a *Conception*, it would have necessarily undergone a process of criticism and reflection; it would not be known im- mediately and certainly any more than any other object of knowledge, and 20 its nature *might* only be discoverable by experimental inductive science. Thus where inexactness and approximation are logically *possible*, they must be assumed to be present, for reflective knowledge of sensational matter is necessarily inexact. Hence Metageometry and the apriority of space are not obviously incompatible—and neither can, without further investigation, be regarded as an argument against the other.

In the "Transcendental Aesthetik", it is assumed that sensational space is precisely similar to the space-conception with which Geometry deals, and thus the accuracy and apodeictic certainty of the latter seems an immediate consequence of the apriority of the former. Throughout this Essay I shall 30 however try to maintain (1) That even if sensational space were subjective, it would not afford sufficient ground for an objection to Metageometry, and vice versa, that Metageometry cannot afford an objection to the subjectivity of space; though, if the latter were established on other grounds, it might reinforce the objection to the Kantian assumption that subjectivity accounts for apodeictic certainty (i.e. it might necessitate a more careful distinction between the subjective and the à priori)—(2) That Geometrical Axioms owe their origin in part only to spatial intuition, the remainder being due to purely logical motives (as is *wholly* the case with Arithmetic)—that the latter element, like Arithmetic, has apodeictic certainty, while the former is only 40 approximate and empirical.

## 41b  Alternative or Supplementary Introduction

WHEN I FIRST determined to write a dissertation, I intended to confine myself to Metageometry and its immediate bearings on Philosophy. But the great interest shewn in Riemann and Helmholtz by Non-Mathematicians springs from the fact that their investigations are supposed to upset Kant; it has seemed to me, on the contrary, that though they undoubtedly destroy that argument which is derived from the apodeictic certainty of Geometry, they do not touch the others; I was therefore led to investigate the psychological and metaphysical contentions for and against Kant's other arguments, so that my subject became very considerably widened. To give it unity, I may as well group its various parts about the "Transcendental Aesthetik".

The psychological problem occurs thus: Kant contended that extension is subjective in a way in which the secondary qualities are not so: that is, there is no counterpart to it in the object. As a necessary corollary from this view, extension is not matter of sensation, for sensation is the direct operation, upon the mind, of the external world. Thus the controversy may be decided by the psychological investigation of the question: Can we explain space-presentation without assuming anything corresponding to it in crude sensation? If so, Kant's position *may* be sound; if not, it *must* be false. This investigation has been very skilfully conducted by Stumpf, with whose position I agree; it is brought into connection with non-Euclidean Geometry by the fact that the latter provides a means of regarding Euclid's geometrical axioms as approximate, and of constructing a consistent system with slightly varying axioms, so that within the errors of observation we are at liberty to choose between Euclid and Helmholtz. This approximativeness and power of slight continuous variations of axioms is the mark of a matter derived from sense, not from logic or from purely subjective processes, and thus the two investigations confirm and strengthen one another.

## 41c  Note. On the Meaning of Apriority as Applied to Space

IN READING THE "Transcendental Aesthetik", it might seem as though Kant meant by apriority nothing more than subjectivity, but this cannot be taken as his real meaning. The word à priori has since been used a great deal, and apparently with many different meanings—sometimes it is thought that the apriority of space is established when it is deduced psychologically from complexes of sensations themselves non-spatial, e.g. motor-sensations (not presentations of motion, for these are already spatial); sometimes it is thought necessary to shew that it does not in any way belong to crude sensation, but is a subjective form which would (perhaps) first appear in *perception*, and so have as little counterpart in the outer world as the Syllogism for example. This seems to be as nearly as possible the view of Kant: he says "In a phenomenon I call that which corresponds to sensation its *matter*; but that which makes it possible to order the manifold of the phenomenon in certain relations I call its *form*." Since this form "*cannot itself be in turn sensation*, it follows that only the matter is given à posteriori, the form must however lie ready à priori in the mind, and can therefore be studied apart from all sensation." Thus *à priori*, to Kant, means much more than subjective—the pure sensation, also, belongs to the subject, and is as much determined by the nature of the subject affected as by that of the object causing the sensation. In this sense the secondary qualities have, since Locke, been regarded as subjective—but to Kant they are not à priori. À priori is that, and that alone, which is neither part of sensation nor assumed for the sole purpose of explaining sensations—or classifying them, as some empiricists would prefer to say. Space, to Kant, is thus à priori in the same sense as number is to modern logicians (*v.* Sigwart, *Logik*, Bd. II, Methodenlehre, §66)—it is not called for by sensation, but is added by a free spontaneous activity of the subject. This being the case, it is plain that space is really put on a different level from empirical data—it does not depend on an outer world whose nature can only become known to us bit by bit through its action on ourselves; but *we* have brought it forth, and in our own self-identity we seem to have a warrant for its permanence and for the accuracy of our knowledge about it. The Kantian position, if it could be maintained, would undoubtedly make space independent of *outer* experience; (I use *outer* of course as referring to not-self, not to spatial externality)—but there would seem to be still an *inner* experience, just as empirical and inductive as the outer, on which it must depend. Of course Kant is right in maintaining that *something* must be presupposed to make experience possible, and that our knowledge of this something cannot, without a *logical fallacy*, be made in turn to rest on experience. But in this statement the solution is already suggested: *logic* alone, it would seem, must be presupposed—understanding logic in the widest sense, as including the whole of the *formal* science of inference, Causation e.g. as well as the Syllogism. Self-knowledge is certainly in some departments quite as difficult and uncertain as knowledge of the outer world; desire, for instance, is unquestionably à priori in the above sense, and yet the whole array of modern psychological fiction is a commentary on the difficulty of knowing our own desires. In short, it is one thing to be *part* of consciousness, another to be the *object* of consciousness.

However, I shall recur to the objections to Kant's general views later on—at present I am primarily concerned in making clear the *meaning* of apriority. Kant's doctrine on space cannot, I think, establish the apodeictic certainty of Geometry[1]; nor, conversely, if this be shaken, can Kant's doctrine be thereby upset. But it is obviously open to attack from the side of Psychology. If it can be shewn that space *does* form part of the matter of sensation (which is a question for Psychology), then Kant's doctrine as above explained falls to the ground (*v.* Stumpf, §1). It does not, however, follow that space is not in *some* sense à priori, and thus, when this position is maintained in modern writers, the word usually has a different meaning from that which I have here attributed to Kant. Thus Erhardt, who has devoted 300 pages to maintaining the truth of the "Transcendental Aesthetik", distinguishes between apriority and Ideality; the former appears to mean to him *mere* subjectivity, the latter *exclusive* subjectivity; the two together, according to him, constitute Kant's doctrine. The former is, in a certain sense, a truism: the space we know is in our consciousness, and is therefore in a certain sense subjective. Only naïve realism can maintain that "real" space exactly resembles presented space; and yet Herr Erhardt is at great pains to combat this view, as though it were held by those who attack Kant. So far he is of course successful; but when he comes to Ideality, he does not appear to realize what his task really is. Undoubtedly Kant maintained ideality, as I shewed above; and Erhardt himself asserts (pp. 304, 305) that Idealism denies the existence of anything similar to space in the objective world and holds space to be merely the form in which we perceive things in themselves non-spatial. Nevertheless he allows a correspondent series of relations among things-in-themselves, allows a "metaphysical distance" (p. 345), and allows the real analogue of space to have something corresponding to three dimensions (p. 352). But such admissions are all that the most determined anti-Kantian can desire—if, as Kant maintained, space were *not* given in sensation at all, there would be no more ground for supposing an external analogue to space-relations than to Barbara.

Thus great confusion exists in the use of the word à priori. In future I shall mean by it what I have endeavoured to shew that Kant meant; views such as Erhardt's, which allow a real analogue to it, I shall speak of as maintaining only its Subjectivity. It will be seen that Geometry cannot decide between them; but on psychological grounds the decision would now-a-days be pretty generally anti-Kantian.

---

1 If, however, Geometry were à priori in Kant's sense, i.e. not concerned with matter of sensation, this fact would shew the actual division between Geometry and other Sciences, e.g. Optics, to be not arbitrary and purely intellectual, but corresponding to a *sharp* division between their subjects; otherwise, a different Geometry and a different Optic *might* be found to give equally good explanations of the actual phenomena by compensating each other, and therefore be admissible. The importance of this point will appear in the sequel.

# 41d  Erhardt, *Metaphysik*, Kap. v, Pp. 226–258

IN CONNECTION WITH Lotze it seems natural to say a few words about the most recent adherent of his views, Herr Erhardt, since he "subscribes almost word for word" the views which I have criticized above. As might be expected from this fact, he appears to have a very narrow acquaintance with the literature of the subject—indeed, except the popular lecture of Helmholtz on which Lotze, as we saw, based his attack, he criticizes only Lobatchewsky and Riemann. He repeats most of Lotze's arguments, so that these remarks may be brief. He *assumes* the straight line, etc., to be à priori conceptions; the Spheredwellers who regard their great circles as straight lines he puts aside as (1) psychologically impossible, since all space-intuition *must* have three dimensions; (2) certain, if they could exist, to set up a Euclidean three-dimensional system; (3) wholly in error, if this did not take place, in treating great circles as straight lines; (4) in any case irrelevant, since two-dimensional Spherical Geometry is not incompatible with Euclid. These views are supported by no new arguments, so it is not necessary to criticize them in detail. Helmholtz's unfortunate analogy, which was intended to make the non-Euclidean system intelligible to non-mathematicians, is certainly responsible for an immense amount of confusion on the part of these latter gentlemen. But his *idea* is, I explained above, correct: the Spheredwellers can't imagine straighter lines than theirs, which cut in two points: believing their surface to be all there is of space, they *will* set up a Geometry totally inconsistent with Euclid. The confusion arises thus: So long as we deal with two-dimensional analogies, we can regard the whole space under consideration as a boundary within a plane space of three dimensions in which Euclidean straight lines are possible; it seems, therefore, to the non-mathematician, mere verbal jugglery to call great circles straight lines and say two of them cut in two points; but when we rise to three dimensions, for which all this is merely introduction, the case is otherwise—our spherical space can no longer be regarded, except for purely abstract mathematical purposes, as a boundary in four dimensions, and the analogue of a great circle becomes really the straightest line we can draw without the questionable aid of the fourth dimension. Thus in such a space the axiom of the straight line really *would* not hold, and there would be a clash with Euclid; and this is all which Helmholtz's much abused analogies were intended to bring forth. To say people in such a space would be mistaken in regarding their lines as straight as Erhardt does (p. 229) is to beg the question, which is just as to the most legitimate conception of the straight line.—Lotze's arguments about parallel lines (which turn on Helmholtz's careless omission of the word "straight") and as to the supposed contradictions which would lead the Spheredwellers to three dimensions and Euclid, are then repeated (p. 230); these I have already answered,

so I need say no more about them.—Erhardt next denies that there is any more contradiction between Euclid and Non-Euclid than between quadrilaterals and triangles. In a sense this is true, just as there is no contradiction between a tall man and a short one; but in Erhardt's sense it is hardly true, since he maintains the apodeictic certainty of Geometry. If any one had maintained that by an à priori necessity people could only see triangles, the discovery of quadrilaterals would be extremely embarrassing to him; if I said (having lived perhaps among the Hottentots) that all men must, by a logical compulsion, be under six foot, there would be a contradiction bet-
10 ween my system and people above that height. So long as Euclidean Geometry is content to be *coordinate* with Non-Euclidean, there is no contradiction; but if it demands a superior position, a quarrel between the rivals must ensue. This however does not probably touch Erhardt's meaning: he probably believes the difference between the two to be verbal, a mere matter of defining the straight line and so forth, as, with Helmholtz's illustration of Sphereland, it to some extent is. And this would still be the case with Solid Geometry, if we could allow ourselves to extend our views to four dimensions; but such extensions, once for all, are no longer Geometry, but mere analysis; the distinction between Euclidean and non-Euclidean Geometry in
20 our actual world is a matter of accurate measurement, but a fourth dimension wholly surpasses all attempts to imagine it, as is acknowledged by every sane person. Thus in three-dimensional Spherical Geometry we are not at liberty to regard straighter lines as in any way possible, and it therefore remains a fact that two straight lines, in the only intelligible sense, meet in two points, which certainly contradicts Euclid if anything can.

Erhardt asserts, even more decidedly than Lotze, as against poor Sphereland, which was never more than an elucidatory analogy, that everything for every conscious being must have three dimensions: "was existieren soll, muss ein dreidimensionaler Körper sein" (p. 232), and this view
30 is repeated many times, sometimes for several pages on end, in varying language—but Erhardt does not, like Lotze, attempt an à priori proof of this startling statement, but relies on Psychology for his defence—though I fail to see how this Science can afford an objection to anything so purely hypothetical as Helmholtz's fairy-tale. However, even if his view were established, it is only by a complete misunderstanding of the whole purpose of the analogy (which is purely formal) that anything important could be supposed proved against Helmholtz.—Next (pp. 235–6) follows an attack, with which I am happy to be able entirely to concur, on Helmholtz's view that rigid physical bodies are necessary to Geometry; I agree here with
40 Erhardt, and not with Helmholtz, but will give my grounds elsewhere.—
Finally, Erhardt professes to agree with the view Helmholtz has put forward as possible to a strict Kantian, that Geometry applies to ideal bodies, but becomes empirical the moment it is used of real objects. Helmholtz himself

has well shewn the difficulties of this view in *Mind*, Vol. III—but this is too wide a question to go into here.

After a criticism of Riemann in which there is much that is valuable, Erhardt returns to more technical questions (p. 240) with the consideration of Lobatchewsky. And here he shews a complete misunderstanding of Metageometry in comparing its premisses to the assumption of a four-cornered circle, from which he does not doubt but that certain propositions might be deduced: "these propositions of course contradict one another, but they are quite correctly deduced from the fundamental conception" (p. 241); while the whole point of Metageometry is that its propositions do *not* contradict one another, and never can, unless those of Euclidean Geometry should, since they can be correlated with these by a unique correspondence, by which any proposition in the one has a single counterpart in the other.—Finally on p. 244, misled by the troublesome word "Krüm-mungsmaass" (which Klein very properly objects to), he confesses that for his part he can think nothing when he tries to think a curved space, though the measure of curvature of a *surface* is perfectly intelligible to him. This is certainly a misunderstanding due to a defective terminology—no one *ought* to speak of a curved space, but it is difficult to make the idea of a measure of curvature of space plain to a non-mathematician in any other way. I should therefore feel very tolerant of Erhardt if he did not impute his own inability to the mathematicians who use the term—as well might he believe them not to understand what they mean by a Theta-Function because he doesn't. He demonstrates his boasted want of comprehension by speaking of spaces with finite measure of curvature as non-congruent (p. 245), in this error again following Lotze.

The points I have criticized in these two, I fear, somewhat too caustic attacks, have been only details in which a want of mathematical knowledge had led to errors, which, for the sake of non-mathematicians, it seemed worth while to set right. I do not mean to deny them both considerable general value; for example, there is great importance in Erhardt's objection (p. 237) to the disjunction of Riemann and other empiricists: Geometrical Propositions are either consequences of general conceptions of magnitudes (*Grössenbegriffen*), or inductions from observation. But in the above remarks it was not my purpose to speak of general views, but of detailed criticism which seemed to me to proceed from critics unequal to the task they had set themselves.

# 42

# The Logic of Geometry [1896]

THIS PAPER APPEARED in *Mind*, n.s. 5 (Jan. 1896): 1–23. It is the earliest extant document in which Russell tries to prove the apriority of general metrical geometry. (Throughout the paper he speaks of "geometry", but his characterization of the discipline makes it clear that he has metrical geometry in mind.) His method is to argue that three axioms—the axiom of congruence (or free mobility), the axiom of dimensions and the axiom of distance (or the straight line)—are necessary for any form of metrical geometry, and thus are à priori. Russell repeats these arguments, with some additions and many minor stylistic changes (as the Textual Notes show), in *An Essay on the Foundations of Geometry* (1897). Of the five lengthy passages in **42** not reprinted in Russell's *Essay*, two merit comment. The first (270: 19–272: 4), on Helmholtz's account of the relation between rigid bodies and the axiom of congruence, is replaced in *1897* by the much briefer §148 since Russell had already dealt with Helmholtz's views at length in §§70–1. The second (278: 5–279: 18), on the axiom of the straight line, is extensively recast as §§162–4, though the overall argument remains the same.

There is clear evidence that **42** was originally part of Russell's lost fellowship dissertation, which he submitted to Trinity College in August 1895 and on the basis of which (together with some successful examination answers) he was elected to a six-year fellowship. The day before his election he wrote to Alys that Whitehead, who with Ward had examined his dissertation, had told him "certain parts, more or less as they stood, were well worth publishing" (9 Oct. 1895). That **42** is the result is confirmed by Alys, who told Mary Gwinn that the paper published in the current (i.e. January) issue of *Mind* was "a part of his Dissertation" (20 Jan. 1896, Bryn Mawr College Library). There is also internal evidence indicating its origin: at 285: 20–1 Russell wrote: "The whole task of our chapter has been...." In revising the chapter for *Mind* he neglected to alter this reference. The extent to which he revised part of his dissertation for publication as **42** cannot be absolutely determined, but in view of the above it seems likely that the changes were minor. The changes must have been made in October or November 1895, for Alys reported to her father on 4 November that Russell was correcting proofs of the article "and I would not on *any* account disturb him!"

Since no manuscript is known, the copy-text is that published in *Mind*. Russell's library includes a bound offprint of the paper: it is not marked in any way.

IN THE PRESENT paper, we are not concerned with the correspondence of Geometry with fact; we are concerned with Geometry simply as a body of reasoning, the conditions of whose possibility we wish to examine. For our present purpose, therefore, we have nothing to do with crude or unformed notions of space; we have to do with the conception of space in its most finished and elaborated form, after thought has done its utmost in transforming the intuitional data. Nevertheless, we shall have occasion to remember, from time to time, that there *is* a space-intuition, and that the nature of this intuition makes the conception of space radically and permanently different, in important respects, from that of any other man- 10 ifold.

### 1. THE AXIOM OF CONGRUENCE

Let us begin with a provisional definition. Geometry, we may say, deals with the comparison and relations of spatial magnitudes. Whether or not geometry has a wider subject-matter than this, we may for the present leave undecided; this much it certainly does deal with. The conception of magnitude, then, is, from the start, a necessary part of Geometry. Some of Euclid's axioms, accordingly, have been classed as arithmetical, and have been supposed to have nothing particular to do with space. Such are the axioms that equals added to or subtracted from equals give equals, and that things 20 which are equal to the same thing are equal to one another. These axioms, it is said, are purely arithmetical, and do not, like the others, ascribe an adjective to space. As regards their use in arithmetic, this is of course true. But if an arithmetical axiom is to be applied to spatial magnitudes, it must have some spatial import, and thus even this class is not, in Geometry, *merely* arithmetical. Fortunately, the geometrical element is the same in all the axioms of this class—in fact we can see at once that it can amount to no more than a definition of spatial magnitude. Again, since the space with which Geometry deals is infinitely divisible, a definition of spatial magnitude reduces itself to a definition of spatial equality, for, as soon as we have this last, 30 we can compare two spatial magnitudes by dividing each into a number of equal units, and counting the number of such units in each.[1] The ratio of the number of units is, of course, the ratio of the two magnitudes.

We require, then, at the very outset, some criterion of spatial equality; without such a criterion, Geometry would become wholly impossible. It might appear, at first sight, as though this need not be an axiom, but might be a mere definition. This, however, is not the case, for two distinct spatial

---

1 Strictly speaking, this method is only applicable where the two magnitudes are commensurable. But if we take infinite divisibility rigidly, the units can theoretically be taken so small as to obtain any required degree of approximation. The difficulty is the universal one 40 of applying to continua the essentially discrete conception of number.

magnitudes are necessarily external to one another, and cannot, therefore, as they stand, be directly compared. Euclid gives the requisite axiom in the form: "Magnitudes which exactly coincide are equal." But this form does not clearly bring out the difficulty, for if they exactly coincide, they are not only equal, but identical. It is only when he uses his axiom (as e.g. Bk. I, Prop. 4) that we discover the real point of it: the two magnitudes have to be *brought* into coincidence by the motion of one or both of them. Hence if mere motion could alter shapes, our criterion of equality would break down. It follows that the application of the conception of magnitude to figures in
10 space involves the following axiom: *Spatial magnitudes can be moved from place to place without distortion*; or, as it may be put, *Shapes do not in any way depend on absolute position in space*.

The above axiom is the axiom of Congruence, or Free Mobility. I propose to prove (i) that the denial of this axiom would involve logical and philosophical absurdities, so that it must be classed as wholly à priori; (ii) that Geometry, if it refused this axiom, would have to set up another far more arbitrary axiom, namely that a shape given in some standard position would in any other position be some definite function of the standard shape and the change of place; (iii) that such an axiom as this last would be a mere
20 convention, since no experience could determine the form of the function to be assumed; and (iv) that Geometry, in setting up this alternative axiom, would be guilty of a philosophic absurdity. The conclusion will be that the axiom cannot be proved or disproved by experience, but is an à priori condition of Geometry. As I shall thus be maintaining a position which has been much controverted, especially by Helmholtz and Erdmann, I shall have to enter into the arguments at some length.

A. *Philosophical Argument*. The denial of the axiom involves absolute position, and an action of mere space, *per se*, on things. For the axiom does not assert that real bodies, as a matter of empirical fact, never change their
30 shape in any way during their passage from place to place; on the contrary, we know that such changes do occur, sometimes in a very noticeable degree, and always to some extent. But such changes are attributed, not to the change of place as such, but to physical causes: change of temperature, pressure, etc. What our axiom has to deal with is not actual material bodies, but geometrical figures, and it asserts that a figure which is possible in any one position in space is possible in every other. Its meaning will become clearer by reference to a case where it does not hold, say the space formed by the surface of an egg. Here, a triangle drawn near the equator cannot be moved without distortion to the point, as it would no longer fit the greater
40 curvature of the new position; a triangle drawn near the point cannot be fitted on to the flatter end, and so on. Thus the method of Superposition, such as Euclid employs in I.4, becomes impossible: figures cannot be freely moved about; indeed, given any figure, we can determine a certain series of

possible positions for it on the egg, outside which it becomes impossible. What I assert is, then, that there is a philosophic absurdity in supposing space in general to be of this nature. On the egg we have marked points, such as the two ends: space is not homogeneous, and if things are moved about in it, it must of itself exercise a distorting effect upon them, quite independently of physical causes; if it did not exercise such an effect, the things could not be moved. Thus such a space would not be homogeneous, but would have marked points, by reference to which bodies would have absolute position, quite independently of any other bodies. Space would no longer be passive, but would exercise a definite effect upon things, and we should have to accommodate ourselves to the notion of marked points in empty space; these points being marked, not by the bodies which occupied them, but by their effects on any bodies which might from time to time occupy them. This want of homogeneity and passivity is, however, absurd; no philosopher has ever thrown doubt, so far as I know, on these two properties of empty space; indeed they seem to flow from the maxim that nothing can act on nothing, for empty space is rather a possibility of being filled than a real thing given in experience. We must, then, on purely philosophical grounds, admit that a geometrical figure which is possible anywhere is possible everywhere, which is the axiom of Congruence.

B. *Geometrical Argument.* Let us see, next, what sort of Geometry we could construct without this axiom. The ultimate standard of comparison of spatial magnitudes must, as we saw in introducing the axiom, be equality when superposed; but need we, from this equality, infer equality when separated? For the more immediate purposes of Geometry, I believe this would be unnecessary. We might construct a new Geometry, far more complicated than any yet imagined, in which sizes varied with motion on any definite law.[2] Suppose the length of an infinitesimal arc in some standard position were $ds$; then in any other position $p$, its length would be $ds \cdot f(p)$, where the form of the function $f(p)$ must be supposed known. But how are we to determine the position $p$? For this purpose, we require $p$'s coordinates, i.e. some measure of distance from the origin. But the distance from the origin could only be measured if we assumed our law $f(p)$ to measure it by. For suppose the origin to be $O$, and $Op$ to be a straight line whose length is required. If we have a measuring rod with which we travel along the line and measure successive infinitesimal arcs, the measuring rod will change its size as we move, so that an arc which appears by the measure to be $ds$ will really be $f(s) \cdot ds$, where $s$ is the previously traversed distance. If, on the other hand, we move our line $Op$ slowly through the origin, and measure each piece as it passes through, our measure, it is true, will not alter, but then we

2 Cp. Cayley's "Sixth Memoir upon Quantics", and Klein's development of it in his *Nicht-Euklidische Geometrie*, Vol. I, Chap. ii.

have no means of discovering the law by which any element has changed its length in coming to the origin. Hence, until we assume our function $f(p)$, we have no means of determining $p$, for we have just seen that distances from the origin can only be estimated by means of the law $f(p)$. It follows that experience can neither prove nor disprove the constancy of shapes throughout motion, since, if shapes were not constant, we should have to *assume* a law of their variation before measurement became possible, and therefore measurement could not itself reveal that variation to us.

Nevertheless, such an arbitrarily assumed law *does* give a mathematically
10 possible Geometry. The fundamental proposition, that two magnitudes which can be superposed in any one position can be superposed in any other, still holds. For two infinitesimal arcs, whose lengths in the standard position are $ds_1$ and $ds_2$, would in any other position $p$ have lengths $f(p) \cdot ds_1$ and $f(p) \cdot ds_2$, so that their ratio would be unaltered. From this constancy of ratio, as we know through Riemann and Helmholtz, the above proposition follows. Hence all that Geometry requires, as a basis for measurement, is an axiom that the alteration of shapes during motion follows a definite known law, such as that assumed above.

This law, since it is a prerequisite of measurement, cannot be derived
20 from experience, but must be arbitrarily assumed. Mathematically, in short, it is a mere convention. But philosophically, as we have seen, any form for the law, except the special form contained in the axiom of Congruence, involves absolute position and an action of empty space *per se* on things. Fortunately, therefore, where experience leaves us in the lurch, we have an à priori ground for accepting the geometrically simplest alternative, viz., that shapes are completely independent of motion in space.

As the axiom of Congruence is the most fundamental of all the axioms of Geometry, and as the Pangeometers have generally held that it is derived entirely from experience of rigid bodies, I may perhaps be pardoned for
30 dwelling on it a little longer. If I am right in contending that this axiom is necessary à priori, Helmholtz's view, that it asserts the rigidity of actual bodies, is already disproved. For, as he rightly points out, such rigidity could only be proved empirically, and the axiom would therefore be itself empirical, as much as the law of gravitation. But if what I have said about its necessity for Geometry is correct, Helmholtz's view involves a logical fallacy: for unless we assume congruence, or the more general axiom suggested above, there would remain no geometrical method of discovering whether or how a body had changed its shape in moving from place to place, and we could thus never discover whether there were rigid bodies or not. Since our
40 own bodies would have to share the change when we moved, there is no reason for supposing that our sensations would reveal the change to us; indeed the whole conception of spatial magnitude becomes meaningless, and there would therefore be nothing left for sensations to tell us about it. If

our measure changed its shape, as it would have to do, in the same manner as the thing measured, we could never discover such change. But, a supporter of Helmholtz might object, unless you assume your measure to be a rigid body, *you* are equally unable to measure things—and rigidity *can* only be known by experience. Unless you assume some bodies, such as the platinum bar in the Exchequer, which, under certain conditions, e.g. constant temperature, are approximately rigid, it becomes impossible to apply your Geometry to concrete things—it is reduced to what Helmholtz mockingly calls "transcendental" as opposed to "physical" Geometry.—This objection is plausible, but I believe we can answer it. (1) In the first place, the conception of rigidity is meaningless until we have the axiom of Congruence. If mere space did not allow, in one place, a shape which it had allowed in another, we should not be able to bring our measure, unchanged, to the new place; if a body, in the passage from the first to the second place, had suffered deformation, we should not be able to estimate the extent of that deformation. Non-rigidity, in an actual body, involves the continued possibility of the old shape, together with an actual departure from it. (2) There are, as a matter of fact, no such things as perfectly rigid bodies, and yet Geometry remains. All bodies change their size with changes of temperature; some change with pressure. If the atomic theory be true, nothing *can* be rigid except the ultimate atoms. It would be odd if the most fundamental postulate of Geometry, on which all spatial measurement depends, were as a matter of fact untrue. (3) To pass to positive objections, Geometry deals, not with matter, but with space. If we admitted Helmholtz's view, the distinction between Physics and Geometry would break down. What our axiom asserts about real bodies is not that their shapes do not change, but that such changes of shape as they do undergo are due to physical, not to geometrical, causes. This makes the investigation of these physical causes possible, by the ordinary inductive methods. We can compare two bodies, first at the same temperature, then at different temperatures, and thus discover the effect of temperature on volume. But such comparison, as we have seen, is only possible by the help of the axiom of Congruence, which alone makes spatial magnitude an intelligible property of a body. What we require is not the existence of actual rigid bodies, but the axiom that bodies, *under precisely similar physical conditions*, preserve their shapes in spite of changing geometrical conditions. The platinum bar in the Exchequer varies in size, but that does not upset our Geometry; we specify a certain temperature at which its size is to be taken, and at this temperature our axiom tells us that its length is constant, in spite of the earth's motion in space. Of course, when we apply Geometry to real bodies, an empirical element appears in the axiom, for it is only empirically and approximately that we can know the physical conditions to be the same in two cases. But geometrical shapes are not necessarily bodies—indeed bodies never have accurate geometrical shapes—and the properties of space need not be confounded with those of matter. Thus there seems no ground for giving to our axiom the untrue sense of affirming the actual existence of rigid bodies. What it does assert, at bottom, is the impossibility of absolute position, and the homogeneity of space.

There remain one or two objections to be answered. First, how do we obtain equality in solids, and in Kant's case of right and left gloves or right- and left-handed screws, where actual superposition is impossible? And second, how can we take Congruence as the only possible basis of spatial measurement, when we have before us the case of time, where no such thing as
10 Congruence is conceivable? I will consider these objections in turn.

(1) How do we measure the equality of solids in Geometry? These could only be brought into actual congruence if we had a fourth dimension to operate in, and from what I have said before of the absolute necessity of this test, it might seem as though we should be left here in utter ignorance. Euclid is silent on the subject, and in all works on Geometry it is assumed as self-evident that two cubes of equal side are equal. This assumption suggests that we are not so badly off as we should have been without congruence as a test of equality in one and two dimensions; for now we can at least be sure that two cubes have all their sides and all their faces equal. Two such
20 cubes differ, then, in no sensible spatial quality save position, for volume, in this case at any rate, is not a sensible quality. They are, therefore, as far as such qualities are concerned, indiscernible; if their places were interchanged, we might know the change by their colour or by some other non-geometrical property; but so far as any property of which Geometry can take cognizance is concerned, everything would seem as before. To suppose a difference of volume, then, would be to ascribe an effect to mere position, which we saw to be inadmissible while discussing congruence; except as regards position, they are geometrically indiscernible, and we may call to our aid the Identity of Indiscernibles to establish their agreement in the one
30 remaining geometrical property of volume. This may seem rather a strange principle to use in Mathematics, and for Geometry their equality is, perhaps, best regarded as a convention; but if we demand a philosophical ground for this convention, it is, I believe, only to be found in the Identity of Indiscernibles. Of course, as soon as we have established this one case of equality of volumes, the rest of the theory follows; as appears from the ordinary method of integrating volumes, by dividing them into small cubes.

Thus congruence *helps* to establish three-dimensional equality, though it cannot directly *prove* such equality; and the same philosophical principle, of the homogeneity of space, by which congruence was proved, comes to our
40 rescue here. But how about right-handed and left-handed screws? Here we can no longer apply the identity of indiscernibles, for the two are very well discernible. As with solids, so here, actual superposition would only be possible if we had a fourth dimension to operate in. But again, as with solids, so

here, Congruence can help us much. It can enable us, by ordinary measurement, to show that the internal relations of both screws are the same, and that the difference lies only in their relations to other things in space. Knowing these internal relations, we can calculate, by the Geometry which Congruence has rendered possible, all the geometrical properties of these screws—radius, pitch, etc.—and can show them to be severally equal in both. But this is all we require. Mediate comparison is possible, though immediate comparison is not. Both can, for instance, be compared with the cylinder on which both would fit, and thus their equality can be proved. A precisely similar proof holds, of course, for the other cases—right and left gloves, spherical triangles, etc. On the whole, these cases confirm my argument; for they show, as Kant intended them to show, the essential relativity of space.

(2) As regards time, no Congruence is here conceivable, for to effect Congruence requires always—as we saw in the case of solids—one more dimension than belongs to the magnitudes compared. No day can be brought into temporal coincidence with any other day, to show that the two exactly cover each other; we are therefore reduced to the arbitrary assumption that some motion or set of motions, given us in experience, is uniform. Fortunately, we have a large set of motions which all roughly agree: the swing of the pendulum, the rotation and revolution of the earth and the planets, etc. These do not exactly agree, but they lead us to the laws of motion, by which we are able, on our arbitrary hypothesis, to estimate their small departures from uniformity; just as the assumption of Congruence enabled us to measure the departures of actual bodies from rigidity. But here, as there, another possibility is mathematically open to us, and can only be excluded by its philosophic absurdity; we might have assumed that the above set of approximately agreeing motions all had velocities which varied approximately as some arbitrarily assumed function of the time, $f(t)$ say, measured from some arbitrary origin. Such an assumption would still keep them as nearly synchronous as before, and would give an equally possible, though more complex, system of Mechanics; instead of the first law of motion, we should have the following: A particle preserves in its state of rest, or of rectilinear motion with velocity varying as $f(t)$, except in so far as it is compelled to alter that state by the action of external forces. Such a hypothesis *is* mathematically possible, but, like the similar one for space, it is excluded by the fact that it involves absolute time, as a determining agent in change, whereas time can never, philosophically, be anything but a passive holder of events, abstracted from change.

I have introduced this parallel from time, not as really bearing on the argument, but as a simpler case which may serve to illustrate my reasoning in the more complex case of space. For since time, in Mathematics, is one-dimensional, the mathematical difficulties are simpler than in Geometry;

and although nothing accurately corresponds to Congruence, there is a very similar mixture of mathematical and philosophical necessity, giving, finally, a thoroughly definite axiom as the basis of time-measurement, corresponding to Congruence as the basis of space-measurement.[3]

(3) The case of time-measurement suggests one last objection which might be urged against the absolute necessity of the axiom of Congruence. Psychophysics has shown that we have an approximate power, by means of what may be called the sense of duration, of immediately estimating equal short times. This, it may be said, establishes a rough measure independent of any assumed uniform motion, and in space also we may be said to have a similar power of immediate comparison. We can see, by immediate inspection, that the sub-divisions on a foot-rule are not grossly inaccurate, and so, it may be said, we both have a measure independent of Congruence, and also could discover, by experience, any gross departure from Congruence. Against this view, however, there is at the outset a very fundamental psychological objection. It appears that all our comparison of spatial magnitudes proceeds by ideal superposition. Thus James says (*Psychology*, Vol. II, p. 152): "Even where we only feel one sub-division to be vaguely larger or less, the mind must pass rapidly between it and the other sub-division, and receive the immediate sensible shock of the *more*", and "so far as the sub-divisions of a sense-space are to be *measured* exactly against each other, objective forms occupying one sub-division must be directly or indirectly superposed upon the other."[4] Even if we waive this fundamental objection, however, others remain. To begin with, such judgments of equality are only very rough approximations, and cannot be applied to lines of more than a certain length, if only for the reason that such lines cannot well be seen together. Thus this method can only give us any security in our own immediate neighbourhood, and could in no wise warrant such operations as would be required for the construction of maps, etc., much less the measurement of astronomical distances. They might just enable us to say that some lines were longer than others, but they would leave Geometry in a position no better than that of the Hedonical Calculus, in which we depend on a purely subjective measure. So inaccurate, in fact, is such a method acknowledged to be, that the foot-rule is as much a need of daily life as of science. Besides, no one would trust such immediate judgments, but for the fact that the stricter test of Congruence to some extent confirms them; if we could not apply this test, we should have no ground for trusting them even as much as we do. Thus we should have, here, no real escape from our absolute dependence upon the axiom of Congruence.

3 It is also important to observe that since time, in the above account, is measured by motion, its measurement presupposes that of spatial magnitudes.

4 Cp. Stumpf, *Ursprung der Raumvorstellung*, p. 68.

One last elucidatory remark is necessary before our proof of the axiom of Congruence can be considered complete. We spoke, above, of the Geometry on an egg, where Congruence does not hold. What, I may be asked, is there, about a thoroughly non-Congruent Geometry, more impossible than this Geometry on the egg? The answer is obvious. The Geometry of non-congruent surfaces is *only* possible by the use of infinitesimals, and in the infinitesimal all surfaces become plane. The fundamental formula, that for the length of an infinitesimal arc, is only obtained on the assumption that such an arc may be treated as a straight line, and that Euclidean Plane Geometry may be applied in the immediate neighbourhood of any point. If we had not our Euclidean measure, which could be moved without distortion, we should have no method of comparing small arcs in different places, and the Geometry of non-congruent surfaces would break down. Thus the axiom of Congruence, as regards three-dimensional space, is necessarily implied and presupposed in the Geometry of non-congruent surfaces; the possibility of the latter, therefore, is a dependent and derivative possibility, and can form no argument against the à priori necessity of Congruence.

It is to be observed that the axiom of Congruence or Free Mobility, as I have enunciated it, includes also the axiom to which Helmholtz gives the name of Monodromy. This asserts that a body does not alter its dimensions in consequence of a complete revolution through four right angles, but occupies at the end the same position as at the beginning. On the mathematical necessity of making a separate axiom of this property of space, there is disagreement among experts; philosophically it is plainly a particular case of Congruence[5] and indeed a particularly obvious case, for a translation really does make some change in a body, namely a change in position, but a rotation through four right angles may be supposed to have been performed any number of times without appearing in the result, and the absurdity of ascribing to space the power of making bodies grow in the process is palpable; everything that was said above on Congruence in general applies with even greater evidence to this special case.

To sum up: the axiom of Free Mobility contains whatever is geometrical in the so-called arithmetical axioms, as well as Euclid's 8th axiom. It supplies a measure of spatial equality for lines, surfaces and angles, and so of spatial magnitude in general, but this is *geometrically* not the only possible way of supplying such a measure. We might suppose that all geometrical figures varied their shapes and sizes in any assumed definite way, so that, say, an elementary line, whose length in a standard position was $ds$, became, in the position $p$ of a length $ds \cdot f(p)$. As, however, the position $p$ could only be defined by the lengths of its coordinates, and these lengths could only be

---

5 As is Helmholtz's other axiom, that the possibility of superposition is independent of the course pursued in bringing it about.

discovered by means of the above assumed law, the law could never be either proved or disproved by Geometry, and would, therefore, be of the nature of an arbitrary convention. This being so, it is open to us, without danger to the validity of Geometry, to choose any form for $f(p)$ which may be convenient; we may therefore make $f(p)$ a constant, unity, by which means we reduce the above axiom to that of Congruence. But when we pass to the philosophical point of view, it appears that the axiom flows from the general principle of the passivity of mere space in relation to objects, so that philosophically it is more than a convention; it is even necessary à priori, and non-Euclidean systems (with the apparent exception of Cayley's) do not, as a matter of fact, ever dispense with it.

## II. THE AXIOM OF DIMENSIONS

We have seen, in discussing the axiom of Congruence, that all position is relative, that is, a position exists only by virtue of relations.[6] It follows that, if positions can be defined at all, they must be uniquely and exhaustively described by some finite number of such relations. If Geometry is to be possible, it must happen that, after enough relations have been given to determine a point uniquely, its relation to any fresh known point must be deducible from the relations already given. Hence we obtain, as an à priori condition of Geometry, logically indispensable to its existence, the axiom that *Space must have a finite integral number of Dimensions*. For every relation required in the definition of a point constitutes a dimension, and a fraction of a relation is meaningless. The number of relations required must be finite, for an infinite number of dimensions would be practically impossible to determine. If we remember our axiom of Congruence, and remember also that space is a continuum, we may state our axiom in the form given by Helmholtz: "In a space of $n$ dimensions the position of a point is uniquely determined by the measurement of $n$ continuous independent variables (coordinates)."[7]

So much, then, is à priori necessary to Geometry. The restriction of the dimensions to three seems, on the contrary, to be wholly the work of experience. This restriction cannot be logically necessary, for as soon as we have formulated any analytical system, it appears wholly arbitrary. Why, we are driven to ask, cannot we add a fourth coordinate to our $x$, $y$, $z$, or give a geometrical meaning to $x^4$? In this more special form, we are tempted to

---

6 The question "Relations to what?", is a question involving many difficulties. It will be touched on later in this article, but can only be answered by abandoning the purely geometrical standpoint. For the present, in spite of the glaring circle involved, I shall take the relations as relations to other positions.

7 *Wissenschaftliche Abhandlungen*, Bd. ii, S. 614.

regard the axiom of dimensions, like the number of inhabitants of a town, as a purely statistical fact, with no greater necessity than such facts have.

Geometry affords intrinsic evidence of the truth of my division of the axiom of dimensions into an à priori and empirical portion. For the extension of the number of dimensions to four, or to $n$, alters nothing in plane and solid Geometry, but only adds new branches which interfere in no way with the old; but *some* definite number of dimensions is assumed in all Geometries, nor is it possible to conceive of a Geometry which should be free from this assumption.

Let us, since the point seems of some interest, and has, to my knowledge, repeat our proof of the apriority of this axiom from a slightly different point of view. We will begin, this time, from the most abstract conception of space, such as we find in Riemann's dissertation. We have, here, an ordered manifold, infinitely divisible and allowing of free mobility. Free mobility involves, as we saw, the power of passing continuously from any one point to any other, by any course which may seem pleasant to us; it involves, also, that, in such a course, no changes occur except changes of mere position; i.e. positions do not differ from one another in any qualitative way. (This absence of qualitative difference is the distinguishing mark of space as opposed to other manifolds, such as the colour- and tone-systems; in these, every element has a definite qualitative sensational value, whereas, in space, the sensational value of a position depends wholly on its relation to our own body, and is thus not intrinsic, but relative.) From the absence of qualitative differences among positions, it follows logically that positions exist only by virtue of other positions; one position differs from another just because they are two, not because of anything intrinsic in either. Position is thus defined simply and solely by relation to other positions. Any position, therefore, is completely defined when, and only when, enough such relations have been given to enable us to determine its relation to any new position, this new position being defined by the same number of relations. Now in order that such definition may be at all possible, a finite number of relations must suffice. But every such relation constitutes a dimension. Therefore, if Geometry is to be possible, it is à priori necessary that space should have a finite integral number of dimensions.

The limitation of the dimensions to three is, as we have seen, empirical; nevertheless, it is not liable to the inaccuracy and uncertainty which usually belong to empirical knowledge. For the alternatives which logic leaves to sense are discrete—if the dimensions are not three, they must be two or four or some other number—so that *small* errors are out of the question. Hence the final certainty of the axiom of three dimensions, though in part due to experience, is of quite a different order from that of (say) the law of Gravitation. In the latter, a small inaccuracy might exist and remain undetected; in the former, an error would have to be so considerable as to be utterly impossible to overlook. It follows that the certainty of our whole axiom is almost as great as that of the à priori element, since this element leaves to sense a definite disjunction of discrete possibilities.

### III. THE STRAIGHT LINE

I have hitherto spoken of relations between points as though the meaning of such relations were self-evident; I have spoken, also, of distances and magnitudes as though these were terms which any one might use unchallenged. The time has now come to examine more minutely into these assumptions.

First of all, what *is* the relation between two points? The answer seems evident: the relation is their distance apart. Well and good: but how is their distance to be measured? It must be measured by some curve which joins the two points, and if it is to have a unique value, it must be measured by a curve which those two points completely define. But such a curve is a straight line, for a straight line is the only curve determined by any two of its points. Hence, *if two points are to have to each other a determinate relation, without reference to any other point or figure in space, space must allow of curves uniquely determined by any two of their points, i.e. of straight lines.*

This is the axiom of the straight line; but we cannot regard the à priori certainty of this axiom as established by so summary an argument. In the first place, our axiom is as yet hypothetical—we have still to discuss whether it is logically possible for the relation between two points to be dependent on the rest of space, or on some part of the rest of space. If this possibility is successfully disposed of, it remains to show, more rigidly than above, that the relation between two points can only have a unique value if it is measured by a curve which those two points completely define. In short, we shall have to consider the conditions for the measurement of distance. Here we shall have a very formidable difficulty in spherical Geometry, which may compel us somewhat to modify our axiom. In the course of the discussion, it will appear that points have no meaning apart from lines, nor lines apart from points; thus our definition of the straight line will become circular, and we shall be forced to admit the necessity of some extra-geometrical aid in framing our idea of the straight line.

(1) What warrant have we for supposing that two points must have to each other a determinate relation, independent of the rest of space? Our argument is already rather risky, since we have said that points can only be determined by their relations to other points, and these others by relations to fresh points, and so on *ad infinitum*. This procedure involves either a circle or an infinite regress,[8] either of which is a logical fallacy, which we are

8 Corresponding to the two possibilities of infinite, and of finite but unbounded space.

not yet in a position to resolve. Hence our reasoning, as resting on this fallacy, is necessarily rather precarious. Nevertheless, we will see what is to be said.

Our great resource, here as always, is the homogeneity of space. It is plain that any two points must have *some* relation to each other, and it follows from the homogeneity of space that two points having the same relation can be constructed in any other part of space. Using the axiom of Free Mobility, we may express this fact thus: The figure formed of the two points can be moved about in space, in any way we choose, without being altered in any way. Consequently, the relation between the two points cannot be altered by motion. But, if that relation were in any way dependent on the position of the two points in space, it would necessarily be altered by change of position. Now relation to other figures in space means nothing but position, or some factor in the determination of position, and is thus necessarily altered by motion.[9] It follows that the relation between the two points, being unaltered by motion, must be independent of the rest of space. Thus two points have to each other a definite relation, uniquely determined by those two points.

But why, it may be asked, should there be only one such relation between two points? Why not several? The answer to this lies in the fact that points are wholly constituted by relations, and have no intrinsic nature of their own. A point is defined by its relations to other points, and when once the relations necessary for definition have been given, no fresh relations to the points used in definition are possible, since the point defined has no qualities from which such relations could flow. Now one relation to any one other point is as good for definition as more would be, since however many we had, they would all remain unaltered in a motion of both points. Hence there can only be one relation determined by any two points.

(2) We have thus disposed of the first objection—two points have one and only one relation uniquely determined by those two points. This relation we call their distance apart. It remains to consider the conditions of the measurement of distance, i.e. how far a unique value for distance involves a curve uniquely determined by the two points.

We are accustomed to the definition of the straight line as the *shortest* distance between two points, which implies that distance might equally well be measured by curved lines. This implication I believe to be false, for the following reasons. When we speak of the length of a curve, we can give a meaning to our words only by supposing the curve divided into infinitesimal

---

9 It may be objected that, if the relation were, for instance, distance from some plane, motion parallel to that plane would not alter the relation. But the axiom of Free Mobility admits of no exceptions, so that the motion of the two points cannot be restricted to motion parallel to that plane. Motion of a general kind will alter any external relation of the figure moved.

rectilinear arcs, whose sum gives the length of an equivalent straight line; thus, unless we presuppose the straight line, we have no means of comparing the lengths of different curves, and can therefore never discover the applicability of our definition. It might be thought, perhaps, that some other line, say a circle, might be used as the basis of measurement. But in order to estimate in this way the length of any curve other than a circle, we should have to divide the curve into infinitesimal circular arcs. Now two successive points do not determine a circle, so that an arc of two points would have an indeterminate length. It is true that, if we exclude infinitesi-
10  mal radii for the measuring circles, the lengths of the infinitesimal arcs would be determinate, even if the circles varied, but that is only because all the small circular arcs through two consecutive points coincide with the straight line through those two points. Thus, even with the help of the arbitrary restriction to a finite radius, all that happens is that we are brought back to the straight line. If, to mend matters, we take *three* consecutive points of our curve, and reckon distance by the arc of the circle of curvature, the notion of distance loses its fundamental property of being a relation between *two* points. For two consecutive points of the arc could not then be said to have any corresponding distance apart—three points would be
20  necessary before the notion of distance became applicable. Thus the circle is not a possible basis for measurement, and similar objections apply, of course, with increased force, to any other curve. All this argument is designed to show, in detail, the logical impossibility of measuring distance by any curve not completely defined by the two points whose distance apart is required. If in the above we had taken distance as measured by circles *of given radius*, we should have introduced into its definition a relation to other points besides the two whose distance was to be measured, which we saw to be a logical fallacy. Besides, how are we to know that all the circles have equal radii, until we have an independent measure of distance?
30    A straight line, then, is not the *shortest* distance, but it is simply *the* distance between two points—so far, this conclusion has stood firm. But suppose we had two or more curves through two points, and that all these curves were congruent *inter se*. We should then say, in accordance with the axiom of Congruence, that the lengths of all these curves were equal. Now it might happen that, although no one of the curves was uniquely determined by the two end-points, yet the common length of all the curves was so determined. In this case, what would hinder us from calling this common length the distance apart, although no unique figure in space corresponded to it? This is the case contemplated by spherical Geometry, where, as on a
40  sphere, antipodes can be joined by an infinite number of geodesics, all of which are of equal length. The difficulty supposed is, therefore, not a purely imaginary one, but one which modern Geometry forces us to face. I shall consequently discuss it at some length.

To begin with, I must point out that my axiom is not quite equivalent to Euclid's. Euclid's axiom states that two straight lines cannot enclose a space, i.e. cannot have more than one common point. Now if every two points, without exception, determine a unique straight line, it follows, of course, that two different straight lines can have only one point in common—so far, the two axioms are equivalent. But it may happen, as in Spherical Space, that two points *in general* determine a unique straight line, but fail to do so when they have to each other the special relation of being antipodes. In such a system, every pair of straight lines in the same plane meet in two points, which are each other's antipodes; but two points, *in* general, still determine a unique straight line.[10] We are still able, therefore, to obtain distances from unique straight lines, except in limiting cases; and in such cases, we can take any point intermediate between the two antipodes, join it by the *same* straight line to both antipodes, and measure its distances from those antipodes in the usual way. The sum of these distances then gives a unique value for the distance between the antipodes.

Thus, even in spherical space, we are greatly assisted by the axiom of the straight line; all linear measurement is effected by it, and exceptional cases can be treated, through its help, by the usual methods for limits. Spherical space, therefore, is not so adverse as it at first appeared to be to the à priori necessity of the axiom. Nevertheless we have, so far, not attacked the kernel of the objection which spherical space suggested. To this attack it is now our duty to proceed.

It will be remembered that, in our à priori proof that two points must have one definite relation, we held it impossible for those two points to have, to the rest of space, any relation which would be unaltered by motion. Now in spherical space, in the particular case where the two points are antipodes, they *have* a relation, unaltered by motion, to the rest of space—the relation, namely, that their distance is half the circumference of the universe. In our former discussion, we assumed that any relation to outside space must be a relation of position—and a relation of position must be altered by motion. But with a finite space, in which we have absolute magnitude, another relation becomes possible, namely, a relation of magnitude. Antipodal points, accordingly, like coincident points, no longer determine a unique straight line. And it is instructive to observe that there is, in consequence, an ambiguity in the expression for distance, like the ordinary ambiguity in angular measurement. If $k$ be the space-constant, and $d$ be one value for the distance between two points, $2\pi k n \pm d$, where $n$ is any integer, is an equally good

10 The distinction, in metageometry, between positive and negative space-constant does not lie, as is generally supposed, in the validity of the axiom of the straight line. For Klein has shown that in elliptic space, which also has positive space-constant, the axiom holds without exception.

value. Distance is, in short, a periodic function like angle. Whether or not such a system is philosophically permissible, I shall consider later—for the present, I am content to point out that such a state of things rather confirms than destroys my contention that distance depends on a curve uniquely determined by two points. For as soon as we drop this unique determination, we see ambiguities creeping into our expression for distance. Distance still has a set of discrete values, corresponding to the fact that, given one point, the straight line is uniquely determined for all other points but one, the antipodal point. It is tempting to go on, and say: If through *every* pair of points there were an infinite number of the curves used in measuring distance, distance would be able, for the same pair of points, to take, not only a discrete series, but an infinite *continuous* series, of values.

This, however, is mere speculation. I come now to the *pièce de résistance* of my argument. The ambiguity, in spherical space, arose, as we saw, from a relation of *magnitude* to the rest of space—such a relation being unaltered by motion of the two points, and therefore falling outside our introductory reasoning. But what is this relation of magnitude? Simply a relation of the *distance* between the two points to a *distance* given in the nature of the space in question. It follows that such a relation *presupposes* a measure of distance, and need not, therefore, be contemplated in any argument which deals with the à priori requisites for the possibility of definite distances.

I have now shown, I hope conclusively, that spherical space affords no objection to the apriority of my axiom. Any two points have one relation, their distance, which is independent of the rest of space, and this relation requires, as its measure, a curve uniquely determined by those two points. I might have taken the bull by the horns, and said: Two points *can* have no relation but what is given by lines which join them, and therefore, if they have a relation independent of the rest of space, there must be one line joining them which they completely determine. Thus James says:[11]

> Just as, in the field of quantity, the relation between two numbers is another number, so *in the field of space the relations are facts of the same order with the facts they relate....* When we speak of the relation of direction of two points toward each other, we mean simply the sensation (?) of the line that joins the two points together. *The line is the relation.... The relation of position between the top and bottom points of a vertical line is that line, and nothing else.*

If I had been willing to use this doctrine at the beginning, I might have avoided all discussion. A unique relation between two points *must*, in this case, involve a unique line between them. But it seemed better to avoid a doctrine not universally accepted, the more so as I was approaching the question from the logical, not the psychological, side. After disposing of the objections, however, it is interesting to find this confirmation of the above theory from so different a standpoint. Indeed, I believe James's doctrine could be proved to be a logical necessity, as well as a psychological fact. For what sort of thing can a spatial relation between two distinct points be? It must be something spatial, and it must be something which somehow bridges the gulf of their disparateness. It must be something at least as real and tangible as the points it relates, since we saw that points are wholly constituted by their relations. There seems nothing which can satisfy all these requirements, except a line joining them. Hence, once more, a unique relation must involve a unique line. That is, linear magnitude is logically impossible, unless space allows of curves uniquely determined by any two of their points.

To sum up: If points are defined simply by relations to other points, i.e. if all position is relative, every point must have to every other point one, and only one, relation independent of the rest of space. This relation is the distance between the two points. Now a relation between two points can only be defined by a line joining them—nay further, it may be contended that a relation can only *be* a line joining them. Hence a unique relation involves a unique line, i.e. a line determined by any two of its points. Only in a space which admits of such a line is linear magnitude a logically possible conception. But, when once we have established the possibility, in general, of drawing such lines, and therefore of measuring linear magnitudes, we may find that a certain magnitude has a peculiar relation to the constitution of space. The straight line may turn out to be of finite length, and in this case its length will give a certain peculiar linear magnitude, the space-constant. Two antipodal points, that is, points which bisect the entire straight line, will then have a relation of magnitude which, though unaltered by motion, is rendered peculiar by a certain constant relation to the rest of space. This peculiarity presupposes a measure of linear magnitude in general, and cannot therefore upset the apriority of the axiom of the straight line. But it destroys, for points having the peculiar antipodal relation to each other, the argument which proved that the relation between two points could not, since it was unchanged by motion, have reference to the rest of space. Thus it is intelligible that, for such special points, the axiom breaks down, and an infinite number of straight lines are possible between them; but unless we had started with assuming the general validity of the axiom, we could never have reached a position in which antipodal points could have been known to be peculiar, or indeed any position which would enable us to give any definition whatever of particular points.

In connection with the straight line, it will be convenient to say a few words about the logical conditions of the possibility of a coordinate system.

Much recent Geometry, more especially that of Cayley and Klein, begins, if I have understood it aright, by presupposing a coordinate system, without considering whether the axioms set forth at the start are sufficient to make such a system possible. I am going to contend, here, that no system of coordinates can be set up without presupposing the straight line as the measure of distance. Cayley and Klein begin with coordinates, and proceed to *define* distance, more or less arbitrarily, as a function of coordinates; this is, I think, a logical fallacy, as I shall now attempt to prove.

In the first place, a point's coordinates constitute a complete definition of it; now a point can only be defined, as we have seen, by its relations to other points, and these relations can only be defined by means of the straight line. Consequently, any system of coordinates must involve the straight line, as the basis of its definitions of points.

This à priori argument, however, though I believe it to be quite sound, is not likely to carry conviction to any one persuaded of the opposite. Let us, therefore, examine coordinate systems in detail, and show, in each case, their dependence on the straight line.

We have already seen that the notion of distance involves the straight line. We cannot, therefore, define our coordinates in any of the ordinary ways, as the distances from three planes, lines, points, spheres, or what not. Polar coordinates are impossible, since—waiving the straightness of the radius vector—the length of the radius vector becomes unmeaning. Von Staudt's projective construction[12] proceeds entirely by the help of straight lines. Triangular coordinates involve not only angles, which must in the limit be rectilinear, but straight lines, or at any rate some well-defined curves. Now curves can only be defined in two ways: either by relation to the straight line, as e.g. by the curvature at any point, or by purely analytical equations, which presuppose an intelligible system of coordinates. What methods remain for assigning these arbitrary values to different points? Nay, how are we to get any estimate of the difference—to avoid the more special notion of distance—between two points? The very notion of a point has become illusory. When we have a coordinate system, we may define a point by its three coordinates; in the absence of such a system, we may define the notion of point *in general* as the intersection of three surfaces or of two curves. Here we take surfaces and curves as notions which intuition makes plain, but if we wish them to give us a precise numerical definition of *particular* points, we must specify the kind of surface or curve to be used. Now this, as we have seen, is only possible when we presuppose either the straight line, or a coordinate system.—It follows that every coordinate system presupposes the straight line, and is logically impossible without it.

I may point out, as a corollary, that the straight line cannot be defined as a

12  V. Klein, *Nicht-Euklid.*, I, p. 338 ff.

curve of the first degree, since this involves a coordinate system. When we have the straight line, it follows from its definition—as a curve determined by two points—that its equation will be of the first degree, but to give this property as a definition is to put the cart before the horse.

The above discussion has shown, particularly in treating of coordinate systems, that points can only be defined by the help of the straight line. But we have defined the straight line as a curve determined by two points. Our logic is therefore circular, and—unless an error has crept into our reasoning—it is *necessarily* circular. This fact is a warning that we have exhausted the powers of geometrical logic, and must turn for aid to something more concrete and self-subsistent than geometrical space.[13]

Before ending this paper, let us briefly sum up the argument we have just concluded. Geometry, as we defined it in the beginning, deals with spatial magnitudes and their relations, while measurement may be defined as the comparison of any magnitude with a unit of its own kind. Starting from these definitions, we saw that all geometry may be regarded as spatial measurement, mediate or immediate. Accordingly it is à priori necessary, if Geometry is to be logically possible, that space should be such as to render possible (subject to the inevitable errors of observation) accurate and unequivocal measurement of spatial magnitudes. The whole task of our paper has been, accordingly, to find the necessary and sufficient conditions of such measurement. We found, first, since spatial magnitudes are given, to begin with, in different places, that comparison of them will only be possible if they are unaltered by the motion necessary for superposition. This led to the Axiom of Free Mobility, which turned out to be equivalent to the homogeneity of space, or, as it may be called, the complete relativity of position.

We then saw that position, being relative, must be defined—if it can be defined at all—by some definite number of relations. Each of these relations constitutes a dimension, so that we obtain the axiom: Space must have a finite integral number of dimensions.

The above definition of dimensions, as the relations necessary to define positions, or points, led naturally to the enquiry: What sort of relations are they which define our points and constitute our dimensions? We found that

---

13  Throughout the above discussions, I have freely used the postulate of Infinite Divisibility. This has sometimes been supposed to involve difficulties, though I have never been able to feel their force. Of course the postulate applies only to the *conception* of space, not to the intuition—as regards the latter, Hume's contentions as to the *minimum sensibile* remain perfectly valid. But the conception of space is that of a continuum, and I am unable to see how a continuum can be other than infinitely divisible. Moreover, the very essence of space, as conceived by Geometry, is relativity and mutual externality of parts, which makes the notion of an atomic unit of finite extension particularly preposterous. Such a limit to divisibility is open to the same objections as a boundary to space—it assigns a reality and power to empty space, such as it cannot conceivably have. On this postulate, therefore, I have no more to say. It seems to me unimpeachable and wholly à priori.

any relation between two points was measured by—nay, actually was—some curve between those points. We found that our need of relations adequate to definition could only be satisfied if two points had, *in general*, a unique relation, called distance, defined by a curve which the two points uniquely determined. This curve is the straight line. In our proof of the necessity of such a relation, however, we supposed that, so far, we had no measure of distance; when the straight line has enabled us to establish distance for every *general* point-pair, we may find one distance bound up in the nature of space. Corresponding to this distance, the curve defining the rela-
10 tion of a point-pair *may* not be unique. This argument, however, only shows a logical possibility—it remains for special mathematics to discuss when or how it is realized.

With the above axioms, we have, I think, all that is à priori necessary to the establishment of a Geometry. A Geometry using no axioms but the above will be wholly à priori, taking nothing from experience but the one fundamental property of space, that points and positions have not an intrinsic, but only a relative nature. This is the quality which distinguishes space from any other manifold—in the colour- and tone-systems, every element has an intrinsic nature, sensationally given, from which the relations be-
20 tween the elements are intellectually constructed. In space, on the contrary, the relations also are sensationally given, and the elements (points) are never given except as terms in a relation. We may then state the problem we have been dealing with above in the following form: Given a manifold in which the elements have not an intrinsic, but only a relative being, what postulates are à priori necessary for its exact quantitative treatment? The postulates required have turned out, as might have been expected, to be exactly those which Euclid and the Pangeometers have in common. The axiom of parallels, the three dimensions, and the axiom of the straight line in the more special form given by Euclid, have not been found to be logically inevitable.
30 These, then, may be supposed to derive their evidence from intuition. Finally, the postulate from which the whole discussion started, the relativity of position, made it impossible to avoid circles in our definitions: points could only be defined by lines, and lines by points. Thus, even in the à priori part of Geometry, we have a space which cannot stand by itself, a thing all relations, without any kernel of thinghood to which the relations can be attached. This forces us to attempt a resolution of the contradiction by abandoning the purely geometrical standpoint; but such an attempt would fall outside the limits of the present paper, and would only be possible on the basis of a general metaphysic.

# 43

# Review of Lechalas, *Étude sur l'espace et le temps* [1896]

THIS REVIEW, PUBLISHED in *Mind*, n.s. 5 (Jan. 1896): 128, was probably written two months earlier, when Russell read Lechalas's book. Georges Lechalas (1851–1919), a French mathematician, philosopher and engineer, was a prolific writer on a wide variety of topics. His admiration of Russell's early work on geometry is reflected in his seventy-one page summary of *An Essay on the Foundations of Geometry* (see Lechalas *1898–99*). In a reply to Couturat's review of the book he praised it as a "work of the first order" and Russell himself as an "eminent Fellow of Trinity College" (*1898*, 746).

Since no manuscript is known, the copy-text is the text in *Mind*. There are no alterations in Russell's copy of *Mind* containing the review.

*Étude sur l'espace et le temps.* By Georges Lechalas. Paris: Félix Alcan, 1896. Pp. iv, 201.

THIS BOOK DEALS with the mathematical and metaphysical, not with the psychological, aspects of space and time. In the first chapter, on geometrical space, the author discusses the nature of geometrical proof. No postulates are required, since, as metageometry shews, all Geometry flows from the mere definition of space, and definitions do not involve the existence of their objects. The justification of a definition lies in the absence of contradiction in its results. Thus general Geometry is apodeictic, but the decision between Euclid and non-Euclid is empirical.

In Mechanics, which is next discussed, we must begin by the choice of a unit-movement, assumed uniform, and chosen from motives of simplicity. We must choose our axes from the same motive; e.g. for axes rotating with the sun, Kepler's laws would be false. This does not involve absolute motion, but only care in the selection of axes. (The difficulty, however, lies in the fact, overlooked by our author, that the axes have to be fixed by reference, not to particular bodies, but to empty space.) The fundamental notion of Dynamics is not force, but mass; the determination of actual masses is empirical, but apart from this, Dynamics follows apodeictically from Geometry.

After a chapter on the Geometry of our universe, which adds little to Chapter I, M. Lechalas discusses the problem of similar worlds and the reversibility of the material universe. The former problem is meaningless, since a proportional change of all temporal and spatial magnitudes would be no change. As to the latter, a reversed world would be unstable and improbable. (This answer does not touch the difficulty—apparently insoluble on a purely mechanical level—which lies in the absence of qualitative difference between past and future in mathematical time.)

From a discussion of Kant's antinomies and Zeno's arguments against motion, the author is led to declare that motion is discontinuous. The difficulties of space have hitherto proved insoluble; as to time, however, the Transcendental Analytic provides a solution, by identifying temporal succession with causation. The discrete irreducible elements of motion, again, afford a natural unit for time-measurement, and correspond to distinct events in the causal chain.

The book is chiefly useful as a bibliography of recent French works on the philosophy of Mathematics; its own solutions almost always evade the fundamental difficulties they are intended to resolve.

# 44

# The *À Priori* in Geometry [1896]

THIS PAPER APPEARED in the *Proceedings of the Aristotelian Society*, o.s. 3, no. 2 (1896): 97–112; this issue was published (to judge from the British Library's date-stamped copy) by July 1896. It was the first paper Russell read to the Society, which had elected him to membership on 17 February 1896. The paper was written shortly afterwards, for he told Alys on 1 March 1896 that he had "finished my Aristotelian paper". He read it to a meeting of the Society on 30 March, and a summary of the paper was published in *The Athenaeum*, no. 3571 (4 April 1896): 451. It is almost certain that the paper was the basis of the fourth lecture in a series of six delivered at Bryn Mawr College in November 1896. According to a report of the fourth lecture in the Philadelphia *Public Ledger and Daily Transcript* (16 Nov. 1896), Russell discussed "the conditions of spatial measurement" and "the three essential axioms of metrical geometry". (See Appendix I.4(c) for the complete report.) The lecture may also have been given at The Johns Hopkins University in December of the same year, as one in a series of five lectures.

Paper 44 complements Paper 42, with which it has a considerable textual overlap (see the Textual Notes). The arguments already presented in 42 for the apriority of the axioms of general metrical geometry are restated more briefly in 44, but are supplemented by a new transcendental argument designed to show that these axioms are necessary conditions for any form of externality. The supplement completes Russell's attempt at a Kantian transcendental deduction of general metrical geometry. Since Russell admits that the approach through the new transcendental argument is "more convincing for exposition" (292: 20), it is unlikely that he would have omitted it from 42 if he had already worked it out in his dissertation. Moreover, the fact that this part of the argument received the most extensive revisions when it was incorporated into *An Essay on the Foundations of Geometry* suggests that Russell's thought about it early in 1896 was still in a formative stage. In the *Essay* Russell transfers his second transcendental argument from general metrical to projective geometry, attempting to show that the axioms of projective geometry are necessary for any form of externality (*1897*, §§123–38). (This opens a gap in his argument in the *Essay*, for, in order to show that general metrical geometry is à priori, he would need to show in addition that the possibility of measurement was a necessary condition of any form of externality.) The required link between the axioms of general metrical geometry and the form of externality was the principle of relativity of position, which, though it occurs in 42, receives much more prominence in 44. Strictly,

289

in order to complete the transcendental deduction of general metrical geometry, Russell would have to show that a form of externality is a necessary condition of experience. The issue is broached in **44** (292: 28–38) in purely Kantian terms, but receives much fuller attention in the *Essay* (§§180–93). The material from **42** omitted in **44** was removed in the interests of brevity: the fact that it was, for the most part, restored in the *Essay* indicates that no change of position was involved.

Since no manuscript is known, the copy-text is that published in the *Proceedings of the Aristotelian Society*. Russell's library at McMaster contains a bound offprint of the paper and the relevant issue of the *Proceedings*: neither is marked in any way.

T HE PURPOSE OF the present paper is purely logical, and aims at applying principles of general logic to geometrical reasoning. The inquiry which I propose to conduct may be divided into two parts: (1) an analysis of the actual reasoning of Geometry, with a view to discovering those essential axioms, and that fundamental postulate, without which this reasoning would become formally impossible; (2) a deduction, from the fundamental nature of a form of externality, of the principles which must be true of any such form, when treated in abstraction as the subject-matter of a special science. Our conclusion, as might be expected, will be the same in both cases: for the two arguments are fundamentally the same, and form together a completed circle. The element in geometrical reasoning, which both methods reveal as necessary to any Geometry, I shall call *à priori*.

As I have ventured to use the word *à priori* in a slightly unconventional sense, I will preface the geometrical inquiry by a few elucidatory remarks of a general nature.

The à priori, since Kant at any rate, has generally stood for the necessary or apodeictic element in knowledge. But modern logic has shown that necessary propositions are always, in one aspect at least, hypothetical. There may be, and usually is, an implication that the connection, of which necessity is predicated, has some existence, but still, necessity always points beyond itself to a *ground* of necessity, and asserts this ground rather than the actual connection. As Bradley points out, "arsenic poisons" remains true, even if it is poisoning no one. If, therefore, the à priori in knowledge be primarily the necessary, it must be the necessary on some hypothesis, and the *ground* of necessity must be included as à priori. But the ground of necessity is, so far as the necessary connection in question can show, a mere fact, a merely categorical judgment. Hence necessity alone is an insufficient criterion of apriority.

To supplement this criterion, we must supply the hypothesis or ground, on which alone the necessity holds, and this ground will vary from one science to another, and even, with the progress of knowledge, in the same science at different times. For as knowledge becomes more developed and articulate, more and more necessary connections are perceived, and the merely categorical truths, though they remain the foundation of apodeictic judgments, diminish in relative number. Nevertheless, in a fairly advanced science such as Geometry, we can, I think, pretty completely supply the appropriate ground, and establish, within the limits of the isolated science, the distinction between the necessary and the merely assertorical.

There are two grounds, I think, on which necessity may be sought within any science. These may be (very roughly) distinguished as the ground which Kant seeks in the *Prolegomena*, and that sought in *Pure Reason*. We may start from the existence of our science as a fact, and analyse the reasoning employed with a view to discovering the fundamental postulate on which its

logical possibility depends: in this case, the postulate, and all which follows from it alone, will be à priori. *Or* we may accept the existence of the subject-matter of our science as our basis of fact, and deduce dogmatically whatever principles we can from the essential nature of this subject-matter. In this latter case, however, it is not the whole empirical nature of the subject-matter, as revealed by the subsequent researches of our science, which forms our ground; for if it were, the whole science would, of course, be à priori. Rather it is that element, in the subject-matter, which makes *possible* the branch of experience dealt with by the science in question.[1] The
10 importance of this distinction will appear more clearly as we proceed.

These two grounds of necessity, in ultimate analysis, fall together. The *methods* of investigation, in the two cases, differ widely, but the *results* cannot differ. For in the first case, by analysis of the science, we discover the postulate on which alone its reasonings are possible. Now, if reasoning in the science is impossible without some postulate, this postulate must be essential to experience of the subject-matter of the science, and thus we get the second ground. Nevertheless, the two methods are useful as supplementing one another, and the first, as starting from the actual science, is the safest and easiest method of investigation, though the second seems the
20 more convincing for exposition.

After these general remarks, I will proceed to Geometry. I propose, first, by an analysis of geometrical reasoning, to prove that its possibility depends on three axioms, which I shall call the axiom of congruence or free mobility, the generalized axiom of dimensions, and the generalized axiom of the straight line, and that the truth of these axioms involves the homogeneity of space and the complete relativity of position. So far the argument proceeds by a mere analysis of Geometry. But passing now to the consideration of space, I shall contend, with Kant, that some form of externality, given either by sensation or by intuition (psychological questions are here irrele-
30 vant), is a necessary condition of our experience of an external world. But I shall contend that the particular form of externality, which we know as Euclidean space, is not necessary; that, on the contrary, all that is necessary is complete relativity of position. This is necessary, because externality cannot be an intrinsic property of anything. I shall then deduce, from the relativity of position, the three axioms which we found essential to Geometry. This will complete the circle of the double argument. The three axioms will be à priori, in the sense that any form of externality, in beings with our laws of thought and a knowledge of an external world, must conform to them. The remaining axioms required to define Euclidean space will remain, for
40 Geometry, empirical, since no geometrical principle and no possibility of

---

1 I use "experience" here in the widest possible sense, the sense in which the word is used by Bradley.

experience of an outer world can prove them to be necessary.

## A. GEOMETRICAL ARGUMENT

Geometry has always possessed, since Euclid, a great advantage—at least for the philosopher—over most of the other sciences, in that it prefaces its reasonings with a definite statement of those axioms which it believes to be fundamental. Until the very end of last century, Euclid's statement, though felt to be unsatisfactory, was believed to be accurate: many attempts were made to *prove* the axiom of parallels, but none to dispense with it. At first by Gauss, however, and then by a whole school of geometricians, an investigation was made into the effects of a denial of the doubtful axiom. It was found that geometries, whose reasonings, granted the premises, were equally cogent and equally free from contradictions, could be constructed on a basis opposed to Euclid. Hence arose the idea, chiefly fostered by Helmholtz, that all the axioms were empirical, and that nothing but conformity to experienced space prompted the acceptance even of those axioms which Metageometry retained. Riemann and Helmholtz believed, in fact, that a Geometry could be constructed without the axioms which they retained, but neither they nor subsequent mathematicians have constructed such a Geometry. Three axioms are always retained in non-Euclidean systems, namely, the axiom of Free Mobility, the axiom that space has a finite integral number of dimensions, and the axiom that any two points have an invariant relation, namely, distance, which is unaltered by a combined motion of the two points as one figure.[2] I will discuss these axioms successively, and endeavour to prove that, without them, spatial magnitude would be unmeaning, and localization would be impossible.

1. *The Axiom of Free Mobility.* Some of Euclid's axioms have been classed as arithmetical, and have been supposed to have nothing particular to do with space. Such are the axioms that equals added to or subtracted from equals give equals, and that things which are equal to the same thing are equal to one another. But if these arithmetical axioms are to be applied to spatial magnitudes, they must have some spatial import, and thus even this class is not, in Geometry, *merely* arithmetical. The spatial element involved in the geometrical use of all these axioms is, in fact, a definition of spatial magnitude.[3] A definition of spatial magnitude, again, since geometrical space is

---

2 *Vide* Sophus Lie, "Ueber die Grundlagen der Geometrie", *Leipziger Berichte*, 1890.

3 I ought to point out that most modern geometers, as adherents of the "projective school", regard magnitude as a conception wholly irrelevant to Geometry, and refuse to admit measurement as an aim of geometrical reasoning. This fact, however, does not invalidate my argument, for the following reasons: (1) Spatial measurement remains a requisite for other sciences and for daily life. (2) The reduction of metrical to projective Geometry is effected,

infinitely divisible, reduces itself to a definition of spatial equality. For, given this last, we can always divide two unequal magnitudes into a number of equal parts, and count the number of such parts in each.

We require, then, at the very outset, if Geometry is to be possible at all, some criterion of spatial equality. Now, two spatial magnitudes, unless they are whole and part, are necessarily external to one another, and cannot, therefore, as they stand, be directly compared. For comparison, therefore, some axiom is required. The requisite axiom is given by Euclid in the form, "Magnitudes which exactly coincide are equal." But this form does not
10 bring out the real point of the difficulty, which we only discover when he uses his axiom (e.g. in Book I, Prop. IV). The two magnitudes have to be *brought* into coincidence by a motion of one or both of them. Hence, if mere motion could alter shapes, our criterion of spatial equality would break down, and Geometry would become impossible. It follows that the application of the conception of magnitude to Geometry involves the following axiom: *Spatial magnitudes can be moved from place to place without distortion*; or, as it may be put, *shapes do not depend in any way upon absolute position in space*.

This is the axiom of Free Mobility, or of Congruence, as it is sometimes
20 called. It has been regarded by Helmholtz and Erdmann as derived empirically from our experience of rigid bodies. But if the above deduction be correct, Helmholtz's view must be mistaken. For the mere notion of spatial magnitude, and hence of a rigid body, as one whose shape remains unaltered through motion, becomes meaningless if the axiom be denied. The axiom, in fact, renders the experience in question possible, and cannot, therefore, be itself logically dependent on this experience. I do not mean to deny, of course, that we are made aware of Free Mobility, psychologically, by experience of approximately rigid bodies, and that, in a world of fluids, much more acute wits might have been needed to discover it. But in that case, the
30 inhabitants of a fluid world would have to do without any Geometry until they discovered the axiom. The facts, I think, may be stated thus: When our axiom has made the conception of a rigid body possible, we find certain bodies, such as the platinum bar in the Exchequer, which approximately answer to this conception. Having eliminated mere motion as a cause of change of shape, we can discover the other causes—change of temperature, etc.—by the ordinary empirical inductive methods. Our actual measure-

---

except in the case of hyperbolic space, by the use of imaginaries, and has therefore a purely technical, not a philosophical, import (*vide* Klein, *Nicht-Euklidische Geometrie*, Göttingen, 1893). (3) Even projective Geometry involves localization, and is even called, by many of its
40 adherents, the Geometry of position; and localization, as I have endeavoured to show, is exactly the same problem as that of spatial measurement. (4) Projective Geometry uses precisely those three axioms which I have regarded as à priori necessary for spatial measurement. (*Vide* Sophus Lie, *op. cit.*)

ments, therefore, which are always effected by means of such approximately rigid bodies as we can discover, must always be empirical and inaccurate. But Geometry, as the science which deals with the conditions of measurement, and discusses shapes rather than actual bodies, will not be rendered empirical by this fact. *Actual* motions must be motions of matter, whose rigidity can be only empirically known; but *geometrical* motions are motions of shapes, and afford the accurate and à priori standard by which alone the empirical inaccuracies become discoverable and acquire a logical meaning.

Having now, I hope, made clear the *meaning* of the axiom of Free Mobility, I will endeavour to elucidate its necessity by discussing two cases where it does not hold, namely, the Geometry of non-congruent surfaces (e.g. an egg), and the measurement of time.

We have, in ordinary Geometry, many elaborate and satisfactory systems for non-congruent surfaces, e.g. for ellipsoids and hyperboloids. Why, I may be asked, is a thoroughly non-congruent Geometry more impossible than such systems? The answer is obvious. The whole of the Geometry of such surfaces is only rendered possible by the use of infinitesimals, and in the infinitesimal all surfaces become plane. The fundamental formula, that for the length of an infinitesimal arc, is only obtained on the assumption that such an arc may be treated as a straight line, and that Euclidean Plane Geometry may be applied in the immediate neighbourhood of any point. If we had not our Euclidean measure, which could be moved without distortion, we should have no method of comparing small arcs in different places, and the Geometry of non-congruent surfaces would break down. The possibility of such systems, therefore, presupposes the axiom of Free Mobility, and can form no argument against its à priori necessity.

It remains to discuss the case of time-measurement. This case is very peculiar, for although time, like space, is homogeneous in all its parts, motion through time is impossible, because time has only one dimension. Superposition, as contemplated in the above criterion of spatial equality, is only possible for magnitudes of at least one dimension less than that of the manifold in question. In space, we cannot superpose two solids; in time, since we have only one dimension altogether, we cannot superpose two times. No event can be made to recur, without alteration, at another place in the time-series, in order to test the equality of its duration with that of some other event. No day can be superposed upon another day. Hence, it would seem, if the above discussion be correct, time-measurement must be impossible. As regards *direct* time-measurement, this is indeed the case. Time is measured *indirectly*, by means of space. We are reduced, in fact, to the more or less arbitrary assumption that some motion, or set of motions, given in experience, is uniform. Equal times, on this assumption, are measured by equal spaces traversed. Fortunately, we have a large set of motions which all roughly agree: the swing of the pendulum, the rotation of the earth, the revolutions of the planets, etc. These do not exactly agree, but they suffice to suggest the laws of motion, by which we are able, on our arbitrary hypothesis, to estimate their small departures from uniformity, just as we were able, by assuming Free Mobility, to measure the departures of actual bodies from rigidity. Philosophically, of course, the assumption is not arbitrary, but mathematically, the only reason we can give for it is, that without it time-measurement would be impossible.

The Axiom of Free Mobility involves, for its truth, the homogeneity of Space, or the complete relativity of position. For if any shape which is possible in one part of space be possible in another, it follows that all parts of space are qualitatively similar, and cannot, therefore, be distinguished by any intrinsic property. Hence, positions in space, if our axiom be true, must be wholly constituted by external relations, i.e. *Position is not an intrinsic, but a purely relative, property of things in space*. If there could be such a thing as absolute position, in short, all Geometry would be impossible. This is the fundamental postulate of Geometry, to which each of the three necessary axioms leads, and from which, conversely, as we shall see in the second part of the argument, each of these axioms can be deduced.

II. *The Axiom of Dimensions.* We have just seen, in discussing the axiom of Free Mobility, that all position is relative, i.e. that a position exists only by virtue of relations. It follows that, if positions are definable at all, they must be uniquely and exhaustively described by some finite number of such relations. If Geometry is to be possible, it must happen that, after enough relations have been given to determine a point uniquely, its relation to any fresh known point must be deducible from the relations already given. Hence we obtain, as an à priori condition of Geometry, logically indispensable to its existence, the axiom that *Space must have a finite integral number of Dimensions*. For every relation required in the localization of a point constitutes a dimension, and a fraction of a relation is meaningless, while an infinite number of dimensions would be practically impossible to determine.

This axiom, like that of Free Mobility, is accepted by all metageometers. It is thus stated, for example, by Helmholtz: "In a space of $n$ dimensions, the position of a point is uniquely determined by the measurement of $n$ continuous variables (co-ordinates)" (*Wissenschaftliche Abhandlungen*, Vol. ii, p. 614). So much, then, is à priori necessary to Geometry. The restriction of the dimensions to three, on the other hand, appears to have no logical necessity, and may be set down as wholly empirical. The extension of the dimensions to four, or to $n$, alters nothing in plane and solid Geometry, and presents no new logical difficulties; but *some* definite number of dimensions is assumed in all Geometries, nor is it possible to conceive of a Geometry which should be free from this assumption.

The limitation of the dimensions to three, though it is empirical, is not liable to the uncertainty and inaccuracy which usually belong to empirical knowledge. For the alternatives which logic leaves to sense are discrete—if the dimensions are not three, they must be two or four, or some other integer—so that *small* errors are impossible. Hence the certainty of the axiom of three dimensions, though in part due to experience, is of quite a different order from that of (say) the law of gravitation. In the latter, a small inaccuracy might exist and remain undetected; in the former an error would have to be so large as to be utterly impossible to overlook. Hence the certainty of our whole axiom is almost as great as that of its à priori element.

III. *The Axiom of the Straight Line.* We have one more axiom to consider, before we have exhausted the logical prerequisites of spatial measurement. This axiom is required to render possible the measurement of a special, but fundamental, spatial relation, namely *distance*.

We have seen that the measurement of spatial magnitudes, at bottom, is the same problem as that of localization, and consists in the determination of spatial relations. I have hitherto spoken of these relations as though their meaning were self-evident, and as though spatial magnitude were a term which any one might use unchallenged. The time has come to examine more minutely into these assumptions.

First of all, what *is* the relation between two points? Obviously their distance apart. Well and good, but how is this to be measured? If it is to be measurable at all, it must be measured by a curve which joins the two points; and if it is to be unique, it must be measured by a curve which those two points completely determine. But such a curve is a straight line, for a straight line is defined as a curve determined by any two of its points. Hence, *if two points are to have to each other a determinate intrinsic relation, without reference to any other point or figure in space, space must allow of curves uniquely determined by any two of their points, i.e. of straight lines.*

This is the axiom of the straight line, but we can hardly regard its necessity for Geometry as established by so summary an argument. Many difficulties must be met before it can be regarded as proved. The chief of these is a mathematical difficulty, arising out of spherical Geometry, for a discussion of which I have not time tonight, but must refer to *Mind*, n.s., No. 17, pp. 16–18 ⟨Paper **42**, 279: 34–283: 21⟩. But the first and obvious difficulty is that of turning the above hypothetical conclusion into a categorical one. Why should Geometry be impossible, if the relation between two points were not independent of the rest of space? Why must our spatial magnitudes be built up out of distances and their relations? Why should not a reference to outside space be always necessary in determining distance?

The answer to this question lies in the axiom of Free Mobility, or its equivalent, the homogeneity of space. To begin with, two points must, if

Geometry is to be possible, have *some* relation to each other, for we have
seen that such relations alone constitute localization. Now, if two points
have a relation to each other, this must be an intrinsic relation. For it follows, from the axiom of Free Mobility, that two points, having the same
relation to each other, can be constructed in any other part of space; if this
were not possible, we have seen that Geometry could not exist. Hence the
two points can traverse all space in a combined motion, without altering
their relation to each other. But, in such a motion, any external relation of
the two points, any relation which involves any other point or figure in
space, must be altered[4]; hence the relation between the two points, being
unaltered, must be an intrinsic relation, a relation involving no other point
or figure in space; and this intrinsic relation we call distance.

It might be thought, perhaps, that the distance between two points involved a reference to the intermediate points on the straight line joining
them, but the above argument shows that this is not the case. For the intermediate points, in a combined motion of the two whose distance we are
discussing, do not accompany the two moving points, and yet the distance
remains unaltered. In any given position of the two points, the fact that the
others are intermediate is deduced from the nature of distance, as measured
by a certain curve on which the other points lie, and not vice versa. Only
when distance, and its measurement by the straight line, have been established, do the intermediate points on the straight line acquire any peculiar
relation to the two whose distance is in question.

Thus the first objection is disposed of. If Geometry is to be possible, any
two points must have to each other a relation independent of the rest of
space. But why only one? Why not several? The answer to this lies in the fact
that, as we saw in discussing Free Mobility, points must be wholly constituted by relations, and can have no intrinsic nature of their own. A point is
defined by its relations to other points, and when once the relations necessary for definition have been given, no fresh relations to the points used in
definition are possible, since the point defined has no properties from which
such relations could flow. Now one relation to any one other point is as good
for definition as more would be, since, however many we had, they would all
remain unaltered in a combined motion of both points. Hence there can be
only one intrinsic relation between any two points.

Hence two points must have one, and only one, relation independent of
the rest of space. But need this relation be measured or defined by a curve
which the two points completely determine?

We are used to the definition of the straight line as the *shortest* distance
between two points, and this definition implies that distance might be

---

4  This is subject, in spherical space, to the modification pointed out in *Mind*, n.s., No. 17, p.
18 ⟨Paper **42**, 281: 24–282: 21⟩.

equally well measured by other curves. This implication I believe to be wholly false. For when we speak of the length of a curve, we can give a meaning to our words only by dividing it into infinitesimal arcs, of which each may be regarded as a straight line, and whose sum gives a straight line equivalent in length to the curve measured. This necessity of the straight line is implied in the mathematical phrase, the *rectification* of curves. Unless we presuppose the straight line, as the measure of the infinitesimal arcs, we can never discover the length of our curve, and hence can never discover the applicability of our definition of the straight line as the *shortest* distance.

Again, let us suppose that some other curve, say a circle, is taken as our 10 measure of distance. Then the distance between any two points becomes indeterminate, for through two points we can draw an infinite number of circles, each of which will give a different distance. To overcome this indeterminateness, we should have to define our measuring circles as circles of given radius. But a given radius involves a measure of distance already given, otherwise we cannot know that two radii are equal. If it is said that we could define our circles as congruent *inter se*, without introducing the notion of a given radius, the choice of our typical circle would be perfectly arbitrary, and could only be effected by introducing, into distance, a relation to some third point, such as the centre of the circle. (For three points are 20 needed to define a circle.) But we have seen that distance must be an intrinsic relation between two points. Hence the circle is impossible as a basis for the measurement of distance. If we seek a last escape from this conclusion, by restricting the direct measurement of distance to infinitesimal arcs, we do, it is true, so long as we exclude circles of infinitesimal radius, get a definite measure for the distance between two consecutive points, and hence for distance in general. But that is only because an infinitesimal arc of a circle is a straight line, and the measurement is effected through the above general method of measuring curves by dividing them into infinitesimal straight lines. Hence, once more, the circle is not available for our present 30 purpose. Similar objections apply, of course, to any other curve. Hence, for the measurement of the intrinsic relation between two points, we require a curve which those two points uniquely determine, i.e. the straight line.[5]

We can now take a further step in the argument, and say: Not only must the intrinsic relation between two points be *measured* by a curve which those

---

5 It is not intended to imply, in the above argument, that two points have no relation but the intrinsic relation of distance. On the contrary, they have also an extrinsic relation, direction, which involves a reference to other straight lines. But direction is meaningless apart from straight lines; it is, in fact, primarily a relation between straight lines, just as distance is a relation between points. The basis of spatial relations therefore remains the simple 40 intrinsic relation of distance, as measured by the straight line. What I had to prove was that two points *have* a relation independent of external reference, not that they have no relation dependent on external reference.

two points uniquely determine, but the relation must actually *be* that curve. If, as we saw in discussing the axiom of Free Mobility, all position is relative, and all spatial magnitudes are spatial relations, then it follows that a curve in space must actually *be* a relation or complex of relations.[6] If I had used this doctrine at the start, I might have greatly shortened the above discussion. But it seemed better to avoid a controverted view in the first introduction of the axiom. Now, however, when the axiom has been shown, to the best of my ability, to be necessary to Geometry, we may argue thus: Two points *can* have no relation but what is given by lines which join them, and therefore, if they have a relation independent of the rest of space, there must be one line joining them which they completely determine. For what sort of thing can a spatial relation between two distinct points be? It must be something spatial, and it must, since points are wholly constituted by their relations, be at least as real and tangible as the points it relates. Only a line joining the points, it would seem, is capable of satisfying these requirements. Hence, once more, an intrinsic relation must involve—nay, must actually *be*—a unique line joining the two points. That is, linear magnitude, and hence Geometry in general, is logically impossible, unless space allows of curves uniquely determined by any two of their points.

To sum up: If, as the possibility of spatial measurement requires, all position is purely relative, then every point must have, to every other, one, and only one, relation independent of the rest of space. This relation is the distance between the two points. Now a relation between two points can only be defined—can only *be*, in fact—a line joining them. Hence, a unique relation involves a unique line, i.e. a line determined by any two of its points. Only in a space which allows of such lines is linear magnitude, or localization in general, a logically possible conception.[7]

The above three axioms, then, are à priori necessary to Geometry. No others can be necessary, since geometries logically as unassailable as Euclid, geometries in which space is perfectly homogeneous, and position is purely relative, have been constructed without any other axioms by the metageometers. The remaining axioms of Euclidean Geometry—the axiom of parallels, the axiom that the number of dimensions is three, and the axiom of the straight line in Euclid's special form (two straight lines cannot enclose a space)—are not essential to the possibility of a Geometry, i.e. are not deducible from the fact that a science of spatial relations and magnitudes is possible. These, then, must be derived from more special experience.

In summing up the argument we have just concluded, we may give it a

---

6 Compare James, *Psychology*, Vol. ii, pp. 149, 150.

7 Spherical Geometry forces us slightly to modify the above axiom, and state it in the form: Any two points must, *in general*, determine a unique straight line. In this form the axiom is no longer equivalent to Euclid's.

more general form, and discuss the conditions of measurement in any manifold, i.e. the qualities necessary to the manifold, in order that magnitudes in it may be determinable, not only as to the more or less, but as to the precise *how much*.

Measurement, we may say, is the application of number to continua, or, if we prefer it, the transformation of mere quantity into number of units. Using *quantity* to denote the vague more or less, and *magnitude* to denote the precise number of units, the problem of measurement may be defined as the transformation of quantity into magnitude.

Now number is discrete, and springs from the pure intellect, while quantity is continuous, and springs from sense. Hence, measurement, which arises from the effort to synthesize this dualism, involves fundamental and unavoidable contradictions. But disregarding these for the moment, let us discuss the conditions which enable us, in using the notion of magnitude, to avoid any other than the unavoidable contradictions.

Number, to begin with, is a whole, consisting of smaller units, all of these units being qualitatively alike. In order, therefore, that a continuous quantity may be expressible as a number, it must, on the one hand, be itself a whole, and must, on the other hand, be divisible into qualitatively similar parts. In the aspect of a whole, the quantity is *intensive*; in the aspect of an aggregate of parts, it is *extensive*. A purely intensive quantity, therefore, is not numerable. On the other hand, a quantity which can be divided at all into parts, must, since it is continuous, be *infinitely* divisible, otherwise the points at which it could be divided would form natural barriers, and destroy its continuity. But, further, it is not sufficient that there should be a possibility of division into mutually external parts; while the parts, to be perceptible as parts, must be mutually external, they must also, to be knowable as *equal* parts, be capable of overcoming their mutual externality. For this, as we have seen, superposition, which involves Free Mobility and perfect homogeneity, is necessary; in time, where superposition is impossible, direct measurement is also impossible, although all the other requisites for measurement are satisfied. Hence, infinite divisibility, free mobility, and homogeneity are necessary for the possibility of measurement in *any* manifold, and these, as we have seen, are equivalent to our three axioms. Hence these axioms are necessary, not only for spatial measurement, but for all measurement. The only manifold given in experience, in which these conditions are satisfied, is space. All other exact measurement—as could be proved, I believe, for every separate case—is effected, as we saw in the measurement of time, by reduction to a spatial correlative. This explains the paramount importance, to exact science, of the mechanical view of nature, which reduces all phenomena to motions in time and space. For number is, of all conceptions, the easiest to operate with, and science seeks everywhere for an opportunity to apply it, but finds this opportunity only by means of spatial equivalents to phenomena.

We come now to the second part of our argument, which may be distinguished from the first part as deductive rather than analytic. This argument starts from the conditions of spatial experience, and deduces the above axioms as necessary consequences of these conditions, while our previous argument started from Geometry as its datum, and arrived, through the axioms, at the necessary conditions of their truth. The conditions for the truth of our essential axioms, as we have seen, resolve themselves into the homogeneity of space, or the complete relativity of position. In our present argument—which may be brief, since it is little more than a repetition, in inverse order, of the geometrical argument—we shall see that the relativity of position is deducible from the fact that we experience an external world, and that our three axioms are deducible from the relativity of position.

All experience of an external world, we may say with Kant, depends on the existence, psychologically, of some form of externality. I shall not enter into the arguments for this view, as I have nothing to add to the stock argument of the Transcendental Aesthetic, that to experience anything as external involves, as a logically prior condition, some form of externality in the mind. Whether this form is given in sensation, or in a pure intuition, is to me wholly irrelevant. All that is relevant is the purely logical point, that, if experience excludes solipsism, if perception presents me with an external world, then this externality cannot be logically dependent on the experience in which it is given, but is itself the logical prerequisite of such an experience. Accepting, then, as a mere experienced fact, the existence of an external world, some form of externality is an à priori condition of our knowledge of such a world.

So far with Kant. But Kant extended this à priori necessity to the whole of Euclidean space, and in this, I think, Metageometry proves that he went too far. For all that his argument proves is, that the properties which must belong to *any* form of externality are à priori. Now Euclidean space, as we have seen, has properties which are not necessary to any form of externality, and are not shared by non-Euclidean spaces. We can see, with very little trouble, that the properties which must belong to any form of the externality are precisely those axioms which are shared by Euclid and Metageometry, and which are à priori necessary to any Geometry. I will give, very briefly, the outlines of this deduction.

In the first place, externality is an essentially relative conception—nothing can be external to itself. To be external to something is to be an other with some relation to that thing. Hence, when we abstract a form of externality from all material content, and study it in isolation, position will appear, of necessity, as purely relative—it can have no intrinsic quality, for our form consists of pure externality, and externality contains no shadow or trace of an intrinsic quality. Hence we derive our fundamental postulate, the relativity of position. From this follows the homogeneity of our form, for any quality in one position, which marked out that position from another, would be necessarily more or less intrinsic, and would contradict the pure relativity. From the homogeneity of our form follows Free Mobility, for our form would not be homogeneous unless it allowed, in every part, shapes, or systems of relations, which it allowed in another. From the relativity of position follows the finite integral number of dimensions. For positions are defined simply and solely by relations to other positions. Any position, therefore, is completely defined when, and only when, enough such relations have been given to enable us to determine its relation to any fresh known position; and every such relation constitutes a dimension. At this point, it is true, a difficulty arises: why should any number of these relations of externality suffice to determine the relations to a fresh known position? This difficulty is serious, and the only answer I can think of lies in the systematic unity of the world. If the relations between one point and a certain number of others never gave indication of its relation to fresh known points, we should have to suppose a system of relations perpetually reaching out into new worlds, and this, while it would throw doubt on the homogeneity of our form, would leave a scrappy world without systematic unity. It is essential to such unity—a unity which, being equivalent to the law of excluded middle,[8] is à priori in a far higher degree than any geometrical principle—that the relation of A to B and of A to C should throw light on the relations of B to C, and our axiom of dimensions is only the special form which this principle takes at the abstract geometrical level.

It is noticeable that the above argument cannot prove the necessity of any particular number of dimensions, and, in particular, cannot prove that there must be more than one dimension. In a space of one dimension, however, as we saw in discussing time, our axiom of Free Mobility would break down. In such a space no figure could be superposed upon any other, and Geometry would be impossible. Hence, also, the measurement of time would be impossible. At the same time, motion would remain possible, unless we adopt the doctrine of the plenum. Nevertheless, the existence of more than one dimension is, I think, an à priori condition of any experience in the least resembling our own. For in a world of only one dimension we could perceive only one point, or one object, throughout our whole lifetime, and the knowledge of a varied world of interrelated objects would be impossible. On this ground, I think, we may regard the existence of two or more dimensions as an essential condition of anything worth the name of experi-

8 *See* Bosanquet's *Logic*, Book ii, Chap. vii.

ence of an external world.

As regards the axiom of the straight line, our argument here may be brief, since it was already deduced above from the relativity of position. Since position is relative, any two points must have *some* relation to each other: since our form of externality is homogeneous, this relation can be kept unchanged while the two points move in the form, i.e. change their relations to other points; hence their relation to each other is an intrinsic relation, independent of their relations to other points. Since our form is merely a complex of relations, a relation of externality must appear in the form, i.e. must
10 be immediately presented, and not a mere inference; hence the intrinsic relation of two points must be a unique figure in our form, i.e., in spatial terms, the straight line joining the two points.

All the above essential axioms, therefore, are deducible from the fundamental properties of any form of externality, or, more generally still, from the mere fact that we have experience of an external world, quite apart from the specific nature of such experience. The special axioms of Euclid, on the contrary, can only be derived from an observation of the special nature of our actual spatial experience, and are therefore, for Geometry, empirical.

Finally, it is interesting to observe that our fundamental postulate, the
20 relativity of position, involves, when we endeavour to study space apart from the matter which it relates, the most glaring contradictions. For, as we have seen, it is only possible to define points by their relations, i.e. by lines, while lines can only be defined by the points they relate. This involves either an infinite regress or a vicious circle, the penalty of our attempt to give thinghood to a mere complex of relations. If this contradiction is inherent in the notion of a form of externality taken in abstraction, it affords no argument against our reasoning, but rather evidence that the difficulties dealt with have been fundamental. To remove the contradiction, we should have to abandon the purely geometrical standpoint, and introduce, to begin with,
30 the notion of matter, as that which is localized in space, as that which is related by spatial relations. With the notion of matter new contradictions are introduced, as is shown by the difficulties of atomism. But these contradictions fall outside the limits of the present paper, and could only be dealt with by a detailed criticism of Physics.

# Part VII

# Political Economy

# General Headnote

THE FIVE PAPERS here, with *German Social Democracy* (1896) and Paper **12**, are evidence of Russell's aspirations in the mid-1890s to become both an economist and analyst of contemporary politics. (A majority of Papers **2–8** are earlier evidence of his political and economic interests.) In 1948 he recalled his indecision in 1894 as to whether to pursue a practical career or a life of the mind:

> I had, however, decided that politics could not be intelligently pursued without the help of economics, and that, *if* I chose politics, I must first become a competent economist. Accordingly, while postponing a fundamental decision, I became a student of economics at the University of Berlin, and for a year I was in doubt whether I should write my Fellowship dissertation on economics or on non-Euclidean geometry. In the end, I chose the latter subject for my dissertation.... And ⟨I decided that⟩ if my dissertation were thought sufficiently well of I would become a philosopher: if not, an economist with a view to politics.   (Russell *1948*, 144)

Russell's uncertainty is expressed in letters to Alys and his friends Sanger and Marsh. To Alys he envisioned himself a civil servant working on economics in his "spare time" (6 March 1894). On 5 June he informed her that the famous Cambridge economist, Alfred Marshall, had given him an extensive reading list and invited him to return for more specialized titles. During his stay at the Paris Embassy he remained undecided about whether to pursue philosophy, economics, or both. Inspired by a wish to do socially useful work and by his reading of the political economists Graham Wallas and Adolph Wagner, Russell confided to Alys on 11 October his desire to seek a Cambridge fellowship in economics as well as philosophy. Even at this early stage of his development his view of economics was defined in ways that would characterize much of his later social writings. For example, he agreed with Wallas that the nurturing of sympathy was crucial for the solution of social questions, and he criticized Wagner for an inadequate understanding of the foundations of economics. He later recalled that at about the same time he had outlined to his Apostolic friends plans for "abandoning mathematical philosophy for economics" (*1967*, 113). While Alys was enthusiastic about the proposal, Ward, McTaggart and others were not. They "*all* urged me to do what I'm good at, rather than fly off to Economics" (Russell to Alys, 4 Nov. 1894; Russell *1967*, 107).

Nevertheless Russell went to the University of Berlin early in 1895 and immersed himself in economics for two months.

Russell never stated explicitly why he and Alys chose Berlin, but reasons can be inferred. Alys had urged him to go to Berlin as part of their plan to collaborate on political and social reform. In August 1893 George Santayana had advised Russell that Berlin had the best German university (see 63: 25–6). From his correspondence with Alys, it is clear that Russell viewed himself as a socialist (12 and 21 Sept. 1894), and Berlin was the centre of the most flourishing socialist movement in Europe. Moreover, there were outstanding economists at the university. Finally, Berlin was an ancestral home of the idealist philosophy to which Russell adhered at the time.

When Russell returned to England in the summer of 1895, he abandoned the idea of doing dissertations in both philosophy and economics and worked exclusively in mathematical philosophy. When he was awarded a fellowship in the autumn of 1895, he determined to devote himself to philosophical aspects of mathematics. Despite this decision, Russell spent another two months in Berlin late in 1895 investigating German social democracy. As late as the summer of the following year, his interest in political and economic questions led him to attend the International Socialist Workers and Trade Union Congress (Russell *1951*, 5). In the same year he demonstrated his commitment to the study of economics and his interest in socialism by assigning the whole of his Trinity Prize Fellowship honorarium, £210 a year for six years, to the new London School of Economics to set up research studentships (Beveridge *1960*, 70). Although Russell did not join the Fabian Society at this time, he proclaimed his political faith in an address at Bryn Mawr College entitled "Socialism as the Consummation of Individual Liberty". A newspaper summary of this lost paper is printed as Appendix I.5.

While Russell was in Berlin he bought two large notebooks called the "Mit Gott" notebooks because these words are printed on the title-page. The first notebook (RA 210.006549–FI) contains the notes used for drafting *German Social Democracy* (1896). The second (RA 210.006550–FI), described in the headnote to **38**, contains Papers **45** and **46**, Chap. 4 of *German Social Democracy*, and other economic, philosophical and mathematical entries. (Many of those on philosophical aspects of mathematics, under the title "Various Notes on Mathematical Philosophy", are printed in *Collected Papers* 2.) The wide range of topics in the second notebook is in keeping with Russell's ambitious plan, formulated after a day of brooding in the Tiergarten in Berlin, to write a series of books "on the philosophy of the sciences from pure mathematics to physiology, and another series of books on social questions". The two series, he hoped, "might ultimately meet in a synthesis at once scientific and practical" (*1967*, 125).

Russell never constructed the synthesis. But even after he had abandoned economics and politics as areas of primary investigation, he remained interested in economic matters. His articles in 1904 in defence of Free Trade (see *Collected Papers* 12) and many articles and books on political theory and behaviour attest to his lifelong concern with economic and political questions.

# 45

# Note on Economic Theory [*c.* 1895]

THIS "NOTE ON Economic Theory" was probably written in Berlin during one of Russell's two visits in 1895 or in London early in 1896. The "Note" consists of attempts to define some of the most significant ideas of British neo-classical economists, particularly Alfred Marshall. The neo-classicists were primarily concerned with short-run analyses of economic behaviour and took contemporary political and economic institutions and resources as given. During the period when he contemplated becoming an economist Russell read Marshall's *Principles* (1890) systematically and often. Other neo-classical economists he read during this period were W. S. Jevons, F. Y. Edgeworth, and C. F. Bastable.

In Russell's general reference to rent he follows Marshall (and other neo-classicists) in extending the concept beyond land to include other factors, especially rent of ability and consumer's rent. The question whether rent of ability was morally legitimate or even a valid term of analysis exercised economists of the 1880s and 1890s. Consumer's rent came to be viewed by Marshall and some of his followers as a concept which could be employed by government as a tool for social reform. Russell is conventionally neo-classical in placing wages and interest on the same level by assuming that they are both related to a calculus of pleasure and pain. He attempts also to incorporate the language of marginal utility theorists, who rejected the labour theory of value of the British classical economists and its reformulation by Marx.

The "Note" appears in one of the "Mit Gott" notebooks (see the headnote to Paper **38**) preceded by seventeen pages of jottings Russell made on some economic works by William Thompson, John Francis Bray, Karl Rodbertus, Anton Menger, Georg Adler and Marx. These jottings consist of quotations varying in length from a few words to almost a page. An example of the latter is an important paragraph from Engels's preface to the first authorized English edition of *The Communist Manifesto* (1888). Scattered among the quotations are Russell's own summaries, questions, comments and comparisons of these economists. Occasionally he made judgments on entire works. For example, he concluded concerning Menger's *Das Recht auf den vollen Arbeitsertrag* (1891): "The book is careful, and good on the Utopia-mongers. But being concerned with a question of right, of jurisprudence and equity, it wholly misses the point of Marx and gives him credit for far less originality than he possessed" (194). Although such evaluations are too short to warrant publication here, they give some clues as to Russell's opinions of the economists he read.

The copy-text is the single-page manuscript (RA 210.006550–F1, 166).

$A$LL INCOME IS derived from one of two sources:

*A.* The monopoly of some useful or desirable good.
*B.* Endurance of pain or abstinence from pleasure in a manner which increases the wealth of others.

The first of these is *Rent* in a general sense, the second is wages (including interest).

    *A.* Includes the Rent of internal and of external goods.

        1. *Internal* goods yield rent of ability, and being non-transferable, cannot be nationalized.
        2. *External* goods yield rent of land, of mines, and of all other 10 monopolies of a productive kind.

    In both classes, the income derived is the excess of the amount produced above that on the margin, i.e. on the worst land or by the most foolish undertaker. This head does not include Consumer's Rent, and analogous categories which come under *B.*

    *B.* Includes

        1. The reward of a disagreeable exertion which produces a desirable result: *wages.*
        2. The reward of an abstinence from present pleasure, in a form which increases the national wealth (i.e. by the increase of produc- 20 tivity through machines): *interest.*

    In both cases, the greatest or marginal self-denial determines the price of the whole, but the greatness of this marginal self-denial is determined by the demand, i.e. by the price which can be paid without neutralizing the gain resulting from the self-denial. The other portions of self-denial get a Rent analogous to Consumer's Rent.

# German Social Democracy,
## as a Lesson in Political Tactics [1896]

THIS LECTURE ON politics was delivered to the Fabian Society on 14 February 1896 at Clifford's Inn, near Fleet Street, London. There the Fabians held meetings, which were restricted to members and invited guests. Russell's lecture was presented soon after he had begun a series of six weekly lectures on German social democracy at the London School of Economics on 6 February. The series was published later in 1896 as *German Social Democracy*, Russell's first book. He cannot have been a very confident speaker at this time, for he recalled to Wood (*1957*, 40) that he was very nervous on the occasion: "I dreaded it, and wished I could break my leg before it." He was apparently not very deft in responding to criticisms and had to be coached afterwards by Graham Wallas. Russell's advice to work with the Liberal Party must have seemed ill-advised to those in the audience who had rejected the Liberals and given their allegiance to the Independent Labour Party. At the same time, he would have irritated the Webbs, who, despairing of the Liberal Party as an organization for reform and viewing the Independent Labour Party as inconsequential, were increasingly drawn to collaboration with Conservative politicians such as A. J. Balfour.

Nevertheless, Russell's call for cooperation between Liberals and Socialists was far from heretical in left-wing circles. Many Gladstonian Liberals were evolving from rigorous individualists into supporters of a New Liberalism which advocated various degrees of collectivism. This development of traditional Liberalism coincided with and was stimulated by the emergence of a number of socialist groups. Party lines were so fluid for much of the 1890s that many reformers hoped for a "Progressive Alliance" between New Liberals and Socialists in the Labour movement. Moreover, many New Liberals saw no incompatability in doctrine between "advanced" Liberalism and Socialism and, indeed, often viewed Socialism as a special form of Liberalism.

The title Russell used in the manuscript has been adopted here. The *Fabian News* used the title "Lessons from Germany in Independent Labour Politics" in both its advertisement and report of the lecture (see the issues of February and March 1896, pp. 1 and 1–2, respectively). The advertisement states that Russell agreed to give the lecture "at very short notice".

One paragraph of the report summarizes material which is not found in the manuscript:

In estimating the effects of this policy ⟨that of uncompromising indepen-
dence⟩ we must remember that, even in democratic countries, there is no
reason to suppose that the majority in Parliament holds the same opinions as
the majority of the nation. The candidate is selected to suit the marginal
voter, the man who may or may not vote, and not to suit the rank and file who
will vote straight in any event. Marginals may be equal in numbers at both
ends of the scale, and then the best candidate is the average politician. But
sometimes they are unequally placed, and then the candidate will be selected
to suit the majority of the marginals.

This paragraph, together with the reference in the *Fabian News* to further details
not present in the manuscript, suggests that a second draft was made. The extensive
revisions in the manuscript alone would seem to have required a fair copy from
which to deliver the lecture.

The twenty-page manuscript, which provides the copy-text, is found in the first
"Mit Gott" notebook (RA 210.006550–FI, 5–35), one of two in which Russell
drafted *German Social Democracy*. Preceding the manuscript is a detailed outline for
the lecture, printed as Appendix 1.2. The lecture has been translated into German
(Russell *1972*, 39–47).

I T IS NOT my purpose, tonight, to discuss the merits of Socialism or of
Communism: such a discussion may be left with advantage to men of
wider knowledge and larger experience. The question which I wish to
discuss, is a purely Machiavellian question, namely: Given Socialism as a
desirable or desired end, what are the best tactics for obtaining it? What
method of political warfare is likely to bring it about soonest, with least
suffering in the process, and in the most satisfactory final form? I do not
intend to treat this question in an abstract spirit, but by putting before you
certain considerations, suggested to me by the differences between German
10 and English politics, as to the advisability of an Independent Labour Party.

German democratic Socialists, from Marx and Lassalle downwards, have
always regarded such a party as absolutely necessary to the success of
Socialism. This necessity they have deduced, not from the exigencies of
tactics, not from empirical observation of political human nature, but from
Marx's à priori doctrine of class-warfare. To judge of the wisdom of their
policy, therefore, we must first make up our minds as to the à priori truth of
this doctrine. If we reject it, we have still to consider the empirical grounds
for and against the policy to which this doctrine leads.

Marx's doctrine of class-warfare is closely connected with his materialis-
20 tic theory of history, with the theory that all political struggles, and all
political parties, are the outcome of economic conditions, and the embodi-
ment of economic interests. If this be so, if every political party is the party
of a class, it follows that the interests of labour will be represented, of necessity, by a labour party, and that this party must always be in conflict with
every party opposed to labour, i.e., in Marxian phrase, with every capitalistic or bourgeois party. No compromise is possible, if this theory be correct,
between labour and capital. And it is this theory, held à priori, though
illustrated by actual history, which has led the German Socialists to form a
party of uncompromising opposition.

30 To the reflective historian, no doubt, there is, in this doctrine, an immense measure of truth. To those actually engaged in the making of history,
however, it has in general been unknown, and has not given their actions
that precision, or that foresight, which the theory supposes. If all men were
immortal, perfectly far-sighted, and actuated exclusively by the economic
motive, the doctrine would, I admit, be rigidly true. But the failure of any
one of these three conditions, I maintain, seriously impairs its truth, and
correspondingly modifies the political tactics by which any particular reformer may best obtain his ends.

The chief of these three conditions is foresight, and it is the excessive
40 estimate of political foresight, to my mind, which principally vitiates Marx's
theory. The gullibility of the ordinary man and its correlative, the possibility of statesmanlike hypocrisy, are alike ignored by Marx. To descend from
the abstract to the concrete: by his own undeniably keen political insight,

312

Marx has taught a corresponding insight to the German bourgeoisie, has shewn the bourgeoisie, from the first, the quarter from which its existence is really threatened, and has given it, therefore, far more effectual weapons, against the interests of labour, than the English bourgeois has ever possessed. Thus even if the doctrine be true, it would seem unwise to proclaim it: for in all human affairs, a motive, which has hitherto operated blindly, is radically transformed when it is made an object for self-consciousness. A theory of human motives, though true up to the moment of discovery, is apt to change men's motives radically as soon as they become aware of its truth;[1] and conversely, a theory which would previously have been false may become true, as soon as it is believed by any considerable number of people. The latter especially has been the case, in Germany, as regards the principle of class-warfare.

But it is rather as a fact than as a theory that the principle of class-warfare is important for my present purpose. For this principle, true or false, regulates the whole policy of German Social Democracy, and dictates its attitude of uncompromising opposition to all other parties. Regarding this principle, then, merely as a political fact, I wish to examine some of the effects of its wide adoption in Germany, and contrast them with the effects of the opposite course, adopted by the large majority of organized working-men in England.

At the time when the Independent Labour Party, under the volcanic influence of Lassalle, first came into being, Bismarck, who had but recently assumed the government of Prussia, found himself violently opposed by almost the whole middle-class, and forced into unconstitutional means of raising the necessary taxation. At this time—in 1863–4—the air was full of revolution, and no one knew whether Bismarck or the Progressives would be victorious. The Progressives, it is true, were very mildly progressive— they were not united as regards reform of the suffrage, and most of their leaders were anxious to keep much power in the hands of the well-to-do citizens. Still, many of their number desired universal suffrage, and in so even a battle as theirs, the support of the working-men would have been well worth any moderate price. One can hardly doubt, for example, that they would have been willing, under pressure, to adopt universal suffrage as an item in their programme; and when this had been obtained, further reforms could have been demanded by labour, as the price of further support.

But, instead of bringing such pressure to bear, Lassalle and his followers refused, under any circumstances, to support so half-hearted a party as the Progressives. These, therefore, seeing that nothing was to be gained by

---

1 A good instance is afforded by the discovery of the decennial period of crises. The discovery gave every one such a feeling of security up to the predicted time, that the next crisis occurred in seven years instead of ten (1866–1873).

adopting more advanced views, gradually became less and less progressive; fearing that an extreme labour party would endanger their existence more than an autocratic government, many of them abandoned their opposition to Bismarck, and left Conservatism victorious. Bismarck had been compelled, it is true, to grant universal suffrage, and had been compelled largely, one may suppose, by the need of popularity with the working-classes. But he had granted this reform, as usually happens with concessions granted for a conservative purpose, in a form which could give little real influence to labour, since the body elected by universal suffrage, the
10 Reichstag, was a body with very limited powers. Moreover the *Prussian* constitution, concerning which the previous conflict had been waged, was left unchanged, and only the *Imperial* constitution was given an appearance of democracy. And to the present day, the advanced Liberal, such as we know him at home, is almost non-existent in Germany: the force which produces him has been transferred to the Socialists, and instead of being urged forward, he has been pushed back by terror of the Red Spectre.

From the standpoint of the champions of labour, again, the effect of isolation has not been wholly beneficial. Lassalle himself was a wise and politic man, who contented himself with demanding one reform at a time and,
20 though very hostile to Liberalism, did not disdain diplomatic dealings with the Conservatives. But his successors, who fell more and more completely under the influence of Marx, failed to perceive the importance of minimizing their opponents' alarm. By being hopelessly in opposition, by being cut off from contact with politicians of other schools, and by the influence of Marx's à priori principle of class-warfare, they lost all sense of what was practicable from moment to moment, they ceased to care for anything but their ultimate goals, and, in short, they developed more and more into mere visionary enthusiasts. By separation from the radicals, the centre of gravity of the party was changed, moderate men abandoned it, and it came more
30 and more into conflict, by its opposition to religion, the family, and the fatherland, with the common sense of the ordinary German Philistine.

Thus, more and more, the fatalistic doctrine of the *Communist Manifesto* has been growing true through being believed: Society has become divided, more and more, into two hostile camps, bourgeoisie and proletariat. Between these two camps, the enmity grows more and more bitter, in proportion as the bourgeoisie grows more and more alarmed; and as the enmity grows more bitter, the radical connecting links become fewer, and compromise becomes increasingly difficult. In Saxony, for example, where the Social Democrats are more numerous than anywhere else, where, in fact,
40 they number about half the population, the Liberal parties have practically disappeared: the Conservatives, and their allies the Antisemites, alone dispute the elections with the Social Democrats. The result of this state of things is, that the Social Democrats are more oppressed in Saxony than in

any other state of the Empire, and that the suffrage for the Saxon Diet is at present being restricted by the Government.

Of course, if it had been true, as Marx seems to have expected, that all except a few rich capitalists would join the Independent Labour Party, as soon as its principles became known to them, then a short and impotent opposition would have quickly given place to a peaceful Socialistic community. But unfortunately for Social Democracy, political parties are not exclusively the parties of classes, but are very often, more often perhaps, the parties of prejudices, and the weak have hitherto been induced to advocate, in the form of prejudices, the interests of the strong. Thus it happens that atheism, reform of the family, etc., frighten away many working-men, especially in the Catholic districts of Germany; while those engaged in agriculture, in East Prussia especially, have still a feudal reverence for their lords, whom they invariably elect, with docile regularity, as the representatives of their wishes and interests in Parliament.

Thus, in spite of the numerical preponderance of labour, the bourgeoisie remains, and is likely long to remain, much the stronger party. The uncompromising attitude of Social Democracy produces a similar attitude on the part of the bourgeoisie, and sets in motion the whole formidable apparatus of the executive. The battle becomes a battle for all or nothing, and no step can be won till all is won. Meantime, all manner of oppression, tyranny and misgovernment are submitted to, because the bourgeoisie dreads Socialism more than it dreads a military dictatorship. If, in the end, Communism should be victorious, it would be suddenly victorious, by means of a revolution or a civil war. Its principles would be tried under the most unfavourable circumstances, and however excellent Communism might be as the result of a process, as a sudden revolutionary product it could hardly be expected to succeed.

But now let us suppose the opposite policy to have been adopted: let us suppose, not that no labour party existed, but that, instead of opposing all parties, it had given a conditional support to the most friendly. (The existence of Second Ballots, by the way, makes this policy, in Germany, peculiarly feasible, since it need never lead to the exclusion of a labour candidate who might otherwise have been elected). By such a policy, the labour party would have made it the interest of all advanced liberals to be a little *more* advanced, so as to comply with the conditions necessary for catching the labour vote. The labour party itself would have been restrained from demanding too much all at once, for fear of losing the support of liberals, and thus that complete estrangement which has occurred in Germany, to the great weakening of both parties, would have been completely averted. On the one occasion when the Socialists were really keen about any immediate reform, in the elections under Bismarck's Socialist Law, they did adopt these tactics: they voted, in the Second Ballots, for all Radicals who would pledge themselves not to vote for any renewal of repressive legislation. The Radicals, it is true, did not vote for Socialists in return; the bulk of the Social Democratic Party were furious at this betrayal, and severely censured their leaders for the policy they had advised. Nevertheless, they have, for the present, continued it, and it is to be hoped they will develop the same line of policy further.

The wisdom of conditional support of the more friendly of two opposing parties, has always been recognized in England, and has, in particular, been a main principle of England's foreign policy. The immense power of this system is well illustrated by Wolsey's diplomacy, which was governed throughout, according to Bishop Creighton, by this one principle. Although England's real strength was immeasurably smaller than that of France or of the Empire, Wolsey succeeded, by holding the balance of power, in raising England's diplomatic importance and prestige to a level with that of the leading nations of the Continent. Had he adopted the policy of the Social Democrats, had he refused to ally himself with any power which would not grant all that England might desire, England would have been forced, as France was forced in 1793, to fight the collective power of Europe—and unless England had been stronger than this collective power, such a policy could only have ended in disaster.

But the mention of 1793 naturally suggests the one really powerful argument, in my opinion, in favour of an independent and more or less Utopian party, an argument which brings us to my second question, namely, how far has the policy of the Social Democrats facilitated the spread of Socialistic opinions? For this argument is, the far greater enthusiasm, energy and self-denial called forth by a wide gospel of human salvation, than by piecemeal measures of petty politic reform. Among a people not naturally political, only two causes seem adequate to call forth a keen political activity in ordinary times, namely, religious fervour, and personal enthusiasm. *Personal* enthusiasm is a precarious motive, for not only does it depend on the existence and the life of its hero, but it also puts almost irresistible temptations to dishonesty in his way. A blindly devoted following may be used so easily for personal aggrandisement, that few can withstand the inducements so to use it. *Religious* enthusiasm, on the contrary, if it has a hero, has usually a dead hero; it is directed to impersonal ends, and is therefore relatively stable; it is inspiring and infectious, and for this reason highly adapted for propaganda; and when once accepted, it leads to more self-denial and more passionate devotion than any other political motive. What Marxian Socialism has done for the German workman, and what a temporizing Socialism emphatically cannot do for the English workman, is, to produce this intense religious fervour, this daily support of faith. With religious fervour has come, of course, the intolerance and sectarian bigotry of all new religions, but also a compactness and fighting strength such as religion or patriotism alone can give. Whether the gain in strength is worth the loss in tolerance and political instinct, whether unanimity is not too dearly bought at the price of uncritical dogmatism, it seems almost impossible to decide. But this, I think, is certain: That the German working-man could never have been roused from his natural lethargy and acquiescence, except by some rare genius such as Lassalle, or by Marx's far-reaching promise of an earthly Paradise. Since no second Lassalle has arisen, the Marxian gospel has become a necessary condition of the effective demand for the rights of labour, and it only remains to deplore its necessity, and to ask whether a labour party, created at such a cost of oppression and internal enmity, is really a gain or a loss to the interests of labour.

In one respect, certainly, it is a gain. Although fear of Socialism has led the German government and the German bourgeoisie into a dogged opposition to Democracy, it has, on the other hand, led to a number of more or less Socialistic measures, designed to pacify labour and diminish the revolutionary party. Bismarck himself, in one of his occasional attacks of frankness, confessed, in the Reichstag, that this motive alone had led people to accept the measures which had been passed up to the time when he spoke. ⟨"If there were no Social Democracy, and if many were not afraid of it, even the moderate progress, which we have hitherto made in Social Reform, would not have been brought about."⟩

The great extension of bureaucratic or State Socialism, also, is directly or indirectly traceable to the influence of Social Democracy or of its founders; and though State Socialism, for the moment, means only an increase in the already excessive powers of the government, the machine which it creates may be a useful preparation for an ultimate democratic socialism.

In these respects, then, the uncompromising attitude of Social Democracy has undoubtedly been effectual in producing reform. So long as the party was weak, it may well have felt—and the failure of Lassalle's negotiations with Bismarck would encourage it to feel—that compromise could only make it the dupe of stronger forces. Now, however, when its adherents are a quarter of the whole nation, it can well afford to treat, on equal terms, with other political parties. Von Vollmar, one of the ablest of its leaders, has strongly urged cooperation with the Radicals, on a basis of five essential and immediately pressing reforms. But unfortunately, the temper of the party has made it impossible to accept his advice, and Social Democrats still refuse to cooperate with any one who is not an out-and-out Communist. If they persist in this policy, they have only two alternatives: either to remain for ever a struggling minority, or, if they ever win a majority of the nation and of the army, to fight their way to victory by revolution and civil war. Sectarian intolerance may have been a necessary stage in their growth, but to persist in it now seems a daily increasing folly. As a friend to peaceful and continued progress, therefore, I must hope that Vollmar's policy will be accepted, that German Socialism will learn to aim first at the possible, and that it will emerge from that sectarian bigotry which, as its own *Communist Manifesto* has warned it, is the natural tomb of all early and one-sided movements for the emancipation of the labouring proletariat.

# 47

# The Uses of Luxury [1896]

THIS PAPER IS dated 17 February 1896 on the last leaf of the manuscript. The title may refer to contemporary debates involving Progressives and Fabians over the provocative economic writings of J. A. Hobson. Russell was being deliberately controversial in delivering a defence of inherited incomes in all likelihood either in the company of the Progressives who frequented the Pearsall Smith ménage as friends of the Russells, or in the presence of the Webbs and their circle. Such a conservative thesis would have been regarded by Progressives and Fabians as immoral and reactionary. Russell's audacity is apparent not only in the fact that his own income at this time was inherited, but even more in his ironic extension (in the opening paragraph) of Hobson's arguments. Hobson held that excessive thrift led to underconsumption by the masses and thence to unemployment and trade depression (see Hobson *1894*).

    The audience for this paper can only be conjectured on the basis of the probable location of its delivery. The strongest, but still ambiguous, clue comes in the reference at 320: 41–2 to Mr. Tate's Gallery being built "next door". Known then as the National Gallery of British Art, the Tate opened on 21 July 1897. Its address, 45 Grosvenor Road (now Millbank), suggests three possible venues for the paper's delivery. If Russell's use of the term "next door" is to be interpreted strictly, then the Pearsall Smiths' London house at 44 must have been the setting. In this case, the audience is likely to have been the Cambridge and Westminster Club, recently formed by the Russells to provide "social evenings" for their friends (as Alys noted in her diary in February 1896). Although Russell and Alys lived then at 90 Ashley Gardens, they could have used the spacious Pearsall Smith house freely. A less likely location is the house at 40 Grosvenor Road of B. F. C. Costelloe, a Progressive politician and the estranged husband of Alys's sister, Mary. Nearby at 41, the third possibility, lived Sidney and Beatrice Webb, leaders of the Fabian Society. According to Janet Beveridge, who interviewed Russell in his old age, the Webbs and Costelloe "were continually in and out of one another's houses. In this way Bertrand Russell found himself swept into the circle of the Webbs and the School of Economics that they were creating" (*1960*, 70).

    The copy-text is the manuscript (RA 220.010530); it consists of twelve leaves.

WE HAVE ALL learnt, from the arguments of Hobson, a new respect for the wits of our parents, whom we used to despise because they imagined luxury to be good for trade. I am not going to discuss Hobson's economic argument, however, and I fear that, if I did, it might militate against my conclusion. I wish, tonight, to leave economics on one side, and reflect, for a moment, that man can, after all, employ his time otherwise than in making money—if, that is to say, he has plenty of money already.

There is a well-worn argument for equality of fortunes, much in favour with Socialists on account of its extreme individualism and atomism. This argument says, that the richer a man is, the less pleasure he can get out of a given amount of money; whence, by a brief and apparently conclusive piece of mathematics, we prove irrefutably that equal division gives the greatest aggregate happiness.

I am far from denying a certain scope to this argument. If, for example, you had a box of chocolate creams to distribute among eighty children, you would do better to distribute them equally all round, than to make one child ill with the whole box, and the others envious with none at all. But if your eighty children were psychological novelists, it might be ultimately for the good of everyone to give them a taste of such poignant emotions as envy and indigestion. Thus even here, the question is not so simple as it looks.

Proceeding, then, to the general case, we may urge, as a possibility, that even if the aggregate of brute happiness, for the moment, were increased by equal division, there would be such a loss in the complexity and variability of individual lives as would, in the end, counterbalance the mathematical gain. For human beings cannot safely be treated as separate atoms, and our argument took no account of such exquisite pleasures as Dr. Watts must have felt in thanking God that he was rich while others are poor.

But leaving aside such pleasures, and the pleasure which the rich, with conscience-quelling unction, attribute to the poor in watching a fox-hunt or a royal drawing-room, there remain some important aspects of civilization, I think, only to be obtained through the freedom which nothing but great wealth or great improvidence can give. Since we are not all gifted with the art of improvidence, then, there will always, if I am right in this, remain some uses for wealth and luxury.

The chief use, I think, arises from its direct and indirect encouragement of art. As regards its direct use, in a country where most people have bad taste—and all countries, I suppose, come under this head—the only way, so far as one can see, in which a good artist can make a living, is by the happy accident of rich patrons. Of course the majority of the rich, like the majority of the nation, will encourage *bad* art: with Mr. Tate's Gallery of Modern British Art growing up next door, I need not enlarge on this sombre fact. But the patronage of some few, perhaps, or some pence from the munificence of those whose taste is usually bad, may, by good luck, fall to the share of the great artist. Thus we get that lack of system which, where general public opinion is bad, seems absolutely necessary for the accidental encouragement of good things. Whistler might seem an instance against me, for few men have received less recognition from the wealthy Philistine: and yet many people, who think "Mr. Whistler doesn't finish his pictures because he can't", have allowed him an occasional order, and preserved him from starvation or the poor-house. But further, there are several reasons why the man of means has more chance of possessing taste than the poor man. He has leisure to be cultivated, and, if he be intelligent, he is likely to occupy his time looking out for new things and new people. If he chooses wrongly, that is an error which is necessary for the *right* choice: for few people can tell, till after an artist is dead, whether he is really great or not: and it is only by encouraging much that is bad, that the good can ever have a chance to creep through. If Lord Palmerston had not endowed Poet Close, Alfred Tennyson and Alfred Austin might have had to forego their butt of malmsey wine.

Put generally, the argument comes to this: That where excellence is so hard to estimate that most people will judge wrong, and where success and honour depend wholly on the opinions of others, there it is advisable to leave rewards to be adjudged by many private individuals separately, in order to avoid a system or a standard almost inevitably pernicious. That further, such individuals are supplied by rich men of leisure, who can afford to spend money even on what *may* be waste, just because a given amount of money, to them, has less utility than to poorer men; and that, finally, there is a little more hope of taste in such men than in those who have to work for their living.

But there are also indirect ways in which wealth encourages art, partly by supplying it with material, partly by making possible a varied and picturesque life. As an instance of the first, I might mention Watteau, whom I accept from Pater's description. According to this description, it would seem as though he had this one talent, of painting courtly gentlemen and aristocratic ladies, in all the splendid immorality of the *ancien régime*. If the whole world had resembled Bedford Park, he might have wandered idly through it, a discontented and melancholy man, useless and perhaps an outcast from society.

As regards the indirect encouragements, I will not go so far as an artist of my acquaintance, and say that two conditions only are necessary for the artist, namely: luxury and immorality. But there can be little doubt, surely, that fine houses, beautiful furniture, careful and well-chosen dresses, and all the other appurtenances of splendour, are an inspiration to many artists, and set a standard which people of less leisure and taste can imitate in a humbler way, thus beautifying life even where luxury cannot penetrate. I

was struck, in Germany, by the dowdiness of the women, the incompetence of the house-keeping, and the hideousness of the furniture, which could not wholly be accounted for by the actual poverty of the people concerned; and I came to the conclusion that it was due to the absence of a rich and idle class, who could afford to plan and scheme, and set a standard to shop-keepers and to the world. Taste is a delicate and economically useless product, which has come in, as James would express it, by the back-door way, and which seems, therefore, incapable of surviving a very severe struggle for existence. Historically, I believe, a good case could be made out, for proving
10 that those nations, which have excelled in art, have usually, at the time of their excellence, only newly emerged into considerable wealth and leisure. This is certainly true of Italy, Holland and Spain at their times of greatness, but I know too little of the history of art to carry my argument further. But some degree of wealth, generally speaking, seems essential to the growth of all economically useless products.

I have laid little stress on the more direct argument, that those who are best fitted for unremunerative but valuable work, have occasionally been enabled to do their work only by the possession of wealth, though this also is important. Many of our poets have belonged to this class, and only in this
20 way, I think, can we account for the very undue share of English poets which falls to the upper or well-to-do classes. Darwin, again, is a stock instance of the uses of wealth. But all these chances, as society grows better organized, will probably be more securely provided for in other ways, than by the improbable inheritance of a fortune.

This, in fact, suggests the one point in which my argument could not be applied in support of the existing House of Lords and Industrial Kings. This one point is, that I would wish wealth to be not hereditary, but the perquisite of certain posts of distinction, whether in the service of the State, in art or literature, in Science or Industry, or, in short, in any branch of
30 useful human activity. In this way, we should not be oppressed by that weight of stupidity which usually accompanies the inheritance of wealth from a freebooting ancestry. In a Socialistic community of the future, in our nearer Utopia, we would have great inequalities of fortune, but not accidental or inherited inequalities. Rather they should be, like Bishops' palaces, the reward of real or supposed merit. In this way, all the above uses of luxury could be preserved, and intensified by the greater intelligence of those who would possess it.

To sum up the above arguments, let us try to put them in a slightly more philosophical shape. What we are all aiming at in politics, blindly or con-
40 sciously, is, philosophically considered, a Utopia, or *Civitas Dei*, in which all those elements of our present life, which we consider excellent, will be intensified, and possessed by all. But it may be that some of those elements, such as the contemplation of Truth or Beauty for their own sakes, involve an

assumption, more or less explicit, that the existing state is already more or less perfect, and that already, as in our ultimate heaven on earth, pure contemplation is the legitimate occupation of "noble mind". Now such an assumption can only be preserved by freedom from daily cares, and by the power of immersing oneself in a pleasant but as yet unreal world. And yet the people who have this power—our poets, painters, and enthusiasts of all kinds—perform, perhaps, the most useful function of all: for they remind us and bring home to us, in a way which is impossible to hard-driven normal humanity, of the glories of that Kingdom of Heaven which *should* be the goal of all our actions, and they shed some of its light back along the painful path by which we are striving to attain to it. There is a cruel Socialist saying that Browning would never have said "God's in his heaven, all's right with the world", if he hadn't had his comfortable two thousand a year. True, I reply, and therefore we must give him his comfortable income, to allow him a truer, a more prophetic, perception of events and the world than can be acquired by those who struggle.

The Good which we pursue has many sides, to be pursued in many ways: and if an essential spur in the pursuit is the delight of attainment, let us give every opportunity to these sensitive and imaginative minds, which can construct, from daily objects, "forms more real than living man, nurslings of immortality".

# 48

# Mechanical Morals and the
# Moral of Machinery [1896]

IT SEEMS LIKELY, from the reference to "the Club" in the first two lines, that this paper was written for the Cambridge and Westminster Club. Russell belonged to only two "clubs" at this time, and the minutes of the other, the Cambridge University Moral Sciences Club, contain no record of this paper. Moreover, its tone, though not its topic, would have been out of keeping with the papers delivered to the Moral Sciences Club. Finally, the paper is dated 23 July 1896, the likely day of its completion and perhaps its delivery. It could not, therefore, have been presented to the Moral Sciences Club, which did not meet during the summer.

The casting of economic questions in the context of larger social concerns, which characterizes Paper **47**, also distinguishes this essay. While less provocative than "The Uses of Luxury", it discusses issues which were central to Fabians and New Liberals in the 1890s. Russell's argument, couched in Marshallian terms, that the "law of diminishing return" had been replaced by the "law of increasing return", was the basis of the optimism Progressives of all varieties felt about future human advances. Expansion in productive powers, brought about by innovations in technology, had, in the estimation of Fabians and New Liberals, rendered obsolete the doctrine of the survival of the fittest and had opened the door to far-reaching reforms.

The copy-text is the manuscript (RA 220.010550); it consists of eleven leaves.

THE PEDANTIC LISTENER—if any such could be imagined in the Club—would perhaps demand or expect from me some definition of my terms. What are morals, he may say, and when are they mechanical? What is machinery, and what do you mean by its moral? The question what makes a machine is doubtless full of interest, and I can imagine a Platonic dialogue in which the lever, the pulley, the eight day clock, the Universe, the old gentleman with periodical anecdotes, and even the Czar of all the Russias, would be given as instances whose common mechanical quality was to be sought. But tempting as such a discussion would be, I will resist: machinery will be left to my hearers, to define as they think fit.　　10

Of Morals, and even of mechanical morals, however, the definition, I think, is tedious and therefore necessary. I mean by morals any motive by which an impulse is restrained or fostered in circumstances where it would otherwise operate or fail to operate. Morals are good when this restraint or encouragement occurs at the right times, and only at the right times; otherwise they are bad. They are not to be confounded with virtue, which is defined as always that which is right, while morals, I fear, may often be wrong. There are three kinds of morals, the instinctive, the conventional, and the rational or reasoned. The instinctive occurs where an impulse is restrained by an instinct, as where maternal affection overcomes the instinct　20 of self-preservation. The conventional occurs wherever the restraining impulse is due to precept, to education, to social sanctions and deference to the opinions of others. Reasoned morality, on the contrary, does not defer blindly to authority, does not believe any precept because that precept is generally accepted, does not bow down before the wisdom of its ancestors; but reflects for itself on the ends of human life, and on the means for attaining those ends in its actual milieu. If the results of reasoned morality coincide with those of instinctive and conventional morality, well and good; if not, these last must be altered. I wish to point ⟨out⟩ how the conflict, which most of us admit, between the different kinds of morals, is due, in large　30 measure, to machinery. Mechanical morals are thus at variance with the moral of machinery.

It is a singular fact that the doctrines of Malthus and Darwin were discovered almost at the very moment when, as applied to human beings, they ceased to be true. For they depend wholly on the law of diminishing return, which the wisdom of a bygone age has embodied in the saying "The fewer the better fare". But, as it happens, the progress of intelligence has introduced the possibility of cooperation and organization, by which an opposite law, that of increasing return, has been brought into the field. The operation of this law is embodied in machinery. Now-a-days, "the more the merrier"　40 is supplemented by "the *more* the better fare". This law, since its action depends on human intelligence, is likely to operate more and more as intelligence grows. But if so, what becomes of the struggle for existence? What of

the survival of the fittest? Where are all the pretty phrases which Darwin-
ians taught us to lisp in the nursery? Where the virtues based on these
phrases? Where the morality which has gathered round the necessity, to
your own survival, of your neighbour's starvation? These are the questions
for a reasoned morality, and these the questions which conventional and
instinctive morality would find it hard to answer.

But how did instinctive and conventional morals grow up? They are fos-
silized remains—so I shall contend—of what might once have been, but
never was, a reasoned and faultless ethic. They are the embodied results, in
10 fact, of that very struggle for existence which their justification must assume, but must now falsely assume. They differ in two respects: in the stage
of that struggle at which they arose, and in ⟨the⟩ kind of feelings by which
they are prompted. Instinctive morality arose in a savage, or even partly a
pre-human, state of society, when "kill in order not to be killed" was the
main principle of morals. This principle was a necessary one, for people not
conforming to it would die young and leave no descendants. Where some
only could survive, some must be killed: efficiency in killing was, therefore,
the condition of all survival, and therefore of all virtue—for to be virtuous,
one must first be alive. But in the state we are supposing, people acted only
20 on instinct: efficiency in killing could only, therefore, be the result of an
instinctive love, for their own sakes, of those acts which produced this efficiency. Hence those virtuous savages who possessed these instincts would
alone survive, and would transmit these instincts to their descendants.
Since excess of virtue above their contemporaries would alone enable them
to survive, the strength of the instincts in question would be intensified in
every generation. Being instincts prompting directly to certain acts, not to
the ends attainable by these acts, they would survive their own utility—
witness the modern love of sport and of duelling.

So much for instinctive morality; conventional morality arose somewhat
30 differently. The advantages of combination having at last led to the survival
of a gregarious instinct, patriotism and a social consciousness would gradually supplement the purely personal instincts of the utter savage. There
would arise a desire to stand well with one's fellows, by which many advantages might be secured: for instance, food in time of famine, a large number
of wives, etc., all of which would increase the number of descendants of
those who succeeded in winning popular esteem. Hence, in the struggle
between different tribes, those which gave honour to qualities useful in
warfare would survive. Hence would arise two things, first, the desire for
the respect of others, secondly, the bestowal of respect upon the qualities
40 useful in the struggle for existence. Out of these two constituents arose, in
remote antiquity—say the stone age, or the dawn of the Christian era, or the
reigns of the Plantagenets—that body of common sense which we call, according to our tastes, conventional morality, virtue, true Christianity,

priggery or hypocrisy. It consists essentially, on the one side, of a moral standard applied to others and honouring those qualities which are helpful in war, and on the other side, of a desire to conform to the moral standard of others, with the conscious or unconscious end of winning their approbation. The precepts of this morality, though based on instincts, are not themselves instinctive, but are taught by education, imitativeness, religion and political institutions. This is the morality which most people, in practice, believe and act upon. Invented for an extinct social order, it is enforced by the inherited strength of instinct, and the accumulated force of religion and the social order. But can it, by any possibility, be adequate to modern needs?            10

If, as I contended at the beginning of this paper, the struggle for existence is rapidly becoming a thing of the past, it cannot now be adequate. If all can survive, and if the survival of all is for the good of all, the art of killing your neighbour is the art of impoverishing yourself. The whole basis of conventional morals is thus sapped. The mere art of keeping alive, formerly the precondition of all virtue, has become unimportant, and the question becomes, not how to keep alive, but how to live. Formerly the alternatives were life or death; now the alternatives are a good or a bad life. A good life, to conventional morality, was one which helped the survival of your group: but this end is now too easily attained to be a basis of morals. Conventional 20 morality, therefore, stands helpless before the problem of determining the good life without reference to survival: to the reasoned attempts to solve the problem, convention opposes the antiquated word "morbid", i.e. opposed to survival—a criterion which is no longer adequate to the issues it attempts to solve.

Some of the effects of this change in the basis of morals may be worth tracing. The law of diminishing return held sway till the invention of steam and the cheapening of ocean transportation: in Napoleon's time it still dominated, and as during the eighteenth century, death to the Frenchman was survival to the Englishman. Hence the morality which Nelson taught 30 his midshipmen: Tell the truth, never be afraid, and hate a Frenchman as you would the devil. The second precept, to the modern mind, is unimportant: the third is grotesque. Though the instinctive and unthinking of all countries continue that hatred of foreign nations which was formerly a virtue, those who have grasped the principles of reasoned morality advocate international arbitration and laugh at the mutual hatreds of civilized nations. The modern love of arbitration is a direct outcome of the law of increasing returns.

Another outcome is the advocacy of women's rights. War being no longer of supreme importance, the less warlike sex may become as useful for the 40 new end of living well, and as capable of realizing that end, as men are: they may therefore attain an equal respect, an equal position in the state, and an equal share in advancing, not the art of keeping alive, but the art of living.

Hence it is no accident that women's rights and steam are twins, that Mary Wollstonecraft was a contemporary of James Watt.

A third outcome is education, and its concomitant, democracy. Increasing returns are won solely by human intelligence: intelligence, therefore, formerly less important than strength, is now more important: that it is more important in war, as well as in business, is due to that very power of combination and machinery which has created increasing returns. That education is desirable, is thus due to the perceived possibility of increasing returns: that education is possible, is due to the wealth which this law
10 creates. That democracy is possible, is due, again, to the diffusion of education.

Democratic Socialism, also, is due to this law: without it, that mitigation of the struggle for life, at which Socialism aims, would be disastrous, and those advantages of cooperation and organization, which it urges, would be non-existent. So much is this the case, that most Socialists are never tired of vilifying Malthus, though they rarely succeed in pointing out why his doctrines are no longer true of civilized man. Under the same head come medicine, sanitation, temperance legislation, and all the many other schemes for enabling the weak to survive.
20 The survival of the weak is still often regarded as a misfortune. But if, as I have urged, modern morals should aim, not at the fact of life, which civilization sufficiently ensures, but at the fullest content of life, the survival of the weak may be highly desirable. For the weak in a Darwinian sense are not, so far as one can see, at all identical with the people whose life is poorest in content, and should, therefore, on modern principles, be allowed to survive.

Finally, from a private point of view, that worldliness, that pushing struggle for success, which was virtuous in our ancestors, and is regarded as moral by our conventional contemporaries, is now no longer needed: we
30 may devote ourselves to the adornment of life, to the growth of roses rather than cabbages, to the pursuit of all that makes life not merely possible, but beautiful, interesting and varied. With this remark I will end this somewhat platitudinous series of "wise saws and modern instances".

**49**

# Review of Schmöle, *Die Sozialdemokratischen Gewerkschaften in Deutschland seit dem Erlasse des Sozialisten-Gesetzes* [1897]

THIS REVIEW APPEARED in *The Economic Journal*, London, 7 (March 1897): 94–5, two months after Russell had read the book. He knew one of the editors of the *Economic Journal*, F. Y. Edgeworth, as the author of a pamphlet on monetary standards he had read in January 1895; but no evidence of a more personal acquaintance between them has been found that would suggest a reason for a request to write the review. The assignment may have come to Russell simply because of the publicity attaching to the publication of *German Social Democracy* in December 1896 (reviewed by the *Economic Journal* the following June). Although by early 1897 Russell was mainly occupied with seeing *An Essay on the Foundations of Geometry* through the press and developing a neo-Hegelian philosophy of science, this review is evidence that he retained an interest in economics and German social democratic ideas and institutions.

Josef Schmöle was a lecturer at the University of Greifswald in Germany. The title of this "preliminary" volume of his book translates as "Social Democratic Unions in Germany Since the Passing of the Socialist Law". The second volume was published in 1898.

As no manuscript has been found, the copy-text is the text in the *Economic Journal*.

*Die Sozialdemokratischen Gewerkschaften in Deutschland seit dem Erlasse des Sozialisten-Gesetzes.* By Josef Schmöle. Vol. I. Jena: Fischer, 1896. Pp. xviii, 211.

GERMAN TRADE UNIONS differ, in their origin, from those of England, in much the same way as the origin of the German constitution differs from that of the English. The English constitution has arisen, bit by bit, out of the needs of the moment. The German constitution was decreed ready-made by the Court at Versailles in 1871. Similarly, English Trade Unions have been obscure in their beginnings and variable in their
10 aims. German Trade Unions, on the contrary, have been almost unchanging in their aims, and sprang into existence by the fiat of the labour leaders in 1868. This difference of origin was rendered possible by the fundamental difference which, as Dr. Schmöle points out in his Introduction, gives the key to the peculiarities of the German labour movement. This difference is that Trade Unions in Germany have been throughout subsidiary to political parties, and regarded mainly as means of political agitation. To supplant Social Democracy, Dr. Max Hirsch, a prominent Liberal, decided, in 1868, to found unions in Germany "on the English model", i.e. on the assumption that the interests of labour and capital are really the same. To supplant Dr.
20 Hirsch, Schweitzer, the successor of Lassalle, obtained, in August of the same year—while Dr. Hirsch was still making preliminary studies in England—the support of the Universal German Working Men's Association for the foundation of socialistic Trade Unions. Dr. Hirsch, on his return, thus found himself anticipated, and his friendly societies—for such they virtually are—have ever since dragged on an obscure and unimportant existence.

It is, accordingly, the Social Democratic Unions alone with which the present volume deals. It is a pity that Dr. Schmöle, in spite of the emphasis which he lays on the pre-eminence of the political movement, has not gone more deeply into the manifold reactions of this movement on German Trade
30 Unionism. For example, much of his space is devoted to the efforts of the police to apply the Coalition Laws to the destruction of Trade Unions, and the counter-efforts of Trade Unionists to evade the laws. The singular fact that none of their energies were devoted to the repeal of these laws, which he leaves unexplained, can only be explained by their adherence to Social Democracy. For Social Democracy is too lofty in its aims to concentrate on any single practicable reform, and has never instituted any special agitation for freedom of combination.

At first the Trade Unions were frankly political. But this frankness cost them their life, for it led to the dissolution of almost all of them at the passing
40 of the Socialist Law (1878). New societies were soon founded, however, which endeavoured to appear non-political; but the slightest appearance of Socialism, even a petition to the Reichstag for regulation of the hours of

labour, would usually afford the police a pretext for their dissolution. The laws under which dissolutions took place were two: First, the Coalition Law by which, in most German states, no two political associations may combine in any way for any common purpose; and, second, the Insurance Law, by which insurance societies can only exist with the permission and under the inspection of the police. The best part of Dr. Schmöle's book is the section devoted to the legal chicaneries by which the police endeavoured to make these two laws applicable to Trade Unions, and the ingenuity with which Trade Unionists sought to evade them. The Courts would appear to have frequently differed from the police in their interpretation of the law, but Dr. Schmöle shows clearly the vacillating and inconsistent character of the various judgments delivered in these matters. This led the Socialists, not unnaturally, to infer that the law depended entirely on the bias of particular judges, a view for which, though our author rejects it, there seem to be excellent grounds.

On the whole, German Trade Unionism impresses one as a very half-hearted movement, and the present work does nothing to alter this impression. The most energetic members, being Social Democrats, have in general but little faith in the efficacy of movements within the capitalistic state— even the organizers often urge men not to expect of the unions what only a Socialist State can give. Almost all the energy and self-sacrifice which in England would have gone to the unions, goes in Germany to Social Democracy. Dr. Schmöle concludes with a hope that this state of things may change as the status of German labour improves, but for such a hope there seem, at present, only the slenderest grounds.

The book is learned and sympathetic, but not sufficiently critical or scientific in its attitude; although its task is a far easier one than the history of English Trade Unionism, it accomplishes hardly any of the objects which Mr. and Mrs. Sidney Webb's book so successfully attains. It abounds in generalities, but contains few useful generalizations. The style is prolix and lacking in concrete detail. In this respect, at any rate, we may hope for an improvement in the treatment of separate trades, which Dr. Schmöle promises in a second part of the present work.

# Appendices

# Appendix I
# Outlines and Reports of Lectures

1.1 Abstract of Paper **13**, "Lövborg or Hedda"

1.2 Outline of Paper **46**, "German Social Democracy, as a Lesson in Political Tactics"

1.3 Syllabus of "The Foundations of Geometry" Lectures

1.4 Reports of "The Foundations of Geometry" Lectures

    1.4(a)   Lecture I
    1.4(b)   Lecture III
    1.4(c)   Lecture IV
    1.4(d)   Lecture V
    1.4(e)   Lecture VI
    1.4(f)    Report of Lectures I–VI

1.5 Report of Lecture, "Socialism as the Consummation of Individual Liberty"

THE WRITINGS PRINTED here are all, in ways to be explained, associated with Russell's career as a thinker and author during the period encompassed by Volume 1. The outlines have a special relevance to Russell as a writer. He confessed in old age: "I do not know how other people write, but I know that in my own case the labour is practically finished by the time I begin the actual writing. The crucial moment for me is when I make a brief synopsis" (*1954*, 4–5). The abstract of Paper **13** was enclosed with a letter sent to Alys on 22 February 1894. She returned it on the 24th, with comments on passages she had numbered on Russell's manuscript. These numbers are not printed here; nor are her comments. The outline of **46** is to be found in the first "Mit Gott" notebook (RA 210.006550–FI, 1–3).

    The syllabus of Russell's lectures on the foundations of geometry at Bryn Mawr College (and repeated in large part at The Johns Hopkins University) in the autumn of 1896 exists in manuscript. It is probably the outline that Alys sent on 1 February 1896 to Carey Thomas, then President of Bryn Mawr, who probably forwarded it to the President of Johns Hopkins. In 1981 it was discovered in the archives of the latter institution. Reports of four of Russell's lectures on geometry at Bryn Mawr have been found in the *Public Ledger and Daily Transcript*, a newspaper published in Philadelphia; they are reprinted here. The reports make it clear that Russell delivered his lectures in a different order than the syllabus promised: the first and third were as planned but the sixth in the syllabus became the fourth in delivery. The reporter of the lectures is not named in the published accounts. There were no reports of the substance of the second and sixth lectures; but the *New York Evening Post* reported on 21 November 1896 that the sixth lecture was given. An omnibus report of the series appearing in a Bryn Mawr journal is also included. (For details of the arrangements for the lecture series, see Armstrong *1969–70*.) Manuscripts of the lectures have not been found. It is probable that they did exist, for Alys wrote to Thomas in the letter cited above that Russell was "fearfully nervous and shy" about delivery of the lectures and "thinks he will have to read" them. The final report, again from the *Public Ledger and Daily Transcript*, concerns a more popular lecture Russell delivered during his visit to Bryn Mawr. The Introduction (sec. III) discusses the possibility of this paper being identical to one declined by the *Forum*.

I.I Abstract of Paper **13**, "Lövborg or Hedda"

*Abstract.* Two questions. (1) How far sexual point of view come in (2) How far spoil discussion if did. Both purely psychological—would be different in different people utterly—On first point have to observe (a) Intellectual attitude antagonistic to sexual, and free discussion does not as is supposed tend to make this stronger but rather weaker. (b) Evening worse than morning: all the passions stronger at night. (c) The frequent meetings with various members of the opposite sex on a basis at least in theory non-flirtatious would tend to make the sexual element much less easily roused than otherwise. [Observations on monasticism, hermits, harlots etc.] (c) Of course in many people, and in most people at times, there is a difference in mental attitude towards *any* member of the opposite sex who is fairly young (unless physically repulsive); but this may merely stimulate to greater activity and to greater interest in such a person's sayings and doings.

This carries over to second point. How far would sexual element spoil discussion if it did come in? For certainly to some extent with some people I suppose it must be admitted it would come in. If there were love only on one side, unreciprocated, my own belief is it would have by no means a harmful influence, for any departure from the traditions of the Society or any failure in discussion would be viewed unfavourably by the person whose opinion would be valued. Let us suppose the most unfavourable case: reciprocal love so strong as to make every thing else seem worthless. This would in the first place be very apt to be so absorbing as to destroy intellectual interests except in subjects immediately connected with the relation of the sexes: in the second place the meeting of the Society would probably become an occasion for seeing each other rather than for contributing to the argument. Little attention would be paid to the proceedings by the pair, and they might become practically lost to the Society. At least this is the pessimistic view.

But this picture is one sided: such a pair probably anxious not to prove the admission of women a mistake: would therefore make effort to discuss as well as formerly: and this effort would I know be successful in many cases though perhaps not always. Indeed the mere exhilaration of each other's presence would in some cases so sharpen all their faculties that their intellects would be even better than usual. And finally, danger in being too purely intellectual. Many questions come up in which experience of passion, of emotion, of feeling in general is absolutely necessary to the formation of a competent judgment: and this I should think is likely to become even more the case in the future. To discuss the march of the Hegelian dialectic may be possible without such experience: but few things can be discussed adequately from a purely intellectual standpoint. [And you might finish up by roundly cursing the monasticism of the Varsity on the ground of diminished experience of life.] [Might observe somewhere that women's views might correct a possible one-sidedness in man's even in matters almost purely intellectual.]

## 1.2 Outline of Paper 46

Notes for a lecture on the Political Teachings
of German Social Democracy, or
*Social Democracy as a Lesson in Political Tactics.*
(German Lessons in Independent Labour Politics).

I.  Accepting the end as good, ought labour to form a separate party? German leaders emphatically say yes.

II.  This has a double effect:

Give examples from
Lecture III.
Diminution of
Fortschrittler.
Conservatism of Liberals. Collapse of opposition to Bismarck.

1. To eliminate moderate men from the labour-party, and so make it more intransigeant and unpractical.
2. To remove the motive to other parties, derived from a conditional support, for advance in the direction of labour's wishes, and to produce a terror which has very reactionary effects.

Instance Saxony.

III.  It thus divides society—as the *Communist Manifesto* says it must—into two hostile camps, bourgeoisie and proletariat; and this division has no tendency to heal itself, but grows continually more bitter as the labour-party grows.

Antisemites,
Agrarians etc.
Suppression and
Socialist Law.

IV.  Unfortunately for the labour-party, many labourers, especially in the country, refuse to join it. Thus the bourgeoisie remains, and is likely long to remain, the stronger party. The uncompromising attitude of the labour-party produces a similar attitude in the other parties, and no single step can be won till all is won.

Quote various
speeches of
Liebknecht.

V.  This necessitates no mitigation at present, and revolution in the end. But even if Communism, as the result of a process, be desirable, as a sudden revolutionary product it could hardly succeed.

England.
*cf.* also the Irish agitation.

VI.  But now suppose the labour-party has conditionally supported the most friendly of the bourgeois parties. In this case, it remains itself apparently unalarming, and yet it can apply a perpetual spur to the bourgeois radicals, as the price of its support. Thus the radicals become more radical, remain more numerous in the country, and proportionately to their numbers, are more represented in Parliament—since Radical and Socialist votes are not divided. Second Ballots would make this policy peculiarly feasible in Germany. Illustration from diplomacy in foreign politics: e.g. Wolsey.

**Religious fervour for Marx.**

VII. Against this advantage, however, must be set the smaller enthusiasm among workmen themselves. If these are not naturally political, only a far-reaching gospel can rouse them—and this is more or less the case in Germany. The times of Schulze-Delitzsch, however, suggest that this objection does not outweigh the advantages. Another advantage is, that terror may produce reforms as well as oppression: Bismarck's "social reform".

**Vollmar.**

VIII. But the stronger Social Democracy grows, the better it can afford to negotiate with other parties. It is therefore most urgently to be desired that it should soon adopt this policy, and save Germany from revolution and civil war. For Germany, a separate labour-party may have been a necessary stage, but cannot profitably be *more* than a stage.

## I.3  Syllabus of "The Foundations of Geometry" Lectures

### Syllabus of Six Lectures on
### The Foundations of Geometry

#### by Bertrand Russell,
#### Fellow of Trinity College in Cambridge

Lectures I and II. History of Metageometry.

   I.    First and second periods:
       (1) Gauss, Lobatchewsky, Bolyai
       (2) Riemann, Helmholtz, Beltrami

  II.   Third period:
       (3) Cayley, Klein, Lie. Discussion of the question how far metrical Geometry is really superseded by projective.

For these two lectures, read Klein's *Vorlesungen über Nicht-Euklidische Geometrie*, Göttingen 1893, if a mathematician. Very few symbols will be used, and the lectures will be comprehensible without much mathematics.

Lectures III and IV. Critical account of some previous philosophical theories of Geometry.

  III.  Kant, Herbart, Riemann, Helmholtz, Erdmann.

  IV.  Lotze and recent French philosophers (Renouvier, Delboeuf, Lechalas,

Calinon, Poincaré).

These lectures and Lectures V and VI will require some knowledge of Logic and general philosophy. Recommended: Erdmann, *Axiome der Geometrie*, Leipzig 1877; Bosanquet, *Logic*, Vol. I, Oxford 1888.

Lectures V and VI. Constructive theory of Geometry.

    V. *Projective Geometry*. Applies equally to Euclidean and non-Euclidean spaces, and so far as truly projective, cannot distinguish between them. Deduction of axioms of projective Geometry from necessary properties of any form of externality. Some such form necessary to experience, and projective Geometry therefore wholly à priori.

    VI. *Metrical Geometry*. Possibility of space-measurement involves three axioms, equivalent to the three axioms of projective Geometry. These three à priori; the other axioms of Euclid empirical. [See *Mind*, N.S. No. 17].

Recommended: Kant's Transcendental Aesthetic, Lotze's *Metaphysic*, Bk. II, Chaps. I and II; Bradley's *Logic*, Bk. I, Chaps. I and II, London 1883.


## I.4  Reports of "The Foundations of Geometry" Lectures


### I.4(a)  "The Foundations of Geometry / The First of a Course of Lectures by Hon. Bertrand Russell", *Public Ledger and Daily Transcript*, Philadelphia, 4 Nov. 1896, 3.

THE FIRST LECTURE of the course on "The Foundations of Geometry," which is to be given by the Hon. Bertrand Russell at Bryn Mawr College through November, was delivered on Monday afternoon last. The lecture was attended by a class of fifteen graduate students in mathematics and philosophy and by men and women professionally interested in the subject discussed, among them being Professor Susan Cunningham and Professor Gummere, of Swarthmore; Professor Frank Morley and Professor Ernest Brown, of Haverford; Professor Edwin Crawley and Mr. Hallett, of the University of Pennsylvania, and the following members of the Bryn Mawr Faculty: President M. Carey Thomas, Professors Scott, Harkness, Mackenzie, Buckingham, Miller, Hodder and Gwinn.

    Mr. Russell gave a short account of the history of the origin of metageometry, and traced the attitude of the different investigators of the subjects from Lobatchewsky, Gauss and the two Bolyais, down to Riemann; and sketched briefly the problem to the discussion of which the lectures are to be devoted, viz.: which of the geometrical axioms are to be described as *à priori* (using the Kantian terms), and which as *empirical*.

    In the evening President Thomas gave a reception in honor of Mr. and Mrs.

Bertrand Russell and Mr. and Mrs. Richard Norton. Among those present were Charles Hartshorne, Philip C. Garrett, Mr. and Mrs. Henry Tatnall, Mr. and Mrs. Henry Scattergood, Mr. and Mrs. F. H. Converse, Mr. and Mrs. Henry T. Townsend, John W. Townsend, Mr. and Mrs. Theodore Ely, Miss Elizabeth P. Smith, Mr. and Mrs. Frank H. Taylor, Mr. and Mrs. Albanus L. Smith, William H. Nicholson, Mr. and Mrs. Edward H. Keiser, James Harkness, Dr. Florence Bascom, Mr. and Mrs. Alfred Hodder, Miss Florence V. Keys, Dr. A. B. Foster, Miss Fredericka M. Kerr, Miss Helen W. Thomas, Mrs. H. W. Smythe, Miss Martha G. Thomas, Miss Elizabeth M. Blanchard, Dr. Harriet Randolph, Miss Madeline V. Abbott, Dr. Charles Wood.

I.4(b) "Philosophy and Geometry / Mr. Russell's Third Lecture before the Graduate Students at Bryn Mawr College", *Public Ledger and Daily Transcript*, 10 Nov. 1896, 2.

BERTRAND RUSSELL, FELLOW of Trinity College, Cambridge, delivered the third of his series of lectures on geometry at Bryn Mawr College yesterday afternoon before the class of graduate students in mathematics. Guests were present from Haverford, Swarthmore and the University of Pennsylvania. Mr. Russell's lecture dealt with the philosophical theories of Kant, Riemann and Helmholtz in regard to the geometrical properties of space. The question how far metageometry, which was of course unknown to Kant, upset Kant's arguments as to a priority of geometrical axioms is one of the most interesting which Mr. Russell has undertaken to discuss. He gave a short account of Kant's argument on the "Transcendental Aesthetic", and emphasized the fact that his doctrine of the distinction between analytic and synthetic judgments has proved untenable for modern logic, though the conception of àpriori judgments is retained.

He then proceeded to criticise somewhat severely the philosophical aspect of Riemann's work, while acknowledging the importance of his mathematical investigations. The remainder of this most interesting lecture was devoted to Helmholtz, with whose theory of the dependence of geometry on mechanics the lecturer seemed to have little sympathy. The next lecture will deal with the condition of spatial measurement.

I.4(c) "Measurement in Space / The Fourth Lecture by Mr. Russell to Bryn Mawr College Students", *Public Ledger and Daily Transcript*, 16 Nov. 1896, 3.

MR. BERTRAND RUSSELL lectured again at Bryn Mawr College on Friday afternoon before the course assembly of students and invited guests. In this, his fourth lecture, which dealt with the conditions of spatial measurement, Mr. Russell discussed the three essential axioms of metrical geometry, the axioms of free mobility, of dimensions and distance, and showed in the first place the impossibility of measurement—that is, of comparison of spatial magnitude—in space which is not homogeneous. He deduced from this that position is not an intrinsic, but a relative, property of things in space.

He next pointed out that it is an à priori condition of geometry that space must have a finite integral number of dimensions, but that the limit of the number of dimensions to three is, to a certain extent, empirical.

In regard to distance, he showed that spatial magnitude would not be possible if two points had not a certain intrinsic relation—a magnitude—the distance between them. Again, distance can only be determined by two points, if there is a definite curve in space completely defined by these two points; that is, linear magnitude is a logically possible conception in space only where two points determine one line.

1.4(d)  "The Foundations of Geometry", *Public Ledger and Daily Transcript*, 18 Nov. 1896, 2.

MR. RUSSELL, IN the fifth lecture of the course he is delivering at Bryn Mawr College, dealt yesterday with the principles and axioms of projective geometry. This geometry has found no exponents as philosophical as Helmholtz and Riemann, and has not been fully discussed from the philosophical standpoint. After a brief explanation of the fundamental ideas of projective geometry, the lecturer discussed the axioms here implied, arriving at the conclusion that projective geometry is wholly a priori, and thus realizes the ideal of Grassmann (which he himself failed to attain) of that department of pure knowledge which is possible without any appeal to special intuition.

The most important of the axioms on which projective geometry relies are those of the relativity and homogeneity of space. All elements—points, lines, planes—have to be regarded as relations between other elements; thus space is simply an aggregate of relations. The persistence of the internal relations of a figure under the operations of projective geometry proves their independence of all external relations and thus proves the homogeneity of space.

1.4(e)  "Bryn Mawr", *New York Evening Post*, 21 Nov. 1896, 20.

THE SIXTH AND concluding lecture of Mr. Russell's course on the "Foundations of Geometry" was delivered on Friday evening (November 20). This lecture closed a most instructive course, which has been followed with interest not only by the members of the mathematical and philosophical departments of Bryn Mawr College, but by visitors from the University of Pennsylvania, Haverford, and Swarthmore. At the conclusion of the lecture Profs. Harkness and Miller expressed the gratitude of the audience on behalf of the departments concerned. After Thanksgiving Mr. Russell will repeat the lectures before the students of the Johns Hopkins University.

I.4(f) "The Russell Lectures", *The Lantern*, Bryn Mawr, Pa., no. 6 (June 1897): 137–8.

UPON THE INVITATION of the Mathematical Department, the Honorable Bertrand Russell, Fellow of Trinity College, Cambridge, delivered a course of six lectures at the college during the month of November, 1896. These lectures were attended by the members of the departments of Mathematics and Philosophy, and by a number of persons from outside the college who were interested in the subject discussed.

Mr. Russell in his first lecture stated that his object was to determine which of the axioms of Geometry were to be regarded as *a priori*, and therefore involved in any conception of space, and which were empirical, or dependent on the experience of some special form of space.

In the succeeding lectures, accordingly, he made a careful examination of the axioms of Euclidean and of projective Geometry, showing as a result of this examination, that there are certain axioms common to both systems, and therefore independent of the nature of the space with which we deal. These axioms, Mr. Russell argued, are *a priori*. On the other hand, he showed that, while these axioms are sufficient so long as only descriptive properties are involved, it is impossible to introduce the idea of metrical relations by means of them. All axioms involving metrical relations have to be deduced from our supposed knowledge of the special space with which we have to deal, and are therefore empirical.

The last lecture of the series was an attempt to prove from the philosophic standpoint two statements. Of these the first is, that assuming the conception of any form of externality, the *a priori* axioms follow; the second, that the conception of some form of externality is necessary, if knowledge is to be possible at all.

Not the least pleasant circumstance in connection with the lectures was the privilege of meeting Mr. Russell at the close of the hour, when questions were asked and answered in regard to any obscure or knotty point.

Those that attended the lectures are now awaiting with interest the appearance of Mr. Russell's book, which is very shortly to be issued by the Cambridge University Press.

*E⟨milie⟩ N⟨orton⟩ M⟨artin⟩, '94*

I.5 Report of Lecture, "Socialism as the Consummation of Individual Liberty" (reported under title: "Bertrand Russell's Lectures on Socialism"), *Public Ledger and Daily Transcript*, 23 Nov. 1896, 3.

AT A MEETING of the Graduate Club of Bryn Mawr College on Saturday evening, in the parlors of Pembroke East, Miss Isabel Maddison, president of the club, presided, and introduced the guest of honor, Bertrand Russell, whom the club had invited to deliver the address of the evening. He spoke upon "Socialism as the Consummation of Individual Liberty."

Mr. Russell spoke of various ways in which State action may increase individual liberty, saying they were all socialistic, and that freedom has always been the ideal of Socialists. German social democracy descends, through Marx, from the English Socialists of 1820–1840, whose premises were those of Rousseau, Bentham and Ricardo, *i.e.*, the individualist doctrines of the rights of man and the universal pursuit of self-interest. German and English Socialism alike, in accordance with this ancestry, advocate State action entirely on the ground that it is capable of increasing the freedom of the individual. A reception followed the address.

# Appendix II
# What Shall I Read?

FROM FEBRUARY 1891 to March 1902 Russell kept a monthly list of books, partial books and some individual papers which he read during that time. This list, which totals 758 entries, bears the printed title "What Shall I Read?" and is subtitled "A Record of Books Read and to Be Read". It is contained in a small, bound book presented to Russell by his maternal grandmother, Lady Stanley of Alderley. The list is confined to books read, rather than to be read. In keeping such a record, Russell was following a well-established practice of many Victorian intellectuals such as Mill, Arnold and Gladstone.

The entries reflect the unusual range of Russell's intellectual interests: in addition to works on philosophy, mathematics and physics, there are many entries noting novels, poems, plays, historical studies, economic treatises and biographies. Well over a hundred entries are French and German titles. A number of entries refer to the same book or part thereof. For example, Gibbon's *Decline and Fall of the Roman Empire* is entered nine times. Russell also read large portions of the canon of such writers as Henry James, Ibsen and Turgenev. Indeed, literary titles comprise the majority, although the list reflects some of the background reading Russell did for the three books (*1896, 1897* and *1900*) he wrote in the nineteenth century.

Many of the philosophy books he read for the Moral Sciences Tripos during 1893–94 are recorded, but none of those for the Mathematical Tripos in 1890–93. (The deletion of the entry in February 1891 of Routh's *Analytical Statics* suggests that Russell intentionally omitted assigned mathematical reading.) He entered many of the titles from the reading list in philosophy that Harold Joachim sent him in September 1892 (see his *1959*, 37). There is no definite evidence that Russell read any of the titles on the reading list in economics that he was given by Alfred Marshall in June 1894. Since neither Marshall's list nor any notes relating to it survive, it is not known what books were suggested. Probably some of the titles entered after June 1894 reflect Marshall's recommendations. It is also probable that the books summarized in the "Mit Gott" notebook (see the headnote to **45**) and listed in the bibliography of Russell *1896* are Marshall's suggestions, even though none of these titles appears in "What Shall I Read?" The Bibliographical Index to this volume and the references in Russell's *1897* and *1900* contain other titles not listed in "What Shall I Read?" For example, Riemann *1867*, on which he made extensive notes in 1895, is not recorded. Hence this appendix cannot be regarded as a complete record for the time covered.

Beginning as early as January 1894, there are some 227 entries marked "A.", indicating that Alys also read those books, probably aloud with Russell. In September 1895 a list begins on the right-hand pages of books Alys read, presumably by herself. Alys also independently kept two lists in the "Locked Diary". One, entitled "Books read together in the first five years after our marriage", coincides almost completely with the entries marked "A." The other list of her own reading from 1895 to 1899 duplicates the list that appears on the right-hand pages in "What Shall I Read?" Alys's lists are not printed here. After he had filled the notebook Russell did not, it seems, begin another. Perhaps the breakdown of his marriage in 1901–02 discouraged him from carrying on an enterprise that, since 1894, had been a joint effort.

Russell used a system of dashes before many entries between February 1891 and April 1895 whose significance has not been determined. Of greater interest is the fact that he often wrote a single word or phrase in the remarks column describing the impact of a particular book upon him. All but one of his comments—two exclamation marks on p. 53 (January 1895)—were heavily deleted. On reconsidering what he had written, Russell decided to cancel these remarks, possibly because he came to think them jejeune. There are thirty-seven cancellations ending in November 1891, many of them so obliterated as to be illegible, and in several cases a second ink obliteration was superimposed on a first. Infra-red and ultra-violet photographic enlargements were used to try to penetrate these markings, but with little success. Cancellations are given in the text only when it is fairly certain that they have been correctly construed.

In printing this document abbreviations in titles and authors' surnames have been expanded. First names are supplied in the author index immediately following. Titles shortened by Russell are not given in full. The capitalization of English titles has been regularized. Italics and double inverted commas have been applied according as the titles are of monographs or parts of larger works. Misspelled words in titles and authors' names are corrected, and the Textual Notes record the corrections. It has not been possible to verify every title. For example, the first two of the three entries ascribed to Sickert—presumably Oswald Sickert, the author of *Helen* (read May 1895) under the pseudonym Oswald Valentine—cannot be found in any standard bibliography.

The black morocco booklet which contains "What Shall I Read?" is box-stamped in gilt on the front and back boards, with a variation of the subtitle gilt-stamped on the front board. The 128 pages are gilt-edged, and the end-papers are in a gold and green floral pattern. The pages have been odd-numbered (by the Russell Archives' staff) on the recto of each leaf. The leaves measure 95 × 115 mm. As the Illustrations show, there are spaces for twelve or thirteen entries per set of facing pages. The book, whose entries form the copy-text, was printed by George Waterston & Sons of Edinburgh and London.

**1891**

| | |
|---|---|
| February | −*Omar Kayyam* [Edw. FitzGerald] ⟨obliterated⟩ |
| | −*Harzreise* and *Norderney* Heine |
| | *Excursion* [Bks. 1–4] Wordsworth |
| March | ⟨"*Analytical Statics*"? "Routh"?, comment obliterated⟩ |
| | *Virginians* Thackeray ⟨"... excellent"⟩ |
| | −*Jack* Daudet ⟨"Good, but ..."⟩ |
| | −*Esmond* Thackeray ⟨"A beautiful book"⟩ |
| April | −*Three Essays on Religion* J. S. Mill ⟨"Admirable (especially first)"⟩ |
| | =*Epipsychidion* Shelley |
| | =*Hedda Gabler* Ibsen ⟨obliterated⟩ |
| | −*The Man v. the State* Herbert Spencer |
| | −*French Revolution* Carlyle ⟨obliterated⟩ |
| | *Fair Maid of Perth* Scott |
| | *Tale of Two Cities* Dickens ⟨obliterated⟩ |
| May | *Life of Shelley* Dowden ⟨"Moderately good"⟩ |
| | *Mountaineering without Guides* Girdlestone ⟨obliterated⟩ |
| | *Mademoiselle Ixe* ⟨Lanoe Falconer⟩ ⟨"Admirable"⟩ |
| | *Amaryllis* ⟨anonymous⟩ ⟨"Very silly"⟩ |
| June | *Japonneries d'Autonne* Pierre Loti ⟨obliterated⟩ |
| | −*Subjection of Women* J. S. Mill ⟨obliterated⟩ |
| | *Egmont* Goethe |
| | *Manfred* Byron |
| | *Macbeth* Shakespeare |
| | *Englische Fragmente* Heine ⟨"Excellent, but rather superficial"⟩ |
| | =*The Egoist* Meredith ⟨"Excellent at first, after ..."⟩ |
| | −*Scenes of Clerical Life* George Eliot |
| | *King John* Shakespeare |
| | Gibbon, Vol. VII |
| July | *Le Tartuffe* Molière |
| | *Le Cid* Corneille |
| | =*Cranford* Mrs. Gaskell ⟨"Charming"⟩ |
| | *Deformed Transformed* Byron ⟨"Caesar excellent; otherwise feeble"⟩ |
| | *Utilitarianism* Mill |
| | −*Triumph of Life* Shelley ⟨"Magnificent"⟩ |
| | −*Revolt of Islam* Shelley ⟨obliterated⟩ |
| | −*Queen Mab* Shelley |
| | *Bourgeois Gentilhomme* Molière |
| | −*Pippa Passes* Browning ⟨"Splendid"⟩ |

| | |
|---|---|
| August | *Fourberies de Scapin* Molière |
| | *Femmes Savantes* Molière |
| | *Malade Imaginaire* Molière |
| | −*Belinda* Miss Edgeworth ⟨"Good"⟩ |
| | =*Wives and Daughters* Mrs. Gaskell ⟨"Excellent"⟩ |
| | *Christmas Eve and Easter Day* Browning |
| | *A Soul's Tragedy* Browning ⟨"Very trifling"⟩ |
| | *Measure for Measure* Shakespeare |
| | *Luria* Browning ⟨"Striking"⟩ |
| | *Men and Women* Browning |
| September | *Heart of Midlothian* Scott ⟨obliterated⟩ |
| | *Literature and Dogma* M. Arnold ⟨obliterated⟩ |
| | =*Autobiography* J. S. Mill |
| | *Representative Government* J. S. Mill |
| | *Dramatis Personae* Browning |
| | *New England Nun* etc. Mrs. Wilkins ⟨"Very clever, but stories too often? too sketchy"⟩ |
| | *Dramatic Lyrics* Browning |
| | *Pauline* Browning |
| | *Strafford* Browning |
| | *Paracelsus* Browning |
| | *King Victor and King Charles* Browning |
| | *Return of the Druses* Browning |
| 24 | *A Blot in the 'Scutcheon* Browning ⟨"Fine"⟩ |
| 25 | *Colombe's Birthday* Browning |
| 25 | *Dramatic Romances* Browning |
| 25 | *In a Balcony* Browning |
| 25 | *Descent of Man* Darwin |
| October | −*Compromise* J. Morley ⟨"Admirable"⟩ |
| | Gibbon, Chap. XLV–LI |
| | −*Far-away Melody* etc. M. E. Wilkins ⟨"Excellent"⟩ |
| | *Vision of Judgment* Byron ⟨"Vastly clever"⟩ |
| | *Monastery* Scott |
| | −*Piccadilly* L. Oliphant ⟨"Excellent"⟩ |
| | =*Dr. Faustus* Marlowe ⟨"Great"⟩ |
| | *Tambourlaine* Part I Marlowe ?⟨sic⟩ |
| November | *Jew of Malta* Marlowe |
| | −*Hero and Leander* Marlowe and Chapman ⟨"Pretty"⟩ |
| | −*North and South* Mrs. Gaskell ⟨"Excellent"⟩ |
| | −*Edward the Second* Marlowe |
| | *Cecilia de Noël* Lanoe Falconer |
| | *La Saisiaz* Browning |
| | *The Two Poets of Croisic* Browning |

| | |
|---|---|
| December | *Dramatic Idyls* Browning |
| | =*Frankenstein* M. W. Shelley |
| | *By Order of the Czar* Hatton |
| | *Emma* Miss Austen |
| | *Lyrics from the Elizabethan Song-Books* [A. H. Bullen] |
| | *Lyrics from the Elizabethan Dramatists* [A. H. Bullen] |
| | *Mansfield Park* Miss Austen |
| | *History of Philosophy* Schwegler |
| | =*Mrs. Lorimer* Lucas Malet |

**1892**

| | |
|---|---|
| January | –*Some Emotions and a Moral* J. O. Hobbes |
| | *Endymion* Keats |
| | *Stella* Goethe |
| | *Sleep and Poetry* Keats |
| | *Isabella or the Pot of Basil* Keats |
| | *Purgatorio* Dante (*finished* January 1892) |
| | *Unsere Naturerkenntnis* Kroman |
| | *Traveller and Deserted Village* Goldsmith |
| | *The Inheritance* Miss Ferrier |
| | *Lady Geraldine's Courtship* Mrs. Browning |
| | *Kreutzer Sonata* Tolstoi |
| | *Trials of a Country Parson* Jessopp |
| | –*Wuthering Heights* Emily Bronte |
| | *Lyrics from Elizabethan Romances* [A. H. Bullen] |
| February | *Davison's Poetical Rhapsody* [A. H. Bullen] |
| | =*Astrophel and Stella* Sir Ph. Sidney |
| | *England's Helicon* [A. H. Bullen] |
| | *Beethoven's Unsterbliche Geliebte* M. Tenger |
| | *The Song Celestial* (Edw. Arnold) |
| March | *Monte Christo* Dumas (père) |
| | *Mornings in Florence* Ruskin |
| | *St. Mark's Rest* Ruskin |
| | –*Love-Letters of a Worldly Woman* Mrs. W. K. Clifford |
| April | =*Notre-Dame de Paris* V. Hugo |
| | *Stones of Venice*, small edn. Ruskin |
| | –*Lord Kilgobbin* Lever |
| | *Vittoria* G. Meredith |
| | *Hamlet* Shakespeare |
| May | –*Le Père Goriot* Balzac |
| | *Maison du Chat-qui-pelote* Balzac |
| | –'*Tis Pity She's a Whore* Ford |

|  |  |
|---|---|
|  | *−The Broken Heart* Ford |
|  | *Flatland* Dr. Abbott |
|  | *−A Maid's Tragedy* Beaumont and Fletcher |
| June | Gibbon, Chap. LII–LV |
|  | *That Lass o' Lowrie's* Mrs. Burnett |
|  | *Grania* Miss Lawless |
| July | *Prometheus Unbound* Shelley |
|  | *Pride and Prejudice* Jane Austen |
|  | *Huck Finn* Mark Twain |
|  | *Henry IV* Pt. I Shakespeare |
|  | *=Lavengro* Borrow |
| August | *−Romany Rye* Borrow |
|  | *Macbeth* Shakespeare |
|  | *Cinq-Mars* A. de Vigny |
|  | *Last Days of Pompei* Lytton |
| September | *Epipsychidion* Shelley |
|  | *Sense and Sensibility* Miss Austen |
|  | *Canterbury Tales* Chaucer |
|  | *Paradiso* Dante |
|  | *−Débâcle* Zola |
| October | *Paracelsus* Browning |
|  | *History of Christianity* Milman |
|  | *=Peer Gynt* Ibsen |
| November | *Revolution and Reaction in Modern France* Dickinson |
|  | *−Achilles in Scyros* Bridges |
|  | *Theaetetus* Plato [Jowett] |
|  | *=Atta Troll* Heine |
| December | *=Life of Shelley* Hogg |
|  | *Symposium* Plato [Jowett] |
|  | *Persuasion* Jane Austen |
|  | *=The Wages of Sin* Lucas Malet |
|  | *−Crotchet Castle* Peacock |
|  | *The Ring and the Book* Browning |
|  | *A Treatise of Human Nature* Vol. I Hume |

## 1893

|  |  |
|---|---|
| January | *−Across the Plains* etc. R. L. Stevenson |
|  | *Heritage of the Kurts* Björnsen |
|  | *Verses to Order* (A. G⟨odley⟩.) |
|  | *Kantische Erkenntnisstheorie* Hölder |
|  | Gibbon, Chap. LV |
|  | *Epipsychidion* Shelley |

|  | |
|---|---|
| | —*In God's Way* Björnsen |
| | —*Tristram Shandy* Sterne |
| February | =*Ordeal of Richard Feveral* Meredith |
| | =*Brand* Ibsen |
| | =*Väter und Söhne* Tourgenieff |
| | —*Daisy Miller* etc. Henry James |
| March | —*Erste Liebe* Tourgenieff |
| | *Mary Barton* Mrs. Gaskell |
| | *As You Like it* Shakespeare |
| April | *Twelfth Night* Shakespeare |
| | *The Country Cousin* F. M. Peard |
| | *Christmas Eve and Easter Day* Browning |
| | *Men and Women* Browning |
| | *Macbeth* Shakespeare |
| | =*Villette* Charlotte Bronte |
| | *Past and Present* Carlyle |
| | Gibbon, Chaps. LVI, LVII |
| | —*Life of Charlotte Brontë* Mrs. Gaskell |
| | *Port Tarascon* Daudet |
| | *Maud* Tennyson |
| | —*Tartarin sur les Alpes* Daudet |
| May | —*Shirley* Charlotte Brontë |
| | —*Bible in Spain* Borrow |
| June | *Evelina* Fanny Burney |
| | *Alastor* Shelley |
| | *Peer Gynt* Ibsen |
| | *Excursion* Wordsworth |
| | =*Die Neue Generation* Tourgenieff |
| | *La petite Fadette* George Sand |
| | =*Die Wildente* Ibsen |
| | *Brand* Ibsen |
| | *The Cenci* Shelley |
| July | —*La Fortune des Rougon* Zola |
| | —*A Study in Temptations* J. O. Hobbes |
| | *Methods of Ethics* H. Sidgwick |
| | —*Docteur Pascal* Zola |
| | —*Jane Eyre* C. Brontë |
| | *Descartes* Liard |
| | *Lieutenant Jergunoff* Tourgenjeff |
| | *Eine Seltsame Geschichte* Turgenjeff |
| | —*Der Raufbold* Turgenjeff |
| | *Geschichte der Religion und Philosophie in Deutschland* Heine |
| | *Discours de la Méthode* Descartes |

| | |
|---|---|
| August | *Lukerja* Turgenjeff |
| | *System der Philosophie* Wundt |
| | −*Sylvia's Lovers* Mrs. Gaskell |
| | *Epipsychidion* Shelley |
| | *Further Determination of the Absolute* McTaggart |
| | *Der Bund der Jugend* Ibsen |
| | =*Rosmersholm* Ibsen |
| | *Cymbeline* Shakespeare |
| September | −*Stützen der Gesellschaft* Ibsen |
| | *Tempest* Shakespeare |
| | *Principles of Logic* Bradley |
| | *Prolegomena* Kant |
| | *Epipsychidion* Shelley |
| | =*Der Katzensteg* Sudermann |
| | *Egmont* Goethe |
| | =*Tagebuch eines Ueberflüssigen* Turgenjeff |
| | *Midsummer Night's Dream* Shakespeare |
| | *Les Précieuses Ridicules* Molière |
| | *Prolegomena to Ethics* Green |
| | *Kate Coventry* Whyte Melville |
| | =*Dunst* Turgenjeff |
| | *Romeo and Juliet* Shakespeare |
| October | *Marmion* Scott |
| | *The Corsair* Byron |
| | −*Elle et Lui* George Sand |
| | *Einleitung in die Philosophie* Paulsen |
| | *Witch of Atlas* Shelley |
| | *Hobbes* Croom Robertson |
| | *Grundlegung zur Metaphysik der Sitten* Kant |
| November | =*Madame Bovary* Flaubert |
| | *De Augmentis* Bks. II–VI Bacon |
| | −*Komödie der Liebe* Ibsen |
| | *Novum Organum* Bacon |
| | =*Anna Karénine* Tolstoi |
| December | *Ein König Lear der Steppe* Turgenjeff |
| | −*Simple Histoire* Gontcharov |
| | *Epipsychidion* Shelley |
| | *Coriolanus* Shakespeare |
| | −*Confession d'un Enfant du Siècle* Alfred de Musset |
| | *Religion of a Literary Man* Le Gallienne |
| | *Die Axiome der Geometrie* Erdmann |

**1894**

| | |
|---|---|
| January | A. *Epipsychidion* Shelley |
| | *Hamlet* Shakespeare |
| | *Neue Novelletten* Kielland |
| | *Christabel* Coleridge |
| | =*Les Messieurs Golovleff* Chtchédrine |
| | *Manfred* Byron |
| | *Méditations, Objections et Réponses* DesCartes |
| | −*Frau Sorge* Sudermann |
| | *Computation or Logic* Hobbes |
| | *Liberty and Necessity* Hobbes |
| | *Hyperion* Keats |
| | *Des Passions de l'Ame* DesCartes |
| | *Spinoza* Pollock |
| February | =*Nightmare Abbey* Peacock |
| | *A Purple Patch* Sickert |
| | *Monadologie* Leibnitz |
| | =*Sex Love* Edward Carpenter |
| | *Règles pour la Direction de l'Esprit* Descartes |
| | *Dialogues between Hylas and Philonous* Berkeley |
| | *The Wild Duck* Ibsen |
| | *Hypothesen welche der Geometrie zu Grunde liegen* Riemann |
| | *Epipsychidion* Shelley |
| March | *Hedda Gabler* Ibsen |
| | −*Frühlingswogen* Turgenjeff |
| April | =*The American* Henry James |
| | =*Madonna of the Future*, etc. Henry James |
| | *Recherche de la Vérité* etc. DesCartes |
| May | *Ethical Studies* Bradley |
| | *Kathy* Sickert |
| | =*Woman* Edw. Carpenter |
| | =*Portrait of a Lady* Henry James |
| June | *Woman* Bebel |
| July | =*One of Our Conquerors* Meredith |
| | −*The Talking Horse* etc. Anstey |
| | *The Coxon Fund* Henry James |
| | −*Faust* Tourgenjeff |
| | *Absolute Geometrie* Frischauf |
| | *Die Nicht-Euklidischen Raumformen* (erste Hälfte) Killing |
| | *Obiter Dicta* Birrell |
| August | *Appearance and Reality* Bradley |
| | "Psychology" (*Encyclopaedia Britannica*) Ward |

|            | |
|------------|---|
|            | *Nicht-Euklid* Klein |
|            | –*Princess Casamassima* Henry James |
| September  | =*The Tragic Muse* Henry James |
|            | =*An Imaginary Portrait (The Child in the House)* Pater |
|            | *Basil* Joanna Baillie |
|            | *The Siege of Corinth* Byron |
|            | –*Miss Brown* Vernon Lee |
|            | –*Headlong Hall* Peacock |
|            | *Marriage* Edw. Carpenter |
|            | *Hereditary Genius* Galton |
|            | –*The Lady of the Aroostook* Howells |
|            | *Psychology* James |
| October    | =*The Bostonians* Henry James |
|            | *Epipsychidion* Shelley |
|            | –*Roderick Hudson* Henry James |
|            | *Political Economy* Bk. III Mill |
|            | –*Vanitas* Vernon Lee |
| November   | –*La Mort d'Ivan Iliitch* Tolstoï |
|            | –*Dimitri Roudine* Turgenjeff |
| December   | A. *Epipsychidion* Shelley |
|            | *Theory of the Content* Sir R. Ball |

**1895**

|            | |
|------------|---|
| January    | *Monetary Standard (Pamphlets)* Edgeworth, Nicholson, etc. |
|            | A. *Economics* Vol. I Marshall *(finished* January 1895*)* |
|            | *Gruppentheorie*, I Abschnitt Sophus Lie (Scheffers) |
|            | A. *Niebelungen Ring* Wagner |
|            | A. *Rise of the Dutch Republic* Motley |
|            | A. *Little Eyolf* Ibsen !! |
|            | A. *Political Economy* Ricardo |
|            | A. *Tristan und Isolde* Wagner |
|            | *Grundlagen der Politischen Oekonomie* Bd. I Ad. Wagner |
| February   | A.=*Lombard Street* Bagehot |
|            | A.–*Die Weber* Hauptmann |
|            | *Gesetze und Elemente des wissenschaftlichen Denkens* Heymans |
|            | *Theorie der Parallellinien* Lobatchewsky |
|            | A. *Tempest* Shakespeare |
|            | A.=*Einsame Menschen* Hauptmann |
|            | *Mechanik in ihrer Entwickelung* Mach |
|            | A.–*Heimath* Sudermann |
|            | A. *Recent Economic Changes* D. A. Wells |

A. *Essay on Population* Malthus
A. *Nora* Ibsen
A. *Ethic of Freethought* Bk. III K. Pearson
A. *Fliegende Holländer* Wagner

March     *Metaphysik* Kap. V und VI Erhardt

A. *Tannhaüser* Wagner
    *Sämmtliche Schriften über Geometrie* Helmholtz
    *Maid Marian* Peacock
A. *Emma* Miss Austen
A. −*Their Wedding Journey* Howells
A. −*A Chance Acquaintance* Howells
A. *Ancient Mariner*, and *Cristabel* Coleridge
A. *Books of Job and Ruth*
A. −*Das Fest auf Solhang* Ibsen
    −*Sonja Kovalevsky* Leffler

April     A. *Venetian Painters* Berenson

A. *History of the Papacy* Creighton
    −*A Vau l'Eau* Huysmans
    *Homogenic Love* Carpenter

May     A. Gibbon, Chaps. LVIII–LXIV

    *Sixth Memoir on Quantics* Cayley
    *Ursprung der Raumvorstellung* Stumpf
    *Darwinism and Race Progress* Haycraft
    *Helen* Sickert
    *Disquisitiones circa superficias curvas* Gauss
    *Saggio*, and *Teoria Fondamentale* Beltrami

June     *Grundlagen der Geometrie*, I und II. 1890 Sophus Lie

A. *Psychology* Vol. II W. James
    *Natural Inheritance* Galton
A. *Imaginary Portraits* Pater
    *Nicht-Euklid*, I and II Klein
    *Comus* Milton
    *Logic* Bosanquet
    *The Art of Fiction* W. Besant and H. James

July     A. *The Origin of Species* Darwin

A. *The Evolution of Sex* Geddes and Thompson

August     *The Cossacks* Tolstoï

A. *The Evolution of Marriage* Letourneau
A. *Economic Studies* Bagehot
    *The Mirror of Music* Makower
    *Othello* Shakespeare
A. *Man and Woman* Havelock Ellis
A. *The Newcomes* Thackeray

| | |
|---|---|
| September | A. *Foreign Exchanges* Goschen |
| | *Logic* Bosanquet |
| | A. *Darwinism and Politics* Ritchie |
| | *Nicht-Euklid* I and II Klein |
| | *Marius the Epicurean* Pater |
| | A. *Enquiry concerning Human Understanding* Hume |
| | A. *Youth of Parnassus* etc. L. Pearsall Smith |
| October | *Lesson of the Master* etc. Henry James |
| | *Modern Love* Meredith |
| | A. *Physics and Politics* Bagehot |
| | A. *Wolsey* Creighton |
| | A. *English Constitution* Bagehot |
| November | A. *Money* Jevons |
| | A. *Lohengrin* Wagner |
| | *L'Espace et le Temps* Lechalas |
| | A. *Marx'sche Werththeorie* Paul Fischer |
| | *Sozial Demokratie und der deutsche Reichstag* Paul Fischer |
| | A. *Soziale Frage auf dem Laude* Kampffmeyer |
| | A. *Arbeiterschutzgesetzgebung* Paul Ernst |
| | *Akademische Nationalökonomie und der Sozialismus* Ad. Wagner |
| | A. *German Socialism and Lassalle* Dawson |
| | A. *Herr Bastiat-Schulze von Delitsch* Lassalle |
| | *Friedrich Engels* Sombart |
| | A. *Capital*, Vol. I Marx |
| | *Feuerbach* etc. Engels |
| | A. *Quintessence of Socialism* Schaeffle |
| December | *Entwickelung des Sozialismus* Engels |
| | *Grundsätze und Forderungen der Sozialdemokratie* Kautsky und Schoenlank |
| | *Geheime Organisation der Sozialdemokratischen Partei* Krieter |
| | A. *Assissen Rede, 1849* Lassalle |
| | A. *Lassalle* Brandes |
| | *Social Democratic Protocols, 1880 and 1887* |
| | A. *Impossibility of Social Democracy* Schaeffle |
| | A. *Offenes Antwortschreiben* Lassalle |
| | A. *Arbeiterprogramm* Lassalle |
| | A. *Zur Arbeiterfrage* Lassalle |
| | *Lassalle* Bernstein |
| | *Der Lassalle'sche Vorschlag* W. Bracke |
| | *Unsere Ziele* Bebel |
| | A. *Bismarck and State Socialism* Dawson |
| | A. *Le Livre de mon ami* Anatole France |

**1896**

| | | |
|---|---|---|
| January | | *Karl Mark'sche Kritik*  Georg Adler |
| | | *Kapital* Bd. III  Marx |
| | | *The Bothie*  Clough |
| | A. | *The Amazing Marriage*  George Meredith |
| February | A. | *Candide*  Voltaire |
| | A. | *The Tragic Comedians*  Meredith |
| | | *Reine Vernunft*  Kant |
| March | | *Un Bulgare*  Tourgenieff |
| | | Various Articles in *Acta Mathematica* II  Cantor |
| | | *Metaphysische Anfangsgründe der Naturwissenschaft*  Kant |
| | | *Essai sur l'Hypothèse des Atomes*  Hannequin |
| | | *Lize*  Tourgenieff |
| | | *Smaller Logic*  Hegel |
| April | | *Concepts of Modern Physics*  Stallo |
| | | Article "Atom", *Encyclopaedia Britannica*  Maxwell |
| | | *Matter and Motion*  Maxwell |
| | A. | *Bouvard et Pécuchet*  Flaubert |
| | A. | *Study of History*  Lord Acton |
| | | *International Trade*  Bastable |
| | A. | *Early Renaissance in England*  Creighton |
| | A. | *La Maison Tellier* etc.  Maupassant |
| | A. | *Bonnie Briar Bush*  Ian Maclaren |
| | A. | *Ferdinand and Isabella*  Prescott |
| | | *Atomistik und Kriticismus*  K. Lasswitz |
| May | | *Analytical Psychology*  Stout |
| | | *Ausdehnungslehre von 1844*  Grassmann |
| | A. | *Phaedo*  Plato (Jowett) |
| | | *Axiome der Geometrie*  Erdmann |
| | | *Synechologie*  Herbart |
| | A. | *Economics*  Marshall |
| | | *Studies in Hegelian Dialectic*  McTaggart |
| June | | *Whist*  Cavendish |
| July | A. | *Frauenbewegung in England und Deutschland*  L.v. Gizycki |
| | A. | *Boyhood Adolescence and Youth*  Tolstoï |
| | A. | *American Commonwealth*  Bryce |
| August | | *First Supper* etc.  Sturges |
| | A. | *Age of Elizabeth*  Creighton |
| | | *L'Infini Mathématique*  Couturat |
| September | | *Embarrassments*  H. James |
| | | *The Europeans*  H. James |
| | | *Stories Revived*  H. James |

|  |  |
|---|---|
| | *Your Money or Your Life*  Edith Carpenter |
| October | *Dolly Dialogues*  Anthony Hope |
| | A. *Cashel Byron's Profession*  Bernard Shaw |
| | A. *Thirty Years' War*  Gardiner |
| | A. *Hajji Baba*  Morier |
| November | *Theory of Knowledge*  Hobhouse |
| | A. *Abraham Lincoln*  Morse |
| | A. *Gaston de Latour*  Pater |
| | A. *The Other House*  H. James |
| | *The Scarlet Letter*  Hawthorne |
| December | A. *Division and Reunion*  Woodrow Wilson |
| | A. *Blithedale Romance*  Hawthorne |
| | *The Sense of Beauty*  Santayana |
| | *Stetigkeit und irrationale Zahlen*  Dedekind |
| | A. *Human Marriage*  Westermarck |
| | *A Modern Instance*  Howells |

## 1897

|  |  |
|---|---|
| January | A. *Wealth against Commonwealth*  H. D. Lloyd |
| | A. *Die Sozialdemokratischen Gewerkschaften*  Schmöle |
| | A. *History of Trade Unionism*  Webb |
| | A. *Aglavaine et Sélisette*  Maeterlinck |
| February | A. *La Révolte*  de L'Isle Adam |
| | A. *John Gabriel Borkman*  Ibsen |
| | *Principes de la Métagéométrie*  Mansion |
| | *Hypothèses dans la Géométrie*  Bonnel |
| | A. *Short History of the English People*  Green |
| | A. *An Unsocial Socialist*  Shaw |
| | A. *Trooper Peter Halket*  Olive Schreiner |
| | *Eaux Printanières*  Tourgenieff |
| | *Récits d'un Chasseur*  Tourgenieff |
| March | A. *Die versunkene Glocke*  Hauptmann |
| | *Greater Logic*  Hegel |
| | A. *Midsummer Night's Dream*  Shakespeare |
| | A. *Measure for Measure*  Shakespeare |
| | A. *Richard III*  Shakespeare |
| | A. *Richard II*  Shakespeare |
| | *Quentin Durward*  Scott |
| | *Natural Philosophy*  Thomson and Tait |
| April | A. *The Greek View of Life*  Dickinson |
| | *Terres Vierges*  Tourgenieff |
| | A. *King John*  Shakespeare |

|  |  |  |
|---|---|---|
| | | *Principia* Newton |
| | | *Applications of Dynamics* J. J. Thomson |
| May | | *Ueber die Fernkraft* Isenkrahe |
| | | *Dynamics in Elliptic Space* Heath |
| | | *Modern Views of Electricity* Lodge |
| | | *Pendennis* Thackeray |
| | | *Confessions of an Opium-Eater* De Quincey |
| | | *Metaphysik* Lotze |
| | A. | *Life and Labour* (Vols. I–IX) Booth |
| June | A. | *Paradise Lost* Milton |
| | A. | Gibbon, Chap. LXV–end |
| | | *Appearance and Reality* Bradley |
| | | *Principien der Galilei–Newton'schen Theorie* C. Neumann |
| | | *Physikalische Grundlagen der Mechanik* Streintz |
| | | *Geschichtliche Entwickelung des Bewegungsbegriffes* L. Lange |
| | | *The Spoils of Poynton* H. James |
| | | *Omar Khayyam* FitzGerald |
| July | | *Spherical Harmonics* Ferrers |
| | | *Electricity and Magnetism* Maxwell |
| | | *Electric Waves* Hertz |
| | | *Atalanta* Swinburne |
| | | *Samson Agonistes* Milton |
| | | *Elasticity* Vol. I Love |
| | | *Bonheur Intime* Tolstoï |
| August | A. | *History of the Popes* Ranke |
| | A. | *Paradise Regained* Milton |
| | | *Mechanical Theory of Heat* Clausius |
| | | *Recent Researches in Electricity* J. J. Thomson |
| | | Papers on Heat Lord Kelvin |
| | | *Theory of Functions* Durège |
| | A. | *Montaigne* Lowndes |
| | A. | *Siècle de Louis XIV* Voltaire |
| September | | *Last Chronicle of Barset* Trollope |
| | | *Manon Lescaut* Prévost |
| October | A. | *What Maisie Knew* H. James |
| | A. | *The Aspern Papers* H. James |
| | A. | *Tentation de Saint Antoine* Flaubert |
| | A. | *Venetian Painters* Berenson |
| | A. | *Makers of Venice* Mrs. Oliphant |
| | A. | *History of England* Ranke |
| | | *Chartreuse de Parme* Stendhal |
| November | | *Le Rouge et le Noir* Stendhal |
| | A. | *The Four Georges* Thackeray |

A.  *On Translating Homer*  Matthew Arnold
A.  *English Humourists*  Thackeray
A.  *Sogno d'un Mattino di Primavera*  D'Annunzio
A.  *Voltaire*  J. Morley
A.  *Rousseau*  J. Morley
    *Les Diverses Grandeurs*  Calinon
December    *Theoretical Mechanics*  Love
    *Elektromagnetische Theorie des Lichtes*  Helmholtz
    *Salammbô*  Flaubert
A.  *Central Italian Painters*  Berenson
A.  *Maud*  Tennyson
    *Annouchka*  Tourgenieff

## 1898

January    *Grammar of Science*  K. Pearson
A.  *Pride and Prejudice*  Jane Austen
    *Kenilworth*  Scott
    *Logic*  Bradley
February    Gifford Lectures I–VI  J. Ward
    *Principien der Mechanik*  Hertz
March  A.  *Prelude*  Wordsworth
    *Properties of Matter*  P. G. Tait
    *Comus*  Milton
    *Infinitesimalmethode*  Cohen
    *Crotchet Castle*  Peacock
    *Universal Algebra*  Whitehead
April  A.  *Contes Cruels*  Villiers de L'Isle Adam
    *Life of Francis Place*  Wallas
A.  *Plays Pleasant and Unpleasant*  Bernard Shaw
    *Was sind und was sollen die Zahlen?*  Dedekind
May    *Industrial Democracy*  Webb
A.  *Frederick the Great*  Carlyle
    *Chances of Death* etc. Vol. I.  K. Pearson
June  A.  *Memoires of the Reign of George II*  H. Walpole
    *Hyperion*  Keats
    *New Essays*  Leibnitz
A.  *Decline and Fall*  Gibbon
July    *Cyrano de Bergerac*  Rostand
    *Essay concerning Human Understanding*  Locke
August  A.  *History of Rome*  Mommsen
A.  *Lord Clive*  Macaulay
A.  *Warren Hastings*  Macaulay

        *Philosophical Works of Leibnitz* (Duncan)

A. *Pitt* Rosebery

A. Plutarch's "Marius" (North)

A. Plutarch's "Sulla" (North)

A. Plutarch's "Alexander" and "Caesar" (North)

A. "M. Brutus" (Plutarch) (North)

        *Classification des Sciences* Goblot

        *Mathematical Theory of Evolution* (4 papers) Karl Pearson

**September**      *Bedeutung des Weber'schen Gesetzes* A. Meinong

        *Mallow and Asphodel* R. C. Trevelyan

A. *Civil Wars in France* Ranke

A. *Das Friedensfest* Hauptmann

**October**        *Die Bernsteinhexe* Meinhold

        *Macaulay's Life* Trevelyan

A. *Peninsula War* Napier

        Leibniz: *Monadology* etc. Latta

        *Leibnitz* Merz

A. *Roman Provinces* Mommsen

**November**  A. *Moll Flanders* Defoe

        *Théodicée* Leibniz

        *The Metaphysical Basis of Ethics* G. E. Moore

**December**  A. *History of Modern Europe* Fyffe

        *Geschichte der Neuern Philosophie*, Vol. II Kuno Fischer

A. *Fifteen Decisive Battles* Creasy

A. *Greek Studies* Pater

**1899**

**January**       *Parmenides* (Jowett)

A. *Charles the Vth* Robertson

A. *Don Quixote* (Shelton)

**February**   A. *Lectures on Ethics* G. E. Moore

        *Philosophischen Schriften von Leibniz* (Gerhardt)

A. *Tom Jones* Fielding

**March**        *Ethics* Spinoza

A. *Miscellanies* Vol. I J. Morley

        *Leibniz und Spinoza* Stein

A. *Gorgias* (Jowett)

A. *Protagoras* (Jowett)

        *Leibniz'sche Monadenlehre* Selver

        *Economic Policy of Colbert* Sargent

        *Theaetetus* (Jowett)

        *Sophist* (Jowett)

|          |                                                                                      |
|----------|--------------------------------------------------------------------------------------|
|          | *Introduction to Analytic Functions*  Harkness and Morley                            |
|          | A.  *England in the Age of Wycliffe*  G. M. Trevelyan                                 |
| April    | A.  *Practical Ethics*  Sidgwick                                                      |
|          | A.  *American Revolution*, Part I  G. O. Trevelyan                                    |
|          | A.  Article "Israel" (*Encyclopaedia Britannica*)  Wellhausen                         |
|          | A.  *Vanity Fair*  Thackeray                                                          |
|          | *Allgemeine Arithmetik*  Stolz                                                        |
|          | A.  *Timaeus*  (Jowett)                                                               |
|          | A.  *Henry IV*, Pts. I and II  Shakespeare                                            |
|          | A.  *Henry V*  Shakespeare                                                            |
|          | A.  *Much Ado*  Shakespeare                                                           |
|          | *Phaedrus*  (Jowett)                                                                  |
|          | A.  *As You Like It*  Shakespeare                                                     |
|          | A.  *Twelfth Night*  Shakespeare                                                      |
|          | A.  *All's Well That Ends Well*  Shakespeare                                          |
| May      | A.  *Hamlet*  Shakespeare                                                             |
|          | A.  *Spain, 1479–1788*  Martin Hume                                                   |
|          | A.  *Measure for Measure*  Shakespeare                                                |
|          | A.  *Troilus and Cressida*  Shakespeare                                               |
|          | *Middlemarch*  George Eliot                                                           |
|          | *Shakspere*  Dowden                                                                   |
|          | A.  *Othello*  Shakespeare                                                            |
|          | A.  *Macbeth*  Shakespeare                                                            |
|          | A.  *Antony and Cleopatra*  Shakespeare                                               |
|          | A.  *Coriolanus*  Shakespeare                                                         |
|          | A.  *King Lear*  Shakespeare                                                          |
|          | A.  *Cymbeline*  Shakespeare                                                          |
|          | A.  *Tempest*  Shakespeare                                                            |
| June     | A.  *Winter's Tale*  Shakespeare                                                      |
|          | A.  *Pericles*  Shakespeare                                                           |
|          | *Lectures on Mathematics* (*Northwestern University*)  F. Klein                       |
| July     | *Mannichfaltigkeitslehre*  G. Cantor                                                  |
| August   | Article "Measurement" (*Encyclopaedia Britannica*)  Sir R. Ball                       |
| September| A.  *Samson Agonistes*  Milton                                                        |
|          | A.  *Comus*  Milton                                                                   |
| October  | *Nicht-Euklid* I and II  Klein                                                        |
|          | *Modern Analytical Geometry*  C. A. Scott                                             |
|          | *La Guerre et la Paix*  Tolstoï                                                       |
|          | *Zwei geometrische Abhandlungen*  Lobatchefskij (Engel)                               |
|          | A.  *Les Romanesques*  Rostand                                                        |
|          | *Euklid bis Gauss*  (Stäckel und Engel)                                               |
|          | *Théorie des Surfaces*, Vols. I and III  Darboux                                      |

| | | |
|---|---|---|
| November | | *Höhere Geometrie*  Klein |
| | | *Theory of Parallels*  Lobatchewsky |
| | | *Science Absolute of Space*  J. Bolyai |
| | A. | *History of the Papacy*  Creighton |
| | A. | *Talks to Teachers*  W. James |
| December | A. | *Invasion of the Crimea*  Kinglake |
| | | *Psychologie der Axiome*  Schultz |

**1900**

| | | |
|---|---|---|
| January | | *Cromwell's Letters and Speeches*  Carlyle |
| | A. | *The Open Road*  (E. V. Lucas) |
| | A. | *Peter the Great*  Waliszewski |
| February | A. | *Peter Binney*  Marshall |
| | A. | *Historical Sketches*  Carlyle |
| | A. | *Canon Law in the Church of England*  Maitland |
| March | A. | *Influence of Sea Power*  Mahan |
| | | *Influence of Sea Power on French Revolution*  Mahan |
| | A. | *Poetry and Religion*  Santayana |
| | A. | *Giovanni Bellini*  R. E. Fry |
| | A. | *Plato and Platonism*  Pater |
| April | A. | *Andromache*  Murray |
| | A. | *Forty-One Years in India*  Ld. Roberts |
| | A. | *Omar Kayyam*  FitzGerald |
| | A. | *The Golden Bough*  Frazer |
| May | | *Rudder Grange*  Stockton |
| | A. | *Introduction to History of Religion*  Jevons |
| | A. | *The War in South Africa*  Hobson |
| | | *Theorie der Functionen*  Dini |
| June | A. | *Early Life of Fox*  Sir G. Trevelyan |
| July | | *Aether and Matter*  Larmor |
| August | | *Geometria di Posizione*  Pieri |
| | | *Mannichfaltigkeitslehre*  Cantor |
| | | *Paradoxien des Unendlichen*  Bolzano |
| | | *Zählen und Messen*  Helmholtz |
| | A. | *Life of Johnson*  Boswell |
| September | | *Formulaire de Mathématiques*, I, II  Peano |
| | | *Rivista di Mathematica*, I–VI |
| | A. | *Cromwell*  Firth |
| | | *Principii di Geometria*  Peano |
| October | | *Was sind und was sollen die Zahlen?*  Dedekind |
| | A. | *Religion of the Semites*  Robertson Smith |
| | A. | *Alexander the Great*  Wheeler |

|  |  |  |
|---|---|---|
|  |  | *Teoria delle Grandezze*  Bettazzi |
| November |  | *Esmond*  Thackeray |
|  |  | "Théorie des Ensembles" (*Mathematische Annalen* 46, 49) Cantor |
|  |  | *Neuere Geometrie*  Pasch |
| December | A. | *History of the Rebellion*  Clarendon |
|  |  | *L'imagination et les mathématiques*  P. Boutroux |

## 1901

|  |  |  |
|---|---|---|
| January |  | *Kant's Cosmogony*  (Hastie) |
|  |  | *Règles*  Descartes |
|  |  | *Parmenides*  (Jowett) |
|  |  | *The Virginians*  Thackeray |
| February |  | *Grundlagen der Geometrie*  Hilbert |
|  | A. | *The Meaning of Good*  Dickinson |
|  | A. | *Hippolytus*  (Murray) |
| March | A. | *Visits of Elizabeth*  Glyn |
| April |  | *Omar Kayyam*  FitzGerald |
|  |  | *Furnée*  Tourgéneff |
|  |  | *Bouvard et Pécuchet*  Flaubert |
|  | A. | *Golden Bough* (2nd ed.)  Frazer |
| May |  | *Pères et Enfants*  Tourgéneff |
| June |  | *The Adversaries of the Sceptic*  Hodder |
| July |  | *Terres Vierges*  Tourgéneff |
|  |  | *Questioni di Parole*  Vailati |
|  |  | *The World and the Individual*  Royce |
|  |  | *Raum und Zeit*  Palágyi |
| August |  | *Naturalism and Agnosticism*  James Ward |
|  |  | *Unleavened Bread*  R. Grant |
|  | A. | *Life of Wolsey*  Cavendish |
| September | A. | *History of England*  Ranke |
|  |  | *Eleanor*  Mrs. H. Ward |
|  |  | *Theorie der Grenzbegriffe*  Kerry |
| October |  | *La Logique de Leibniz*  Couturat |
|  | A. | *Italian Art*  Berenson |
|  | A. | *Greek Literature*  Murray |
|  | A. | *Laches*  (Jowett) |
|  | A. | *Charmides*  (Jowett) |
|  | A. | *Euthydemus*  (Jowett) |
|  | A. | *Historical Essays*, 3rd Series  Freeman |
| November |  | *Spinoza's Ethics*  Joachim |
| December | A. | *Letters from John Chinaman*  G. L. Dickinson |

          A.  *History of Greece*  Bury
          A.  *Evan Harrington*  Meredith
          A.  *Memoirs of Grammont*
          A.  *Memoir of Colonel Hutchinson*  ⟨Lucy Hutchinson⟩

**1902**

January        A.  *History of American Literature*  Barrett Wendell
                 A.  *Polyphemus* etc.  R. C. Trevelyan
                 A.  *Westeuropa*  Philippson
                     *Sherlock Holmes*  Conan Doyle
February      A.  *French Revolution*  Morse Stephens
                     *La Vie des Abeilles*  Maeterlinck
                 A.  *Diamond Necklace. Mirabeau*  Carlyle
                 A.  *French Revolution*  Carlyle
March             *Harry Richmond*  Meredith
                 A.  *Autobiography*  Gibbon
                     *Leibniz' System*  Cassirer

# Author Index to
# "What Shall I Read?"

FOLLOWING THE AUTHOR'S name are the dates of the entries in which his name is found. "5/92" indicates an entry of May 1892. Multiple entries within a given month are indicated by superscript numbers placed at the end of the date, thus: 5/92[2]. First names or initials have been supplied where lacking. The index includes one title: the Bible.

# Annotation

# 1 Greek Exercises

The annotations include the fourteen comments Russell made in 1894 when he transcribed "Extracts from My Journal" for Alys, and the three notes he added to the text in 1948 or 1949.

5:5 **religion in which I have been brought up** In the "Extracts" Russell inserted an exclamation mark after this phrase.

5:10 **my people** Russell refers to his surviving immediate family at Pembroke Lodge, who had taken responsibility for him on the deaths of his parents: his grandmother, the Countess Russell (known as Lady John Russell—see A9: 13), his aunt, Lady Agatha Russell, and his uncle, the Hon. Rollo Russell (who had returned to live at Pembroke Lodge with his infant son, Arthur, following his first wife's death in 1886).

5:11 **Mr. Ewen** In 1894 Russell noted that he was "a tutor, who left a little before this time". John F. Ewen "was an agnostic, and an acquaintance of ⟨Edward⟩ Aveling and Mrs. Aveling (Marx's daughter). It was from him, in that connection, that I first heard of Marx. It was also from him, not in the same connection, that I first heard of non-Euclidean geometry. I liked him very much—more than any of my many tutors. I imagine that he left because he was suspected of undermining my faith" (Russell, note to letter from Ewen, 3 Jan. 1890).

5:14–27 2 "This is one I afterwards scratched out, being very much ashamed of it: it proves the wickedness of letting people pass through the morbid period without telling them it is a necessary and common phase, and nothing more" (1894 comment).

5:15 **an article in the *Nineteenth Century*** James Sully's "Genius and Insanity" (1885).

5:18 **discern in myself** "I grew up without the means of comparing myself with other boys, so that I could only infer, in round about ways, whether I was a genius or a dunce, and was really ignorant how I stood" (1894 note).

5:18–19 **sexual passion ... resisting** Russell's 1894 note: "the episode of the housemaid I once told thee ⟨Alys⟩ of". See Russell *1967*, 39.

5:20 **this tutor's** The Southgate crammer. See A10: 25.

5:23 **when up a tree** Russell noted in 1894: "literally, not metaphorically!" As a

373

child Russell enjoyed causing concern by hanging upside down from the top of a large beech tree (Russell *1967*, 37).

5: 35 **the present laws of nature** The laws of conservation of mass and conservation of energy.

5: 37 **nebular hypothesis** Russell much later wrote with admiration of Laplace's "famous nebular hypothesis" of the origin of the solar system (*1935*, 57–8).

6: 28 **evolution** In *Religion and Science* Russell recalled: "When I was a boy, I had a tutor who said to me, with the utmost solemnity: 'If you are a Darwinist, I pity you, for it is impossible to be a Darwinist and a Christian at the same time'" (*1935*, 76).

7: 10 **Miss Bühler** Dora Bühler (d. late 1903 or early 1904), who had come to Pembroke Lodge at age nineteen, had been Russell's lively Swiss governess. Russell became attached to her, as Frank Russell's diary indicates: "I hear the most fearful wailing going on next door from Bertie and Miss B. at their approaching separation: there is one of the chief evils of the governess system" (20 Sept. 1883). She is mentioned often and with affection in Russell's 1894 correspondence with Alys.

7: 11–12 **Unitarian Chapel at Ealing ... Mr. Muirhead** John Henry Muirhead (1855–1940), a liberal idealist philosopher who briefly considered becoming a Unitarian minister. From 23 October 1887 until July 1888 Muirhead preached at Ealing in the Lyric Hall, not a chapel as Russell supposed. Russell later corresponded with him concerning inclusion of some of Russell's books in the Muirhead Library of Philosophy, published by George Allen & Unwin Ltd. Muirhead wrote the letter of introduction to Russell used by the representative of the Government University at Peking when Russell was invited to lecture there in 1920.

7: 33 **Herbert Spencer** In a series of studies of nature and man, Spencer (1820–1903) sought to synthesize all knowledge through the concept of evolution. See A26: 9 and A37: 40–1.

9: 6–10: 1 **9** "This seems to me rather good, considering I had not read a syllable of any book on the subject, but had thought it all out for myself—beyond having just heard that there was a Greatest Happiness Principle, and having wondered why anything so obvious was called a principle, or how any one could dispute it—I myself no longer believe in it now" (1894 note).

9: 12–13 **people made happy** "Prig!" was Russell's 1894 comment after this phrase.

9: 13 **Granny** Lady Frances Anna Maria Elliot (1815–1898), the second daughter of the 2nd Earl of Minto; in 1841 she became the second wife of Lord John Russell (1792–1878), who was created Earl Russell in 1861. Her grandson wrote that Lady Russell "was the most important person to me throughout my childhood. She was a Scotch Presbyterian, Liberal in politics and religion (she became a Unitarian at the age of seventy), but extremely strict in all matters of morality" (Russell *1967*, 20).

9: 18–19 **divine nature of conscience** Russell's 1894 note: "this is a fallacious and very Spencerian argument".

10: 1 **for my life** "Prig again!" was Russell's 1894 comment.

10: 3 **Argyll's *Reign of Law*** George Douglas Campbell (1823–1900), 8th Duke of

Argyll, landowner, naturalist and politician. A cabinet colleague of Lord John Russell in the 1850s and 1860s, he resigned from politics over Gladstone's Irish Land Bill in 1881. His voluminous writings covered many fields and included *The Reign of Law* (1866), which was widely discussed and much reprinted. In it he defended a teleological view of nature and attacked Darwin's theory of evolution on scientific rather then theological grounds. The chapter on "The Supernatural" to which Russell refers is Chap. 1.

10: 9–10 **reduced Kepler's laws to one** Newton's single law of universal gravitation permitted the derivation of Kepler's earlier three laws of planetary motion.

10: 12 **vortex theory** One view of the constitution of matter current in the late nineteenth century was that atoms consisted of permanent vortices in a perfectly fluid ether.

10: 22–4 **Life ... seem.** Henry Wadsworth Longfellow, "A Psalm of Life", *The Poetical Works* (*1882*, 9). Russell's copy is inscribed "To Bertrand from his affectionate uncle Rollo Russell Christmas. 1884." Longfellow, a favourite poet of his grandmother, came to Pembroke Lodge in Russell's boyhood.

10: 25 **Southgate** "Just before my sixteenth birthday, I was sent to an Army crammer at Old Southgate ..." (Russell *1967*, 42). The crammer was B. A. Green's University and Army Tutors. In preparation for a scholarship examination to Trinity College, Cambridge, Russell remained at Green's a year and a half.

11: 22 **my future happiness I expect** In 1894 Russell noted: "these remarks mostly apply to my present life!"

12: 9 **Wordsworth's "Intimations"** William Wordsworth, "Ode: Intimations of Immortality from Recollections of Early Childhood" (1807).

12: 13 **I do wrong every night** "For though I had long ceased to believe in the efficacy of prayer, I was so lonely and so in need of some supporter such as the Christian God, that I took to saying prayers again when I ceased to believe in their efficacy: the need only arose when I no longer believed in its satisfaction: as a boy I didn't pray, because I felt no need" (1894 note).

12: 13 **Argyll ... says** *The Reign of Law*, Chap. 2, "Law: Its Definitions".

13: 17 **Argyll alludes** *The Reign of Law*, Chap. 6, "The Reign of Law in the Realm of the Mind".

13: 24 **Buddha's nirvana** Russell learned of Buddhism from his brother, Frank, who had become a Buddhist (Russell *1967*, 46), and possibly from his father's *An Analysis of Religious Belief* (1876).

14: 9 **Marshall** "A former tutor" (1948 or 1949 note).

14: 10–16 **Broom Hall ... Frank ... Teddington** "Where my brother was living" was Russell's 1948 or 1949 note about Broom Hall. John Francis Stanley Russell (1865–1931), 2nd Earl Russell, engineer, barrister and minor public servant, was married three times without issue. He became a leading advocate of divorce reform in Britain. A fairly diligent member of the House of Lords, he was the first peer to declare himself a member of the Labour Party. Throughout the First World War Frank used his position in support of his brother and the conscientious objectors, although not himself a pacifist. Teddington (up the Thames from Richmond) was the location of Broom Hall, where Frank lived from 1887 to 1890.

14: 23–5 **Parcus deorum ... erro.** Horace, *The Odes*, Bk. 1, Ode XXXIV. C. E. Bennett (in Horace *1934*) translates: "I, a chary and infrequent worshipper of the gods, what time I wandered, the votary of a foolish wisdom...."

14: 35 **Baillie** James Hugh ("Jimmie") Baillie (1872–1956) was a boyhood friend who stayed with Russell at Pembroke Lodge. He later moved to Vancouver, where Russell met him again in 1929. Russell corresponded with Baillie's family as late as the 1960s.

15: 2 **motto to *The Reign of Law*** The book took as its motto Tennyson's *In Memoriam A. H. H.*, Prologue, st. 7 and part of st. 8.

15: 21 **Mr. Mauchlen** Russell's 1894 note was: "the Presbyterian Minister". The Rev. John Mauchlen (1854–1901) was pastor of the Presbyterian Church at Richmond. While a student at Edinburgh University he had been moved to evangelicalism by the Moody and Sankey mission.

15: 27–8 **she must ... die some day** "When she did in fact die, which was after I was married, I did not mind at all" (Russell *1967*, 22).

15: 29–30 **the support of religion** "See why I didn't want our children to have religion and morality muddled up" (1894 note).

17: 9 **"fanfaron de crimes"** A boaster of crimes.

17: 11 **Williams** Russell noted in 1948 or 1949 that Williams was "a budding parson".

17: 16 **"despitefully use me and persecute me"** Adapted from Matt. 5: 44.

18: 7 **Grimm's law** A phonetic law, formulated by Jacob Grimm (of fairy-story fame), which explains systematic correspondences between the sounds of equivalent words in different Indo-European languages by means of a regular shifting of consonants. The law plainly aroused Russell's interest. The "Greek Exercises" notebook contains fourteen pages of classified lists of Greek, German, Latin and English vocabulary designed to test the law's accuracy. Russell's aim, as he explains at the outset, was to confirm that "the law in German mostly fails in the beginning of words ... except with dentals." He concludes with the following note: "It appears from these lists that in modern German Grimm's Law does not hold with initials, except among the Dentals (the English, or Low German form being used instead); but I would not have the conceit to deny Grimm's Law for High German, for modern German may very likely be a mixture of High and Low German, since those who speak it extend to the Baltic, where Low German used to be spoken. August 1888."

18: 11 **The Duke ... speaks** *The Reign of Law*, Chap. 2, "Law: Its Definitions".

18: 20 **The Duke ... says** *The Reign of Law*, Chap. 6, "The Reign of Law in the Realm of the Mind".

18: 35 **... only cunning casts in clay,** Tennyson, *In Memoriam A. H. H.*, cxx, st. 2. Russell's copy, *The Works of Alfred Lord Tennyson Poet Laureate* (1886), is inscribed on the flyleaf: "Bertrand Russell from his loving Aunt Maude ⟨Stanley⟩ Christmas 1886."

mile west of Pembroke Lodge.

43: 39 **Dysart** William John Manners Tollemache (1859–1935), 9th Earl of Dysart. The reception was held to mark Dysart's return to his ancestral home, Ham House, for the summer (*Richmond Herald*, 23 May 1890, 3).

44: 1 **Ham** A hamlet lying immediately to the south-west of Petersham.

44: 5 **Lilly Blyth** Lillian Blyth (1864–1942), close friend of the Russell family and daughter of the Rev. Frederic Cavan Blyth, for many years curate of St. Peter, Petersham.

44: 7 **Ruskin's *Modern Painters*** The most important nineteenth-century study of landscape painting was *Modern Painters* (5 vols., 1843–60), by John Ruskin (1819–1900). From the references on 10 and 16 June 1890 it appears that Russell read the edition of 1888 (see A50: 5).

44: 15 **Rochat** See 45: 38, where Rochat is said to have become "an entire prohibitionist". This suggests that he was Louis-Lucien Rochat, a pastor from Geneva, who wrote four tracts on the misuse of alcohol between 1888 and 1899. Frank Russell recorded in his journal for 19 December 1883: "Made Rochat's, Bertie's tutor's acquaintance today; he is an ungainly Swiss youth and is soon going". Russell's letters of 1884 to Frank mention Rochat's taking him on various trips. And in part of a passage deleted from his autobiography, Russell wrote: "I remember a Swiss Protestant tutor, whom I had when I was eleven ..." (RA 210.007050–FI).

44: 21 ***Past and Present*** Thomas Carlyle's *Past and Present* (1843) is a work of historical imagination in which the social obligations of the twelfth century are contrasted with the chaos of modern individualism.

44: 22 **Robson** Henry Cumming Robson (1856–1945), B.A. (Cantab., 1882), M.A. (1885), fellow of Sydney Sussex College and lecturer in mathematics 1890–1923, and college bursar 1896–1923. Between taking his degree and returning to his college in 1890, he taught at Wren's coaching establishment at Powis Square in Notting Hill, London, where Russell went to see him three times a week (see 61: 11–12). *The Times*'s obituary noted significantly that "As a teacher of mathematics he was thorough and painstaking, and his method was well adapted to the needs of all but the ablest men" (27 Jan. 1945, 6).

44: 23 **Metrodora** Probably the name of a boat which was moored on one of the Pen Ponds in Richmond Park. The largest of the Pen Ponds is commonly referred to as "the Pond". In a passage cancelled from the first typescript of the third volume of his *Autobiography*, Russell wrote: "There were in Richmond Park two large ponds very close together, and on the larger we had a boat. I took my two young friends, Jimmie Bailey ⟨Baillie⟩ and Maud Burdett, to an island in the middle of the large pond, where, after playing for a time, we found that the boat had drifted away. We drew lots as to who should swim to the boat, and the lot fell to me. We made Maud conceal herself while I swam and subsequently dressed" (RA 210.147509–FI, fol. 78).

44: 26 **lines** A word game.

44: 27–8 **the Newton** Isaac Newton's *Principia Mathematica* (1687), possibly in an edition recommended by *The Student's Guide to the University of Cambridge, Part II,*

*Mathematical Tripos* (*1880*, 16), which lists editions by Evans and Main respectively: *The First Three Sections of Newton's Principia* (Newton *1871*) and *Newton's Principia; First Book* (Newton *1883*).

**44:28 Routh** Edward John Routh (1831–1907), fellow of Peterhouse, Cambridge. His *Treatise on the Dynamics of a System of Rigid Bodies* (1860), which Russell was studying, came out in two parts in its fourth edition: *Elementary* (1882) and *Advanced* (1884).

**44:34 Baby** Arthur Russell (1886–1943), Rollo's son by his first wife, Alice Sophia. "When I was fourteen, my Uncle Rollo's first wife died, leaving a new-born son; he, also, was brought up by my grandmother until his father's second marriage in 1891 ..." (Russell and Russell *1937*, 1: 32). At 48:41 Baby is said to be ill, and the kindergarten has to go on without him. The next day, "Arthur seemed to have bronchitis but today he seems well" (49:15).

**44:36 Johnson to M'Pherson** The letter belongs to an exchange with James Macpherson, who claimed authenticity for *Fragments of Ancient Poetry, Collected in the Highlands of Scotland* and *The Poems of Ossian*. See Boswell *1887*, 2:298.

**44:39 Mr. Ross** Probably the son of the East India Company merchant, George Ross, who lived at Edge Hill in Wimbledon.

**44:39 the Elphinstones'** The family of Sir Howard Elphinstone (1804–1893), 2nd Baronet Elphinstone of Sowerby. Sir Howard lived in Wimbledon and had close connections with Trinity College, Cambridge.

**45:4 Caroline Fitzmaurice** Caroline, Lady Edmond Fitzmaurice (1866–1911), sister of Russell's schoolboy friend at Southgate, Edward FitzGerald. Russell briefly experienced romantic longings for her when he went to Paris in 1889 with the FitzGerald family. Caroline became a translator of Italian literary works. She married, in 1889, the younger son of the 4th Marquess of Lansdowne, Lord Edmond Fitzmaurice, an historian and Liberal politician. The marriage was annulled in 1894. In 1901 she married Fillipo de Filippi, an Italian pathologist and explorer.

**45:14 Fitz** Edward Arthur ("Fitz") FitzGerald (1871–1931). See Russell *1967*, 43–4, and "A History of My Friendship for Fitz", this volume, 60–1. There is additional history of Russell's relationship with Fitz in letters of September and October 1894 to Alys. The extent of his later disillusionment with Fitz is revealed in a description of an afternoon with Mabel Edith Scott and her mother while Russell was in his last term at Southgate: "Though the whole crew were vile, they were to my mind such a relief from Fitz that that day stands out as one of the few tolerable ones" (25 Oct. 1894). Even after Russell realized Fitz's moral deficiencies, he endured him for years because his complex psychology was intriguing.

**45:14 Fred** Possibly Frederick Morshead (1836–1914), for many years a house master at Winchester. Frank Russell referred to him affectionately as "surely the ideal of a schoolmaster" (*1923*, 60). He was popularly known as "Fred" or "Freddy". Another possibility is Frederick Fraser (b. 1855), brother of Margaret and Maria Fraser and son of Alexander Campbell Fraser (see A43:31).

**45:23 the Hamiltons** The family of Alexander Charles Hamilton (1840–1920), who was the eldest son of Margaret Dillon Hamilton, an aunt of Russell's mother. Hamilton became the 10th Baron Belhaven and Stenton in 1893.

45:24 **Dickens** Possibly the Rev. Henry Compton Dickins (1838–1920), a tutor at Winchester up to 1868 and soon afterwards vicar of a poor parish in the town of Winchester, where he continued to be associated with the school. Frank Russell remembered Dickins, whom he continued to see often long after he had left school, as a "most lovable, most amusing, and most honest man" (*1923*, 76). Dickins performed the marriage service at the wedding of Frank to Mabel Edith Scott (see A48:22).

45:24 **Miss Fane** Unidentified.

45:38 **prohibitionist** Russell took the pledge in the spring of 1893, though by that time he was already abstemious. On 11 October 1894 he wrote Alys: "... I tasted alcohol (in the shape of beer) for the first time since the Society's dinner in June 1892."

45:41 **Simeons at Datchet** The family of Stephen Louis Simeon (1857–1937), who became Principal Clerk in the House of Commons in 1913. Between 1882 and 1894 he published six translations.

46:1 **Irish people called Dennehy** Perhaps William Francis Dennehy (d. 1918) and his family. Dennehy was an Irish historian, antiquarian and man of letters.

46:8–9 **Chapter on Motion in three Dimensions** Routh *1882*, Chap. 5.

46:12 **Kingston** Kingston-upon-Thames is about three miles upstream from Petersham.

46:13–14 **Ady Villiers** Frances Adelaide Villiers (1862–1934), eldest daughter of the Rev. Henry Montagu Villiers and Lady Victoria ("Toza") Russell, who was Lord John Russell's daughter by his marriage to Adelaide Lister.

46:15 **Dante, in the bolge of the hypocrites** The eighth circle of Nether Hell in the *Divine Comedy* (Malbowges) is divided into ten trenches, or bowges, of which the sixth contains hypocrites. See *The Inferno*, Canto XXIII. Russell's grandmother "was extremely fond of reading Dante" (MacCarthy and Russell *1910*, 258).

46:16 **poems of Hamilton Aïdé's** Charles Hamilton Aïdé (1826–1906), celebrated in his time for versatile accomplishments in the arts, was known for such widely anthologized lyrics as "Love, the Pilgrim", "Lost and Found" and "George Lee".

46:18 **Earl's elder brother** Possibly the reference is to Lionel Earle or Sydney Earle, older brothers of Maxwell Earle. They were the sons of Maria Theresa Earle, née Villiers, a cousin of Ady Villiers's father.

46:24 **Boughey** Anchitel Harry Fletcher Boughey (1849–1936), B.A. 1872, M.A. 1875, fellow of Trinity College. In 1890 he was one of four Trinity College tutors to whom "the newly arrived student or 'freshman,' should habitually apply for direction" on various matters, including lodgings (*The Student's Guide to the University of Cambridge*, "Introduction", *1893*, 12).

46:26 **Kew Coteries** Perhaps the Kew Institute, where lectures were given.

46:26 **Lowell** James Russell Lowell (1819–1891), essayist, poet and a professor at Harvard University.

46: 32 *Biglow Papers* "John P. Robinson" appears in Lowell's *The Biglow Papers* (1848), first series, no. III, "What Mr. Robinson Thinks"—a dialect satire on the political crudity of an ordinary Yankee: "But John P. / Robinson he / Sez they didn't know every thin' down in Judee."

47: 11–12 **questions in Routh about angular momentum** Possibly those in Routh *1882*, Chap. 5, §268.

47: 14 **Salvationists** The Salvation Army, founded in 1878 by the former Methodist and revivalist, William Booth. By early 1890 it was deeply involved in controversial schemes to convert, by a simple Christian message and promise of social amelioration, great numbers of the poor, particularly in London.

47: 29 **Wordsworth's ode** William Wordsworth's "Ode: Intimations of Immortality from Recollections of Early Childhood" (1807) argues for immortality through transmigration of souls. See the "Greek Exercises", entry 21.

47: 36 **Auntie had a meeting** The Richmond Liberal Association held a meeting on capital punishment in Channing Hall on 30 May.

48: 16–17 **the Moretons in Petersham** Unidentified.

48: 18 **Johnson … hanging** Johnson told Boswell that Americans "are a race of convicts, and ought to be thankful for any thing we allow them short of hanging" (Boswell *1887*, 2: 312).

48: 22 **Mabel** Frank Russell's first wife, Mabel Edith, née Scott (1869–1908), whom he had married on 6 February 1890. Frank later told his brother that he had married in response to Mabel's threat to end their affair, which was becoming notorious (Russell to Alys, 19 Oct. 1894). The marriage was soon in difficulties. She left him on 6 May and, after a brief reconciliation, on 12 June took up residence at Pembroke Lodge (see 51: 10–11) for what was to be a three months' separation. She sued for a judicial separation in 1891, but was unsuccessful in this as well as in various other attempts at litigation, which were instituted primarily to extract money. Only after Frank married for a second time, in 1900 in Nevada, without a divorce acceptable in English law, did Mabel (in 1901) succeed in having the marriage dissolved. While the divorce was proceeding, Frank was convicted of bigamy under English law and spent three months in prison. These matrimonial adventures earned Frank the sobriquet "the wicked Earl".

48: 30 **the Levens** The family of the Earl of Leven and Melville. See A43: 31.

48: 30 **the Freres** The family of the controversial statesman and colonial administrator, Sir Bartle Frere (1815–1884), consisting of his son (the 2nd Baronet) and four unmarried daughters. They lived at Wimbledon, close to Richmond Park.

48: 36–8 **Browning … "Abt Vogler"** "Abt Vogler (after he has been extemporizing upon the musical instrument of his invention)" by Robert Browning (1812–1889) appeared in his *Dramatis Personae* (1864).

49: 1–2 **Frank's new works at Teddington** Frank's electrical firm, Swinburne & Co., originally occupied a shed on the grounds of Broom Hall (see A14: 10–16). When larger facilities were required, the operation moved to vacant buildings near the Teddington railway station.

49: 8–9 **Lady Elizabeth Biddulph with three Adeane daughters** Lady Elizabeth (1834–1916) was born Elizabeth Yorke, daughter of the 4th Earl of Hardwicke. The 1st Baron Biddulph was her second husband. She was the widow of Henry Adeane, Russell's first cousin once removed in the Stanley line.

49: 9 **Lady S. Palmer** Lady Sophia Palmer (1852–1915), later comtesse de Franqueville. She was the third daughter of Roundell Palmer, 1st Earl of Selborne, a distinguished Liberal statesman and reformer of the English legal system.

49: 9 **Lady Huntingtower** The mother of the 9th Earl of Dysart (see A43: 39), Katherine Elizabeth Camilla Tollemache (1820–1896), née Burke, was the widow of Lord Huntingtower (who had predeceased his father, the 8th Earl of Dysart).

49: 12–13 **O'Brien ... Madame and Miss Raffalovich** William O'Brien (1852–1928), Irish Nationalist M.P., journalist, historian, essayist and novelist. Mme Raffalovich was the wife of Hermann Raffalovich, a Russian Jew who emigrated to France. Their daughter Sophie (1860–1960), who married O'Brien (see A50: 19), was an undistinguished writer of Irish travels and tales.

49: 15 **Arthur** See A44: 34.

49: 17 **vis viva** The mass of a body times the square of its velocity. There are a number of problems about vis viva and angular momentum in Chap. 5 of Routh *1882*. Russell may also have been working through Chap. 6 ("On Momentum"), which includes angular momentum, or Chap. 7 ("Vis Viva").

49: 30 **halma** A board game.

49: 30 **questions in Vis Viva** Here Russell appears to have reached Chap. 7 in Routh *1882*.

49: 31 **Maie** Georgina Marie, sister of Maud Burdett. See A43: 19.

49: 32 **Clarke** Possibly William Clarke (1852–1901), distinguished Fabian journalist with the *Daily Chronicle* and editor of the *Progressive Review*, who was also a Unitarian, a leader in the South Place Ethical Society and a vehement pro-Boer.

49: 32 **Swift MacNeill** John Gordon Swift MacNeill(1849–1926), Irish Nationalist M.P., polemicist and historian.

50: 2 **Tintoret** Jacopo Tintoretto (1518–1594), the Venetian painter. Ruskin discusses him in *1888*, Vol. 2, Pt. 3, Sec. 2, Chap. 3, "Of Imagination Penetrative".

50: 5 **a note** Ruskin *1888*, 2: 260–1. Ruskin added many notes to the 1883 edition of Vol. 2 of *Modern Painters*. This note concerns Pt. 3, Sec. 2, Chap. 2, "Of Imagination Associative", §6.

50: 15–16 **Read a canto of Dante** *Divine Comedy*, Canto XXV, Hell Circle VIII, Bowge vii; the opening passage reads: "Al fine delle sue parole il ladro / Le mani alzò...."

50: 16 **Uncle William (Minto)** William Hugh Elliot, 3rd Earl of Minto (1814–1891), brother of Countess Russell.

50: 19 **O'Brien's wedding** Writing about his wedding to Sophie Raffalovich, a recent biographer of O'Brien says: "That affair was a great Irish event in London, with Archbishop Croke officiating and Dillon as best man, in the presence of Parnell and more than eighty Irish M.P.'s—the last amicable gathering of what was the great

Irish Parliamentary party" (J. V. O'Brien *1976*, 101). Russell was invited to O'Brien's wedding doubtless because his family had long advocated redress of Irish grievances and were staunch supporters of Home Rule. Lord John Russell was dedicated to what he called "the great and holy cause" of Ireland (Prest *1972*, 61). Justin MacCarthy counted Lady Russell and her daughter, Agatha, among "our very earliest friends in England" (J. McCarthy *1905*, 311). See also A51: 26 and A54: 17.

50: 21 **a small church** St. Charles Borromeo.

50: 22 **Brompton** The Brompton Oratory is the most noted church of traditional English Catholics.

50: 22 **The music** The male choir sang Gounod's "Kyrie" and Handel's "Hallelujah"; the string band played Scotson Clark's "Marche aux Flambeaux" and Mendelssohn's "Wedding March" (*Manchester Guardian*, 12 June 1890, 6).

50: 27 **Dillon** John Dillon (1851–1927), Irish Nationalist M.P. Except for Parnell, he was the most important Irish politician from the late Victorian period to the end of World War I.

50: 28 **the bride** Sophie Raffalovich. See A49: 12–13.

50: 38 **Balfour** Arthur James Balfour (1848–1930), Chief Secretary for Ireland, 1887–90, and hence responsible for suppressing nationalist agitation; Prime Minister, 1902–05; created 1st Earl of Balfour in 1922. He was a minor philosopher, whom Russell reviewed in 1914 and 1923; see also Paper **37**, esp. 229–34.

50: 38–39 **National League** The Irish National League (1882–91) was founded by Parnellites to emphasize Home Rule rather than land reform, but was used after 1886 by Dillon and O'Brien to give financial support to tenants evicted by Anglo-Irish landlords.

51: 1 **Alexandra Hotel** At that time a well-known hotel off Hyde Park.

51: 2 **Parnell** Charles Stewart Parnell (1846–1891), "the uncrowned king of Ireland", who created the Irish Nationalist Party dedicated to Home Rule. By that measure (as put forth in two bills by Gladstone in 1886 and 1893), Ireland would have been given a separate parliament in Dublin, over which Westminster would still have exercised substantial control. Despite the moderate nature of that policy, Russell was correct in recalling that "It is hardly possible, nowadays, to imagine the bitterness of the Irish question in the late 80's and early 90's" (Russell and Russell *1937*, I: 27).

51: 5 **Mrs. Cobb** Bessie Cobb, wife of the Radical M.P., Henry Cobb, who was a dedicated Home Ruler and a particularly persistent opponent of coercive legislation against Ireland.

51: 7 **Mr. Buller's** Charles William Dunbar-Buller (1847–1924), nephew of the Radical politician, Charles Buller, and friend of Countess Russell. In 1890 he married Georgiana Anne Elizabeth Dunbar.

51: 9 **Walton** Mabel's mother lived at The Hurst, Walton-on-Thames.

51: 15 **the mother** Maria Selina, Lady Scott, widow of Sir Claude Scott, 4th Baronet. She had a reputation as an adventuress even before Frank married her daughter, Mabel Edith. Chagrined by failures to gain money from Frank for her daughter, Lady Scott, in 1896, circulated documents designed to besmirch his character. In 1897 she was convicted of criminal libel and sentenced to eight months in prison.

51:18 **divorce should be made much easier** The Matrimonial Causes Act of 1857, though it abolished divorce by private act of Parliament, reinforced inequalities in the law by declining to recognize equal grounds of divorce for men and women. It was the extreme difficulty which Mabel would experience in gaining a divorce, or even a judicial separation, that prompted Russell's observation at 52:27–8 that Mabel had only "the prospect of life-long misery ... before her."

51:21 **Met** The Metropolitan railway line.

51:22–23 **Hurst's, G Whewell's Court** During 1890–92 Russell's rooms at Trinity were G5, Whewell's Court. The previous occupant had been Bertram Preston Hurst (B.A. 1890, M.A. 1897).

51:24 **Little-go** The colloquial name for the Previous Examination, which was taken by those intending to go up to Cambridge before they were admitted. The *Cambridge University Reporter*, 14 October 1890, 74–9, records Russell as having been "examined and approved" in the Previous Examination of October 1890. He was placed in the first class in both parts of the examination, as well as in his additional subject, which was mechanics. The "Little-Go" was contrasted with the "Great-Go", the final examination for the B.A.

51:25 **the Butlers** The Rev. Henry Montagu Butler (1833–1918), Master of Trinity College from 1886 to 1918, and his second wife, Agnata Frances. His first wife, Georgina Elliot, had been a distant relative of Countess Russell.

51:26 **Grandmama** Russell's maternal grandmother, Henrietta Maria (née Dillon), Lady Stanley of Alderley (1807–1895). She lived at 40 Dover Street, London, with her unmarried daughter, Maude. Lady Stanley's house was a salon for intellectuals and politicians. Since after 1886 she and her family were Liberal Unionists and therefore opposed to Home Rule, the political atmosphere at Dover Street differed significantly from that at Pembroke Lodge. Lady Stanley helped found Girton College, Cambridge.

51:26 **Miss Fawcett** Philippa Fawcett (1868–1948), daughter of the famous feminist, Millicent Fawcett, and the Cambridge political economist and Liberal statesman, Henry Fawcett. She was renowned at Cambridge for placing above the senior wrangler in the Mathematical Tripos in 1890, but because of her sex her ranking was not official. She had a noted career as principal assistant in the Education Department of the London County Council.

51:28 **Deerbrook** In this romance Mr. Hope is induced by a match-making lady to marry the beautiful Hester Ibbotson instead of her sister, Margaret, whom he loves. The novel works out the moral consequences of the misalliance. The author of *Deerbrook* (1839) was Harriet Martineau (1802–1876), a well-known novelist and popularizer of Malthus, Ricardo and Comte; she was an advocate of humanitarian reforms.

51:29 **Mabel's stay** See A48:22.

51: 40 **Tosti's "Goodbye"** A song by Sir Francesco Paolo Tosti (1847–1916), who was born in Italy but moved to London in 1876 where he became singing teacher to the royal family. "Goodbye", a sentimental lament for the ephemeral, was a favourite drawing-room song of the period. For the lyrics and score, see Johnson and Dean *1899*, 3: 822–5.

51: 42–52: 1 **Shelley's short lyrics** For a discussion of some of Shelley's short lyrics, see "The Importance of Shelley" in Russell *1961*.

52: 24 **went to Windsor** Probably to the home of Mabel's sister, Lina Mary Scott (Mrs. Dick Russell), who herself had been involved in a celebrated nullity case.

52: 31 *Sesame and Lilies* John Ruskin, *Sesame and Lilies* (1865). There are two lectures, "Sesame: of King's Treasuries", dealing with the art of reading, and "Lilies: of Queens' Gardens", discussing education and the duties of women of the privileged class.

52: 37 **the formula** The equation $\rho = y^2/2x$ is found in Routh *1882*, 174, where $\rho$ is the radius of curvature, $x$ a second derivative (or acceleration), and $y$ a first derivative (or velocity). Both $x$ and $y$ are represented by Taylor series with higher-order terms neglected. Russell may have been attempting a problem such as those in §§201–2.

52: 40 **Aunt Maude** Russell's spinster aunt, the Hon. Maude Alethea Stanley (1832–1915); according to Russell, "a perfect aunt" (Russell and Russell *1937*, 1: 23), and according to Frank Russell, "the beloved confidant of the whole family" (*1923*, 9).

53: 3–4 **the Bedfords' box at Covent Garden** The 9th Duke of Bedford, Francis Charles Hastings Russell (1819–1891), was Russell's first cousin once removed. (Bedford's father, Lord William Russell, and Lord John Russell were brothers.) He married Lady Elizabeth Sackville-West. The 11th Duke sold the area known as Covent Garden, which had long been one of the Bedford estates. The Bedfords' lease on the Royal Opera House, Covent Garden, had specified "one private Box, plus its own lobby, retiring room, fireplace, chimney stack, staircase and entrance".

53: 4 **Mr. and Miss Pearsall Smith** Logan Pearsall Smith (1865–1946) and Alys Pearsall Smith (1867–1951), children of the Philadelphia Quakers Robert and Hannah, evangelist and popular religious writer respectively. In 1889 the family settled into a house near Fernhurst, Sussex. Their new home, Friday's Hill, was located close to Hindhead in Surrey, where Rollo Russell lived. Logan became a literary critic; Alys, a dedicated temperance reformer and feminist, was Russell's wife from 1894 to 1921. Russell first met Alys in the summer of 1889 and later claimed that he fell instantly in love with her (Russell *1967*, 76), although the present journal entry gives no indication of this feeling.

53: 5 **Gounod's *Roméo et Juliette*** An opera by Charles François Gounod (1818–1893), first presented in 1867. *The Times* announced on 18 June 1890 a production by the Royal Italian Opera Company under the direction of Augustus Harris and featuring Nellie Melba (1861–1931), a world-famous coloratura soprano, and Jean de Reszke (1851–1925), a Polish tenor of equal renown.

53: 15 **Mr. Spencer Holland** Spencer Holland (1855–1936), barrister and writer on public issues.

53: 16 **F. G. H.** Unidentified.

53: 16 **Rowland Hill** Rowland Hill (1849–1945) was a Bedford Unitarian preacher.

53: 18–19 **George Russell** George William Erskine Russell (1853–1919), nephew of Lord John Russell, miscellaneous author and minor Liberal politician.

53: 19 **George Lefevre** George John Shaw-Lefevre (1832–1928), 2nd Baron Eversley, Liberal cabinet minister 1881–84 and 1892–95.

53: 19 **H. H. Fowler M.P.** Henry H. Fowler (1830–1911), Viscount Wolverhampton, 1908; Liberal Imperialist and a cabinet minister, 1892–95, in the Gladstone–Rosebery administration.

53: 19 **Uncles Minto and Henry Elliot** Uncle Minto was Uncle William (Minto) (see A50: 16). The Rt. Hon. Sir Henry Elliot (1817–1907), a noted diplomat, was his younger brother. Countess Russell was their sister.

53: 20 **Ethel Portal** Ethel M. Portal "was a daughter of my great-aunt Lady Charlotte Portal. In adolescence I had greatly admired her because she was an atheist…. ⟨In 1905⟩ I discovered that she had returned to the bosom of the Church…. Nevertheless I still liked her" (from Russell's note on a letter from Ethel Portal, 1 Sept. 1905, RA 736.080918–19).

53: 20 **Herbert Paul** Herbert Paul (1853–1935), historian, man of letters and Liberal politician.

53: 24 **expect her back** In fact Mabel never returned to Pembroke Lodge.

53: 28 **Miss Martineau** See A51: 28.

53: 32–3 **Lagrange's equations … oscillations** Routh *1882*, Chap. 8, is on Lagrange's equations. The reference to small oscillations suggests that Russell had got at least as far as Chap. 9, which is on this topic—or maybe as far as the early chapters (2 and 3) of Routh *1884*. Russell's entry the next day suggests that he was already well into Routh *1884*.

54: 1–2 **easy questions … under any forces** This suggests that Russell was now working on Chap. 4 ("Motion of a Body under No Forces") and Chap. 5 ("Motion of a Body under Any Forces") of Routh *1884*.

54: 5 **read some of Dante** Russell is probably referring to the passage in the *Divine Comedy* in which the poets pass into Bowge vii of Hell to find a thief stung by a serpent, reduced to ashes, and then restored to himself (Canto XXIV).

54: 8 **Lyulph and Maizie** Russell's maternal uncle and aunt. Edward Lyulph Stanley (1839–1925) was a barrister, M.P., and member of the London School Board (see Jones *1979*). In 1873 he married Mary Katherine ("Maizie") Bell (1839–1929), daughter of the great steel magnate, Sir Lothian Bell. In 1903 Lyulph became the 4th Baron Stanley of Alderley and 4th Baron Sheffield. Russell recalled: "He was an ardent supporter of free trade, and (what is really remarkable) he took the chair for me at a meeting during the War, when my pacifism made me unpopular and many of my relations fought shy of me" (Russell and Russell *1937*, 1: 25).

54: 8–9 **the Lubbocks** Sir John Lubbock (1834–1913), 1st Baron Avebury, financier, politician and entomologist. In 1884 he married his second wife, Alice Augusta Lane-Fox-Pitt-Rivers (d. 1947), a daughter of Russell's maternal aunt, Alice.

54: 9  **Sir (John?) Morier**  Sir Robert Morier (1826–1893), an important diplomat and ambassador, a close friend and colleague of Lord Odo Russell (a first cousin once removed of Bertrand Russell). He was much admired by Lord John Russell, who had sensed his abilities "long before they were known to the world" (Peel *1920*, 240). Morier was a brother-in-law of Bertrand Russell's aunt, Georgiana Peel, who remembered that "as a young man, he was often to be seen at Pembroke Lodge" (*ibid.*). Morier died of complications arising from gout.

54: 9  **Mr. Wright**  Robert Samuel Wright (1839–1904), a High Court judge who was knighted in 1891. He was a friend of Russell's Grandmother Stanley and Aunt Maude. Frank Russell claimed he was "the kindest soul that ever breathed" (*1923*, 54).

54: 9  **Mr. Reid or Reeve**  Probably Henry Reeve (1813–1895), Liberal journalist and man of letters who moulded the foreign policy of *The Times* from 1840 to 1855. In 1855 he became editor of the *Edinburgh Review*.

54: 13  **John Morley**  Lord Morley of Blackburn (1838–1923), Liberal statesman, biographer and essayist. On 9 September 1894 Morley, then Chief Secretary for Ireland and a cabinet member, wrote to Countess Russell offering to make her grandson his private secretary. Having accepted just eleven days earlier Lord Dufferin's offer of an honorary appointment to the British Embassy in Paris, Russell reluctantly declined. He wrote to Alys from Paris that he was "ever so sorry to have been already established here when J. Morley's offer came: that would have been 1000 times more interesting ..." (12 Sept. 1894).

54: 17  **I used to be a Unionist**  Since Countess Russell had been a firm, early supporter of Gladstone's 1886 Home Rule bill, this declaration points up the degree of political debate prevailing at Pembroke Lodge.

54: 29–30  **that's federalism**  A reference to Joseph Chamberlain's abortive scheme of late 1885 to create local parliaments for the national groupings of Britain, rather than to single out Ireland for the more sweeping policy of Home Rule.

54: 42–3  **when God ... wine.**  There is no biblical evidence that God promised "plenty of wine", but presumably Morier was referring to the fact that, after the flood, Noah planted a vineyard and got shamefully drunk (Gen. ix: 20–1).

55: 8–9  **the *Mill on the Floss***  George Eliot, *The Mill on the Floss* (1860), Bk. IV, "The Valley of Humiliation", Chap. 3, "A Voice from the Past". Maggie Tulliver vows to renounce her selfishness upon reading certain passages from Thomas à Kempis's *The Imitation of Christ* (*c.* 1427). See Paper **14**.

56: 24–5  **"He told me ... Who made God?"**  J. S. Mill, *Autobiography*, Chap. 2: "and he ⟨Mill's father⟩ impressed upon me from the first, that the manner in which the world came into existence was a subject on which nothing was known: that the question, 'Who made me?' cannot be answered, because we have no experience or authentic information from which to answer it; and that any answer only throws the difficulty a step further back, since the question immediately presents itself, 'Who made God?'" (*1873*, 42–3 = Mill *1963*–, 1: 45).

57: 3–4 **Agnosticism ... Mill** See Mill *1873*, 45–6 = *1963*–, 1: 47–8.

57: 8 **(Cambridge).** Russell was now in his first term at Trinity College, Cambridge.

57: 14–15 **not perceptibly shy ... agreeable society** Despite the way Russell perceived himself, C. P. Sanger remembered him "as a very shy undergraduate" when he went into residence (Sanger *1929*, 678). The "agreeable society" Russell had begun to enjoy must have been enhanced when, eight days after this entry, he first attended a meeting of the Cambridge Moral Sciences Club (becoming a member on 27 February 1891—see Pitt *1981*). On the change Russell reports in his character, see also Paper **11**.

57: 21–2 **The people ... are ... unsatisfactory** *Cf.* Russell *1967*, 56: "From the moment that I went up to Cambridge at the beginning of October 1890 everything went well with me. All the people then in residence who subsequently became my intimate friends called on me during the first week of term."

57: 22–3 **the Llewelyn Davies's** Russell refers to Crompton (1868–1935) and Theodore (1871–1905), the two youngest sons of the distinguished theologian, advanced social thinker and fellow of Trinity College, John Llewelyn Davies (1826–1916). Russell considered Crompton his "closest friend at the University, and ever after" (Russell *c.1944*, 1). He became a prominent lawyer and, according to Russell, drafted the Anglo-Irish peace treaty of 1921. He was Russell's lawyer throughout the turbulent proceedings for divorce (completed in 1934) from Dora Black, his second wife. Theodore was regarded as a promising and even influential civil servant in the Treasury. He died tragically by drowning. Their sister, Margaret Llewelyn Davies (1861–1944), was a prominent socialist and feminist and for many years a correspondent with Russell on public issues.

57: 38 **Trevelyan** Either Sir Charles Philips Trevelyan (1870–1958), President of the Board of Education in the Labour governments of 1924 and 1929–31, or Robert Calverley Trevelyan (1872–1951), a minor poet. It was probably the latter, as Russell wrote that "Bob, the second ⟨brother⟩, was my special friend" (*1967*, 64). Although he writes here of making the acquaintance of a Trevelyan in his first term, in his *Autobiography* Russell recounts meeting both Charles and Robert at a dinner in December 1889 at Cambridge, just after he had finished his scholarship examination (*1967*, 56). It was only later (in 1893 or 1894) that he got to know the "considerably younger" brother, George Macaulay Trevelyan (1876–1962), the distinguished historian and the Master of Trinity College when Russell was elected to a fellowship there in 1944.

57: 39 **McTaggart** John McTaggart Ellis McTaggart (1866–1925), British neo-Hegelian philosopher. In 1890 he was a graduate student at Trinity, having taken first-class honours in the Moral Sciences Tripos in 1888. He became a fellow of Trinity in 1891 and one of the most important of the younger neo-Hegelians. Russell claimed he was "even shyer" than himself and described their first meeting: "I heard a knock on my door one day—a very gentle knock. I said: 'come in' but nothing happened. I said, 'come in', louder. The door opened, and I saw McTaggart standing on the mat.... ⟨H⟩e was too shy to come in, and I was too shy to ask him to come in.... For two or three years, under his influence, I was a Hegelian" (*1967*, 63).

58: 1 **Waldegrave** Probably John Waldegrave (1868–1901), third son of the 3rd Baron Radstock. He was admitted to Trinity in 1888 (LL.B. 1891) and became a barrister. He was killed in the Boer War.

58: 1 **Buckler** William Hepburn Buckler (1867–1952). He was born in Paris of American parents and was admitted to Trinity in 1887 (B.A. 1890, LL.B. 1891, M.A. 1924). He was subsequently with the U.S. diplomatic service and published *The Origin and History of Contract in Roman Law down to the End of the Republican Period* (1895).

58: 1 **Crawford** Probably Lawrence Crawford (1867–1951), admitted to King's (from Glasgow) in 1887 (B.A. 1890, M.A. 1894, D.SC. [Glasgow] 1899). He subsequently taught mathematics at Birmingham University and the University of Cape Town.

58: 8 **Gaul** Percy Cory Gaul (1867–1925), admitted to Trinity in 1885 (B.A. [second wrangler] 1889; Math. Trip., Pt. II, 1st class, 1890; M.A. 1893). He was subsequently a fellow of Trinity Hall and a lecturer in mathematics at Cambridge, 1895–1902.

58: 12 **Scholarship Essay and General Paper** Probably Russell is referring to the "Examination for Major and Minor Scholarships, Exhibitions, and Sizarships", which was held on 10 December 1890 and following days (*Cambridge University Reporter*, 28 Oct. 1890, 148–9). Russell wrote the "General Questions" on 15 December and, two days earlier, the "English Essay", for which he selected the topic "The genius and character of James Boswell". The examination question papers are in the possession of Mrs. Halpern (see the Illustrations).

58: 20–1 **Shelley's two** "Ye hasten to the dead" is found in Russell's copy of Shelley as "Ye hasten to the grave" (Shelley *1885*, 3: 85). Each of the volumes is inscribed: "Bertrand Russell from H. M. Stanley of Alderley 1890". "Lift not the painted veil" (3: 34) is marked, as is the other sonnet.

59: 17 **spring of 1889** See entry 22 of the "Greek Exercises".

59: 19–20 **"sunset ... silentness"** Shelley, "Alastor; or, the Spirit of Solitude", ll. 6–7 and 11–12. The full verse paragraph is marked in Russell's copy.

59: 39–40 **Wordsworth's ode ... day".** "Ode: Intimations of Immortality from Recollections of Early Childhood", st. 5, ll. 19–20.

60: 22 **Green's** Boyle Arthur Green (d. 1919), M.A., was the proprietor of the Southgate crammer that Russell attended. Green was remembered by a friend as having "accomplished by tact, persuasion and kindness" what a predecessor had "achieved by sternness" (*Palmer's Green and Southgate Gazette*, 12 Aug. 1927, 8). In congratulating Russell on his fellowship, Green told him: "I very seldom get a pupil of intelligence" (13 Oct. 1895).

60: 26 **Carlyle, Tennyson, Shelley, Byron** See "Books That Influenced Me in Youth" in Russell *1961*.

61: 20 **his sister** Caroline Fitzmaurice. See A45: 4.

61: 26 **when he came here** Probably a reference to Pembroke Lodge, where Russell would have gone between Cambridge terms.

61: 39 **I dreamt last night** Russell recalled this dream in his *Autobiography* (*1967*, 84).

61: 40 **my mother** Katharine Louisa Russell (1842–1874), Viscountess Amberley, fourth daughter of the 2nd Baron Stanley of Alderley. She married Russell's father, Viscount Amberley, in 1864. She and her husband were advanced mid-Victorian social thinkers on subjects such as women's suffrage and contraception. Russell claimed in his *Autobiography* that he remembered virtually nothing about her. In *The Amberley Papers* (1937), he co-edited with his third wife a collection of his parents' letters.

62: 2 **Neschdanoff in Turgenjeff** Aleksey Nezhdanov, a young, idealistic socialist in Turgenev's *Virgin Soil* (1877), believes revolution to be the panacea for Russia's ills but is haunted by Hamlet-like anxieties.

62: 12 **"I can give not what men call Love"** Shelley's poem, "One word is too often profaned", in Palgrave *1890*, 198–9.

62: 16 **Tripos List** Russell was bracketed seventh wrangler in the Mathematical Tripos (Pt. 1) list, which was published in the *Cambridge University Reporter*, 13 June 1893, 1014. See also *The Times*, 14 June 1893, 5.

62: 17 **Walt** Walt Whitman (1819–1892), American poet, with whom Alys Pearsall Smith corresponded. See Strachey *1980*, 65ff.

62: 25–6 **my little essay** Paper **10**.

62: 41 **occasional correspondence** The "occasional correspondence" began on 16 August 1893 with a letter from Alys. But see A63: 20.

62: 42 *vertraulich* "Intimate".

63: 1 **McTaggart's paper** J. M. E. McTaggart, *The Further Determination of the Absolute* (1893), a privately printed pamphlet.

63: 3 **mysteriously disappeared** McTaggart's pamphlet was found soon after and mailed to Alys on 5 September. Russell's copy is now in the library of Bernard Berenson at I Tatti, Italy.

63: 4 **two letters from Alys and written two** Alys's two letters are dated 16 and 23 August 1893; Russell's, 19 and 25 August.

63: 12 **Miss Stephens** Unidentified.

63: 20 **tear up her letters** On 9 October 1893 Russell told Alys: "Even when you wrote to say that you would come here ⟨i.e., her second visit to Cambridge that summer, *c.* 20 July⟩, although your letter was delightful because of the confidence it showed, I made a supreme effort and tore it up, thinking it silly to indulge a hopeless sentiment."

63: 24 **Santayana** George Santayana (1863–1952), Spanish-born American philosopher and man of letters. Russell's brother had known him since a trip to America in 1885. "I admired him as much as I disagreed with him", Russell recalled (*1967*, 211).

63: 25 **Berlin** Russell attended lectures on economics at the University of Berlin in early 1895.

**63: 28–9 the one Drayton** Michael Drayton's sonnet begins: "Since there's no help, come let us kiss and part" (*Idea. In Sixtie Three Sonnets*, 1619). The sonnet is marked in Russell's copy of Palgrave's *Golden Treasury* (*1890*, 36).

**63: 32 Bôw-Tree** The Bô-Tree house, in which these events took place, was an elaborate construction built about twenty-five feet up a tree by Robert Pearsall Smith and equipped with windows, chairs and even a sofa. It was called the "Bô-Tree House" because it was under such a tree that the Buddha found enlightenment. The Bô-Tree house is described at length, with a water-colour illustration, in Hannah Whitall Smith's Circular Letter No. 56 (7 Sept. 1891) to her family and friends (letter in the possession of Mrs. Halpern).

**64: 34–5 Et depuis ... joie.** "And since then I am transported with joy."

**65: 3 O Love they wrong thee much** The second (and last) stanza of the anonymous poem, "Omnia Vincit"; the whole poem is marked in Russell's copy of Palgrave's *Golden Treasury* (*1890*, 6).

**65: 13 July 20–21, ⟨1894,⟩ midnight.** In his *Autobiography* (*1967*, 84), where he includes another version of this entry, Russell claims he showed these reflections "to nobody, not even Alys, until a much later date." Nevertheless Alys saw them, for she made a diary entry herself on the same page, dated 21 July, beginning "It made me very happy to read this."

**65: 27 the tragedies** The various tragedies of the Russell family are catalogued in Russell *1967*, 83–4.

**65: 29 P. L.** Pembroke Lodge.

**65: 31 the fear of heredity** As a result of being told stories of family madness intended to discourage his marriage to Alys, Russell became very interested in the topic of heredity. The next month he acquired a copy of Francis Galton's *Hereditary Genius* (1892) and read and annotated it in September. The next year he read and praised Galton's *Natural Inheritance* (1889). Galton, he wrote Alys, "discovers all his laws from statistics à priori. It is *most* beautiful!" (15 June 1895). Much later he commented: "I am quite convinced that family tradition plays a very considerable part in the phenomena which Galton and his disciples attribute to heredity" (Russell *1929*, 147).

**66: 8 Dr. Anderson** Dr. William Anderson (*c*.1838–1901), of The Little Green, Richmond, was the Russell family doctor (referred to, though not by name, in Russell *1967*, 83–4). He consistently seems to have given professional opinions in support of Countess Russell's wishes.

**66: 8 Here** Friday's Hill, the home of the Pearsall Smiths, where Russell stayed from 16 July to 17 August 1894. See Russell *1967*, 86.

**66: 16 Received at Paris** Russell had arrived in Paris on 10 September 1894 to take up his post as attaché at the British Embassy. He had asked Alys to forward the "locked diary" to him so that he might read her entries.

**66: 17–18 a d—d cypher telegram** Russell told Alys that his work at the Embassy "consists of copying dispatches, varied occasionally by a telegram to cipher or decipher" (25 Sept. 1894). At the end of his letter of 6 October, Russell told her: "But here comes a cypher Telegram—blast it—which I must decypher at once—and then the Post will be gone."

66: 20 **Phipps** Sir Edmund Constantine Henry Phipps (1840–1911), Secretary of the British Embassy in Paris in 1892 and Minister Plenipotentiary in 1893 and until late 1894, when he was posted to Brazil. Russell described him as the only official at the Embassy who looked at all like a diplomat. Phipps was an "older man, with sunken eyes, and rather fierce looking moustache and whiskers; he walks with a slight stoop, as if, Atlas-like, he bore all the cares of the state on his back, and looks altogether one's idea of a very responsible official ..." (Russell to Alys, 11 Sept. 1894).

66: 20–2 **Rosebery ... France** Archibald Philip Primrose (1847–1929), 5th Earl of Rosebery, Liberal cabinet minister in a number of posts, twice Foreign Secretary, and successor to Gladstone as Prime Minister (March 1894–June 1895). The possible rupture of diplomatic relations with France to which Russell alludes concerned the abortive British attempt to get the European great powers and the United States to intervene in the Sino-Japanese War and thereby avoid a complete Japanese victory. The attempt failed because the United States and Germany, but not France, refused to take part. Ironically, Russia, Germany and France intervened in 1895 to overturn the punitive peace settlement Japan had imposed upon China. Russell adds slight details in his letter of 7 October 1894 to Alys. For two nights he was "kept busy till 12 o'clock with telegrams" (8 Oct. 1894).

66: 23 **Sanger's** Charles Percy Sanger (1871–1930), lifelong friend to Russell, was bracketed second wrangler in the Mathematical Tripos (Pt. 1) of 1893. He was the author of *The Place of Compensation in Temperance Reform* (1901) and wrote the biography of Russell in the *Encyclopaedia Britannica* (1929). He practised law and occasionally lectured at the London School of Economics.

66: 25 **Wagner on Psychology of Economic Action** Adolph Wagner (1835–1917), *Grundlegung der politischen Oekonomie* (1892–94), I: Pt. 1, Bk. 1, §§1–2, pp. 73–120. Russell recorded reading the first volume of Wagner's *Grundlegung* in January 1895, but at the time of this diary entry he had been writing summaries of and commentaries on Wagner's views. Russell told Alys that he found Wagner "so bad" that he was encouraged to write a fellowship dissertation in economics. "If Wagner is considered a good book, there must be an immense lot to be done in the way of a philosophical basis for economics" (11 Oct. 1894).

66: 27–8 **abstract intellectual nature of my passions** Russell wrote Alys: "... intellect is a great safe-guard, because it makes one's passions more abstract and less ephemeral, less absorbed in the satisfaction of the moment, which is all that sensual pleasures can give. It is lucky for us that my mind is not more concrete and artistic and pictorial as thee would wish it to be—all my thoughts being about abstractions, my passions too are very abstract, and it is often surprising to me to find how my love for thee is reinforced by several highly abstract passions—the love of sanity, of health, of independence, in women especially, and a corresponding set of hatreds"

(6 Oct. 1894).

**66: 29 Spinoza in Pater** The only extended writing on Spinoza by Walter Pater (1839–1894) is in "Sebastian van Storck", one of his *Imaginary Portraits* (1887). In "What Shall I Read?" Russell recorded that he read "An Imaginary Portrait (The Child in the House)" in September 1894. Perhaps he went on to read other portraits. His remark about Spinoza does not fit that philosopher, but rather van Storck. Pater's portrait is of a man of Spinoza's time who is imagined as having taken the self-abnegating aspect of Spinoza's ethic to an extreme and whose ego consequently seems to have dried up. See Small *1978*.

**66: 34 reading James** Russell read the first volume of *The Principles of Psychology* (1890) by William James (1842–1910) in September 1894. James's distinction between visualizers and non-visualizers (*1890*, 2: 56–7) appealed to Russell, who wrote by the description of the non-visualizer: "This would do for a description of my own case, except in the case of childish memories, and a few others of strong emotional interest." See also Wood *1957*, 48.

**67: 10 our decision** Apparently the decision to marry but to take precautions against having children.

**67: 26 How like a winter hath my absence been** Shakespeare, sonnet 97.

## 10  Die Ehe

**69: 1–21 Unfolded ... in himself.** Walt Whitman, "Autumn Rivulets", *Leaves of Grass* (1855).

## 11  Self-Appreciation

**73: 14 Fabian ideal** Russell wrote in *Roads to Freedom*: "In England Marx has never had many followers. Socialism here has been inspired in the main by the Fabians (founded in 1883), who threw over the advocacy of revolution, the Marxian doctrine of value, and the class war. What remained was State Socialism and a doctrine of 'permeation'" (*1918*, 71). Russell joined the Fabian Society in 1897. After his conversion experience in 1901 (see Russell *1967*, 146), he found the Fabians too authoritarian and undemocratic. He resigned from the Society in 1903 because he opposed the Webbs' support of imperialism and Chamberlain's crusade for tariff reform.

**73: 35 Spinoza and Lassalle attract me** Benedictus de Spinoza (1632–1677), rationalist philosopher. Russell described Spinoza as "the noblest and most lovable of the great philosophers. Intellectually, some others have surpassed him, but ethically he is supreme" (*1945*, 569). The persistence of Russell's admiration of Spinoza is shown by the fact that at the age of ninety-two Russell declared: "Spinoza has been a great influence in my life and an influence of a practical sort" (Russell *1964*, 12–13).

Ferdinand Johann Gottlieb Lassalle (1825–1864) was the father of German socialism. (See also A312: 11.) Like the English Fabians, he wished to transform the state rather than overthrow it. Russell found Lassalle appealing perhaps because he was "far more English than Marx" (*1896*, 42) and espoused a "rather aristocratic Socialism" (*1934*, 443). "The secret of his influence", wrote Russell, "lay in his overpowering and imperious will, in his impatience of the passive endurance of evil, and in his absolute confidence in his own power. His whole character is that of an epicurean god, unwittingly become a man, awakening suddenly to the existence of evil, and finding with amazement that his will is not omnipotent to set it right" (*1896*, 42).

## 12  Can We Be Statesmen?

79: 1  **our brother Sidgwick**  Henry Sidgwick (1838–1900), Knightbridge Professor of Moral Philosophy at Cambridge (1883–1900), author of *The Methods of Ethics* (1874), and an active member of the Society, 1856–65. Russell called him "the last survivor of the Benthamites" and noted that he did not receive the respect he deserved from the young people at Cambridge: "We called him 'Old Sidg' and regarded him merely as out of date" (*1959*, 38).

79: 20  **Local Option**  The choice given to a local authority to allow the electorate to vote on liquor licensing.

79: 23  **middle axioms**  The term "middle axiom", though used in the nineteenth century, is now rarely found. Russell used it somewhat earlier, in Paper **30** (205: 19). It seems to have been established in philosophical usage by Bacon, who used it to refer to principles mid-way in generality between statements of "bare experience" and the most abstract and general first principles. The middle axioms are "the true and solid and living axioms, on which depend the affairs and fortunes of men" (*Novum Organum*, Bk. I, CIV; Bacon *1857–74*, 1: 205). Mill also, in his essay on Bentham, used the term in a context closely similar to Russell's. Mill argued that although people may disagree on fundamental moral principles (such as the principle of utility), they may achieve a consensus on intermediate principles, or middle axioms. Such middle axioms also have the advantage of proposing simpler and more immediate ends than those proposed by, e.g., the principle of utility (Mill *1963–*, 4: 110–11). In a letter of 3 April 1902 Russell presented Gilbert Murray with a criticism linking middle axioms to Sidgwick's ethical theory (see Russell *1967*, 157–8).

79: 28  **my *Chronicle* tells me**  In the lead editorial of the London *Daily Chronicle*, 18 Nov. 1893, 4. The *Daily Chronicle* had been active in raising relief funds for 300,000 miners who were locked out by their employers for four months over the attempt by the latter to cut wages by twenty-five per cent. The miners won their point after intervention on 13 November 1893 by Prime Minister Gladstone. Russell contributed to the strike fund (see the letters from Logan Pearsall Smith in Russell *1967*, 94).

79: 34  **Principles such as Mill's**  J. S. Mill, "On Liberty" (1859) (Mill *1963–*, 18: 223–4).

80: 23 **Gladstone** William Ewart Gladstone (1809–1898), statesman and four-time prime minister, was known as "the People's William" because from the mid-1860s he engaged in speaking crusades outside Parliament.

81: 17 **Home Rule** Gladstone's second Home Rule bill was defeated in September 1893.

82: 1–2 **Darwin's fortune** The affluence of Darwin's family enabled him, for example, to serve without pay on the voyage of the *Beagle*.

## 13 Lövborg or Hedda

84: 38 **Mrs. Grundy** A proverbial figure of conventional propriety.

85: 34–5 **early Christian hermits** During their separation later in 1894, Russell wrote Alys: "... in old days when I was unhappy I was perpetually haunted by impure imaginings, like the early Christian hermits I put in my paper last February" (26 Oct. 1894).

85: 37 **Gibbon** Edward Gibbon, *The History of the Decline and Fall of the Roman Empire* (1776–88), Vol. 3, Chap. 37, Pt. 1.

87: 25 **the Souls** The Souls were an informal group of aristocratic and upper-class men and women drawn together in the 1890s by common literary and aesthetic tastes. Arthur Balfour was the most famous, although George Curzon and Margot Asquith were also significant, as was H. G. Wells (whom they lionized).

87: 29 **a Goetheish fancy** Russell probably refers either to Goethe's sentimental romance, *The Sorrows of Young Werther* (1774), in which Werther is doomed by his passion for Charlotte, or to Wilhelm Meister's impulsive loves in Goethe's philosophical romance, *Wilhelm Meister's Apprenticeship* (1795–96).

88: 11 **as we found last Saturday** At their previous meeting, on 24 February 1894, the Apostles had discussed a paper by C. P. Sanger entitled "Which Wagner?" The contrast was between the composer Richard Wagner and the economist Adolph Wagner—more broadly, between art and social reform.

88: 12 **McTaggart's Absolute** See A63: 1. Russell wrote to Alys: "The odd thing about the absolute is that it always goes against the *Chronicle* whatever that paper may happen to say. Also when anybody else uses it McTaggart says it can't be used" (25 Feb. 1894).

88: 14 **G. A.** God Almighty.

88: 41 **Our brother Trevelyan** Robert Calverley ("Bob") Trevelyan (see A57: 38).

## 14 Cleopatra or Maggie Tulliver

92: 4 **Descartes's "remède** *Les Passions de l'âme* (1649), art. CXLVIII: "Que l'exercise de la vertu est un souverain remède contre les passions." [Translation: "That the exercise of virtue is a sovereign remedy against the passions."] In his library copy Russell marked the text following this proposition and wrote "Stoicism" in the margin (Descartes *1824–26*, 4: 161 = *1911*, 1: 398–9).

92:12 **English aesthetes** In September 1894 Russell read Walter Pater's "imaginary portrait" "The Child in the House" (1878), with its prose of exquisite sensibility. "Logan Pearsall Smith indoctrinated me with the culture of the nineties—Flaubert, Walter Pater, and the rest", wrote Russell (*1967*, 80). "The rest" would include Oscar Wilde, and perhaps the French poets Paul Verlaine and Arthur Rimbaud.

92:21 **Whitmaniacs** Swinburne used this term in "Whitmania" (1887).

92:26–7 **Mr. Carr Bosanquet's words** Robert Carr Bosanquet (1871–1935) was an archaeologist and Professor of Classical Archaeology at the University of Liverpool (1906–20). In 1890–94 he was a student at Trinity College, Cambridge. His *Letters and Light Verse* (1938) includes some early writing. The source of "sane lusty and adequate" may be a Cambridge University publication of the 1890s. On 1 October 1895 Russell noted to Alys that he had come upon Carr Bosanquet: "He has been digging up pots in Greece, and is trying for his Fellowship on the results of his digging."

92:27–8 **"Without shame ... sex" says Walt** Russell quotes incorrectly from the "Enfans D'Adam" section of Walt Whitman's *Leaves of Grass* (1855). The lines should read: "Without shame the man I like knows and avows the deliciousness of his sex, / Without shame the woman I like knows and avows hers."

In 1950 Alys sent Russell a copy published in Philadelphia in 1882, inscribed to her by Whitman, and further inscribed: "For Bertie from Alys / 1894–1950 / From a former Arch-Prig to the / other former Arch-Prig!" Most of the pages in "The Children of Adam" section are cut out, as Arch-Prigs may well have done to its most explicitly sexual passages. (See Leithauser *1975*.)

The second passage, from "Song of the Open Road" ("Poem of the Road"), reads: "No diseased person—no rum-drinker or venereal taint is permitted here."

92:31–2 **Sidgwick ... "consensus of common sense"** For Henry Sidgwick, see A79:1. For the "consensus of common sense", which formed an important part of Sidgwick's philosophical method in *The Methods of Ethics* (1890), see Bk. II, Chap. 4, §2; Bk. III, Chap. I, §5; Bk. III, Chap. 11; and elsewhere.

92:39 **as Spinoza says** *Ethics* (1677), Bk. IV, prop. 7.

94:40 **"scorn delights ... days"** John Milton, "Lycidas" (1638), l. 72. Lines 65–6, 68, 72–4 are marked in Russell's 1890 copy of Palgrave. Russell would have seen the line quoted in a footnote to Sidgwick *1890*, 156.

95:17 **Mr. Gilfil** Mr. Gilfil appears in George Eliot's "Mr. Gilfil's Love-Story" in *Scenes of Clerical Life* (1858).

96:2 **Dostojewski's *Crime and Punishment*** Russell seems to have read the German translation, as this is how Dostoevsky's name was rendered in German. There is no other record than this paper of Russell's having read the book by this time. His library copy, a German translation, is not marked.

96:15 **Princess Casamassima** "What Shall I Read?" records for 1894 seven of Henry James's fiction titles, among them *The Princess Casamassima* (August) and *Roderick Hudson* (October). Russell wrote to Alys of the Princess: "He has drawn her in both books with a tantalizing mystery ..." (25 Oct. 1894). But while the Princess, as an example of "morbid effects", seems less well suited than does Verena Tarrant in *The Bostonians*, which Russell read in October, the Princess Casamassima must still be the example he wants. The princess, in the novel of that title, does indeed suffer severe disappointment by anarchists she thought she had befriended. The "morbid effects" are Russell's, not James's, interpretation of the results.

97: 3  **McTaggart will say**  McTaggart held that from the ultimate point of view, that of the Absolute, the moral categories of good and evil are transcended.

97: 8  **what James calls**  William James, *The Principles of Psychology* (*1890*, I: 179), where the phrase is "making a luxury of intellectual defeat").

97: 39–41  **McTaggart ... personal immortality ... Time**  On 29 October 1894 Russell wrote Alys: "For a few months last autumn, after reading Green and McTaggart I believed in immortality—but Green's mistakes were soon evident to me, and since then I have had no solution—I believe no other is possible." The work by McTaggart was *The Further Determination of the Absolute* (1893). In it McTaggart presented for the first time his views on immortality (McTaggart *1934*, 216), as well as an early dialectical version of his famous argument for the unreality of time (*1934*, 215–16). A more developed account of the latter appeared in "Time and the Hegelian Dialectic" (1893), which Russell also read (Russell to Alys, 12 Oct. 1893).

97: 43–98: 1  **a more Bradleian view of the Subject**  See Bradley, *Appearance and Reality* (1893), Chaps. 9, 10.

98: 6  **a mere fluid nucleus of Feeling**  Bradley *1893*, 524–6 (= *1930*, 464–6), argues that it is a mistake to identify the self with a "finite centre of feeling" (a passage marked by Russell; compare similar phrases on the following pages) because this ignores the unity which the self forms with the rest of Reality. "A mere fluid nucleus of Feeling" seems to be Russell's attempt to express the Bradleian idea that the self does not have (de)finite limits.

98: 8  **Spinozistic monism**  "Spinoza's metaphysic is the best example of what may be called 'logical monism'—the doctrine, namely, that the world as a whole is a single substance, none of whose parts are logically capable of existing alone" (Russell *1945*, 577).

98: 41  **old Kantian rule**  The categorical imperative: "So act that the maxim of your will could always hold at the same time as a principle establishing universal law" (*Critique of Practical Reason*, Kant *1956*, 30; *1867–68*, 5: 32).

## 15  Is Ethics a Branch of Empirical Psychology?

100: 16–17  **undermined Hume's**  Russell refers to David Hume's scepticism about induction. It is discussed in his *Treatise of Human Nature* (1739–40), Bk. I, Pt. iii, "Of Knowledge and Probability".

102: 11  **our brother Moore**  Russell is referring to views put forward by G. E. Moore in a paper, "Can We Mean Anything, When We Don't Know What We Mean?", read to the Apostles on 23 January 1897 (Moore papers, Cambridge University Library). Although in that paper Moore explicitly attacked only the identification of the good with the pleasant, some of his arguments could easily be applied against the identification of the good with the desired. Russell was not present at that meeting, but it is likely that he would have heard of the paper's content from those who were, and he would in any case have been generally familiar with the direction of Moore's thinking.

102: 15 **Mr. Bradley** Bradley, *Appearance and Reality*: "We may speak of the good, generally, as that which satisfies desire" (*1893*, 402 = *1930*, 356). The passage is marked in Russell's copy of Bradley *1893*.

102: 33–4 **the ontological argument** In an ontological argument a thing's existence is said to be proved by showing that existence is part of its essence, or definition. Although used most famously by St. Anselm and others in an attempt to prove the existence of God, the British absolute idealists sometimes appealed to the ontological argument for a proof of the existence of the Absolute, and it is to this version of the argument that Russell refers here (see Spadoni *1976*).

102: 39 **When Sigmund refuses Valhalla** An incident in Act I of Richard Wagner's musical drama *The Valkyries*, in *The Ring of the Nibelungs* cycle (1853).

104: 32–3 **Moore ... definition of the good** Moore gives no explicit definition of "good" in his paper, "Can We Mean Anything, When We Don't Know What We Mean?" Indeed, the view for which he became famous was that "good" is the name of an indefinable, non-natural property. At the time Russell wrote this paper, however, it appears that Moore had not yet properly formulated this view. And, while it is clear that he rejected any straightforward identification of the good with the pleasant, it is not clear that he would have rejected a more comprehensive definition of "good". Indeed, certain passages in Moore's paper imply that he would have countenanced such a definition, and such could well have been the impression conveyed to Russell by those who attended the meeting at which Moore read his paper.

## 16 Seems, Madam? Nay, It Is

106: 7–9 **How charming ... Apollo's lute.** The Younger Brother speaks these lines in Milton's *Comus* (1637), ll. 476–8.

106: 15–16 **rigid Science of Mr. F. W. H. Myers** F. W. H. Myers (1843–1901) was one of the founders of the Society for Psychical Research in 1882 and the person with whom it was most closely associated. The Society was formed to inquire, by scientific means, into data and questions that would normally be considered beyond the scientist's ken. The appeal of the Society for intellectuals perplexed by their abandonment of traditional Christianity is revealed by the fact that Henry Sidgwick was another founder and that Arthur Balfour and William James were, in succession, presidents. Russell's observation can only be construed as ironic or even sarcastic.

106: 18 **McTaggart and Mr. Bradley** According to both McTaggart and Bradley, the moral categories apply only in the realm of appearance, where they depend upon a partial point of view, which the Absolute transcends.

106: 32–3 **"God's in ... the world"** Browning's *Pippa Passes* (1841), Pt. 1, ll. 117–18. Russell has substituted "wrong" for "right".

107: 4–11 **Full many a glorious morning** ... Shakespeare, sonnet 33, ll. 1–8.

107: 16–19 **McTaggart ... explicit** McTaggart published early versions of his well-known arguments against the reality of time in "Time and the Hegelian Dialectic" (*1893a*) and *The Further Determination of the Absolute* (1893). The phrase "a harmony which must some day become explicit" occurs in the latter (McTaggart *1934*, 211).

107: 28 **"my grief lies onward and my joy behind"** Shakespeare, sonnet 50, l. 14.

108: 16–18 **That I shall never ... love** John Keats, sonnet, "When I have fears that I may cease to be", ll. 10–12. This sonnet appears in Palgrave *1890*, 272.

108: 19 **"fair creature of an hour"** Keats, "When I have fears that I may cease to be", l. 9.

108: 20–1 **"Time will come ... away"** Shakespeare, sonnet 64, l. 12.

108: 21–2 **"This thought ... lose"** Shakespeare, sonnet 64, ll. 13–14.

108: 33–4 **"He's a good fellow ... well."** Edward FitzGerald's translation of the *Rubáiyát of Omar Khayyám* (1859), LXIV. Recorded in "What Shall I Read?", February 1891, June 1897 and twice thereafter.

109: 34–9 **"When poetry ... worthless."** F. H. Bradley, *Appearance and Reality* (*1893*, 3–4 = *1930*, 3).

110: 17–23 **"Some in one way ... truth"** Bradley *1893*, 5–6 = *1930*, 5. The correct quotation is: "Some in one way and some in others ... both chastens and transports us...."

111: 3 **"where all is rotten ... fish"** Bradley *1893*, xv = *1930*, xiv.

111: 14–17 **"The man ... contemptible."** Bradley *1893*, 6 = *1930*, 5.

## 17 Was the World Good before the Sixth Day?

113: 1–2 **Our brother Moore ... work** During the autumn term of 1898 G. E. Moore delivered a set of ten lectures entitled "The Elements of Ethics" at the London School of Ethics and Social Philosophy. The lectures have not been published; a photocopy of the typescript in the Moore papers, with Russell's annotations and some responses from Moore, is in the Russell Archives.

113: 5–6 **"The London School of Ethics and Social Philosophy"** The London School of Ethics and Social Philosophy was founded in 1897 at the Passmore Edwards Settlement in Tavistock Place to provide instruction in philosophy at the university level. It gained the support of a number of distinguished philosophers: Bernard Bosanquet served as president and Henry Sidgwick as a vice-president.

113: 25 **Moore contends** Moore argues that beauty is of value independently of the existence of consciousness, i.e. that a purely material beautiful world is of more value than a purely material ugly one ("The Elements of Ethics", Lecture 4, 129–31; Lecture 5, 160–2).

114: 3 **the Berkeleian theory** George Berkeley (1685–1753), Irish philosopher who was both an empiricist and idealist. Russell refers here to his maxim that to be is to be perceived.

114: 11–12 **as Moore says** Moore does not deal with the utilitarian account of beauty in "The Elements of Ethics", though what he says there would be compatible with the view Russell ascribes to him. It is possible that Russell is referring to other unpublished writings of Moore's, or to a view Moore expressed in conversation.

## 18 Paper on Epistemology I

121: 40 **according to Wundt:** Wilhelm Wundt (1832–1920), German philosopher, physiologist and psychologist. Wundt's distinction between form and matter is made in his *System der Philosophie* (*1889*, 240–1), which Russell had read in August 1893.

## 19 Paper on Epistemology II

126: 3 **axiom of parallels** Euclid's statement of this axiom, the fifth postulate, is equivalent to saying that, given a straight line $AC$ and a point $B$ not on $AC$, there is one and only one straight line through $B$ parallel to $AC$. The axiom, and the unsuccessful attempts to derive it from Euclid's other axioms, were at the centre of the debates which led to non-Euclidean geometry. Euclid's axiom may be denied in two ways: (1) by asserting that there is no line through $B$ parallel to $AC$, or (2) by asserting that there is more than one line through $B$ parallel to $AC$. The hyperbolic geometry of Bolyai and Lobatchewsky results from replacing the parallel axiom by (2). The spherical geometry of Riemann results from replacing the parallel axiom by (1) and denying the Euclidean requirement that between any two points there is a unique straight line.

126: 5 **Meta-Geometry** This term for non-Euclidean geometry seems to have originated with Stallo (*1882*, 214, 258), although Helmholtz (*1878*, 212 = *1882–95*, 2: 640) had earlier referred to "'metamathematical investigations'—as to wider kinds of geometry". By 1893 the term was in fairly wide currency, being used by Ward in his metaphysics lectures (see Russell's lecture notebooks, 1: 89) and by Delboeuf (*1893*, 450), to mention two sources known to Russell.

126: 8–11 **Lobatchewsky … analysis** Nikolai Ivanovich Lobatchewsky (1793–1856), Russian mathematician, a seminal figure in the development of non-Euclidean geometry. The hyperbolic geometry he, and independently János Bolyai, developed was the first consistent system incorporating the negation of Euclid's parallel postulate (see A126: 3). Russell's use of "analysis" and "synthesis" stems ultimately from an addition to Bk. XIII of Euclid's *Elements* (*1908*, 3: 442–3), but was in general philosophical use when Russell wrote. In synthesis a proposition is established by showing that it is a consequence of what has already been admitted (e.g. a consequence of the axioms); in analysis a proposition is established by showing that it has consequences which are admitted to be true. In Russell's example, the constancy of the measure of curvature is established analytically by showing that it has free mobility (which is already admitted) as a consequence.

126: 11–16 **the possibility of ... fulfilled** The central thesis of Russell's fellowship dissertation, and its published elaboration *An Essay on the Foundations of Geometry* (1897), was that only those geometries are possible that have a constant measure of curvature. See Russell *1959*, 39.

126: 36 **Helmholtz endeavours** Hermann Ludwig Ferdinand von Helmholtz (1821–1894), German scientist with diverse achievements in biology, mathematics, physics and philosophy. His main writings on geometry are collected in his *Wissenschaftliche Abhandlungen* (3 vols., 1882–95), of which Russell's library contains the first two volumes (1882–83). The geometrical papers in these volumes are very heavily annotated (though some of the annotations belong to a slightly later period). Helmholtz's "elaborate analogy" occurs in his paper "Ueber die Thatsachen, die der Geometrie zum Grunde liegen" (*1868*, 219–20 = *1882–95*, 2: 637–8). The analogy is also referred to in Helmholtz's "The Origin and Meaning of the Geometrical Axioms" (*1876*, 311 = *1884*, 2: 18–19). Helmholtz's papers were required reading for Ward's metaphysics course (see Russell's lecture notebooks, 1: 90).

127: 1–2 **Helmholtz defines** Helmholtz *1876*, 304.

127: 16 **flat-fish** Helmholtz supposes two-dimensional creatures, "surface-beings", on the surface of a sphere (*1876*, 304–5). "Flat-fish" is the term used by Clifford, *The Common Sense of the Exact Sciences* (*1886*, 220ff.).

127: 22 **W. K. Clifford even hints** In Clifford *1886*, 223n.2.

127: 35 **Helmholtz's distinction** "Ueber den Ursprung und Sinn der geometrischen Sätze; Antwort gegen Herrn Professor Land" (*1878*, 212–13, 217–21 = *1882–95*, 2: 640–1, 648–55; Russell marked the passage on 640–1 with a question mark and a pencilled "No!"). Kant's doctrine can be found in his *Critique of Pure Reason* (1781), "Transcendental Aesthetic", sec. I, "Space".

128: 14–15 **He says accordingly** Helmholtz *1876*, 319–20 = *1884*, 2: 30.

128: 24 **"topogenous moment"** Helmholtz *1878*, 223 = *1882–95*, 2: 657.

128: 28 **measurement** Ward underlined this word and wrote in the margin: "It would then have all the uncertainty and inexactness of empirical knowledge."

129: 4 **the first axiom** Euclid's first axiom (or common notion) may be stated: "Things which are equal to the same thing are also equal to one another."

129: 9–25 *Metaphysical exposition of number ... Transcendental exposition of number* Russell's subheadings parallel those of Kant's "Transcendental Aesthetic".

129: 13 **Mill thought** *A System of Logic* (1843), Bk. III, Chap. 24, §5 (= Mill *1963*–, 7: 610–13).

## 20 Paper on Bacon

132: 9 **Prerogative Instances** In *Novum Organum* (1620), Bk. II, Aph. 22–51.

132: 10–11 **as with Aristotle** Russell seems here to have relied on Stout's lectures (see lecture notebooks, 2: 88). For Aristotle's theory of induction, see *Topics*, especially Bk. IV for the role of genera.

132: 27–9 **Mill's method of Agreement and Difference ... Concomitant Variations** The methods of agreement, difference and concomitant variation formed part of Mill's taxonomy of the methods of experimental inquiry. They were "regulated" by, respectively, the first, second and fifth of his canons of induction. See Mill, *A System of Logic* (1843), Bk. III, Chap. 8.

132: 30 **Galileo's Method** See *Dialogue concerning the Two Chief World Systems* (1632) and *Dialogue concerning Two New Sciences* (1638), Day Three.

134: 4–6 **"a real ... another"** Locke, *An Essay concerning Human Understanding* (1690), III.iii.17.

134: 11 **Mill's Objections** Mill *1843*, Bk. V, Chap. 3, §7. For Mill on the plurality of causes, see *ibid.*, Bk. III, Chap. 10.

134: 23 **Mill's objection** Mill *1843*, Bk. III, Chap. 22, §4.

134: 29–31 **an early work ... *Novum Organum*** This passage owes much to Stout's lectures on the history of philosophy, at which Russell recorded the following remark: "As to atomism, seems to waver: in a very early writing even criticizes common conception of atom as too gross ... seems almost to point to conception of atom as mere centre of force. But seems to have receded from this view, for in *Novum Organum* regards atom as possibly visible by good microscope" (lecture notebooks, 2: 97). The work to which Stout and Russell refer is possibly Bacon's *The Wisdom of the Ancients* (1609), section XVII of which deals with atomism (*Works, 1857–74*, 6: 729–31). Bacon suggests that ancient stories about Cupid were in fact metaphorical descriptions of the atom, in particular that Cupid's archery is a metaphor for the atom's action at a distance.

134: 32 **says (Aph. 8)** *Novum Organum*, Bk. II.

134: 34–5 **Latent Process he says (Aph. 6)** *Novum Organum*, Bk. II.

137: 19–21 **"to resolve nature ... the rest."** *Novum Organum*, Bk. I, Aph. 51; Bacon *1857–74*, 4: 58.

137: 22–3 **"so concerned ... structure."** *Novum Organum*, Bk. I, Aph. 57; Bacon *1857–74*, 4: 60.

139: 4 **"monstrous and deformed"** *Novum Organum*, Bk. I, Aph. 64; Bacon *1857–74*, 4: 65.

139: 8 **Gilbert** William Gilbert (1544–1603), English scientist and physician, best known for his discovery of the earth's magnetism, published in *De Magnete* (1600). He was repeatedly criticized by Bacon, who thought his work showed signs of overhasty generalization.

## 21 Paper on History of Philosophy

141: 27–8 **mere Identity and Contradiction** The laws of identity and non-contradiction.

142: 21–4 **"The … substance"** *An Essay concerning Human Understanding* (1690), IV.vi.7.

142: 26 **He says a changeling** *An Essay concerning Human Understanding* (1690), III.vi.22.

142: 37–143: 4 **Thus he says … matter.** *Essay*, IV.iii.6 (note). This is Russell's paraphrase of an extract, added to the fifth edition (1706) of the *Essay*, from Locke's first letter to Stillingfleet (1697). The extract reads: "First, we experiment in ourselves thinking. The idea of this action or mode of thinking is inconsistent with the idea of self-subsistence, and therefore has a necessary connexion with a support or subject of inhesion: the idea of that support is what we call substance; and so from thinking experimented in us, we have a proof of a thinking substance in us, which in my sense is a spirit…. ⟨T⟩he general idea of substance being the same every where, the modification of thinking, or the power of thinking, joined to it, makes it a spirit, without considering what other modifications it has, as, whether it has the modification of solidity or no. As, on the other side, substance, that has the modification of solidity, is matter, whether it has the modification of thinking, or no" (Locke, *Works, 1824*, 2: 80).

143: 34–40 **Thus there are three … (p. 389)** *A Treatise of Human Nature* (1739–40), I.iii.6; Green and Grose ed., *1890*, 1: 389. The three distinct elements occur in the previous section (*1890*, 1: 385).

144: 25 **Hylas … as Fraser does in a note** Berkeley, *Three Dialogues between Hylas and Philonous in Opposition to Sceptics and Atheists* (1713). Hylas represents Berkeley's antagonist. Fraser's note occurs in Berkeley *1871*, 1: 317n.29.

145: 5–6 **"permanent possibility of sensation"** Mill, *An Examination of Sir William Hamilton's Philosophy* (1865); Mill *1963*–, 9: 183.

## 22 Paper on Epistemology III

147: 2–3 **as Kant shewed** *The Critique of Pure Reason* (1781), "Transcendental Analytic", Bk. II, Chap. 2, §3, First Analogy.

147: 22 **vortices** Helmholtz had shown that, in a rotating ideal fluid, vortex tubes could form closed indestructible rings. This result led William Thomson, 1st Baron Kelvin, to hypothesize that material atoms were such vortex rings formed from the ether. (See Thomson *1867, 1891* and Thomson and Tait *1879–83*, 1: §345.) The theory fell into disrepute because it had difficulty in explaining inertia. Still, the theory was attractive because it avoided the difficulties faced by the view that atoms were inelastic solids.

147: 34 **centres of force** Another means of avoiding the problems of inelastic solid atoms was to suppose that matter consists of unextended centres of force. Such a theory had been proposed in the eighteenth century by Boscovich and was taken up in the nineteenth by Cauchy and Faraday.

147: 39 **intuit** Ward commented: "Though intuited is this any better understood than action at a distance?"

148: 5–7 **On the other hand ... atomic theory** Ward commented: "Centre of force seems inadequate when rotations are involved", to which Russell replied: "[No]".

148: 17 **Wundt says** Wundt, *System der Philosophie* (*1889*, 290–1).

148: 22 **Wundt admits** Ward commented: "Explain. You give no references. *Cf.* Wundt. *System* p. 373 ff.", to which Russell replied "*cf. System* p. 291".

148: 34 **"felt background"** Bradley, *Appearance and Reality* (1893). The phrase occurs on pp. 109, 174, 461 and 521 (= *1930*, 94, 153, 408, 461, respectively), but the idea is more fully presented in Chap. 9. The phrase occurs also in Bradley *1893a*, 213, a reply to Ward *1893*. This exchange was referred to in Ward's metaphysics course (see Russell's lecture notebooks, 1: 104, 106).

148: 40–1 **as well as force?** Ward commented at the end of this section: "The implication of Cause and Substance in the two cases of Body and Mind is an interesting problem. That the two cases are not coordinate may be shewn from the fact that we start from experience (?) of personal identity on the one side and from continuous occupation of a definite position or a continuous series of positions on the other".

149: 37 **perceptions are copies of them** Ward underlined "perceptions" and noted: "Not in the case of secondary qualities".

150: 2 **Malebranche** Nicolas Malebranche (1638–1715), French philosopher. In his *De la Recherche de la vérité* (1674–75) he put forward the doctrine of "vision in God", according to which the immediate objects of perception are the ideas, or archetypes, in God's mind of corporeal objects.

150: 8–9 **The problem ... existence.** Ward commented: "It does so because the knowledge of the external world turns out to be an intellectual construction to an extent that Locke had failed to realise".

150: 24–5 **What sort of existence? ... objects?** Ward underlined this passage and noted: "*Cf.* asking 1) Of what nature is this object as compared or contrasted with that? 2) What is the common nature of objects *quâ* objects? 3) What is it which to me is object apart from its objectivity for me? 4) If objectivity is correlative to subjectivity in general what are the relata *per se*?"

## 23 Paper on Descartes

152: 32–3 **objections ... "principium cognoscendi" ... "principium essendi"** The objection Russell refers to is Mersenne's third objection (second set of objections) to the *Méditations* (1640–42) (Descartes, *Oeuvres, 1824–26*, 1: 403–4 = *1911*, 2: 26–7). Descartes does not use these phrases in his reply or, apparently, elsewhere. It is very likely, in view of some manuscript notes on Descartes which Russell made at this time (RA 220.010320), that Russell got the terms from Erdmann's *Geschichte der Philosophie* (*1878*, 2: 15–16). Erdmann does not attribute the terminology to Descartes, but cites Descartes's replies to the second, fourth and sixth sets of objections (*1824–26*, 1: 426–7 = *1911*, 2: 30–51; 2: 38–40, 333–4 = *1911*, 2: 96–122, 258) for the distinction.

153: 7–9 **Descartes ... existence** Ward wrote in the margin against this passage:

"Yes, this is odd".

153: 9–11 **for imagination ... exists (Med.** vi) "⟨Q⟩uand je considère attentive- ment ce que c'est que l'imagination, je trouve qu'elle n'est autre chose qu'une cer- taine application de la faculté qui connoît, au corps qui lui est intimement présent, et partant qui existe" (Descartes *1824–26*, 1: 322–3).

153: 21 **occasionalist** Occasionalism was the doctrine, held by Geulincx and Malebranche, that mind and body, being separate substances, could (and did) inter- act only through God's intervention and not directly. The view that Descartes ought to have embraced occasionalism occurs in the notes Russell took at Ward's lectures on the history of philosophy (lecture notebooks, 2: 27–8).

153: 23 **treatise on the Passions** *Les Passions de l'âme* (1649).

154: 12 *Passions de l'Âme* Much of Pt. 1 of this work is concerned with the in- teraction of soul and body. See especially art. xxxiv.

## 24 A Critical Comparison of the Methods of Bacon, Hobbes and DesCartes

157: 5–6 **Aristotle's induction** See A132: 10–11.

157: 28 **Prerogative Instances** See A132: 9.

157: 39–42 **"the knowledge ... effects"** Hobbes, *De Corpore* (1655), 1.6.1; *English Works, 1839–45*, 1: 65–6.

158: 1–2 **The shortest way ... vice versa.** *De Corpore*, 1.6.1; Hobbes *1839–45*, 1: 66.

158: 9–14 **Thus** *square* **... cause of a square".** *De Corpore*, 1.6.4; Hobbes *1839–45*, 1: 69.

158: 17–19 **The causes ... namely** *motion.* *De Corpore*, 1.6.5: "But the causes of universal things (of those, at least, that have any cause) are manifest of themselves, or (as they say commonly) known to nature; so that they need no method at all; for they have all but one universal cause, which is motion" (Hobbes *1839–45*, 1: 69).

158: 20 **he says elsewhere** *De Corpore*, 1.3.9: "Now *primary* propositions are no- thing but definitions, or parts of definitions" (Hobbes *1839–45*, 1: 37).

159: 29–30 **"selon les règles ... de la nature"** Descartes, *Discours de la méthode* (1637), Pt. v; *Oeuvres, 1824–26*, 1: 184. Haldane and Ross translate: "according to the laws of mechanics, which are identical with those of Nature" (Descartes *1911*, 1: 115).

160: 24–5 **When we come ...** *Règles.* Russell noted in the margin: "[Not true, or at any rate greatly exaggerated, says Stout.]"

161: 2 **second objections** The objections by Mersenne, printed in Descartes *1824–26*, 1: 409 = *1911*, 2: 29; for Descartes's reply, see 1: 446–50 = *1911*, 2: 48–51.

## 25 Paper on Bacon

163: 2 **Peter Ramus** Anglo-Latin name of Pierre de la Ramée (1515–1572), French logician, educational reformer and philosopher. He is known principally for his wide-ranging attacks on Aristotle and scholasticism which divided sixteenth-century philosophers into bitterly opposed factions.

163: 3 **his thesis** Russell refers to Ramus's lost master's thesis (1536), which, according to a popular but probably spurious story, was called *Quaecumque ab Aristotele dicta essent, commentitia esse* [Whatever Aristotle has said is a fabrication].

163: 9–10 **fourth figure** In Aristotelian syllogistic (*Prior Analytics*, Bk. I, Chaps. 4–7), syllogisms are divided into three figures according to the position of the middle term in the two premisses. The fourth figure, in which the middle term is the predicate in the major premiss and the subject in the minor, was added by Aristotle's pupil Theophrastus and does not occur in Aristotle's work, although there is evidence that Aristotle knew of fourth-figure syllogisms. Ramus's attack on Aristotelian syllogistic occurs in his *Aristotelicae animadversiones* (1543), especially Bk. VII. Ramus's positive account of syllogistic, which he calls "first judgment" and which forms only one part of the art of dialectic, can be found in his *Dialecticae* (1556), Bk. II. Here syllogistic is divided into the explicated syllogism (second and first figures) and the contracted syllogism (an enthymematic version of the third figure), while the fourth figure is dropped entirely.

163: 15–16 **He taught Logic ... Vergil and Cicero.** Since Ramus held that his art of dialectic was appropriate for the treatment of any type of discourse, in his *Dialecticae institutiones* (1543) he frequently used extracts from poets and orators as examples.

163: 30 **Digby** Everard Digby (c.1550–1592), English divine and philosopher. His lectures may well have been attended by Bacon. Logically orthodox, he published a highly eclectic metaphysical system, drawing on scholastic, Platonic and occult sources, in *Theoria analytica* (1579). His attack on Ramist method, *De duplici methodo* (1580), was the occasion of Temple's reply, which Russell mentions below. See A164: 35.

163: 30 **Temple** Sir William Temple (1555–1627), English philosopher and the most active champion of Ramism in England; subsequently Provost of Trinity College, Dublin. His most important contribution to the Ramist cause was his annotated edition (1584) of Ramus's *Dialecticae*.

164: 5–8 **His view of method ... highest principle.** See *De duplici methodo*. Digby's "bipartite" method of abstraction and deduction is directly opposed to Ramus's view that a single method, that of descent from "general" to "special", is universally applicable.

164: 14 **he sums up his position** It has not proved possible to locate this claim in Digby's writings, though it was standard scholastic doctrine at the time. Russell's preparatory notes for this essay (RA 220.010050) attribute this view to Digby. But the attribution is not made in Rémusat *1875*, on which Russell's notes are largely based.

164: 25–6 **Philosophia Prima** Bacon, *De Augmentis Scientiarum* (1623), Bk. III, Chap. I; *Works, 1857–74*, 4: 337.

164: 28 **hierarchy of angels** Bacon, *The Advancement of Learning* (1605), Bk. I; *1857–74*, 3: 296.

164: 35 **Mildapettus** *Ad Everardum Digbeium Anglum admonitio de unica P. Rami methodo reiectis caeteris retinenda* (1580) by Franciscus Mildapettus Navarrenus. ("Navarrenus" was a reference to the fact that Ramus had studied at the Parisian College of Navarre.) The work is a defence of Ramist method in reply to Digby's *De duplici methodo*.

164: 37 **he was the first** In fact an English translation of Ramus's *Dialecticae* had been published by Roland MacIlmaine in 1574, and Continental editions of Ramus's writings had circulated in England even earlier.

164: 39 **Buchanan** George Buchanan (1506–1582), Scottish historian, scholar and poet. At one time it was widely believed that, as Principal (1566–70) of St. Leonard's College, Buchanan was responsible for the introduction of Ramism at St. Andrews (see Waddington *1855*, 396; Mullinger *1873–1911*, 2: 410); but since nothing definite is known of Buchanan's work at St. Leonard's, the belief lacks solid support. Indeed, there is little reason (apart from his studies in France) to suppose that Buchanan was a Ramist at all, especially since his reform plan for St. Andrews recommended the study of Aristotle for logic.

165: 8–11 **The Ethics ... Supreme Evil.** Presumably Russell refers here to Temple's *Pro Mildapetti de unica methodo defensione contra Diplodophilum, commentatio ... huc accessit nonnullarum e physicis et ethicis quaestionum explicatio, uná cum epistola de Rami Dialectica ad Joannem Piscatorem Argentinensem* (1581), in which Temple, who reveals his identity for the first time, replies to Digby's *Admonitioni Francisci Mildapetti responsio* (1580) as well as to Georgius Lieblerus's defence of Aristotelian ethics against Ramus.

165: 30 **"perfect Induction"** See Aristotle, *Prior Analytics*, 68b 15 ff.

166: 3 **Baconian induction** See Bacon, *Novum Organum*.

166: 33 **"Dinglichkeit"** "Thinghood".

166: 36–167: 2 **But as to final causes ... action** *Novum Organum*, Bk. II, Aph. 2: "But of these the final cause rather corrupts than advances the sciences, except such as have to do with human action" (*1857–74*, 4: 120).

166: 37–8 **"Forms ... immutable."** *Novum Organum*, Bk. II, Aph. 9: "let the investigation of Forms, which are (in the eye of reason at least, and in their essential law) eternal and immutable, constitute *Metaphysics* ..." (*1857–74*, 4: 126).

167: 3–4 **"perfectly continuous ... the sense"** *Novum Organum*, Bk. II, Aph. 6: "For what I understand by ⟨Latent Process⟩ is not certain measures or signs or successive steps of process in bodies, which can be seen; but a process perfectly continuous, which for the most part escapes the sense" (*1857–74*, 4: 124).

167: 11 **Mill ... four canons** See Mill, *A System of Logic* (1843), Bk. III, Chap. 8, for the canons of induction. Mill, in fact, lists five canons, but the third is a composite of the first two, which presumably is why Russell does not accord it independent status. The method of agreement is "regulated" by the first canon; the method of differences by the second; and the method of concomitant variations by the fifth.

167: 38 **Galileo's view of Induction** See A132: 30.

## 26 Paper on DesCartes I

170: 12–13 **"every subject is considered corporeal"** Hobbes's second objection to Descartes's *Méditations* (1640–42): "les sujets de tous les actes semblent être seulement entendus sous une raison corporelle, ou sous une raison de matière ..." (*Oeuvres, 1824–26*, 1: 469). [Haldane and Ross translate: "the subjects of all activities can be conceived only after a corporeal fashion, or as in material guise ..." (Descartes *1911*, 2: 62).]

170: 19 *idea* Hobbes's fifth objection to Descartes's *Méditations* (*1824–26*, 1: 478–82 = *1911*, 2: 66–8).

170: 22–3 **"anything immediately conceived by the mind"** Reply to Hobbes's fifth objection: "je prends le nom d'idée pour tout ce qui est conçu immediatement par l'esprit" (*1824–26*, 1: 481). [Haldane and Ross translate: "I take the term idea to stand for whatever the mind directly perceives ..." (Descartes *1911*, 2: 67–8).]

170: 24–30 **Reasoning, says Hobbes ... DesCartes misses ... by them.** Hobbes's fourth objection and Descartes's reply (*1824–26*, 1: 476–8 = *1911*, 2: 65–6).

170: 33–5 **Hobbes says the idea ... producing.** Hobbes's tenth objection and Descartes's reply (*1824–26*, 1: 488–93 = *1911*, 2: 71–3).

170: 35–8 **Hobbes says error ... positive** Hobbes's twelfth objection and Descartes's reply (*1824–26*, 1: 494–6 = *1911*, 2: 74–5).

170: 38–42 **Hobbes objects ... objection.** Hobbes's fourteenth objection and Descartes's reply (*1824–26*, 1: 498–500 = *1911*, 2: 76–7). Russell inserted this passage in the margin of his paper. Underneath it he wrote in pencil: "[Stout objects to this criticism but made it himself in lecture]". Certainly Russell recorded the criticism at Stout's lectures, for his notes (lecture notebooks, 2: 150) contain the following: "Hobbes says if no triangle anywhere, can't see how it has essence. Descartes says essence and existence are distinguished by all the world. [Ought to have accepted objection: his ontological argument depends on it.]" But as it was often Russell's practice to include his own comments on the lectures in square brackets, the criticism may not have been Stout's.

171: 2 **DesCartes says** Reply to Hobbes's eighth objection (*1824–26*, 1: 486 = *1911*, 2: 70).

171: 6 **Hobbes also objects** Hobbes's thirteenth objection (*1824–26*, 1: 496–7 = *1911*, 2: 75–6).

172: 20 **DesCartes then asks** *Discours de la méthode* (1637), Pt. IV; *1824–26*, 1: 159 = *1911*, 1: 101.

172: 34–8 **A Perception ... it properly.** Principle XLV: "J'appele claire celle qui est présente et manifeste à un esprit attentif; de même que nous disons voir clairement les objets, lorsqu'étant présents à nos yeux ils agissent assez fort sur eux, et qu'ils sont disposés à les regarder; et distincte, celle qui est tellement précise et différente de toutes les autres, qu'elle ne comprend en soi que ce qui paroît manifestement à celui qui la considère comme il faut" (*1824–26*, 3: 90). [Haldane and Ross translate: "I term that clear which is present and apparent to an attentive mind, in the same way as we assert that we see objects clearly when, being present to the regarding eye, they operate upon it with sufficient strength. But the distinct is that which is so precise and different from all other objects that it contains within itself nothing but what is clear" (Descartes *1911*, 1: 237).]

173: 15 **God** Below the line in which "God" appears, which comes at the bottom of the manuscript leaf, Russell wrote in pencil: "*cf*. Rule xii: Proposition 'I am therefore God is' one in which can't form clear perception of either without the other, as of figure without extension". Russell's copy of Descartes has a vertical pencilled line against the passage he refers to (*1824–26*, 2: 274 = *1911*, 1: 43).

173: 27–8 *principium cognoscendi ... principium essendi* See A152: 32–3.

175: 3 **Hylas** Berkeley, *Three Dialogues* (1713). Hylas represents Berkeley's antagonists.

177: 6 **"mélange confus"** It seems likely that Russell got this phrase from Ward's lectures on the history of philosophy. It occurs in Russell's lecture notebooks (2: 21), in a discussion of Descartes's rejection (in the sixth Meditation) of the view that the soul is to the body as a pilot to a boat. In that passage Descartes uses the phrase "et tellement confondu et mêlé" (*1824–26*, 1: 336 = *1911*, 1: 192), which may have given rise to "mélange confus".

177: 25–6 **"turn towards the body"** Descartes (in the sixth Meditation) maintains that in imagination the mind "se tourne vers le corps" (*1824–26*, 1: 325 = *1911*, 1: 186). Russell's passage owes much to Ward, who also could not understand what Descartes meant (see Russell's lecture notebooks, 2: 22).

## 27 Paper on Descartes II

179: 4–5 **every concept ... *necessary* existence** Descartes's reply to the first set of objections to the *Méditations* (1640–42) (*Oeuvres*, *1824–26*, 1: 390 = *1911*, 2: 20).

179: 9 **he does say somewhere** It has not proved possible to find a passage in which Descartes says that "we are compelled to think God". Indeed, in Meditation v he says "il ne soit pas nécessaire que je tombe jamais dans aucune pensée de Dieu" (Descartes *1824–26*, 1: 315). [Haldane and Ross translate: "... it is not necessary that I should at any time entertain the notion of God ..." (Descartes *1911*, 1: 182).] Possibly Russell had in mind Descartes's view that the idea of God is innate (Meditation III; *1824–26*, 1: 290 = *1911*, 1: 170).

179: 10 **Kant points out** *The Critique of Pure Reason* (1781), "Transcendental Dialectic", Bk. II, Chap. 3, sec. 4.

179: 21–2 **We *must* think the Absolute** See A102: 33–4. For Russell's acceptance of the ontological argument for the Absolute, see Spadoni *1976*.

179: 25 **Anselm** *Proslogion*, Chaps. 2–4.

179: 33 **Leibnitz** See, e.g., *The Monadology* (1714), §§38ff.

180: 1 **In Aristotle** *De anima*, Bk. II, Chap. 2.

180: 20–3 **in a letter ... manner.**" Letter to Princess Elizabeth of Bohemia, January 1646: "c'est lui aussi qui a disposé toutes les autres choses qui sont hors de nous, pour faire que tels et tels objets se présentassent à nos sens à tel et tel temps, à l'occasion desquels il a su que notre libre arbitre nous détermineroit à telle ou telle chose, et il l'a ainsi voulu ..." (Descartes *1824–26*, 9: 374). [Kenny translates: "... it is He who has disposed all the other things outside us so that such and such objects would present themselves to our senses at such and such times, on the occasion of which He knew that our freewill would determine us to such or such an action; and He so willed ..." (Descartes *1970*, 189).]

181: 9 **there is a passage** Descartes *1824–26*, 1: 195–6 = *1911*, 1: 120–1.

181: 14–15 **"from certain seeds ... our souls"** *Discours de la méthode* (1637), Pt. VI: "j'ai tâché de trouver en général les principes ou premières causes de tout ce qui est ou qui peut être dans le monde, sans rien considérer pour cet effet que Dieu seul qui l'a créé, ni les tirer d'ailleurs que de certaines semences de vérités qui sont naturellement en nos âmes" (*1824–26*, 1: 194–5). [Haldane and Ross translate: "I have first tried to discover generally the principles or first causes of everything that is or that can be in the world, without considering anything that might accomplish this end but God Himself who has created the world, or deriving them from any source excepting from certain germs of truths which are naturally existent in our souls" (Descartes *1911*, 1: 121).]

182: 3 **Locke's polemic** *An Essay concerning Human Understanding* (1690), Bk. I ("Of Innate Notions").

182: 5–6 **Hobbes's objections** Reply to Hobbes's Tenth Objection (Descartes *1824–26*, 1: 492–3 = *1911*, 2: 72).

182: 6 **hereditary gout** In *Notae in programma* (1647). This work is not included in the Cousin edition of the *Oeuvres*, which Russell owned. The relevant passage can be found in the Adam and Tannery edition (Descartes *1897–1910*, 8: 357–8).

182: 9 **as Hobbes would have it ... do** Hobbes's Tenth Objection to the *Méditations* (Descartes *1824–26*, 1: 491 = *1911*, 2: 72–3).

182: 14–15 **"the inventions and creatures of the understanding"** Russell probably had in mind a passage from the first of Locke's letters to Stillingfleet (1697). In talking of the general idea of substance Locke wrote: "For general ideas come not into the mind by sensation or reflection, but are the creatures or inventions of the understanding, as, I think, I have shown; and also, how the mind makes them from ideas, which it has got by sensation and reflection: and as to the ideas of relation, how the mind forms them, and how they are derived from, and ultimately terminate in, ideas of sensation and reflection, I have likewise shown" (*Works, 1824*, 3: 19). That Locke's account of ideas of relation is essentially similar to his account of general ideas is shown by an earlier passage in the letter (*1824*, 3: 11).

182: 27 **his illustration** *Les Passions de l'âme* (1649), Pt. II, art. CXLVII. Against this passage Russell wrote in the margin of his copy: "Emotions are due to the soul"

(Descartes *1824–26*, 4: 160 = *1911*, 1: 398).

183: 2 **Passions** *Les Passions de l'âme*, Pt. II, art. CXLVIII; Pt. III, art. CCXII.

183: 10 **Spinoza's intellectual love of God** The key term in Spinoza's *Ethics* (1677), it is discussed in Bk. V, props. 32–7. The interpretation of the "intellectual love of God" is much disputed. Russell probably, at this early stage in his study of Spinoza, understood the term as suggesting a mode of contemplative living as independent as possible of the passions. (For this interpretation, Russell may have been indebted to Pollock *1880*, 300; he had read the book in January 1894.) The term was to have more profound meaning for him as he became immersed in Bradley's metaphysics and its conception of the self.

183: 14 **three provisional rules of conduct** *Discours de la méthode*, Pt. III; Descartes *1824–26*, 1: 146–53 = *1911*, 1: 95–8. In fact Descartes gives four maxims.

183: 20 **Geulinx's** Arnold Geulincx (1624–1669), Flemish philosopher, prominent in his day for his writings on ethics, metaphysics and logic. Now he is best known for his occasionalist theory of action. See A153: 21.

184: 2–5 **Ethics ... Bouillier** Francisque Bouillier, *Histoire de la philosophie cartésienne* (*1854*, 1: 288): "L'éditeur de l'*Éthique* de Geulincx, le pseudonyme Philarète, explique d'ailleurs dans une note son sentiment avec une précision qui ne laisse rien à désirer: 'Deus has res diversissimas (motum materiae et arbitrium voluntatis meae), inter se devinxit, ut cum voluntas vellet; motus talis adesset qualem vellet, et contra cum motus adesset, voluntas vellet sine ulla alterius in alterum causalitate vel influxu.' Il se sert même, pour faire comprendre cette correspondance, de la comparaison de deux horloges dont plus tard se servira Leibniz en faveur de son harmonie préétablie." [Translation: "The editor of Geulincx's *Ethics*, writing under the pseudonym Philaretus, elsewhere explains his thinking in a note whose precision leaves nothing to be desired: 'These two completely separate things (the motion of matter and the decision of my will) God has bound together in such a way that whenever my will chooses there is at hand whatever kind of motion it desires, and conversely, whenever a motion presents itself my will is in accord, and this without any causal determination of the one upon the other.' In order to clarify this correspondence, he brings in the illustration of the two clocks which Leibniz would later employ in support of his theory of a pre-established harmony."] In fact, these remarks are Geulincx's, not Philaretus's (see Geulincx *1891–93*, 3: 212).

184: 13 **Malebranche** See A150: 2.

184: 20–2 **Leibnitz ... praises the schoolmen** *Theodicy* (1710), §§385–6; but see §§382–4 for Leibniz's attitude to the schoolmen's version of this doctrine.

## 28  Paper on Hobbes

186: 9 **is said** By John Aubrey, as reported by Croom Robertson, *Hobbes* (*1886*, 17–18), which Russell read in October 1893.

186: 14 **Hobbes translated Thucydides** Hobbes's translation of *The History of the Peloponnesian War* was published in 1629.

186: 17–21 **Euclid ... the proof** This story also comes from Aubrey, via Croom Robertson *1886*, 31. Russell has the date wrong: the event occurred on Hobbes's second visit to the Continent (not the third), which makes the year 1629.

186: 26 **Gassendi** Pierre Gassendi (1592–1655), French sceptical and epicurean philosopher, now chiefly known for his objections to Descartes's *Méditations*, which he wrote in 1641. It is Gassendi's epicurean atomism which Russell thinks may have influenced Hobbes; although Gassendi, unlike Hobbes, did not extend his theory to cover the activities of the soul.

186: 35–8 **"the knowledge ... of the effects."** Hobbes, *De Corpore* (1655), 1.6.1; *English Works*, *1839–45*, 1: 65–6. The word "cause" is only implicit in Hobbes's definition, though it does occur in an earlier version of the definition (*De Corpore* 1.1.2; Hobbes *1839–45*, 1: 3).

187: 17–19 **"the voice ... imposed"** *Human Nature* (1650), Chap. 5, §2; Hobbes *1839–45*, 4: 20.

187: 22–3 **"signs of our conceptions"** *De Corpore*, 1.2.5; Hobbes *1839–45*, 1: 17.

187: 27–8 **"of two appellations ... negation"** *Human Nature*, Chap. 5, §9: "of two *appellations* by the help of that little verb *is*, or something equivalent, we make an *affirmation* or *negation*" (Hobbes *1839–45*, 4: 23).

187: 32–3 **"true and false ... things"** *Leviathan* (1651), Chap. 4; Hobbes *1839–45*, 3: 23.

187: 33–5 **"the first truths ... others"** *De Corpore*, 1.3.8; Hobbes *1839–45*, 1: 36.

187: 38 **"when we expect ... be"** *Leviathan*, Chap. 4; Hobbes *1839–45*, 3: 23.

188: 9–10 **a definition resolves ... exemplifies it** *De Corpore*, 1.6.14; Hobbes *1839–45*, 1: 83–4.

188: 20–4 **"if we consider ... may be filled."** *De Corpore*, 11.7.2: "If therefore we remember, or have a phantasm of any thing that was in the world before the supposed annihilation of the same; and consider, not that the thing was such or such, but only that it had a being without the mind, we have presently a conception of that we call *space*: an imaginary space indeed, because a mere phantasm, yet that very thing which all men call so. For no man calls it space for being already filled, but because it may be filled ..." (Hobbes *1839–45*, 1: 93).

188: 24–5 **"the phantasm ... simply"** *De Corpore*, 11.7.2; Hobbes *1839–45*, 1: 94.

188: 26 **Kant's "form of the external sense"** *The Critique of Pure Reason* (1781), A26=B42.

188: 28–9 **"the causes ... motion."** *De Corpore*, 1.6.5: "But the causes of universal things (of those, at least, that have any cause) are manifest of themselves, or (as they say commonly) known to nature; so that they need no method at all; for they have all but one universal cause, which is motion" (Hobbes *1839–45*, 1: 69).

188: 38–9 **"the manner ... conceived"** *De Corpore*, 11.8.2; Hobbes *1839–45*, 1: 103.

189: 3–4 **"the continual relinquishing ... another"** *De Corpore*, 11.8.10; Hobbes *1839–45*, 1: 109.

189: 8 **"the phantasm of before and after in motion"** *De Corpore*, 11.7.3; Hobbes

*1839–45*, 1: 95.

189: 14 **Zeno's antinomy** Russell refers to Zeno's "arrow paradox" designed to show the impossibility of motion. A free adaptation of the paradox runs as follows: In an instant no motion is possible. Thus at each instant of its flight the arrow is at rest. Thus the arrow is always at rest. See Russell *1914*, 178–80, for some old formulations and a modern solution.

189: 16 **Quantity of motion is defined** *De Corpore*, II.8.18; Hobbes *1839–45*, I: 115.

189: 17–19 **Newton's first law ... is stated** *De Corpore*, II.8.19; Hobbes *1839–45*, I: 115.

189: 30–1 **"cause simply taken ... they be"** *De Corpore*, II.9.3: "But a CAUSE simply, or *an entire cause*, *is the aggregate of all the accidents both of the agents how many soever they be*, *and that of the patient*, *put together* ..." (Hobbes *1839–45*, 1: 121). Alternatively, *De Corpore*, II.9.3, where Hobbes says, under the heading "Cause simply taken", "The cause, therefore, of all effects consists in certain accidents both in the agents and in the patients" (*1839–45*, 1: 121); or *De Corpore*, II.10.1: "*entire cause* ... consist ⟨s⟩ in the sum or aggregate of all the accidents, as well in the agent as in the patient" (*1839–45*, 1: 128).

189: 41 **"Computation or Logic"** The title of Pt. 1 of *De Corpore*.

190: 5–6 **"All mutation is motion"** Section heading of *De Corpore*, II.9.9; Hobbes *1839–45*, 1: 126.

190: 13 **Possible ... ignorance** This passage seems to derive mainly from Stout's lectures on Hobbes. In his lecture notes on Hobbes, Russell wrote: "Word possible then simply a name for our ignorance: no sphere of real possibility" (lecture notebooks, 2: 120). In *Leviathan*, Chap. 11, Hobbes writes: "Ignorance of natural causes, disposeth a man to credulity, so as to believe many times impossibilities: for such know nothing to the contrary, but that they may be true; being unable to detect the impossibility" (Hobbes *1839–45*, 3: 92).

191: 4–10 **(1) the subject ... besides sight.** *Human Nature*, Chap. 2, §4: "That the subject wherein colour and image are inherent, is *not* the *object* or thing seen. That there is nothing *without us* (really) which we call an *image* or colour. That the said image or colour is but an *apparition* unto us of the *motion*, agitation, or alteration, which the *object* worketh in the *brain*, or spirits, or some internal substance of the head. That as in *vision*, so also in conceptions that arise from the *other senses*, the subject of their *inherence* is not the *object*, but the *sentient*" (Hobbes *1839–45*, 4: 4).

191: 20–8 **"Not every thought ... moved."** *Leviathan*, Chap. 3; Hobbes *1839–45*, 3: 11–12.

191: 36–9 **one might say ... sense** Russell here echoes F. H. Bradley's critique of associationism. See Bradley *1883*, Bk. II, Pt. II, Chap. 1, §10.

192: 2–7 **these motions ... the motion** Russell here freely, but not inaccurately, adapts *De Corpore*, IV.25.12; Hobbes *1839–45*, 1: 406–7.

193: 21–2 **"Pity is ... calamity".** *Human Nature*, Chap. 9, §10; Hobbes *1839–45*, 4: 44.

193: 30–1 **But in explaining ... imagination** *Human Nature*, Chap. 9, §10; Hobbes *1839–45*, 4: 45.

193: 39–41 **"hath no name ... anybody"** *Human Nature*, Chap. 9, §13: "There is a passion that hath *no name*; but the sign of it is that distortion of the countenance which we call *laughter*, which is always *joy*: but what joy, what we think, and wherein we triumph when we laugh, is not hitherto declared by any" (Hobbes *1839–45*, 4: 45).

193: 43–194: 1 **"to see ... laugh"** *Human Nature*, Chap. 9, §21; Hobbes *1839–45*, 4: 53.

194: 7 **Hood** Thomas Hood (1799–1845), English comic poet, best known for his use of puns and word-play.

## 29 On the Distinction between the Psychological and Metaphysical Points of View

196: 9–10 **besides their existence ...** *meaning* Russell's distinction between the existence, nature and meaning of ideas is taken from Bradley *1883*, Bk. I, Chap. I, §4.

196: 21–2 **"a vague mass of the felt"** Bradley uses the phrase "an indefinite mass of the felt" in "Consciousness and Experience" (*1893a*, 215). The same idea is expressed in similar words (though none are quite so close to the version Russell gives) in Bradley *1893*, e.g. at 87–96 (= *1930*, 74–82).

197: 3 **Cassim** Ali Baba's brother in "The History of Ali Baba and the Forty Thieves" from *The Thousand and One Nights*. Cassim returned to the thieves' cave for more treasure but was so excited by the gold that he forgot the password, "Open Sesame", and was trapped in the cave where he was found and murdered by the thieves. It was McTaggart who compared this task of metaphysics to the attempt to stitch him back together again ("Further Determination", *1934*, 254).

## 30 On Pleasure

202: 2–13 **In popular ... produce.** Against this passage Sidgwick wrote: "good: but does not notice distinction of desired/desirable."

202: 34 **Veronese** Paolo Veronese (1528–1588), Venetian painter.

202: 34 **ordinary division into physical and mental** Sidgwick commented that this was "open to objection" but did not elaborate.

203: 5–6 **the contrary ... to be the case** "I doubt this" was Sidgwick's comment here.

203: 18 **pleasures of self-approbation** Sidgwick added: "The imagined approbation of God not merely 'self' must be a prominent motive in such acts of fanatical asceticism."

203: 19 **Simon Stylites** St. Simeon Stylites (c. 390–459), best known of the ascetics who lived on pillars.

203: 21 **on easier terms** Sidgwick noted: "Still he imagined that his mortification of the flesh was in a special sense in harmony with God's will."

203: 24–5 **this energy ... requires it** "I fear this mitigation may be only transient", Sidgwick noted.

204: 15 **Mr. Worldly Wiseman** A character in Bunyan's *Pilgrim's Progress* (1678) who attempts to dissuade Christian from continuing his journey to the Celestial City. Bunyan, however, gives no evidence for supposing that Mr. Worldly Wiseman intended to repent on his death bed.

205: 3 **as Mill does** In *Utilitarianism* (Mill *1963*–, 10: 210–11). Russell has marked parts of this passage in his copy (Mill *1888*, 11–12).

205: 9–11 **No doubt ... neutral feeling** Against this Sidgwick confusingly observed: "I am afraid my experience is that this attitude of introspective scrutiny is much more effective in interfering with pains than in interfering with pleasures."

205: 15 **middle axioms of Hedonism** See A79: 23.

## 31 On the Foundations of Ethics

208: 13 **the Categories** Russell refers to Kant's view of the categories as the à priori forms of all possible experience. See Kant's *The Critique of Pure Reason* (1781), "Transcendental Analytic", Bk. I, Chap. 2, §2.

208: 29 **Green** In the *Prolegomena to Ethics* (1883) of Thomas Hill Green (1836–1882), British idealist philosopher and advanced liberal theorist. Green is generally recognized as the first major figure in the British neo-Hegelian movement. His teaching at Oxford exerted a marked influence on younger neo-Hegelians and liberal social reformers.

209: 8 **McTaggart's pamphlet** McTaggart, *The Further Determination of the Absolute* (1893).

209: 23–4 **another theorem of McTaggart's** The alleged proof of this theorem is given in a letter of 18 May 1892 from McTaggart to an unnamed correspondent. See Dickinson *1931*, 88–9. The correspondent may have been C. P. Sanger, who reported the proof to Russell in a letter of 16 July 1892.

209: 33 **Bk. III, Chap. II** Bk. III is "The Moral Ideal and Moral Progress" and Chap. 2 is "Characteristics of the Moral Ideal".

210: 23–4 **as Sidgwick points out** Henry Sidgwick, *The Methods of Ethics* (*1890*, Bk. I, Chap. 6, §3, 82–6).

210: 29 **his objection** Green *1883*, §221, argues that, even if desire is only for pleasure, the sum of all imaginable pleasures cannot be desired because (1) each pleasant feeling "is one, and is over before another can be enjoyed", (2) "A sum of pleasures is not a pleasure", and (3) the sum of all imaginable pleasures is "not a possible state of feeling".

210: 32 **On Free Will** Green *1883*, Bk. II, Chap. I.

210: 33 **using natural as Green does** Green *1883*, §2, contrasts the natural with the moral.

210: 36–7 **as indeed Green himself sees** See Green *1883*, Bk. I, Chap. I.

## 32 The Relation of What Ought to Be to What Is, Has Been or Will Be

213: 32 **materially equivalent** Sidgwick was puzzled by this term: "Does it mean 'capable of being inferred from'?", he wrote.

213: 42–3 **brought about by circumstances** Sidgwick wrote against this remark: "not enough. Would it not be still absurd to say that the earth ought to remedy the obliquity of its axis, even if 'circumstances' *might* bring the change about".

## 33 The Relation of Rule and End

216: 3 **the nature of Feeling** Sidgwick wrote against this phrase: "This does not recognize the biological conception of the End as 'Life'—*cf.* Spencer ⟨*The Principles of Ethics*⟩ chap. i and ii."

216: 9 **End or Ends** Sidgwick added: "But if Good Will is 'The Good' is it not therefore the Ultimate End of rational action?"

216: 17–22 **[An ethical ... itself]**. Sidgwick wrote against this passage: "Ingenious, but surely we require to distinguish 'Perfect character' as ulterior ends⟨?⟩ from volition as realizing 'Good Will' in itself."

216: 20 **radically from the Kantian view** Sidgwick commented: "It is plain from Kant's later treatise that he did not recognise this difference so far as moral perfection is concerned".

216: 29–32 **According to Kant ... the volition.** Sidgwick wrote: "I should agree that it cannot be conceived as *sole* end in acting, but not that it cannot be conceived as an indispensable element of it".

216: 32–7 **[This objection.... imperfect.]** Sidgwick replied: "But may not perfection lie in movement rather than rest? *cf.* perfect circle".

## 34 On the Definition of Virtue

219: 8–11 **For example ... virtuous actions.** Sidgwick wrote "*good*" against this passage.

219: 25–6 **I think we shall ... as virtuous** Sidgwick commented in the margin: "surely, in cases of fanaticism, not without qualification."

219: 34 **exclude selfish considerations altogether** Sidgwick underlined this phrase and commented in the margin: "renders conduct entirely⟨?⟩ unselfish identical with that to which predominant inclination prompts. [To get the phrase more in harmony with Kant's view of selflove]".

220: 6–7 **that virtue consists ... character** Sidgwick commented: "But surely the difference between Virtue with/without conflict might apply equally in either case?"

220: 7–8 **On this view ... objective rightness** Sidgwick asked: "Why more than on the other view?"

220: 14-19 **And I think … approve.** Sidgwick commented: "Do you mean that the common sense ideal of Perfection *includes* the first view? If so, why? [*I* should say because certain acts are better in their results if done from other motives]".

220: 24-5 **But it is thought dangerous … abeyance** Sidgwick commented: "Perhaps we may say that, in order to allow Conscience to be in abeyance without danger, we require a perfect adaptation of the individual to his environment".

220: 25 **Wordsworth says … cast.** From "Ode to Duty" (1807), st. 2, ll. 9-16. Russell's second and sixth lines contain misquotations. The lines should read: "Be on them; who, in love and truth," and "Who do thy work, and know it not:", respectively.

220: 39 **when Godwin censures Fénelon** Russell freely adapts a passage from William Godwin's *Enquiry concerning Political Justice* (1793), Bk. II, Chap. 2. Godwin supposes a hypothetical case in which a rescuer has to choose between saving Fénelon or his chambermaid (1793 ed.) or his valet (1796 and 1798 eds.) from a burning house. Godwin argues that it would be just for the rescuer to choose to save the "more valuable" life of Fénelon.

## 35 The Ethical Bearings of Psychogony

223: 22 **as facilitating the propagation of the species** By this passage Sidgwick wrote: "perhaps more important as preventing resentments leading to feuds".

223: 39 **of the species?** Sidgwick remarked: "? 'when struggle for existence severe' for a woman's life is a part of the society".

224: 3-4 **maximising of Life (in Herbert Spencer's phrase)** In fact, the phrase appears not to have been Spencer's. It does not occur in any of Spencer's works which Russell is known to have read, though the idea is expressed clearly enough in the first volume of *The Principles of Ethics* (1892), §§6, 8, 16, 48.

224: 29 **that pleasure springs from life-preserving actions** Spencer, *The Principles of Psychology* (1855), §124; *The Principles of Ethics*, §§33, 36.

## 36 Ethical Axioms

228: 2-5 **And this objectivity … feelings).** Sidgwick replied: "might conceivably be objective and differ from individual to individual".

228: 29-31 **but self-realization … self-sacrifice** Sidgwick commented: "but what is commonly called selfsacrifice is sacrifice of one's own good."

## 37 The Free-Will Problem from an Idealist Standpoint

230: 1 **Mr. Balfour** Arthur James Balfour (1848-1930), 1st Earl of Balfour, British politician and sometime philosopher. (See A50: 38.) Educated at Cambridge, he had been a student of Sidgwick's and a member of the Apostles. In his first book, *A*

*Defence of Philosophic Doubt* (1879), Balfour used a form of epistemological fallibilism to argue that the claims of both science and religion were alike open to doubt. He took the argument a stage further in *The Foundations of Belief; Being Notes Introductory to the Study of Theology* (1895), his best-known philosophical work, where he argued for the claims of authority, as well as those of reason, as a foundation for belief. His conclusion was that theism forms a more satisfactory basis than naturalism for both scientific and theological belief. Russell may have become acquainted with Balfour's views on the insufficiency of naturalism as a basis for ethics two years before he wrote Paper **37**. The first chapter of *The Foundations of Belief* is devoted to this topic and was read to the Ethical Club at Cambridge on 4 March 1893. The lecture had been advertised in the *Cambridge Observer* (31 Jan., 2), with which Russell was associated, and then reported there (7 Mar., 2). The report noted that McTaggart and Sidgwick participated in the discussion following the lecture.

230:3 **Naturalism** Balfour *1895* uses "naturalism" loosely as a generic term to cover empiricism, positivism and agnosticism.

230:6 **Mr. T. H. Green** See A208:29.

230:12–13 **"original work ... school of thinkers"** Balfour *1895*, 137n.

230:15–17 **"he does not know ... upon its merits."** Balfour *1895*, 137.

230:26 **in a foot-note** Balfour *1895*, 147n.

230:38–40 **"that moral impoverishment ... produce"** Balfour *1895*, 22.

231:25 **"unusually obstinate attempt to think clearly"** In fact, the quotation is not from Bradley but from William James: "Metaphysics means nothing but an unusually obstinate effort to think clearly" (*The Principles of Psychology, 1890,* 1: 145).

232:11–13 **If we are doomed ... honour.** Shakespeare, *Henry V,* IV.iii.20–2. Russell misquotes the first line, which should read "mark'd" instead of "doomed".

232:16 **Ibsen's *Ghosts*** Henrik Ibsen's tragedy *Ghosts* (1881) traces the breakdown of Oswald Alving's sanity as a result of congenital syphilis. Ibsen uses this disease as a metaphor for the harm and debilitation caused by inherited traditions and conventions.

232:41–233:1 **This view was upheld by Kant** See his *Groundwork of the Metaphysic of Morals* (*1964*, Chap. 3, 114 = Kant *1867–68*, 4:294) and *Critique of Practical Reason* (*1956*, Chap. 3, 102–3 = Kant *1867–68*, 5:103–4).

## 38 Note on Ethical Theory

No annotations.

## 39 Are All Desires Equally Moral?

243:11 **the Socratic maxim** See Plato, *Protagoras*, 352c.

## 40  Review of Heymans

**251: 4–11 "The subject ... philosophy."** "Der Zweck des vorliegenden Buches ist ein doppelter: für den Nichtphilosophen soll es ein Lehrbuch der Erkennt-nisstheorie, für den Philosophen aber eine durch Beispiele erläuterte Abhandlung über die Methode sein. Das Bestreben, Beides in einem Buche zu vereinen, wurzelt in meiner Ueberzeugung, dass eben jene empirische Forschungs- und Beweis-methode, deren gutes Recht in der Philosophie ich den Fachgenossen gegenüber zu vertheidigen wünsche, sich auch als Darstellungsmethode ganz besonders demjeni-gen empfiehlt, der wissenschaftlich gebildete Männer in die Philosophie ein-zuführen hat" (Heymans *1890–94*, Vorwort).

**251: 12 Mill's Canons of Induction** See A167: 11.

**251: 20–3 "The exact ... consciousness"** "*Die exacte, durch empirische Unter-suchung des gegebenen Denkens zu ermittelnde Feststellung und Erklärung der causalen Beziehungen, welche das Auftreten von Ueberzeugungen im Bewusstsein bedingen, ist die Aufgabe der Erkenntnistheorie*" (Heymans *1890–94*, 3).

**251: 29 "Gedankensexperiment"** "Thought-experiment".

**251: 30–1 "irreducible psychical laws suffering no exception"** "Wir werden in der That finden dass dieses möglich ist; und zwar dass dieselben sich sämmtlich auf zwei fundamentale, nicht weiter reducirbare und keine Ausnahme erleidende psychische Gesetze zurückführen lassen" (Heymans *1890–94*, 67). [Translation: "We shall find that this in fact is possible, and indeed that they are all reducible to two fundamental psychical laws which are not further reducible and admit of no exceptions."] Russell gives p. 69 in his review.

**251: 38–9 Euclidean system ... Transcendental Aesthetic** In the "Transcen-dental Aesthetic" Kant maintained that geometry (by which he is usually inter-preted to have meant Euclidean geometry) is a synthetic à priori science. See *The Critique of Pure Reason* (1781), B40–1.

**251: 40–1 a confusion ... à priori** For Russell's distinction between the à priori and the subjective, see *An Essay on the Foundations of Geometry* (*1897*, 2–4).

**252: 6 White Queen's practice** In Carroll's *Through the Looking-Glass* (1872), Chap. 5.

**252: 21 Riehl's hypothesis** Alois Riehl (1844–1924), Austrian neo-Kantian phi-losopher. Heymans *1890–94*, 226, quotes Riehl's *Der philosophische Kriticismus* (*1876–87*, 2: 143) as his source.

**253: 2 Heymans observes in answer to Helmholtz** In Heymans *1890–94*, §46. For Helmholtz's position, see "The Origin and Meaning of Geometrical Axioms" (1876).

**253: 12–13 Klein's definition of axioms in general** See Klein, *Nicht-Euklidische Geometrie* (*1893*, I: 356), where he writes: "Ich schreibe den Axiomen die Bedeutung zu, dass sie *Forderungen* vorstellen, vermöge deren wir uns über die Ungenauigkeit der Anschauung oder über die Begrenztheit der Genauigkeit der Anschauung zu unbegrenzter Genauigkeit erheben." [Translation: "To axioms I ascribe the meaning that they represent *demands*, by means of which we raise ourselves above the inexactitude of perception or above the limitation of exactitude of perception, to unlimited exactitude."]

253: 35-6 **Hume's difficulties with the *minimum sensibile*** In his *Treatise of Human Nature* (1739–40), I.ii.1–4, Hume argued that an analysis of our impressions and ideas always comes to an end when we reach visible or tangible elements of finite size anything smaller than which we cannot experience or imagine. We therefore have no idea of infinite divisibility.

254: 6 **criticism of the views of Mill** In Heymans *1890–94*, §§71–4. J. S. Mill's views of causation are to be found in his *System of Logic* (1843), Bk. III, Chap. 10.

254: 6 **Jevons** William Stanley Jevons (1835–1882), British economist and logician. See his *The Principles of Science* (*1874*, I: 250–312) for his views on causality; Heymans *1890–94* discusses them in §68.

254: 7 **Hamilton's hypothesis** Sir William Hamilton (1788–1856), Scottish philosopher and logician. His hypothesis about causation is quoted by Heymans (*1890–94*, 373) and can be found in Hamilton's *Lectures on Metaphysics and Logic* (*1859–60*, 2: 377). Heymans discusses the hypothesis in §§83–7.

254: 23 **the first law** Newton's statement of the first law reads: "That every body perseveres in its state of resting, or of moving uniformly in a right line, as far as it is not compelled to change that state by external forces impressed upon it" (Newton *1969*, 22).

254: 35-6 **the superannuation of the idea of force ... energy** In Hamiltonian mechanics the concept of energy plays a role similar to that of force in Newtonian mechanics. Later Kirchhoff (*1876*) and, most notably, Hertz (*1894*) attempted to derive mechanics from the fundamental concepts of space, time and mass—without essential reference to either force or energy.

254: 38-9 **Kant ... regulative ... constitutive** See *The Critique of Pure Reason*, A178–9 = B221–2, for the distinction between these two kinds of principles. See the "Review of Hannequin" in *Collected Papers* 2 for a Russellian example of the distinction. There he writes: "We cannot say bodies are organized *ad infinitum*, but only that it is the business of science to organize them without end." The first clause denies that there is a constitutive principle with regard to the organization of bodies, and the second affirms that there is a regulative one.

255: 18 **Mach and others** Ernst Mach (1838–1916), Austrian physicist and positivist philosopher; see his *Science of Mechanics* (1883) and *The Analysis of Sensations* (1886). The "others" probably include Richard Avenarius (1843–1896), German positivist philosopher, and Gustav Robert Kirchhoff (1824–1887), German physicist.

255: 20 **Lange's geometrical theory of formal logic** Friedrich Albert Lange (1828–1875), German neo-Kantian philosopher. For his logical views, see his *Logische Studien* (1877). In 1925 Russell wrote an introduction for a new edition of the English translation of Lange's *History of Materialism* (1866).

## 41  Observations on Space and Geometry

258: 1  **Quelle blague que la Géométrie!** "What a joke geometry is!" Russell's use of this quotation (from Flaubert *1886*, 258) is not entirely disingenuous. His correspondence with Alys and C. P. Sanger in October and November 1894 refers frequently to his disillusionment with his research on geometry.

259: 9  *de gustibus* etc. *De gustibus non est disputandum.* ["Matters of taste are not to be disputed."]

259: 14–15  **as Kant himself insists** *The Critique of Pure Reason* (1781), B40.

260: 2  **When I first determined to write a dissertation** On 10 June 1894 Russell had reported to Alys his intention to write on "The Epistemological Bearings of Metageometry". It is not known when his subject became widened.

260: 4–5  **Riemann and Helmholtz** Georg Friedrich Bernhard Riemann (1826–1866), German mathematician. His *1867*, which helped bring non-Euclidean geometry into prominence, not only marked an important mathematical development but also attempted a new clarification of the conceptual bases of geometry. For Helmholtz, see A126: 36.

260: 21  **Stumpf** Carl Stumpf (1848–1936), German psychologist and philosopher. In his *Über den psychologischen Ursprung der Raumvorstellung* (1873), he argued that spatial intuition was present at birth and that extension was part of the content of sensation.

261: 4–6  **"In a phenomenon ... form."** *The Critique of Pure Reason*, B34. Russell followed the text of the second edition: "In der Erscheinung nenne ich das, was der Empfindung correspondirt, die *Materie* derselben, dasjenige aber, welches macht, dass das Mannigfaltige der Erscheinung in gewissen Verhältnissen geordnet werden kann, nenne ich die *Form* der Erscheinung" (Kant *1867–68*, 3: 56).

261: 6–9  **"cannot itself be ... sensation."** The italics are Russell's. The original text of *The Critique of Pure Reason*, A20=B34, is: "Da das, worinnen sich die Empfindungen allein ordnen und in gewisse Form gestellt werden können, nicht selbst wiederum Empfindung sein kann, so ist uns zwar die Materie aller Erscheinungen nur *a posteriori* gegeben, die Form derselben aber muss zu ihnen insgesammt im Gemüthe *a priori* bereit liegen, und dahero ⟨sic⟩ abgesondert von aller Empfindung können betrachtet werden" (Kant *1867–68*, 3: 56).

261: 17  **Sigwart** Christoph Sigwart (1830–1904), German philosopher and logician. Russell seems to have made extensive notes on his two-volume *Logik* (1873–78), telling Alys: "I hope thee admired the neatness and ant-like industry betrayed by the abstract of Sigwart! I have found him especially very useful indeed, so far as he is intelligible" (29 Oct. 1894). Only three pages of notes survive (RA 220.010330).

261: 37  **modern psychological fiction** The idea to which Russell refers, that a complete and undistorted knowledge of mental states, desires and motives is not given by introspection, was becoming commonplace by the end of the nineteenth century. It is difficult to be sure which authors Russell has in mind. In his journal

(62: 2), however, he mentions Nezhdanov in Turgenev's *Virgin Soil* in almost exactly this connection. Other authors whom he may have had in mind include George Eliot, George Meredith, Henry James and Fyodor Dostoyevsky. The fact that he originally wrote "novel" and altered it to "fiction" (T259: 37) suggests that even playwrights such as Ibsen, in whose work he was intensely interested, might be included.

262: 5 **Stumpf** Stumpf *1873*, §1 ("Kant's Theorie der subjectiven Formen").

262: 8–10 **Erhardt ... Ideality** Franz Erhardt (1864–1930), German neo-Kantian philosopher. The 300 pages Russell refers to constitute Chap. 5 ("Die Apriorität des Raumes") and Chap. 6 ("Die Idealität des Raumes") of Erhardt's *Metaphysik* (1894). These chapters do not defend the Transcendental Aesthetic as a whole, but only the account of space found there (occupying less than twenty pages of Kant's *Critique*). Russell's extensively annotated copy of Erhardt's *Metaphysik* is in the Russell Archives (REC. ACQ. 521).

262: 19 **Erhardt himself asserts** In the margin of his copy of Erhardt *1894*, 304, Russell wrote "*cf.* p. 345" (the passage to which he refers below at 262: 23–4); and on 305 Russell wrote: "But we must surely assume in the real world what Helmholtz calls 'topographical ⟨sic⟩ moments'."

262: 23–5 **allows ... three dimensions** (p. 352). Against the relevant passage (Erhardt *1894*, 352) Russell wrote: "The various admissions in this section seem to contradict former sections, and reduce apriority of space to mere assertion that in so far as we perceive space it is, like everything else in perception, part of subjective consciousness and in this sense subjective,—which is not a very weighty discovery." Erhardt's discussion continues on the next page, where Russell noted: "The existence of such correlata between our perception and the external world gives space as much objectivity as can belong to anything in consciousness, and reduces Erhardt's contention to a truism, i.e. that what is *in* consciousness is not *out* of consciousness."

262: 23–4 **"metaphysical distance"** Erhardt *1894*, 345: "metaphysischen Abstand". Russell underlined the phrase and wrote in the margin: "Helmholtz's 'topographical ⟨sic⟩ moment' *cf.* p. 304".

262: 28 **Barbara** The mnemonic name of that valid first-figure syllogistic mood in which both premisses and the conclusion are universal affirmative propositions.

262: 40 **the sequel** It is not clear what Russell is referring to here. It does not seem to be any subsequent passage in "Observations on Space and Geometry". The relation of geometry to the empirical sciences (e.g. optics), which he would have found discussed in Clifford *1886*, was important in Poincaré's conventionalism. (Poincaré discussed the relation of optics to geometry in his *1892*, a paper cited by Ward in his metaphysics lectures. See Russell's lecture notebooks, 1: 90.) The connection between the apriority and subjectivity of space, on the one hand, and the apodeictic certainty of geometry, on the other, is discussed by Russell in *An Essay on the Foundations of Geometry* (1897), §§53–5.

263: 2 **Lotze** Rudolph Hermann Lotze (1817–1881), German physician and idealist philosopher. His criticism of non-Euclidean geometry is to be found in his

*Metaphysik* (1879), Bk. II, Chap. 2. In the previous section of "Observations on Space and Geometry", Russell attacked Lotze's criticism. Russell's critique of Lotze is to be found in his *1897*, §§85–97 (where it is considerably expanded).

263: 3–4 **"subscribes almost word for word"** "Zur Vervollständigung und Bestätigung meiner eigenen Darlegungen über die Nicht-Euklidische Geometrie verweise ich vor allen Dingen auf die eingehende Kritik Lotzes (Metaph., 2. Buch, 2. Kap., S. 233–267), welche ich fast Wort für Wort unterschreibe ..." (Erhardt *1894*, 258n.). [Translation: "For supplementation and confirmation of my treatment of non-Euclidean geometry I refer ⟨the reader⟩ chiefly to the detailed critique of Lotze (Metaphysics, Bk. II, Chap. 2, pp. 233–267), which I endorse almost word for word...."]

263: 8 **Lobatchewsky** See A126: 8–11.

263: 17–18 **Helmholtz's unfortunate analogy** See Helmholtz, "On the Origin and Meaning of the Geometrical Axioms" (1876).

263: 37 **as Erhardt does (p. 229)** "Denn nehmen wir an, dass die Kugelbewohner die Kreisbögen fälschlich für gerade Linien halten können, weil sie nach der Voraussetzung von der dritten Dimension, in welcher die Krümmung der Bögen liegt, nichts wissen, so wird diese irrtümliche Auffassung in eben dem Momente zerstört werden, in welchem sie entdecken, dass zwischen bestimmten zwei Punkten der Kugeloberfläche mehr als eine kürzeste Gerade gezogen werden kann" (Erhardt *1894*, 229). [Translation: "For if we suppose that the spheredwellers mistakenly take the arcs of circles for straight lines because they, *ex hypothesi*, know nothing of the third dimension in which the curvature of the arcs lies, this erroneous view will be shattered the moment they discover that between two fixed points on the surface of the sphere more than one shortest straight line can be drawn."] Beside this passage Russell commented: "This begs the question".

263: 39–42 **Lotze's arguments ... repeated (p. 230)** Lotze's arguments are to be found in his *1879*, §§132–3. The same criticism, with references to Lotze, is made in Erhardt *1894*, 230. Against Lotze's two points Russell wrote in the margin of his copy of Erhardt: "Helmholtz should have said, and probably meant, parallel *straight* lines" and "Lotze's arguments referred to rest on a misunderstanding", respectively. More detailed criticism can be found in Russell *1897*, §§93–4. Helmholtz's "careless omission of the word 'straight'" to qualify "parallel lines" is a reference to the following passage: "Parallele Linien würden die Bewohner der Kugel gar nicht kennen. Sie würden behaupten, dass jede beliebige zwei geradeste Linien, gehörig verlängert, sich schliesslich nicht nur in einem, sondern in zwei Punkten schneiden müssten" (Helmholtz *1876*, 305 = *1884*, 2: 9–10). [Translation: "The spheredwellers would not know of parallel lines at all. They would maintain that any two straightest lines whatever must, if suitably extended, ultimately intersect not in one, but in two points."] In his *1897*, 102n., Russell quoted the whole passage, italicizing "geradeste" ["straightest"], to show that in context Helmholtz meant parallel straight lines. Erhardt (*1894*, 230) quoted only the second sentence, omitting the first three words. Lotze and Erhardt both argue that parallel lines (albeit not straight

ones) could be known to the spheredwellers, that is they could know the "parallels"
of latitude.

264: 1 **Erhardt next denies** "... zu behaupten, dass zwischen der Euklidischen
Geometrie und derjenigen der Kugelbewohner ein unvereinbarer Gegensatz be-
stehe, der die alleinige Gültigkeit der ersteren aufhebe, ist ungefähr ebenso richtig,
als wenn man sagen wollte, die Sätze vom Viereck widersprechen denen vom
Dreieck" (Erhardt *1894*, 231). [Translation: "... to maintain that between Euclidean geometry and that of the spheredwellers there exists an irreconcilable antagonism, which the exclusive validity of the first overcomes, is roughly as accurate
as if one were to say that propositions about rectangles contradict those about
triangles."] Russell wrote in the margin of his copy: "This is true, but not the point.
If any one had maintained that we *must* see only triangles by an à priori necessity,
quadrilaterals would be a very awkward fact for him."

264: 28–9 **"was existieren ... sein"** (**p.** 232) "Whatever may be taken as existing
must be a three-dimensional body". The full passage reads: "Zunächst ist die Existenz zweidimensionaler Wesen ein Unding; zweidimensionale Flächen giebt es nur
als eine mathematische Abstraktion und nicht in Wirklichkeit und kann es in
Wirklichkeit auch gar nicht geben. Was existieren soll, muss ein dreidimensionaler
Körper sein, an dem wir zwar Flächen zu unterscheiden imstande sind, die aber
abgesondert für sich keine Existenz haben können" (Erhardt *1894*, 232). [Transla-
tion: "In the first place, the existence of two-dimensional beings is an absurdity.
Two-dimensional planes exist only as a mathematical abstraction and not in reality.
Whatever may be taken as existing must be a three-dimensional body, in which we
are indeed able to distinguish planes, but such as can have no separate existence of
their own."] Russell commented in the margin: "This is a large order."

264: 37 **Next ... an attack** "Helmholtz behauptet nämlich, dass die geometrischen
Axiome gar nicht allein über Verhältnisse des Raumes sprechen, sondern zugleich
auch über das mechanische Verhalten unserer festesten Körper bei Bewegungen ..."
(Erhardt *1894*, 235). [Translation: "Helmholtz claims that the geometrical axioms
treat not only of spatial relations, but also of the mechanical behaviour of solid bodies
in motion...."] Russell commented in the margin: "This view of Helmholtz's is rot".

264: 41–265: 1 **Erhardt professes ... *Mind*, Vol.** III Erhardt *1894*, 237. The
hypothesis that "Geometry applies to ideal objects and becomes empirical the moment it is used of real objects" was suggested by Land, "Kant's Space and Modern
Mathematics" (*1877*, 38–46). Helmholtz admits that such a distinction between a
geometry based on transcendental intuition and physical geometry is possible for a
Kantian, but he argues that, since empirical science is the arbiter of truth, either the
two geometries must be identical or the ideal geometry false. See Helmholtz, "The
Origin and Meaning of Geometrical Axioms (II)" (*1878*, 217–21).

265: 5–10 **And here ... conception"** (**p.** 241) Again "Observations on Space and
Geometry" closely follows Russell's marginal comment, "This paragraph shews a
complete misunderstanding of Meta-Geometry", written sprawlingly down the
right-hand margin of Erhardt *1894*, 241. The passage Russell quotes reads in Ger-

man: "Diese Sätze widersprechen einander natürlicherweise, aber aus dem zu Grunde gelegten Begriff sind sie ganz richtig abgeleitet ..." (Erhardt *1894*, 241).

**265: 12 can be correlated ... by a unique correspondence** The first relative consistency proof for a non-Euclidean geometry was provided for hyperbolic geometry by Beltrami in 1868. But the decisive contribution was made three years later by Klein *1871*, who recognized the projective nature of the models devised by Beltrami (now known as "Beltrami-Klein models").

**265: 14–17 Finally ... Klein ... to him.** "Um nun zunächst auf diesen allerletzten Punkt einzugehen, so muss ich offen bekennen, dass ich mir unter einem gekrümmten Raume absolut nichts zu denken vermag; ich verstehe zwar sehr gut, inwiefern man von dem Krümmungsmasse einer Fläche sprechen und demselben je nach der Beschaffenheit der Fläche einen positiven oder negativen Wert beilegen kann. Was aber der Begriff des Krümmungsmasses bei dem Raume bedeuten soll, ist mir völlig unverständlich" (Erhardt *1894*, 244). [Translation: "Now to take this final point first, I must candidly confess that by a curved space I am able to understand absolutely nothing. To be sure, I understand very well the extent to which one can speak of the measure of curvature of a surface and ascribe to this measure a positive or negative value, according to the nature of the surface. But what the concept of the measure of curvature of space is supposed to mean is completely unintelligible to me."] Russell's marginal note reads: "The word Krümmungsmaass is, as Klein observes, very misleading—but the projective treatment of the subject makes the *idea* perfectly plain."

Felix Klein (*1849–1925*) was a German mathematician noted for his work on geometry and the theory of functions. His influential "Erlanger Programm" (*1872*) proposed the use of transformation groups as a means of systematizing the study of different systems of geometry. Klein's criticism of the term "Krümmungsmass" ("measure of curvature"), which he said "lässt er einem Missverständnisse freien Lauf" ["gives free rein to a misunderstanding"], occurs in his *Nicht-Euklidische Geometrie* (*1893*, I: 159–60). ("Krümmungsmaass" is now usually spelled with a single "a", but Russell follows Klein's spelling here.)

# 42  The Logic of Geometry

**267: 22–3 ascribe an adjective to space** Russell, following Bradley *1893*, Chap. 2, uses "adjective" to refer to properties. In his *1897*, x–xi, he seems to use "adjective" to mean "essential property", for "adjective" is used on the pages cited to summarize the contents of §§61 and 80, both of which mention "essential properties" but not "adjectives". At one place (*1897*, 15) he writes that axioms "in the most desirable form" are "adjectives of the conception of space". The two uses are, of course, compatible because geometrical axioms involve the essential properties of space.

**268: 2 Euclid gives the requisite axiom** It is not known with certainty which edition of Euclid Russell used. Russell's citation of this axiom as "Euclid's 8th" (275: 33) and the form in which he quotes it, however, suggest his edition was that by

Robert Potts, which was recommended for the Cambridge Mathematical Tripos. Potts (*1845*, 6) gives the eighth axiom as "Magnitudes which coincide with one another, that is, which exactly fill the same space, are equal to one another." T. L. Heath (Euclid *1908*, I: 155) lists this as Common Notion No. 4 (or Axiom 7) but in this form: "Things which coincide with one another are equal to one another." In his commentary he notes that Euclid's use of it in the proof of Prop. 4 of Bk. I "leaves no room for doubt that he regarded one figure as actually *moved* and *placed upon* the other" (Euclid *1908*, I: 225). This is the point of Russell's remark at 268: 5–6.

268: 25 **Helmholtz** See A126: 36. The position referred to here is developed in his "Ueber die thatsächlichen Grundlagen der Geometrie" (Helmholtz *1882–95*, 2: 610–17). Russell *1897*, §§66–71, offers a detailed discussion and criticism of Helmholtz's position.

268: 25 **Erdmann** Benno Erdmann (1851–1921), German mathematician and philosopher. Erdmann defends the same empiricist position as Helmholtz in Chap. 2 of *Die Axiome der Geometrie: eine philosophische Untersuchung der Riemann–Helmholtz'schen Raumtheorie* (1877). Russell *1897*, §§74–82, criticizes his defence of it.

270: 15 **Riemann and Helmholtz** For Riemann see A260: 4–5. In his dissertation, *Ueber die Hypothesen, welche der Geometrie zu Grunde liegen* (1867), Riemann assumed the truth of the quadratic formula for the infinitesimal arc length. Helmholtz proved it in "Ueber die Thatsachen, die der Geometrie zum Grunde liegen" in 1868 (Helmholtz *1882–95*, 2: 618–39).

270: 28 **Pangeometers** Non-Euclidean geometers. The term seems to have originated with Lobatchewsky *1856*.

270: 31 **Helmholtz's view** It is found in his "Ueber die thatsächlichen Grundlagen der Geometrie". Russell *1897*, §§69–73, criticizes it.

271: 8 **Helmholtz mockingly** See "The Origin and Meaning of Geometrical Axioms (II)" for his discussion of "physical geometry and the supposed transcendental geometry" (Helmholtz *1878*, 220 = *1882–95*, 2: 652).

272: 6 **Kant's case of right and left gloves** See §13 of his *Prolegomena to Any Future Metaphysics* (1783) for his discussion of this and related examples. Right and left gloves are congruent, though their difference cannot be made intelligible by reference to any concept but only by means of intuition, which shows their relationship to space as a whole. Kant uses these examples in an attempt to show that things-in-themselves do not have spatial qualities.

272: 11 **How do we measure the equality of solids …?** Russell had asked C. P. Sanger about Euclid's answer to this question in a letter of 29 September 1894.

274: 17 **James says** In quoting W. James, Russell inverted the sentences in the original, omitting "And" from the beginning of the first sentence and the following from the end of the second sentence: "and the mind must get the immediate feeling of an outstanding *plus*" (James *1890*, 2: 152). The passage is marked in Russell's copy with two vertical lines and the instruction "Quote".

274: 42 **Stumpf** See A260: 21.

275: 20 **Monodromy** Helmholtz gives the axiom in "Ueber die thatsächlichen Grundlagen der Geometrie" (*1882-95*, 2: 615); Russell *1897*, 24, gives a translation.

275: 33 **Euclid's 8th axiom** See A268: 2. (Heath [Euclid *1908*, 1: 155] gives "The whole is greater than the part" as Common Notion No. 5 [or Axiom 8], which is obviously not what Russell had in mind.)

275: 41 **Helmholtz's other axiom** While Helmholtz's axiom set for geometries of constant curvature (*1866, 1868*) contains a distinct axiom of monodromy, it does not contain a distinct axiom to the effect that congruence is "independent of the course pursued in bringing it about". It is likely, however, that Russell has in mind Helmholtz's second axiom, which concerns rigid bodies. This axiom, if shorn of its existential claims (already criticized by Russell), asserts that the relation between the $2n$ coordinates of any point-pair in a rigid body is the same for any congruent point-pair and is independent of the movement of the rigid body. See Helmholtz *1882-95*, 2: 622.

276: 27-9 **"In a space ... (coordinates)."** Helmholtz: "Im Raume von $n$ Dimensionen ist der Ort jedes Punktes bestimmbar durch Abmessung von $n$ continuirlich veränderlichen, von einander unabhängigen Grössen ..." (*1882-95*, 2: 614).

277: 13-14 **Riemann's dissertation** Riemann *1867*.

277: 21 **colour- and tone-systems** Riemann merely mentions the colours as forming a manifold. Helmholtz *1876*, 309-10 (= *1884*, 2: 16-17), during the course of a discussion of Riemann's work, develops the examples more fully.

281: 2 **Euclid's axiom** Potts (*1845*, 6) gives as Axiom 10, "Two straight lines cannot inclose a space." Heath (Euclid *1908*, 1: 154-6) gives no such axiom but admits that this requirement was a common interpolation and one which Euclid himself relied on (*1908*, 1: 195-6).

281: 36-7 **the ordinary ambiguity in angular measurement** This is the ambiguity in measuring the angle with rays $\overrightarrow{O\,A}$ and $\overrightarrow{O\,B}$. This angle, if taken to be between zero and $2\pi$ radians, is $\theta$. It may equally well be $2\pi+\theta$, or $4\pi+\theta$, or in general $2\pi n+\theta$, if $n$ full rotations around $O$ are allowed (a full rotation is $2\pi$ radians). In ordinary language, the ambiguity is that one cannot in principle know whether any full rotations have preceded the angle to be measured and are to be included in its measurement.

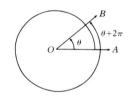

282: 30-6 **Just as ... *nothing else.*** The parenthetical question mark after "sensation" is not in James's text. Russell also added one in the margin of his copy of James *1890*. The full passage reads: "But just as, in the field of quantity, the relation between two numbers is another number, so *in the field of space the relations are facts of the same order with the facts they relate. If these latter be patches in the circle of vision, the former are certain other patches between them.* When we speak of the relation of direction of two points toward each other, we mean simply the sensation of the line that joins the two points together. *The line is the relation;* feel it and you feel the relation, see it and you see the relation; nor can you in any conceivable way think the latter except by imagining the former (however vaguely), or describe or indicate the one except by pointing to the other. And the moment you have imagined the line, the relation stands before you in all its completeness, with nothing further to be done. Just so the relation of *direction* between two lines is identical with the peculiar sensation of shape of the space enclosed between them. This is commonly called an angular relation. ¶If these relations are sensations, no less so are the relations of position. *The relation of position between the top and bottom points of a vertical line is that line*, and nothing else" (James *1890*, 2: 149–50).

This passage is heavily marked in Russell's copy. In the margin, against James's claim that *"The line is the relation"*, Russell wrote: "how about relations of magnitude, i.e. ratios, of lines etc. (*v.* p. 151)".

284: 1 **that of Cayley and Klein** Arthur Cayley (1821–1895), British mathematician and Sadlerian Professor of Mathematics at Cambridge, 1863–95. His main work was on invariants and the theory of matrices. For Klein, see A265: 14. Cayley (*1859*), and following him Klein (*1871*), defined a distance-function on point-pairs of projective space. Cayley's distance-function was unusual in that it was complex-valued, i.e. it is always the case that for some point-pairs the "distance" between the points will have a non-zero imaginary part. Klein demonstrated that Cayley's distance-function, when restricted to an appropriately chosen region of projective space, does define a real-valued metric function. See Russell *1897*, §§34–7, for more extensive criticism of the projective definition of distance.

284: 22–3 **Von Staudt's projective construction** Karl Georg Christian von Staudt (1798–1867), German mathematician, whom Russell (*1903*, 421) hails as "the true founder of non-quantitative Geometry". His projective construction may be found in §8 of *Geometrie der Lage* (1847); Russell *1897*, §§112–14, reproduces it.

285: 41 **Hume's contentions as to the *minimum sensibile*** See A253: 35–6.

## 43 Review of Lechalas

288: 29–32 **Kant's antinomies ... Transcendental Analytic** For Kant's antinomies see *The Critique of Pure Reason* (1781), A421–60 = B448–88. It is the first antinomy which is relevant to Lechalas's argument (see Lechalas *1896*, 142ff.). Zeno's arguments, as well as Russell's later view of them, can be found in Russell's *Our Knowledge of the External World* (1914), Chaps. 6 and 7; Lechalas discusses them in §2 of Chap. 5. For the "solution" provided by Kant in the "Transcendental Analytic", see his *Critique*, A129–211 = B232–56, and Lechalas *1896*, Chap. 6, §1. 288: 30 **the author is led to declare** Lechalas *1896*, 140–1.

## 44 The *À Priori* in Geometry

291: 17 **modern logic has shown** Russell refers here primarily to Bradley's work in logic. His analysis of necessary propositions is given in *The Principles of Logic* (*1883*, 181–94 = *1922*, 197–208).

291:22 **Bradley points out** Bradley *1883*, 42n. = *1922*, 43n.

291:40-1 **the ground which Kant seeks** The two methods which Russell outlines were known as the analytic and synthetic methods, respectively. In his *Prolegomena to Any Future Metaphysics* (1783), Kant proposed using the terms "regressive" for the analytic method and "progressive" for the synthetic method (terms Russell adopted in his *1907*, using "regressive method" to characterize his own work on the foundations of mathematics). The analytic method dominates Kant's *Prolegomena*, while the synthetic method is employed throughout (at least) the first edition of *The Critique of Pure Reason* (1781). Kemp Smith *1918*, 44-50, has a full discussion of the differences between the two methods.

292:28 **I shall contend, with Kant** See Kant, *The Critique of Pure Reason*, A26-30 = B42-5.

292:41-2 **I use "experience" ... Bradley** Bradley's two most characteristic doctrines about experience are that experience is an indissoluble amalgam of content and awareness and that the real consists entirely and exclusively of experience. See *Appearance and Reality, 1893*, 144, 241-2, 455-60 (= *1930*, 127, 213, 403-7, respectively).

293:9 **Gauss** Carl Friedrich Gauss (1777-1855), German mathematician. Gauss's earliest results in non-Euclidean geometry are contained in his letters, which were not published until the 1860s (Gauss *1860-65*). Russell *1897*, 10, gives an account of them.

293:13-14 **by Helmholtz ... axioms were empirical** This view is to be found in all of Helmholtz's writings on geometry, but see especially "On the Origin and Meaning of Geometrical Axioms" (1876) for his argument in support of this position.

294:8 **The requisite axiom is given by Euclid** See A268:2.

294:20 **Helmholtz and Erdmann** See A268:25.

294:37 **the use of imaginaries** See A284:1.

296:32-4 **"In a space ... (co-ordinates)."** For the original German, see A276:27-9.

300:39 **James** See A282:30-6.

302:18 **Transcendental Aesthetic** That part of *The Critique of Pure Reason* (A19-49 = B33-91) in which Kant attempts to determine the à priori elements in sensory knowledge.

303:35 **the doctrine of the plenum** The doctrine that space is completely occupied.

303:42 **Bosanquet's** *Logic* Bernard Bosanquet (1848-1923), British neo-Hegelian philosopher. Chap. 7 of Bk. II of his *Logic* (1888) is entitled "The Relation of Knowledge to Its Postulates"; see the *Logic*, 211-12.

304:32 **difficulties of atomism ... Physics** Russell takes up these difficulties, already alluded to in 267:38-41 and 301:5ff., in a number of papers in *Collected Papers* 2, e.g. the "Review of Hannequin", "On Some Difficulties of Continuous Quantity" and "On the Relations of Number and Quantity".

## 45 Note on Economic Theory

309: 3 **abstinence from pleasure** The abstinence theory was the most important contribution to economic analysis of Nassau Senior, who advanced it as a justification for the income earned by capital. The theory attempted to refute the classical labour theory of value by making capital as well as labour responsible for the real costs which contribute to value. Marshall adopted the concept of abstinence but substituted the neutral word "waiting" (*1895*, 314–15).

308: 8 **rent of ability** Rent of ability was much debated among social scientists in the late 1880s and 1890s. Russell follows Marshall (*1895*, 702–4) in defining this aspect of rent as the product of exceptional or rare natural abilities which are nontransferable and therefore cannot be nationalized. The idea of a rent of ability was attacked by the Fabians, who, denying its utility in economic analysis, claimed that such a rent either was a reward for superior status or depended upon supply and demand, and thus was seldom morally legitimate. Russell appears to side with Marshall.

309: 13–22 **on the margin ... marginal self-denial** Russell is employing the theory of marginal utility, which was developed in the 1870s independently by Jevons, the Austrian economist Carl Menger, and the French economist Léon Walras to replace the labour theory of value. The theory of diminishing marginal utility was first employed to define the equilibrium position of consumers and to justify the assumption that demand curves slope downwards. Each consumer achieves an optimum allocation of his resources when a given unit of expenditure in one direction yields the same increment of satisfaction as in any other direction. If the price of any good (say) rises, less of it must be purchased in conformity with the equi-marginal rule. Subsequently, the marginal principle was extended to form the marginal productivity theory of distribution.

309: 14 **Consumer's Rent** A concept developed by Marshall (*1895*, 200–9) to explain the difference between the actual price of a commodity and the amount a consumer would pay to avoid being deprived of it. Marshall hoped that, by a judicious application of taxes and bounties, the consumer's rent available to the whole community would be increased, and that it would serve as the basis of a theory of welfare economics. In this he was disappointed, although the principle is still utilized in, for example, benefit-cost analysis.

## 46 German Social Democracy, as a Lesson in Political Tactics

312: 10 **an Independent Labour Party** The name of the mildly socialist, non-revolutionary party which Keir Hardie created in Britain in 1893. Russell uses the term to denote any labour party that will avoid alliance with parties that do not primarily represent the working class.

312: 11 **Marx and Lassalle** Karl Marx (1818–1883), social philosopher, author of *Das Kapital* (3 vols., 1867–94) and advocate of proletarian revolution. His most significant organization, the International Working Men's Association, was founded in 1864. Ferdinand Lassalle (1825–1864) formed in 1863 the first broadly-based German socialist organization, the Universal German Working Men's Association (a forerunner of the Social Democratic Party). Until the early 1870s his influence in Germany was much more widespread than Marx's. Lassalle diverged from Marx on a number of important issues. He wished to advance German, as opposed to international, working-class interests and believed that universal suffrage obtained without revolution would lead to extensive reforms for German workers. (See Marx, "Critique of the Gotha Programme", in Marx *1978*, 533–4, 538.) At a theoretical level, Russell claimed, Lassalle's "more thorough Hegelianism" and consequently his "respect for the State" separated him from Marx and the Marxist Social Democrats (*1896*, 51). See also A73: 35.

312: 29  **party of uncompromising opposition**  The Marxist domination of the Social Democratic Party was finally achieved in 1891, when the Erfurt Programme was adopted—thereby eradicating the last vestige of the Lassalleans.

313: 22  **the Independent Labour Party**  I.e. the Universal German Working Men's Association.

313: 23  **Bismarck**  Otto von Bismarck (1815–1898): architect of German unification, 1864–71; Chief Minister of Prussia, 1862–71; Chancellor of the German Empire, 1871–90.

313: 26  **the necessary taxation**  During 1862–65 the Progressives refused to pass the military budget for the royal army. Bismarck collected the taxes illegally, was popularly vindicated by the Austro-Prussian War, and received retroactive sanction by the passage of a Bill of Indemnity in 1866.

313: 27  **the Progressives**  They were split by Bismarck's victorious wars. The minority that refused to support the Indemnity Bill formed the German Progressive Party after 1867, while the majority helped to create the National Liberal Party.

313: 40  **decennial period of crises**  Developed by such mid-Victorian economists as Jevons and John Mills, the theory traced the occurrence of economic crises every ten years from 1836 to 1866 to abnormal fluctuations in credit.

314: 10–11  *Prussian* **constitution**  For the plutocratic, three-class nature of the Prussian constitution, see Russell *1896*, 86–7.

314: 12–13  *Imperial* **constitution ... appearance of democracy**  The Reichstag's democratic character was largely vitiated since it could not control the Chancellor or military expenditure, and it shared the legislature with the Bundesrat (an assembly of ambassadors from the various states from which the executive of the Empire was chosen).

314: 28  **the radicals**  Progressives who were prepared by the 1890s to support collectivist reforms such as those advocated by the New Liberals in Britain during the same period.

314: 41  **the Antisemites**  The popular designation for the Christian Social Party, led by Adolf Stöcker.

315: 1  **Saxon Diet**  For events in Saxony, see Russell *1896*, 86.

315: 42 **Bismarck's Socialist Law** The legislation passed in October 1878 restricting socialist political activity while permitting socialists to sit in the Reichstag. The legislation was renewed periodically until 1890. Russell discusses it in his *1896*, 92–115 (Lecture IV).

315: 43 **Second Ballots** In electoral districts where no party won an absolute majority during a general election, run-off elections were held between the two parties that had led the polling on the first ballot.

316: 10–11 **Wolsey's diplomacy ... according to Bishop Creighton** Thomas Wolsey (1471?–1530), cardinal and statesman. As Lord Chancellor from 1515 to 1529 under Henry VIII, Wolsey was the architect of British foreign policy until his disgrace in 1529. His fall was occasioned by the ultimate collapse of his balance of power policies and failure to get an annulment of the King's marriage to Catherine of Aragon. Russell had read Mandell Creighton's *Cardinal Wolsey* (1888) in October 1895.

316: 13 **the Empire** The Holy Roman Empire.

316: 18 **France ... in 1793** By spring 1793 revolutionary France, governed by the National Convention, had been invaded by allied troops of the First Coalition, which was composed of Britain, Austria, Spain, Holland and Sardinia.

317: 14–15 **more or less Socialistic measures** Bismarck, from 1881 to 1889, enacted numerous reforms (such as accident insurance and old age pensions) intended to kill socialism with kindness.

317: 18 **he spoke** Bismarck's speech of 26 November 1884, as quoted by Russell *1896*, 135.

317: 29–30 **failure of Lassalle's negotiations with Bismarck** Lassalle met with Bismarck a number of times in 1863 and early 1864 in an attempt to convince him to grant universal suffrage and state credit to workers' cooperatives.

317: 33–5 **Von Vollmar ... pressing reforms.** Georg von Vollmar (1850–1922), Social Democratic leader in Bavaria. He anticipated the revisionist leader, Eduard Bernstein, in opposing orthodox Marxism by advocating, rather than revolution, cooperation with existing radical parties to achieve gradual reform. For the five reforms, see Russell *1896*, 134–5.

## 47 The Uses of Luxury

320: 1 **the arguments of Hobson** J. A. Hobson (1858–1940), economist and New Liberal theorist, claimed that capitalists oversaved—primarily by paying low wages for workers. Workers thereby lacked the purchasing power to buy all the goods produced, and the resulting underconsumption was the root cause of depression. Hobson thus challenged a central tenet of economists from Adam Smith to J. S. Mill: that supply could not exceed demand. Unlike capitalists obsessed with saving, the aristocracy had promoted a high degree of purchasing power by lavish spending. In this paper, however, Russell does not wish to follow Hobson in arguing that extreme inequality in the distribution of incomes would lead to depression and was immoral.

Hobson's remedy was to redistribute wealth by reform, which would increase general consumption and not permit luxury for a few.

320: 19 **psychological novelists** Russell probably had in mind such novelists as George Eliot and Henry James, with whose works he was well acquainted. See also A261: 37.

320: 27 **Dr. Watts** Isaac Watts, D.D. (1674–1748), wrote in Song IV of *Divine Songs* (1715):

> Whene'er I take my Walks abroad,
> How many Poor I see?
> What shall I render to my God
> For all his Gifts to me?

320: 41–2 **Mr. Tate's Gallery of Modern British Art** This is a wry glance at the art collection of Sir Henry Tate (1819–1899), the benefactor. His collection, formed at Park Hill, Streatham, was the basis of the Tate Gallery when it opened in 1897.

321: 6–7 **"Mr. Whistler ... can't"** This is probably not a quotation but Russell's report of common opinion. James Abbott McNeill Whistler (1834–1903), whose exhibition of lithographs had opened at the Fine Arts Society in December 1895, was notorious for his inability to complete his canvases, while his critics complained that those he did complete were unfinished. Russell may have had in mind the protracted and well-publicized Eden case, then in appeal, in which Sir William Eden sued Whistler for delivery of a commissioned portrait of Eden's wife.

321: 15 **Poet Close** Lord Palmerston (Henry John Temple, 1784–1865) is commended for attempting as Prime Minister to give the poet John Close (1816–1891) a Civil List pension. Close's talent was negligible, but he convinced enough patrons of his worth that the prime ministerial action was taken. When in 1861 Close's poetry was ridiculed in the London papers, the pension was withdrawn. The poets laureate Alfred Tennyson (1809–1892) and Alfred Austin (1835–1913) owed their "butt of malmsey wine" to the fact that patronage entails risk.

321: 30–1 **Watteau ... Pater's description** Walter Pater writes in the "imaginary portrait", "A Prince of Court Painters: Extracts from an Old French Journal" (1885): "Antony Watteau reproduces that gallant world, those patched and powdered ladies and fine cavaliers, so much to its own satisfaction, partly because he despises it ..." (Pater *1900–01*, 8: 33).

321: 34 **Bedford Park** The Bedford Park garden suburb, just north of Turnham Green station in London, was designed by Norman Shaw and begun in 1875. It was noted for its artistic population.

321: 37–8 **an artist of my acquaintance** At this time Russell was acquainted with James Abbott McNeill Whistler, Walter Sickert (1860–1942), William Rothenstein (1872–1945), and Roger Fry (1866–1934). Whistler Russell had known in Paris, Sickert had been a contributor to the *Cambridge Observer* (with which Russell had been associated), Rothenstein had painted Alys's portrait, and Fry had designed Russell and Alys's neo-classical bookplate.

322: 7 **James** The reference is to the philosopher William James (see A66: 34), whose works Russell was then reading and whose fresh turn of phrase was remarkable. In *The Principles of Psychology* James speaks of how a habitual judgment is overturned: "But its overturning is due to a back-door and not to a front-door process" (*1890*, 2: 673).

322: 21 **Darwin** Charles Darwin (1809–1882). Although by the mid-1890s Russell looked upon himself as a socialist, he never believed in complete equality of incomes. On 8–9 October 1894 he had written to Alys that such income equality might "cut off all the flowers of civilization—The Shelleys and Darwins and so on, who could not have existed at all if they'd had to work for their living...." Russell reiterated this idea, once again instancing Darwin, in his *1951a*, 216–17. Nevertheless, he added, geniuses would have to have independent means of support if "universal mediocrity" were not to prevail and progress to cease.

323: 3 **"noble mind"** Milton uses the phrase in "Lycidas", l. 71: "(That last infirmity of noble mind)".

323: 12–13 **"God's ... the world"** The line is from Robert Browning's *Pippa Passes*, Pt. I, ll. 117–18.

323: 20–1 **"forms ... immortality"** Shelley, *Prometheus Unbound*, I. Russell marked in his copy these lines spoken by the Fourth Spirit (*1885*, 2: 87).

## 48 Mechanical Morals and the Moral of Machinery

325: 1–2 **the Club** The Cambridge and Westminster Club. See the headnote to Paper *47*.

325: 33 **Malthus and Darwin** For Malthus see A28: 14; for Darwin see A322: 21.

325: 40–1 **"the more ... better fare"** "The more the merrier; the fewer, the better fare" is how Palsgrave *1852*, 885, gives the complete proverb.

327: 11–12 **the struggle for existence ... past** Like other New Liberal theorists, Russell's dismissal of this popular Spencerianism was an attack on such Social Darwinist writers as Benjamin Kidd and Karl Pearson, who maintained struggles between nations and races are inevitable. See "The Politics of a Biologist", *Collected Papers* 12.

327: 28 **cheapening of ocean transportation** From the 1870s on, technological innovations in metal steamers, such as the replacement of the paddle by the screw and the introduction of compound engines, had revolutionized ocean transport, allowing e.g. for the rapid inundation of Europe by cheap American wheat.

327: 30 **morality which Nelson taught** When in 1793 Horatio Nelson assumed command of the *Agamemnon* to fight against Jacobin France, he is said to have exhorted one of his midshipmen: "First, you must always implicitly obey orders ... secondly, you must consider every man your enemy who speaks ill of your king; and, thirdly, you must hate a Frenchman as you do the devil" (Southey *1909*, 59).

327: 37 **modern love of arbitration** Arbitration as a means of preventing wars was increasingly advocated by the numerous European and American peace societies since the Napoleonic wars. Interest in arbitration was increased beginning in the middle of the century by a rapidly growing fear among many groups in various western countries that most wars in the future might well become world wars. The focus of peace advocates on arbitration was strengthened in 1889 by the formation of two groups, the Inter Parliamentary Union and the Universal Peace Congress, both of which met annually. Popular faith in arbitration as a method of avoiding conflict reached its peak before 1914 in The Hague Peace Conferences of 1899 and 1907.

328: 1–2 **Mary Wollstonecraft ... James Watt** *A Vindication of the Rights of Woman* (1792) by Mary Wollstonecraft (1759–1797) attacked the repressive conventions of the day. James Watt (1736–1819), the Scottish engineer, substantially advanced steam-engine technology, establishing his main patents from the late 1760s to the early 1780s.

328: 15–16 **Socialists are never tired of vilifying Malthus** Socialists, particularly Marx and Engels, viewed the Malthusian claim—that population growth outstrips growth in food production by a geometrical to an arithmetical ratio—merely as a cynical rationalization by capitalists who wished to keep wages low. Moreover, they argued that Malthus's view of human nature was false. Marx claimed that the problem of poverty was caused not by over-population but by the inequitable distribution of goods, inevitable under capitalist conditions of production. Russell claims that most socialists miss the point in their attack on Malthus by failing to grasp that it is the law of increasing return that renders Malthus obsolete—although this criticism is to be found in Marx.

328: 33 **"wise saws ... instances"** Shakespeare, *As You Like It*, ii.vii.156.

## 49 Review of Schmöle

330: 8 **Court at Versailles in 1871** The Prussian victory over France in 1870 gave Bismarck the opportunity to create the German Empire. The ceremony marking its inception was held at Versailles in January 1871. Prussia dominated the Empire with the King of Prussia as Kaiser.

330: 17 **Dr. Max Hirsch** Max Hirsch (1832–1905), a publisher and Progressive politician. In 1868 he and his fellow Progressive, Franz Duncker (1822–1888), founded the Hirsch–Duncker trade unions, which existed until 1933. Opposed to class conflict and committed to reform by cooperation with the government, these unions never attracted many workers and, after 1875, were overshadowed by Marxist unions.

330: 20 **Schweitzer** Johann Baptist von Schweitzer (1833–1875) was a prominent follower of Lassalle (for whom see A312: 11). In 1867, three years after Lassalle's death, Schweitzer became President of the Universal German Working Men's Association. The trade unions he established worked with Bismarck until 1871, when Schweitzer was expelled from the Association because he allegedly collaborated too closely with the Chancellor. By 1875 Schweitzer's unions had become Marxist bodies affiliated to the Social Democratic Party.

330: 24 **his friendly societies** A comparison to the German equivalent of the mutual insurance companies founded by British workers to provide assistance to members and their families in financial distress.

331: 29 **Mr. and Mrs. Sidney Webb's book** *The History of Trade Unionism* (1894). During the autumn of 1894 Alys sent Russell her abstracts of the Webbs' book. He found these summaries so interesting that he revised his prejudice against Mrs. Webb, whom he had described to Alys as one who could "never become first-rate, or more than a shadow of her husband" (5 Sept. 1894). Later Russell's view became so complimentary that he claimed "she had the ideas and he did the work" (*1967*, 95).

# Textual Notes

# Textual Principles and Methods

RUSSELL'S WRITINGS VARY greatly, not only in subject matter but also in respect to the form in which the text survives. Some items survive only in print; others exist only in manuscript. A large number are preserved in both manuscript and printed forms, sometimes more than one of each; in certain cases typescripts or proofs are also available. In addition, Russell made marginal notes in his own copies of some of his publications. Thus the preparation of this edition involves a wide variety of editorial decisions. The purpose of the first section below is to indicate the main principles and methods which are being followed, with particular reference to this volume. Later volumes will contain a statement of any special textual problems which apply therein. The second section describes the main methods used to produce a text as authentic in content as possible and containing the minimum of inconsistencies in the handling of formal matters. The final section explains and justifies the copy-text decisions made in this volume. A separate "Guide to the Textual Notes" begins on page 455.

## I. PRINCIPLES

Since Wood's widely read biography (*1957*, 50), Russell has been seen, somewhat incorrectly, as a writer who rarely revised his drafts. He himself claimed that, if the content needed serious revision, he would compose the work anew; otherwise, no amount of revision, he had found through experience, would improve the style (*1956b*, 194–5). "Of course", he said, "I always compose each sentence fully in my head before beginning to write it out" (*1930a*, 11). This description of his writing process is not borne out by most of the papers printed in the present volume, or by many in succeeding volumes, despite its applicability to his later, popular articles. Instead, the early papers reveal considerable revision. Russell acknowledged as much for his early career: "I wrote very carefully, with many corrections, until I had passed the age of thirty, i.e. down to and including the year 1902" (*1930a*, 11). Revisions in manuscript are not the only place in which Russell's second thoughts are found; revisions in printed texts raise the problem of the choice of the text to be printed when both manuscript and printed versions are available. Thus editorial decisions have to be taken both in preparing a text for printing here and also in indicating textual variants.

### Substantives and Accidentals

Any text has two main features: its substantives and its accidentals. The substantive features are the words themselves and their order; the accidental features are the ways in which the words are spelled, divided, capitalized, italicized, punctuated and arranged in paragraphs. Changes in the accidentals generally do not fundamentally affect the meaning of the text, although on occasion they clearly do. The substantives and accidentals of holograph manuscripts are seldom a problem for editorial theory; there is little disputing the original authority of what is in the author's hand. Where print is concerned, however, the authority of any variants is doubtful, unless they appear in the author's hand on preserved proofs. Knowledge of an author's thought and style, as well as of publishing circumstances, usually suffices for editorial decisions on the probable authority of the substantive variants. When such decisions on the author's intentions are made, and provided a work's historical place in his *oeuvre* is respected, the substantive variants to be adopted are the final ones, because they reflect the author's settled judgment on what he wished to say.

Accidental variants, which can be important, are more troublesome. In his manuscript an author will place the substantives in a pattern of accidentals that is his own. He may also alter some of his accidentals in the publishing process; but the difficulty arises that others involved in that process may make other alterations.

Russell brought to the expression of his thought a system of accidentals that is, for the most part, settled as early as 1895. Although in typescripts and proofs he would make occasional changes to his original punctuation, the accidentals of his first drafts seem to have been carefully considered. The sense and elegance of his expression are enhanced by his precision in punctuation. For him, one of the merits of an outstanding literary style is its rhythm: "All the artistic qualities of writing (except in China) are intended to appeal to the ear, not to the eye, and can therefore only be appreciated either by reading aloud or at least by pronouncing each word to oneself as one reads" (Russell *1927*, p. E1). He remarks on the importance of rhythm in all of his writings on composition.

### Russell's Writing and Proofreading Practices

Following standard practice, we use the term "copy-text" to refer to the document which appears to be closest to the author's accidentals. The choice of this document is affected both by Russell's writing conventions and the available versions of the text. Two main cases arise.

(1). When both manuscript and printed versions are available, the manuscript is designated as the copy-text because of the certainty of its accidentals (as opposed to the possible intervention by other hands in the printing process). It supplies the kinds of accidentals which we call "mechanical": spelling, word-division, distinctions of mention from use, italicization and accenting of foreign terms, the display (if any) of quotations and lists of points for discussion, parenthetical commas (which appear either in pairs or not at all), and the authorial equivalent of house style in punctuation. "Non-mechanical accidentals" covers all other kinds, such as changes in punctuation designed to alter sense or style, paragraphing, and the capitalization of concept words. These accidentals have been adopted from the printed version, *rather than* the manuscript, when internal evidence of the text or external evidence (such as correspondence) makes it likely that Russell passed proofs.

(2). When two or more printed versions survive but no manuscript or typescript, the printed version over which he seems to have devoted the most care is the one chosen as the copy-text. Thus, for instance, a version appearing in one of his own collections of articles is usually preferred to an earlier, periodical version of the same article. These general copy-text decisions are supported by an analysis of his writing and proofreading habits.

As a proofreader Russell was especially watchful, no doubt in part because he was accustomed to the demands of proofreading mathematics. Several of his corrected book proofs are extant, from *The Philosophy of Leibniz* (1900) to *Portraits from Memory* (1956). They show precise corrections of departures from his manuscript or typescript. Very few typographical errors escape his notice. Mere house style he lets stand, but he continues to revise his punctuation, especially for restrictive and non-restrictive phrases and clauses. The few galley proofs of his essays that survive (they are confined chiefly to publications in *The Dial* in the 1920s) tend to confirm the conclusion, drawn from his book proofs, that when Russell read proofs, his scrutinizing and revising of them were such that the printed texts, where they depart from his manuscript, reflect his final intentions both for substantives and for non-mechanical accidentals. His own confidence in the authority of his printed texts is expressed in a letter to his publisher written in his ninety-seventh year. Having received requests to reprint some of his writings with alterations (presumably of substantives), he was "anxious that my writings not be altered" and asked that permission not be given to do so (4 Aug. 1968, George Allen & Unwin).

*Paragraphing and Spelling*

Russell also had strong opinions about his paragraphing. For example, when he discovered in his proofs that the paragraphing of *The Problems of Philosophy* (1912) had been altered, he complained to Gilbert Murray, an editor of the Home University Library:

> In some cases it didn't seem to matter much, but in others it destroyed the style. I generally put quite a different sort of sentence at the end of a paragraph from any that I should put in the middle—I make the ones in the middle obviously incomplete. I hope Perris ⟨the house editor⟩ or whoever it is won't insist. (9 Nov. 1911, Bodleian Library)

Even about spelling Russell held firm views. He once said: "... there is no point whatever in being able to spell anything.... If it is thought that print, at least, ought to be spelled conventionally, it is always possible to keep ⟨proof⟩readers for the purpose" (*1928*, 95–6). Nevertheless, he was very conventional in his spelling, and he preferred English forms.

## II.  REGULARIZATION

The purpose of regularizing and house styling the copy-texts is to maximize authenticity and minimize inconsistency in mechanical accidentals. A serious attempt is made here to restore Russell's mechanicals in his printed copy-texts, while the regularizing and house styling of his manuscript copy-texts is limited to removing features that would prove typographically distracting. The texts are nevertheless relatively unmodernized. We discuss house style relating to the papers as a whole before considering the problems specific to manuscripts and to printed copy-texts.

*House Style*

Typographical modifications have been made to various features of the copy-texts as printed here. Titles of papers are given a consistent capitalization, and any terminal period removed. (The original form of the title is given either in the headnote to a paper or in the textual notes.) Section headings are centred and sub-section headings italicized. Figures below 100 are spelled out, and the number of dots in ellipses is modernized.

Quotations in Russell's text have been checked for accuracy. Neither substantive nor accidental errors are corrected in his text, but, in the case of substantive errors, the correct text of the quotation is found in the Annotation. The Annotation also provides translations of foreign language quotations. The quotations which are displayed in the copy-text are set off uniformly and references following them are given a standard format.

Russell's bibliographical references are emended to a common format. Footnote indicators have been replaced by a continuous numeration through each paper. Russell used various typographical techniques to distinguish the different elements of references; but they are not modern techniques and are inconsistently applied. For example, the original form of the reference at 293: 35, as printed in the *Proceedings of the Aristotelian Society*, was: "*Vide Sophus Lie, Die Grundlagen der Geometrie*, Leipziger Berichte, 1890." Not only are the author's name and the publication title italicized, but some of the remaining data are presented in a way that, to those who do not know German, looks as if they might form a publisher's name. The reader might assume that he is being referred to a monograph. The reference is actually to an article by Lie in the serial *Berichte über die Verhandlungen der Sächsischen Gesellschaft der Wissenschaften zu Leipzig*, known informally as the "Leipziger Berichte". Russell's provision of only the year 1890 is insufficient by modern standards. Rather than intervene substantially in Russell's references, however, we have relied on the Bibliographical Index to inform the reader of the volume and page numbers.

### Manuscripts

As the illustrations show, Russell's manuscripts are remarkably legible. The rarity of errors and inconsistencies reflects his keen attention to detail and his relatively settled mechanical accidentals. His handwriting sometimes causes difficulty, particularly in distinguishing between "u" and "m" and between the upper- and lower-case forms of certain other letters (discussed below under capitalization). Demonstrable slips of the pen have been rectified. The original foliation of the manuscripts has not been indicated in the texts as printed.

While his spelling includes various alternative English forms, it is seldom unconventional. In Volume I certain archaisms appear, like "negligeable", "developement", "excentric" and "shew". These are distinguished from simple errors (the standard of correctness being the *Oxford English Dictionary*) and are retained. The unit for the regularization of spelling is the individual paper. Certain words are therefore spelled differently in different papers, since his spelling was still, to some degree, in flux during the period represented by this volume. A list of spelling errors is on page 499; corrections to proper names, however, appear individually in the textual notes, with unusual but not incorrect forms (such as "DesCartes") being retained in the text.

Russell was aware of the problem of capitalizing concept words; see, for example, his query to Moore regarding "Good/good", quoted in the head-note to Paper **15**. However, he was not consistent in practice: he usually capitalized such words on their first occurrence, but did not do so later in the text. No attempt has been made to impose consistency. When capitalization is used to indicate the name, or part of the name, of an organization, Russell's practice is rendered consistent, as with "the Society" in Papers **13** and **17**. In fact, his upper-case "S" is sometimes indistinguishable from his lower-case "s". The same problem is encountered with his "A" and his "G". Silent editorial judgment is the only solution in cases of ambiguity.

Foreign words and phrases like "*Ding an Sich*" (150: 13) and "*cogito ergo sum*" (161: 1) have been italicized (in keeping with Russell's mature preferences and standard printing practice), unless they are enclosed in quotation marks in the copy-text. Editorial italicization has been recorded in the textual notes when it might be mistaken for a use–mention distinction (which, indeed, Russell often indicated by italics). In addition, accents have been corrected or supplied where needed. The copy-text readings in Volume I which required emendation are: "Romeo" (53: 5), "$\psi\upsilon\chi\hat{\eta}$" (180: 2), "Fénélon" (220: 39, 220: 41), "Géometrie" (258: 1), "A priori" (261: 14) and "Korper" (264: 29).

We have silently expanded all abbreviations that would normally be expanded in print. Russell's common abbreviations will be found listed on page 500. The textual notes record the abbreviations of the names of people, places and organizations where they occur first in a given paper. For example, in "A Locked Diary" (**9**) he often referred to people by their initials. When we are certain to whom he refers, these initials have been expanded; the initials can be recovered from the textual notes. (Particular care had to be taken to differentiate the initials used for Russell's grandmothers; see T43: 25 and T52: 39–40.) The initials "P.L." have not been expanded because he seems to have called Pembroke Lodge by these initials. Little mathematical or logical symbolism occurs in this volume. We have set mathematical letters in italics throughout, following the practice of printing mathematics which had long been established by Russell's day.

Although Russell was fairly consistent in the mechanical kinds of punctuation in his manuscripts, certain inconsistencies were noticed. Since these are both inadvertent and exceptional, they have been emended according to the following rules and are not recorded individually in the textual notes:

—single quotation marks (at 17: 9, 26: 17, 26: 19, 29: 5, 47: 17–18 and 262: 23–4) are altered to double quotation marks, and double quotation marks are supplied where missing around quoted conversations (at 54: 24

and 54: 41);

—a period is supplied where needed (at 43: 28, 66: 22, 95: 29, 150: 21, 154: 9, 208: 15, 208: 22, 243: 1 and 309: 15);

—a comma is supplied if missing before and (if needed) after "etc.";

—a colon is supplied where missing before quoted conversations (at 54: 27–8, 64: 18, 64: 21, 64: 24 and 64: 25);

—the order of punctuation and closing quotation marks has been made consistent with Russell's style, i.e. the punctuation mark is set before the quotation marks only if the punctuation mark is part of the original quotation;

—a dash instead of a period at the end of a paragraph is changed to (or interpreted as) a period.

## Printed Copy-Texts

Russell's careful proofreading creates confidence in his printed copy-texts in respect to non-mechanical accidentals. Hence only mechanical accidentals needed to be regularized in order to approach full fidelity to his settled preferences. Essentially such regularization is equivalent to the replacement of the printer's house style. Emendation of such accidentals has been undertaken silently, for the most part, because the changes are generally minor. Russell's preferred forms have been used as the standard—the capitalization of names of organizations, for example, and word-division. He consistently did not mark for italicization terms such as "à priori", "i.e." and "e.g."; such italics have been removed from these texts, as has the comma following "i.e." and "e.g." (in accordance with his preference).

A few problems have been presented by spelling. We have applied to printed copy-texts the conventions followed in manuscripts. Spelling is the major subject of regularization of printed copy-texts. Those printed in the United States differ in spelling from those printed in Britain, although both may differ from Russell's manuscripts. American spelling is converted to Russell's preference; if his preference is unknown, then the conversion is to English spelling in the O.E.D. As it happens, there are no American copy-texts published in this volume, although they will occur in later ones. As in the case of manuscripts, the capitalization of names of organizations is regularized, e.g. "Exchequer" at 294: 33. Word-division is regularized to Russell's preferences.

Corrections of typographical errors are listed on page 499. The original pagination of the texts has not been indicated.

### III. COPY-TEXT DECISIONS IN VOLUME I

The present volume raised few difficulties in the choice of copy-texts and their emendation through the adoption of variant readings. Thirty-six of the papers are available only in single manuscripts. The choice of the copy-text among two or more texts was theoretically necessary on nine occasions (Papers **1**, **3**, **4**, **9**, **15**, **16**, **38**, **42** and **44**). Four papers posed problems regarding their final substantive readings.

In 1894 and again in 1948 or 1949 Russell made a transliteration-*cum*-translation of some of the entries in Paper **1**, the "Greek Exercises". The transliterations differ in some substantives from the original text. We decided not to emend the copy-text to incorporate these variants, on the ground that a diary entry cannot be altered much later without losing its historical character. The variants have, however, been included in the textual notes to indicate what Russell later understood himself to have intended.

Paper **15** contains a paragraph that also appears in Paper **38**. There is no doubt about the copy-text in each case. The substantive variants between the two texts of the paragraph are listed in the textual notes to **15**.

Although Paper **16** was written in 1897, it was not published until 1957, in *Why I Am Not a Christian*. There are several variants between the manuscript and typescript, and even more between them and the several editions of the book. But the later variants have no authority. Russell made no attempt to revise the essay. Moreover, an essay written in 1897 could not be revised sixty years later and retain its historical character. The variants are due solely to misreading his early handwriting (starting with the date) and to corruptions introduced in *Why I Am Not a Christian*.

Paper **42**, which appeared in *Mind* in 1896, is a chapter from Russell's then recently successful dissertation. Most of the paper is recognizable in revised form in his *Essay on the Foundations of Geometry* (1897). The revisions of 1897 are part of the process of improving his thoughts in that paper; and so are the further revisions in the 1901 French translation of his *1897*. However, the absorption of a short, self-contained paper in a much longer book resulted in a very different text. To ignore the integrity of the original paper would be to ignore part of the history of the publication of Russell's views and to inhibit any appraisal of the response to them and, therefore, of their effect upon his early reputation. The material which Russell took from **42** and revised in writing *1897* appears in various places in the book and has thematic connections with, and sometimes is made dependent upon, material elsewhere in the book. It would be misleading to incorporate in **42** the changes that Russell intended to be seen only in the wider context of the book. Thus we have taken the substantives from *Mind* and given the variants from *1897* in the textual notes, since they are an important record of Russell's changing thought.

Similar considerations apply to Paper **44**. Passages in **42** reappear, in altered form, in **44**, and considerable portions of **44** reappear in his *1897* and again in his *1901*. We regarded each of these stages of revision as creating a separate work and, as with **42**, decided to publish the earliest preserved text, leaving the later stages for a possible critical edition of his *1897*. The only emendations of the texts to include revisions in *1897* are of one or two accidentals, where *1897* appeared more trustworthy as to Russell's original intentions. In lieu of a critical edition of his *1897*, the revisions Russell made in incorporating **42** and **44** in that book are presented in the textual notes.

# Guide to the Textual Notes

THE TEXTUAL NOTES provide a complete record of the available evidence of the progression of Russell's thought from cancelled readings in first drafts through revisions of manuscripts, typescripts and proofs, to revisions in later printings and in marginalia. Comparison of different versions of a passage, as reconstructed from the textual notes, enables one to evaluate his change in a line of thought or of a particular word or phrase, and to gain a fuller appreciation of his creative process and literary style.

The cancelled readings and other changes appearing on, or prior to, the copy-text (the basis for our text) are authorial alterations. They are distinguished from variants, which are the changes between the copy-text and any succeeding texts. Since the authorial alterations can be as revealing of the process of composition as the variants, a full register of substantive authorial alterations is included in the textual notes.

The textual notes also record editorial emendations of Russell's text.

## Format

For each paper a brief physical description of the copy-text and any other pertinent textual documents is provided. In the case of holograph or typed documents the description offers an exact statement of their foliation (the numbering of the leaves), the paper size, and whether they are written in pencil or ink, typed or printed. Italic numbers in the foliation refer to unnumbered leaves, and a number in parenthesis refers to a leaf's initial numbering in cases of alteration. Other major features—such as a change in the type of paper used—are described when present. Also included in the description is an identification of the symbols used in the textual notes to denote the various texts of the paper at hand. The most common symbol is "CT", the abbreviation for "copy-text".

All of the textual notes are recorded in one comprehensive register. This feature allows the reader to find in a single place all of the available evidence for the determination of the substantives of a given passage. Information on archival locations and file numbers of manuscripts and typescripts will be found in the headnotes to the papers.

## Record of Authorial Alterations

The most frequent kind of note concerns authorial alterations. A precise vocabulary has been devised to cover insertions of words, words written over words, and deletions of words. Whenever practicable, we use such terms as *"inserted"*, *"inserted in margin"*, *"above deleted"*, *"before deleted"*, *"after deleted"*, and *"written over"* to describe the physical appearance of the alteration. The term *"replaced"* is employed when the alteration does not easily lend itself to description by the other terms. We have combined alterations when it appears that they are parts of a larger alteration. The presence of illegible words is rarely recorded. Ignored too are false starts, letters written over the same letters, words written over the same words, and incomplete words (except when they are part of a larger alteration or are otherwise thought to be of interest). If there is more than one level of revision, usually only the immediately prior reading is recorded.

Each note is comprised of a number of distinct components, as in the following example:

49: 6  morning CT] *after deleted* evening

First the note is keyed to a passage in the volume at hand of the *Collected Papers*. In "49: 6 morning" we have a page/line reference to and reading from the present volume. This reading coincides with the final reading in the copy-text, as the symbol "CT" indicates. A right-hand square bracket completes this component of the note. The next component is a phrase describing the physical appearance of the alteration in the copy-text. Editorial comments, which are always to the right of the square bracket, are in italic, unless probable ambiguity with an italic reading requires that they be in roman. The final component is the prior reading. The complete note is to be understood as follows: "At p. 49, line 6, the reading 'morning' is from the copy-text, where it appears immediately after the deleted word 'evening'."

*Record of Variants*

Another kind of note deals with a variant reading in a second text of a paper. Typical of such notes is this one:

284: 18  involves CT] is impossible without 97

Here the reading in the present volume and the copy-text is to be compared with the (later) reading in the text designated "97". Consultation of the paragraph introducing the textual notes of the paper in which p. 284 falls shows that "97" refers to *An Essay on the Foundations of Geometry*, where Russell specified a stronger relationship in his subject matter than he did in the copy-text.

*Record of Editorial Emendations*

A less frequent kind of note records editorial emendations. Departure from the copy-text may take place for any of the following reasons: a text subsequent to the copy-text was revised by Russell to incorporate a final intention; the copy-text was changed because it was obviously wrong; or the copy-text was regularized. Not all of these types of emendation can be illustrated from the present volume, to which the following examples are confined.

The source of an emendation may be another text of the paper at hand. Consider the following note:

> 108: 32 It has always been 56+] It has been always been CT

The reading in the text denoted by "56" (identified in the textual notes to Paper **16** as a typescript made in 1956) is judged to be preferable to that in the copy-text. The plus sign indicates that the reading is common to all subsequent texts examined. The note

> 285: 20 paper] chapter CT

shows that the reading in the present volume is different from that in the copy-text. That no text is cited as the source of the different reading indicates that the word "chapter" in the copy-text was editorially altered to the word "paper" in this volume. (The reason for the emendation is provided in the headnote to Paper **42**.) Finally, the same format is found when the copy-text is regularized or house-styled. The note

> 48: 29 Aunt Agatha] A. A. CT *Also at 50: 18, 52: 25.*

records the editorial expansion in three places of a copy-text abbreviation of a proper name.

*Compound Textual Notes*

Complex situations in the documents sometimes require the use of compound textual notes. For example, multiple levels of revision in a passage from the manuscript of Paper **46** are indicated by this note:

> 312: 36 seriously impairs CT] *replaced* seriously modifies] *above deleted* vitiates

Another example is taken from Paper **42**:

> 284: 22–3 Von Staudt's projective construction[12] proceeds entirely by the help of straight lines.] Von Standt's ... lines. CT] *sentence and footnote omitted in 97*

This note records (1) a correction to the spelling of von Staudt's name in the copy-text, and (2) the fact that the passage and its footnote were deleted in Russell *1897*. The ellipsis is used to avoid repetition of words common to the text of *Collected Papers* 1 and the copy-text. In providing full substantive variant readings, the assumption is that the reader does not have the variant text at hand. Since the paragraphs of a text usually reappear continuously, page numbers to variant editions are rarely needed to enable the reader to trace the text in detail. However, that is not so with Papers **42** and **44**, the reappearance of whose paragraphs in his *1897* is not continuous. The provision of the table on 486–7 charting the intersection of the two papers with *1897* obviates any need in this case to provide page numbers with the source of the variant readings.

*Compound Textual Notes for Paper* **1**

Another illustration of a compound note is in order because of the special features of the notes to the "Greek Exercises". Here is an illustration:

8: 31  idea of self-preservation 48] εἰδιας οφ σελφ-πρεσεφησχεν CT] *after de-leted* δοξης τοὺ φρη βουλομαι [doctrine of free will]

This note is to be understood as follows: "At p. 8, line 31, the reading 'idea of self-preservation' is shared by the 1948 (or 1949) transliteration of the copy-text reading: 'εἰδιας οφ σελφ-πρεσεφησχεν'; the copy-text reading is found after the de-leted words 'δοξης τοὺ φρη βουλομαι', which can be translated 'doctrine of free will'." (Foreign-language quotations in the editorial apparatus of this edition are usually followed by an English translation in square brackets.)

Finally, some of the notes are explanatory in nature. They focus, for example, on difficulties in reading the manuscripts, Russell's usage of Greek, the reason for an editorial emendation, or the limits of passages contained on leaves inserted in the manuscript.

# 1 Greek Exercises

The text of the "Greek Exercises" uses for the most part a system of phonetic spelling employing English words written in Greek characters. While the idea itself is not an original one, Russell displayed considerable ingenuity in rendering various English vowel and consonantal combinations. A short extract will serve as illustration: «εἰ χαφ θε φερι γρητεστ φια θατ μει λειφ μη χιραφτα βι ρουινδ βει μει χαφιν λοστ θε σαπωρτ οφ φιλιζεν. εἰ δισεια οφ ὡρλ θινς θατ μει φιλιζεν σχυδ νοτ σπρεδ, φωρ εἰ, οφ ὡρλ πιπλ, ὡρτ, ὡιν τυ μει ἐδευκησχεν ...» (15: 28–31). The text, however, is not wholly English written in Greek characters. At certain places, particularly in the early entries, Russell used a number of common Greek words and tried his hand at composing in Greek.

At the time he composed the "Greek Exercises" he was clearly in the early stages of his exposure to the Greek language, for he is repeatedly guilty of elementary mistakes in the formation of nouns, adjectives and verbs, as well as in the use of pronouns and prepositions. The following are offered as examples: εἰ ὁ θεος ἐστι ποιητα των νομυς [if God is maker of the laws, 6: 20]; εἰ ποιω θελειν ἐγω βελιφδ [I do wish I believed, 7: 16]; οἱ μειστονες ἀνθρωποι [the greatest men, 8: 10]; ἐν ἑαυτου [in itself, 10: 16]. In addition, his inexperience in the language more than once led him astray in his choice of Greek words—οὐρανος instead of κοσμος for "universe" (12:25), πολις [city-state] for "state of mind" (13: 28). It must be remembered, however, that the early entries of the "Greek Exercises" were composed before he began attending B. A. Green's University and Army Tutors at Southgate (see 11: 17–18, 3 May 1888, and 14: 27, 20 May 1888), so that we are probably presented with the results of Russell's efforts at self-instruction.

The notebook ("CT"), which measures 176 × 227 mm., is paginated 1–96; pp. 1–49 comprise the "Greek Exercises". They are written chiefly in pencil. In the notes that follow, "94" refers to the "Extracts from my Journal", which Russell sent Alys on 13 September 1894 and which are part of Mrs. Halpern's collection of Pearsall Smith family papers. "48" refers to the mainly interlinear transliteration and translation that Russell made of many of the entries in 1948 or 1949.

The following entries were transliterated in 1948 or 1949: §1 (5: 1–13), §§3–12 (5: 28 –12: 10), §15 (incomplete, 13: 34–14: 20), §16 (incomplete, 14:26–15: 1, ending at "Memoriam."), §§17–19 (15: 16–17: 23) and §20 (incomplete, 17: 33–18: 29, ending at "me." and 18: 39–19: 2, beginning at "it is").

After he made the transcription, Russell had it typed for inclusion in his *Autobiography* (1967). (Selections also appeared in *My Philosophical Development* [1959].) The typescript was an inaccurate one, and was the beginning of considerable corruption in the text of the transliteration before it was printed; for further extensive revision of the chapter text of the *Autobiography* required that it be repeatedly retyped, with a concomitant loss of accuracy in the transmission of the whole text. A certain amount of editing preceded publication, and further passages were excised. It would seem that no typescript or proof of the "Greek Exercises" was ever read against Russell's transcription.

Apart from deliberate omissions of entries and parts of entries in *1959* and *1967*, there are unmarked deletions of text (some of them surely unintended), inadvertent word substitutions, and dozens of instances of unauthentic punctuation. Some of the more serious errors are these: at 5:3 "especially religious ones" is omitted; at 7:10 the date is incorrectly given as April 6 instead of April 9; at 8:30–1 "and in the second place, to civilization and education, which introduces great refinements of the idea of self-preservation" is omitted; at 10:34 "or of that particular section of the species" is omitted; at 14:5 "even the whole prayer was more or less a solemn farce to me" is omitted; and at 18:10 "planet" reads "plant". There are fewer errors in the extracts printed in *1959*.

Since the variants in the typescripts and printed versions do not show any sign of being deliberately made by Russell, presentation of a full collation of them is unnecessary.

5:2  eight 48] ἤτ CT] *after deleted* σιξ [six]
5:2  I shall write 48] γραψω CT] I am going to write 94
5:3  now 48] νυν CT] at present 94
5:23  in particular] εν πετιχλα CT] particularly 94
5:29, 5:30, 6:4  God ] *In the first instance Russell wrote* Γοδ, *in the second* θεω; *at the end of the exercise he wrote* γοδ. *Although he knew the upper case gamma, we assume in our transliteration (in keeping with Russell's own rendition throughout 48) that by* γοδ *he meant* God .
5:31  belief ] βιλιφ CT] believing 48
5:34–5  we ... We 48] *In both instances CT reads* ὑμεις, *meaning* you , *whereas* ἡμεις *means* we ; *but the second instance is followed by an attempt at a Greek verb* (γιγνομεν) *which has a first person plural ending. Since Russell cannot be trusted in his use of Greek pronouns, and since* we *is more natural in the context, we assume that Russell intended the first person plural in both instances.*
5:36  energy 48] ἐνεργον CT] *above deleted* φωρς [force]
6:2  come 48] χαμ CT] *replaced* χαμς

[comes]
6:7  uniformity 48] εὐνιφωρμιτι CT] *after deleted* ἀχσχ [acti⟨on⟩]
6:34  we must not give it] οὐ δε διδοναι δει CT] we cannot give it 48
6:37  living things 48] ζωα CT
7:10  April] ἤπριλ CT] *after deleted* με [May]
7:13  himself 48] αὐτο CT *Russell probably intended the third person singular reflexive pronoun* ἑαυτον.
8:3  energy 48] ἐνεργης CT] *In 48 Russell first wrote* energies *but altered it to* energy to *agree with the verb* is employed .
8:31  idea of self-preservation 48] εἰδιας οφ σελφ-πρεσεφησχεν CT] *after deleted* δοξης τοῦ φρη βουλομαι [doctrine of free will] *Russell used the genitive singular of* δοξη *in the cancelled phrase; hence it is assumed that, in its replacement, he also intended the genitive singular of* εἰδεια [sic], *rather than the plural of the English equivalent.*
8:33  Many of them 48] μενι οφ θεμ CT] *above deleted* ὠρλμωστ παντες [almost all]
9:8  this 94, 48] *The CT's* αὐτο *is a mistake for a form of the demonstrative pronoun.*
9:14  says 94, 48] *The CT's* ἐφη *is a mistake for the present tense form.*
9:16  depend mostly upon 48] διπενδ μωσττλι ἀπον CT] depend on 94
9:22  maximum of happiness 48] μαξιμυμ οφ χαπινες CT] maximum happiness 94
9:23–4  my own individual happiness 48] μει ὠν ἰνδιφιδευελ χαπινες CT] my own happiness 94
9:26  as long as 48] ἀς λον ἀς CT] while 94
10:3  Argyll's] Ἀγειλς CT] Argyle's 48 *Also at 11:24.*
10:16  out in that way] αὐτ ἐν θατ ἤ CT] is not that but 48
11:8  tea 48] τῖ CT] *after deleted* δινα [dinner]
11:11  are horrified 48] ἀ χοριφειδ CT] *after deleted* λουχ [look]
11:17  I am going 48] ἐιμι βεινειν CT] I am to go 94
12:12–13  I feel that I] εἰ φιλ θατ εἰ CT] I feel I 94
13:39–40  moreover it is one of which 48] μωρωφα ἰτ ἐστι ἀν οφ ἰζ CT] of which moreover 94
13:40  in the greatest need 48] ἰν θε γρητεστ νῖδ CT] very much in need 94

14:25 erro.] ἔρρω. CT] *before deleted* νυγχ
  ρετ. [nunc ret⟨rorsum⟩]
14:33 done so 48] δαν σω CT] *after deleted*
  νοτ [not]
14:40 over] ὠφα CT] *all* 48
15:21 among 48] ἀμον CT] *with* 94
15:22 difficult for anyone to 48] διφευχαλτ
  φωρ ἐνιυαν τυ CT] difficult to 94
15:22 walk 94] ὠρχ CT] work 48
15:27 when 48] ἐν CT] where 94
15:29 my life 48] μει λειφ CT] I 94
16:5 *June* 48] ζουν CT] *after deleted* μη
  [May]
16:27 truth 48] τρυθ CT] *above deleted* ιτ [it]
17:6 capacity 48] χαπασιτι CT] *after deleted*
  χηπαβιλιτι [capability]
17:9 near 48] νια CT] *after deleted* νηα
17:33 comerging] χωμερζιν CT] converging
  48

18:5 Of all] ὁφ ὠρλ CT] *after deleted* ἰν θις εἰ
  [In this I]
18:11 Argyll] Ἀγειλ] Argyle 48 *Also at*
  *18:20.*
18:34 imagine] ἰμαζιν CT] *after deleted* ση
  [say]
19:16 monster] μονστα CT] *after deleted*
  δισχωρ [discor⟨d⟩]
19:19 Oh for] ὠ φωα CT] *replaced* χου λον
  εἰ φωρ [How long I for]
19:20 of answer or] ὁφ ἀνσα ὠρ CT] *above
  deleted* ορ προμις οφ [or promise of]
20:23 '89] ἤτι νειν CT] *replaced* ἤτι ητ ['88]
21:6 speaking] σπἳχιν CT] *after deleted* ἀ φο
  [a vo⟨ice⟩]
21:7 man] μαν CT] *above deleted* ἀς [us]
21:23 Whether] ἐθα CT] *above deleted* ἰφ
  [If]

## 2–8 Essay Notebook

The manuscript notebook ("CT") is paginated 1–51, followed by six blank leaves. It
measures 180 × 228 mm. and is written in
ink. Papers **3** and **4** were typed in the late
1940s, but as the typescripts do not show
any evidence of having been approved by
Russell, they have not been collated.

## 2 How Far Does a Country's Prosperity Depend on Natural Resources

24:6 condition CT] *after deleted* state
24:12 it CT] *written over* is
24:14 one CT] *before deleted* of the forces
24:24 requires CT] *above deleted* includes
24:25 before which CT] *replaced* and before
  these

24:37–8 difference CT] *after deleted* Natural
24:39 If CT] *after deleted* But
25:3 are now CT] *replaced* is now a
25:12 Natural Laws, CT] *before deleted*
  both by observing the errors of the past,

## 3 Evolution as Affecting Modern Political Science

25:23 and the causes of human happiness
  CT] *inserted*
25:25 causes CT] *above deleted* courses of
  action
25:26 most CT] *inserted before* to happiness
25:32 for the moment CT] *inserted*
25:32 to be CT] *above deleted* as being
26:11 Politics, CT] *before deleted* which
26:11 practical CT] *inserted*
26:12 false assumption CT] *after deleted*
  fallacy
26:18 revelations CT] *before deleted* that
  were

26:19 "laissez-faire" CT] *before deleted* is
  slightly of a different
26:22 would CT] *before deleted* allow
26:26 then, CT] *written over* and
26:29 progress CT] *after deleted* free
26:34 combining the two CT] *above deleted*
  this effecting this
26:34–5 our present subject CT] *replaced*
  the scope of the present
26:42–3 it calls CT] *Russell sometimes uses
  the singular pronoun (and verb) when the
  referent or the subject is grammatically
  plural.*

27: 4  would CT] *written over* is
27: 11  Houyhnhnms] Houhnyhms CT
27: 22  individual CT] *above deleted* own
27: 23  them; CT] *before deleted* and
27: 26  either. CT] *before deleted* Other forces

must be brought to bear; on
27: 27  endeavour CT] *before deleted* as surely
27: 27  make our CT] *inserted*
27: 28  and not CT] *after deleted* until

## 4 State-Socialism

28: 13  tend to prosperity CT] *after deleted* produce a better state of things
28: 13  comfort, CT] *before deleted* had
28: 14–15  deduction CT] *replaced* deductions
28: 26  increase CT] *before deleted* to the
28: 29  seemed CT] *after deleted* appeared

28: 39  refused CT] *replaced* , while refusing
28: 39  looked CT] *replaced* while looking
29: 22  its application to CT] *inserted*
29: 24  it CT] *after deleted* Socialistic legislation
29: 38  unemployed. CT] *replaced* unemployed which are

## 5 The Advantages and Disadvantages of Party Government, and the Conditions Necessary for Its Success

30: 3  system CT] *written over* scheme
30: 11  at CT] *above deleted* towards
30: 14  society. CT] *replaced* society which
30: 25  natural CT] *after deleted* the
30: 32  condition CT] *before deleted* of the condition
30: 38  today CT] *written over* one day
30: 38  tomorrow CT] *inserted*
30: 39  opposite CT] *before deleted* the next
30: 41  Government CT] *before deleted* , as it
31: 11  when it CT] *replaced* when its
31: 19  Repeal of the CT] *inserted*
31: 19  was CT] *written over* were
31: 31  one CT] *inserted*
31: 31  other CT] *before deleted* party
31: 38  be always consistent CT] *replaced* fulfill the desired consistency

31: 39  Instead CT] *after deleted* Rarely,
31: 42  pressure. CT] *before deleted* or as again in the case of the
31: 43  independent CT] *after deleted* an
32: 14  solely CT] *inserted*
32: 16  improved CT] *after deleted* remedied
32: 21  affairs CT] *above deleted* policy
32: 22  be carried out CT] *after deleted* continue
32: 24  questions CT] *after deleted* policy
32: 28  changes CT] *inserted*
32: 31  a CT] *after deleted* the
32: 33  them CT] *replaced* their ways of thought
32: 34  distortions CT] *before deleted* of party
32: 34  of deserting CT] *replaced* to desert
32: 38  which CT] *written over* whose

## 6 "The Language of a Nation Is a Monument to Which Every Forcible Individual in the Course of Ages Has Contributed a Stone."

33: 28  as CT] as *inserted in pencil before* the medieval
33: 29  of the latter CT] *after deleted* which
33: 30  old CT] *written over* new
33: 41  express ideas before CT] *after deleted* before
34: 2  in the period CT] *after deleted* within the las
34: 2–3  their developement CT] *replaced in pencil* the developement of words
34: 3  which CT] *after deleted* has
34: 8  much CT] *after deleted* quite

34: 11  shown CT] *above deleted* expressed
34: 13  part CT] *after deleted* standard
34: 29  Semitic] Semetic CT
34: 32  Rome CT] *after deleted* the
34: 36  dead CT] *after deleted* dead
34: 43  their CT] *after deleted* its
35: 8  its permanent form. CT] *replaced* the permanent form of the
35: 9  ancestors. CT] *before deleted* Seeing that our words are of such permanent influence,
35: 11  on their CT] *after deleted* by their

## 7 Contentment; Its Good and Bad Points

35:25 murmurs CT] *after deleted* feels the increased
35:35 life CT] *after deleted* real
36:3 stand CT] *replaced* stands
36:10 incentive CT] *after deleted* great

36:17 new gods to replace CT] *after deleted* something new to replace
36:18 accumulated CT] *after deleted* "dust of antique time"
36:20 requirements CT] *after deleted* needs

## 8 Destruction Must Precede Construction

36:24 *title inserted in another hand*
36:34 yet CT] *before deleted* it is certain that
36:35 must CT] *above deleted* would
36:36 is CT] *after deleted* are
36:36 mould CT] *after deleted* develop into
37:6 action. CT] *before deleted* Hence reforms are always looked upon
37:6 regeneration CT] *after deleted* a
37:8 if CT] *above deleted* where
37:10 To CT] *replaced* Thus to
37:16 any CT] *after deleted* anything

37:23 theory CT] *above deleted* system
37:25 nearly CT] *inserted in margin*
37:27 reason CT] *after deleted* all
37:35 heretics CT] *before deleted* iconoclasts,
37:36–7 a purer faith. CT] *replaced* purer teachings
37:39 replace, CT] *before deleted* and if he is the first to put forward any views in his
37:40 apply CT] *above deleted* introduce
37:43 degree CT] *above deleted* amount

## 9 "A Locked Diary"

Three versions of the text exist for the entry of 20–21 July 1894, i.e. 65:13–66:14. In addition to the diary itself ("CT"), there is a contemporary holograph document consisting of a single sheet written in pencil (RA 710.055228) and denoted by "94". There are thirteen accidental variants, mostly of punctuation, between 94 and CT, and one substantive variant. The cancellations in 94 and the variants show that 94 preceded CT. Russell included 94 in the first volume of his *Autobiography* (1967), and the relevant pages (84–5) of the first printing of this edition ("67") have been collated with CT and 94. Further impressions and other editions have not been collated, since there is no reason to suppose that Russell read proofs or otherwise specially intervened in the printed texts of these editions. (Indeed, it is doubtful that he read proofs of the first British edition.) CT has been emended at one place (65:19) to prefer a formal variant from 94. The rest of the text has required various other editorial emendations, such as regularization of the dates of the diary entries.

The covers of the diary measure 198 × 230 mm.; the pages are 187 × 222 mm. Most of the entries are written in ink.

43:14 Channing Hall] Ch. H. CT *Also at 49:20 (as* Ch. Hall*).*
43:14 Farrington] F. CT *Also at 45:13, 49:25, 52:6.*
43:20 Uncle Rollo] U. R. CT *Also at 43:32, 43:38, 44:6, 46:25, 46:26, 47:13–14, 47:18, 49:10, 49:18, 50:14, 53:3, 53:10, 53:14.*
43:25 Granny's] Gr.'s CT *Also at 44:32 (as* Gr.*) and at 51:8 (as* G.*).*
44:5 Lilly Blyth] Lilly Blythe CT
44:39 Elphinstones'] Elphistone's CT
44:39 Maud Burdett] Maud B. CT *Also at 45:24, 46:24–5, 47:12, 49:18–19, 49:32, 53:38–9.*
45:24 Dickens CT] *Russell seems first to have written a long dash (as was his custom when he did not know a person's name—cf. 54:11), and then to have written* Dickens *over it.*
45:38 Rochat] R. CT *Also at 45:40.*
46:13–14 Ady Villiers] Ady V. CT
46:22 Euclid] Euc. CT
47:32 a short and imperfect CT] *replaced* an imperfect
47:34 believe CT] *written over* belief
48:5 the CT] *written over* on
48:29 on the ponds with Aunt Agatha CT]

*above deleted* to Robson

48: 29  Aunt Agatha] A. A. CT *Also at 50: 18, 52: 25.*

49: 6  morning CT] *after deleted* evening

49: 23  Frank] Fr. CT

51: 1  Alexandra Hotel] Alexandre H. CT

51: 5  MacNeill] Mac-Neill CT

51: 9  Agatha] A. CT

51: 17  allows CT] *replaced* allowed

51: 23  lunched CT] *after deleted* dine

52: 22  Mabel] M. CT

52: 32  *Der Trompeter* CT] *in German script after deleted* Sesame and Lilies, but

52: 39–40  Grandmama] Gra. CT *Also at 53: 26 (as* G'ma) *and at 55: 2 (as* Gr'ma).

53: 1  and CT] *after deleted* then

53: 16  Silas Farrington's] S. F's CT

53: 18  George CT] *after deleted* among others

53: 19  Uncles] U's. CT

53: 23  Miss Fraser] Miss F. CT

53: 37  questions CT] *inserted*

54: 4  Centre of Gravity] C.G. CT

54: 19  Aunt] A. CT *Also at 54: 22.*

54: 27  Lyulph] Ly. CT *Also at 55: 3.*

54: 27–8  Sir John Lubbock] Sir J. L. CT *Also at 54: 29.*

54: 43  said CT] *before deleted* well

55: 2  Morier] M. CT

55: 36  yet CT] *after deleted* but

55: 42–56: 1  disappointment of the CT] *inserted*

56: 8  have to CT] *inserted*

56: 9  His CT] *replaced* his *Also at 56: 10.*

57: 23  Llewelyn] Llewellyn CT

58: 12  Scholarship] Schol. CT

60: 1  *December* 5. 1892. 1 a.m.] *In CT, the date appears at the end of the entry.*

60: 12  no CT] *written over* know

60: 26  Shelley] Shelly CT

60: 32  mutually CT] *inserted*

61: 25  She has apostatized since. CT] *in-*

serted *after* in him

61: 32  though CT] *written over* or

61: 39  Alys] A. CT *Also at 62: 1, 62: 2, 62: 21, 63: 4, 66: 16, 66: 26, 66: 31, 66: 31, 67: 12, 67: 24.*

62: 1  (Alys's birthday.) CT] *in Alys's handwriting*

62: 8–9  has been CT] *inserted*

62: 17  me CT] *written over* my

62: 35  to CT] *inserted*

62: 36  spiritual CT] *after deleted* pure

62: 36  communion. CT] *before deleted* This came to a medical point where the discussion of course ended as we had not the means of deciding it.

63: 2  our CT] *inserted*

63: 28  Shakespeare's] Shakspeare's CT

63: 31  the first morning CT] *replaced* the morning of the

63: 32  Bôw-Tree CT] *written over* Bôo-Tree

63: 32–3  few demands on life and those were CT] *replaced* only one demand on life and that was

64: 12  more CT] *after deleted* so

64: 29  without CT] *inserted*

64: 39  power CT] *after deleted* the

64: 43  effects. CT] *before deleted* But for her I fear.

65: 19  is), 94, 67] is) CT

65: 25  my subsequent CT, 67] the subsequent 94

66: 5  of CT] *before deleted* P.L.,

66: 8  Dr. Anderson 67] Dr. A. CT, 94

66: 16  *Wednesday ... B. R.* CT] *Russell wrote this line at the foot of the page following Alys's entry of 2 October.*

66: 18–19  England, Germany,] England Germany CT

66: 20  Rosebery] Roseberry CT

66: 39–40  because ... impressions CT] *inserted*

67: 18  in marriage CT] *inserted*

## 10 Die Ehe

The manuscript ("CT") is foliated 1–3, measures 120 × 185 mm. and is written in ink. It is signed "B.R."on the last leaf.

69: 9  poems CT] *after deleted* inimitable

69: 25  new and wider CT] *above deleted* en-

larged sphere of

70: 1  compensate for CT] *after deleted* obviate the

70: 10  better CT] *written over* worse

70: 12  under the tyranny of Respectability CT] *replaced* bound by respectability

70: 18 lead CT] *after deleted* break through
70: 25 one who lives CT] *inserted*
70: 27 judge of CT] *replaced* pronounce on
70: 30 disapproval CT] *above deleted* opinion
71: 3 speech CT] *above deleted* word
71: 5 stated CT] *above deleted* postulated

## 11 Self-Appreciation

"CT" stands for the only known version of the text, that in *The Golden Urn*, no. 1 (March 1897): 30–1.

72: *title* Self-Appreciation] SELF-APPRECIATIONS. / I. ORLANDO. CT
73: 35 Lassalle] Lasalle CT

## 12 Can We Be Statesmen?

The manuscript ("CT") is foliated *1*, 1a-b, 2, 2a, 3–5, measures 221 × 285 mm. and is written in ink. It is signed "B. Russell." on the last leaf.

78: *title* Can We Be Statesmen?] Can we be Statesmen? CT
79: 4 should I wish to CT] *above deleted* if possible
79: 5 to consider CT] *after deleted* if possible to discover
79: 5 briefly CT] *inserted*
79: 6 , as a matter of fact, CT] *inserted*
79: 7 most of us CT] *after deleted* we
79: 14 seem CT] *before deleted* likely to be
79: 20 appeal CT] *after deleted* describe
79: 23–80: 9 A rather more … zero. CT] *inserted as fos. 1a–b; originally the insertion was to follow* existing community *(79: 11)*
79: 23 A rather more systematized method proceeds CT] *above deleted* These deductions are practically made usually
79: 23 more systematized CT] *above deleted* less primitive
79: 23 middle axioms. CT] *before deleted* : such as that the State ought not to interfere with a man for his own good
79: 27 for CT] *written over* as
79: 28 by the Coal-Strike CT] *inserted*
79: 35 good, CT] *before deleted* are I thin
79: 36 are CT] *inserted at both occurrences*
79: 38 not only are CT] *inserted*
79: 38 no two cases] no two cases are CT
79: 40 within CT] *above deleted* in
79: 42 Further CT] *inserted*
79: 43 action CT] *before deleted* of the State
80: 7 bad CT] *inserted in margin*
80: 8 practice CT] *before deleted* make it
most
80: 8 way CT] *before deleted* I
80: 8 value CT] *after deleted* practical
80: 9 zero CT] *after deleted* nothing
80: 10 The CT] *written over* This
80: 14 posterity CT] *before deleted* to the end of the world
80: 16 Government CT] *after deleted* the
80: 21 voter CT] *written over* man
80: 24 reasoning CT] *after deleted* mental
80: 24 people's mandate CT] *above deleted* popular voice
80: 25 abandon CT] *after deleted* I think
80: 26–7 Perhaps something might be done by substituting CT] *replaced* I think the first step is to substitute
80: 30 progress. CT] *before deleted* and may accept
80: 32 might perhaps CT] *above deleted* can only
80: 32 used CT] *before deleted* I think
80: 33 at all. CT] *before deleted* For example pure empirical Utilitarianism can give no argument for education or development: on the contrary increase of knowledge is increase of sorrow; by education new wants are produced with at first no means of satisfying them. But if progress and development require greater sensitiveness and greater knowledge, if we can not approach our ideal without them, then although a temporary increase of pain may be caused by education we have a ground for believing such pain to be counterbalanced by some future gain, even though social Science may be unable to point out how this is to happen. Again if the pleasures which can survive as the ideal is ap-

proached are not sensual, but are such as indulgence in sensual pleasures destroys, we have a presumption at least against the desirability of a drunken nation, *(not continued on any further page of extant manuscript)*

80: 34–81: 28 Progress ... suggest one. CT] *inserted as fos. 2a–3 (the original fol. 3 not being extant)*

80: 36 such progress CT] *above deleted* it

80: 36 consists CT] *before deleted* in the main

80: 36 sensitiveness, CT] *before deleted* an education of knowledge and of feeling (the former however having its value for ourselves only as a means to the latter).

80: 40 of self-development CT] *above deleted* to perfection

81: 14 know CT] *after deleted* have

81: 16 nation CT] *above deleted* state

81: 17 nation CT] *after deleted* state

81: 17 no such CT] *after deleted* there seems

81: 18 progress CT] *before deleted* or the re-

verse

81: 19 in this instance CT] *inserted*

81: 21 event CT] *before deleted* tendency] *above deleted* event

81: 22 from CT] *written over* for

81: 24 the tendency CT] *after deleted* if it

81: 24 conquers CT] *above deleted* exists

81: 27 perhaps CT] *above deleted* I hope

81: 29 And I CT] *after deleted* The most definite

81: 30 branch CT] *after deleted* definite

81: 35 sources CT] *above deleted* means

81: 36 the same CT] *after deleted* differen

81: 43 throughout CT] *after deleted* among

82: 1 all CT] *written over* the

82: 5 ought to CT] *above deleted* must

82: 9 side. CT] *before deleted* B. Russell *This marks the original end of the paper.*

82: 10 Philosophy of History CT] *after deleted* theory

82: 19 methods CT] *above deleted* ways by which we arrive at our conclusions

## 13  Lövborg or Hedda

The manuscript ("CT") is foliated 1–6, 6a, 7, 7a, 8–9, measures 221 × 282 mm. and is written in ink. It is signed "B. Russell." on the last leaf.

84: 1 The CT] *written over* It

84: 5 advantages CT] *above deleted* difficulties

84: 5 difficulties CT] *above deleted* advantages

84: 11 will CT] *written over* would

84: 12 exist, CT] *before deleted* and be

84: 15 purely CT] *inserted*

84: 15–16 questions CT] *before deleted* purely

84: 19 dealing CT] *before deleted* exactly

84: 19 average CT] *after illegible deletion] above deleted* normal

84: 21 is by CT] *replaced* by

84: 22 rather CT] *after inserted and deleted* but

84: 24 nature and CT] *inserted*

84: 27 derive CT] *above deleted* make

84: 27 intellectual CT] *before pencil deletion* interests

84: 29 resemble CT] *after deleted* are found

84: 35 as to CT] *after deleted* as to

84: 35 point CT] *replaced* points

84: 37 to the Society in the eyes CT] *above deleted* from the point of view

84: 42 got CT] *written over* had

84: 42 and CT] *after deleted* for

84: 42 election CT] *after deleted* first

85: 4 it is CT] *inserted*

85: 5 has CT] *inserted*

85: 10 than would otherwise be the case CT] *inserted in pencil*

85: 11 felt. CT] *before deleted* But

85: 11–13 There is ... at least. CT] *inserted*

85: 13 But CT] *inserted*

85: 15 promise CT] *after deleted* under

85: 17 discuss it, but CT] *replaced* discuss, but

85: 17 unartificial CT] *above deleted* natural

85: 27 almost CT] *inserted in pencil*

85: 29 to passion CT] *inserted*

85: 32 likely to CT] *after deleted* prone to

85: 32 when an opportunity occurs CT] *inserted*

85: 39 Just as CT] *before deleted* this conduct succeeded in accentuating the coarsest forms of the sexual by

85: 39  the hermit CT] *replaced* a hermit

85: 41  makes CT] *after deleted* leads to its

85: 41–2  and makes the form taken by the passion a better and healthier one CT] *above deleted* to the arousing of sexual passion and I believe (though this is really irrelevant)

86: 2  occasionally CT] *above deleted* sometimes

86: 2  In CT] *after pencil deletion* First:] *above deleted* The

86: 3  there CT] *after deleted* feel

86: 7–8  so far as I have been able to observe, CT] *above deleted* usually

86: 9  seems to me CT] *in pencil above pencil deletion* I should consider] *after deleted* could be

86: 11  of one CT] *pencil replacement of* for

86: 11  for another CT] *in pencil above pencil deletion* on the part of either man or woman

86: 20  I have a right CT] *above deleted* it is necessary

86: 21  might CT] *in pencil above pencil deletion* would probably

86: 25  exact CT] *inserted*

86: 30–40  This however ... subject discussed. CT] *inserted as fol. 6a*

86: 36  chosen CT] *after pencil deletion* their

86: 38  feeble CT] *inserted*

86: 40  or with their interest in the subject discussed CT] *in pencil above ink deletion* or with the keenness of their interest in the argument

86: 41  But] —But CT

86: 42  make CT] *written over* be a

87: 4  together CT] *inserted*

87: 11  hearthrug CT] *above deleted* speech

87: 15  often CT] *above deleted* sometimes

87: 15–16  completely CT] *inserted*

87: 17  fairly often CT] *above deleted* occasionally

87: 18  some CT] *above deleted* the case of

87: 18  mutual CT] *above deleted* prosperous

87: 21  most CT] *inserted*

87: 22  in CT] *after deleted* by

87: 23–42  There is one ... utter destruction. CT] *inserted as fol. 7a*

87: 23  more CT] *inserted in pencil*

87: 27  apostolic CT] *inserted*

87: 27  would CT] *after deleted* of

87: 29–30  respected CT] *before pencil deletion* intellectually

87: 32–5  Of course ... elected, CT] *replaced* And though of course many men at the present day hold this view about women in general, if one can imagine one of this class of men to be apostolic (and the days when apostolic men could belong to this class are rapidly passing away, if not already passed),

87: 37  either CT] *inserted*

87: 41  best CT] *after deleted* very

88: 1  mention CT] *after deleted* say a few

88: 1–2  very important advantages CT] *above deleted* reasons

88: 2  should CT] *after deleted* have

88: 3  be CT] *inserted in pencil*

88: 6  largely CT] *inserted in pencil*

88: 8  I am CT] *after deleted* When we discussed

88: 17  unable CT] *after deleted* able

88: 17  alone. CT] *before deleted* and masculin

88: 18  to CT] *inserted in pencil*

88: 20  discussions CT] *after deleted* such

88: 26  some CT] *before deleted* amount of] *in pencil above deleted* a certain

88: 30  corrected CT] *before deleted pencil insertion* by women

88: 38  it is difficult CT] *above deleted* we cannot help

88: 38  not to be CT] *above deleted* being

88: 41  Our CT] *replaced* And our

88: 43  more CT] *after pencil deletion* perhaps even] *before deleted* much] *above deleted* quite as much

89: 2  for CT] *in pencil above pencil deletion* when I can have

89: 8  not radically CT] *in pencil above pencil deletion* scarcely

89: 11  a great part CT] *replaced* far the greater part

89: 12  very strongly CT] *inserted in pencil*

89: 13  the brethren CT] *after deleted* other members

## 14 Cleopatra or Maggie Tulliver

The manuscript ("CT") is foliated 1-3, 3a, 4-7, 8[*bis*], 8a, 9, 10, 10a, 11, 11a, 12, measures 221 × 286 mm. and is written in ink. It is signed "B. Russell" on the last leaf.

92: 1 say CT] *written over* says
92: 3 of CT] *written over* or
92: 6 to CT] *inserted in margin*
92: 19 sentiment CT] *above deleted* passion
92: 19-20 professions CT] *before deleted* only
92: 26-7 Carr Bosanquet's] Carr B's CT
92: 29 with us CT] *after deleted* allowed
92: 34 particular CT] *inserted*
92: 37 (final CT] *after deleted* of a
92: 39 I shall CT] *before deleted* endeavour to
93: 3-18 Before beginning ... conclusions. CT] *inserted on fol. 3a*
93: 3 may observe CT] *after deleted* will observe
93: 13 ethically CT] *inserted*
93: 14 Good CT] *written over* good
93: 16 try to tackle CT] *after deleted* begin the regular dis
93: 16 my CT] *above deleted* the
93: 26 relative to CT] *after deleted* for
93: 27-8 in the first place CT] *replaced* , first,
93: 28-32 And the wish ... equally pleasurable. CT] *inserted on fol. 3a*
93: 28 the wish for CT] *inserted*
93: 29 is pleasant CT] *after deleted* gives pleasure,
93: 31 reinforces CT] *written over* enforces
93: 32 equally pleasurable CT] *after deleted* all
93: 32-3 But this class does not consist exclusively of desires for pleasure— CT] *replaced* but not exclusively—
93: 35 an immediate CT] *replaced* a
93: 37 the CT] *written over* we
94: 8-9 as is shown by the match-making instinct in women CT] *replaced* as the match-making instinct in women shews
94: 12 the object of CT] *inserted*
94: 13 power CT] *after deleted* for
94: 14-15 the desire, which thus CT] *replaced* us, and the desire,
94: 16-19 and generally speaking ... ethi-

cally considered CT] *inserted*
94: 22 similar CT] *above deleted* the same
94: 24 deciding us CT] *after deleted* determining our
94: 32 will say nothing for the moment CT] *replaced* have said and will say nothing
94: 34 at any rate at our present level CT] *inserted*
94: 39 it is the command CT] *after deleted* for
94: 42 theoretical CT] *above deleted* abstract
95: 1 be CT] *inserted*
95: 4 conduct CT] *inserted*
95: 5 possible CT] *above deleted* easy
95: 6 strong CT] *above deleted* a weak
95: 11 men are the men CT] *replaced* man is the man
95: 12 them CT] *written over* him
95: 13 them CT] *written over* him
95: 13 their CT] *written over* his
95: 19 worse still CT] *before deleted* (I am describing a case of which I have bitter experience)
95: 24 in daily life CT] *above deleted* to live with
95: 35-96: 24 The effects ... to hold. CT] *inserted as new fos. 8-8a to replace the following, which begins at the foot of fol. 7 and ends at the head of fol. 9:* All these remarks are dry and general, but I don't know how else to treat the subject, unless I were to illustrate my meaning by some particular instance. ⟨*end of fol. 7*⟩ ¶I might take as a good example of a conflict of passions Wronsky, in Anna Karenina: the struggle between ambition and love, when he sits down to endeavour to decide calmly between them, is powerfully described. Let us put ourselves in his place—most people, in view of the rest of the book, would agree that he decided wrongly, and yet—how could he have decided otherwise? Let us imagine him with a clear intellect, able to get outside him and look on critically. It would tell him, if he were wise and knew himself, that under the circumstances love could bring little satisfaction—that it would remain imperfect, and perpetually harassing by contrast

with his ideal—that it would remain passion, and not pass into emotion—that he
would be sure to regret his frustrated
ambition—and that the pleasure would be
at best only an episode, while the resulting
pain would *not* be an episode but would
last the rest of his life. And yet it is impossible to deny such a passion as his love for
Anna without putting something very
satisfying in its place—*mere* ambition
would no longer suffice. I think, if he had
been sufficiently cold-blooded, he would
have put himself deliberately in the way of
falling in love with someone else
instead—(though I confess I should despise a man who did—). A simple pre-
scription would, in the early stages, be
very likely to secure the result—by absence and solitude it is easy to nurse susceptibility, and then a little beauty and
sympathy combined would probably effect enough of a cure to make that course
better than the other. As to what Anna
should have done, I don't know—I think
⟨*end of original fol. 8*⟩ in her case there was
no solution, and that, with a little less
jealousy, her actual course would have
been as good as any other.—

95: 35 too great repression of passions CT]
*above deleted* repressed passion

95: 38 never CT] *after deleted* always

95: 43 are CT] *above deleted* remain

96: 2 Dostojewski's CT] *Russell followed
closely the spelling of this name in his German edition of Dostojewskij's* Schuld und
Sühne (*c.1888*).

96: 2 *Crime and Punishment*] crime and
punishment CT

96: 5 nervousness. CT] *before deleted* or]
*before deleted note in tiny script* [or anything
else that

96: 18 laziness or CT] *inserted*

96: 20–1 the little thought that is possible
easily shows them to be valueless CT] *replaced* which the little thought that is possible easily shows to be worthless

96: 22 they are invaluable. CT] *replaced*
their worth is inestimable.

96: 22 invaluable. CT] *before deleted* A Powerful Love, when resisted by a man, turns
normally to profligacy—when a woman

resists it, it turns more readily to brutal
cynicism, prudishness and hatred of men
as a class—always supposing, in both
cases, that they avoid insanity, which I
have gathered from doctors to be quite a
likely alternative.

96: 25 a passion CT] *after deleted* the

96: 30–1 by which I am sure very much may
be done CT] *inserted*

96: 34 strangle CT] *above deleted* check

96: 36–7 tomorrow CT] *after deleted insertion* for ever

96: 41–2 because only then is deliberate
choice possible CT] *inserted*

97: 3 McTaggart] McT CT *Also at* 97: 39,
98: 22.

97: 5 take CT] *inserted*

97: 5 where CT] *written over* when

97: 6 compels CT] *above deleted* forces

97: 6 level CT] *after deleted* plane] *after deleted* point

97: 7–8 the objections to what James calls
CT] *replaced* James's objections to what
he calls] *replaced* James's objections to

97: 10 judge CT] *after deleted* think

97: 11 as CT] *inserted*

97: 13 and in proportion as CT] *inserted*

97: 14 i.e. when the desire conflicts with the
general body of desires. CT] *inserted*

97: 15–36 No reason ... difficulty of Ethics.
CT] *inserted as fol. 10a*

97: 25 confusion—] confusion CT

97: 25–6 we are dealing with the desire,
which is a fact, not with its object, which
is not a fact CT] *inserted*

97: 27 judge CT] *above deleted* condemn

97: 30 If CT] *replaced* As I said above, if

97: 31 individuals CT] *above deleted* people

97: 32 ethics CT] *after deleted* morality

97: 33 wish to do, CT] *before deleted* the

97: 35 is CT] *above deleted* remains

97: 36 Ethics. CT] *before deleted* B. Russell.

97: 37 had CT] *written over* have

98: 1 Subject CT] *above deleted* Self

98: 6 the Subject CT] *above deleted* Self

98: 10 Hatred and CT] *replaced* Hatred to

98: 12–19 Also all I said ... becomes easy.
CT] *inserted as fol. 11a*

98: 14–15 knowledge CT] *before deleted*
, rational

98: 18 Thus CT] *inserted*

98: 24 However CT] *before deleted* this
98: 26 required CT] *above deleted* necessary
98: 27 necessarily of the Self CT] *replaced* so limited

98: 30 my conduct CT] *after deleted* not
98: 34 necessarily CT] *inserted*
98: 34–5 completely CT] *inserted*
98: 36 the CT] *written over* our

## 15 Is Ethics a Branch of Empirical Psychology?

The manuscript ("CT") is foliated 1–10. Folios 1–6 (ending at 102: 6) measure 207 × 334 mm.; fos. 7–10, which are of a thinner stock, measure 201 × 329 mm. The essay is written in ink. The last leaf is signed "B. Russell." The passage at 104: 13–31 was taken from Paper **38**, "Note on Ethical Theory", second paragraph. The textual notes provide a collation of CT with **38**.

99: *title* Is Ethics a Branch of Empirical Psychology? CT] *replaced* On Ethics as a Branch of Empirical Psychology.
100: 3 good CT] *written over* true
100: 3 true CT] *after deleted* good
100: 3 are due, in a sense, to CT] *above deleted* depend on
100: 9 , as the objectively true, CT] *inserted*
100: 23 objective CT] *inserted*
100: 25 having CT] *above deleted* with
100: 25 , with CT] *replaced* : only with
100: 26 Hence CT] *above deleted* Thus
100: 31 judgments CT] *after deleted* knowledge] *above deleted* cognitions
101: 3 is CT] *above deleted* expresses
101: 7–8 an ethical CT] *after deleted* the content of
101: 8 considered CT] *after deleted* is not
101: 10–11 the result CT] *after deleted* this ethical justifiction is
101: 12 knowledge CT] *written over* desire
101: 14 in CT] *above deleted* for
101: 25 assertion CT] *above deleted* knowledge
101: 28–9 our criterion of the good CT] *replaced* our guide in life *with* criterion of the good *inserted in pencil*] *replaced* the guide of life

101: 31 criterion of the good CT] *in pencil above pencil deletion* guide in life
101: 39 in the same terms CT] *replaced* in same terms
102: 21 desires CT] *after deleted* and erroneous
102: 24 since CT] *after deleted* moreover
102: 38 accept CT] *after deleted* take
102: 43 the name CT] *after deleted* calling such
103: 23 good and bad CT] *inserted*
103: 23 in CT] *before deleted* relation to
103: 27 error, CT] *before deleted* but
103: 40 this is fortunate, CT] *inserted*
104: 12 quarter. CT] *After* quarter. *Russell inserted the following:* [see back of preceding page] . *The preceding page was fol. 9; fol. 9ᵛ contains the penultimate paragraph of the paper.*
104: 15 chooses CT] *after deleted* places
104: 16 a CT] *replaced* as
104: 16–17 hand, CT] *before deleted* an ethic
104: 19 action, CT] *after deleted* desire,
104: 19–20 action, and CT] *replaced* action, CT, **38**
104: 22 the contrast CT] contrast **38**
104: 23 desire alone CT] only desire **38**
104: 24 must be CT] is **38**
104: 25 contrast CT] distinction **38**
104: 26 most of us CT] we **38**
104: 27 dislike CT] we dislike **38**
104: 29–30 good in his conduct CT] virtuous **38**
104: 31 possible. CT] possible. What want of harmony may remain, will be the fault of the world; a conflict of desires would no longer be possible. **38**

## 16 Seems, Madam? Nay, It Is

The manuscript ("CT") is foliated 1–14. Folios 1–2 (ending at 106: 38) and 10–14 measure 224 × 286 mm.; fos. 3–9 (ending at 109: 19), which use a much cheaper stock (almost newsprint), measure 201 × 253 mm. The essay is written in ink. The last leaf is signed "B. Russell".

When, early in 1956, Paul Edwards wrote

Russell about collecting his anti-religious writings for *Why I am Not a Christian* (1957), Russell responded affirmatively and soon sent him this essay to consider including, Edith Russell typing it from the manuscript. Russell corrected some errors in the typescript (denoted here by "56"). Four substantive variants emerge from a collation of CT and 56, although two are corrections of slips of the pen in CT. These variants are reported below. Not reported below are several further corruptions of the text when it was published. Edwards had a new typescript made of the entire copy for *1957*, including **16**. The American and British publishers each set type for the book (the contents were not exactly the same), and as a result there are numerous accidental as well as some substantive variants between the first editions and between them and 56. Since these variants have no authority, they are not reported here. Some examples, however, are the following: at 107: 39, "R" is printed "Reality"; at 110: 43 "inspiriting" is printed "inspiring"; and at 111: 12–13 the words "that some attempts would still be made to understand the world, and that it is possible" are omitted after "probable", which itself is altered to "probably". Since these variants are common to both first editions, it is likely that they derive from Edwards's new typescript.

105: *title* Seems, Madam? Nay, It Is] Seems, Madam? Nay it is CT, 56
106: 6 the CT] *inserted*
106: 10 those CT] *written over* these
106: 11 pretensions CT] *above deleted* claims
106: 12 , for the most part, CT] *inserted*
106: 12 acquired CT] *inserted after deleted* claimed
106: 18 whimsies CT] *replaced* whims
106: 19 consolation CT] *before pencil deletion* —the last power of the powerless— *The deletion was ignored in 56.*
106: 21 our modern CT] *above deleted* the
106: 24 "I know that CT] *inserted*
106: 31 and regards CT] *replaced* regarding
107: 13 will be; CT] *replaced* will be. In this all depends upon
107: 29 it may be ... behind" CT] *inserted*

107: 30 imagine CT] *above deleted* conceive of
107: 41 could CT] *above deleted* were to
108: 3 follows from CT] *above deleted* is a result of
108: 5 as concerns CT] *after deleted* as far] *after deleted* from the
108: 9 after death CT] *inserted*
108: 10–11 and for whose satisfaction CT] *in pencil above pencil deletion* and which
108: 11 we should be CT] *in pencil after pencil deletion* would make us
108: 12 grateful CT] *before pencil deletion* to it
108: 23 doctrine of a CT] doctrines of 56+
108: 23 Whatever CT] *after deleted* No evil from which we suffer now—and it is the base prerogative of evil
108: 25 evil CT] *inserted*
108: 31–2 good men CT] *replaced* the good
108: 32 It has always been 56+] It has been always been CT
108: 41 world CT] *inserted in pencil*
109: 2 appearance CT] *after deleted* experience
109: 6 the CT] *in pencil above pencil deletion* this
109: 7 of Reality CT] *inserted in pencil*
109: 9 that CT] *inserted*
109: 14 cannot CT] *replaced in pencil* can no longer
109: 15 experience CT] *above deleted* world
109: 23 , in extreme cases, CT] *inserted*
109: 25 like CT] *in pencil above pencil deletion* as we use
109: 39 What metaphysics CT] *after deleted* This claim for metaphysics
109: 43 we are informed CT] *replaced* metaphysics informs
110: 2 the aesthetic CT] *replaced* aesthetic
110: 2 allow CT] *in pencil above pencil deletion* admit
110: 9 the CT] *inserted*
110: 11 such CT] *above deleted* these
110: 13 the experiences CT] *after deleted* such
110: 16 philosophy CT] *after deleted* religi
110: 33 than others to CT] *inserted*
111: 7 that 56+] than CT

## 17 Was the World Good before the Sixth Day?

The manuscript ("CT") is foliated 1–9, measures 223 × 288 mm. and is written in ink. It is signed "B. Russell" on the last leaf.

112:*title* Was the World Good before the Sixth Day?] Was the World good before the sixth day? CT

113: 9 as CT] *above deleted* since

113: 10 so CT] *inserted*

113: 11 shadows CT] *after deleted* people

113: 14 according to CT] *inserted*

113: 15 he persuaded CT] *after deleted* informs me that

113: 16 one of the wise and good CT] *above deleted* a brother

113: 18 of Moore's mission, CT] *inserted*

113: 18 more overwhelming CT] *above deleted* greater

113: 31 judge CT] *before deleted* better

113: 32 to be better CT] *inserted*

113: 43 taken CT] *above deleted* urged

114: 7 unable to see CT] *after deleted* deaf to its cries, like the politicians when Ireland is silent.

114: 9 This course would CT] *before deleted* , of course

114: 22 do not CT] *inserted*

114: 24 is CT] *above deleted* be

114: 27 as a means. CT] *before deleted* When a tile falls on one's head, and kills one, it is bad as a means; when it falls on the head of one's aged parent, it is similarly good.

115: 1 be CT] *inserted*

115: 9 horrid CT] *above deleted* hideous

115: 9 quite CT] *inserted in margin*

115: 14 this emotion CT] *after deleted* it

115: 15 we shall say, CT] *inserted*

115: 36 many of the CT] *inserted*

116: 5 first, CT] *replaced* in the first place,

116: 25 such CT] *inserted*

## 18 Paper on Epistemology I

The manuscript ("CT") is unfoliated, measures 220 × 284 mm. and is written in ink. Each leaf is signed "B. Russell." in the upper right-hand corner.

121: 4 their CT] *written over* the

121: 4 contradictions. CT] *before deleted* involved

121: 15 unified. CT] *before deleted* It must treat Science as Science treats particular facts

121: 18 explaining CT] *after deleted* reducing

121: 19 the CT] *inserted*

121: 31 datum CT] *written over* data

121: 31 is CT] *after deleted* are

121: 31 perceptions CT] *above deleted* sensations

121: 33 immediate CT] *after deleted* the

121: 41–122: 1 general CT] *inserted*

122: 2 time. CT] *before deleted* though a variation of these entails that of the matter.

122: 2 general CT] *inserted*

122: 2–3 properties of CT] *before deleted* this purely

122: 3 are CT] *before deleted* thus a

122: 5 suppose CT] *above deleted* require

122: 6 their CT] *written over* there

122: 9 apply] applies CT

122: 15 pass. CT] *replaced* pass: the predicates of existential judgments such as Hot! or Red! (which judgments have no explicit subject).

122: 17 The constituents of CT] *inserted*

122: 24 such as CT] *after deleted* of

122: 27 by thought CT] *inserted*

122: 31–2 the interval CT] *after deleted* these occur at

122: 35 the elements CT] *after deleted* if our sensa

122: 37 succession,] succession CT

123: 12 in thought CT] *inserted*

123: 12–13 this objective CT] *inserted*

## 19 Paper on Epistemology II

The manuscript ("CT") is foliated 1–11, measures 221 × 285 mm. and is written in ink. The verso of fol. 9 was originally its recto and has the conclusion of a long cancellation on fol. 8.

125: 10  what CT] *above deleted* the
125: 16  can CT] *above deleted* do
125: 18  the time can remain unchanged CT] *replaced* we can imagine the time unchanged
125: 21–2  at astronomic time CT] *replaced* again at the mathematical time
125: 23  this CT] *written over* them
125: 31  and so CT] *before deleted* action
126: 7  are CT] *above deleted* is
126: 18  (algebraical) CT] *above deleted* (analytical) *at both occurrences*
126: 19  These CT] *replaced* To these
126: 32  would CT] *above deleted* can
126: 33  to CT] *inserted*
126: 35  have CT] *inserted in margin*
126: 38  a new meaning, CT] *before deleted* one applicable
127: 5  picturing them CT] *before deleted* (vorstellen)
127: 10–11  he has eliminated CT] *inserted*
127: 41  intuition CT] *replaced* intuitions
128: 4  thereby CT] *after deleted* by
128: 14  meaning. CT] *before deleted* If I were to translate all the results of analytical geometry by making my three coordinates mean respectively tom-cats, she-wolves and dragons I should arrive at a perfectly self-consistent but perfectly absurd series of propositions.
128: 23  objective CT] *inserted*
128: 35  perceptions, CT] *before deleted* not merely an imagination which a
128: 38  contradicted by experience CT] *before deleted* or now required experience for their justification
128: 39  admit. CT] *before deleted* When a

child is told on beginning Euclid that two straight lines cannot enclose a space, it does not begin drawing straight lines with a ruler or looking about for straight lines in nature; such a proceeding would be perfectly fruitless, first because in experience no line could be straight, and secondly because no line could be produced to infinity: but having called up a picture in its mind of two lines as nearly straight as possible, it finds them diverging more and more: and any diminution in the divergence appears only possible by a lapse from straightness. This in itself does not afford adequate ⟨*concluded on fol.* 9$^v$⟩ ground for believing in the axiom, but is I believe what actually happens in such a case.

128: 41  fit CT] *above deleted* be fitted
128: 41  into] in to CT
129: 3  but CT] *after deleted* rather
129: 11  number is not produced by this CT] *replaced* but by this number is not produced
129: 13  rise to CT] *inserted*
129: 15  constituents CT] *above deleted* objects
129: 17  things CT] *after deleted* objects
129: 21  apprehend CT] *replaced* have apprehended
129: 24  ⟨of⟩] *word editorially supplied (Alan Wood's typescript supplies a queried* of *in pencil)*
129: 30  one and two CT] *replaced* adding one to two
129: 39  time CT] *before deleted*, since

## 20  Paper on Bacon

The manuscript ("CT") is foliated *1–3, 1–2, 1, 1, 1–2, 1–2, 1–4*, measures 221 × 285 mm. and is written in ink. It is signed "B. Russell." on the last leaf.

132: 6  have CT] *above deleted* bear
132: 9–10  in the investigation. The CT] *replaced* in investigating. These
132: 11  Aristotle. CT] *before deleted insertion* But in drawing up instances
132: 11  applied CT] *after deleted* always
133: 6  rather than why; CT] *before deleted* to arrive at simplicity of description

133: 9  every CT] *above deleted* any
133: 21  schoolmen CT] *written over* scholars
134: 7  in this CT] *after deleted* but
134: 16  the CT] *written over* its
134: 26  in CT] *written over* on
135: 14  consistency CT] *above deleted* density
136: 2  *E* CT] *written over* D
136: 24  as final causes CT] *inserted*
136: 35  the CT] *inserted*
137: 10  as possible CT] *after deleted* in a
137: 25  unduly. CT] *replaced* unduly and lead to error

138: 7  most CT] *written over* more

138: 8  most forcibly CT] *after deleted* the

138: 16  some CT] *before deleted* people

139: 9  theology CT] *above deleted* faith

## 21 Paper on History of Philosophy

The manuscript ("CT") is foliated 1–2, 1–2, 1–2, 1–2, 1–2, measures 222 × 283 mm. and is written in ink.

141: 8  attributes CT] *after deleted* merely

141: 10  individuals CT] *before deleted* as such

141: 16  at CT] *inserted*

141: 22  perform CT] *written over* play

143: 25  difficulties CT] *written over* difficulty

143: 31  as why CT] *after deleted* such

143: 36  qualities CT] *written over* quality

144: 20  idea, CT] *before deleted* we believe in

144: 20  questions of CT] *inserted*

144: 27  merely CT] *inserted*

144: 33  in vain. CT] *after deleted* probably

144: 33  Berkeley maintains CT] *after deleted* Berkeley is thoroughly sensationalist: all knowledge of existence springs from sense and is of sensible qualities except con-

cerning God. If this be true, it seems an unavoidable consequence that only sensible qualities necessarily exist. Locke's substratum in which these inhere is not known by sense, but by thought; and a thorough-going sensationalist must deny the possibility of knowledge of existence obtained in such a manner. Thus from Hume's point of view it is intelligible why Berkeley's arguments should be both unanswerable and unconvincing. *Across this passage Russell wrote:* THIS must be rewritten. Berkeley admits inferences as to existence but maintains matter to be a self-contradictory conception.

144: 36  conception CT] *above deleted* idea

144: 38  the existence CT] *after deleted* my consciousn

144: 40  Self CT] *before deleted* of

145: 8  an odd blend CT] *replaced* a blend

## 22 Paper on Epistemology III

The manuscript ("CT") is foliated *1*–3, 1–2, 1–2, 1–2, measures 220 × 282 mm. and is written in ink.

147: 39  contact CT] *after deleted* impact

148: 1  conception CT] *after deleted* explanation of

148: 21  something CT] *above deleted* it is some

148: 23  and CT] *before deleted* surely

148: 34  and when CT] *after deleted* and subject and object as depending on

148: 35  enters CT] *after deleted* becomes consc

148: 35  definite CT] *inserted*

148: 39  But CT ] *inserted*

149: 13  principle CT] *after deleted* idea of

149: 21  homogeneity CT] *after deleted* perfect

149: 23–4  causes heterogeneous from their effects CT] *replaced* a cause heterogeneous from its effect

149: 27  physics CT] *after deleted* metaph

149: 34  of what nature CT] *replaced* what

150: 6–7  on the rationalist side CT] *inserted*

150: 10  Kant holds that CT] *before deleted* we have knowledge which refers to external things, but

150: 17  ever CT] *inserted*

150: 20–1  intercourse.] intercourse CT (*manuscript damaged, accounting for missing period*)

150: 24  sort of CT] *inserted*

## 23 Paper on Descartes

The manuscript ("CT") is foliated *1*, *1*, *1*–2, *1*, *1*, measures 221 × 282 mm. and is written in ink.

152: 19  criterion CT] *inserted*

153: 10  body which is] body with which is CT

153: 39  has CT] *written over* is
154: 5  be CT] *after deleted* by
154: 25  Being; CT] *before deleted* which idea cannot have sprung from myself

154: 32  by CT] *above deleted* upon
154: 32  conditioned CT] *above deleted* contingent
154: 33  as CT] *after deleted* has

## 24 A Critical Comparison of the Methods of Bacon, Hobbes and DesCartes

The manuscript ("CT") is foliated 1–15, measures 221 × 281 mm. and is written in ink. It is signed "B. Russell." on the last leaf.

156: 5  profess, CT] *before deleted* a resemblance
156: 8  differences CT] *after deleted* obvious
156: 9–10  allowed no place to induction CT] *replaced* allowed it no place at all
156: 11  built CT] *before deleted* of
156: 35  existence CT] *after deleted* the real
156: 38  the actual world CT] *after deleted* nature
157: 9  observations CT] *after deleted* the
157: 14  and general CT] *inserted*
157: 16  some such basis CT] *above deleted* it
157: 24  phenomenon CT] *above deleted* particular nature

158: 5  (or rather concepts) CT] *inserted*
158: 31  possibilities CT] *written over* possibility
158: 36  the type, while CT] *replaced* the type of the Sciences, while
158: 38  rationalist CT] *before deleted* he is
159: 3  especially CT] *before deleted* of
159: 8  of it CT] *inserted*
159: 14  have occurred CT] *after deleted* certainly
159: 22  mechanics CT] *after deleted* physical
159: 29  règles CT] *above deleted* lois
159: 30  mêmes que CT] *inserted*
160: 6  a very CT] *after deleted* an almost
160: 13  natures CT] *after deleted* form
161: 4  his CT] *written over* the
161: 11  , he tells us, CT] *inserted*
161: 33  the CT] *inserted on both occurrences*

## 25 Paper on Bacon

The manuscript ("CT") is foliated 1–2, 1–4, 1–2, 1, 1, 1–2, 1–2, measures 220 × 282 mm. and is written in ink. It is signed "B. Russell." on the last leaf.

163: 5  upheld CT] *after deleted* believed
163: 8  invented the doctrine of CT] *in pencil above pencil deletion* made great contributions to
164: 9  it frames CT] *inserted*
164: 14  activity.] activity— CT
164: 35  Mildapettus] Mildepettus CT
165: 36  classes of CT] *replaced* examples of a
165: 38  more Aristotelian CT] *replaced* better

166: 5  inapplicable CT] *after deleted* entirely
166: 23  flux CT] *after deleted* constant
166: 31–2  sensible world on the physical side CT] *after deleted* sensible into
166: 33  *thing* CT] *after deleted* belief in the
167: 15  combine CT] *written over* seem
167: 18  of Induction CT] *inserted*
167: 29  step, though it is CT] *replaced* point, but
168: 10  from our hypothesis CT] *inserted*
168: 12  is CT] *above deleted* was *Also at 168: 13, 168: 14.*
168: 23  in CT] *written over* on
168: 26  method.] method— CT
168: 26  the CT] *inserted*

## 26 Paper on DesCartes

The manuscript ("CT") is foliated 1–2, 1–2, 1–2, 1, 1–2, 1, 1–3, 1–2, 1–2, measures 221 × 284 mm. and is written in ink.

170: 35  error CT] *after deleted* the

170: 38  Hobbes] H. CT
170: 38–42  Hobbes … objection. CT] *inserted in margin*
171: 14  change from CT] *before deleted* analysis to a

171: 27 deny CT] *after deleted* think
171: 33–4 kind of CT] *inserted*
171: 34 does CT] *above deleted* is
172: 28 this CT] *replaced* the existence of God
173: 10 out CT] *after deleted* ought
173: 15 with CT] *above deleted* by
174: 5 state CT] *after deleted* say
174: 18 can always be avoided by CT] *replaced in pencil* is always
174: 26 body CT] *after deleted* material
175: 11 sometimes CT] *after deleted* often
175: 14 , e.g. ] e.g. CT
175: 14–15 e.g. substances than their attributes CT] *inserted*

175: 16 as the most real being CT] *inserted*
175: 26 its essence CT] *replaced* the essence of mind
175: 37 universal CT] *after deleted* blind
175: 42 him CT] *after deleted* DesCartes
176: 31 principle CT] *replaced* principles
176: 32 substance CT] *after deleted* existence of the
177: 15 material CT] *above deleted* external
177: 19–20 But perceptions ... senses. CT] *inserted in margin*
177: 25–6 "turn towards the body" CT] *replaced* "turn towards or away from certain objects

## 27 Paper on Descartes II

The manuscript ("CT") is foliated 1–2, 1, 1, 1–2, 1, 1, 1–2, 1–2, 1–2, measures 221 × 284 mm. and is written in ink.

179: 4 involves existence CT] *replaced* is thought as existing
179: 13–16 Suppose ... ghosts exist. CT] *inserted in margin*
179: 33 that CT] *above deleted* the being
179: 34 existence,] existence; CT
179: 34 preferring ... "perfect being"; CT] *inserted in margin before marginal deletion* necessity and possibility involves existence
180: 14 were CT] *after deleted* are
180: 15 of CT] *inserted*
180: 17 instant CT] *replaced* same instant that the mind
180: 27–8 in the case of CT] *above deleted* as applied to
180: 35 applying CT] *above deleted* using
180: 36 extension CT] *after deleted* motion
181: 1 be CT] *inserted in pencil in another hand*
181: 9 *Method* CT] *above deleted* Meditations

181: 10–11 or more CT] *inserted*
181: 12 reasoning CT] *replaced* reason
181: 16 propositions CT] *after deleted* judgments
181: 37 parallel: CT] *before deleted* the
182: 7 when CT] *above deleted* on
182: 17–18 with the enquiry into its logical order CT] *replaced* and the logical order
182: 22 on ethical CT] *replaced* of ethical
182: 27 his illustration of CT] *inserted*
182: 30 Descartes' CT] *The apostrophe was added in pencil, possibly not by Russell.*
183: 2 sections] section CT
183: 7 permit] *in pencil above pencil deletion* allow
183: 8 always CT] *inserted*
183: 22 Finite things CT] *after deleted* Thought and extension exist only as
183: 29 as one CT] *before deleted* and indivisible
184: 4 Bouillier] Bouiller CT
184: 13 Geulinx,] Geulinx CT
184: 13 Descartes CT] *after deleted* Cartes
184: 24 world, CT] *replaced* world. Eve
184: 28 rest of the CT] *inserted*

## 28 Paper on Hobbes

The manuscript ("CT") is foliated 1–2, 1, 1–2, 1–5, 1, 1–2, 1–4, measures 221 × 282 mm. and is written in ink.

186: 29 about CT] *inserted*
186: 29 1651] *The last digit of this date is illegible.*

186:32 Civil War CT] *after deleted* Eng
189:6 and later CT] *replaced* though and
189:27 body CT] *before deleted* which led to its
189:28 different CT] *after deleted* due not
189:30 agent CT] *after deleted* producer
189:32 any of CT] *inserted*
189:33 agent CT] *above deleted* patient
190:6 no motion CT] *after deleted* he says that
190:9 a CT] *above deleted* equal
190:10 operations CT] *before deleted* with
190:38 Hobbes uses CT] *after deleted* When the thing is no longer present,
191:4–5 perceived CT] *after deleted* seen
191:23 our CT] *inserted*
191:25 one another] *The manuscript is blotted and partially illegible; on another is a possible reading though* one another *is the reading in Hobbes.*
191:38 if it is sensuous CT] *inserted*

192:12 it consists CT] *after deleted* he compares life to a
192:21 lower CT] *after deleted* higher to a lower
192:30 king CT] *in pencil above pencil deletion* sovereign
192:33–4 very defective CT] *after deleted* of course
193:17 the world CT] *above deleted* society
193:17 And the partial CT] *after deleted* Self-assertion and self-denial become one in such a state; and
193:30 ourselves CT] *above deleted* us
193:39–40 but is always joy CT] *inserted*
193:41 from CT] *after deleted* say
194:2–3 except that ... minute CT] *inserted in margin*
194:3 minute;] minute.; CT
194:13 small CT] *inserted*
194:15 However, CT] *after deleted* Perhaps

## 29 On the Distinction between the Psychological and Metaphysical Points of View

The manuscript ("CT") is foliated 1–7, measures 222 × 285 mm. and is written in ink. It is signed "B. Russell" on the last leaf.

196:6 in Astronomy CT] *inserted*
196:6–7 try to discover CT] *above deleted* endeavour to find out
196:8 their CT] *written over* the
196:8 composition CT] *before deleted* of such states
196:22 I CT] *written over* we
196:25 pure CT] *inserted*
196:27 we shall do CT] *replaced* it would be
196:36 contains knowledge CT] *above deleted* is
196:38 is CT] *before deleted* equally
196:41 mind CT] *before deleted* of

197:5 element of consciousness CT] *above deleted* state of mind
197:7 state of mind CT] *above deleted* desire
197:14 craving CT] *above deleted* desire
197:15–16 and he has ... correct. CT] *above deleted* etc. etc.
197:16 moral CT] *above deleted* rational
197:19 bridged CT] *above deleted* healed
197:26 every idea CT] *replaced* in every proposition
197:28 whereas CT] *after deleted* but
197:35 any CT] *inserted*
197:39 circular CT] *after deleted* necessarily
198:10 or CT] *after deleted* on
198:14 immediately CT] *before deleted* (if not mor

## 30 On Pleasure

The manuscript ("CT") is foliated 1–5(6), 6, measures 221 × 284 mm. and is written in ink. It is signed "B. Russell." on the last leaf.

201:*title* On Pleasure:] On Pleasure. CT

202:2 desirable CT] *above deleted* agreeable
202:4 loosely CT] *before deleted* to denote the
202:7 desirability CT] *above deleted* agreeableness

202: 10 take the CT] *replaced* be used in
202: 17 an CT] *above deleted* the
202: 23 at all times CT] *after deleted* always
202: 24 most obvious CT] *above deleted* best
202: 25 sources of pleasure CT] *replaced* pleasures
202: 31 necessarily CT] *inserted*
202: 31 pleasures CT] *after deleted* many
202: 39 that CT] *written over* these
203: 1 purely CT] *after deleted* in
203: 3 often CT] *inserted*
203: 5 other sources of enjoyment CT] *after deleted* pleasures
203: 13 subject. CT] *replaced* subject of the work of
203: 17 external events CT] *replaced* the external events of their life
203: 36 may be called CT] *above deleted* are

204: 4 pleasures, CT] *before deleted* (which for ethical Hedonism is all that is really required)
204: 13 additional pain CT] *inserted*
204: 14 live CT] *written over* life
204: 43 in imagination. CT] *before deleted* This argument is the same as the argument that it is absurd to speak of a sum of pleasures:
205: 2 preferring CT] *replaced* the preference of
205: 12 neither] Neither CT
205: 13 unpleasant. But CT] *replaced* unpleasant, but as
205: 17 introspection CT] *after deleted* this
205: 18 frequently CT] *inserted*
205: 18 seldom CT] *above deleted* not

## 31 On the Foundations of Ethics

The manuscript ("CT") is foliated 1–5, measures 120 × 185 mm. and is written in ink. It is signed "B. Russell." on the last leaf.

208: 7 attainable CT] *written over in pencil* attained
208: 15 of it CT] *inserted*
208: 20 it is CT] *after deleted* the
208: 24 the pursuit CT] *replaced* it
208: 26 particular CT] *above deleted* individual
208: 26 does CT] *above deleted* need
208: 26 as CT] *inserted in pencil*
208: 27 first CT] *after deleted* second
208: 29 to CT] *written over* a
208: 34 other CT] *before pencil deletion* passion
208: 37 then CT] *inserted*
209: 2 mar CT] *in pencil above pencil deletion*

destroy
209: 2 There will CT] *after deleted* It will ther
209: 17 spirits CT] *after illegible deletion*
209: 23 parenthetically CT] *inserted*
209: 31 happiness. CT] *before deleted* As an example one might quote the alleged increase of suicide due to education.
209: 38 a particular CT] *inserted*
209: 39 on which they differ CT] *inserted*
209: 40 suggests CT] *above deleted* produces
210: 1 it is CT] *after deleted* no one
210: 6–7 than Green's view CT] *inserted*
210: 13 happiness CT] *after deleted* greater
210: 19 either CT] *written over* neither
210: 35 latter CT] *inserted*
211: 2 But this CT] *above deleted* This however

## 32 The Relation of What Ought to Be to What Is, Has Been or Will Be

The manuscript ("CT") is foliated 1–3, measures 221 × 283 mm. and is written in ink. It is signed "B. Russell." on the last leaf.

212: *title* The Relation of What Ought to Be to What Is, Has Been or Will Be] The Relation of what ought to be to what is, has been or will be. CT
213: 2 A CT] *written over* I

213: 3 such CT] *inserted*
213: 7 true CT] *after deleted* equally
213: 12 by ourselves] be ourselves CT
213: 13 regarded as CT] *inserted*
213: 31 must CT] *before deleted* logically
213: 31 unless CT] *before deleted* they are
213: 36 be derived] by derived CT
213: 42–3 and that ... circumstances CT] *inserted*

214: 6 we find CT] *after deleted* our argument
214: 7 such other CT] *replaced* other such
214: 9 ¶The notion CT] *after deleted* ¶The notion of *ought* seems to imply that any

## 33 The Relation of Rule and End

The manuscript ("CT") is foliated *1–3*, measures 219 × 284 mm. and is written in ink. It is signed "B. Russell." on the last leaf.

216: 24 a moral act CT] *after deleted* an act
216: 26 Will.] Will: CT] *before deleted* an act is moral or immoral or morally indifferent according as the Will is determined by some motive of the agent is to act morally, to act in a manner recognized by the agent as opposed to morality, or is directed to an end which is not considered in an ethical light at all. Thus it is the nature of the Will alone which determines whether an

agent to whom it is applicable acts for some purpose which presents itself to him as desirable, and to require that such purpose shall be *good*.
214: 23 be CT] *inserted*

act is moral or not.
216: 27 actual volition CT] *after deleted* will
216: 32 and CT] *written over* as
216: 43 conformity to virtue in the immediate future CT] *replaced* future conformity to virtue
217: 3 in the Kantian sense CT] *inserted*
217: 10 volition CT] *above deleted* will
217: 13 further result. CT] *before deleted* And this further result cannot be action, for then the same difficulty would reappear.
217: 15 regarded CT] *after deleted* conceive
217: 17 consciously CT] *inserted*

## 34 On the Definition of Virtue

The manuscript ("CT") is foliated *1–6*, measures 220 × 284 mm. and is written in ink. It is signed "B. Russell." on the last leaf.

219: 7 about it CT] *inserted*
219: 12 irksome to me, CT] *before deleted* but that I do it
219: 13 benevolent CT] *replaced* natural benevolence
219: 15 merely CT] *inserted*
219: 19 it CT] *written over* is
219: 21 then CT] *inserted*
219: 29 virtuous; CT] *after deleted* to be regar
219: 32 sacrifice ought CT] *before deleted* to spring
219: 33 an emotional CT] *replaced* a
219: 41 temperance CT] *above deleted* it
219: 43 so CT] *inserted*

220: 2 are CT] *written over* were
220: 7 particular CT] *above deleted* individual
220: 7 On CT] *above deleted* According to
220: 8 first CT] *inserted*
220: 9 to promote CT] *after deleted* towards
220: 18 other CT] *inserted*
220: 33 dread power CT] *inserted*
220: 38 disapprove of CT] *above deleted* censure
221: 1 more virtuous CT] *above deleted* better
221: 4 considerable CT] *inserted*
221: 4 act,] act CT] *before deleted* it is usually supposed that the motive was a sense of duty, and
221: 4 usually CT] *inserted*
221: 15 morally CT] *after deleted* virtuously
221: 21 should then CT] *replaced* shall

## 35 The Ethical Bearings of Psychogony

The manuscript ("CT") is foliated *1–6*, measures 222 × 286 mm. and is written in ink. It is signed "B. Russell." on the last leaf.

223: 6 ethical CT] *inserted in pencil*

223: 7 considerable CT] *replaced* a considerable regulative
223: 16 parents CT] *above deleted* mother
223: 23 complex, CT] *before deleted* as tribes grew into nations

223: 23–4 more and more CT] *before deleted* extra

223: 27 prudence and CT] *inserted*

223: 29 may CT] *inserted*

223: 36 children CT] *inserted*

223: 37 bring them up CT] *replaced* bring up children

224: 10–11 usually considered CT] *before deleted insertion* ipso facto

224: 11 than CT] *written over* that

224: 13 not materially different CT] *replaced* no different

224: 19 choose to CT] *inserted in pencil above pencil deletion* do

224: 23 determined CT] *after deleted* accepted

224: 24 Psychogony.] Psychogony—CT] *before deleted* If for example we are Hedonists, we shall on the whole accept existing morality if we regard life as on the whole pleasurable, since existing morality tends on the whole to maximise life; while if we are pessimists we shall on the whole reject existing morality so as to minimise life (though this rejection is liable to numerous restrictions). Again an intuitionist would have to face the question how in other times and countries intuitions differing from his own exist or have existed on moral questions: he would have to explain how an organic morality

224: 27 or reject CT] *inserted*

224: 33 proof of the CT] *inserted*

224: 34 is CT] *inserted before deleted* stands

224: 36 are likely to CT] *above deleted* must

224: 39–40 these needs CT] *before deleted* that

225: 1 acting (as we think) virtuously CT] *above deleted* doing so

225: 1 those very CT] *replaced* the

## 36 Ethical Axioms

The manuscript ("CT") is foliated *1–4*, measures 221 × 284 mm. and is written in ink. It is signed "B. Russell." on the last leaf.

227: 5 of error, CT] *before deleted* in a moral judg

227: 9 at any rate CT] *inserted*

227: 14 will and act CT] *after deleted* continually

227: 15–16 or even to abstain from acting, CT] *inserted*

227: 40 the CT] *inserted*

227: 43–228: 2 (since ... conduct). CT] *The parentheses were added in pencil. It is probable that they were inserted by Russell, since his pencil revisions also appear at 228: 6 and 228: 10. Sidgwick also marked the manuscript in pencil, but it was not his practice to use parentheses for this purpose.*

228: 6 I think CT] *inserted in pencil*

228: 8 precept CT] *before deleted* to guide us

228: 10 one CT] *inserted in pencil above pencil deletion* a maxim

228: 13 imagined CT] *inserted*

228: 18 his own imagined CT] *replaced* imagine his own

228: 18 by his act CT] *after deleted* to be best obtainable

228: 25 any CT] *after deleted* the

228: 26 merely CT] *inserted*

228: 33 this CT] *written over* it

228: 34 question CT] *after deleted* princi

## 37 The Free-Will Problem from an Idealist Standpoint

The manuscript ("CT") is foliated 1–5, 5a–b, 6–9, 9a, 10, 10a, 11–16, 16a, 17–24, measures 221 × 286 mm. and is written in ink. It is signed "B. Russell" on the last leaf. The manuscript bears pencil marks and occasional revisions in another hand, over which Russell usually wrote in ink when he wished to adopt them. It has proved impossible to determine the order of composition of the inserted leaves and the renumbered leaves (5b and 10a in particular appear to have been renumbered from 5 and 10). Probably some of the original draft leaves were discarded. There is also the possibility that Russell made use of the manuscript of November 1894 that he wrote for Mary Costelloe.

230: 2 must CT] *after deleted* are

230: 4 There CT] *above deleted* It] *after deleted* As

230: 5 to begin with CT] *above deleted* in this Chapter

230: 5 choice CT] *before deleted* of the late Mr. T. H. Green

230: 5 representative CT] *before deleted* and champion

230: 7 champion. CT] *before deleted* This choice of a

230: 8 school. CT] *replaced* shool ⟨sic⟩, and it cannot be denied English Philosophy, since

230: 8–9 But we cannot deny, however we may honour Mr. T. H. Green as a pioneer, CT] *replaced* But, however we may honour Mr. T. H. Green as a pioneer, we cannot deny

230: 14 very accurately to CT] *inserted*

230: 19 work CT] *above deleted* views

230: 19 to whose views CT] *after deleted* who hold the views

230: 21 treatment CT] *after deleted* determinism

230: 23 chief CT] *above deleted* main

230: 26 , in a foot-note CT] *replaced* is in a note,

230: 34 who are CT] *above deleted* being

230: 35 fit only for the Middle Ages CT] *above deleted* for which the time has gone by

230: 38 cannot face CT] *above deleted* dreads

231: 9 join. CT] *replaced* join, the more so,

231: 11 suggesting CT] *above deleted* raising

231: 11 refuse CT] *after deleted* deny

231: 19 in abuse of CT] *after deleted* , and abuse you as

231: 22 "up to date man" CT] *above deleted* scientist

231: 22 abuse Metaphysics, CT] *after deleted* break down before a little metaphysical criticism

231: 27 Free Will] Free-Will CT

231: 27 point out CT] *before deleted* , however imperfectly,

231: 28 each of CT] *above deleted* both

231: 30 this CT] *written over* that

231: 31–232: 13 solution ... honour." CT] *inserted as fos. 5a and 5b*

231: 32 this country CT] *Above this phrase someone (possibly Russell) has written* Eng in pencil.

231: 33 and has been CT] *after deleted* and teaches

231: 39 controversy CT] *after deleted* error

231: 42 discussion CT] *above deleted* argument

231: 43 , as we shall see, CT] *inserted*

232: 2 these CT] *written over* the *in Alys's hand*

232: 2 broader senses, CT] *inserted in Alys's hand above deleted* latter pair

232: 5 usually CT] *inserted*

232: 5–6 the doctrine—more properly called fatalism—CT] *replaced* , in general, more properly called fatalism; fatalism is the doctrine

232: 9 driven CT] *above deleted* forced] *after deleted* compelled

232: 16 works CT] *above deleted* plays

232: 23 ourselves. We CT] *replaced* ourselves; we

232: 23 , in different characters, CT] *inserted*

232: 27 cause. Our CT] *replaced* cause; our

232: 28 , however, is CT] *replaced* is, however,

232: 29–30 So much as to the two meanings of Determination. CT] *inserted in Alys's hand*

232: 31–3 There remain ... abandoned. CT] *before deleted* We come next to the two senses of Freedom. The old sense, called Liberty of Indifference, has now been almost universally abandoned, and is really, pretty much what is commonly meant by caprice.] *replaced* We come next to the two senses of Freedom. The old sense, which has now been universally abandoned, has been called Liberty of Indifference. In this sense, it is, really, pretty much what is meant by caprice.

232: 33 was CT] *written over* is

232: 34 held CT] *written over* hold

232: 34 man CT] *above deleted* person

232: 34 could CT] *written over* can

232: 34–5 by a sheer act of will, CT] *inserted*

232: 35 act CT] *after deleted* be

232: 36 character, CT] *before deleted insertion* they said,

232: 40 simply CT] *before deleted* and

233: 1 Ethic. The CT] *replaced* Ethic; the

233:2 in his view CT] *above deleted* according to him

233:7 that CT] *after deleted* it to

233:8 Transcendental Ego CT] *before deleted* , or pure reason,

233:9 able CT] *before deleted* to determine

233:15 we CT] *after deleted* it

233:20 We may even CT] *after deleted* Nay, if caprice really existed, it would

233:21 that CT] *inserted*

233:22 ends—but CT] *replaced* ends; and

233:23 bondage! CT] *before deleted* For to pursue my own ends means no more than seek what I most desire, to do as I like in fact; and who would wish for a liberty which is never realized except when he abstains from doing as he does what he doesn't like?

233:23 Not only, then, is this Liberty of Indifference, CT] *replaced* This Liberty of Indifference, then, is not only

233:26 compulsion. A CT] *replaced* compulsion; a

233:27 Such laws— CT] *after deleted* Such laws, although they are self-imposed, will suffice, as I shall proceed to shew, for the science of Psychology. Yet,

233:27-8 Such laws—being, in truth, nothing but the resolution consistently to pursue certain ends—will CT] *replaced* Yet, being, in truth, nothing but the determination consistently to pursue certain ends, they will

233:28 resolution CT] *above deleted* determination

233:29 our CT] *above deleted* his

233:29 them CT] *inserted*

233:31-234:11 But how ... evident, CT] *inserted as fol. 9a*

233:31-2 But how CT] *after deleted* But how such a freedom be real

233:33 , for this occasion only, to make himself CT] *replaced* to make himself, for this occasion only,

234:17 points out CT] *above deleted* holds

234:24 these, CT] *before deleted* can be

234:26-34 (1) Cause ... Gravitation was CT] *inserted as fol. 10a before deleted* ¶To make plain the sense in which such laws suffice for Psychology, it will be necessary to make a few general remarks about the

general nature of scientific laws, and also about the meanings of the word *cause*. Let us consider some science, such as Astronomy, in which the "Reign of Law" has been thoroughly established, and chance and caprice have long ago disappeared. A cause, here, may have one of two meanings which must be considered separately.

234:26 Cause CT] *above deleted* It

234:29 loose. It regards CT] *replaced* loose; we regard

234:30 or not CT] *inserted*

234:32 rests CT] *above deleted* is

234:35 he CT] *inserted before* saw

234:37 facts. Finally, CT] *replaced* facts; and at last

234:37-8 , according to the same formula, CT] *inserted*

234:38 also CT] *inserted*

234:38 round the sun CT] *above deleted* too

235:2 it. Hence CT] *replaced* it; hence

235:6 say CT] *written over* said

235:6 that CT] *inserted*

235:6 is CT] *above deleted* was

235:8 has taken CT] *replaced* takes

235:10 cause and effect CT] *after deleted* both

235:12 total CT] *inserted*

235:13 the impact CT] *inserted*

235:14-17 In this sequence ... laws of science. CT] *replaced* The laws of science are certain uniformities, in this sequence of cause and effect, by which, when we know the cause, we can discover the effect, and when we know the effect we can discover the cause.

235:22 past eclipses and transits CT] *replaced* the eclipses and transits of past times

235:24 relation. We CT] *replaced* relation—we

235:24 that CT] *before deleted* one

235:24 determines CT] *above deleted* produces

235:29 , in all hitherto observed sequences, CT] *inserted*

235:35 this CT] *before deleted* much

235:37 future CT] *after deleted* past] *above deleted* future

235:37 past CT] *below ink deletion* future

*written in pencil in another hand*

236: 6–7 will ... relation CT] *replaced* has more power than the other *The replacement has been written in ink over a pencil insertion in another hand.*

236: 19 complain of CT] *above deleted* fret over *The word* complain *has been written first in pencil in another hand.*

236: 20–1 There are cases where such a complaint would be justified— CT] *replaced* The cases where such a complaint would have a real ground, would be the

236: 21–2 interposes CT] *written over* interposed

236: 22 desires. The CT] *replaced* desires—the

236: 23–4 the deafness ... devoted CT] *replaced* the defeat of a cause to which we had devoted our lives, the deafness of a Beethoven,

236: 28 are. Such a complaint would be the more unreasonable, CT] *replaced* are—the more so,

236: 35–6 To answer CT] *after deleted* For this

236: 38–43, 237: 39–43 I ought ... article. CT] *inserted as fol. 16a*

236: 42 we have just CT] *after deleted* I have just

237: 20 we cannot CT] *after deleted* , even here,

237: 21 considering, at the same time, CT] *above deleted* taking into account

237: 24 world CT] *after deleted* external

237: 24 his CT] *above deleted* our

237: 27 laws. Now CT] *replaced* laws—now

237: 35 when CT] *above deleted* as long as

237: 42 considered CT] *after deleted* which is

238: 2 we are CT] *above deleted* a man is

238: 3 we are CT] *replaced* he is *Also again on this line and at 238: 4.*

238: 3–4 in proportion CT] *inserted*

238: 6–7 of Free Will, which is the more special subject of this Essay. We CT] *replaced* we proposed to ourselves at the beginning; we

238: 9 , before taking leave of the subject,

CT] *above deleted* at the en

238: 19 the pure CT] *after deleted* but

238: 19–20 , not in any prevision of desirable consequences, but CT] *inserted*

238: 20 in the will alone CT] *replaced* alone in the will

238: 22 purpose CT] *above deleted* end

238: 31–2 The motives ... are always desires CT] *replaced* The motives to will are always, even in what are called acts of self-sacrifice, desires

238: 42 may CT] *inserted*

239: 1 for, CT] *inserted*

239: 2 test CT] *above deleted* proof

239: 2 only CT] *inserted*

239: 7 is CT] *above deleted* be

239: 7 that CT] *above deleted* which

239: 7–8 realization of desired ends, CT] *replaced* satisfaction of desire,

239: 11 pleasure. As CT] *replaced* pleasure; as

239: 17 desired. The CT] *replaced* desired, and the

239: 18 , not the mere feeling of attainment, but CT] *inserted*

239: 19 the actual world CT] *above deleted* fact

239: 19 object of our desire. CT] *replaced* desired object.

239: 19 object of our desire. CT] *before deleted* Now in all cases of a conflict of desires, what occurs is, that two incompatible things both seem good to us, and to renounce either would be felt as a loss. Most of us have what are called different "universes" of desire; that is, we have a number of desires tending towards one end, and a number of other desires tending towards

239: 20 We may CT] *replaced* Hence we may

239: 24 proposed CT] *inserted*

239: 26 unimpeded CT] *after deleted* able

239: 30 in harmony CT] *replaced* harmony

239: 31 the precept CT] the *written over* a

239: 36 In CT] *above deleted* With

239: 39 may CT] *after deleted* shall

239: 40 , however slight, CT] *inserted*

## 38 Note on Ethical Theory

The manuscript ("CT") measures 220 × 347 mm. and is written in ink. With the exception of the last sentence, the second paragraph reappears in Paper 15, "Is Ethics a Branch of Empirical Psychology?", at 104: 13–31. A collation of the passages will be found in the textual notes to 15.

241: 28 those] these CT
241: 35 it CT] *inserted*

## 39 Are All Desires Equally Moral?

The manuscript ("CT") is paginated 1–3, measures 224 × 287 mm. and is written in ink.

242: *title* Are All Desires Equally Moral?]
  Are all desires equally moral? CT
243: 7 desired CT] *above deleted* which

would satisfy it
243: 19 satisfaction CT] *inserted after* This
243: 31 these things CT] *replaced* them
244: 6 of mind CT] *inserted*
244: 13 pleasure CT] *inserted*
244: 14 2 is a harmony,] 2 is a harmony CT

## 40 Review of Heymans

"CT" stands for the only known version of the text, that in *Mind*, n.s. 4 (April 1895): 245–9.

251: 33 (p. 67).] (p. 69). CT *The passage*

*Russell refers to here is on p. 67 of Heymans 1890–94. Since Russell's handwritten 7 was often confused with his 9 (see the headnote to 16), it seems likely that the printer simply misread Russell's manuscript.*

## 41 Observations on Space and Geometry

The relevant pages of the manuscript notebook ("CT") are foliated *i*, 1–13, 30–8. It measures 166 × 206 mm. and is written in ink.

258: 1 Quelle CT] *replaced* La Géometrie, quelle
258: 6 *Principles of Psychology,* II, p. 150n.]
  Principles of Psychology p. 150. CT
258: 7 Introduction] I. Introduction. CT
258: 8 manner CT] *above deleted* way
258: 16 their explanation or classification. CT] *replaced* an explanation or classification of them.
258: 25 any questionable implication CT] *replaced* any implication as to its nature
258: 26 in part CT] *after pencil deletion* being
258: 29 spring CT] *written over* sprang
258: 30 similarity CT] *above deleted* uniformity
258: 32 something like CT] *inserted in pencil*
258: 32 *matter* CT] *before deleted* of sensation
258: 33 while CT] *inserted*
258: 35 fascinating in CT] *replaced* fas-

cinating about
258: 36 insight CT] *after deleted* apparent
258: 36–7 are subjective CT] *altered in pencil from* are ascribed to the subject
258: 38 are CT] *above deleted* form
258: 38–9 externally-caused CT] *inserted*
259: 8 value is CT] *above deleted* judgments are
259: 12 , in the case of space, CT] *inserted*
259: 21 experimental CT] *written over* empirical
259: 22 are logically CT] *above deleted* is
259: 22 they CT] *written over* it
259: 23 be present CT] *after deleted* exist
259: 23 reflective knowledge of sensational matter CT] *replaced* sensational knowledge of reflective matter
259: 25 and CT] *above deleted* hence
259: 26 regarded CT] *after deleted* declared
259: 28 -conception CT] *inserted*
259: 30 former CT] *written over* latter
259: 34 the latter CT] *in pencil above pencil deletion* this
259: 37 and the CT] *replaced* and

259: 38 only CT] *inserted*

259: 38 the CT] *written over* and

259: 40 while CT] *inserted*

260: 2 first CT] *inserted*

260: 9 contentions CT] *above deleted* arguments

260: 20 This CT] *written over* I

260: 22 brought CT] *after deleted* interesting to

260: 26 Helmholtz] Helmholz CT

260: 36 psychologically CT] *inserted*

260: 37 these are CT] *replaced* this is *with* is *deleted in pencil*

261: 2 have CT] *written over* be

261: 7 in turn CT] *above deleted* again

261: 8 à priori CT] *inserted*

261: 9 sensation." CT] *before deleted* It is to be observed that Kant never (to my knowledge) uses the word *phenomenon* of anything below the stage of perception.

261: 10 subjective CT] *after deleted* psychologically

261: 13 to Kant CT] *inserted*

261: 34 e.g. CT] *inserted*

261: 37 array CT] *inserted*

261: 37 psychological CT] *after deleted* analytical

261: 37 fiction CT] *written over* novel

261: 37-8 is a commentary on CT] *above deleted* proves

261: 38 In short, CT] *inserted*

261: 40 objections CT] *after deleted* general

262: 2 thereby CT] *inserted*

262: 4-5 as above explained CT] *inserted*

262: 8 from that which I have here attributed to Kant CT] *inserted in pencil*

262: 9-10 "Transcendental Aesthetik"] Tr. Ae. CT

262: 10 distinguishes CT] *after deleted* seems to give a

262: 10 Ideality CT] *after deleted* subjectivity

262: 16 held CT] *in pencil above pencil deletion* denied

262: 16 attack CT] *after deleted* maintain

262: 17 Ideality CT] *replaced* the Ideality of

262: 18 what CT] *written over* that

262: 19 himself CT] *inserted in pencil*

262: 20 denies the existence of CT] *in pencil above pencil deletion* combats the position that

262: 20 space CT] *before pencil deletion* exists

262: 23-4 "metaphysical distance"] *In CT Russell used single quotes in this case only, perhaps suggesting more than simple quotation.*

262: 27 no more ground CT] *replaced* no ground whatever

262: 28-9 Barbara. Thus] Barbara.—Thus CT *Russell originally ran this paragraph on with the next. Then he indicated his need for a paragraph break by writing* N.P. *before* Thus .

262: 28 analogue CT] *after deleted* groun

262: 31 speak of CT] *after deleted* call

262: 35-40 If ... sequel. CT] *inserted on the opposing page, i.e. fol. $10^v$*

262: 38-9 be found to CT] *inserted in pencil*

262: 40 The importance ... sequel. CT] *inserted in pencil*

263: 8 only Lobatchewsky and Riemann. CT] *replaced* no one except Lobatchewsky.

263: 12-13 certain, if they could exist, CT] *replaced* if they could exist, certain

263: 13-14 wholly in error, if this did not take place, CT] *replaced* if this did not take place, as wholly in error

263: 14 in any CT] *after deleted* as

263: 26-7 in which Euclidean straight lines are possible CT] *inserted*

263: 28 say two of them CT] *replaced* say they

263: 37 as Erhardt does (p. 229) CT] *inserted*

263: 38-9 the straight CT] *replaced* straight

264: 2 more CT] *inserted*

264: 2 than CT] *above deleted* as

264: 4 in Erhardt's sense CT] *replaced* to Erhardt

264: 29 (p. 232) CT] *written over* (p. 332)

264: 36 important CT] *inserted*

264: 39 rigid CT] *after deleted* fixed

264: 39 are CT] *above deleted* were

265: 9-10 (p. 241) CT] *inserted*

265: 17 surface CT] *underlined in pencil*

265: 18 a misunderstanding CT] *inserted*

265: 24 demonstrates CT] *after deleted* shews

265: 25 (p. 245) CT] *inserted*

## 42 The Logic of Geometry

The textual notes contain a collation of the copy-text, *Mind*, n.s. 5 (Jan. 1896): 1–23, denoted by "CT", with the closely related passages in *An Essay on the Foundations of Geometry* (1897), denoted by "97". Parts of Paper **42** also reappear in altered form in **44**. The table below summarizes the intersection of these three texts.

There is a greater overlap between Paper **42** and 97 than there is between Paper **44** and 97. However, there are passages which occur only in 97 and **44** (e.g. 291: 13–292: 20 of **44** reappears as §§6–8 of 97). In fact, **44** presents a somewhat compressed version of the general argument of **42**, supplemented by additional material concerning the relativity of position. The version in 97 is verbally closer to **42**, but incorporates the new material from **44**.

When parallel passages are to be found in all three texts, the more distantly related passage is enclosed in parentheses. When **42** or **44** contains a passage which has no equivalent in either of the other two texts, its page and line numbers are given in the table as the only entry on the line. The intersection of **42** and **44** is not reported in the notes, but may be ascertained in summary from the table.

It is convenient, for the purposes of making such a comparison, to use the article numbers by which *An Essay on the Foundations of Geometry* is structured, rather than its page numbers. The former also facilitate comparison with the revised edition (published only in French) of 1901. It should be noted that many of the closely related passages in 97 incorporate new material and are therefore longer than the corresponding passages in **42** and **44**.

| 97 *An Essay on the Foundations of Geometry* | 42 "The Logic of Geometry" | 44 "The *À Priori* in Geometry" |
|---|---|---|
| | 267: 1–11 | |
| | | 291: 1–12 |
| §6 | | 291: 13–38 |
| §7 | | 291: 39–292: 10 |
| §8 | | 292: 11–20 |
| | | 292: 21–293: 25 |
| §143 | 267: 12–33 | (293: 26–294: 3) |
| §144, 1st ¶ | 267: 34–268:12 | (294: 4–18) |
| | | 294: 19–296: 18 |
| §144, 2nd (and last) ¶ | 268: 13–26 | |
| §145 | 268: 27–269: 20 | |
| §146 | 269: 21–270: 18 | |
| | 270: 19–272: 4 | |
| §149 | 272: 5–10 | |
| §150 | 272: 11–273: 13 | |
| §151 | 273: 14–274: 4 | |
| §152 | 274: 5–39 | |
| §153 | 275: 1–17 | |
| §154 | 275: 17–31 | |
| | 275: 32–276: 11 | |
| §158 | 276: 12–29 | (296: 19–35 [to "p. 614)."]) |

| §159 | 276: 30–277: 9 | (296: 35–41) |
| §160 | 277: 10–35 | |
| §161 | 277: 36–278: 4 | (296: 42–297: 9) |
| | 278: 5–20 [ to "argument."] | 297: 10–30 [ to "argument."] |
| | 278: 20–279: 3 | |
| | | 297: 30–40 |
| §163 | | 297: 41–298: 12 |
| | | 298: 13–23 |
| | 279: 4–18 | |
| §165 | 279: 19–28 | (298: 26–35 [from "But why"]) |
| §166, 1st ¶ | 279: 29–33 | (298: 24–6 [to "space."]) |
| | | 298: 36–8 |
| §167, 1st 10 lines | 279: 34–280: 4 [to "definition."] | (298: 39–299: 9) |
| §167, remainder | 280: 4–29 | |
| | | 299: 10–33 |
| §168 | 280: 30–43 | |
| §169 | 281: 1–23 | |
| §170 | 281: 24–282: 12 | |
| §171 | 282: 13–21 | |
| §172 | 282: 22–283: 14 | (299: 34–300: 19) |
| §175, 1st 10 lines of 1st ¶ | 283: 15–23 | (300: 20–7) |
| §175, remainder of 1st ¶ | 283: 23–41 [from "But,"] | |
| §176 | 283: 42–284: 40 | |
| | 284: 41–286: 39 | |
| §177 | | 300: 28–37 |
| §178, 1st 2 ¶¶ | | 300: 38–301: 9 |
| | | 301: 10–15 |
| §178, 3rd (and last) ¶ | | 301: 16–302: 1 |
| | | 302: 2–304: 34 |

267: 12 I. THE AXIOM OF CONGRUENCE CT] I. *The Axiom of Free Mobility.* 97

267: 13–17 Let us begin ... Geometry. CT] **143.** Metrical Geometry, to begin with, may be defined as the science which deals with the comparison and relations of spatial magnitudes. The conception of magnitude, therefore, is necessary from the start. 97

267: 25 import, CT] *footnote added in 97:* [1]Contrast Erdmann, op. cit. p. 138.

267: 27 in fact we can see at once CT] we can see at once, in fact, 97

267: 28 magnitude. CT] *footnote added in 97:*

[2]Cf. Erdmann, op. cit. p. 164.

267: 35 Geometry CT] metrical Geometry 97 *Also at* 268: 16, 268: 24, 276: 30.

267: 37–268: 7 This, however ... both of them. CT] In part this is true, but not wholly. The part which is merely a definition is given in Euclid's eighth axiom: "Magnitudes which exactly coincide are equal." But this gives a sufficient criterion only when the magnitudes to be compared already occupy the same position. When, as will normally be the case, the two spatial magnitudes are external to one another—as, indeed, must be the case, if they are distinct, and not whole and part—the two magnitudes can only be made to coincide by a motion of one or both of them. In order, therefore, that our definition of spatial magnitude may give unambiguous results, coincidence when superposed, if it can ever occur, must occur always, whatever path be pursued in bringing it about. 97

268: 10 axiom CT] *footnote added in 97:* [2]Cf. Erdmann, op. cit. p. 50.

268: 12 *depend on* CT] *depend upon* 97

268: 13 Congruence, or Free Mobility CT] Free Mobility 97

268: 13 Free Mobility CT] *footnote added in 97:* [3]*Also called the axiom of congruence. I have taken congruence to be the definition of spatial equality by superposition, and shall therefore generally speak of the axiom as Free Mobility.*

268: 16-22 have to ... philosophic absurdity. CT] be unable, without a logical absurdity, to establish the notion of spatial magnitude at all. 97

268: 33 change CT] changes 97

268: 35 figures CT] *footnote added in 97:* [1]For the sense in which these figures are to be regarded as material, see criticism of Helmholtz, Chapter II. §§69 ff.

269: 4 space CT] the space formed by its surface 97

269: 15-18 no philosopher ... experience. CT] space must, since it is a form of externality, allow only of relative, not of absolute, position, and must be completely homogeneous throughout. To suppose it otherwise, is to give it a thinghood which no form of externality can possibly possess. 97

269: 20 Congruence CT] Free Mobility 97 *Also at 273: 1, 273: 5, 273: 24, 274: 6, 274: 14, 274: 39, 275: 3, 275: 14, 275: 25, 276: 13, 276: 25.*

269: 25-8 For the more ... definite law.[2] CT] It has been urged by Erdmann that, for the more immediate purposes of Geometry, this would be unnecessary[1]. ⟨*footnote:* [1]Op. cit. p. 60.⟩ We might construct a new Geometry, he thinks, in which sizes varied with motion on any definite law. Such a view, as I shall show

below, involves a logical error as to the nature of magnitude. But before pointing this out, let us discuss the geometrical consequences of assuming its truth. 97

269: 29 $ds \cdot f(p)$] $ds.f(p)$ CT *Dot raised also at 270: 13, 270: 14 and 275: 39.*

269: 32 measure CT] measurement 97

269: 38 $f(s) \cdot ds$] $f(s)\, ds$ CT

269: 40 then CT] now 97

269: 41-2 *Nicht-Euklidische Geometrie*] *Vorlesungen über Nicht-Euklidische Geometrie* CT *Also at 294: 38. Klein's lectures were first published in two volumes in 1890 as* Nicht-Euklidische Geometrie, I. Vorlesung *and* Nicht-Euklidische Geometrie, II. Vorlesung. *Russell slightly misquoted the title. He did so also in the syllabus of lectures called "The Foundations of Geometry" (see App. I.3, 338: 31) as well as in his 1897, 9n. He had acquired a copy of the second printing of both volumes in July 1894, read them in August 1894, June and September 1895, and October 1899, and had them bound together in his library. His copy bears his frequent annotations. At 294: 38 the date has been emended from 1890 to 1893 to make it consistent with Russell's other references to Klein 1893.*

270: 8 us CT] *footnote added in 97:* [1]The view of Helmholtz and Erdmann, that mechanical experience suffices here, though geometrical experience fails us, has been discussed above, Chapter II. §§73, 82.

270: 9 *does* CT] *does, at first sight,* 97

270: 16 requires, CT] requires, it would seem, 97

272: 5 There remain one or two objections to be answered. CT] **149.** There remain, however, a few objections and difficulties to be discussed. 97

272: 6 case CT] cases 97

272: 6 gloves CT] hands, 97 *Also at 272: 11.*

272: 6 or CT] or of 97

272: 7-8 And second CT] Secondly 97

272: 10 I will consider these objections in turn. CT] Thirdly, it might be urged that we can immediately estimate spatial equality by the eye, with more or less accuracy, and thus have a measure independent of congruence. Fourthly, how is metrical Geometry possible on non-congruent surfaces, if congruence be the basis of spatial measurement? I will discuss these objections successively. 97

272: 11  solids in Geometry CT] solids 97

272: 13  in, CT] *footnote added in 97:* [1]Contrast Delboeuf, L'ancienne et les nouvelles géométries, II. Rev. Phil. 1894, Vol. xxxvii. p. 354.

272: 18  one and two CT] one or two 97

272: 22  indiscernible; if CT] indiscernible. If 97

272: 27  congruence; except CT] Free Mobility. Except 97

272: 32  convention CT] definition 97 *Also at* 272: 33.

272: 34  Indiscernibles. CT] Indiscernibles. We can, without error, make our *definition* of three-dimensional equality rest on two-dimensional congruence. For since direct comparision as to volume is impossible, we are at liberty to *define* two volumes as equal, when all their various lines, surfaces, angles and solid angles are congruent, since there remains, in such a case, no *measurable* difference between the figures composing the two volumes. 97

272: 42–3  As with solids, so here, actual superposition would only be possible if we had a fourth dimension to operate in. But again CT] But 97

273: 3  relations CT] relation 97

273: 12  show CT] *footnote added in 97:* [1]Prolegomena, §13. See Vaihinger's Commentar, II. pp. 518–532 esp. pp. 521–2. The above was Kant's whole purpose in 1768, but only part of his purpose in the Prolegomena, where the intuitive nature of space was also to be proved.

273: 29  , $f(t)$ say, 97] $f(t)$ say, CT

273: 36  excluded CT] excluded logically by the comparative nature of the judgment of quantity, and philosophically 97

273: 38  holder of events CT] form 97

273: 40  really CT] directly 97

274: 5–6  one last objection which might be urged against CT] the third of the above objections to 97

274: 9  This, it may be said, CT] This 97

274: 10  we may be said to CT] , it may be said, we 97

274: 16  It appears CT] It has been urged 97

274: 40  It is also important to observe that since CT] On the subject of time measurement, cf. Bosanquet's Logic, Vol. i. pp. 178–183. Since 97

275: 1  One last elucidatory CT] 153. (4) One last elucidatory 97

275: 1–2  the axiom of Congruence CT] this axiom 97

275: 17  Congruence. CT] congruence as the test of equality. 97

275: 18  Congruence or Free Mobility CT] Free Mobility 97

275: 22–4  On the mathematical … disagreement among experts CT] The supposed mathematical necessity of making a separate axiom of this property of space has been disproved by Sophus Lie (v. Chap. I. §45) 97

275: 39  $ds \cdot f(p)$] $ds.F(p)$ CT

276: 12  II. THE AXIOM OF DIMENSIONS CT] *footnote added in 97:* [1]This deduction is practically the same as that in Sec. A, but I have stated it here with more special reference to space and to metrical Geometry.

276: 16  described CT] defined 97

276: 18  relation CT] relations 97

276: 18  must be CT] are 97

276: 24  for CT] since 97

276: 26  axiom CT] axiom, for metrical Geometry, 97

276: 27  Helmholtz CT] Helmholtz (v. Chap. I. §25) 97

276: 27  a point CT] every point 97

276: 31–2  experience CT] *footnote added in 97:* [2]Cp. Grassmann, Ausdehnungslehre von 1844, 2nd ed. p. XXIII.

276: 37–8  article, but can only be answered by abandoning the purely geometrical standpoint. CT] chapter, and answered, as far as possible, in the fourth chapter. 97

277: 4  For CT] For while 97

277: 6  new branches which interfere CT] a new branch which interferes 97

277: 7  old; but *some* CT] old, *some* 97

277: 9  assumption CT] *footnote added in 97:* [1]Delboeuf, it is true, speaks of Geometries with $m/n$ dimensions, but gives no reference (Rev. Phil. T. xxxvi. p. 450).

277: 10  interest, and has, to my knowledge,

never been noticed before, CT] interest, 97

277: 13–14 Riemann's dissertation. CT] Riemann's dissertation or in Erdmann's extents 97

277: 15 free mobility. CT] *footnote added in 97:* [4]In criticizing Erdmann, it will be remembered, we saw that Free Mobility is a necessary property of his extents, though he does not regard it as such.

277: 23 relation CT] spatial relation 97

277: 40 out of the question. CT] *footnote added in 97:* [1]Cf. Riemann, Hypothesen welche der Geometrie zu Grunde liegen, Gesammelte Werke, p. 266; also Erdmann, op. cit. p. 154.

278: 2 our whole axiom CT] our whole axiom, that the number of dimensions is three, 97

279: 22 own. CT] *footnote added in 97:* [1]See the end of the argument on Free Mobility, §155 ff.

279: 27 motion CT] combined motion 97

279: 29 disposed of the first objection CT] established our first proposition 97

280: 28 Besides CT] Moreover 97

280: 30 it is CT] is 97

280: 4 axiom of Congruence CT] definition of spatial equality 97

281: 11 line.[10] CT] *no footnote in 97*

281: 15 distances CT] distance 97

281: 37 $k$ CT] $1/k^2$ 97

282: 1–3 Whether or not such a system is philosophically permissible, I shall consider later—for the present, I am content to point out that CT] Thus 97

282: 16 motion CT] a motion 97

282: 21 distances. CT] *footnote added in 97:* [1]Nor in any argument which, like those of projective Geometry, avoids the notion of magnitude or distance altogether. It follows that the propositions of projective Geometry apply, without reserve, to spherical space, since the exception to the axiom of the straight line arises only on metrical ground.

282: 34 sensation (?) CT] sensation 97 *See A282: 30–6.*

283: 7–10 must be something which ... relations. CT] must, since points are wholly constituted by their relations, be some-

thing at least as real and tangible as the points it relates. 97

283: 10–11 all these requirements CT] these requirements 97

283: 27 linear magnitude CT] magnitude 97

283: 40 any CT] a 97

283: 40 enable CT] have enabled 97

283: 41 definition CT] quantitative definition 97 *Also at 284: 9.*

283: 2–3 to say a few words about CT] to discuss 97

283: 43 logical conditions of the possibility CT] conditions 97

283: 43 coordinate CT] metrical coordinate 97 *Also at 284: 16 (see also T284: 9).*

284: 1–8 Much recent Geometry ... attempt to prove. CT] The projective coordinate system, as we have seen, aims only at a convenient nomenclature for different points, and can be set up without introducing the notion of spatial quantity. But a metrical coordinate system does much more than this. It defines every point quantitatively, by its quantitative spatial relations to a certain coordinate figure. Only when the system of coordinates is thus metrical, *i.e.*, when every coordinate represents some spatial magnitude, which is itself a relation of the point defined to some other point or figure—can operations with coordinates lead to a metrical result. When, as in projective Geometry, the coordinates are not spatial magnitudes, no amount of transformation can give a metrical result. I wish to prove, here, that a metrical coordinate system necessarily involves the straight line, and cannot, without a logical fallacy, be set up on any other basis. The projective system of coordinates, as we saw, is entirely based on the straight line; but the metrical system is more important, since its quantities embody actual information as to spatial magnitudes, which, in projective Geometry, is not the case. 97

284: 9 coordinates CT] metrical coordinates 97 *Also at 284: 28.*

284: 12 system CT] metrical system 97

284: 18 involves CT] is impossible without 97

284: 22–3 Von Staudt's projective construction¹² proceeds entirely by the help of straight lines.] Von Standt's ... lines. CT] *sentence and footnote omitted in 97*

284:26 defined CT] metrically defined 97

285:20 paper] chapter CT

## 43 Review of Lechalas

"CT" stands for the only known version of the text, that in *Mind*, n.s. 5 (Jan. 1896): 128.

286:1 1896] 1895 CT

## 44 The *À Priori* in Geometry

The textual notes contain a collation of the copy-text, *Proceedings of the Aristotelian Society*, o.s. 3, no. 2 (1896): 97–112, denoted by "CT", with the closely related passages in *An Essay on the Foundations of Geometry* (1897), denoted by "97". For a summary of the intersection of **44** and 97, see the table at the beginning of the textual notes to Paper **42**. The intersection of **44** and **42** is not reported below, but may be ascertained in summary from the table.

Paragraphs in 97 which are closely related to **44** but which are extensively revised are given in full below.

291:12 *à priori*] a priori CT *Also at 291:13. These are the only instances of* à priori *whose italicization in CT has been retained.*

291:14 preface the geometrical inquiry by CT] give 97

291:41 sought in *Pure Reason* CT] which he seeks in the *Pure Reason* 97

292:10 proceed. CT] *footnote added in 97:*
²Where the branch of experience in question is essential to all experience, the resulting apriority may be regarded as absolute; where it is necessary only to some special science, as relative to that science.

293:26–294:3 I. *The Axiom of Free Mobility* ... parts in each. CT] I. *The Axiom of Free Mobility.* **143.** Metrical Geometry, to begin with, may be defined as the science which deals with the comparison and relations of spatial magnitudes. The conception of magnitude, therefore, is necessary from the start. Some of Euclid's axioms, accordingly, have been classed as arithmetical, and have been supposed to have nothing particular to do with space. Such are the axioms that equals added to

or subtracted from equals give equals, and that things which are equal to the same thing are equal to one another. These axioms, it is said, are purely arithmetical, and do not, like the others, ascribe an adjective to space. As regards their use in arithmetic, this is of course true. But if an arithmetical axiom is to be applied to spatial magnitudes, it must have some spatial import,¹ ⟨*footnote:* ¹Contrast Erdmann, op. cit, p. 138.⟩ and thus even this class is not, in Geometry, *merely* arithmetical. Fortunately, the geometrical element is the same in all the axioms of this class—we can see at once, in fact, that it can amount to no more than a definition of spatial magnitude². ⟨*footnote:* ²Cf. Erdmann, op. cit. p. 164.⟩ Again, since the space with which Geometry deals is infinitely divisible, a definition of spatial magnitude reduces itself to a definition of spatial equality, for, as soon as we have this last, we can compare two spatial magnitudes by dividing each into a number of equal units, and counting the number of such units in each¹. ⟨*footnote:* ¹Strictly speaking, this method is only applicable where the two magnitudes are commensurable. But if we take infinite divisibility rigidly, the units can theoretically be taken so small as to obtain any required degree of approximation. The difficulty is the universal one of applying to continua the essentially discrete conception of number.⟩ The ratio of the number of units is, of course, the ratio of the two magnitudes. 97

294:4–18 We require ... in space. CT]
**144.** We require, then, at the very outset, some criterion of spatial equality: without

such a criterion metrical Geometry would become wholly impossible. It might appear, at first sight, as though this need not be an axiom, but might be a mere definition. In part this is true, but not wholly. The part which is merely a definition is given in Euclid's eighth axiom: "Magnitudes which exactly coincide are equal." But this gives a sufficient criterion only when the magnitudes to be compared already occupy the same position. When, as will normally be the case, the two spatial magnitudes are external to one another—as, indeed, must be the case, if they are distinct, and not whole and part—the two magnitudes can only be made to coincide by a motion of one or both of them. In order, therefore, that our definition of spatial magnitude may give unambiguous results, coincidence when superposed, if it can ever occur, must occur always, whatever path be pursued in bringing it about. Hence, if mere motion could alter shapes, our criterion of equality would break down. It follows that the application of the conception of magnitude to figures in space involves the following axiom[2]: ⟨footnote: [2]Cf. Erdmann, op. cit. p. 50.⟩ *Spatial magnitudes can be moved from place to place without distortion;* or, as it may be put, *Shapes do not in any way depend upon absolute position in space.* 97

294: 33  Exchequer] exchequer CT
294: 39  1893] 1890 CT  *See T269: 41–2.*
296: 19–35  II. *The Axiom of Dimensions ...* Vol. ii, p. 614). CT] II. *The Axiom of Dimensions*[1]. ⟨footnote: [1]This deduction is practically the same as that in Sec. A, but I have stated it here with more special reference to space and to metrical Geometry.⟩ **158.** We have seen, in discussing the axiom of Free Mobility, that all position is relative, that is, a position exists only by virtue of relations[2]. ⟨footnote: [2]The question: "Relations to what?" is a question involving many difficulties. It will be touched on later in this chapter, and answered, as far as possible, in the fourth chapter. For the present, in spite of the glaring circle involved, I shall take the

relations as relations to other positions.⟩ It follows that, if positions can be defined at all, they must be uniquely and exhaustively defined by some finite number of such relations. If Geometry is to be possible, it must happen that, after enough relations have been given to determine a point uniquely, its relations to any fresh known point are deducible from the relations already given. Hence we obtain, as an *à priori* condition of Geometry, logically indispensable to its existence, the axiom that *Space must have a finite integral number of Dimensions.* For every relation required in the definition of a point constitutes a dimension, and a fraction of a relation is meaningless. The number of relations required must be finite, since an infinite number of dimensions would be practically impossible to determine. If we remember our axiom of Free Mobility, and remember also that space is a continuum, we may state our axiom, for metrical Geometry, in the form given by Helmholtz (v. Chap. 1. §25): "In a space of *n* dimensions, the position of every point is uniquely determined by the measurement of *n* continuous independent variables (coordinates).'" ⟨footnote: [1]Wiss. Abh. Vol. II. p. 614.⟩ 97
296: 35–41  So much ... assumption. CT]
¶**159.** So much, then, is *à priori* necessary to metrical Geometry. The restriction of the dimensions to three seems, on the contrary, to be wholly the work of experience[2]. ⟨footnote: [2]Cp. Grassmann, Ausdehnungslehre von 1844, 2nd ed. p. XXIII.⟩ This restriction cannot be logically necessary, for as soon as we have formulated any analytical system, it appears wholly arbitrary. Why, we are driven to ask, cannot we add a fourth coordinate to our *x, y, z,* or give a geometrical meaning to $x^4$? In this more special form, we are tempted to regard the axiom of dimensions, like the number of inhabitants of a town, as a purely statistical fact, with no greater necessity than such facts have. ¶Geometry affords intrinsic evidence of the truth of my division of the axiom of dimensions into an *à priori* and empirical

portion. For while the extension of the number of dimensions to four, or to $n$, alters nothing in plane and solid Geometry, but only adds a new branch which interferes in no way with the old, *some* definite number of dimensions is assumed in all Geometries, nor is it possible to conceive of a Geometry which should be free from this assumption[3]. ⟨*footnote:* [3]Delboeuf, it is true, speaks of Geometries with *m/n* dimensions, but gives no reference (Rev. Phil. T. xxxvi. p. 450).⟩ 97

296: 42–297: 9  The limitation ... à priori element. CT] **161**. The limitation of the dimensions to three is, as we have seen, empirical; nevertheless, it is not liable to the inaccuracy and uncertainty which usually belong to empirical knowledge. For the alternatives which logic leaves to sense are discrete—if the dimensions are not three, they must be two or four or some other number—so that *small* errors are out of the question[1]. ⟨*footnote:* [1]Cf. Riemann, Hypothesen welche der Geometrie zu Grunde liegen, Gesammelte Werke, p. 266; also Erdmann, op. cit. p. 154.⟩ Hence the final certainty of the axiom of three dimensions, though in part due to experience, is of quite a different order from that of (say) the law of Gravitation. In the latter, a small inaccuracy might exist and remain undetected; in the former, an error would have to be so considerable as to be utterly impossible to overlook. It follows that the certainty of our whole axiom, that the number of dimensions is three, is almost as great as that of the *à priori* element, since this element leaves to sense a definite disjunction of discrete possibilities. 97

297: 41–298: 12  The answer ... we call distance. CT] **163**. (1) The possibility of spatial measurement allows us to infer the existence of a magnitude uniquely determined by any two points. The proof of this depends on the axiom of Free Mobility, or its equivalent, the homogeneity of space. We have seen that these are involved in the possibility of spatial measurement; we may employ them, therefore, in any argument as to the conditions of this possibility. ¶Now to begin with, two points must, if Geometry is to be possible, have *some* relation to each other, for we have seen that such relations alone constitute position or localization. But if two points have a relation to each other, this must be an intrinsic relation. For it follows, from the axiom of Free Mobility, that two points, forming a figure congruent with the given pair, can be constructed in any part of space. If this were not possible, we have seen that metrical Geometry could not exist. But both the figures may be regarded as composed of two points and their relation; if the two figures are congruent, therefore, it follows that the relation is quantitatively the same for both figures, since congruence is the test of spatial equality. Hence the two points have a quantitative relation, which is such that they can traverse all space in a combined motion without in any way altering that relation. But in such a general motion, any external relation of the two points, any relation involving other points or figures in space, must be altered[1]. ⟨*footnote:* [1]This is subject, in spherical space, to the modification pointed out below, in dealing with the exception to the axiom of the straight line. See §§168–171.⟩ Hence the relation between the two points, being unaltered, must be an intrinsic relation, a relation involving no other point or figure in space; and this intrinsic relation we call distance[2]. ⟨*footnote:* [2]In speaking of distance at once as a quantity and as an intrinsic relation, I am anxious to guard against an apparent inconsistency. I have spoken of the judgment of quantity, throughout, as one of comparison; how, then, can a quantity be intrinsic? The reply is that, although measurement and the judgment of quantity express the result of comparison, yet the terms compared must exist before the comparison; in this case, the terms compared in measuring distances, *i.e.* in comparing them *inter se*, are intrinsic relations between two points. Thus, although the *measurement* of distance involves a reference to other distances, and its expression as a magnitude requires such a reference, yet its existence does not depend on any external reference, but exclusively on the two points whose distance it is.⟩ 97

298: 24–6 Thus ... space. CT] **166.** (2) We have thus established our first proposition—two points have one and only one relation uniquely determined by those two points. This relation we call their distance apart. It remains to consider the conditions of the measurement of distance, *i.e.*, how far a unique value for distance involves a curve uniquely determined by the two points. 97

298: 26 But why only one? CT] ¶**165.** But why, it may be asked, should there be only one such relation between two points? 97

298: 27 , as we saw ... points must be CT] points are 97

298: 28 can have CT] have 97

298: 28 own. CT] *footnote added in 97:* ¹See the end of the argument on Free Mobility, §155 ff.

298: 31 properties CT] qualities 97

298: 34–5 be only one intrinsic relation between CT] only be one relation determined by 97

298: 39–299: 9 We are used to ... the *shortest* distance. CT] **167.** We are accustomed to the definition of the straight line as the *shortest* distance between two points, which implies that distance might equally well be measured by curved lines. This implication I believe to be false, for the following reasons. When we speak of the length of a curve, we can give a meaning to our words only by supposing the curve divided into infinitesimal rectilinear arcs, whose sum gives the length of an equivalent straight line; thus unless we presuppose the straight line, we have no means of comparing the lengths of different curves, and can therefore never discover the applicability of our definition. 97

299: 34–300: 19 We can now ... of their points. CT] **172.** I have now shown, I hope conclusively, that spherical space affords no objection to the apriority of my axiom. Any two points have one relation, their distance, which is independent of the rest of space, and this relation requires, as its measure, a curve uniquely determined by those two points. I might have taken the bull by the horns, and said: Two points *can* have no relation but what is given by lines which join them, and therefore, if they have a relation independent of the rest of space, there must be one line joining them which they completely determine. Thus James says²: ⟨*footnote:* ²Psychology, Vol. II. pp. 149–150.⟩ "Just as, in the field of quantity, the relation between two numbers is another number, so in the field of space the relations are facts of the same order with the facts they relate....... When we speak of the relation of direction of two points towards each other, we mean simply the sensation of the line that joins the two points together. *The line is the relation......* The relation of position between the top and bottom points of a vertical line is that line, and nothing else." ¶If I had been willing to use this doctrine at the beginning, I might have avoided all discussion. A unique relation between two points *must* in this case, involve a unique line between them. But it seemed better to avoid a doctrine not universally accepted, the more so as I was approaching the question from the logical, not the psychological, side. After disposing of the objections, however, it is interesting to find this confirmation of the above theory from so different a standpoint. Indeed, I believe James's doctrine could be proved to be a logical necessity, as well as a psychological fact. For what sort of things can a spatial relation between two distinct points be? It must be something spatial, and it must, since points are wholly constituted by their relations, be something at least as real and tangible as the points it relates. There seems nothing which can satisfy these requirements, except a line joining them. Hence, once more, a unique relation must involve a unique line. That is, linear magnitude is logically impossible, unless space allows of curves uniquely determined by any two of their points. 97

300: 20–7 To sum up ... conception.⁷ CT]

175. To sum up: If points are defined simply by relations to other points, *i.e.*, if all position is relative, *every point must have to every other point one, and only one, relation independent of the rest of space. This relation is the distance between the two points.* Now a relation between two points can only be defined by a line joining them—nay, further, it may be contended that a relation can only *be* a line joining them. Hence a unique relation involves a unique line, *i.e.*, a line determined by any two of its points. Only in a space which admits of such a line is linear magnitude a logically possible conception. 97

300: 28–37 The above three axioms ... more special experience. CT] **177**. The above three axioms, we have seen, are *à priori* necessary to metrical Geometry. No others can be necessary, since metrical systems, logically as unassailable as Euclid's, and dealing with spaces equally homogeneous and equally relational, have been constructed by the metageometers, without the help of any other axioms. The remaining axioms of Euclidean Geometry—the axiom of parallels, the axiom that the number of dimensions is three, and Euclid's form of the axiom of the straight line (two straight lines cannot enclose a space)—are not essential to the possibility of metrical Geometry, *i.e.*, are not deducible from the fact that a science of spatial magnitudes is possible. They are rather to be regarded as empirical laws, obtained, like the empirical laws of other sciences, by actual investigation of the given subject-matter—in this instance,

experienced space. 97

300: 35 space)—are 97] space), are CT

300: 38 the argument we have just concluded CT] the distinctive argument of this Section 97

301: 1–2 manifold CT] continuous manifold 97

301: 2 magnitudes CT] quantities 97

301: 16 Number CT] Now a number 97

301: 22–3 numerable. On the other hand ... *infinitely* divisible, otherwise CT] numerable—a purely extensive quantity, if any such could be imagined, would not be a single quantity at all, since it would have to consist of wholly unsynthesized particulars. A measurable quantity, therefore, is a whole divisible into similar parts. But a continuous quantity, if divisible at all, must be *infinitely* divisible. For otherwise 97

301: 24 destroy CT] so destroy 97

301: 29–32 superposition ... are satisfied. CT] we require superposition, which involves Free Mobility and homogeneity——the absence of Free Mobility in time, where all other requisites of measurement are fulfilled, renders direct measurement of time impossible. 97

301: 33–4 *any* manifold CT] *any* continuous manifold 97

301: 34–5 Hence these axioms are necessary CT] These axioms are necessary, therefore 97

301: 39 measurement of time CT] case of time 97

302: 1 phenomena. CT] *footnote added in 97:* [1]Cf. Hannequin, Essai critique sur l'hypothèse des atomes, Paris, 1895, passim.

## 45 Note on Economic Theory

The manuscript measures 220 × 347 mm. and is written in ink.

No textual notes.

## 46 German Social Democracy, as a Lesson in Political Tactics

The manuscript ("CT") is paginated 5, 7–9, 11–13, 15–17, 19, 21, 23, 25, 27–9, 31, 33, 35, measures 220 × 347 mm. and is written in ink.

312: 2 Communism: such CT] *replaced* Communism. Such

312: 2 with advantage CT] *inserted*

312: 4 Machiavellian] Macchiavellian CT

312: 7 final CT] *inserted*
312: 8 treat CT] *after deleted* discuss
312: 8 spirit CT] *after deleted* form
312: 8 putting CT] *after deleted* suggesting
312: 12 necessary CT] *above deleted* essential
312: 22–3 if every political party is the party of a class, CT] *inserted*
312: 27 it is CT] *inserted*
312: 35 I admit CT] *above deleted* no doubt
312: 36 seriously impairs CT] *replaced* seriously modifies] *above deleted* vitiates
312: 39–40 excessive estimate CT] *above deleted* exaggeration
312: 41–2 The gullibility of the ordinary man and its correlative, the possibility of statesmanlike hypocrisy, are alike ignored by Marx. CT] *replaced by pencil changes* Marx never allows for the gullability of the ordinary man; its correlative, statesman-like hypocrisy, seems to him, therefore, a useless method of political warfare.
313: 1 Marx CT] *above deleted* he
313: 2 the bourgeoisie CT] *above deleted* it
313: 3 far more effectual weapons CT] *replaced* a far more effectual policy
313: 7–8 self-consciousness. A CT] *replaced* self-consciousness, and a true
313: 9 truth; CT] *replaced* truth.
313: 10–13 and conversely, ... class-warfare. CT] and conversely, *was inserted in pencil immediately after* truth; *the rest was written on the opposing page (p. 8) with double asterisks to signal its placement in the text.*
313: 15–16 regulates CT] *after deleted* is the principle
313: 20 large CT] *inserted*
313: 20–1 organized working-men in England. CT] *replaced* English organized working-men.
313: 23 , who CT] *inserted*
313: 24 Prussia, CT] *replaced* Prussia and
313: 26 raising CT] *after deleted* carrying on
313: 29 most CT] *after deleted* almost
313: 35–6 programme; and when this had been obtained, further reforms could have been demanded by labour, as the price of further support. CT] *replaced* programme. *with* and when this had been *inserted after* programme *and with* obtained ... support. *inserted on the opposing page (p. 12)*

313: 37 , instead of bringing such pressure to bear, CT] *inserted*
314: 2 an extreme CT] *above deleted* the
314: 3 abandoned CT] *after deleted* became gr
314: 8 purpose, CT] *before deleted insertion* not compelled by a popular agitation,
314: 9 influence CT] *above deleted* power
314: 15 instead CT] *after deleted* instead the terror of these has
314: 17 From CT] *after deleted* Again
314: 17 standpoint CT] *after deleted* point of view
314: 17–18 of isolation CT] *inserted*
314: 19–21 and, though ... Conservatives CT] *inserted on the opposing page (p. 16)*
314: 22–3 the importance of minimizing their opponents' alarm. By CT] *replaced* how important it was to minimize their opponents' alarm, and by
314: 27 mere CT] *inserted*
314: 28 visionary enthusiasts. CT] *before deleted* It is said that conspirators in exile, by associating only with each other, lose all sense of the mass of opposition against which they have to contend, and some-thing of this kind happened to the earlier German Socialists.
314: 30–1 by its opposition ... fatherland CT] *replaced* especially by its atheism and its views on marriage
314: 33 growing true through being believed CT] *replaced* growing true because it has become believed] *above deleted* realizing itself
314: 37 fewer CT] *before deleted* and fewer
314: 38 for example, CT] *inserted*
315: 1 the CT] *replaced* their
315: 3 seems to have CT] *inserted*
315: 6 peaceful CT] *inserted*
315: 9–10 and the weak have hitherto been induced to advocate, in the form of preju-dices, the interests of the strong. CT] *replaced* and the weak have hitherto been led to adopt, in the form of prejudices, the interests of the strong.] *above deleted* and the powerful have hitherto had great suc-cess in imprinting their own interests, as prejudices, upon the weak.
315: 13 for CT] *written over* from
315: 14–15 whom they invariably elect,

with docile regularity, as the representatives of their wishes and interests in Parliament. CT] *replaced* whom they are good enough regularly to elect, as their representatives, in Parliament.

315:26 excellent CT] *after deleted* much

315:30 instead CT] *after deleted* it

315:32 by the way, CT] *inserted*

315:34 By CT] *after deleted* In the

315:36 necessary for catching CT] *replaced* on which they would catch

316:1 not to vote for any renewal CT] *replaced* to vote for its abolition

316:2 in return; CT] *replaced* in the Second Ballots; and

316:3 betrayal, CT] *before deleted* and determined, for the future,

316:5 and CT] *after deleted* with

316:10 governed CT] *inserted*

316:13 holding CT] *before deleted* obtaining

316:21 But the mention CT] *after deleted* ¶Or again, consider the advantage which the Irish Vote derives, both in the United Kingdom and in America, from allying itself always with one or other party. If it held rigidly aloof, if it refused to negotiate except on a basis of perfect agreement

316:23–5 an argument … Socialistic opinions? CT] *inserted on the opposing page (p. 28)*

316:25 For this CT] *replaced* This

316:28 keen CT] *above deleted* lasting

316:36 for this reason CT] *in pencil above pencil deletion* therefore

316:42 religious CT] *after deleted* the

317:2 instinct CT] *after deleted* insight] *above deleted* sense

317:6 Marx's CT] *after deleted* the

317:7 earthly Paradise CT] *in pencil above pencil deletion* end to all his wrongs

317:12 Socialism CT] *in pencil above pencil deletion* Social Democracy

317:14–15 more or less Socialistic measures, CT] *replaced* measures of Social Reform, all more or less Socialistic, and

317:25 government CT] *after deleted insertion* monarchical

317:25 the machine which it creates CT] *above deleted* it

317:29 well CT] *inserted*

317:30 it to feel CT] *above deleted* this feeling

317:42 a daily CT] *replaced* daily

317:42–3 As a friend to peaceful and continued progress, therefore, I must hope CT] *replaced* All friends to peaceful and continued progress must hope

317:43 that Vollmar's policy CT] *below deleted insertion* German Socialists will be a

318:3 tomb CT] *after deleted* grave

## 47　The Uses of Luxury

The manuscript ("CT") is foliated 1–12, measures 224 × 286 mm. and is written in ink. It is signed "B. Russell" on the last page. A number of revisions in this paper were made by Alys, usually in pencil.

320:13 irrefutably CT] *after deleted* conclusive

320:28 have felt CT] *replaced* feel

320:28 was CT] *above deleted* is

320:29–30 , with conscience-quelling unction, CT] *inserted*

320:31 royal CT] *inserted by Alys in pencil*

320:32 nothing but CT] *inserted*

320:33 improvidence CT] *before deleted* alone

320:41 Tate's] Tait's CT

320:43 the patronage of CT] *inserted*

321:4 Whistler CT] *after deleted* Mr.

321:5 few men have CT] *written over* no man has

321:6 many CT] *after pencil deletion* how

321:12 right CT] *underlined in pencil after deleted* success of the

321:28 also CT] *before deleted* many

321:31 According to CT] *inserted by Alys in pencil before pencil deletion* From] *above deleted* By

321:34 whole CT] *inserted*

321:34 idly CT] *inserted*

321:35 it, CT] *before deleted* as a

322:2–3 which could not wholly be accounted for by CT] *inserted by Alys in pencil above pencil deletion* to a degree which

322:3 concerned; CT] *inserted by Alys in*

*pencil above pencil deletion* concerned
could not wholly account for;
322: 7 express it CT] *above deleted* say
322: 11 only newly CT] *inserted by Alys in pencil above pencil deletion* lately
322: 12 Italy, CT] *above deleted* Venice,
322: 14 generally speaking CT] *above deleted* certainly
322: 16 laid CT] *written over* layed *by Alys in pencil*
322: 21 well-to-do CT] *inserted*
322: 25 my argument CT] *after deleted* I should fail
322: 33 nearer CT] *above deleted* ideal
322: 33 fortune, CT] *after deleted* wealth,

322: 40 *Civitas Dei* CT] *Alys wrote* Siv *in pencil above* Civitas *which was written over in pencil by Russell*
322: 42 possessed by CT] *above deleted* present to
323: 4 preserved CT] *above deleted* maintained
323: 12 would never have CT] *altered in pencil by Alys from* wouldn't have
323: 14 allow CT] *above deleted* give
323: 15–16 can be acquired by those who struggle. CT] *replaced by Alys in pencil* those who struggle can acquire.
323: 19 every opportunity CT] *inserted*
323: 20 , from daily objects, CT] *inserted*

## 48 Mechanical Morals and the Moral of Machinery

The manuscript ("CT") is foliated 1–11, measures 220 × 285 mm. and is written in ink. It is signed "B. Russell" on the last leaf.

324: *title* Mechanical Morals and the Moral of Machinery] Mechanical Morals and the moral of Machinery. CT
325: 5 and CT] *written over* I
325: 11 of CT] *inserted*
325: 11 however, CT] *before deleted* I think,
325: 13 or fostered CT] *inserted*
325: 14 or fail to operate CT] *inserted*
325: 14–15 or encouragement CT] *inserted*
325: 17 as always CT] *replaced* always as
325: 17 , I fear, CT] *inserted*
325: 17 often CT] *inserted*
325: 22 deference CT] *after deleted* to
325: 27 its CT] *inserted after deleted* the
325: 29 ⟨out⟩ how] how how CT
325: 34 very CT] *inserted*
325: 35 For CT] *inserted*
326: 3–4 , to your own survival, CT] *inserted*
326: 16 young CT] *above deleted* out
326: 21 , for their own sakes, CT] *inserted*
326: 24 their CT] *above deleted* your
326: 24 them CT] *above deleted* you

326: 33 many CT] *inserted*
326: 38–9 for the respect of CT] *above deleted* to stand well with
326: 41 antiquity CT] *above deleted* ages
326: 41 say the stone age, or CT] *replaced* the stone age,
327: 1 on CT] *after deleted* of
327: 1 side CT] *above deleted* hand
327: 1–2 moral standard CT] *after deleted* morality
327: 5 , though based on instincts, CT] *inserted*
327: 5 themselves CT] *inserted*
327: 12 it CT] *above deleted* this
327: 17–18 alternatives were CT] *written over* alternative was
327: 22 to the CT] *above deleted* before the
327: 27 sway CT] *after deleted* absolute
327: 31 Tell CT] *replaced* To tell
327: 35 those CT] *written over* the
328: 2 Wollstonecraft] Wolstonecraft CT
328: 8 education CT] *above deleted* intelligence
328: 8 desirable, CT] *after deleted* possible,
328: 13 at CT] *inserted*
328: 20 often CT] *written over* so

## 49 Review of Schmöle

No textual notes.

# Appendix I  Outlines and Reports of Lectures

I.I.
337: 30  each other's] each others' CT
1. 4(b)
341: 18  Riemann and Helmholtz] Reimann
  and Helmholz CT
341: 27  Riemann] Reimann CT

341: 28  Helmholtz] Helmholz CT
1.4(c)
342: 8  three] there CT
1.4(d)
342: 22  Grassmann] Grossmann CT

# Appendix II  What Shall I Read?

347: 3  *Norderney*] Nordeney CT
348: 36  *Tambourlaine*] Tambourline CT
349: 22  Jessopp] Jessop CT
350: 2  Dr. Abbott] Dr. Abbot CT
352: 20  Whyte Melville] White Melville CT
353: 40  Birrell] Birrel CT

355: 43  Anatole] Anatolle CT
357: 22  de L'Isle Adam] de L'Isle-Adam CT
357: 40  *Embarrassments*] Embarassments CT
358: 21  Maeterlinck] Metterlinck CT
359: 17  FitzGerald] Fitzgerald CT *Also at*
  *349: 2, 363: 21 and 364: 15.*

# Misspellings in the Copy-Texts

The corrected spelling is at the passage referred to.

51: 3  aquaintance
61: 25  apostasized
187: 27  appelations
64: 16  beach
28: 20, 48: 37, 79: 10  benifit
70: 4  bigotted
24: 5  coexistant
26: 21  competion
26: 39  compulsary
132: 28  concommittant
92: 31  concensus
203: 11  conoisseurs
96: 4–5, 163: 35  excentricity
264: 7  embarassing
312: 14  empiral
35: 11  excercised
87: 18  exhileration
50: 2  favorite
95: 27  guage
61: 17  gullability
322: 27  heriditary
138: 38  innacurate

64: 42  innoculated
121: 14  intelligble
28: 30  lessenned
43: 2  lilaac
328: 18  medecine
35: 25  murmers
328: 15  non-existant
263: 40  ommission
128: 18, 260: 29  oneanother
30: 5  peacable
24: 28, 26: 30, 110: 21, 161: 6  principle
202: 25  principal
159: 26  quantitavely
203: 16  rapt
62: 14  repitition
260: 21  skillfully
32: 11  substatially
52: 10  superceded
54: 40  teatotaller
203: 9  tecnique
34: 3, 81: 22  tendancy
291: 13  unconvential
61: 35  inorthodox
32: 9  vigourously
60: 4  week

# Regularization of Spelling

A dictionary is kept of Russell's spelling preferences. In Volume 1 the following preferred
forms were substituted for the forms in
printed copy-texts, which are recorded to the
right of the bracket.

characterize] characterise
connection] connexion
coordinates] co-ordinates
emphasizes] emphasises
generalize] generalise
localize] localise
organize] organise

prerequisites] pre-requisites
presupposes] pre-supposes
realize] realise
specialize] specialise
synthesize] synthesise
tonight] to-night

## Expansion of Abbreviations

Russell's manuscript abbreviations of common words are listed below. In this transcription, raised letters, as in "ab$^f$", are systematically lowered and preceded by an apostrophe thus: "ab't". The period or underlining that usually accompanies raised letters is ignored. Capitalizaton is reported, but is usually irrelevant to the abbreviation. Uncommon abbreviations and abbreviations of proper names are found in the Textual Notes, keyed to their occurrence in the text.

about] ab't
actions] ac'ns
although] altho'
and] &
angular] $<$'lar
between] betw.
circles] $\odot$'s
circumstances] circums.
corresponding] corr'g.
could] c'd
definition] def
differences] diff'ces
different] diff't
distinction] dist'n
equations] eq'ns
explanations] expl'ns
first] 1'st
fourth] 4'th
general] gen'al
Geometrical] Geom'al
Geometry] Geom'y
important] imp't
increase] incr.
knowledge] kn.
Lady] L'y
Lord] L'd
Mathematics] Math's
Metageometry] Meta'y
morning] mg.

non-mathematician] non-mathemat'ian
non-mathematicians] non-math'ns
number] n'o
objection] obj'n
observations] obs'ns
observe] obs.
phenomena] phen'a
Philosophy of History] Phil. of Hist.
point] pt.
Proposition] Prop.
Propositions] Props.
quadrilaterals] quads.
Received] Rec'd
Relation] Rel'n
relative] rel've
requires] reqs.
required] req'd
revolution] rev'n
rotation] rot'n
second] 2'nd
should] sh'd
Sensation] Sens'n
sixth] 6'th
society] soc'y
Spherical] Spher'al
straight] str.
Street] Str.
subjective] subj've
therefore] ∴
three-dimensional] 3-dim'al
though] tho'
third] 3'rd
Transcendental Aesthetik] Tr. Ac./Trans.
   Aesth./Transc. Aesth.
triangles] $\triangle$'s
ultimate] ult.
Uncles] U's
Utilitarian principles] Ut'an princ's
which] wh.
would] w'd

# Bibliographical Index

THE WORKS REFERRED to by Russell and by the author–date system in editorial matter are cited here in full. The italicized year following the author's name is that of the edition described, or that of first publication. Where relevant, an index of the pages on which the work is mentioned follows the citation. Page numbers in roman type indicate Russell's text in the papers and in Appendix I; page numbers in italic type indicate editorial matter.

Not every entry warranted complete bibliographical data. For example, while §100 of Cicero's *De amicitia* is mentioned on p. 23, it is not known what edition Russell used. Such information is not necessary, since the allusion to the section applies to all modern editions. In some other cases, such as the editorial references to Ibsen *1881*, Mach *1883* and Tolstoi *1873–77*, the provision of full data would be unnecessary and even misleading, for we have no knowledge of what editions Russell may have consulted. Moreover, we wished to give the titles in their English translation. Finally, complete bibliographical data are not given for pre-1800 editions, unless a quotation used by Russell or in the commentary can be traced to such an edition.

The presence of a work in Russell's library at McMaster University is noted by the phrase "(Russell's library.)", where a large proportion of the volumes once owned by him are housed. For volumes that are elsewhere, the location is added in the parenthesis. Sometimes that location is McMaster, since some volumes have been acquired which were once owned by him.

The Bibliographical Index excludes papers by Russell printed in this volume, unless he himself refers to them in those papers.

AÏDÉ, CHARLES HAMILTON, *1882*. "Love, the Pilgrim", "Lost and Found" and "George Lee". In his *Songs without Music: Rhymes and Recitations*. London: David Bogue.
Referred to: *385*.

AMBERLEY, JOHN RUSSELL, VISCOUNT, *1876*. *An Analysis of Religious Belief*. 2 vols. London: Trübner. (Russell's library.)
Referred to: *375*.

ANON. "Omnia Vincit". In Palgrave *1890*, 6.
Referred to: 65, *396*.

ANSELM. *Proslogion*.
   Referred to: *414*.
ARGYLL, GEORGE DOUGLAS CAMPBELL, DUKE OF, *1866*. *The Reign of Law*. London: Strahan.
   Referred to: 10, 11, 12, 13, 15, 18, *374–5, 376*.
ARISTOTLE. *De anima*.
   Referred to: *415*.
—— *Prior Analytics*.
   Referred to: *411, 412*.
—— *Topics*.
   Referred to: *407*.
ARMSTRONG, WILLIAM M., *1969–70*. "Bertrand Russell Comes to America, 1896". *Studies in History and Society*, 2: 29–39.
   Referred to: *336*.
AUSTEN, JANE, *1813*. *Pride and Prejudice*. 3 vols. London: T. Egerton.
   Referred to: *77*.
BACON, FRANCIS, *c.1603*. "Of the Interpretation of Nature". Reprinted in his *1857–74*, 3: 215–52.
   Referred to: *131*.
—— *1605*. *The Advancement of Learning*. Reprinted in his *1857–74*, 3: 253–491.
   Referred to: *412*.
—— *1609*. *The Wisdom of the Ancients*. Reprinted in his *1857–74*, 6: 603–764.
   Referred to: *407*.
—— *1620*. *Novum Organum*. Reprinted in his *1857–74*, 4: 39–248.
   Referred to: 134, 137, 139, 166n., 167, *399, 406, 407, 412*.
—— *1623*. *De Augmentis Scientiarum*. Reprinted in his *1857–74*, 4: 275–498 and 5: 3–119.
   Referred to: *412*.
—— *1857–74*. *The Works of Francis Bacon*. Edited by James Spedding, Robert Leslie Ellis, and Douglas Denon Heath. 14 vols. London: Longman, *et al*.
   Referred to: *399, 407, 412*.
BALFOUR, ARTHUR JAMES, EARL OF, *1879*. *A Defence of Philosophic Doubt; Being an Essay on the Foundations of Belief*. London: Macmillan.
   Referred to: *422–3*.
—— *1895*. *The Foundations of Belief; Being Notes Introductory to the Study of Theology*. London: Longmans, Green.
   Referred to: 229, 230, 233–4, *423*.
BELTRAMI, EUGENIO, *1868*. "Saggio di interpretazione della geometria non-euclidea". *Giornale di matematiche*, 6: 284–312.
   Referred to: *430*.
BERKELEY, GEORGE, *1713*. *Three Dialogues between Hylas and Philonous*. Reprinted in his *1871*, 1: 258–360.
   Referred to: 144, 175, *408, 414*.

—— *1871. The Works of George Berkeley, D.D.* Edited by Alexander Campbell Fraser. 4 vols. Oxford: Clarendon Press. (Russell's library.)
Referred to: 144, *408.*

BEVERIDGE, JANET, *1960. An Epic of Clare Market; Birth and Early Days of the London School of Economics.* London: George Bell & Sons.
Referred to: *307, 319.*

Bible.
Referred to: 6, 10, 55, *376, 392.*

BISMARCK, OTTO VON, *1884.* Speech. Germany, Reichstag, *Stenographische Berichte über die Verhandlungen des Reichstags,* Vol. 79, 6th Legislatursperiode: 1st session (1884–85), 1: 24–7.
Referred to: 317, *437.*

BLAKISTON, GEORGIANA, *1980. Woburn and the Russells.* London: Constable.
Referred to: *xx.*

BOSANQUET, BERNARD, *1888. Logic; or, the Morphology of Knowledge.* 2 vols. Oxford: Clarendon Press. (Russell's library.)
Referred to: 303n., 340, *434, 489.*

BOSANQUET, ROBERT CARR, *1938. Letters and Light Verse.* Edited by Ellen S. Bosanquet. Gloucester: Printed by John Bellows.
Referred to: *401.*

BOSWELL, JAMES, *1887. Boswell's Life of Johnson, including Boswell's Journal of a Tour of the Hebrides, and Johnson's Diary of a Journey into Northern Wales.* Edited by George Birkbeck Hill. 6 vols. Oxford: Clarendon Press. 1st ed., 1791.
Referred to: 43, 44, 48, 49, 50, *381, 384, 386.*

BOUILLIER, FRANCISQUE, *1854. Histoire de la philosophie cartésienne.* 2 vols. Paris: Durand, *et al.*
Referred to: 184, *416.*

BRADLEY, F. H., *1883. The Principles of Logic.* London: Kegan Paul, Trench. (Russell's copy: McMaster.)
Referred to: 196, 291, 340, *418, 419, 433, 434.*

—— *1893. Appearance and Reality.* London: Swan Sonnenschein; New York: Macmillan. (Russell's library.)
Referred to: *xxii,* 109, 110, 111, 148, 230, *402, 403, 404, 409, 419, 430, 434.*

—— *1893a.* "Consciousness and Experience". *Mind,* n.s. 2: 211–16. Reprinted in his *1914,* 192–8.
Referred to: 196, *409, 419.*

—— *1914. Essays on Truth and Reality.* Oxford: Clarendon Press. (Russell's library.)

—— *1922. The Principles of Logic.* 2nd ed., revised. 2 vols. London: Oxford University Press. (Russell's library.)
Referred to: *433, 434.*

—— *1930. Appearance and Reality.* 2nd ed., 9th impression, corrected. Oxford:

Clarendon Press.
Referred to: *402*, *403*, *404*, *409*, *419*, *434*.

BROWNING, ROBERT, *1841*. *Pippa Passes*. London: Edward Moxon.
Referred to: 106, 323, *404*, *439*.

—— *1864*. "Abt Vogler". In his *Dramatis Personae*. London: Chapman and Hall. Pp. 67–74.
Referred to: 48, *386*.

BUCKLE, HENRY THOMAS, *1857–61*. *History of Civilization in England*. 2 vols. London: J. W. Parker and Son.
Referred to: *377*.

BUCKLER, WILLIAM HEPBURN, *1895*. *The Origin and History of Contract in Roman Law down to End of the Republican Period*. London: C. J. Clay & Sons.
Referred to: *394*.

BUNYAN, JOHN, *1678*. *The Pilgrim's Progress*.
Referred to: *420*.

BYRON, GEORGE GORDON, LORD, *1812*. *Childe Harold's Pilgrimage*. 4th ed. London: John Murray.
Referred to: *377*.

*The Cambridge Observer.*
Referred to: *xxx*, *423*.

CARLYLE, THOMAS, *1843*. *Past and Present*. London: Chapman & Hall. (Russell's library.)
Referred to: *4*, 44, *383*.

CARROLL, LEWIS, [pseud.], *1872*. *Through the Looking Glass and What Alice Found There*. London: Macmillan.
Referred to: 252, *424*.

CAYLEY, ARTHUR, *1859*. "A Sixth Memoir on Quantics". *Philosophical Transactions of the Royal Society of London*. Series A. Mathematical and Physical Sciences, 149: 61–90. Reprinted in his *1889–97*, 2: 561–92.
Referred to: 269n., *433*.

—— *1889–97*. *The Collected Mathematical Papers of Arthur Cayley*. 13 vols. Vols. 8–13 edited by A. R. Forsyth. Cambridge: Cambridge University Press.

CICERO. *De amicitia.*
Referred to: *23*.

CLIFFORD, WILLIAM KINGDON, *1878*. "On the Nature of Things-in-Themselves". *Mind*, 3: 57–67. Reprinted in his *1879*, 274–86.
Referred to: *377*.

—— *1879*. *Lectures and Essays*. Edited by Leslie Stephen and Frederick Pollock. 2 vols. London: Macmillan.

—— *1886*. *The Common Sense of the Exact Sciences*. Edited by Karl Pearson. 2nd ed. London: Kegan Paul, Trench. (Russell's library.)
Referred to: *406*, *427*.

—— *1946*. *The Common Sense of the Exact Sciences*. Edited by Karl Pearson.

Newly edited by James R. Newman. Preface by B. Russell. New York: Alfred A. Knopf. (Russell's library.)
Referred to: *377*.

COUTURAT, LOUIS, *1896*. *De l'Infini mathématique*. Paris: Félix Alcan. (Russell's library.)

—— *1898*. "*Essai sur les fondements de la géométrie par Bertrand Russell*". *Revue de métaphysique et de morale*, 6: 354–80.
Referred to: *287*.

COWPER, WILLIAM. "To Mary". In Palgrave *1890*, 225–7.
Referred to: *4*.

CRAWSHAY-WILLIAMS, RUPERT, *1970*. *Russell Remembered*. London and New York: Oxford University Press.
Referred to: *xxii*.

CREIGHTON, MANDELL, *1888*. *Cardinal Wolsey*. London and New York: Macmillan.
Referred to: 316, *437*.

*The Daily Chronicle*, London. Leading article on the miners' strike, 18 Nov. 1893: 4.
Referred to: 79, *399*.

DANTE ALIGHIERI, *1889*. *Dante's Divine Comedy: The Inferno*. Translated by John A. Carlyle. 5th ed. London: George Bell & Sons. (Russell's library.)
Referred to: 46, 48, 50, 54, *385*, *387*, *391*.

DELBOEUF, J., *1893*. "L'Ancienne et les Nouvelles Géométries. Première étude. L'espace réel est-il l'espace géométrique euclidien?" *Revue philosophique de la France et de l'étranger*, 36: 449–84.
Referred to: *405*, *489*, *493*.

—— *1894*. "L'Ancienne et les Nouvelles Géométries. II. Les nouvelles géométries ont leur point d'attache dans la géométrie euclidienne." *Revue philosophique de la France et de l'étranger*, 37: 353–83.
Referred to: *489*.

DENONN, LESTER E., *1943*. "Recollections of Three Hours with Bertrand Russell". *Correct English*, 44 (Dec.): 14–19.
Referred to: *249*.

—— *1963*. "Bibliography of the Writings of Bertrand Russell to 1962". In Schilpp *1963*, 2: 743–828.
Referred to: *xxi*.

DESCARTES, RENÉ, *c.1628*. *Règles pour la direction de l'esprit*. Reprinted in his *1897–1910*, 10: 349–488.
Referred to: 159, 160, 161, *410*, *414*.

—— *1637*. *Discours de la méthode*. Reprinted in his *1897–1910*, 6: 1–78, 540–83.
Referred to: 160, 172, 173, 181, 183, *410*, *413*, *415*, *416*.

—— *1640–42*. *Méditations*. Reprinted in his *1897–1910*, 7: 1–90, 9A: 1–72.
Referred to: 152–3, 160, 161, *169*, 170, 173, 174, 175, *409*, *410*, *413*, *414*,

Referred to: *95, 401.*

—— *1860. The Mill on the Floss.* 3 vols. Edinburgh and London: William Blackwood and Sons.
Referred to: *55, 90, 392.*

—— *1878–85. The Works of George Eliot.* Cabinet Edition. 24 vols. Edinburgh and London: William Blackwood and Sons.
Referred to: *380.*

—— *The Spanish Gypsy.* In her *1878–85*, Vol. 24.

EMERSON, RALPH WALDO, *1883–87. The Works of Ralph Waldo Emerson.* Standard Library Edition. 14 vols. Boston and New York: Houghton, Mifflin.
Referred to: *380.*

—— "Nominalist and Realist". In his *1883–87*, 3: 213–36.

ERDMANN, BENNO, *1877. Die Axiome der Geometrie: eine philosophische Untersuchung der Riemann–Helmholtz'schen Raumtheorie.* Leipzig: Leopold Voss.
Referred to: *340, 431, 487, 488, 490, 491, 492, 493.*

ERDMANN, JOHANN EDUARD, *1878. Grundriss der Geschichte der Philosophie.* 2 vols. Berlin: Wilhelm Hertz. (Russell's library.)
Referred to: *409.*

ERHARDT, FRANZ, *1894. Metaphysik.* Vol. 1: *Erkenntnistheorie.* Leipzig: O. R. Reisland. (Russell's copy: McMaster.)
Referred to: *256, 262–5, 427, 428, 429, 430.*

EUCLID *1908. The Thirteen Books of Euclid's Elements.* Translated by T. L. Heath. 3 vols. Cambridge: Cambridge University Press.
Referred to: *126, 268, 294, 405, 431, 432.*

—— *See also* POTTS *1845.*

FARRINGTON, REV. SILAS, *1876. The Ideal of Religion: A Lecture.* London: Thomas Scott.
Referred to: *381.*

—— *c.1880. The Upper Brook Street Free Pulpit.* Manchester: A. Heywood & Son.
Referred to: *381.*

—— *1894. Are You Saved?* London: Essex Hall.
Referred to: *381.*

FEINBERG, BARRY, ed., *1967. A Detailed Catalogue of the Archives of Bertrand Russell.* London: Continuum 1.
Referred to: *xxi.*

FLAUBERT, GUSTAVE, *1886. L'Éducation sentimentale, histoire d'un jeune homme.* Paris: G. Charpentier.
Referred to: *258, 426.*

FRANKLIN, BENJAMIN, *1732–46. Poor Richard's Almanack.*
Referred to: *43, 382.*

FRISCHAUF, JOHANNES, *1872. Absolute Geometrie nach Johann Bolyai.* Leipzig: B. G. Teubner. (Russell's library.)
Referred to: *247.*

GALILEO GALILEI, *1632. Dialogue concerning the Two Chief World Systems.*
Referred to: *407.*

—— *1638. Dialogues concerning Two New Sciences.*
Referred to: *407.*

GALTON, SIR FRANCIS, *1889. Natural Inheritance.* London: Macmillan.
Referred to: *396.*

—— *1892. Hereditary Genius: An Inquiry into Its Laws and Consequences.* 2nd ed.
London and New York: Macmillan. (Russell's copy: McMaster.)
Referred to: *396.*

GASKELL, PHILIP, *1972. A New Introduction to Bibliography.* Oxford: Clarendon
Press.
Referred to: *xxxii.*

—— *1978. From Writer to Reader: Studies in Editorial Method.* Oxford: Clarendon
Press.
Referred to: *xxxii.*

GAUSS, CARL FRIEDRICH, *1860–65. Briefwechsel zwischen C. F. Gauss und H. C.
Schumacher.* Edited by C. A. F. Peters. 6 vols. Altona: Gustav Esch.
Referred to: *247, 293, 434.*

GEULINCX, ARNOLD, *1675. Ethica.* Reprinted in his *1891–93,* 3: 1–271.
Referred to: *184, 416.*

—— *1891–93. Opera philosophica.* Edited by J. P. N. Land. 3 vols. The Hague:
Martinus Nijhoff.
Referred to: *416.*

GIBBON, EDWARD, *1776–88. The History of the Decline and Fall of the Roman Empire.* 6 vols. London: W. Strahan and T. Cadell. (Russell's library.)
Referred to: *85, 345, 400.*

GILBERT, WILLIAM, *1600. De Magnete.*
Referred to: *407.*

GOBLOT, EDMOND, *1898. Essai sur la classification des sciences.* Paris: Félix Alcan.

GODWIN, WILLIAM, *1793. An Enquiry concerning Political Justice, and Its Influence
on General Virtue and Happiness.* 2nd ed., 1796. 3rd ed., 1798.
Referred to: *220, 422.*

GOETHE, JOHANN WOLFGANG VON, *1774. The Sorrows of Young Werther.*
Referred to: *400.*

—— *1795–96. Wilhelm Meister's Apprenticeship.*
Referred to: *400.*

—— "Mason-Lodge". In Carlyle *1843,* 293–4.
Referred to: *4.*

GRASSMANN, HERMANN GUNTHER, *1878. Die Ausdehnungslehre von 1844, oder die
lineale Ausdehnungslehre.* 2nd ed. Leipzig: Otto Wigand.
Referred to: *489, 492.*

GREEN, THOMAS HILL, *1883. Prolegomena to Ethics.* Edited by A. C. Bradley. Oxford: Clarendon Press.

Referred to: *206*, *208–11*, *420*, *421*.

HALPERN, BARBARA STRACHEY: *see* STRACHEY, BARBARA.

HAMILTON, SIR WILLIAM, *1859–60*. *Lectures on Metaphysics and Logic*. Edited by Henry L. Mansel and John Veitch. 4 vols. Edinburgh and London: William Blackwood and Sons.
Referred to: *425*.

HANNEQUIN, ARTHUR, *1895*. *Essai critique sur l'hypothèse des atomes dans la science contemporaine*. Paris: G. Masson.
Referred to: *495*.

HELMHOLTZ, HERMANN LUDWIG FERDINAND VON, *1866*. "Ueber die that-sächlichen Grundlagen der Geometrie". *Verhandlungen des naturhistorisch-medizinischer Verein zu Heidelberg*, 4: 197–202. Reprinted in his *1882–95*, 2: 610–17.
Referred to: 276, 296, *431*, *432*.

—— *1868*. "Ueber die Thatsachen, die der Geometrie zum Grunde liegen". *Abhandlungen der königlichen Gesellschaft der Wissenschaften zu Göttingen*, 15: 193–221. Reprinted in his *1882–95*, 2: 618–39.
Referred to: *406*, *431*, *432*.

—— *1876*. "The Origin and Meaning of Geometrical Axioms". *Mind*, 1: 301–21. In German in his *1884*, 2: 1–31.
Referred to: *124*, 126–7, 263, *406*, *424*, *428*, *432*, *434*.

—— *1878*. "The Origin and Meaning of Geometrical Axioms. (II.)". *Mind*, 3: 212–25. German original in his *1882–95*, 2: 640–60, as "Ueber den Ursprung und Sinn der geometrischen Sätze; Antwort gegen Herrn Professor Land".
Referred to: *124*, 126–7, 264–5, 271, *405*, *406*, *429*, *431*.

—— *1882–95*. *Wissenschaftliche Abhandlungen*. 3 vols. Leipzig: Johann Ambrosius Barth. (Russell's library: Vols. 1–2.)
Referred to: 276n., *405*, *406*, *431*, *432*.

—— *1884*. *Vorträge und Reden*. 2 vols. Braunschweig: F. Vieweg.
Referred to: *406*, *428*, *432*.

HERTZ, HEINRICH RUDOLPH, *1894*. *Die Prinzipien der Mechanik*. Preface by H. von Helmholtz. (Gesammelte Werke von Heinrich Hertz, Vol. 3.) Leipzig: Johann Ambrosius Barth. (Russell's library.)
Referred to: *425*.

HEYMANS, GERARDUS, *1890–94*. *Die Gesetze und Elemente des wissenschaftlichen Denkens: ein Lehrbuch der Erkenntnisstheorie in Grundzügen*. 2 vols. Leiden: S. C. Van Doesburgh.
Referred to: *249–50*, 251–5, *424*, *425*, *484*.

HOBBES, THOMAS, *1650*. *De Corpore Politico*. Reprinted in his *1839–45*, 4: 77–228.
Referred to: 186.

—— *1650a*. *Human Nature*. Reprinted in his *1839–45*, 4: 1–76.
Referred to: 186, 187, 191, 193–4, *417*, *418*, *419*.

—— *1651. Leviathan.* Reprinted in his *1839–45*, Vol. 3.
  Referred to: 186–7, 191, *417*, *418*.
—— *1655. De Corpore.* Reprinted in his *1839–45*, Vol. 1.
  Referred to: 157–8, 186, 187, 188, 189, 190, 192, *410*, *417*, *418*, *419*.
—— *1679. Behemoth.* Reprinted in his *1839–45*, 6: 161–418.
  Referred to: 186.
—— *1839–45. The English Works of Thomas Hobbes of Malmesbury.* Edited by Sir
  William Molesworth. 11 vols. London: John Bohn; Vols. 7–11, London:
  Longman, Brown, Green, and Longmans. (Russell's library.)
  Referred to: *410*, *417*, *418*.
—— *See also* THUCYDIDES *1629.*
HOBSON, JOHN ATKINSON, *1894. The Evolution of Modern Capitalism: A Study of
  Machine Production.* London: Walter Scott.
  Referred to: *319*.
HORACE *1934. The Odes and Epodes.* Translated by C. E. Bennett. Revised ed.
  London: William Heinemann.
  Referred to: 14, *376*.
HUME, DAVID, *1890. A Treatise of Human Nature.* 2 vols. Edited by T. H. Green
  and T. H. Grose. London: Longmans, Green. (Russell's library.) 1st ed.,
  1739–40.
  Referred to: 100, *140*, 143–4, *402*, *408*, *425*.
IBSEN, HENRIK, *1881. Ghosts.*
  Referred to: 232, *423*.
—— *1890. Hedda Gabler.*
  Referred to: *83*.
—— *c.1890. Nora; oder, ein Puppenheim.* Translated into German by W. Lange.
  Leipzig: Philipp Reclam. (Russell's library.)
  Referred to: *68*.
*The Inquirer* (London). [Report of B. Russell's fellowship dissertation.] 19 Oct.
  1895.
  Referred to: *xxii*.
JAMES, HENRY, *1876. Roderick Hudson.* Boston: James R. Osgood.
  Referred to: *401*.
—— *1886. The Bostonians.* 3 vols. London: Macmillan.
  Referred to: *402*.
—— *1886a. The Princess Casamassima.* 3 vols. London and New York: Macmil-
  lan.
  Referred to: 96, *401*, *402*.
JAMES, WILLIAM, *1890. The Principles of Psychology.* 2 vols. London: Macmillan.
  (Russell's library: 1891 [i.e. 3rd] printing.)
  Referred to: 66, *90*, 97, 258, 274, 282, 282n., 300n., *398*, *402*, *423*, *431*,
  *432–3*, *439*.
JEVONS, WILLIAM STANLEY, *1874. The Principles of Science: A Treatise on Logic and*

*Scientific Method*. 2 vols. London: Macmillan.
Referred to: *254, 425*.

JOHNSON, HELEN KENDRICK, AND FREDERICK DEAN, *1899*. *The World's Best Music, Embracing Famous Songs and Those Who Made Them*. 6 vols. New York: The University Society.
Referred to: *390*.

JONES, ALAN W., *1979*. *Lyulph Stanley: A Study in Educational Politics*. Waterloo, Ont.: Wilfrid Laurier University Press.
Referred to: *391*.

KANT, IMMANUEL, *1768*. *Von dem ersten Grunde des Unterschiedes der Gegenden im Raume*. Reprinted in his *1867–68*, 2: 383–91.
Referred to: *489*.

—— *1781*. *The Critique of Pure Reason*.
Referred to: 188, *247*, 251, *256*, 259–62, 288, 291, 340, 341, *406*, *408*, *414*, *417*, *420*, *424*, *425*, *426*, *427*, *433*, *434*.

—— *1783*. *Prolegomena to Any Future Metaphysics*.
Referred to: 160, *247*, 291, *431*, *434*, *489*.

—— *1867–68*. *Immanuel Kant's sämmtliche Werke*. Edited by G. Hartenstein. 8 vols. Leipzig: Leopold Voss. (Russell's library.)
Referred to: 402, *423*, *426*.

—— *1956*. *Critique of Practical Reason*. Translated by Lewis White Beck. New York: Liberal Arts Press. 1st ed., 1788.
Referred to: *402*, *421*, *423*.

—— *1964*. *Groundwork of the Metaphysic of Morals*. Translated by H. J. Paton. New York: Harper & Row. 1st ed., 1785.
Referred to: *423*.

KEATS, JOHN, *1817*. "When I have fears that I may cease to be". In Palgrave *1890*, 272.
Referred to: 108, *404*.

KELVIN, 1ST BARON: *see* THOMSON, WILLIAM.

KILLING, WILHELM KARL JOSEPH, *1885*. *Die nicht-Euklidischen Raumformen in analytischer Behandlung*. Leipzig: B. G. Teubner. (Russell's library.)
Referred to: *247*.

KIRCHHOFF, GUSTAV ROBERT, *1876*. *Vorlesungen über mathematische Physik*. 2 vols. Leipzig: B. G. Teubner.
Referred to: *425*.

KLEIN, FELIX, *1871*. "Ueber die sogenannte nicht-Euklidische Geometrie". *Mathematische Annalen*, 4: 573–625.
Referred to: *430*, *433*.

—— *1893*. *Nicht-Euklidische Geometrie*. Transcribed by Fr. Schilling. 2 vols. 2nd printing. Göttingen: no publisher. (Russell's library.) 1st ed., 1890.
Referred to: *247*, 269n., 284n., 294n., 339, *424–5*, *430*, *488*.

LALANDE, ANDRÉ, *1890*. "Remarques sur le principe de causalité". *Revue phi-*

*losophique de la France et de l'étranger*, 30: 225–48.
Referred to: *146*.

LAND, J. P. N., *1877*. "Kant's Space and Modern Mathematics". *Mind*, 2: 38–46.
Referred to: *124, 429*.

LANGE, FRIEDRICH ALBERT, *1877*. *Logische Studien: ein Beitrag zur Neubegründung der formalen Logik und der Erkenntnisstheorie*. Iserlohn: J. Baedeker.
Referred to: *255, 425*.

—— *1925*. *The History of Materialism and Criticism of Its Present Importance*. 3rd ed. Translated by Ernest Chester Thomas. Introduction by B. Russell. London: Kegan Paul, Trench, Trubner; New York: Harcourt, Brace. 1st German ed., 1866.
Referred to: *425*.

LECHALAS, GEORGES, *1896*. *Étude sur l'espace et le temps*. Paris: Félix Alcan.
Referred to: *287, 288, 433*.

—— *1898*. "L'Axiome de libre mobilité, d'après M. Russell". *Revue de métaphysique et de morale*, 6: 746–58.
Referred to: *287*.

—— *1898–99*. "Les Fondements de la géométrie, d'après M. Russell". *Annales de philosophie chrétienne*, 38 (1898): 646–60; 39 (1899): 75–93, 179–97, 317–34.
Referred to: *287*.

LEIBNIZ, GOTTFRIED WILHELM VON, *1710*. *Theodicy*.
Referred to: *416*.

—— *1714*. *The Monadology*.
Referred to: *415*.

LEITHAUSER, GLADYS, *1975*. "Arch-Priggery: A Note on Bertrand and Alys Russell's Copy of Whitman's 'Leaves of Grass'". *Russell*, no. 19: 15–17.
Referred to: *401*.

LEVY, PAUL, *1979*. *Moore: G. E. Moore and the Cambridge Apostles*. London: Weidenfeld and Nicolson.
Referred to: *76, 83, 91, 112*.

LIE, MARIUS SOPHUS, *1890*. "Ueber die Grundlagen der Geometrie". *Berichte über die Verhandlungen der Sächsichen Gesellschaft der Wissenschaften zu Leipzig*, 42: 284–321, 355–418.
Referred to: 293n., 294n., *454*.

LIVY. *History of Rome*.
Referred to: *23*.

LOBATCHEWSKY, NIKOLAI IVANOVICH, *1856*. "Pangéométrie; ou, précis de géométrie fondée sur une théorie générale et rigoureuse des parallèles". In (as translated from the Russian) *Collection of Scientific Papers Written by Professors of the Imperial University of Kazan in Commemoration of the 50th Year of Its Existence*. Kazan: 1856. 1: 227–340.
Referred to: *431*.

LOCKE, JOHN, *1690*. *An Essay concerning Human Understanding*. Reprinted in his

*1824*, Vols. 1–2.
Referred to: *131*, 134, 142–3, 182, *407, 408, 415*.

—— *1697. A Letter to ... Edward [Stillingfleet] Ld. Bishop of Worcester, concerning Some Passages Relating to Mr. Locke's Essay of Humane Understanding.* Reprinted in his *1824*, 3: 1–96.
Referred to: *408, 415*.

—— *1824. The Works of John Locke.* 12th ed. 9 vols. London: C. and J. Rivington, et al. (Russell's library.)
Referred to: *408, 415*.

LONGFELLOW, HENRY WADSWORTH, *1882*. "A Psalm of Life". In *The Poetical Works of Henry Wadsworth Longfellow.* London: Frederick Warne. P. 9. (Russell's library.)
Referred to: *375, 377*.

LOTZE, HERMANN, *1879*. *Metaphysik; drei Bücher der Ontologie, Kosmologie und Psychologie.* 2nd ed. (System der Philosophie, Pt. 2.) Leipzig: S. Hirzel. (Russell's library: 1884 printing.)
Referred to: *247*, 340, *427–8*.

LOVE, A. E. H., *1897*. *Theoretical Mechanics. An Introductory Treatise on the Principles of Dynamics. With Applications and Numerous Examples.* Cambridge: at the University Press.

LOWELL, JAMES RUSSELL, *1848*. "What Mr. Robinson Thinks". In his *The Biglow Papers.* Cambridge, Mass.: George Nichols.
Referred to: 46, *386*.

MACAULAY, THOMAS BABINGTON, *1842*. "Horatius: A Lay Made about the Year of the City CCCLX". In his *Lays of Ancient Rome.* London: Longman, Brown, Green and Longmans. Pp. 39–76.
Referred to: 43, *382*.

MACCARTHY, DESMOND, AND AGATHA RUSSELL, eds., *1910*. *Lady John Russell: A Memoir with Selections from Her Diaries and Correspondence.* London: Methuen. (Russell's library: 1926 ed.)
Referred to: *385*.

McCARTHY, JUSTIN, *1904*. *An Irishman's Story.* London: Macmillan.
Referred to: *388*.

MACH, ERNST, *1883*. *The Science of Mechanics.*
Referred to: *425*.

—— *1886. The Analysis of Sensations.*
Referred to: *425*.

MACPHERSON, JAMES, *1760*. *Fragments of Ancient Poetry, Collected in the Highlands of Scotland, and Translated from the Gaelic or Erse Language.*
Referred to: *384*.

—— *1762. The Poems of Ossian.*
Referred to: *384*.

McTAGGART, J. McT. E., *1893*. *The Further Determination of the Absolute.* Pri-

Green, Longman, Roberts & Green. Reprinted in his *1963–*, Vol. 9.
Referred to: *145, 408*.

—— *1871. Principles of Political Economy, with Some of Their Applications to Social Philosophy.* 7th ed. London: Longmans, Green, Reader, and Dyer. Reprinted in his *1963–*, Vols. 2–3.
Referred to: *379*.

—— *1873. Autobiography.* London: Longmans, Green, Reader, and Dyer. (Russell's library.) Reprinted in his *1963–*, Vol. 1.
Referred to: *56, 392–3*.

—— *1888. Utilitarianism.* 10th ed. London and New York: Longmans, Green. (Russell's library.) Reprinted in his *1963–*, 10: 203–59.
Referred to: *420*.

—— *1963–. Collected Works of John Stuart Mill.* Edited by John M. Robson. Toronto: University of Toronto Press.
Referred to: *379, 393, 399, 406, 408, 420*.

MILTON, JOHN, *1637. Comus.*
Referred to: *403*.

—— *1638.* "Lycidas". In Palgrave *1890*, 79–85.
Referred to: *401, 439*.

—— *1644. Areopagitica.*
Referred to: *380*.

—— *1667. Paradise Lost.*
Referred to: *61, 380*.

MOORE, GEORGE EDWARD, *1897.* "Can We Mean Anything, When We Don't Know What We Mean?" Unpublished manuscript. Moore papers, Cambridge University Library.
Referred to: *402, 403*.

—— *1898.* "The Elements of Ethics". Unpublished typescript. Moore papers, Cambridge University Library.
Referred to: *112, 404, 405*.

MULLINGER, JAMES BASS, *1873–1911. The University of Cambridge from the Earliest Times (to the Decline of the Platonist Movement).* 3 vols. Cambridge: Cambridge University Press.
Referred to: *412*.

NEWTON, ISAAC, *1687. Philosophiae Naturalis Principia Mathematica.* (Russell's library: 3rd ed., 1726.)
Referred to: *44, 383*.

—— *1871. The First Three Sections of Newton's Principia and the Ninth and Eleventh Sections.* Edited by J. H. Evans. 5th ed., edited by P. T. Main. Cambridge School and College Text Books. London: George Bell and Sons.
Referred to: *384*.

—— *1883. Newton's Principia; First Book, Sections I, II, III, with Notes and Illustrations, and a Collection of Problems Principally Intended as Examples of*

*Newton's Methods*. Edited by Percival Frost. 4th ed. London: Macmillan.
Referred to: *384*.
—— *1969. A Treatise of the System of the World*. Introduction by I. Bernard Cohen.
[Facsimile reprint of 2nd ed., London: 1731.] London: Dawsons.
Referred to: *425*.
O'BRIEN, JOSEPH V., *1976. William O'Brien and the Course of Irish Politics,
1881–1918*. Berkeley, Los Angeles and London: University of California
Press.
Referred to: *387–8*.
O'BRIEN, WILLIAM, *1890. When We Were Boys*. London: Longmans, Green.
Referred to: *43, 382*.
OMAR KHAYYÁM, *1859. Rubáiyát of Omar Khayyám, the Astronomer-Poet of Persia*.
Translated by Edward FitzGerald. London: B. Quaritch.
Referred to: *404*.
*The Oxford English Dictionary*.
Referred to: *449, 451*.
PALGRAVE, FRANCIS TURNER, ed., *1888. The Golden Treasury of the Best Songs and
Lyrical Poems in the English Language*. London and New York: Macmillan.
(Russell's library.)
Referred to: *380*.
—— *1890. The Golden Treasury of the Best Songs and Lyrical Poems in the English
Language*. London and New York: Macmillan. (Russell's library.)
Referred to: *395, 396, 401, 404*.
PALSGRAVE, JEAN, *1852. L'Éclaircissement de la langue française*. Paris: Imprimerie
Nationale.
Referred to: *439*.
PATER, WALTER, *1878*. "Imaginary Portrait. The Child in the House". Reprinted
as *An Imaginary Portrait*. Oxford: privately printed by H. Daniel, 1894. Re-
printed in his *1900–01*, 8: 172–96.
Referred to: *398*.
—— *1885*. "A Prince of Court Painters: Extracts from an Old French Journal".
Reprinted in his *1900–01*, 4: 3–44.
Referred to: *321, 438*.
—— *1886*. "Sebastian van Storck". Reprinted in his *1887* and in his *1900–01*,
4: 79–115.
Referred to: *66, 398*.
—— *1887. Imaginary Portraits*. London and New York: Macmillan.
Referred to: *66, 398*.
—— *1900–01. The Works of Walter Pater*. 8 vols. London and New York: Mac-
millan.
Referred to: *438*.
PEARSALL SMITH: *see* SMITH, ALYS W. PEARSALL, or SMITH, LOGAN PEARSALL.
PEEL, ETHEL, ed., *1920. Recollections of Lady Georgiana Peel*. London: John Lane,

The Bodley Head; New York: John Lane.
Referred to: *392*.

PHAEDRUS. *Liber fabularum.*
Referred to: *23*.

PITT, JACK, *1981*. "Russell and the Cambridge Moral Sciences Club". *Russell*, n.s. 1: 103–18.
Referred to: *393*.

PLATO. *Protagoras.*
Referred to: *423*.

POINCARÉ, HENRI, *1892*. "Non-Euclidean Geometry". *Nature*, 45: 404–7.
Referred to: *427*.

POLLOCK, SIR FREDERICK, *1880*. *Spinoza: His Life and Philosophy.* London: C. Kegan Paul. (Russell's library: 1899 ed.)
Referred to: *416*.

POTTS, ROBERT, *1845*. *Euclid's Elements of Geometry, Chiefly from the Text of Dr Simson, with Explanatory Notes.* Cambridge: Cambridge University Press; London: John W. Parker.
Referred to: *431*, *432*.

PREST, JOHN M., *1972*. *Lord John Russell.* London and Basingstoke: Macmillan.
Referred to: *388*.

*Principia Latina.*
Referred to: 43, *382*.

RAMUS, PETER, *1536*. *Quaecumque ab Aristotele dicta essent, commentitia esse.*
Referred to: 163, *411*.

—— *1543*. *Aristotelicae animadversiones.*
Referred to: *411*.

—— *1543a*. *Dialecticae institutiones.*
Referred to: *411*.

—— *1556*. *Dialecticae libri duo, Audomari Talaei praelectionibus illustrati.*
Referred to: *411*.

—— *1574*. *The Logike of the Moste Excellent Philosopher P. Ramus Martyr, newly translated and in divers places corrected after the mynde of the author per M[agistrum] Roll[andum] Makylmenaeum Scotum rogatu viri honestissimi M[agistri] Aegidii Hamlini.*
Referred to: *412*.

—— *1584*. *Dialecticae libri duo, scholiis Guilielmi Tempellii Cantabrigiensis illustrati.*
Referred to: *411*.

REID, STUART JOHNSON, *1895*. *Lord John Russell.* London: Sampson Low, Marston.
Referred to: *xxi*.

RÉMUSAT, CHARLES FRANÇOIS MARIE, COMTE DE, *1875*. *Histoire de la philosophie en Angleterre depuis Bacon jusqu'à Locke.* 2 vols. Paris: Didier.
Referred to: *162*, *411*.

RICARDO, DAVID, *1817*. *On the Principles of Political Economy, and Taxation.* London: J. Murray. (Russell's library: 1891 ed.)
Referred to: *378*.

RIEHL, ALOIS, *1876–87*. *Der philosophische Kriticismus und seine Bedeutung für die positive Wissenschaft.* 2 vols. Leipzig: Wilhelm Engelmann.
Referred to: *424*.

RIEMANN, GEORG FRIEDRICH BERNHARD, *1867*. "Ueber die Hypothesen, welche der Geometrie zu Grunde liegen". *Abhandlungen der königlichen Gesellschaft der Wissenschaften zu Göttingen*, 13: 133–50. Reprinted in his *1876*, 254–69.
Referred to: *247, 277, 345, 426, 431, 432, 490*.

—— *1876*. *Bernhard Riemann's gesammelte mathematische Werke und wissenschaftlicher Nachlass.* Edited by R. Dedekind. Leipzig: B. G. Teubner.
Referred to: *490, 493*.

ROBERTSON, GEORGE CROOM, *1886*. *Hobbes.* Edinburgh and London: William Blackwood and Sons.
Referred to: *416, 417*.

ROSENBAUM, S. P., *1969*. "G. E. Moore's *The Elements of Ethics*". *University of Toronto Quarterly*, 38: 214–32.
Referred to: *112*.

ROUTH, EDWARD JOHN, *1860*. *An Elementary Treatise on the Dynamics of a System of Rigid Bodies.* Cambridge and London: Macmillan.
Referred to: *384*.

—— *1882*. *The Elementary Part of a Treatise on the Dynamics of a System of Rigid Bodies. Being Part I. of a Treatise on the Whole Subject.* 4th ed., revised and enlarged. London: Macmillan.
Referred to: *44, 46, 47, 48, 49, 384, 385, 386, 387, 390, 391*.

—— *1884*. *The Advanced Part of a Treatise on the Dynamics of a System of Rigid Bodies. Being Part II. of a Treatise on the Whole Subject.* 4th ed., revised and enlarged. London: Macmillan.
Referred to: *384, 391*.

—— *1891–92*. *A Treatise on Analytical Statics.* 2 vols. Cambridge: Cambridge University Press.
Referred to: *345*.

RUSKIN, JOHN, *1865*. *Sesame and Lilies: Two Lectures.* London: Smith, Elder.
Referred to: *52, 390*.

—— *1888*. *Modern Painters.* Complete Edition. 6 vols. Sunnyside, Orpington, Kent: George Allen. 1st ed., 1843–60.
Referred to: *44, 45, 46, 49–50, 52, 383, 387*.

RUSSELL, BERTRAND ARTHUR WILLIAM, 3RD EARL, *1878–79*. "[Questions and Answers on English Constitutional History]". Unpublished manuscript notebook. RA 220.010000.
Referred to: *xv*.

—— *1893–94*. "[Lecture Notebooks]". Unpublished manuscript notebooks. 2

vols. RA 220.010040 and 220.010050.

Referred to: *118, 120, 124, 131, 140, 146, 151, 155, 162, 201, 212, 215, 218, 223, 226, 405, 406, 407, 409, 410, 413, 414.*

—— *c.1895.* "Note on the Logic of the Sciences". Unpublished manuscript. RA 210.006550, p. 164.

Referred to: *240.*

—— *1896. German Social Democracy.* London, New York and Bombay: Longmans, Green. 2nd ed., 1965.

Referred to: *xxxiii, 242, 306, 307, 310, 311, 329, 345, 399, 436, 437.*

—— *1896a.* "The Logic of Geometry". *Mind,* n.s. 5: 1–23. (Paper **42** in this volume.)

Referred to: 297, 298n., 340.

—— *1896b.* [Review of Hannequin *1895.*] *Mind,* n.s. 5: 410–17.

Referred to: *xxxii, 434.*

—— *1896c.* "On Some Difficulties of Continuous Quantity". Unpublished manuscript. RA 220.010540.

Referred to: *xxxii, 434.*

—— *1896–98.* "Various Notes on Mathematical Philosophy". Manuscript notebook. RA 210.006550–FI. Published in part in his *1959.*

Referred to: *xxxiv.*

—— *1897. An Essay on the Foundations of Geometry.* Cambridge: Cambridge University Press. *See also* his *1901.*

Referred to: *xxii, xxxiii, 124, 246–8, 256–7, 266, 287, 289–90, 329, 345, 406, 424, 427, 428, 430, 431, 432, 433, 434, 452, 453, 456, 457, 458, 486–95 passim.*

—— *1897a.* "On the Relations of Number and Quantity". *Mind,* n.s. 6: 326–41.

Referred to: *xxxiii, xxxiv, 434.*

—— *1897b.* [Review of Couturat *1896*]. *Mind,* n.s. 6: 112–19.

Referred to: *xxxiii.*

—— *1898.* [Review of Love *1897*]. *Mind,* n.s. 7: 404–11.

Referred to: *xxxiv.*

—— *1898a.* "An Analysis of Mathematical Reasoning". Unpublished manuscript. RA 230.030300–FI, 2.

Referred to: *xxxiv.*

—— *1898b.* "Les Axiomes propres à Euclide, sont-ils empiriques?" *Revue de métaphysique et de morale,* 6: 759–76.

Referred to: *xxxiv.*

—— *1898c.* [Review of Goblot *1898*]. *Mind,* n.s. 7: 567–8.

Referred to: *xxxiv.*

—— *1899.* "The Classification of Relations". Unpublished manuscript. RA 220.010570.

Referred to: *xxxiv.*

—— *1900. A Critical Exposition of the Philosophy of Leibniz, with an Appendix of*

*Leading Passages*. Cambridge: Cambridge University Press. 2nd ed., 1937.
Referred to: *345, 447*.

—— *1901*. *Essai sur les fondements de la geómétrie*. Revised ed. Translated into French by Albert Cadenat. Annotated by B. Russell and Louis Couturat. Paris: Gauthier-Villars.
Referred to: *452, 453, 486*.

—— *1903*. *The Principles of Mathematics*. Cambridge: Cambridge University Press. 2nd ed., 1937.
Referred to: *250, 433*.

—— *1907*. "The Regressive Method of Discovering the Premisses of Mathematics". Read to the Cambridge Moral Sciences Club. In his *Essays in Analysis*. Edited by Douglas Lackey. London: George Allen & Unwin, 1973. Pp. 272–83.
Referred to: *434*.

—— *1907a*. "The Politics of a Biologist". *Albany Review*, n.s. 2 (Oct.): 89–98. Review of G. Chatterton-Hill, *Heredity and Selection in Sociology*.
Referred to: *439*.

—— *1912*. *The Problems of Philosophy*. (Home University Library of Modern Knowledge.) London: Williams and Norgate.
Referred to: *448*.

—— *1914*. *Our Knowledge of the External World as a Field for Scientific Method in Philosophy*. Chicago and London: Open Court. 2nd ed., 1926.
Referred to: *418, 433*.

—— *1918*. *Roads to Freedom: Socialism, Anarchism, and Syndicalism*. London: George Allen & Unwin.
Referred to: *398*.

—— *1925*. "Introduction: Materialism, Past and Present". In Lange *1925*, v–xix.
Referred to: *425*.

—— *1927*. "Is Literature a Dead Art?". *The Forward*, New York, 10 April: p. E1.
Referred to: *446*.

—— *1928*. "Behaviourism and Values". In his *Sceptical Essays*. London: George Allen & Unwin. Pp. 89–98.
Referred to: *448*.

—— *1929*. *Marriage and Morals*. London: George Allen & Unwin.
Referred to: *396*.

—— *1930*. "Bertrand Russell Tells How He Was Educated as a Child". *The Forward*, New York, 9 March: pp. E1–2.
Referred to: *4*.

—— *1930a*. Letter to J. K. Piercy. In Piercy, ed. *Modern Writers at Work*. New York: Macmillan. Pp. 9–12.
Referred to: *445*.

—— *1934*. *Freedom and Organization: 1814–1914*. London: George Allen & Unwin.

Referred to: *399*.

—— *1935*. *Religion and Science*. London: Thornton Butterworth.
Referred to: *374*.

—— *1938*. "My Religious Reminiscences". *Rationalist Annual*, pp. 3–8. Reprinted in his *1961a*, 31–6.
Referred to: *3*.

—— *1944*. "My Mental Development". In Schilpp *1963*, 1: 1–20.
Referred to: *3*.

—— *c.1944*. "C. D." Unpublished manuscript. RA 220.017270.
Referred to: *393*.

—— *1945*. *A History of Western Philosophy, and Its Connection with Political and Social Circumstances from the Earliest Times to the Present Day*. New York: Simon and Schuster. New ed., London: George Allen & Unwin, 1961.
Referred to: *398, 402*.

—— *1946*. "Preface". In Clifford *1946*, v–x.
Referred to: *377*.

—— *1948*. "A Turning Point in My Life". In *The Saturday Book*. Edited by Leonard Russell. London: Hutchinson. 8: 142–6.
Referred to: *306*.

—— *1951*. "George Bernard Shaw". *Virginia Quarterly Review*, 27: 1–7.
Referred to: *307*.

—— *1951a*. *New Hopes for a Changing World*. London: George Allen & Unwin.
Referred to: *439*.

—— *1954*. "How I Write". *The Writer*, n.s. 14 (Sept.): 4–5.
Referred to: *335*.

—— *1956*. *Portraits from Memory, and Other Essays*. London: George Allen & Unwin.
Referred to: *447*.

—— *1956a*. "Lord John Russell". In his *1956*, 109–13.
Referred to: *xxi*.

—— *1956b*. "How I Write". In his *1956*, 194–7. [To be distinguished from his *1954*.]
Referred to: *445*.

—— *1957*. *Why I Am Not a Christian, and Other Essays on Religion and Related Subjects*. Edited by Paul Edwards. London: George Allen & Unwin.
Referred to: *105, 452, 471*.

—— *1957a*. *Why I Am Not a Christian, and Other Essays on Religion and Related Subjects*. Edited by Paul Edwards. New York: Simon and Schuster.
Referred to: *471*.

—— *1959*. *My Philosophical Development*. London: George Allen & Unwin.
Referred to: *xvi, 3, 119, 247, 345, 399, 406, 459–60*.

—— *1961*. "Books That Influenced Me in Youth". In his *Fact and Fiction*. London: George Allen and Unwin. Pp. 9–46.

Referred to: *377, 380, 390, 394.*

—— *1961a. The Basic Writings of Bertrand Russell: 1903–1959.* Edited by Robert E. Egner and Lester E. Denonn. London: George Allen & Unwin.

—— *1964. The Life and Times of Bertrand Russell.* London: British Broadcasting Corporation. "Shot List" [transcript of filmed interview], reel I. RA 430.065345.
Referred to: *398.*

—— *1967. The Autobiography of Bertrand Russell.* Vol. I: *1872–1914.* London: George Allen and Unwin.
Referred to: *xiii, xviii, xxii, 3, 22, 41, 76, 306, 307, 373, 374, 375, 376, 377, 380, 382, 384, 390, 393, 394, 395, 396, 398, 399, 401, 441, 459–60, 463.*

—— *1968. The Autobiography of Bertrand Russell.* Vol. 2: *1914–1944.* London: George Allen and Unwin.
Referred to: *72.*

—— *1969. Dear Bertrand Russell ...; A Selection of His Correspondence with the General Public, 1950–1968.* Edited by Barry Feinberg and Ronald Kasrils. London: George Allen and Unwin.
Referred to: *382.*

—— *1969a. The Autobiography of Bertrand Russell.* Vol. 3: *1944–1967.* London: George Allen & Unwin.
Referred to: *383.*

—— *1972. Politische Schriften.* Vol. I: *Was wir tun können.* Translated into German by Achim v. Borries. (Bertrand Russell Studienausgabe.) Munich: Nymphenburger.
Referred to: *311.*

—— *1984. Theory of Knowledge: The 1913 Manuscript.* Edited by Elizabeth Ramsden Eames in collaboration with Kenneth Blackwell. (The Collected Papers of Bertrand Russell, Vol. 7.) London: George Allen & Unwin.
Referred to: *xv.*

—— AND PATRICIA RUSSELL, eds., *1937. The Amberley Papers: The Letters and Diaries of Lord and Lady Amberley.* 2 vols. London: Hogarth Press.
Referred to: *xvi, xxi, 384, 388, 390, 391, 395.*

—— See also WHITEHEAD, ALFRED NORTH, AND BERTRAND RUSSELL.

RUSSELL, FRANCIS ALBERT ROLLO, *1892. Epidemics, Plagues and Fevers: Their Causes and Prevention.* London: E. Stanford.
Referred to: *381–2.*

RUSSELL, JOHN FRANCIS STANLEY, 2ND EARL, *1923. My Life and Adventures.* London and New York: Cassell.
Referred to: *384, 385, 390, 392.*

*Russell: The Journal of the Bertrand Russell Archives.*
Referred to: *xxi.*

SAMUELS, ERNEST, *1979. Bernard Berenson: The Making of a Connoisseur.* Cambridge, Mass., and London: The Belknap Press of Harvard University Press.

Referred to: *xxii, 72.*

SANGER, CHARLES PERCY, *1901. The Place of Compensation in Temperance Reform.* London: P. S. King & Son.

Referred to: *397.*

—— *1929.* "Russell, Bertrand Arthur William". In *The Encyclopaedia Britannica.* 14th ed. New York and London: Encyclopaedia Britannica. 19: 678.

Referred to: *393, 397.*

SANTAYANA, GEORGE, *1953. Persons and Places.* Vol. 3: *My Host the World.* New York: Charles Scribner's Sons.

Referred to: *xvii.*

SCHEFFEL, JOSEPH VIKTOR VON, *1854. Der Trompeter von Säkkingen. Ein Sang vom Oberrhein.* 2 vols. Stuttgart: J. B. Metzler.

Referred to: *43, 52, 53, 382.*

SCHILPP, PAUL ARTHUR, ed., *1963. The Philosophy of Bertrand Russell.* (The Library of Living Philosophers, Vol. 5.) 4th ed. 2 vols. New York and London: Harper & Row. 1st ed., 1944.

SCHMÖLE, JOSEPH, *1896–98. Die Sozialdemokratischen Gewerkschaften in Deutschland seit dem Erlasse des Socialisten-Gesetzes.* 2 vols. Jena: Gustav Fischer.

Referred to: *329, 330–1.*

SHAKESPEARE, WILLIAM. *Antony and Cleopatra.*

Referred to: *90.*

—— *As You Like It.*

Referred to: *72, 440.*

—— *Hamlet.*

Referred to: *61, 105.*

—— *Henry V.*

Referred to: *43, 382, 423.*

—— *Othello.*

Referred to: *96.*

—— Sonnet 33.

Referred to: *107, 404.*

—— Sonnet 50.

Referred to: *107, 404.*

—— Sonnet 64.

Referred to: *108, 404.*

—— Sonnet 97.

Referred to: *67, 398.*

—— *The Tempest.*

Referred to: *109.*

SHELLEY, PERCY BYSSHE, *1885. The Complete Poetical Works of Percy Bysshe Shelley.* Edited by William Michael Rossetti. 3 vols. London: John Slark. (Russell's library.)

Referred to: *394, 439.*

SMITH, LOGAN PEARSALL, *1950. A Portrait of Logan Pearsall Smith, Drawn from his Letters and Diaries*. Introduced by John Russell. London: Dropmore.
Referred to: *72*.

SMITH, NORMAN KEMP, *1918. A Commentary to Kant's 'Critique of Pure Reason'*. London: Macmillan.
Referred to: *434*.

SOUTHEY, ROBERT, *1909. The Life of Nelson*. London and New York: Cassell.
Referred to: *439*.

SPADONI, CARL, *1976.* "'Great God in Boots!—the Ontological Argument is Sound!'" *Russell*, nos. 23–4: 37–41.
Referred to: *403, 414*.

SPENCER, HERBERT, *1855. The Principles of Psychology*. London: Longman, Brown, Green, and Longmans.
Referred to: *422*.

—— *1873. The Study of Sociology*. London: H. S. King.
Referred to: *26, 37, 377, 380*.

—— *1876–96. The Principles of Sociology*. 3 vols. (A System of Synthetic Philosophy, Vols. 6–8.) London: Williams and Norgate.
Referred to: *377*.

—— *1884. The Man versus the State*. London and Edinburgh: Williams and Norgate.
Referred to: *377*.

—— *1892–93. The Principles of Ethics*. 2 vols. (A System of Synthetic Philosophy, Vols. 9–10.) London: Williams and Norgate. (Russell's library.)
Referred to: *421, 422*.

SPINOZA, BENEDICTUS DE, *1677. Ethics*.
Referred to: *92, 401, 416*.

STALLO, JOHN BERNARD, *1882. The Concepts and Theories of Modern Physics*. London: Kegan Paul, Trench.
Referred to: *405*.

STRACHEY, BARBARA, *1980. Remarkable Relations: The Story of the Pearsall Smith Family*. London: Victor Gollancz.
Referred to: *42, 395*.

*The Student's Guide to the University of Cambridge*. 4th ed. Cambridge: Deighton, Bell; London: George Bell and Sons, 1880. 5th ed., 1893.
Referred to: *383, 384, 385*.

STUMPF, CARL, *1873. Über den psychologischen Ursprung der Raumvorstellung*. Leipzig: S. Hirzel. (Russell's library.)
Referred to: *262, 274n., 426, 427*.

SULLY, JAMES, *1885.* "Genius and Insanity". *Nineteenth Century*, 17: 948–69.
Referred to: *5, 373*.

SWIFT, JONATHAN, *1726. Gulliver's Travels*.
Referred to: *378*.

SWINBURNE, ALGERNON CHARLES, *1887*. "Whitmania". *Fortnightly Review*, n.s. 42: 170–6.
Referred to: *401*.

TEMPLE, WILLIAM [Franciscus Mildapettus Navarrenus, pseud.], *1580*. *Ad Everardum Digbeium Anglum admonitio de unica P. Rami methodo reiectis caeteris retinenda.*
Referred to: 164, *412*.

—— *1581*. *Pro Mildapetti de unica methodo defensione contra Diplodophilum, commentatio ... Huc accessit nonnullarum e physicis et ethicis quaestionum explicatio, una cum Epistola de Rami Dialectica ad Joannem Piscatorem Argentinensem.*
Referred to: *412*.

—— *See also* RAMUS *1584.*

TENNYSON, ALFRED, LORD, *1886*. *In Memoriam A. H. H.* In *The Works of Alfred Lord Tennyson, Poet Laureate.* London: Macmillan. Pp. 247–86. (Russell's library.)
Referred to: 14–15, 18–19, 376, 377.

THOMAS À KEMPIS, *c.1427*. *The Imitation of Christ.*
Referred to: 55, 392.

THOMSON, WILLIAM, *1867*. "On Vortex Atoms". *Proceedings of the Royal Society of Edinburgh*, 6: 94–105.
Referred to: *408*.

—— *1891*. "Steps Toward a Kinetic Theory of Matter". In his *Popular Lectures and Addresses*. 3 vols. London and New York: Macmillan. I: 225–59.
Referred to: *408*.

—— AND PETER GUTHRIE TAIT, *1879–83*. *Treatise on Natural Philosophy*. New ed. 2 parts. Cambridge: Cambridge University Press. (Russell's copy: Pt. 1, 1896 printing; Pt. 2, 1890 printing; in Geophysical Institute Library, University of Alaska.)
Referred to: *408*.

*The Thousand and One Nights.*
Referred to: *419*.

THUCYDIDES *1629*. *Eight Bookes of the Peloponnesian Warre.* Translated by Thomas Hobbes.
Referred to: 186, *416*.

TODHUNTER, ISAAC, *1859*. *Plane Geometry for the Use of Colleges and Schools.* Cambridge: Macmillan.
Referred to: *4*.

TOLSTOI, LEO, *1873–77*. *Anna Karenina.*
Referred to: 90, *468–9*.

TURGENEV, IVAN, *1877*. *Virgin Soil.*
Referred to: 62, *395*, *427*.

VAIHINGER, HANS, *1881–92*. *Commentar zu Kants Kritik der reinen Vernunft.* 2 vols. Stuttgart: W. Spemann.

Referred to: *489*.

VALENTINE, OSWALD, [pseud.]: *see* SICKERT, OSWALD VALENTINE.

VIRGIL. *The Aeneid*.
Referred to: *23*.

VON STAUDT, KARL GEORG CHRISTIAN, *1847*. *Geometrie der Lage*. Nürnberg: Bauer und Raspe.
Referred to: *433*.

WADDINGTON, CHARLES TZAUNT, *1855*. *Ramus (Pierre de la Ramée), sa vie, ses écrits et ses opinions*. Paris: Ch. Meyrueis.
Referred to: *412*.

WAGNER, ADOLPH HEINRICH GOTTHILF, *1892–94*. *Grundlegung der politischen Oekonomie*. 2 vols. Leipzig: C. F. Winter.
Referred to: 66, *90*, *397*.

WAGNER, RICHARD, *1853*. *The Ring of the Nibelungs*.
Referred to: *403*.

WARD, JAMES, *1893*. "'Modern' Psychology: A Reflexion". *Mind*, n.s. 2: 54–82.
Referred to: *409*.

WATTS, ISAAC, *1715*. *Divine Songs Attempted in Easy Language for the Use of Children*.
Referred to: *438*.

WEBB, SIDNEY, AND BEATRICE WEBB, *1894*. *The History of Trade Unionism*. London: Longmans.
Referred to: 331, *441*.

WHITEHEAD, ALFRED NORTH, AND BERTRAND RUSSELL, *1910–13*. *Principia Mathematica*. 3 vols. Cambridge: at the University Press. 2nd ed., 1925–27.
Referred to: *xviii*.

WHITMAN, WALT, *1882*. *Leaves of Grass*. Philadelphia: David McKay. (Russell's and Alys's copy: Charles E. Feinberg Collection, Library of Congress.) 1st ed., 1855.
Referred to: 68, 69, 92, *398*, *401*.

WOLLSTONECRAFT, MARY, *1792*. *A Vindication of the Rights of Woman*.
Referred to: *440*.

WOOD, ALAN, *1957*. *Bertrand Russell: The Passionate Sceptic*. London: George Allen & Unwin.
Referred to: *4*, *310*, *398*, *445*.

WORDSWORTH, WILLIAM, *1807*. "Ode to Duty". Reprinted in his *1890*, 294–5, and in Palgrave *1888*, 204–5.
Referred to: 220, *422*.

—— *1807a*. "Ode: Intimations of Immortality from Recollections of Early Childhood". In his *1890*, 313–17, and in Palgrave *1888*, 301–6.
Referred to: *4*, 12, 20, 47, 59, *375*, *377*, *386*, *394*.

—— *1890*. *The Poetical Works of Wordsworth*. London: Frederick Warne. (Russell's library.)

WUNDT, WILHELM MAX, *1889*. *System der Philosophie*. Leipzig: Wilhelm Engel-
mann.
   Referred to: 121–2, 148, 247, 405, 409.
XENOPHON. *Anabasis*.
   Referred to: 4.

# General Index

PAGE NUMBERS IN roman type refer to Russell's text in the papers and appendices. Page numbers in italics refer to editorial matter, which is indexed less exhaustively than Russell's text. The only references indexed from the Textual Notes are to major authorial alterations and variants.

For authors, see also the Bibliographical Index.

Married women are entered under their married names. With few exceptions, titled persons are entered under their titles. Cross-references are provided for maiden names of married women and family names of titled persons.

## A

the Absolute *403, 404, 414*
  Bradley on *403–4*
  McTaggart on 88, 107, *400, 402, 403–4*
absolute idealism: *see* neo-Hegelianism
absolute position: *see under* position
abstinence theory (economics) 309, *435*
Adeane, Lady Elizabeth: *see* Biddulph, Lady Elizabeth
Adeane, Henry *387*
Adeane daughters 49, *387*
Adler, Georg *308*
aesthetes 92
aesthetic emotion 110, 114–16
aesthetics 50, 66–7, 109–10
agnosticism 57, 59
  Mill on 57
Aïdé, Hamilton 46, *385*
Alexandra Hotel 51, *388*
Alfred, King *250*
Ali Baba *419*
Allotments Bill (1886) 32, *379*
Allotments Bill (1887) 32, *380*
Amberley, Viscount *xvi, xx,* 83, *381, 382, 395*
Amberley, Viscountess *xvi, xx,* 61, 83, *382, 385, 395*
America 48, 66, 72, *395, 397*
Americans: Samuel Johnson on 48, *386*
analysis *405–6*
  Descartes's use of 159, 161, 171, 173

Galileo's use of 168
Hobbes's use of 158
anarchism 36, *380*
Anderson, Dr. William 66, *396*
Anglo-Irish Peace Treaty (1921) *393*
angular measurement 281, *432*
angular momentum: BR's study of 47, *387*
animal spirits: Descartes on 154, 176, 177
Anselm 179, *403*
antinomies, Kant's
  in ethics 219–20
  in geometry 304
  Lechalas on 288, *433*
Antisemites: *see* Christian Social Party
The Apostles (The Society) *xx, xxii,* 77, 78, 83, 90, *105,* 112, 113, 114, 246, *385, 399, 400, 402, 422*
  BR elected to 76
  BR "takes wings" from 99
  described *xviii,* 76
  election of women to 84–9, 337
appearance
  and reality *105,* 106–11
  world of 108–9; in Bradley and McTaggart *403–4*
  *see also* external world
apriority
  of arithmetic 129–30, 254, 259, 261, 301; in Heymans 251–2
  of axiom of congruence 268–76, 285–6,

Hobbes on 158, 186, 188, 189, 190, 191, 192
law(s) of 8, 189, 254, 273, 296, *425*; in Heymans 254–5
Lechalas on 288
and matter 161, 255; in Descartes 154, 177
relative 254
and time 125, 274, 295–6
motives *215*
Argyll on 18
and free will 7, 17, 18
theory of 313
motor-sensations: Heymans on 251, 252, 253
Muirhead, J. H. 7, 12–13, *374*
murder 8, 9
Murray, Gilbert *399*
music: BR's reaction to 50, 51
Myers, F. W. H. 106, *403*
mysticism 196, 209
and aesthetics 110
Spinoza on 192
Temple on 164

# N

Napoleon 95, 98, 327, *378*
Napoleonic Wars 28, *378*, *440*
National Convention (French) *437*
National Gallery of British Art *319*
National Liberal Party (German) *436*
nations: prosperity of 24–5
natural resources 24–5
natural selection 10
Sidgwick on *222*
naturalism: Balfour on 230, *423*
nature
ancient view of 166
Argyll on *375*
Aristotle on 136
Bacon on 136–7, 156
beauty of 21, 56, 57
BR's worship of *4*, 14, 20–1, 56–7, 59, 60, 61, 73
Democritus on 137
Descartes on 181
laws of 234–5, 237, *374*; Argyll on 10, 11, 12, 18; discovery of 25; and free will 7, 17–18; and God 5–6, 10, 12, 20; and miracles 10, 11; reducible to one 10
love of, in Cowper *380*
Malthus on 28
mechanical view of 301

Plato on 137
and political science 25–7
Ricardo on 28
"sadness of" 56
Adam Smith on 28
and survival 224
uniformity of, in Hume 144
worship of 34
nebular hypothesis 5, *374*
Nelson, Horatio 327, *439*
neo-Hegelianism *105*, 307
see also Bradley; Green, T. H.; McTaggart
neo-Platonism: in England 164
Neschdanoff: see Nezhdanov, Aleksey
Nevada *386*
Newnham College, Cambridge *381*
Newton, Sir Isaac 11, 95, 152, 189, 234, *249*, *250*, *375*
Nezhdanov, Aleksey 62, *395*, *427*
nihilism 36
nirvana 13, 47
Noah *392*
nominalism: Hobbes on 157, 170, 186, 187–8
noumena: in Kant 150
number
and abstraction 129; in Mill 129
apriority of 129–30, 254, 261, 301
and continuity 129, 267, 293–4, 301, *491*
and counting 129
metaphysical exposition of 129
and psychology 129; in Heymans 251
transcendental exposition of 129–30
see also arithmetic

# O

object: see subject
O'Brien, Sophie 49, 50, *387*
O'Brien, William 49, 50, 51, *387–8*
occasionalism *410*
Descartes and 153, 154, 180
Geulincx on 183–4
ontological argument 102
and the Absolute *403*
Anselm on 179, *403*
Descartes on 141, 154, 170, 175, 179, 184, *414*
Leibniz on 141, 179, 184
Spinoza on 141, 179
oppression 35
optimism 107
Orlando *72*
Othello 96
Oxford University 186, *420*

# W

wages 309
Wagner, Adolph *xxii*, 66, *90*, *215*, *247*, *306*, *397*, *400*
Wagner, Richard *400*
Waldegrave, John 58, *394*
Wallas, Graham *306*, *310*
Walras, Léon *435*
war 30, 327, 328
Ward, James *xviii*, *206*
    attack of, on Kant *124*
    and BR's dissertation *246*, *266*, *306*
    comments on BR's papers *406*, *408–10*
    courses by *118*, *119*, *120*, *124*, *140*, *146*, *151*, *195*, *405*, *414*, *427*
Watt, James 328, *440*
Watteau, Antony 321, *438*
Watts, Isaac 320, *438*
wealth
    equality of 81–2, 320, 322
    inherited 322
    uses of 320–3
    *see also* income
Webb, Beatrice and Sidney *310*, *319*, *398*, *441*
Wedd, Nathaniel 78, *91*
"Wedding March" (Mendelssohn) *388*
Wedgwood, Ralph *83*
weights and measures 37
Wells, H. G. *400*
Whigs *xx*
Whistler, James Abbott McNeill 321, *438*
White Queen 252
Whitehead, A. N. *xviii*, *246*, *249–50*, *266*
Whitman, Walt 62, 68, *395*, *401*
Whitmaniacs 92, *401*
Wilde, Oscar *401*
will
    acts of *93*, 216–17, 227, 233, 236; in Descartes *174*
    and causation 232–3, 235–6
    and conscience 213
    Descartes on *174*, *177*, 182–3
    Kant on *215*, 216, 233, 238
    universal 103, 237–8, 243
    *see also* free will
Williams, Mr. 17, *376*

Winchester School *xxi*, *384*, *385*
Windsor 52, 53, *390*
Wiseman, Mr. Worldly 204, *420*
Wittgenstein, Ludwig *xv*
Wollstonecraft, Mary 328, *440*
Wolseley, General *379*
Wolsey, Thomas 316, 339, *437*
Wolverhampton, Viscount: *see* Fowler, Henry H.
women
    and Apostolic discussion 85, 88
    and capital punishment 47
    effect of love on 86–7
    equality of 87, 327–8
    function of 223
    in Germany 322
    ideal qualities of 61
    nature of 84, 96
    objections of, to marriage 69–71
    opinions of 88; in marriage 67
    rights of 67, *83*, 327–8
    and self-sacrifice 95
Wood, Alan *119*, *162*, *310*
Wordsworth, William 20, *377*, *386*
workhouses 29, *379*
working class 28
    in Belgium 45
    in Germany 317
    Malthus on 28
    Ricardo on 28
World War I *375–6*, *381*, *388*, *391*
worlds, similar: Lechalas on 288
Wren's Coaching Establishment *383*
Wright, Sir Robert Samuel 54, *392*
Wronsky, Count *91*, *468–9*
Wundt, Wilhelm 148, *405*

# Y

Yorke, Lady Elizabeth: *see* Biddulph, Lady Elizabeth
Young, Miss 52

# Z

Zeno's paradoxes 189, *418*
    Lechalas on 288, *433*